# Lecture Notes in Computer Science 8782

Commenced Publication in 1973
Founding and Former Series Editors:
Gerhard Goos, Juris Hartmanis, and Jan van Leeuwen

T0236172

Sherman S.M. Chow   Joseph K. Liu
Lucas C.K. Hui   Siu Ming Yiu (Eds.)

# Provable Security

8th International Conference, ProvSec 2014
Hong Kong, China, October 9-10, 2014
Proceedings

 Springer

Volume Editors

Sherman S.M. Chow
Chinese University of Hong Kong
Department of Information Engineering
Rm. 808 Ho Sin Hang Engineering Building
Sha Tin, N.T., Hong Kong, China
E-mail: smchow@ie.cuhk.edu.hk

Joseph K. Liu
Institute for Infocomm Research
A*STAR
1 Fusionopolis Way Singapore 138632, Singapore
E-mail: ksliu@i2r.a-star.edu.sg

Lucas C.K. Hui
Siu Ming Yiu
The University of Hong Kong
Department of Computer Science
Chow Yei Ching Building
Pokfulam Road
Hong Kong, China
E-mail:{hui, smyiu}@cs.hku.hk

ISSN 0302-9743       e-ISSN 1611-3349
ISBN 978-3-319-12474-2       e-ISBN 978-3-319-12475-9
DOI 10.1007/978-3-319-12475-9
Springer Cham Heidelberg New York Dordrecht London

Library of Congress Control Number: 2014951517

LNCS Sublibrary: SL 4 – Security and Cryptology

*Typesetting:* Camera-ready by author, data conversion by Scientific Publishing Services, Chennai, India

Printed on acid-free paper

Springer is part of Springer Science+Business Media (www.springer.com)

# Preface

The 8th International Conference on Provable Security (ProvSec 2014) was held in Hong Kong, October 9–10, 2014. The conference was organized by The University of Hong Kong.

This year we have received 68 submissions from 20 different countries. This figure is the second highest since the first ProvSec in 2007. Each submission was reviewed by at least three, and on the average 3.2, Program Committee members. The committee decided to accept 25 papers (including seven short papers). The program also included two invited talks given by Dr. Michel Abdalla titled "Password-Based Authenticated Key Exchange: An Overview" and by Dr. Duncan Wong titled "Practical and Provably Secure Attribute Based Encryption."

We would like to thank all the people who contributed to the success of ProvSec 2014. First, we would like to thank all authors for submitting their works to ProvSec 2014. We deeply thank the 41 Program Committee members (coming from 20 different countries) as well as the external reviewers for their volunteer work of reading and discussing the submissions.

We also thank the Information Security and Forensics Society, which provides an excellent platform for user registration using Paypal and credit card, the general co-chairs Dr. Lucas C.K. Hui and Dr. S.M. Yiu, and the local organizing staff, especially Ms. Catherine Chan, for their unlimited support for ProvSec. This conference could not have been successful without their great assistance.

Last but not least, we would like to thank EasyChair for providing a user-friendly interface for us to manage all submissions and proceedings files.

October 2014

Sherman S.M. Chow
Joseph K. Liu

# Organization

ProvSec 2014 was organized by the Center for Information Security and Cryptography, Department of Computer Science, The University of Hong Kong, and Department of Information Engineering, The Chinese University of Hong Kong.

## Steering Committee

Feng Bao    Huawei, Singapore
Xavier Boyen    Queensland University of Technology, Australia
Yi Mu    University of Wollongong, Australia
Josef Pieprzyk    Queensland University of Technology, Australia
Willy Susilo    University of Wollongong, Australia

## Program Co-chairs

Sherman S.M. Chow    Chinese University of Hong Kong, Hong Kong SAR
Joseph K. Liu    Institute for Infocomm Research, Singapore

## General Co-chairs

Lucas C. K. Hui    University of Hong Kong, Hong Kong SAR
Siu-Ming Yiu    University of Hong Kong, Hong Kong SAR

## Local Organizing Committee

Catherine K.W. Chan    University of Hong Kong, Hong Kong SAR
T.W. Chim    University of Hong Kong, Hong Kong SAR
Leo C.Y. Yeung    University of Hong Kong, Hong Kong SAR
Russell W.F. Lai    Chinese University of Hong Kong, Hong Kong SAR
Yongjun Zhao    Chinese University of Hong Kong, Hong Kong SAR
Tao Zhang    Chinese University of Hong Kong, Hong Kong SAR

## Sponsoring Institution

Information Security and Forensics Society, Hong Kong SAR

# Program Committee

| | |
|---|---|
| Elena Andreeva | KU Leuven, Belgium |
| Man Ho Au | Hong Kong Polytechnic University, Hong Kong SAR |
| Reza Azarderakhsh | Rochester Institute of Technology, USA |
| Joonsang Baek | Khalifa University (KUSTAR), UAE |
| Paulo Barreto | University of São Paulo, Brazil |
| Olivier Blazy | Ruhr-Universität Bochum, Germany |
| Andrej Bogdanov | Chinese University of Hong Kong, Hong Kong SAR |
| Zhenfu Cao | Shanghai Jiao Tong University, China |
| Sanjit Chatterjee | Indian Institute of Science, India |
| Liqun Chen | Hewlett-Packard Laboratories, UK |
| Xiaofeng Chen | Xidian University, China |
| Seung Geol Choi | United States Naval Academy, USA |
| Sherman S. M. Chow | Chinese University of Hong Kong, Hong Kong SAR |
| Nico Döttling | Aarhus University, Denmark |
| Georg Fuchsbauer | Institute of Science and Technology Austria, Austria |
| David Galindo | LORIA-CNRS, France |
| Sanjam Garg | University of California at Berkeley, USA |
| Matt Henricksen | Institute for Infocomm Research, Singapore |
| Xinyi Huang | Fujian Normal University, China |
| Stanislaw Jarecki | University of California at Irvine, USA |
| Aniket Kate | Saarland University, Germany |
| Mirosław Kutyłowski | Wroclaw University of Technology, Poland |
| Alptekin Küpçü | Koç University, Turkey |
| Jin Li | Guangzhou University, China |
| Joseph K. Liu | Institute for Infocomm Research, Singapore |
| Shengli Liu | Shanghai Jiao Tong University, China |
| Mark Manulis | University of Surrey, UK |
| Sarah Meiklejohn | University College London, UK |
| Kazuhiko Minematsu | NEC Corporation, Japan |
| Atsuko Miyaji | Japan Advanced Institute of Science and Technology |
| Reza Reyhanitabar | EPFL, Switzerland |
| Reihaneh Safavi-Naini | University of Calgary, Canada |
| Jacob Schuldt | Royal Holloway, University of London, UK |
| Alice Silverberg | University of California at Irvine, USA |
| Willy Susilo | University of Wollongong, Australia |
| Koutarou Suzuki | NTT, Japan |
| Tsuyoshi Takagi | Kyushu University, Japan |
| Berkant Ustaoğlu | Izmir Institute of Technology, Turkey |
| Cong Wang | City University of Hong Kong, Hong Kong SAR |
| Duncan Wong | City University of Hong Kong, Hong Kong SAR |
| Wun-She Yap | Universiti Tunku Abdul Rahman, Malaysia |
| Rui Zhang | Chinese Academy of Sciences, China |
| Zongyang Zhang | AIST, Japan |

# External Reviewers

Abusalah, Hamza
Chevalier, Celine
Chin, Ji-Jian
Dutta, Ratna
Emura, Keita
Etemad, Mohammad
Farshim, Pooya
Futa, Yuichi
Han, Jinguang
Hanser, Christian
Hanzlik, Lucjan
Kakvi, Saqib A.
Kamath, Chethan
Khoo, Khoongming
Khurana, Dakshita
Kluczniak, Kamil
Koza, Michał

Kraschewski, Daniel
Krzywiecki, Łukasz
Kılınç, Handan
Liang, Kaitai
Liu, Liang
Liu, Zhenhua
Morozov, Kirill
Mukherjee, Sayantan
Namazi, Mina
O'Neill, Adam
Omote, Kazumasa
Pan, Jiaxin
Polychroniadou,
    Antigoni
Rao, Vanishree
Sakai, Yusuke
Schanck, John

Shen, Jiachen
Silverman, Joseph
Su, Chunhua
Tang, Qiang
Thomson, Susan
Tibouchi, Mehdi
Vergnaud, Damien
Wang, Haijiang
Wang, Licheng
Wang, Lihua
Watson, Gaven J.
Xagawa, Keita
Yamada, Shota
Zhang, Jiang
Zhang, Yinghui
Zhang, Yuexin
Zhao, Yongjun

# Invited Talks (Abstracts)

# Password-Based Authenticated Key Exchange: An Overview

Michel Abdalla

ENS, Paris, France[*]

**Abstract.** Password-based authenticated key exchange (PAKE) protocols are a particular case of authenticated key exchange protocols in which the secret key or password used for authentication is not uniformly distributed over a large space, but rather chosen from a small set of possible values (a four-digit pin, for example). Since PAKE protocols rely on short and easily memorizable secrets, they also seem more convenient to use as they do not require an additional cryptographic devices capable of storing high-entropy secret keys. In this survey, we consider the problem of designing authenticated key exchange protocols in the password-based setting. In particular, we discuss the different security goals that one can consider as well as different ways of realizing these goals. Finally, we recall some of the most recent results in the area and discuss some of the issues regarding the implementation of these protocols.

**Keywords.** Password-based authentication, key exchange.

---

[*] DI/ENS, CNRS, and INRIA.

# Practical and Provably Secure Attribute Based Encryption

Duncan S. Wong

Exploratory Research Laboratory
ASTRI
duncanwong@astri.org

We discuss about the properties that are crucial to making an Attribute-Based Encryption scheme practical, and investigate the techniques, which could be used for constructing a provably secure Ciphertext-Policy Attribute-Based Encryption (CP-ABE) scheme, which possesses the properties we identified that could make the scheme practical. In CP-ABE, a user's decryption key is associated with attributes which in general are not related to the user's identity, and the same set of attributes could be shared between multiple users. From the decryption key, if the user created a decryption blackbox for sale, this malicious user could be difficult to identify from the blackbox. Hence in practice, a useful CP-ABE scheme should have some tracing mechanism to identify this 'traitor' from the blackbox. In addition, being able to revoke compromised keys is also an important step towards practicality, and for scalability, the scheme should support an exponentially large number of attributes. We refer to these three important properties as (1) blackbox traceability, (2) revocation, and (3) large universe. In this talk, we also describe one of the first CP-ABE schemes of this type achieving the sub-linear overhead, and at the same time, attaining the fully collusion-resistant traceability against policy-specific decryption blackbox against selective attackers in the standard model. We also discuss about the proofing techniques, as well as the techniques applied in the construction of our CP-ABE scheme for achieving large attribute universe, and retaining highly expressivity on policies.

# Table of Contents

## Protocol

## Public Key Encryption

## Proxy Re-Encryption

## Predicate Encryption

## Attribute-Based Cryptosystem

## Short Papers

## Short Papers

## Author Index

# Password-Based Authenticated Key Exchange:
# An Overview

Michel Abdalla

ENS, Paris, France*

**Abstract.** Password-based authenticated key exchange (PAKE) protocols are a particular case of authenticated key exchange protocols in which the secret key or password used for authentication is not uniformly distributed over a large space, but rather chosen from a small set of possible values (a four-digit pin, for example). Since PAKE protocols rely on short and easily memorizable secrets, they also seem more convenient to use as they do not require an additional cryptographic devices capable of storing high-entropy secret keys. In this survey, we consider the problem of designing authenticated key exchange protocols in the password-based setting. In particular, we discuss the different security goals that one can consider as well as different ways of realizing these goals. Finally, we recall some of the most recent results in the area and discuss some of the issues regarding the implementation of these protocols.

**Keywords.** Password-based authentication, key exchange.

## 1    Introduction

Authenticated key exchange is an extremely useful tool in cryptography, allowing users to establish a common secret which they can then use in applications to achieve both privacy and authenticity. While several means of authentication have been proposed, most of them rely on either the existence of a public-key infrastructure or the availability of pairwise high-entropy secret keys.

Password-based authenticated key exchange (PAKE) protocols are a particular case of authenticated key exchange protocols in which the secret key or password used for authentication is not uniformly distributed over a large space, but rather chosen from a small set of possible values (a four-digit pin, for example). Since PAKE protocols rely on short and easily memorizable secrets, they also seem more convenient to use as they do not require an additional cryptographic devices capable of storing high-entropy secret keys.

Due to their practicality, password-based key exchange protocols have been very popular over the years. Unfortunately, the vast majority of protocols found in practice do not account for the fact that passwords have low entropy and are often subject to the so-called *dictionary* attacks. These are attacks in which an adversary tries to break the security of a scheme by a brute-force method, by

---

* DI/ENS, CNRS, and INRIA.

S.S.M. Chow et al. (Eds.): ProvSec 2014, LNCS 8782, pp. 1–9, 2014.

trying all possible combinations of secret keys in a given small set of values (i.e., the dictionary). Although not very effective in the case of high-entropy keys, dictionary attacks can be very damaging when the secret key is a password since the attacker has a non-negligible chance of winning. Such attacks are usually divided in two categories: *off-line* and *online* dictionary attacks.

To address the problem of dictionary attacks, several protocols have been designed to be secure even when the secret key is a password. The goal of these protocols is to restrict the adversary's success to online dictionary attacks only, in which the adversary must be present and interact with the system in order to be able to verify whether its guess is correct. The security in these systems usually relies on a policy of invalidating or blocking the use of a password if a certain number of failed attempts has occurred.

In this survey, we consider the problem of designing authenticated key exchange protocols in the password-based setting. First, we recall in Section 2 the first seminal work in this area, namely the encrypted key exchange (EKE) protocol by Bellovin and Merritt [13], together with its main variants. As the security of existing EKE-based protocols relies on idealized models, such as the random-oracle model [12], we review in Section 3 the main PAKE schemes with a proof of security in the standard model. Finally, in Section 4, we briefly discuss other issues such as universal composability, adaptive security, and recall some of the most recent results in the area.

## 2  The Encrypted Key Exchange Protocol and Its Variants

The seminal work in the area of password-based key exchange is the encrypted key exchange (EKE) protocol of Bellovin and Merritt [13] (see Fig. 1). In their protocol, two users execute an encrypted version of the Diffie-Hellman key exchange protocol [23], in which each flow is encrypted using the password shared between these two users as the symmetric key. Intuitively, since the elements to which the encryption function is applied are chosen uniformly at random from the underlying group, an adversary eavesdropping on the communication cannot learn any additional information which would allow him to perform an off-line dictionary attack.

Due to the simplicity of the EKE protocol, several other protocols were soon proposed in the literature based on it [14, 31, 36, 40]. Unfortunately, due to the lack of a proper security model for the analysis of PAKE schemes, these protocols were only heuristically secure.

It was only in 2000 that Bellare, Pointcheval, and Rogaway [10], as well as Boyko, MacKenzie, and Patel [17], proposed security models for PAKE schemes and proved variants of the EKE protocol, under ideal assumptions, such as the random-oracle model [12]. In addition to these, several other protocols were proposed in the literature based on EKE protocol [6, 18, 19, 37], each with its own instantiation of the encryption function. Currently, the simple password-authenticated key exchange protocol in [6] (to which we refer as SPAKE) is among the most efficient PAKE schemes based on the EKE protocol.

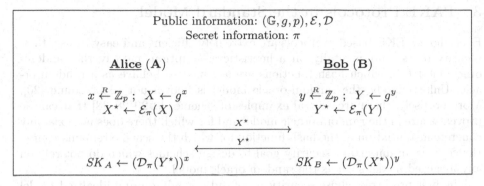

**Fig. 1.** The encrypted key exchange protocol [13]. The protocol uses symmetric encryption and decryption algorithms $\mathcal{E}$ and $\mathcal{D}$ and works over a finite cyclic group $\mathbb{G}$ of prime order $p$ generated by an element $g$.

The SPAKE scheme is a variation of the EKE protocol, in which the encryption function $\mathcal{E}_\pi(.)$ is replaced with a simple one-time pad function. More specifically, whenever a user **A** wants to send the encryption of a value $X \in \mathbb{G}$ to a user **B**, it does so by computing $X \cdot h_1{}^\pi$, where $h_1$ is an element in $\mathbb{G}$ associated with user **A** and the password $\pi$ is assumed to be in $\mathbb{Z}_p$. The session identifier is defined as the transcript of the conversation between **A** and **B** together with their identities, and the session key is set to be the hash (random oracle) of the session identifier, the password $\pi$, and the Diffie-Hellman key. The full description of SPAKE is given in Fig. 2.

$$
\boxed{
\begin{array}{c}
\text{Public information: } (\mathbb{G}, g, p), h_1, h_2, H \\
\text{Secret information: } \pi \in \mathbb{Z}_p \\[4pt]
\underline{\textbf{Alice (A)}} \qquad\qquad\qquad\qquad \underline{\textbf{Bob (B)}} \\[4pt]
x \xleftarrow{R} \mathbb{Z}_p\,;\; X \leftarrow g^x \qquad\qquad\qquad y \xleftarrow{R} \mathbb{Z}_p\,;\; Y \leftarrow g^y \\
X^* \leftarrow X \cdot h_1{}^\pi \qquad\qquad\qquad\qquad Y^* \leftarrow Y \cdot h_2{}^\pi \\
\xrightarrow{\quad X^* \quad} \\
\xleftarrow{\quad Y^* \quad} \\
K_A \leftarrow (Y^*/h_2{}^\pi)^x \qquad\qquad\qquad K_B \leftarrow (X^*/h_1{}^\pi)^y \\
SK_A \leftarrow H(\mathbf{A}, \mathbf{B}, \pi, X^*, Y^*, K_A) \qquad SK_B \leftarrow H(\mathbf{A}, \mathbf{B}, \pi, X^*, Y^*, K_B)
\end{array}
}
$$

**Fig. 2.** SPAKE: A simple password-based key exchange protocol [6]. SPAKE works over a finite cyclic group $\mathbb{G}$ of prime order $p$ generated by an element $g$.

As shown in [6], SPAKE is a secure PAKE scheme in the random-oracle model [11] according to the definition in the indistinguishability-based model of Bellare, Pointcheval, and Rogaway [10] if the computational Diffie-Hellman problem is intractable in $\mathbb{G}$.

# 3   PAKE Protocols in the Standard Model

Even though EKE-based protocols are extremely efficient and easy to use, their security relies fundamentally on a heuristic assumption, namely the random-oracle model, in which hash functions are assumed to behave as a random oracle. Unfortunately, the random-oracle model is known not to be sound [20]. More precisely, there are several examples of schemes [9, 20, 28, 38] that can be proven secure in the random-oracle model and for which there does not exist any concrete instantiation of the hash function for which the scheme remains secure. Hence, it is an important security goal to design schemes which do not rely on any idealized model such as the random-oracle model.

The first protocols whose security proof did not rely on any idealized model were proposed by Katz, Ostrovsky, and Yung (KOY) [34] based on the decisional Diffie-Hellman assumption and by Goldreich and Lindell [27], who proposed a solution based on general assumptions. While the former KOY protocol assumed the existence of a common reference string, the protocol by Goldreich and Lindell did not rely on any trusted setup assumption. Later, Gennaro and Lindell [26] abstracted and generalized (under various indistinguishability assumptions) the KOY protocol using the concept of smooth projective hash functions [22], which became the basis of several other protocols [5, 7, 8, 16] in the literature. To understand how the Gennaro-Lindell protocol works, let us first review the concept of smooth projective hash functions.

**Smooth Projective Hash Functions.** One of the main tools used in the Gennaro-Lindell (GL) protocol is the notion of smooth projective hash functions (SPHF, [22, 26]), which can be seen as a special type of zero-knowledge proof system for an NP language. More precisely, the definition of SPHF requires the existence of a domain $X$ and an underlying NP language $L$ such that it is computationally hard to distinguish a random element in $L$ from a random element in $X \setminus L$. For instance, in the particular case of the PAKE scheme in [21], the language $L$ is defined as the set of triples $\{(c, \ell, \pi)\}$ such that $c$ is an encryption of the password $\pi$ with label $\ell$ under a public key given in the common reference string (CRS). The semantic security of the encryption scheme guarantees computational indistinguishability between elements from $L$ and elements from $X$.

One of the key properties that make SPHF so useful is that, for a point $x \in L$, the hash value can be computed using either a *secret* hashing key hk, or a *public* projected key hp (depending on $x$ [26] or not [22]) together with a witness $w$ to the fact that $x \in L$. Another important property of these functions is that, given the projected key hp, their output is uniquely defined for points $x \in L$ and statistically indistinguishable from random for points $x \in X \setminus L$. Moreover, without the knowledge of the witness $w$ to the fact that $x \in L$, the output of these functions on $x$ is also pseudo-random.

**Overview of the GL Protocol.** Now that we have informally introduced the SPHF concept, we can finally review the GL PAKE protocol, whose detailed

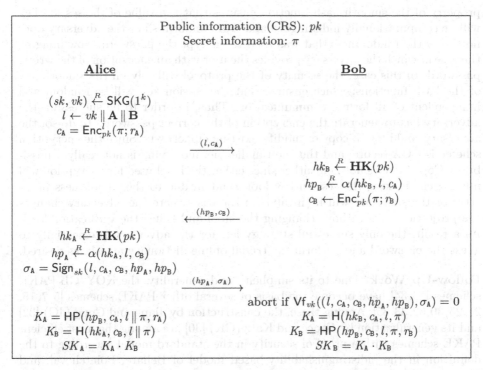

**Fig. 3.** An overview of the Gennaro-Lindell PAKE protocol [26]. (KG, Enc, Dec) are the key generation, encryption, and decryption algorithms of a labeled public-key encryption scheme [39]. (SKG, Sign, Vf) are the key generation, signing, and verification algorithms of a one-time signature scheme [24]. (HK, $\alpha$, H, HP) are the key generation, key projection, hashing, and projected hashing algorithms of a family of smooth projective hash functions for the language $L$ consisting of triples $\{(c, \ell, \pi)\}$ such that $c$ is an encryption of the password $\pi$ with label $\ell$.

description is given in Fig. 3. At a high level, the players in the GL protocol exchange CCA-secure encryptions of the password, under the public-key found in the common reference string, and then compute the session key by combining smooth projective hashes of the two password/ciphertext pairs. More precisely, the players first exchange ciphertexts consisting of encryption of their respective passwords with respect to the label $\ell$ containing their identities and the verification key for a one-time signature scheme. Next, each player chooses a hashing key for a smooth projective hash function for the language $\{(\mathsf{Enc}_{pk}^l(\pi), \ell, \pi)\}$ and sends the corresponding projected key to the other player. Each player can thus compute the output of its own hash function with the help of the hashing key, and the output of the other one using its knowledge of the randomness that was used to generate the ciphertext of the password. To avoid attacks in which the adversary generates new projection keys without modifying the corresponding ciphertexts and projection keys, **A** also signs the transcript of the conversation.

To understand informally why this protocol is secure, first consider the case in which the adversary plays a passive role. In this case, the pseudo-randomness property of the smooth hash function ensures that the value of the session key will be computationally indistinguishable from uniform since the adversary does not know the randomness that was used to encrypt the password. Now imagine the case in which the adversary provides the user with an encryption of the wrong password. In this case, the security of the protocol will rely on the smoothness of the hash functions, which ensures that the session key will be random and independent of all former communication. Thus, in order to be successful, the adversary has to generate the encryption of the correct password. To do so, the adversary could try to copy or modify existing ciphertexts. Since the encryption scheme is CCA-secure, and thus non-malleable, modifying is not really a possibility. Copying does not help either since either the label used for encryption will not match (making the session key look random due to the smoothness property) or the signature will be invalid (in the case where the adversary changes the projection keys without changing the label and hence the verification key). As a result, the only successful strategy left for the adversary is essentially to guess the password and perform the trivial online dictionary attack, as desired.

**Follow-Up Work.** Due to its simplicity and generality, the KOY/GL PAKE schemes [26,34] have become the basis of several other PAKE schemes [5,7,15, 21,25,30,32,33,35]. Among these, the construction by Jiang and Gong (JG) [32] and its generalization by Groce and Katz (GK) [30] are among the most efficient PAKE schemes with a proof of security in the standard model according to the definition in the indistinguishability-based model of Bellare, Pointcheval, and Rogaway [10]. In particular, the GK/JG protocol only requires the exchange of 8 group elements and a total of 3 rounds. More recently, this result has been slightly improved in [4].

## 4    Further Considerations

To conclude this survey, we now discuss some additional issues that one should take into account when designing and implementing PAKE schemes, such as universal composability and adaptive security.

**Universal Composability.** Most of the existing PAKE protocols, including the ones mentioned so far, have proofs either in the indistinguishability-based security model of Bellare, Pointcheval, and Rogaway (BPR) [10] or in the simulation-based of Boyko, MacKenzie, and Patel (BMP) [17]. Even though these models provide a security level that is sufficient for most applications, they fail to consider some realistic scenarios such as participants running the protocol with different but possibly related passwords. To surmount these deficiencies, Canetti, Halevi, Katz, Lindell, and MacKenzie [21] proposed an ideal functionality for PAKE protocols in the UC framework which makes no assumption on the distribution on passwords used by the protocol participants. Since the KOY/GL protocol is not known to achieve UC security, the authors of [21] also provided a new scheme based on the GL construction [26] that securely realizes the ideal functionality for PAKE under static corruptions .

Since the work of Canetti, Halevi, Katz, Lindell, and MacKenzie [21], several new constructions have appeared in the literature achieving UC security under static corruptions [15, 30, 35]. Among these, the work of Benhamouda *et al.* [15] is the most efficient one, only requiring only the exchange of 12 group elements in total.

**Adaptive Security.** While the protocols in [15, 21, 30, 35] already achieve a stronger notion of security than those in the BPR and BMP models, they are only known to be secure in the presence of static adversaries, when the set of corrupted players is known in advance. However, in reality, the adversary may be able to corrupt parties adaptively and learn their internal states. To address this issue, Barak, Canetti, Lindell, Pass, and Rabin (BCLPR) proposed in [8] a simple and intuitive construction that uses general techniques from multi-party computation. Even though their solution is very elegant, their protocol is quite inefficient due to its generality. Since then, several new constructions have been proposed [2, 3, 5]. While the construction in [2] is the most efficient and only requires a single round, the one in [3] has been proven secure even without assuming reliable erasures.

**Trusted Setups.** All of the PAKE protocols discussed in this survey have security proofs in idealized models or assume the existence of a trusted common reference string. There are, however, PAKE protocols which do not assume any trusted setup assumption [27, 29]. While these results are outstanding from a theoretical point of view, they are of limited interest for practice due to their lack of efficiency.

**Acknowledgments.** The text of this survey was extracted from the *Habilitation à diriger des recherches* (HDR) thesis by the author [1] and contains some minor updates to take into account more recent work in the area. Its contents are based on joint work with Fabrice Benhamouda, Olivier Blazy, Emmanuel Bresson, Céline Chevalier, Dario Catalano, Olivier Chevassut, Pierre-Alain Fouque, Louis Granboulan, and David Pointcheval.

# References

1. Abdalla, M.: Reducing the need for trusted parties in cryptography. HDR thesis, École normale supérieure (2011)
2. Abdalla, M., Benhamouda, F., Blazy, O., Chevalier, C., Pointcheval, D.: SPHF-friendly non-interactive commitments. In: Sako, K., Sarkar, P. (eds.) ASIACRYPT 2013, Part I. LNCS, vol. 8269, pp. 214–234. Springer, Heidelberg (2013)
3. Abdalla, M., Benhamouda, F., Pointcheval, D.: Removing erasures with explainable hash proof systems. Cryptology ePrint Archive, Report 2014/125 (2014), http://eprint.iacr.org/2014/125
4. Abdalla, M., Benhamouda, F., Pointcheval, D.: SPOKE: Simple password-only key exchange in the standard model. Cryptology ePrint Archive, Report 2014/609 (2014), http://eprint.iacr.org/2014/609

5. Abdalla, M., Chevalier, C., Pointcheval, D.: Smooth projective hashing for conditionally extractable commitments. In: Halevi, S. (ed.) CRYPTO 2009. LNCS, vol. 5677, pp. 671–689. Springer, Heidelberg (2009)
6. Abdalla, M., Pointcheval, D.: Simple password-based encrypted key exchange protocols. In: Menezes, A. (ed.) CT-RSA 2005. LNCS, vol. 3376, pp. 191–208. Springer, Heidelberg (2005)
7. Abdalla, M., Pointcheval, D.: A scalable password-based group key exchange protocol in the standard model. In: Lai, X., Chen, K. (eds.) ASIACRYPT 2006. LNCS, vol. 4284, pp. 332–347. Springer, Heidelberg (2006)
8. Barak, B., Canetti, R., Lindell, Y., Pass, R., Rabin, T.: Secure computation without authentication. In: Shoup, V. (ed.) CRYPTO 2005. LNCS, vol. 3621, pp. 361–377. Springer, Heidelberg (2005)
9. Bellare, M., Boldyreva, A., Palacio, A.: An uninstantiable random-oracle-model scheme for a hybrid-encryption problem. In: Cachin, C., Camenisch, J. (eds.) EUROCRYPT 2004. LNCS, vol. 3027, pp. 171–188. Springer, Heidelberg (2004)
10. Bellare, M., Pointcheval, D., Rogaway, P.: Authenticated key exchange secure against dictionary attacks. In: Preneel, B. (ed.) EUROCRYPT 2000. LNCS, vol. 1807, pp. 139–155. Springer, Heidelberg (2000)
11. Bellare, M., Rogaway, P.: Entity authentication and key distribution. In: Stinson, D.R. (ed.) CRYPTO 1993. LNCS, vol. 773, pp. 232–249. Springer, Heidelberg (1994)
12. Bellare, M., Rogaway, P.: Random oracles are practical: A paradigm for designing efficient protocols. In: Ashby, V. (ed.) ACM CCS 1993, pp. 62–73. ACM Press (November 1993)
13. Bellovin, S.M., Merritt, M.: Encrypted key exchange: Password-based protocols secure against dictionary attacks. In: 1992 IEEE Symposium on Security and Privacy, pp. 72–84. IEEE Computer Society Press (May 1992)
14. Bellovin, S.M., Merritt, M.: Augmented encrypted key exchange: A password-based protocol secure against dictionary attacks and password file compromise. In: Ashby, V. (ed.) ACM CCS 1993, pp. 244–250. ACM Press (November 1993)
15. Benhamouda, F., Blazy, O., Chevalier, C., Pointcheval, D., Vergnaud, D.: New techniques for SPHFs and efficient one-round PAKE protocols. In: Canetti, R., Garay, J.A. (eds.) CRYPTO 2013, Part I. LNCS, vol. 8042, pp. 449–475. Springer, Heidelberg (2013)
16. Bohli, J.M., Gonzalez Vasco, M.I., Steinwandt, R.: Password-authenticated constant-round group key establishment with a common reference string. Cryptology ePrint Archive, Report 2006/214 (2006), http://eprint.iacr.org/2006/214
17. Boyko, V., MacKenzie, P.D., Patel, S.: Provably secure password-authenticated key exchange using Diffie-Hellman. In: Preneel, B. (ed.) EUROCRYPT 2000. LNCS, vol. 1807, pp. 156–171. Springer, Heidelberg (2000)
18. Bresson, E., Chevassut, O., Pointcheval, D.: Security proofs for an efficient password-based key exchange. In: Jajodia, S., Atluri, V., Jaeger, T. (eds.) ACM CCS 2003, pp. 241–250. ACM Press (October 2003)
19. Bresson, E., Chevassut, O., Pointcheval, D.: New security results on encrypted key exchange. In: Bao, F., Deng, R., Zhou, J. (eds.) PKC 2004. LNCS, vol. 2947, pp. 145–158. Springer, Heidelberg (2004)
20. Canetti, R., Goldreich, O., Halevi, S.: The random oracle methodology, revisited (preliminary version). In: 30th ACM STOC, pp. 209–218. ACM Press (May 1998)
21. Canetti, R., Halevi, S., Katz, J., Lindell, Y., MacKenzie, P.: Universally composable password-based key exchange. In: Cramer, R. (ed.) EUROCRYPT 2005. LNCS, vol. 3494, pp. 404–421. Springer, Heidelberg (2005)

22. Cramer, R., Shoup, V.: Universal hash proofs and a paradigm for adaptive chosen ciphertext secure public-key encryption. In: Knudsen, L.R. (ed.) EUROCRYPT 2002. LNCS, vol. 2332, pp. 45–64. Springer, Heidelberg (2002)
23. Diffie, W., Hellman, M.E.: New directions in cryptography. IEEE Transactions on Information Theory 22(6), 644–654 (1976)
24. Even, S., Goldreich, O., Micali, S.: On-line/off-line digital signatures. Journal of Cryptology 9(1), 35–67 (1996)
25. Gennaro, R.: Faster and shorter password-authenticated key exchange. In: Canetti, R. (ed.) TCC 2008. LNCS, vol. 4948, pp. 589–606. Springer, Heidelberg (2008)
26. Gennaro, R., Lindell, Y.: A framework for password-based authenticated key exchange. In: Biham, E. (ed.) EUROCRYPT 2003. LNCS, vol. 2656, pp. 524–543. Springer, Heidelberg (2003), http://eprint.iacr.org/2003/032.ps.gz
27. Goldreich, O., Lindell, Y.: Session-key generation using human passwords only. In: Kilian, J. (ed.) CRYPTO 2001. LNCS, vol. 2139, pp. 408–432. Springer, Heidelberg (2001), http://eprint.iacr.org/2000/057
28. Goldwasser, S., Kalai, Y.T.: On the (in)security of the Fiat-Shamir paradigm. In: 44th FOCS, pp. 102–115. IEEE Computer Society Press (October 2003)
29. Goyal, V., Jain, A., Ostrovsky, R.: Password-authenticated session-key generation on the internet in the plain model. In: Rabin, T. (ed.) CRYPTO 2010. LNCS, vol. 6223, pp. 277–294. Springer, Heidelberg (2010)
30. Groce, A., Katz, J.: A new framework for efficient password-based authenticated key exchange. In: Al-Shaer, E., Keromytis, A.D., Shmatikov, V. (eds.) ACM CCS 2010, pp. 516–525. ACM Press (October 2010)
31. Jablon, D.P.: Extended password key exchange protocols immune to dictionary attacks. In: 6th IEEE International Workshops on Enabling Technologies: Infrastructure for Collaborative Enterprises (WETICE 1997), June 18-20, pp. 248–255. IEEE Computer Society, Cambridge (1997)
32. Jiang, S., Gong, G.: Password based key exchange with mutual authentication. In: Handschuh, H., Hasan, A. (eds.) SAC 2004. LNCS, vol. 3357, pp. 267–279. Springer, Heidelberg (2004)
33. Katz, J., MacKenzie, P.D., Taban, G., Gligor, V.D.: Two-server password-only authenticated key exchange. In: Ioannidis, J., Keromytis, A., Yung, M. (eds.) ACNS 2005. LNCS, vol. 3531, pp. 1–16. Springer, Heidelberg (2005)
34. Katz, J., Ostrovsky, R., Yung, M.: Efficient password-authenticated key exchange using human-memorable passwords. In: Pfitzmann, B. (ed.) EUROCRYPT 2001. LNCS, vol. 2045, pp. 475–494. Springer, Heidelberg (2001)
35. Katz, J., Vaikuntanathan, V.: Round-optimal password-based authenticated key exchange. In: Ishai, Y. (ed.) TCC 2011. LNCS, vol. 6597, pp. 293–310. Springer, Heidelberg (2011)
36. Lucks, S.: Open key exchange: How to defeat dictionary attacks without encrypting public keys. In: Workshop on Security Protocols. École Normale Supérieure (1997)
37. MacKenzie, P.D.: The PAK suite: Protocols for password-authenticated key exchange. Contributions to IEEE P1363.2 (2002)
38. Nielsen, J.B.: Separating random oracle proofs from complexity theoretic proofs: The non-committing encryption case. In: Yung, M. (ed.) CRYPTO 2002. LNCS, vol. 2442, pp. 111–126. Springer, Heidelberg (2002)
39. Shoup, V.: ISO 18033-2: An emerging standard for public-key encryption (December 2004), http://shoup.net/iso/std6.pdf, final Committee Draft
40. Steiner, M., Tsudik, G., Waidner, M.: Refinement and extension of encrypted key exchange. ACM SIGOPS Operating Systems Review 29(3), 22–30 (1995)

# Adaptive versus Static Security in the UC Model*

Ivan Damgård and Jesper Buus Nielsen

Aarhus University

**Abstract.** We show that for certain class of unconditionally secure protocols and target functionalities, static security implies adaptive security in the UC model. Similar results were previously only known for models with weaker security and/or composition guarantees. The result is, for instance, applicable to a wide range of protocols based on secret sharing. It "explains" why an often used proof technique for such protocols works, namely where the simulator runs in its head a copy of the honest players using dummy inputs and generates a protocol execution by letting the dummy players interact with the adversary. When a new player $P_i$ is corrupted, the simulator adjusts the state of its dummy copy of $P_i$ to be consistent with the real inputs and outputs of $P_i$ and gives the state to the adversary. Our result gives a characterization of the cases where this idea will work to prove adaptive security. As a special case, we use our framework to give the first proof of adaptive security of the seminal BGW protocol in the UC framework.

## 1 Introduction

When defining and proving security of cryptographic protocols we want to capture properties that would make our protocols applicable in real applications. Two aspects are particularly important in this respect. First, a protocol usually is a part of larger system and therefore we want a protocol to remain secure when composed, not only with itself, but also with an arbitrary environment. Second, a protocol must remain secure, even if some of the players are corrupted by an adversary. In a real scenario, one should expect that the choice of which players to attack is made while the protocol is running, i.e., we would like to have security against adaptive corruption rather than static, where the choice is made before the protocol starts.

Capturing these goals in a definition is notoriously a difficult task, and this may be the reason why general protocols for multiparty computation [12,3,9] were found a long time before we had generally accepted definitions of security for which composition results could be shown.

In 1991, Micali and Rogaway [14] as well as Beaver[2] put forward definitions. Like virtually all subsequent work, these definitions use simulation-based security: given only what the adversary is supposed to learn, it should be possible to simulate his view

* Supported by European Research Council Starting Grant 279447. Supported by Danish Council for Independent Research via DFF Starting Grant 10-081612. Supported by the Danish National Research Foundation and The National Science Foundation of China (under the grant 61061130540) for the Sino-Danish Center for the Theory of Interactive Computation, and also by the CFEM research centre (supported by the Danish Strategic Research Council) within which part of this work was performed.

S.S.M. Chow et al. (Eds.): ProvSec 2014, LNCS 8782, pp. 10–28, 2014.
© Springer International Publishing Switzerland 2014

of the protocol. However, it was not until the work around 2000 of Canetti [5] (the universal composition (UC) framework) and independently Pfitzmann, Schunter and Waidner [16] (reactive simulation) that security under arbitrary concurrent composition could be expressed. A recent related, but different approach known as "constructive cryptography" was initiated recently by Maurer [13]. This framework is also simulation-based and gives security under composition, but is technically different from the UC model in several ways.

It turns out that achieving adaptive security under, e.g., the UC definition is highly non-trivial for protocols that are based on cryptographic assumptions (although the problem can be solved at some loss of efficiency using so-called non-committing encryption [7]).

Since these complications are tightly linked to the use of encryption in the protocol, it was for a while believed in the folklore that for protocols that are information theoretically secure, static and adaptive security should be equivalent. This is not the case, however, there are natural examples of information theoretically secure protocols that are statically secure but not adaptively secure, as shown in [10].

In [6], a systematic study of the relation between static and adaptive security was conducted. This was limited to definitions allowing only sequential, rather than concurrent composition. They found that, in most cases, static and adaptive security are not equivalent. However, there was one important exception, namely that in the definition from [14] (called the MR definition in the following), static and adaptive security are equivalent.

*Our contribution.* It is natural to then ask what we can say about definitions that allow for concurrent composition, such as UC. In view of the example from [10], one should of course not expect adaptive to be equivalent to static in general; but it may be possible to identify a class of protocols where equivalence holds, and where therefore we can prove static security and get adaptive security only by verifying that the protocol is in this class.

One might perhaps hope that the positive result from [6] on the MR definition could help us, but this is not clear at all: the MR definition allows the simulator to be infinitely powerful, where a UC simulator must be polynomial time. It considers only secure function evaluation, where UC considers general reactive functionalities; and finally the MR definition requires a protocol to have a certain "committal round" where all the inputs become fixed, where the UC definition makes no such requirement.

In this paper, we borrow a high-level idea from the equivalence proof in [6], which can be loosely described as follows: to do adaptive simulation, we start by running the static simulator for the case where no player is corrupted. As soon as a corruption occurs, we try to "rescue the situation" such that we can continue running the static simulator having corrected for the fact that a new player has been corrupted. We continue in this way until the protocol halts.

Our technical contribution is to first identify the constraints on the static simulator and the target functionality that one needs to make this work in the UC model and second to resolve the difficulties arising from the differences between the MR and UC definitions. As a result, we show that for a certain class of unconditionally secure protocols and target functionalities, static security implies adaptive security in the UC model. The constraints we need on the static simulator and the target functionality are quite natural and allow the result to be applied, for instance, to a wide range of protocols for honest majority based on secret sharing, including the BGW protocol from [3]. The result also holds if the protocol uses one or more auxiliary functionalities, as long as they satisfy the same constraint. The result therefore also covers the on-line phase of several recent protocols in the pre-processing model [4,15,11].

To avoid confusion related to security of the BGW protocol, we want to clarify the relation between our result and the recent security proof for this protocol, given by Lindell and Asharov [1]. They prove static security and then notice that BGW satisfies the MR definition, which by the result from [6] implies adaptive security (in the MR definition). While this is true, it does not imply security in the UC model: first, as we mentioned, an MR simulator has unbounded computing time while a UC simulator must be polynomial time. Second, the equivalence result from [6] depends crucially on the simulator being unbounded. Therefore there is currently no proof that the BGW protocol is adaptively UC secure. However, using our result, such a proof can be derived from the proof of static security. We make an assumption on the structure of the circuit to be computed, namely that each output value is produced by a multiplication gate – this can easily be achieved by adding dummy multiplications by 1 if needed. This certainly simplifies the proof, but might in fact even be essential to get an efficient adaptive simulator. It is so far open whether this is the case. However, we find find it intriguing that even for a well known protocol like BGW, that is generally believed to be "clearly" adaptively secure, a proof of this is a non-trivial step beyond static security.

From a more high-level point of view, our result "explains" why an often used proof technique for such protocols works, namely where the simulator runs in its head a copy of the honest players using dummy inputs and generates a protocol execution by letting the dummy players interact with the adversary. When a new player $P_i$ is corrupted, the simulator patches the state of its dummy copy of $P_i$ to be consistent with the real inputs and outputs of $P_i$ and gives the state to the adversary. Our result gives a characterisation of the cases where this idea will work.

Since one of the constraints we impose on the static simulators is that one can *efficiently* patch from a static simulation of a small set of parties to a static simulation of a larger set of parties, our framework does not give adaptive security for free compared to current proof strategies. However, our framework abstracts current proof techniques and once and for all lifts all the technical details that are common for most proofs. We hope and believe that our result will make it easier to prove adaptive UC security, as it reduces the task to proving static security and checking whether the constraints we require are satisfied.

## 2   The UC Framework

In this section we sketch the UC framework and define some shorthand notation which we believe will make the upcoming proofs more clear.

In the framework from [5] the security of a protocol is defined by comparing its real-life execution to an ideal evaluation of its desired behavior. The protocol $\pi$ is modeled by $n$ interactive Turing Machines (ITMs), $\pi = \{P_1, \ldots, P_n\}$, called the *parties*. In addition an *ideal functionality* is given. An ideal functionality is just an ITM. All parties can send messages to $\mathcal{R}$ and receive messages from $\mathcal{R}$, using perfectly secure channels. The input-output behavior of $\mathcal{R}$ models the communication resource available to the parties in the protocol, and can, e.g., model perfectly secure, synchronous communication or authenticated asynchronous communication, but can be arbitrarily complex. In the *execution* of $\pi$ using communication resource $\mathcal{R}$ also an adversary $\mathcal{A}$ is present and an environment $\mathcal{Z}$ modeling the environment in which $\mathcal{A}$ is attacking the protocol. The environment gives inputs to honest parties, receives outputs from honest parties, and can communication with $\mathcal{A}$ at arbitrary points in the execution. The adversary can see and control the communication by interacting with $\mathcal{R}$.[1] The adversary can additionally corrupted parties adaptively. When a party is corrupted, the adversary learns the entire execution history of the corrupted party, including the random bits used, and will from the point of corruption send messages on behalf of the corrupted party. Both $\mathcal{A}$ and $\mathcal{Z}$ are PPT ITMs.

At the beginning of the protocol all parties, the communication resource, the adversary, and the environment is given as input the security parameter $k$ and random bits. Furthermore the environment is given an auxiliary input $z$. At some point the environment stops activating with parties and outputs some bit. This bit is taken to be the output of the execution. We use $\text{EXEC}_{\pi,\mathcal{R},\mathcal{A},\mathcal{Z}}(k,z)$ to denote the output of $\mathcal{Z}$ in the execution. We let $\text{EXEC}_{\pi,\mathcal{R},\mathcal{A},\mathcal{Z}}$ denote the distribution ensemble $\{\text{EXEC}_{\pi,\mathcal{R},\mathcal{A},\mathcal{Z}}\}_{k\in\mathbb{N},z\in\{0,1\}^*}$.

One particular adversary is the so-called *dummy adversary* $\mathcal{D}$. It simply works as a channel between $(\pi,\mathcal{R})$ and $\mathcal{Z}$. As examples, if $\mathcal{R}$ outputs a message $m$ to $\mathcal{D}$, $\mathcal{D}$ simply outputs $m$ to $\mathcal{Z}$, specifying that it is from the communication resource, and if $\mathcal{Z}$ instructs to corrupt $\mathsf{P}_i$, $\mathcal{D}$ will do so, and return the obtained information to $\mathcal{Z}$. We use $\text{REAL}_{\pi,\mathcal{R},\mathcal{Z}}(k,z)$ to denote $\text{EXEC}_{\pi,\mathcal{R},\mathcal{D},\mathcal{Z}}(k,z)$.

Second an *ideal evaluation* is defined, which is just another protocol plus communication resource being attacked by an adversary in an environment. In the ideal evaluation again an ideal functionality $\mathsf{F}$ is present. However, now the input-output behavior of $\mathsf{F}$ is a specification of the desired input-output behavior of the protocol. Also present is an adversary $\mathcal{S}$ (a.k.a. the *simulator*), the environment $\mathcal{Z}$, and $n$ so-called *dummy parties* $\mathsf{D}_1,\ldots,\mathsf{D}_n$ – all PPT ITMs. The only job of the dummy parties is to take inputs from the environment and send them to the ideal functionality and *vice versa*. We call $\delta = \{\mathsf{D}_1,\ldots,\mathsf{D}_n\}$ the *dummy protocol*. Again the leakage seen by the adversary and the influence that the adversary can except is defined by the input-output behavior of $\mathsf{F}$, i.e., by which messages $\mathsf{F}$ sends to $\mathcal{S}$ and and how $\mathsf{F}$ responds to messages from $\mathcal{S}$. Note that $\delta$ executed with $\mathsf{F}$ as communication resource is a trivially secure protocol with the same input-output behavior as the ideal functionality $\mathsf{F}$. For an environment $\mathcal{Z}$ we use $\text{EXEC}_{\delta,\mathsf{F},\mathcal{S},\mathcal{Z}}(k,z)$ to denote the output of $\mathcal{Z}$ after the execution. Since $\delta$ is a fixed protocol we can omit it in the notation. We let $\text{IDEAL}_{\mathsf{F},\mathcal{S},\mathcal{Z}}(k,z) = \text{EXEC}_{\delta,\mathsf{F},\mathcal{S},\mathcal{Z}}(k,z)$.

---

[1] The leakage seen and influence allowed by $\mathcal{A}$ is defined by the input-output behavior of $\mathcal{R}$. If $\mathcal{R}$ models only authenticated communication it would send the transmitted messages also to $\mathcal{A}$. If it models secure communication it would not. If it models asynchronous communication it could let $\mathcal{A}$ specify any delivery pattern, if it models synchronous communication it would impose restrictions on the delivery patterns $\mathcal{A}$ may specify.

We recall the definition of UC security. It can be proven that it is sufficient to prove security against the dummy adversary, so we phrase the version where the adversary is fixed to be $\mathcal{D}$.

**Definition 1** ([5]). *We say that $\pi$ securely realizes $F$ in the $\mathcal{R}$-hybrid model if there exists a PPT simulator $S$ such that for all PPT environments $\mathcal{Z}$ we have that $\text{IDEAL}_{F,S,\mathcal{Z}}$ and $\text{REAL}_{\pi,\mathcal{A},\mathcal{Z}}$ are computationally indistinguishable. We say that there is statistical security if $\text{IDEAL}_{F,S,\mathcal{Z}}$ and $\text{REAL}_{\pi,\mathcal{A},\mathcal{Z}}$ are negligibly close for all environments $\mathcal{Z}$, i.e., $\mathcal{Z}$ is not restricted to PPT. We say there is perfect security if $\text{IDEAL}_{F,S,\mathcal{Z}} = \text{REAL}_{\pi,\mathcal{A},\mathcal{Z}}$ for all environments $\mathcal{Z}$.*

We use $A \diamond B$ to denote a system containing the two ITMs $A$ and $B$ and also use this notation for larger systems. In the UC framework two ITMs $A$ and $B$ in the same system of ITMs communicate by writing designated messages on the tapes of each other, specifying the message and the identity of the sender. We would like a more convenient terminology for this communication mechanism, so we will talk about $A$ and $B$ being equipped by incoming ports (inports) and outgoing ports (outports). A port is just a bit string pn, naming the port, plus a direction. Ports are connected by identity of name and opposition of direction. I.e., if $A$ has an outport pn and $B$ has an identically named inport pn then we say that $A$ can send messages to $B$ on pn. I.e., saying that $A$ sends $m$ on pn, in $A \diamond B$, is equivalent to saying that $A$ writes $(\text{pn}, m)$ on a tape of $B$. Since ports are connected by names we clearly have that $A \diamond B = B \diamond A$.

Execution of an interactive system of ITMs works in a "sequentialized concurrent" way, where only one ITM is active at a time. The activation is passed from one ITM to the next when a message is sent to that ITM. Initially the environment is activated. Which ITMs can write and read on which tapes and how activation is passed is specified in great detail in the UC framework, but we will not need to address the particularities to prove our result.

When a system of ITMs is closed, i.e., there are no outports without an identically named inport, then it can be executed as described above, and we use the system also to denote the family of random variables describing its execution, i.e., $\delta \diamond F \diamond S \diamond \mathcal{Z} = \text{EXEC}_{\delta,F,S,\mathcal{Z}}$ and $\pi \diamond \mathcal{R} \diamond \mathcal{D} \diamond \mathcal{Z} = \text{EXEC}_{\pi,\mathcal{R},\mathcal{D},\mathcal{Z}}$.

If an interactive system has no protocol, then this will sometimes tacitly mean that the protocol is the dummy protocol. Equivalently, a missing adversary sometimes denotes the dummy adversary, i.e., $F \diamond S := F \diamond \delta \diamond S$ and $\pi \diamond \mathcal{R} := \pi \diamond \mathcal{R} \diamond \mathcal{D}$.

If two interactive systems are open, but would become closed by adding an environment to the system, then we compare them by comparing them in *all* environments, i.e., a missing environment designates *all* environments. Formally, if $F \diamond S \diamond \mathcal{Z} = \pi \diamond \mathcal{R} \diamond \mathcal{Z}$ for all environments $\mathcal{Z}$, we write $F \diamond S \overset{\text{perf}}{\equiv} \pi \diamond \mathcal{R}$. If $F \diamond S \diamond \mathcal{Z}$ and $\pi \diamond \mathcal{R} \diamond \mathcal{Z}$ are negligibly close for all environments $\mathcal{Z}$, we write $F \diamond S \overset{\text{stat}}{\equiv} \pi \diamond \mathcal{R}$. If $F \diamond S \diamond \mathcal{Z}$ and $\pi \diamond \mathcal{R} \diamond \mathcal{Z}$ are negligibly close for all PPT environments $\mathcal{Z}$, we write $F \diamond S \overset{\text{comp}}{\equiv} \pi \diamond \mathcal{R}$. These notions can be refined by restricting the class of environments. For instance, we write $F \diamond S \overset{\text{comp}}{\equiv}_{\text{Env}} \pi \diamond \mathcal{R}$ to mean that $F \diamond S \diamond \mathcal{Z}$ and $\pi \diamond \mathcal{R} \diamond \mathcal{Z}$ are negligibly close for all PPT environments $\mathcal{Z} \in \text{Env}$.

We can rephrase the definition with the new notation as follows. We say that $\pi$ *securely realizes* $F$ in the $\mathcal{R}$-hybrid model if there exists a PPT simulator $S$ such that

$\mathsf{F} \diamond \mathcal{S} \overset{\text{comp}}{\equiv} \pi \diamond \mathcal{R}$. We say that there is statistical security if $\mathsf{F} \diamond \mathcal{S} \overset{\text{stat}}{\equiv} \pi \diamond \mathcal{R}$. We say that there is perfect security if $\mathsf{F} \diamond \mathcal{S} \overset{\text{perf}}{\equiv} \pi \diamond \mathcal{R}$.

We will sometimes further overload notation like $\pi \diamond \mathcal{R} \diamond \mathcal{D} \diamond \mathcal{Z}$ and use it to denote the random variable describing the *trace* of the execution, i.e., $(k, z)$ plus the ordered list of the random tapes of all ITMs plus the ordered list of pairs $(\text{name}, m)$ specifying which messages were sent on which ports and in which order.

## 3    Adaptive versus Static Security Revisited

In this section, we show a general proof strategy for proving adaptive security. The idea is to first prove static security and then construct, from the simulator $\mathcal{S}$ we built, a new simulator $\mathcal{S}'$ for the adaptive case. Roughly speaking, the strategy for $\mathcal{S}'$ is to follow the algorithm of $\mathcal{S}$, but every time a new player $\mathsf{P}_i$ is corrupted, $\mathcal{S}'$ cooks up a view for $\mathsf{P}_i$ that "looks convincing", gives this to the environment, patches the state of $\mathcal{S}$ accordingly and continues.

It turns out that there is a class of unconditionally secure protocols and functionalities where this idea works and our goal will be to characterize this class and point out what the procedure run by $\mathcal{S}'$ to handle corruptions must satisfy. We will consider the case of perfect security first and later show that the results are also true in some cases for statistical security.

So we will assume we are given protocol $\pi$, communication resource functionality $\mathcal{R}$, ideal functionality $\mathsf{F}$, and simulator $\mathcal{S}$ such that $\pi \diamond \mathcal{R} \overset{\text{perf}}{\equiv} \mathcal{S} \diamond \mathsf{F}$ for all static, unbounded environments that corrupts only subsets from some adversary structure $\mathbb{A}$. We write $\pi \diamond \mathcal{R} \overset{\text{perf}}{\equiv}_{\mathbb{A},\text{static}} \mathcal{S} \diamond \mathsf{F}$. We will assume synchronous protocols only.

We will need the following notation.

**Definition 2.** *For an ITM $A$ (ITM) that is part of an interactive system $\mathcal{IS}$, the view of $A$ is a random variable, written $V_A(\mathcal{IS})$, and is defined to be the ordered concatenation of all messages exchanged on the ports of $A$ and of the random choices of $A$, i.e., a random trace of $\mathcal{IS}$ restricted to the values seen by $A$. We use $V_A(\mathcal{IS}|E)$ to denote the view when conditioned on some event $E$ occurring, and $V_A(\mathcal{IS})_j$ to denote the view truncated to contain only the values associated with the first $j$ rounds – we only consider synchronous protocols, so the notion of round is well defined.*

**Definition 3.** *For a player $\mathsf{P}_i$ in a protocol $\pi$ running with communication resource $\mathcal{R}$, and environment $\mathcal{Z}$, the conversation of $\mathsf{P}_i$ is a random variable, written $\text{Conv}_{\mathsf{P}_i}(\mathcal{Z} \diamond \pi \diamond \mathcal{R})$, and is defined to be the ordered concatenation of all messages $\mathsf{P}_i$ exchanges with honest players and $\mathcal{R}$. For a set $C$ of parties we let $\text{Conv}_C(\mathcal{Z} \diamond \pi \diamond \mathcal{R})$ be the set of $\text{Conv}_{\mathsf{P}_i}(\mathcal{Z} \diamond \pi \diamond \mathcal{R})$ for $\mathsf{P}_i \in C$. Likewise, the conversation of $\mathcal{Z}$, written $\text{Conv}_\mathcal{Z}(\mathcal{Z} \diamond \pi \diamond \mathcal{R})$, is the ordered concatenation of all messages $\mathcal{Z}$ exchanges with honest players in $\pi$ and $\mathcal{R}$. For conversations, we denote truncation and conditioning on events in the same way as for views.*

Note that the conversation of a party is a substring of its view. Also note that when a player $\mathsf{P}_i$ is corrupted, its view becomes a substring of the conversation of $\mathcal{Z}$, because $\mathcal{Z}$ learns from the (up to now) honest $\mathsf{P}_i$ the entire view of $\mathsf{P}_i$ up to the corruption. We may think of $\mathrm{Conv}_{\mathcal{Z}}(\mathcal{Z} \diamond \pi \diamond \mathcal{R})$ as the total information $\mathcal{Z}$ gets from attacking the protocol. Recall, however that $\mathcal{Z}$ also chooses the inputs of honest players and learns their outputs.

We will need to assume that the ideal functionality has a certain behavior. First it must ensure that whenever it receives input or gives output, the time at which this happens is publicly known, i.e., the functionality leaks the information that a party just received an output as well as the the name of that party. The second demand is meant to capture the idea that the functionality should treat players who are corrupt but behave honestly in the same way as if they were honest. We give an intuitive explanation after the definition.

**Definition 4.** *The ideal functionality F is said to be* input-based *if the following is satisfied:*

**Honest Behavior Equivalence:** *Consider executions of F where some set A is corrupted from the start and where a fixed (ordered) set of inputs $I_F$ are given to F during the execution[2]. In any such execution the outputs produced by F and its state at the end has the same distribution, in particular the distributions do not depend on the corruptions that occur during the execution.[3]*

**Publicly known Input-Output Provision:** *Each time F receives an input from $P_i$, F leaks a message specifying that some input from $P_i$ has been received.[4] Each time F sends a private output to $P_i$, it also leaks a message, specifying that an output was given, but not the value.*

The "honest behavior equivalence" condition is essentially to the notion of a "well-formed ideal functionality" [8] and can be intuitively explained as follows: an ideal functionality knows which players are corrupt and its actions may in general depend arbitrarily on this information. The condition puts a limitation on this: Consider first an execution where all players outside $A$ remain honest and F gets $I_F$ as input. Compare this to a case where $P_i \notin A$ is corrupted, but F still gets the same inputs. This means in particular that $P_i$ sends the same inputs, so he "behaves honestly" towards F. Therefore, the demand we make loosely speaking means that as long as a corrupt player behaves honestly towards the functionality, the actions it takes will be the same as if that player had been honest.

Our results will also be valid for a slightly more general case where the outputs produced by F do not have to be the same in all executions, but the outputs in one

---

[2] Notice that these inputs will arrive from different parties, depending on whether the player giving input is honest or is controlled by the adversary/environment in the given execution.

[3] Note that technically, in the UC framework F is informed of corruptions, so its state contains information about who is corrupted and when. So strictly speaking, the state cannot be exactly the same in all cases. However, we require that up to the fact that different sets of corrupted players are stored, the state is exactly the same. This can be formalized by saying that $F = F_{\mathrm{wrap}}(F_{\mathrm{core}})$ for a core functionality $F_{\mathrm{core}}$ which has *honest behavior equivalence* in the strict sense plus a wrapper $F_{\mathrm{core}}$ who is informed who is corrupted but does not forward it to the core, but otherwise acts as a channel between its environment and the core.

[4] By leaking a message we mean that the message is sent on the port connected to the adversary/simulator.

execution can be efficiently computed from $I_F$ and the outputs in any other execution. For simplicity we do not treat this general case explicitly in the following.

We also need to make some assumptions on how the simulator $S$ behaves, more precisely on how it decides on the inputs it sends to F on behalf of corrupted players (recall that once a player is corrupted, the simulator gets to decide which inputs this player provides to F). We will assume that $S$ uses a standard technique to decide on these inputs, namely at the time where the input is given, it looks at the conversation of the corrupt player and decides on its input based on this. This is formalized as follows:

**Definition 5.** *The simulator $S$ is* conversation-based *if the following is satisfied:*

**Conversation-based inputs:** *If $S$ sends an input $x$ to F on behalf of $P_i$ in round $j$, it computes $x$ as $x = \text{Inp}_i(c)$ where $\text{Inp}_i$ is a PPT function depending only on the protocol and $c = \text{Conv}_C(Z \diamond S \diamond F)_j$, where $C$ is the set of corrupted parties.*

**Honest behavior implies correct inputs:** *If $P_i$ is corrupt but has followed the protocol honestly then it is always the case that $\text{Inp}_i(c)$ equals the corresponding input $P_i$ was given from the environment. By a corrupt $P_i$ following the protocol honestly, we mean that the environment decides the actions of $P_i$ by running a copy of the code of the honest $P_i$ on the inputs and messages that $P_i$ receives in the protocol and a uniformly independently chosen random tape.[5]*

**Corruption-consistent input functions:** *Consider the conversations $c = \text{Conv}_C(Z \diamond S \diamond F)_j$ of some corrupted parties, and consider the conversations $c' = \text{Conv}_{C'}(Z \diamond S \diamond F)_j$ of some other set of corrupted parties, where both $C$ and $C'$ are allowed to be corrupted and $C \subset C'$. For all such $c, c'$ and all input functions $\text{Inp}_i$ for parties in $C$, it must be the case that $\text{Inp}_i(c) = \text{Inp}_i(c')$.*

Note that input functions only have to be defined on conversations that actually occur in $\pi$. Also note that the corruption consistency of the input functions model the following reasonable intuition: consider a run of $\pi$ that leads to certain inputs. Now suppose we run $\pi$ again with the same random coins, however some players that were honest before are now corrupted, but are told to play honestly. Since all players make the same moves in the two cases, it is reasonable to expect that the resulting inputs should be the same, and this is what the corruption-consistency of the input functions implies. This is in some sense the requirement that the input functions are "well-formed".

A typical example of an input function is where $P_i$ provide inputs by secret-sharing them using polynomials of degree at most $t$. Here the input function reconstructs the input from the shares held by honest players using Lagrange interpolation. If the protocol guarantees that the shares are consistent with some polynomial of degree at most $t$, even if $P_i$ is actively corrupt, then the input function only has to be defined on such sets of shares and is indeed corruption consistent.

Now, suppose we are given an adaptive environment $Z$ and we want to show that the protocol is secure with respect to this environment. For this, we need to think about

---

[5] It is slightly tricky to formally and *generally* define what "following the protocol honestly" means, as an actively corrupted party takes all its instructions from the environment. However, in our context the definition we give here will do, where we make a structural requirement on the environment that it contains a copy of the honest party.

how we can use a static simulator $\mathcal{S}$. Of course, we cannot just run it against $\mathcal{Z}$ because $\mathcal{S}$ does not know how to handle corruptions that occur in the middle of the protocol. So instead, we will construct a family of static environments from $\mathcal{Z}$.

For each set $A$ that $\mathcal{Z}$ may corrupt, we construct an environment $\mathcal{Z}_A$. Informally, what $\mathcal{Z}_A$ does is that it corrupts set $A$, but initially, it lets all players in $A$ play honestly. It runs internally a copy of $\mathcal{Z}$ and lets it interact with the protocol as usual, where the only difference is that players in $A$ are run honestly by $\mathcal{Z}_A$ instead of running by themselves. When $\mathcal{Z}$ corrupts a player in $A$, $\mathcal{Z}_A$ gives control of that player to $\mathcal{Z}$ and continues, if the corrupted player is not in $A$, $\mathcal{Z}_A$ outputs guess 0 and terminates. If $\mathcal{Z}$ outputs a guess $c \in \{0, 1\}$ without corrupting anyone outside $A$, then $\mathcal{Z}_A$ outputs the same guess $c$. A formal description is found below.

---

### Agent $\mathcal{Z}_A$

Static environment constructed from $\mathcal{Z}$.

1. Initially corrupt set $A$. Set up internally a (honest) copy $\mathsf{P}'_j$ of each player $\mathsf{P}_j \in A$. Also set up internally a copy of $\mathcal{Z}$.
2. When the system executes and some $\mathsf{P}_j \in A$ is activated, then if $\mathsf{P}_j$ has not been corrupted by $\mathcal{Z}$ (see next item) $\mathcal{Z}_A$ does the following: $\mathcal{Z}_A$ gives a copy of the messages received by $\mathsf{P}_j$ to its internal copy $\mathsf{P}'_j$ and runs its code to decide (honestly) what to send.
3. If $\mathcal{Z}$ decides to corrupt $\mathsf{P}_j \in A$, $\mathcal{Z}_A$ gives the current state of $\mathsf{P}'_j$ to $\mathcal{Z}$ and gives (passive or active) control of $\mathsf{P}_j$ to $\mathcal{Z}$. Note that this means that after this point any messages meant for $\mathsf{P}_j$ (from $\mathcal{R}$ or from other players) are forwarded to $\mathcal{Z}$ and $\mathcal{Z}_A$ runs the code of $\mathcal{Z}$ to determine what messages $\mathsf{P}_j$ should send.
4. If $\mathcal{Z}$ decides to corrupt $\mathsf{P}_j \notin A$, $\mathcal{Z}_A$ halts and outputs the guess 0.
5. If $\mathcal{Z}$ halts (having corrupted no player outside $A$) with guess $c \in \{0, 1\}$, $\mathcal{Z}_A$ halts and outputs guess $c$.

---

We know that $\mathcal{S}$ can do perfect simulation against any of the $\mathcal{Z}_A$ we just defined and this will be the basis of the adaptive simulator we construct later. Before we can construct the adaptive simulator, we need some auxiliary lemmas on how $\mathcal{S}$ behaves when interacting with the $\mathcal{Z}_A$'s.

Some notation: In the following s will denote an ordered sequence of players, and $A(\mathbf{s})$ will denote the set of players that occur in s. $E_\mathbf{s}$ will be the event that the first $|\mathbf{s}|$ corruptions done by the environment are exactly those in s (in the specified order). Below, when we write views or conversations with subscript s, for instance as in $V_\mathcal{Z}(\mathcal{Z}\diamond \pi \diamond \mathcal{R}|E_\mathbf{s})_\mathbf{s}$, this means that if a corruption outside s occurs, we truncate the view at the point where this corruption happens.

Finally, consider the copy of $\mathcal{Z}$ that is run internally by $\mathcal{Z}_{A(\mathbf{s})}$ where we execute $\mathcal{Z}_{A(\mathbf{s})} \diamond \mathcal{IS}$ for some interactive system $\mathcal{IS}$ (such as $\pi \diamond \mathcal{R}$). We then let $V_\mathcal{Z}(\mathcal{Z}_{A(\mathbf{s})} \diamond \mathcal{IS}|E_\mathbf{s})$ be its view, conditioned on $E_\mathbf{s}$. Since $\mathcal{Z}_{A(\mathbf{s})}$ runs $\mathcal{Z}$ "in the head" it is clear that $V_\mathcal{Z}(\mathcal{Z}_{A(\mathbf{s})} \diamond \mathcal{IS}|E_\mathbf{s})$ can be deterministically and easily extracted from $V_{\mathcal{Z}_{A(\mathbf{s})}}(\mathcal{Z}_{A(\mathbf{s})} \diamond \mathcal{IS}|E_\mathbf{s})$, we will write this as

$$V_{\mathcal{Z}}(\mathcal{Z}_{A(\mathbf{s})} \diamond \mathcal{IS}|E_{\mathbf{s}}) = \mathrm{Extr}(V_{\mathcal{Z}_{A(\mathbf{s})}}(\mathcal{Z}_{A(\mathbf{s})} \diamond \mathcal{IS}|E_{\mathbf{s}}))\,.$$

We can now show that assuming $E_{\mathbf{s}}$ occurs, then $\mathcal{S}$ can be used to perfectly simulate (a part of) the view $\mathcal{Z}$ sees in the protocol, because it can simulate the view of $\mathcal{Z}_{A(\mathbf{s})}$:

**Lemma 1.** *Assuming $\mathcal{R}$ is input based, we have*

$$V_{\mathcal{Z}}(\mathcal{Z}_{A(\mathbf{s})} \diamond \mathcal{S} \diamond \mathsf{F}|E_{\mathbf{s}}) \stackrel{\mathrm{perf}}{\equiv} V_{\mathcal{Z}}(\mathcal{Z} \diamond \pi \diamond \mathcal{R}|E_{\mathbf{s}})_{\mathbf{s}}\,.$$

*Proof.* We have $V_{\mathcal{Z}_{A(\mathbf{s})}}(\mathcal{Z}_{A(\mathbf{s})} \diamond \mathcal{S} \diamond \mathsf{F}) \stackrel{\mathrm{perf}}{\equiv} V_{\mathcal{Z}_{A(\mathbf{s})}}(\mathcal{Z}_{A(\mathbf{s})} \diamond \pi \diamond \mathcal{R})$, since $\mathcal{S}$ is a good static simulator. So the two distributions are also the same when conditioning on $E_{\mathbf{s}}$, that is, we have

$$V_{\mathcal{Z}_{A(\mathbf{s})}}(\mathcal{Z}_{A(\mathbf{s})} \diamond \mathcal{S} \diamond \mathsf{F}|E_{\mathbf{s}}) \stackrel{\mathrm{perf}}{\equiv} V_{\mathcal{Z}_{A(\mathbf{s})}}(\mathcal{Z}_{A(\mathbf{s})} \diamond \pi \diamond \mathcal{R}|E_{\mathbf{s}})\,. \tag{1}$$

The two distributions remain equal if we apply the same deterministic function to both of them, so if we apply Extr on both sides of (1) we get

$$V_{\mathcal{Z}}(\mathcal{Z}_{A(\mathbf{s})} \diamond \mathcal{S} \diamond \mathsf{F}|E_{\mathbf{s}}) \stackrel{\mathrm{perf}}{\equiv} V_{\mathcal{Z}}(\mathcal{Z}_{A(\mathbf{s})} \diamond \pi \diamond \mathcal{R}|E_{\mathbf{s}})\,. \tag{2}$$

Moreover, from the point of view of $\mathcal{Z}$ (and still conditioning on $E_{\mathbf{s}}$), the only difference between $\mathcal{Z}_{A(\mathbf{s})} \diamond \pi \diamond \mathcal{R}$ and $\mathcal{Z} \diamond \pi \diamond \mathcal{R}$ is that in the first case the parties in $A$ are run honestly by $\mathcal{Z}_{A(\mathbf{s})}$ until $\mathcal{Z}$ wants to corrupt them while in the second case they run as honest players in $\pi$. This makes no difference to $\mathcal{R}$ since it is input based (by the honest behavior equivalence property) and hence it makes no difference to $\mathcal{Z}$ either. So we have

$$V_{\mathcal{Z}}(\mathcal{Z}_{A(\mathbf{s})} \diamond \pi \diamond \mathcal{R}|E_{\mathbf{s}}) \stackrel{\mathrm{perf}}{\equiv} V_{\mathcal{Z}}(\mathcal{Z} \diamond \pi \diamond \mathcal{R}|E_{\mathbf{s}})_{\mathbf{s}}\,. \tag{3}$$

The lemma now follows from (2) and (3). $\qquad\blacksquare$

We also need to consider a connection between simulation against several different $\mathcal{Z}_{A(\mathbf{s})}$'s: For a sequence of players $\mathbf{s}$, we can append a player $\mathsf{P}_i$ (who is not in $\mathbf{s}$) at the end of the sequence. We write this new sequence as $\mathbf{s}, i$, and define $E_{\mathbf{s},i}$ and $A(\mathbf{s}, i)$ as before.

**Lemma 2.** *Assuming $\mathcal{R}$ is input based, we have*

$$V_{\mathcal{Z}}(\mathcal{Z}_{A(\mathbf{s})} \diamond \mathcal{S} \diamond \mathsf{F}|E_{\mathbf{s},i}) \stackrel{\mathrm{perf}}{\equiv} V_{\mathcal{Z}}(\mathcal{Z}_{A(\mathbf{s},i)} \diamond \mathcal{S} \diamond \mathsf{F}|E_{\mathbf{s},i})_{\mathbf{s}}\,.$$

*Proof.* Since $\mathcal{S}$ is a good static simulator, we have by a similar argument as in the proof of Lemma 1 that

$$V_{\mathcal{Z}}(\mathcal{Z}_{A(\mathbf{s})} \diamond \mathcal{S} \diamond \mathsf{F}|E_{\mathbf{s},i}) = \mathrm{Extr}(V_{\mathcal{Z}_{A(\mathbf{s})}}(\mathcal{Z}_{A(\mathbf{s})} \diamond \mathcal{S} \diamond \mathsf{F}|E_{\mathbf{s},i})) \tag{4}$$

$$\stackrel{\mathrm{perf}}{\equiv} \mathrm{Extr}(V_{\mathcal{Z}_{A(\mathbf{s})}}(\mathcal{Z}_{A(\mathbf{s})} \diamond \pi \diamond \mathcal{R}|E_{\mathbf{s},i})) \tag{5}$$

$$= V_{\mathcal{Z}}(\mathcal{Z}_{A(\mathbf{s})} \diamond \pi \diamond \mathcal{R}|E_{\mathbf{s},i})\,. \tag{6}$$

Note that, assuming $E_{\mathbf{s},i}$ occurs, the only difference between $\mathcal{Z}_{A(\mathbf{s})} \diamond \pi \diamond \mathcal{R}$ and $\mathcal{Z}_{A(\mathbf{s},i)} \diamond \pi \diamond \mathcal{R}$ is that in the latter case $\mathsf{P}_i$ is run honestly by $\mathcal{Z}_{A(\mathbf{s},i)}$ whereas in the former it plays honestly as party in the protocol. As $\mathcal{R}$ is input based, this makes no difference to $\mathcal{R}$ and hence also no difference to the view of $\mathcal{Z}$ as long as we only consider what happens up to the point where $\mathsf{P}_i$ is corrupted. So we have

$$V_{\mathcal{Z}}(\mathcal{Z}_{A(\mathbf{s})} \diamond \pi \diamond \mathcal{R}|E_{\mathbf{s},i}) \overset{\text{perf}}{\equiv} V_{\mathcal{Z}}(\mathcal{Z}_{A(\mathbf{s},i)} \diamond \pi \diamond \mathcal{R}|E_{\mathbf{s},i})_{\mathbf{s}} . \qquad (7)$$

Using again that $\mathcal{S}$ is a good static simulator, it follows in that same way as before that

$$V_{\mathcal{Z}}(\mathcal{Z}_{A(\mathbf{s},i)} \diamond \pi \diamond \mathcal{R}|E_{\mathbf{s},i})_{\mathbf{s}} \overset{\text{perf}}{\equiv} V_{\mathcal{Z}}(\mathcal{Z}_{A(\mathbf{s},i)} \diamond \mathcal{S} \diamond \mathsf{F}|E_{\mathbf{s},i})_{\mathbf{s}} . \qquad (8)$$

The lemma now follows from (6), (7) and (8).

We now want to show that if we consider both the view of $\mathcal{Z}$ and the inputs and outputs that $\mathsf{F}$ exchanges, we still have a similar result as in the previous lemma. This does not have to be true in general, but is indeed true if $\mathcal{S}$ is conversation-based and if $\mathsf{F}$ is input-based:

**Lemma 3.** *Let* $\mathrm{St}_{\mathsf{F}}(\cdot)$ *be the state of* $\mathsf{F}$ *after running in some interactive system. Then, if $\mathcal{S}$ is conversation-based and $\mathsf{F}$ is input-based, we have*

$$(V_{\mathcal{Z}}(\mathcal{Z}_{A(\mathbf{s})} \diamond \mathcal{S} \diamond \mathsf{F}|E_{\mathbf{s},i}), \ \mathrm{St}_{\mathsf{F}}(\mathcal{Z}_{A(\mathbf{s})} \diamond \mathcal{S} \diamond \mathsf{F}|E_{\mathbf{s},i}))$$

$$\overset{\text{perf}}{\equiv} (V_{\mathcal{Z}}(\mathcal{Z}_{A(\mathbf{s},i)} \diamond \mathcal{S} \diamond \mathsf{F}|E_{\mathbf{s},i})_{\mathbf{s}}, \ \mathrm{St}_{\mathsf{F}}(\mathcal{Z}_{A(\mathbf{s},i)} \diamond \mathcal{S} \diamond \mathsf{F}|E_{\mathbf{s},i})_{\mathbf{s}}) .$$

*Proof.* We already have from Lemma 2 that the view of $\mathcal{Z}$ has the same distribution in the two systems. We then prove the lemma by arguing that because $\mathcal{S}$ is conversation-based, all inputs sent to $\mathsf{F}$ follow deterministically from the view of $\mathcal{Z}$ and will be the same in both systems, so since $\mathsf{F}$ is input-based, the distribution of its state must be the same as well.

In more detail, consider a view $v$ for $\mathcal{Z}$ that occurs with non-zero probability (in both systems). Note first that by public input-output provision of $\mathsf{F}$, one can infer from $v$ in which rounds inputs were provided to $\mathsf{F}$ or outputs were sent, so these must be the same in the two systems. Consider a particular input and say it comes from player $\mathsf{P}_j$. We do a case analysis:

$\mathsf{P}_j \notin A(\mathbf{s}, i)$ In this case $\mathsf{P}_j$ is honest throughout in both systems. This means $\mathcal{Z}$ provides the input directly to $\mathsf{F}$ so the input occurs in $v$ and is the same in both systems.

$\mathsf{P}_j = \mathsf{P}_i$ In the system $\mathcal{Z}_{A(\mathbf{s})} \diamond \mathcal{S} \diamond \mathsf{F}$, $\mathsf{P}_i$ is honest and $\mathcal{Z}$ provides directly to $\mathsf{F}$ the input, say $x$, that occurs in $v$. In $\mathcal{Z}_{A(\mathbf{s},i)} \diamond \mathcal{S} \diamond \mathsf{F}$, $\mathsf{P}_i$ is corrupt but is told to play honestly on input $x$ as provided by $\mathcal{Z}$. Then $\mathcal{S}$ decides on the input to $\mathsf{F}$ using the input function on the conversations of the corrupted parties, and this will result in $x$ by the "honest behavior implies correct input" property.

$\mathsf{P}_j \in A(\mathbf{s})$ **and has not been corrupted by** $\mathcal{Z}$ **when the input is provided** In    this case, in both systems $\mathcal{Z}$ provides input $x$ to $\mathsf{P}_j$ who plays honestly and $\mathcal{S}$ decides the input to $\mathsf{F}$ using the input function on the conversations of the corrupted parties, which will be $x$, again by the "honest behavior implies correct input" property.

$\mathsf{P}_j \in A(\mathbf{s})$ **and has been corrupted by** $\mathcal{Z}$ **when the input is provided** In this case $\mathcal{S}$ will in both systems decide on the input using the input function on the conversations of the corrupted parties. Note first that the messages a corrupted party has exchanged with all players that $\mathcal{Z}$ has not corrupted yet is part of $v$ and is therefore the same in both systems (this includes at least all players outside $A(\mathbf{s})$). However, from the point of view of $\mathcal{S}$, the conversation of a corrupted party is *not* the same in the two systems: in $\mathcal{Z}_{A(\mathbf{s})} \diamond \mathcal{S} \diamond \mathsf{F}$, it consists of messages exchanged with players outside $A(\mathbf{s})$, while in $\mathcal{Z}_{A(\mathbf{s},i)} \diamond \mathcal{S} \diamond \mathsf{F}$ it consists of a subset of these messages, namely those exchanged with players outside $A(\mathbf{s}, i)$. However, since the input functions are corruption-consistent, the input computed by $\mathcal{S}$ is nevertheless the same in the two systems.

In the following, we will consider a situation where we execute the system $\mathcal{Z}_{A(\mathbf{s})} \diamond \mathcal{S} \diamond \mathsf{F}$ until a point where $E_{\mathbf{s},i}$ has occurred. At this point, $\mathcal{Z}_{A(\mathbf{s})}$ would halt. However, by Lemma 3, as far as $\mathcal{Z}$ and the state of $\mathsf{F}$ is concerned, we might as well have been running $\mathcal{Z}_{A(\mathbf{s},i)} \diamond \mathcal{S} \diamond \mathsf{F}$, and unlike $\mathcal{Z}_{A(\mathbf{s})}$, $\mathcal{Z}_{A(\mathbf{s},i)}$ would be able to continue even after $\mathsf{P}_i$ is corrupted. So if we could somehow "pretend" that in fact it was the latter system we ran, we would not have to stop when $\mathsf{P}_i$ is corrupted.

To help us do this trick, we consider an execution of $\mathcal{Z}_{A(\mathbf{s},i)} \diamond \mathcal{S} \diamond \mathsf{F}$ where $E_{\mathbf{s},i}$ occurs. Say that the values of $V_{\mathcal{Z}}(\mathcal{Z}_{A(\mathbf{s},i)} \diamond \mathcal{S} \diamond \mathsf{F}|E_{\mathbf{s},i})_{\mathbf{s}}$ and $\mathrm{St}_{\mathsf{F}}(\mathcal{Z}_{A(\mathbf{s},i)} \diamond \mathcal{S} \diamond \mathsf{F}|E_{\mathbf{s},i})_{\mathbf{s}}$ are $v$ and $w$. We then define $D_{v,w}$ to be the joint distribution of the states of $\mathcal{Z}_{A(\mathbf{s},i)}$ and $\mathcal{S}$ at the point where $\mathsf{P}_i$ is corrupted, given $v$ and $w$. Note that since we assume that $E_{\mathbf{s},i}$ occurred, the state of $\mathcal{Z}_{A(\mathbf{s},i)}$ consists of a state of $\mathcal{Z}$ that is fixed by $v$ and a view of $\mathsf{P}_i$ who has been playing honestly so far. So we can think of the output of $D_{v,w}$ as a view of $\mathsf{P}_i$ plus a state of $\mathcal{S}$.

**Lemma 4.** *Consider an execution of the system $\mathcal{Z}_{A(\mathbf{s},i)} \diamond \mathcal{S} \diamond \mathsf{F}$ until a point where $E_{\mathbf{s},i}$ has occurred. Let*

$$V_{\mathcal{Z}}(\mathcal{Z}_{A(\mathbf{s},i)} \diamond \mathcal{S} \diamond \mathsf{F}|E_{\mathbf{s},i})_{\mathbf{s}} = v \text{ and } \mathrm{St}_{\mathsf{F}}(\mathcal{Z}_{A(\mathbf{s},i)} \diamond \mathcal{S} \diamond \mathsf{F}|E_{\mathbf{s},i})_{\mathbf{s}} = w \,.$$

*Let* io$_{\mathcal{S}}$ *be the string of inputs and outputs $\mathcal{S}$ has exchanged with $\mathsf{F}$, and let* $\mathrm{Conv}_{\mathcal{Z}}$ *be the conversation of $\mathcal{Z}$ in the execution. Then one can sample from the distribution $D_{v,w}$ if given* io$_{\mathcal{S}}$ *and* $\mathrm{Conv}_{\mathcal{Z}}$*. In particular, $D_{v,w}$ depends only on* io$_{\mathcal{S}}$ *and* $\mathrm{Conv}_{\mathcal{Z}}$*.*

*Proof.* Recall that $\mathcal{Z}_{A(\mathbf{s},i)}$ consists of a copy of $\mathcal{Z}$ and copies of players in $A(\mathbf{s}, i)$. However, since $E_{\mathbf{s},i}$ occurs, all players in $A(\mathbf{s})$ have been corrupted earlier by $\mathcal{Z}$, so their entire view until they were corrupted by $\mathcal{Z}$ is part of $\mathrm{Conv}_{\mathcal{Z}}$.

The sampling procedure we claim is now very simple: for each possible set of coins for $\mathsf{P}_i$ and for $\mathcal{S}$, we will test if these coins are consistent with the values of io$_{\mathcal{S}}$ and $\mathrm{Conv}_{\mathcal{Z}}$ we are given. We do the test by simulating $\mathsf{P}_i$ and $\mathcal{S}$ running as part of the system $\mathcal{Z}_{A(\mathbf{s},i)} \diamond \mathcal{S} \diamond \mathsf{F}$. This is possible because the given values io$_{\mathcal{S}}$ and $\mathrm{Conv}_{\mathcal{Z}}$ specify the entire communication that $\mathsf{P}_i$ and $\mathcal{S}$ should have with $\mathsf{F}$ and $\mathcal{Z}$. If the current random coins lead to $\mathsf{P}_i$ or $\mathcal{S}$ sending a message that is inconsistent with io$_{\mathcal{S}}$, $\mathrm{Conv}_{\mathcal{Z}}$, we throw away this set of coins. Finally, we choose randomly a set of coins among those that survived and output the resulting view of $\mathsf{P}_i$ and state of $\mathcal{S}$.

Note that we only prove that one can sample from $D_{v,w}$, we do not claim that one can sample *efficiently* from this distribution. In fact, this does not hold in general. In view of the result of Lemma 4, we will write $D_{\mathrm{io}_{\mathcal{S}},\mathrm{Conv}_{\mathcal{Z}}}$ instead of $D_{v,w}$ in the following. We can now specify the final tool we need to build an adaptive simulator, namely the sampling we have just seen must be possible to do efficiently:

**Definition 6.** *Consider a probabilistic algorithm* Patch *that takes as input strings* $\mathrm{io}_S$ *and* $\mathrm{Conv}_Z$ *of the form as specified in Lemma 4.* Patch *is said to be a* good sampling function *if it satisfies the following:*

- *It is polynomial time computable.*
- *The output* $\mathrm{Patch}(\mathrm{io}_S, \mathrm{Conv}_Z)$ *is distributed according to* $D_{\mathrm{io}_S, \mathrm{Conv}_Z}$.

We are now finally ready to specify the main result of this section:

**Theorem 1.** *Assume we are given a simulator $S$ for protocol $\pi$ and functionality $F$ such that $\pi \diamond \mathcal{R} \stackrel{\mathrm{perf}}{\equiv}_{\mathbb{A}, static} S \diamond F$. Assume further that $S$ is conversation-based, $F$ and $\mathcal{R}$ are input-based, and that we are given a good sampling function* Patch. *Then there exists a simulator $S'$ such $\pi \diamond \mathcal{R} \stackrel{\mathrm{perf}}{\equiv}_{\mathbb{A}, adaptive} S \diamond F$, i.e., $\pi \diamond \mathcal{R} \diamond \mathcal{Z} \stackrel{\mathrm{perf}}{\equiv}_{\mathbb{A}, adaptive} S \diamond F \diamond \mathcal{Z}$ for all for all adaptive and synchronous environment $\mathcal{Z}$ corrupting only subsets from $\mathbb{A}$.*

*Proof.* We specify the algorithm of our adaptive simulator $S'$. To do this, suppose that if we are given a string $\mathrm{io}_S$ containing inputs and outputs that $S$ has exchanged with $F$ on behalf of corrupted players in a set $A$. Suppose we are also given the inputs and outputs $\mathrm{io}_i$ that some honest player $P_i$ has exchanged with $F$ in the same execution. Then we can merge these strings in a natural way: we define $\mathrm{Merge}(\mathrm{io}_S, \mathrm{io}_i)$ to be the string that contains, for every protocol round, the inputs to $F$ that occur in either $\mathrm{io}_S$ or $\mathrm{io}_i$, and also outputs from $F$ that occur in either $\mathrm{io}_S$ or $\mathrm{io}_i$. Note that $\mathrm{Merge}(\mathrm{io}_S, \mathrm{io}_i)$ is a string of inputs and outputs that $S$ might have exchanged with $F$ if $A \cup P_i$ had been the corrupted set (and $P_i$ had behaved honestly).

---

**Agent $S'$**

Adaptive simulator constructed from $S$.

1. Set s be the empty sequence. Set $\mathrm{io}_S$, $\mathrm{Conv}_Z$ to be the empty strings. Set up a copy of $S$ in its initial state. Tell $S$ as input (in the preamble) that the empty set is the corrupted set.
2. Whenever $S'$ is activated, if the input is a request to corrupt a new player $P_i$, it goes to the next step. Otherwise, it runs $S$ on the input received and sends the output $S$ produces on the corresponding output port of its own. Messages exchanged with $\mathcal{Z}$ are appended to $\mathrm{Conv}_Z$, inputs/outputs exchanged with $F$ are appended to $\mathrm{io}_S$.
3. Set $\mathrm{s} = \mathrm{s}, i$. Send a request to corrupt $P_i$ to $F$ and get s string $\mathrm{io}_i$ back. Set $\mathrm{io}_S = \mathrm{Merge}(\mathrm{io}_S, \mathrm{io}_i)$. Compute $(v_i, \mathrm{St}') = \mathrm{Patch}(\mathrm{io}_S, \mathrm{Conv}_Z)$. Put $S$ in state $\mathrm{St}'$, send $v_i$ to the environment, append $v_i$ to $\mathrm{Conv}_Z$ and go to Step 2.

---

To see that this simulation works, note first that it is obvious that $\mathrm{Conv}_Z$ contains at all times the conversation of $\mathcal{Z}$ so far, and that $\mathrm{io}_S$ contains at all times the inputs and outputs we have exchanged with $F$ so far.

We can now show the following

**Claim:** whenever $S'$ enters step 2 the state of $Z, S$ and $F$ are distributed exactly as in a run of $Z_{A(s)} \diamond S \diamond F$ where $E_s$ occurs.

We show this by induction: the claim is trivial when we enter step 2 the first time since here $s$ is empty. So consider a later stage where we enter step 2, and write the current $s$ as $s = s', i$. The previous time we entered step 2, by induction hypothesis, the state of $Z, S$ and $F$ were distributed exactly as in a run of $Z_{A(s')} \diamond S \diamond F$ where $E_{s'}$ occurs. During the following execution of step 2, $S'$ simply ran $S$, so when the $i$'th player is corrupted, the state of the state of $Z, S$ and $F$ were distributed exactly as in a run of $Z_{A(s')} \diamond S \diamond F$ where $E_{s',i}$ occurs. Now, by Lemma 3, the views (and hence state) of $Z$ and the state of $F$ are distributed as in a run of $Z_{A(s',i)} \diamond S \diamond F$ where $E_{s,i}$ occurs.

Then Patch was run and the claim now follows by assumption on Patch, if we show that the inputs $\text{Conv}_Z, \text{io}_S$ we use have the distribution they would have in $Z_{A(s',i)} \diamond S \diamond F$, given the current values of the view of $Z$ and the state of $F$. This is trivially true for $\text{Conv}_Z$ as it follows deterministically from the view of $Z$. For $\text{io}_S$, note that the inputs to $F$ that occur in this string also follow deterministically from the view of $Z$, we argued this in the proof of Lemma 3. But since $F$ is input-based, the resulting outputs from $F$ will be the same regardless of whether we run $Z_{A(s)}$ or $Z_{A(s',i)}$, and so $\text{io}_S$ has the desired distribution.

We can now argue that $V_Z(Z \diamond \pi \diamond R) \stackrel{\text{perf}}{\equiv} V_Z(Z \diamond S' \diamond F)$ which clearly implies the theorem.

We will consider the executions of step 2 one by one. In the first execution, by the above claim, the state of $Z, S$ and $F$ are distributed exactly as in a run of $Z_{A(s)} \diamond S \diamond F$ where $E_s$ occurs. But here $s$ is the empty sequence so $E_s$ always occurs. In step 2, we simply run $S$, so by Lemma 1, we obtain a perfect simulation of $Z$'s view until the point where is halts or corrupts the first player. In particular, in the latter case, that player is chosen with the distribution we would also see in a real execution of the protocol. When we have executed step 3, again by the claim, the state of $Z, S$ and $F$ are distributed exactly as in a run of $Z_{A(s)} \diamond S \diamond F$ where $E_s$ occurs, and where $s$ now contains one player. Again by Lemma 1, while executing step 2 we obtain a perfect simulation of $Z$'s view from the point where it corrupts the first player until the point where is halts or corrupts the second player.

Repeating this argument at most $n$ times (since $Z$ can corrupt only so many players), we see that we get a perfect simulation of the entire view of $Z$.

**Using Theorem 1.** In order to use Theorem 1 on a concrete protocol, one has to first construct a static simulator $S$, verify that is is conversation-based and that the target functionality $F$ is input-based. This is usually quite easy. Then one has to construct an efficient procedure Patch. This may seem harder because the formal definition is quite technical and involves two static environments constructed from an arbitrary adaptive environment.

We therefore give an explanation in more "human" language of what Patch must be able to do. Recall that when Patch is called, players in the sequence $s$ were corrupted earlier and a new player $P_i$ has just been corrupted. We know $\text{io}_S$, i.e., all the inputs and outputs that players in $s, i$ have exchanged with the functionality $F$, and we know $\text{Conv}_Z$, that is, the protocol execution as seen by $Z$ until now. Patch now has two tasks that must be solved efficiently:

The first one is to construct a complete view of $P_i$ playing honestly in the protocol until now, and this must be consistent with $io_S$ and $Conv_Z$. In particular, $io_S$ contains the inputs and outputs $P_i$ has exchanged with $F$ and $Conv_Z$ contains the messages that $P_i$ has sent to players who were corrupted earlier. The reason why this can be feasible for, e.g., protocols based on secret sharing is that the corrupted players (actually, $Z$) have seen less than $t$ shares of the secrets of $P_i$. This leaves the secrets undetermined, so when we now learn the actual secret values of $P_i$ (from $io_S$), we are able to create a full set of shares that is consistent with the secrets and the shares of the corrupt players.

The second task is to create a new state for the simulator $S$. This must be the state as it would have looked if we had run $S$ with all players in $s, i$ being corrupt from the start, but where $P_i$ plays honestly until the current point in time.

We point out that UC proofs in the existing literature often use a strategy for building a static simulator $S$ that actually makes both tasks easier: Initially, $S$ sets up a internally copies of the honest players in the protocol, and gives them dummy inputs. It now simulates by letting these "virtual players" execute the protocol with the corrupt players (controlled by $Z$). The state of $S$ is simply the state of the virtual players. Now, when $P_i$ is corrupted, Patch will compute how the view of the virtual copy of $P_i$ should change, now that we know its actual inputs, and will then update the state of the other virtual players to make everything consistent, including $io_S$ and $Conv_Z$. This creates the required view of $P_i$ and the new state of $S$ is the state of the updated virtual players, except that of $P_i$. It is not hard to see that if one can show that Patch generates correctly distributed states for the internal players, given $io_S$ and $Conv_Z$, then Theorem 1 applies and we get adaptive security.

**Extension to Statistical Security.** It is not clear that Theorem 1 is true for statistical security in general. But it not hard to see that it holds in an important special case: suppose we can define an "error event" $E$ such that $E$ occurs with negligible probability, and we can make a static simulator $S$ that simulates perfectly if $E$ does not occur. Then we can redo the proof of Theorem 1 while conditioning throughout on $E$ not occurring. We leave the details to the reader.

# 4    Adaptive UC Security of the BGW Protocol

*The protocol.* For simplicity we will only consider security of the passively secure version of BGW. The analysis extend to the active case using known fairly standard arguments from secret-sharing. We assume the reader is familiar with the protocol but as a reminder, each secret value $a$ in the computation is secret shared using a polynomial $f_a$ of degree at most $t$ of finite field $\mathbb{F}$, where the protocol is secure against corruption of $t$ of the $n$ players, and where $t < n/2$. Each player $P_i$ then holds $f_a(i)$, and $f_a(0) = a$.

To add secret shared values $a, b$, each player $P_i$ locally computes $f_a(i) + f_b(i)$ which effectively means we now have secret shared $a + b$ using polynomial $f_a + f_b$.

To multiply secret shared values $a, b$, each player $P_i$ locally computes $f_a(i)f_b(i) = (f_a f_b)(i)$, and secret shares this value using a random polynomial $g_i$, i.e., he sends $g_i(j)$ to each player $P_j$. Let $r_1, ..., r_n$ be the Lagrange coefficients with the property that $\sum_{i=1}^n r_i h(i) = h(0)$ for any $h$ of degree less than $n$. Then each player $P_j$ computes

$c_j = \sum_{i=1}^n r_i g_i(j)$. If we define $f_c = \sum_{i=1}^n r_i g_i$, then since the degree of $f_a f_b$ is less than $n$, it is not hard to see that $f_c(0) = f_a(0) f_b(0) = ab$ and that $f_c(j) = c_j$ so that we have effectively secret shared the product $c = ab$[6].

Note that since each honest player contributes a random polynomial $g_i$, this protocol ensures that the polynomial used to secret share the product is a random polynomial of degree at most $t$ with the only constraint that it determines $ab$ as the secret.

To compute a function securely, players secret share their inputs, work their way through an arithmetic circuit computing there desired function and finally open the results, by broadcasting their shares. For simplicity we will assume that each player $P_i$ has a single input $x_i$ and we want to compute a single public output $y$.

*The functionality.* The natural functionality one would expect this protocol to implement is one that gets input from all players, computes the desired function and outputs the results to everyone. Such a functionality is clearly input based: as long as the inputs it gets are the same, the result will be the same, regardless of who is corrupted.

*The simulator.* A static simulator for the protocol is very easy to describe: if the player set $A$ is corrupted from the start, then the simulator sets up internally dummy players $\tilde{P}_i$ for each $P_i \notin A$ and gives them dummy inputs. The dummy players will execute the code prescribed by the protocol.

The simulator now lets the dummy players execute the protocol with the players in $A$, who are controlled by the environment. When a player in $A$ secret shares his input, the simulator reconstructs the input from the shares that are sent to the honest (dummy) players, and passes these inputs to the functionality. This gives a perfect simulation of all steps up to the phase where outputs are opened: the environment never sees more than $t$ shares of any value held by honest players, and hence in its view, there is no difference between dummy and real players.

When an output $y$ is about to be opened, the simulator gets the correct output $y$ from the functionality. The players hold a polynomial $f_{y'}$ that represents the output, but of course we cannot expect that $y' = y$ since $y'$ was computed from dummy inputs. The simulator therefore computes a polynomial $g$ of degree at most $t$ with the property that $g(0) = y - y'$ and $g(i) = 0$ for all $P_i \in A$. Note that if less than $t$ players are corrupted these constraints do not determine $g$, so a random polynomial satisfying the constraints is chosen.

The simulator now pretends that in fact the polynomial $f_y = f_{y'} + g$ is held by the players, which is possible as only the state of dummy players need to be changed. Now the opening will indeed determine the correct $y$.

It is very easy to see that this is a perfect static simulator and that it is conversation based.

*An assumption on the circuit.* Before we continue we describe an assumption we will make on the structure of the circuit: we will assume that each output comes directly

---

[6] This is actually not quite the original BGW multiplication protocol, but it is simpler to consider this variant for our purposes. As discussed in the introduction, it is in fact unclear where the protocol can be proven adaptively secure without this modification.

out of a multiplication gate. This will make the proof below much easier and is perhaps even essential. This can be assumed essentially without loss of generality: we can just add multiplication by dummy value 1 if needed. The effect of this assumption is that the polynomial that is opened is random of degree at most $t$ with the only constraint that it determines the correct output. In particular it is independent of all random choices made by players earlier.

*Patching the views.* We now show how to construct the procedure Patch that is required before we can use our main theorem to conclude adaptive security. So we assume that a player $P_k$ may be corrupted in any round during the protocol. If this happens, the simulator learns the true value of the input $x_k$ and then it has to show the internal state of $P_k$ to the environment. For this, we patch the state of $\tilde{P}_k$ so that it is consistent with $x_k$ and the rest of the values shown to the environment during the execution. Also the state of the remaining dummy players must be patched to be consistent with the state we created for $P_k$. We can then continue the static simulation from this point.

We describe here the case where $P_k$ gets corrupted after the protocol is completed. Then, handling corruption at an earlier stage will simply consist of only doing a smaller part of the patching steps (namely up to the point where the player gets corrupted). Basically, the way to patch the state is to recompute every honest dummy player's share which is affected by the input of $P_k$, while not changing any of the shares that corrupted players have seen. This is done as follows:

- *Input Sharing.* Based on $x_k$ we compute a new random secret sharing of $x_k$ which is consistent with the (strictly less than $t$) shares shown to the environment and $f_{x_k}(0) = x_k$ and updates the shares of the dummy players to be consistent with $f_{x_k}$.
- *Addition or Multiplication by a constant.* Here the players only do local computations so we can simply recompute all the shares of dummy players which were affected by $f_{x_k}$.
- *Multiplication.* The first round in the processing of a multiplication gate only has local computations and hence, we recompute local value as above. Then in the second round, new shares are distributed of the product of two polynomials $f_a f_b$. If $f_{x_k}$ is involved in one of these polynomials, we compute a new random secret sharing of $f_a(0)f_b(0)$ as it did for $x_k$ in input sharing. In the third and last round the simulator is again able to recompute the shares of the dummy parties by local computations. Recall that the recombination vector is independent of $(f_a f_b)(X)$; it is the same for all polynomials of degree at most $n$, so it is indeed possible to redo this step with the new product.
- *Output Reconstruction.* We are given the correct output value $y$. Note that the environment has already seen (points on) a polynomial $f_y$ that was created earlier. Therefore we must patch the state such that $P_k$ ends up holding $f_y(k)$ as his share. Recall that in the real protocol, $f_y$ is produced by the multiplication gate protocol. Our patching procedure applied to this gate produces a polynomial $f_i$ for each player, and then the local recombination step determines a polynomial $f = \sum_{i \in S} r_i f_i$. Since the patching never changes the shares of players in $C$, we have $f_{y_j}(i) = f(i)$ for each $P_i \in C$. But we also need that $f_{y_j}(k) = f(k)$, and this is not guaranteed.

To correct for this, note that there must exist an honest player $P_{i_0}$ such that $r_{i_0} \neq 0$, otherwise the corrupt players could reconstruct the product on their own. We now choose a random polynomial $g$ of degree at most $t$, subject to

$$g(0) = 0, \quad g(i) = 0 \text{ for all } P_i \in C, \text{ and } g(k) = r_{i_0}^{-1}(f_{y_j}(k) - f(k)).$$

This is possible since at most $t - 1$ players could be corrupted before $P_k$, so we fix the value of $g$ in at most $t + 1$ points. We now adjust the state of dummy player $\tilde{P}_{i_0}$, such that we replace its polynomial $f_{i_0}$ by $f_{i_0} + g$. This keeps the state of $P_{i_0}$ internally consistent because $f_{i_0}(0) = (f_{i_0} + g)(0)$, and the shares of players in $C$ are unchanged. However, we have now replaced $f$ by $f + r_{i_0}g$, and clearly $(f + r_{i_0}g)(k) = f_{y_j}(k)$ as desired.

It is not hard to see that Patch as described above indeed produces polynomials for $P_k$ and the remaining dummy players that are random, subject to the constraint that they are consistent with $x_k$, and the adversary's view so far. We therefore conclude that the protocol is adaptively secure.

*Is the assumption on the circuit necessary?* The intuitive reason why the above proof technique needs the assumption that every output value comes from a multiplication gate is as follows: When Patch is started, the environment has already been shown $P_k$'s share of the output $y$, and this share is a result of a random choice that was made by the static simulator earlier. But now Patch produces a view for $P_k$ starting from the input $x_k$ and working its way forward through the protocol, making several random choices underway. This also leads to a share of $y$, but there is no reason to expect that it will agree with the one the environment has seen, as it should. However, because the polynomial used for $y$ is produced from independent random choices from all honest players, we can adjust the random choice of a dummy player so that $P_k$'s view will indeed lead to the right share of $y$.

One way to see this is on a higher level is as follows: what Patch needs to do is find random choices for $P_k$ and the dummy players that are solutions to a set of equations that describe what the choices must satisfy (namely the resulting views are consistent with $x_k$ and the view of the environment). The multiplication gate assumption implies that the equations are linear and easy to solve, and so certainly simplifies the proof.

If we do not make this assumption, the resulting equations do still have a solution, because static security implies adaptive security in the MR definition, and this essentially means that there is a patching procedure, which however is not guaranteed to be efficient. At the time of writing, it is open whether an efficient solution exists. Note that since the local computations of players involve multiplications, it is not clear that the equations one needs to solve are linear.

# References

1. Asharov, G., Lindell, Y.: A full proof of the bgw protocol for perfectly-secure multiparty computation. IACR Cryptology ePrint Archive 2011, 136 (2011)
2. Beaver, D.: Foundations of secure interactive computing. In: Feigenbaum, J. (ed.) CRYPTO 1991. LNCS, vol. 576, pp. 377–391. Springer, Heidelberg (1992)

3. Ben-Or, M., Goldwasser, S., Wigderson, A.: Completeness theorems for non-cryptographic fault-tolerant distributed computation (extended abstract). In: Proceedings of the Twentieth Annual ACM Symposium on Theory of Computing, pp. 1–10 (1988)
4. Bendlin, R., Damgård, I., Orlandi, C., Zakarias, S.: Semi-homomorphic encryption and multiparty computation. In: Paterson, K.G. (ed.) EUROCRYPT 2011. LNCS, vol. 6632, pp. 169–188. Springer, Heidelberg (2011)
5. Canetti, R.: Universally composable security: A new paradigm for cryptographic protocols. In: 42nd Annual Symposium on Foundations of Computer Science, Las Vegas, Nevada, October 14-17, pp. 136–145. IEEE (2001)
6. Canetti, R., Damgård, I., Dziembowski, S., Ishai, Y., Malkin, T.: Adaptive versus non-adaptive security of multi-party protocols. J. Cryptology 17(3), 153–207 (2004)
7. Canetti, R., Feige, U., Goldreich, O., Naor, M.: Adaptively secure multi-party computation. In: Proceedings of the Twenty-Eighth Annual ACM Symposium on the Theory of Computing, Philadelphia, Pennsylvania, May 22-24, pp. 639–648 (1996)
8. Canetti, R., Lindell, Y., Ostrovsky, R., Sahai, A.: Universally composable two-party and multi-party secure computation. In: Proceedings of the Thirty-Fourth Annual ACM Symposium on the Theory of Computing, Montreal, Quebec, Canada, pp. 494–503 (2002)
9. Chaum, D., Crépeau, C., Damgård, I.: Multiparty unconditionally secure protocols (extended abstract). In: Proceedings of the Twentieth Annual ACM Symposium on Theory of Computing, Chicago, Illinois, May 2-4, pp. 11–19 (1988)
10. Cramer, R., Damgård, I., Dziembowski, S., Hirt, M., Rabin, T.: Efficient multiparty computations secure against an adaptive adversary. In: Stern, J. (ed.) EUROCRYPT 1999. LNCS, vol. 1592, pp. 311–326. Springer, Heidelberg (1999)
11. Damgård, I., Pastro, V., Smart, N., Zakarias, S.: Multiparty computation from somewhat homomorphic encryption. In: Safavi-Naini, R., Canetti, R. (eds.) CRYPTO 2012. LNCS, vol. 7417, pp. 643–662. Springer, Heidelberg (2012)
12. Goldreich, O., Micali, S., Wigderson, A.: How to play any mental game or a completeness theorem for protocols with honest majority. In: Proceedings of the Nineteenth Annual ACM Symposium on Theory of Computing, New York City, May 25-27, pp. 218–229 (1987)
13. Maurer, U.: Constructive cryptography – A new paradigm for security definitions and proofs. In: Mödersheim, S., Palamidessi, C. (eds.) TOSCA 2011. LNCS, vol. 6993, pp. 33–56. Springer, Heidelberg (2012)
14. Micali, S., Rogaway, P.: Secure computation. In: Feigenbaum, J. (ed.) CRYPTO 1991. LNCS, vol. 576, pp. 392–404. Springer, Heidelberg (1992)
15. Nielsen, J.B., Nordholt, P.S., Orlandi, C., Burra, S.S.: A new approach to practical active-secure two-party computation. In: Safavi-Naini, R., Canetti, R. (eds.) CRYPTO 2012. LNCS, vol. 7417, pp. 681–700. Springer, Heidelberg (2012)
16. Pfitzmann, B., Schunter, M., Waidner, M.: Secure reactive systems. Technical Report RZ 3206. IBM Research, Zürich (May 2000)

# Impossibility of Surjective Icart-Like Encodings

Mehdi Tibouchi

NTT Secure Platform Laboratories, Japan
tibouchi.mehdi@lab.ntt.co.jp

**Abstract.** Many cryptographic protocols based on elliptic curves rely on the possibility of representing integer values or bit strings as elliptic curve points, or vice versa, in an invertible way. The most practical approach proposed to achieve this for an elliptic curve $E/\mathbb{F}_q$ has been the use of (piecewise) algebraic maps $f\colon \mathbb{F}_q \to E(\mathbb{F}_q)$ called (deterministic, constant-time) "encoding functions", for which numerous constructions have been proposed in recent years, starting with the very simple encoding of Boneh and Franklin (CRYPTO 2001), which maps a value $u \in \mathbb{F}_q$ to $\big((u^2 - b)^{1/3}, u\big)$ on the elliptic curve $E\colon y^2 = x^3 + b$ over $\mathbb{F}_q$, $q \equiv 2 \bmod 3$. That encoding is almost a bijection between $\mathbb{F}_q$ and $E(\mathbb{F}_q)$, which makes it very convenient for security proofs, as well as for applications like covertness, but it is only defined for a very limited class of elliptic curves, all of them supersingular, and hence quite inefficient.

Since then, many other encoding functions have been proposed, and constructions are known for all elliptic curves. They fit into two broad families: Icart-like encodings, which are generalizations of the original Boneh–Franklin encoding starting with a construction due to Icart (CRYPTO 2009), and SWU-like encodings, related to the Shallue–van de Woestijne construction (ANTS 2006). So far, however, almost none of these numerous encodings has replicated the very useful bijectivity property of the Boneh–Franklin encoding.

In this paper, we focus on Icart-like encodings, and investigate the possibility of constructing such encodings $f\colon \mathbb{F}_q \to E(\mathbb{F}_q)$ that are almost bijective like Boneh and Franklin's, or achieve a weaker property like "almost surjectivity" (in the sense that $\#f(\mathbb{F}_q) = q + o(q)$). And we show that the lack of such constructions is no wonder: almost surjective Icart-like encoding cannot exist to non-supersingular elliptic curves.

## 1 Introduction

**Hashing to Elliptic Curves.** Many elliptic curve-based, and particularly pairing-based, cryptographic protocols require hashing to an elliptic curve group $\mathbb{G}$: they involve one or more hash functions $\mathfrak{H}\colon \{0,1\}^* \to \mathbb{G}$ mapping arbitrary values to points on the elliptic curve. For example, in the Boneh-Franklin identity-based encryption scheme [4], the public key for identity id $\in \{0,1\}^*$ is a point $Q_{\mathrm{id}} = \mathfrak{H}(\mathrm{id})$ on the curve. This is also the case in many other pairing-based cryptosystems including IBE and HIBE schemes [1,23,27], signature and identity-based signature schemes [3,5,6,10,42], identity-based signcryption schemes [7,32], passwords-based

S.S.M. Chow et al. (Eds.): ProvSec 2014, LNCS 8782, pp. 29–39, 2014.

authentication protocols such as SPEKE [29] and PAK [8], as well as various signature schemes based on the hardness of the discrete logarithm problem, like [11], when they are instantiated over elliptic curves.

In all of those cases, the hash functions are modeled as random oracles in security proofs, but instantiating them in practice is not so easy. Boneh and Franklin used an elliptic curve of a quite special form:

$$E\colon y^2 = x^3 + b \tag{1}$$

over a finite field $\mathbb{F}_q$ with $q \equiv 2 \pmod 3$, and defined their hash function $\mathfrak{H}\colon \{0,1\}^* \to E(\mathbb{F}_q)$ as $\mathfrak{H}(m) = f(\mathfrak{h}(m))$ for some random oracle $\mathfrak{h}$ to $\mathbb{F}_q$ (for which reasonable candidates can be proposed) and the function $f\colon \mathbb{F}_q \to E(\mathbb{F}_q)$ defined by:

$$f(u) = \big((u^2 - b)^{1/3}, u\big).$$

The function $f$ is almost a bijection between $\mathbb{F}_q$ and $E(\mathbb{F}_q)$ (it is injective and only misses the point at infinity), which makes it easy to establish that the hash function $\mathfrak{H}$ is indifferentiable from a random oracle, and hence let security proofs go through. Unfortunately, the curve (1) is supersingular, and hence unsuitable for most applications as it requires much larger parameters than usual to achieve the same security, due to the Menezes–Okamoto–Vanstone attack [33].

**Elliptic Curve Point Encodings.** Later on, the problem of constructing "encoding functions" $f$ using algebraic techniques to map base field elements $u \in \mathbb{F}_q$ to elliptic curve points $f(u) \in E(\mathbb{F}_q)$ for more general classes of elliptic curves $E/\mathbb{F}_q$ received considerable amount of attention. A number of methods [37,41,34,9,30,18,14,12,20,2] have been proposed to construct such functions $f$, including, in particular, a method due to Shallue and van de Woestijne [36] which applies to essentially all isomorphism classes of elliptic curves, and one due to Icart [28] which is a broad generalization of the Boneh–Franklin appraoch.

In fact, as observed by Farashahi et al. [15], one can roughly classify proposed constructions into two types: Icart's function and its variants, collectively known as "Icart-type encodings" on the one hand, and Shallue and van de Woestijne's construction and its variants, known as SWU-type encodings (or Skałba-type encodings in the terminology of [38, Ch. 3]). The classification of Farashahi et al. was somewhat informal, but can be formalized as follows, as suggested in [38,39].

For Icart-type encodings, which comprise about half of all proposed constructions (including [4,28,30,14,12,13]), there exists a diagram:

$$\begin{array}{ccc}
 & C & \\
{\scriptstyle \pi}\swarrow & & \downarrow{\scriptstyle h} \\
\mathbb{P}^1 & \cdots\cdots\cdots\cdots\!\!\!\!\!\raisebox{1pt}{$\rightarrow$} & E \\
 & {\scriptstyle f = h \circ \pi^{-1}} &
\end{array} \tag{2}$$

where $h\colon C \to E$ is a covering of $E$ over $\mathbb{F}_q$, and $\pi\colon C \to \mathbb{P}^1$ induces a *bijection on points* (it is an *exceptional cover* of $\mathbb{P}^1$ in the terminology of Fried [21]). The map

$f \colon \mathbb{F}_q \subset \mathbb{P}^1(\mathbb{F}_q) \to E(\mathbb{F}_q)$ can then be defined on points as $h \circ \pi^{-1}$. Recently, Couveignes and Lercier [13] proposed a more systematic study of a subset of such constructions, which they call "parametrizations", where the morphism $\pi$ is required to be multiradical.

The other class, SWU-type encodings (including [37,36,41,9,18,20,2]), arise from several coverings:

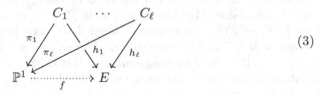

(3)

where the $\pi_i$'s are no longer bijections on points, but simply satisfy that $\pi_1\big(C_1(\mathbb{F}_q)\big) \cup \cdots \cup \pi_\ell\big(C_\ell(\mathbb{F}_q)\big) = \mathbb{P}^1(\mathbb{F}_q)$. The map $f \colon \mathbb{F}_q \subset \mathbb{P}^1(\mathbb{F}_q) \to E(\mathbb{F}_q)$ can then be defined on points as $f(u) = h_i\big(\pi_i^{-1}(u)\big)$ for the first index $i$ such that $u \in \pi_i\big(C_i(\mathbb{F}_q)\big)$. For all existing constructions of this type, the function fields of the coverings $\pi_i$ are linearly disjoint quadratic extensions of $\mathbb{F}_q(u)$, so that membership in the images $\pi_i\big(C_i(\mathbb{F}_q)\big)$ (and their various Boolean combinations) can be determined efficiently by evaluating quadratic characters.

Constructions of the same form have also been considered for obtaining maps $f \colon \mathbb{F}_q \to X(\mathbb{F}_q)$ to points on curves $X/\mathbb{F}_q$ of higher genus (especially hyperelliptic curves of genus 2, since they are the most cryptographically significant).

**Using Point Encodings.** Unfortunately, almost none of the constructions mentioned above achieves the property that the Boneh–Franklin function had of being almost a bijection. For example, it was shown in [16,19] that Icart's function reaches a proportion of $\approx 5/8$ of all points on its target curves, and similar techniques can be used to prove that each individual construction reaches a constant fraction of all curve points, strictly less than 1. The only exception besides Boneh–Franklin is the genus 1 Fouque–Tibouchi encoding [20], whose target curve is also supersingular.

A consequence of this lack of surjectivity is that the encoding functions to ordinary curves cannot be used with the Boneh–Franklin hash function construction to obtain indifferentiable hashing. If $f \colon \mathbb{F}_q \to E(\mathbb{F}_q)$ is Icart's function, or any of the other encodings to ordinary curves, then $\mathfrak{H}(m) = f\big(\mathfrak{h}(m)\big)$ is easy to distinguish from a random oracle even when $\mathfrak{h}$ is modeled as a random oracle to $\mathbb{F}_q$, just by checking whether the point falls in the relatively small image or not (testing for that is easy due to the algebraic nature of $f$).

It was shown by Brier et al. [9] in the case of Icart's function and by Farashahi et al. [15] in general that indifferentiable hashing can nonetheless be achieved with all of those functions $f$ using the more involved construction

$$\mathfrak{H}(m) = f\big(\mathfrak{h}_1(m)\big) + f\big(\mathfrak{h}_2(m)\big), \tag{4}$$

where $\mathfrak{h}_1$ and $\mathfrak{h}_2$ are independent random oracles to $\mathbb{F}_q$. However, this comes at the efficiency cost of requiring *two* evaluations of the function $f$ (which usually have a complexity of one base field exponentiation each) instead of one for almost surjective constructions like Boneh and Franklin's.

More recently, another application of point encoding functions to elliptic curves has surfaced: the problem of representing curve points as uniform random bit strings, in order to obtain covertness guarantees for elliptic curve cryptographic protocols used in anonymity or censorship circumvention applications (e.g. to make network traffic using ECC indistinguishable from random traffic). One idea, introduced by Bernstein et al. in [2], is to use an *injective* encoding function $f\colon \mathbb{F}_q \to E(\mathbb{F}_q)$ (examples of which have been proposed by Farashahi [14], Fouque et al. [17] and Bernstein et al. themselves), and represent a random point in $E(\mathbb{F}_q)$ as its unique preimage under $f$ if it exists, using rejection sampling on points which are not in the image of $f$. We then proposed a variant of that idea in [40], supporting arbitrary curves and avoiding rejection sampling by taking preimages under $F\colon (u, v) \mapsto f(u) + f(v)$ instead (which is almost surjective and has the requisite statistical properties by the results of Farashahi et al.).

**Almost Surjective Encodings.** It is easy to see that both elliptic curve hashing and uniform bit string representation would be greatly simplified and significantly enhanced, from a performance viewpoint, if one could construct "almost surjective" encodings like Boneh and Franklin's to a larger class of elliptic curves, particularly ordinary (i.e. non-supersingular) curves. More precisely, if an encoding function $f\colon \mathbb{F}_q \to E(\mathbb{F}_q)$ has a large image in the sense that

$$\#f(\mathbb{F}_q) \geq \#E(\mathbb{F}_q) \cdot \big(1 - \mathrm{negl}(q)\big) = q \cdot \big(1 - \mathrm{negl}(q)\big), \tag{5}$$

then it is *regular*, i.e. the distribution of $f(u)$ for a close to uniform $u \in \mathbb{F}_q$ is statistically close to uniform in $E(\mathbb{F}_q)$. If it admits the algebraic description discussed above (of the form (2) or (3) with geometric maps of bounded degrees), it is then easy to check using the framework of Brier et al. [9] that, like in the Boneh–Franklin case, $\mathfrak{H}\colon m \mapsto f\big(\mathfrak{h}(m)\big)$ is a hash function construction indifferentiable from a random oracle when $\mathfrak{h}$ is modeled as a random oracle to $\mathbb{F}_q$: this is simpler and typically twice as fast as construction (4). Similarly, one gets an efficient close-to-uniform bit string representation algorithm for points in $E(\mathbb{F}_q)$ by simply taking preimages under $f$: this is like Bernstein et al.'s approach without the need for rejection sampling, and our approach without the overhead from the more complicated function $F$.

In many ways, "almost surjective" encodings, if they exist, are thus optimal from an efficiency standpoint and make simpler constructions possible. But we know no example of them at all to ordinary curves. It is thus natural to ask whether such functions can exist.

The goal of this paper is to partially settle this question in the negative. More precisely, we prove that almost surjective encodings *of Icart-type* (2) can only exist to elliptic curves which are supersingular, even if we relax the surjectivity condition (5) to something weaker like $\#f(\mathbb{F}_q) = q + o(q)$. We conjecture that the impossibility result also holds for SWU-type encodings, but that case is not covered by our proof.

## 2  Almost Surjective Encodings of Icart Type

The original method proposed by Boneh and Franklin for hashing to the (supersingular) elliptic curve $E\colon y^2 = x^3 + b$ over $\mathbb{F}_q$ with $q \equiv 2 \pmod 3$ was considerably simpler that other approaches considered later in the literature, including in the previous sections of this paper: namely, simply map a value $u \in \mathbb{F}_q$ to the well-defined curve point $((u^2 - b)^{1/3}, u) \in E(\mathbb{F}_q)$. This map is essentially bijective, and its inverse $(x, y) \mapsto y$ can also be used for efficient point representation without rejection sampling.

The important property of that map, making those particularly simple constructions possible, is that it is almost surjective: it reaches all but negligibly few points on $E(\mathbb{F}_q)$ (in that case, all but one), and in particular, its image size is $q + o(q)$. It is thus natural to ask whether a similar map can be constructed for a more general class of elliptic curves, particularly ordinary curves, and this section aims to settle that question in the negative.

More precisely, consider an elliptic curve $E/\mathbb{F}_q$ and an encoding $f\colon \mathbb{F}_q \to E(\mathbb{F}_q)$ of *Icart type*, i.e. constructed, like Icart's function [28] and Boneh and Franklin's function above, as described in (2): there exists a (smooth, proper, geometrically integral) curve $C/\mathbb{F}_q$ and branched covers $h\colon C \to E$, $\pi\colon C \to \mathbb{P}^1$ defined over $\mathbb{F}_q$ such that $\pi$ induces a bijection on points $C(\mathbb{F}_q) \xrightarrow{\sim} \mathbb{P}^1(\mathbb{F}_q)$. The encoding $f$ is then defined on $\mathbb{F}_q \subset \mathbb{P}^1(\mathbb{F}_q)$ as $h \circ \pi^{-1}$.

We assume further that the genus $g_C$ of the covering curve and the degree $n = [C : E]$ of the covering $h$ are small compared to $q$; for example, the following bound is sufficient (although usual constructions impose the stronger requirement that $g_C$ and $n$ be bounded independently of $q$):

$$q^{1/2} > 5(n+1)!g_C. \tag{6}$$

Then, we claim that if $f$ is almost surjective, then $E$ must be supersingular. More precisely, we will prove the following.

**Theorem 1.** *Let $E$, $C$ and $f$ be as above, and assume that the bound (6) is satisfied. Then, at least one of the following assertions hold:*

*1. $\#f(\mathbb{F}_q) \le (1 - \frac{1}{2n})q$ (and in particular, $f$ is not almost surjective); or*
*2. $\#E(\mathbb{F}_q) = q + 1$ (and in particular, $E$ is supersingular).*

Moreover, while we have assumed that $\pi$ induces a bijection on points, it will be clear from the proof below that this is automatically satisfied whenever $\pi$

itself is almost surjective (which is certainly necessary if we hope to define the encoding $f$ in the manner described above).

The proof idea is as follows. As has been observed in previous papers about the image size of elliptic curve encodings [16,19,20], the Chebotarev density theorem for function fields can be used to obtain estimates on $\#f(\mathbb{F}_q) = \#h\big(C(\mathbb{F}_q)\big) - 1$ in terms of Galois-theoretic properties of the covering $h$. Indeed, if we denote by $(\widehat{G}, G)$ the arithmetic-geometric monodromy pair of the covering (i.e. $\widehat{G}$ is the Galois group of the Galois closure of $\mathbb{F}_q(C)/\mathbb{F}_q(E)$ and $G$ is the subgroup that fixes the field of constants), we have an estimates of the form $\#f(\mathbb{F}_q) = \big(1 - \frac{\#S_0}{\#G}\big)q + O(q^{1/2})$, where $S_0$ is the subset of elements in $\widehat{G}$ that induce the Frobenius automorphism on the field of constants (hence $S_0$ is contained in a coset of $G$) and have no fixed point when regarded as permutations of $\{1, \ldots, n\}$. The implicit constant in the big $O$ depends only on $n$ and $g_C$. A consequence of that estimate is that $f$ can only be almost surjective if $S_0 = \varnothing$, and it was observed by H. W. Lenstra that this condition formally implies that $h$ is a bijection on points over $\mathbb{F}_q$.

A more detailed proof with precise estimates is given in §4 after the necessary background has been introduced in §3.

# 3 Background on the Chebotarev Density Theorem and Exceptional Covers

Consider $h\colon X \to Y$ a branched covering of $\mathbb{F}_q$-curves (i.e. a finite separable morphism) of degree $n = [X : Y]$, and denote by $\widetilde{h}\colon \widetilde{X} \to Y$ its Galois closure. The curve $\widetilde{X}$ need not be defined over $\mathbb{F}_q$: in general, it is defined over a certain extension $\mathbb{F}_{q^m}$. The arithmetic-geometric monodromy pair $(\widehat{G}, G)$ of the covering $h$ is given by $\widehat{G} = \mathrm{Gal}\big(\mathbb{F}_{q^m}(\widetilde{X})/\mathbb{F}_q(Y)\big)$ and $G = \mathrm{Gal}\big(\mathbb{F}_{q^m}(\widetilde{X})/\mathbb{F}_{q^m}(Y)\big)$. $G$ is a normal subgroup of index $m$ in $\widehat{G}$ and the quotient $\widehat{G}/G \cong \mathrm{Gal}(\mathbb{F}_{q^m}/\mathbb{F}_q)$ is cyclic, generated by the Frobenius automorphism $\phi_q\colon x \mapsto x^q$ of $\mathbb{F}_{q^m}$.

As we have mentioned, our approach relies on the Chebotarev density theorem to estimate the size of the image of $h$ on points. We use the following effective estimate due to Kumar Murty and Scherk [31], where for any subset $S \subset \widehat{G}$ stable under conjugation, we let $N_Y(S)$ be the number of unramified $\mathbb{F}_q$-points $y$ of $Y$ such that the Frobenius conjugacy class $\sigma_y \subset \widehat{G}$ of $\widetilde{h}$ at $y$ is contained in $S$. The number of unramified $\mathbb{F}_q$-points of $Y$ is denoted by $N_Y$ (hence, $N_Y = N_Y(\widehat{G}) = N_Y(\phi_q G)$), and $g_{\widetilde{X}}, g_Y$ are the genera of the curves $\widetilde{X}, Y$ respectively.

**Lemma 1.** *Let $\mathscr{C} \subset \widehat{G}$ be a conjugacy class whose restriction to the quotient $\widehat{G}/G = \mathrm{Gal}(\mathbb{F}_{q^m}/\mathbb{F}_q)$ is $\phi_q$. Then:*

$$\left| N_Y(\mathscr{C}) - \frac{\#\mathscr{C}}{\#G} N_Y \right| \le 2 g_{\widetilde{X}} \frac{\#\mathscr{C}}{\#\widehat{G}} q^{1/2} + 2(2g_Y + 1)\#\mathscr{C} q^{1/2} + 4\#\mathscr{C} \cdot (g_{\widetilde{X}} + \#\widehat{G}).$$

Now, we can give an estimate of the size of the image of $h$ on points in those terms. Indeed, an unramified $\mathbb{F}_q$-point $y$ of $Y$ is in $h(X(\mathbb{F}_q))$ if and only if any element in the Frobenius class $\sigma_y$ (whose restriction to $\mathrm{Gal}(\mathbb{F}_{q^m}/\mathbb{F}_q)$ is necessarily $\phi_q$, since $y$ is defined over $\mathbb{F}_q$) acts on the geometric fiber at $y$ with at least one fixed point, and moreover, the number of fixed points is the number of $\mathbb{F}_q$-points of $X$ above $y$.[1] As a result, there are exactly $N_Y(S_1 \cup \cdots \cup S_n)$ unramified points in $h(X(\mathbb{F}_q))$, where $S_k \subset \phi_q G$ is the set of elements in $\widehat{G}$ whose restriction to $\mathrm{Gal}(\mathbb{F}_{q^m}/\mathbb{F}_q)$ is $\phi_q$ and which have exactly $k$ fixed point when considered as permutations of the $n$-element transitive $\widehat{G}$-set $\widehat{G}/H$ ($H = \mathrm{Gal}\big(\mathbb{F}_{q^m}(\widetilde{X})/\mathbb{F}_q(X)\big)$). As a result, we obtain:

**Corollary 1.** *Write $s_0 = \#S_0/\#G$. We have:*

$$\big|\#h(X(\mathbb{F}_q)) - (1-s_0)\cdot\#Y(\mathbb{F}_q)\big| \leq 2(g_{\widetilde{X}} + 2g_Y\#\widehat{G} + \widehat{G})q^{1/2} + 4(\#\widehat{G}+1)(g_{\widetilde{X}} + \#\widehat{G}).$$

*Proof.* Let $S_+ = S_1 \cup \cdots \cup S_n = \phi_q G \setminus S_0$. As we have seen, the number of unramified points in $h(X(\mathbb{F}_q))$ is $N_Y(S_+)$. Therefore, if we denote by $d$ the number of points in $Y$ ramified in the covering, we have:

$$\big|\#h(X(\mathbb{F}_q)) - (1-s_0)\cdot\#Y(\mathbb{F}_q)\big| \leq \big|\#h(X(\mathbb{F}_q)) - N_Y(S_+)\big| +$$
$$\big|N_Y(S_+) - (1-s_0)N_Y\big| + (1-s_0)\cdot\big|N_Y - \#Y(\mathbb{F}_q)\big| \leq 2d + \big|N_Y(S_+) - (1-s_0)N_Y\big|.$$

Now, the Riemann–Hurwitz formula for $\widetilde{X} \to Y$ ensures that $d \leq (2g_{\widetilde{X}} - 2) - (2g_Y - 2)\#\widehat{G} \leq 2(g_{\widetilde{X}} + \#\widehat{G})$. Moreover, applying Lemma 1 to each of the conjugacy classes forming a partition of $S_+$ and summing, we get, since $1 - s_0 = \#S_+/\#G$:

$$\big|N_Y(S_+) - (1-s_0)N_Y\big| \leq 2g_{\widetilde{X}}\frac{\#S_+}{\#\widehat{G}}q^{1/2} + 2(2g_Y + 1)\#S_+q^{1/2} + 4\#S_+ \cdot (g_{\widetilde{X}} + \#\widehat{G})$$
$$\leq 2(g_{\widetilde{X}} + 2g_Y\#\widehat{G} + \#\widehat{G})q^{1/2} + 4\#\widehat{G} \cdot (g_{\widetilde{X}} + \#\widehat{G}),$$

where we have used the trivial bound $\#S_+ \leq \#\widehat{G}$. The stated result follows immediately.

We can see from this result that two important cases should be distinguished: $s_0 = 0$ on the one hand, and $s_0 > 0$ on the other hand.

In the first case, we say that $h$ is an *exceptional cover* [25]. All permutations in $\phi_q G$ have at least one fixed point, and it is then an elementary group-theoretic result that they all have *exactly one* fixed point[2] (see [22, Lemma 13.1]); as a result, all unramified $\mathbb{F}_q$-points of $Y$ have exactly one $\mathbb{F}_q$-point of $X$ lying

---

[1] One can in fact state a more general result that also gives the number of $\mathbb{F}_q$-points of $X$ above ramified $\mathbb{F}_q$-points $y$, see e.g. [24, Lemma 2.2].

[2] In particular, when $X \to Y$ is a nontrivial covering which is *geometric* (i.e. $G = \widehat{G}$), $\phi_q G = G$ contains the identity which has $n > 1$ fixed points, and therefore it can never happen that $s_0 = 0$. This observation dates back to Jordan, and has many interesting consequences [35].

above them, and one can show that the same is true for ramified points as well. Hence, the following holds (this is a special case of [24, Lemma 2.3]; see also [25, Theorem 1.1] for a more general statement, also due to Lenstra, that applies to higher dimensional varieties as well).

**Lemma 2 (H. W. Lenstra).** *If $s_0 = 0$, then $h$ induces a bijection $X(\mathbb{F}_q) \xrightarrow{\sim} Y(\mathbb{F}_q)$.*

In the second, non-exceptional case, we clearly have $s_0 \geq 1/\#G \geq 1/n!$, but it turns out that a much stronger bound holds, as has been shown by Guralnick and Wan [26, Lemma 3.4].

**Lemma 3 (Guralnick–Wan).** *If $s_0 \neq 0$, then $s_0 \geq 1/n$.*

Finally, we will use the following technical upper bound on the genus $g_{\widetilde{X}}$ of the Galois closure in terms of $n$ and the genera $g_X, g_Y$ of $X$ and $Y$ themselves. It follows from the Riemann–Hurwitz formula and Hilbert's formula for the degree of the ramification divisor.

**Lemma 4 ([25, Lemma 4.5]).** $g_{\widetilde{X}} \leq 1 + \#G \cdot \dfrac{g_X - 1 - (n-2)(g_Y - 1)}{2}$.

## 4   Proof of Theorem 1

We now turn to the proof of Theorem 1. Denote by $(\widehat{G}, G)$ the arithmetic-geometric monodromy group pair of the covering $h\colon C \to E$, by $\widetilde{h}\colon \widetilde{C} \to E$ the Galois closure of the covering, and by $s_0$, as above, the proportion of elements in $\phi_q G$ which have no fixed point as permutations of the $n$-element $\widehat{G}$-set $\widehat{G}/H$ (where $H$ is the Galois group of $\widetilde{C} \to C$).

As we have just seen, two cases can happen: either $h\colon C \to E$ is an exceptional cover ($s_0 = 0$) or not ($s_0 \neq 0$). In the first case, Lemma 2 ensures that $h$ induces a bijection on points $C(\mathbb{F}_q) \xrightarrow{\sim} E(\mathbb{F}_q)$. Since, on the other hand, $\pi\colon C \to \mathbb{P}^1$ also induces a bijection on points over $\mathbb{F}_q$, we get $\#E(\mathbb{F}_q) = \#C(\mathbb{F}_q) = \#\mathbb{P}^1(\mathbb{F}_q) = q + 1$, and thus, assertion 2 of Theorem 1 is satisfied.

In the second, non-exceptional case, Lemma 3 ensures that $s_0 \geq 1/n$. As a result, Corollary 1 gives (denoting the genus of $\widetilde{C}$ by $g_{\widetilde{C}}$):

$$
\begin{aligned}
\#f(\mathbb{F}_q) &\leq h\big(C(\mathbb{F}_q)\big) \\
&\leq (1 - 1/n) \cdot \#E(\mathbb{F}_q) + 2(g_{\widetilde{C}} + \#\widehat{G})q^{1/2} + 4(\#\widehat{G} + 1)(g_{\widetilde{C}} + \#\widehat{G}) \\
&\leq (1 - 1/n) \cdot q + \gamma q^{1/2} + \gamma^2 \quad \text{with} \quad \gamma = 2(g_{\widetilde{C}} + \#\widehat{G} + 1),
\end{aligned}
$$

using the Hasse–Weil bound on $\#E(\mathbb{F}_q)$. Hence:

$$
\#f(\mathbb{F}_q) - \left(1 - \frac{1}{2n}\right)q \leq -\frac{1}{2n}q + \gamma q^{1/2} + \gamma^2. \tag{7}
$$

Now, the largest root $t_+$ of the quadratic polynomial $\frac{1}{2n}T^2 - \gamma T - \gamma^2$ is given by:

$$
t_+ = n \cdot \left(\gamma + \sqrt{\gamma^2 + 2\gamma^2/n}\right) \leq n\gamma \cdot (1 + \sqrt{2}) \leq 5n \cdot (g_{\widetilde{C}} + \#\widehat{G} + 1),
$$

since we necessarily have $n \geq 2$ in this case. Moreover, by Lemma 4, we have $g_{\widetilde{C}} \leq 1 + \#G \cdot \frac{g_C - 1}{2}$, so if we bound $\#G$ and $\#\widehat{G}$ trivially by $n!$, we get:

$$t_+ \leq 5n \left( 2 + n! \frac{g_C + 1}{2} \right) \leq 5n \cdot n! g_C + 10n \leq 5(n+1)! g_C.$$

Therefore, by condition (6), we have $q^{1/2} > t_+$, and as a result, the right-hand side of (7) is negative and assertion 1 holds, which completes the proof.

# References

1. Baek, J., Zheng, Y.: Identity-based threshold decryption. In: Bao, F., Deng, R., Zhou, J. (eds.) PKC 2004. LNCS, vol. 2947, pp. 262–276. Springer, Heidelberg (2004)
2. Bernstein, D.J., Hamburg, M., Krasnova, A., Lange, T.: Elligator: Elliptic-curve points indistinguishable from uniform random strings. In: Gligor, V., Yung, M. (eds.) ACM CCS (2013)
3. Boldyreva, A.: Threshold signatures, multisignatures and blind signatures based on the Gap-Diffie-Hellman-group signature scheme. In: Desmedt, Y.G. (ed.) PKC 2003. LNCS, vol. 2567, pp. 31–46. Springer, Heidelberg (2002)
4. Boneh, D., Franklin, M.: Identity-based encryption from the Weil pairing. In: Kilian, J. (ed.) CRYPTO 2001. LNCS, vol. 2139, pp. 213–229. Springer, Heidelberg (2001)
5. Boneh, D., Gentry, C., Lynn, B., Shacham, H.: Aggregate and verifiably encrypted signatures from bilinear maps. In: Biham, E. (ed.) EUROCRYPT 2003. LNCS, vol. 2656, pp. 416–432. Springer, Heidelberg (2003)
6. Boneh, D., Lynn, B., Shacham, H.: Short signatures from the Weil pairing. In: Boyd, C. (ed.) ASIACRYPT 2001. LNCS, vol. 2248, pp. 514–532. Springer, Heidelberg (2001)
7. Boyen, X.: Multipurpose identity-based signcryption (a swiss army knife for identity-based cryptography). In: Boneh, D. (ed.) CRYPTO 2003. LNCS, vol. 2729, pp. 383–399. Springer, Heidelberg (2003)
8. Boyko, V., MacKenzie, P.D., Patel, S.: Provably secure password-authenticated key exchange using Diffie-Hellman. In: Preneel, B. (ed.) EUROCRYPT 2000. LNCS, vol. 1807, pp. 156–171. Springer, Heidelberg (2000)
9. Brier, E., Coron, J.-S., Icart, T., Madore, D., Randriam, H., Tibouchi, M.: Efficient indifferentiable hashing into ordinary elliptic curves. In: Rabin, T. (ed.) CRYPTO 2010. LNCS, vol. 6223, pp. 237–254. Springer, Heidelberg (2010)
10. Cha, J.C., Cheon, J.H.: An identity-based signature from Gap Diffie-Hellman groups. In: Desmedt, Y.G. (ed.) PKC 2003. LNCS, vol. 2567, pp. 18–30. Springer, Heidelberg (2003)
11. Chevallier-Mames, B.: An efficient CDH-based signature scheme with a tight security reduction. In: Shoup, V. (ed.) CRYPTO 2005. LNCS, vol. 3621, pp. 511–526. Springer, Heidelberg (2005)
12. Couveignes, J.M., Kammerer, J.-G.: The geometry of flex tangents to a cubic curve and its parameterizations. J. Symb. Comput. 47(3), 266–281 (2012)
13. Couveignes, J.-M., Lercier, R.: The geometry of some parameterizations and encodings. arXiv:1310.1013 (2013)

14. Farashahi, R.R.: Hashing into Hessian curves. In: Nitaj, A., Pointcheval, D. (eds.) AFRICACRYPT 2011. LNCS, vol. 6737, pp. 278–289. Springer, Heidelberg (2011)
15. Farashahi, R.R., Fouque, P.-A., Shparlinski, I., Tibouchi, M., Voloch, J.F.: Indifferentiable deterministic hashing to elliptic and hyperelliptic curves. Math. Comp. 82(281), 491–512 (2013)
16. Farashahi, R.R., Shparlinski, I.E., Voloch, J.F.: On hashing into elliptic curves. J. Math. Cryptology 3, 353–360 (2010)
17. Fouque, P.-A., Joux, A., Tibouchi, M.: Injective encodings to elliptic curves. In: Boyd, C., Simpson, L. (eds.) ACISP 2013. LNCS, vol. 7959, pp. 203–218. Springer, Heidelberg (2013)
18. Fouque, P.-A., Tibouchi, M.: Deterministic encoding and hashing to odd hyperelliptic curves. In: Joye, M., Miyaji, A., Otsuka, A. (eds.) Pairing 2010. LNCS, vol. 6487, pp. 265–277. Springer, Heidelberg (2010)
19. Fouque, P.-A., Tibouchi, M.: Estimating the size of the image of deterministic hash functions to elliptic curves. In: Abdalla, M., Barreto, P.S.L.M. (eds.) LATINCRYPT 2010. LNCS, vol. 6212, pp. 81–91. Springer, Heidelberg (2010)
20. Fouque, P.-A., Tibouchi, M.: Indifferentiable hashing to Barreto-Naehrig curves. In: Hevia, A., Neven, G. (eds.) LATINCRYPT 2012. LNCS, vol. 7533, pp. 1–17. Springer, Heidelberg (2012)
21. Fried, M.D.: Global construction of general exceptional covers. In: Mullen, G.L., Shiue, P.J. (eds.) Finite Fields: Theory, Applications, and Algorithms. Contemporary Mathematics, vol. 168, pp. 69–100. American Mathematical Society (1994)
22. Fried, M.D., Guralnick, R.M., Saxl, J.: Schur covers and Carlitz's conjecture. Israel J. Math. 82, 157–225 (1993)
23. Gentry, C., Silverberg, A.: Hierarchical ID-based cryptography. In: Zheng, Y. (ed.) ASIACRYPT 2002. LNCS, vol. 2501, pp. 548–566. Springer, Heidelberg (2002)
24. Guralnick, R.M.: Rational maps and images of rational points of curves over finite fields. Irish Math. Soc. Bull. 50, 71–95 (2003)
25. Guralnick, R.M., Tucker, T.J., Zieve, M.E.: Exceptional covers and bijections on rational points. Int. Math. Res. Not., Article ID 004, 19 pages (2007)
26. Guralnick, R.M., Wan, D.: Bounds for fixed point free elements in a transitive group and applications to curves over finite fields. Israel J. Math. 101, 255–287 (1997)
27. Horwitz, J., Lynn, B.: Toward hierarchical identity-based encryption. In: Knudsen, L.R. (ed.) EUROCRYPT 2002. LNCS, vol. 2332, pp. 466–481. Springer, Heidelberg (2002)
28. Icart, T.: How to hash into elliptic curves. In: Halevi, S. (ed.) CRYPTO 2009. LNCS, vol. 5677, pp. 303–316. Springer, Heidelberg (2009)
29. Jablon, D.P.: Strong password-only authenticated key exchange. SIGCOMM Comput. Commun. Rev. 26, 5–26 (1996)
30. Kammerer, J.-G., Lercier, R., Renault, G.: Encoding points on hyperelliptic curves over finite fields in deterministic polynomial time. In: Joye, M., Miyaji, A., Otsuka, A. (eds.) Pairing 2010. LNCS, vol. 6487, pp. 278–297. Springer, Heidelberg (2010)
31. Kumar Murty, V., Scherk, J.: Effective versions of the Chebotarev density theorem for function fields. C. R. Acad. Sci. Paris 319, 523–528 (1994)
32. Libert, B., Quisquater, J.-J.: Efficient signcryption with key privacy from Gap Diffie-Hellman groups. In: Bao, F., Deng, R., Zhou, J. (eds.) PKC 2004. LNCS, vol. 2947, pp. 187–200. Springer, Heidelberg (2004)
33. Menezes, A., Okamoto, T., Vanstone, S.A.: Reducing elliptic curve logarithms to logarithms in a finite field. IEEE Transactions on Information Theory 39(5), 1639–1646 (1993)

34. Sato, H., Hakuta, K.: An efficient method of generating rational points on elliptic curves. J. Math.-for-Industry 1(A), 33–44 (2009)
35. Serre, J.-P.: On a theorem of Jordan. Bull. Amer. Math. Soc. 40(4), 429–440 (2003)
36. Shallue, A., van de Woestijne, C.E.: Construction of rational points on elliptic curves over finite fields. In: Hess, F., Pauli, S., Pohst, M. (eds.) ANTS 2006. LNCS, vol. 4076, pp. 510–524. Springer, Heidelberg (2006)
37. Skałba, M.: Points on elliptic curves over finite fields. Acta Arith. 117, 293–301 (2005)
38. Tibouchi, M.: Hachage vers les courbes elliptiques et cryptanalyse de schémas RSA. PhD thesis, Univ. Paris 7 and Univ. Luxembourg (2011), Introduction in French, main matter in English
39. Tibouchi, M.: Indifferentiable deterministic hashing to elliptic and hyperelliptic curves. In: Batina, L., et al. (eds.) ECC 2013 (2013)
40. Tibouchi, M.: Elligator Squared: Uniform points on elliptic curves of prime order as uniform random strings. In: Christin, N., Safavi-Naini, R. (eds.) Financial Cryptography (to appear, 2014), http://eprint.iacr.org/2014/043
41. Ulas, M.: Rational points on certain hyperelliptic curves over finite fields. Bull. Pol. Acad. Sci. Math. 55(2), 97–104 (2007)
42. Zhang, F., Kim, K.: ID-based blind signature and ring signature from pairings. In: Zheng, Y. (ed.) ASIACRYPT 2002. LNCS, vol. 2501, pp. 533–547. Springer, Heidelberg (2002)

# On the Practical Security Bound of GF-NLFSR Structure with SPN Round Function

Guangyao Zhao[1], Lei Cheng[2], Chao Li[1,2], Ruilin Li[3], and Xuan Shen[2]

[1] College of Computer,
National University of Defense Technology, Changsha 410073 Hunan,
People's Republic of China
securityzgy@163.com
[2] College of Science, National University of Defense Technology,
Changsha 410073 Hunan, People's Republic of China
{chenglei_1111,academic_lc,shenxuan_08}@163.com
[3] College of Electronic Science and Engineering,
National University of Defense Technology,
Changsha 410073 Hunan, People's Republic of China
securitylrl@gmail.com

**Abstract.** At ACISP 2009, Choy *et al.* proposed the generalised Feistel nonlinear feedback shift register structure (GF-NLFSR). The main feature of GF-NLFSR containing $n$ sub-blocks is that it can be parallelized up to $n$-round for implementation, and meanwhile the provable security bound against differential cryptanalysis (DC) and linear cryptanalysis (LC) can be provided for $n+1$ rounds. Thus, it maybe suit for the lightweight encryption environment, such as RFID tags, smart cards, and sensor nodes. The practical security bound of GF-NLFSR with SPN round function was further studied by Yap *et al.* at Africacrypt 2010, where a differential bound for $2nr$-round was provided, while for the linear bound, only partial results for $n = 2, 4$ were presented. In this paper, we eliminate such discrepancy between the practical differential and linear bound of GF-NLFSR with SPN round function by demonstrating that a unified bound could be proved using the "divide and conquer" strategy. We further find a relationship between the truncated differential characteristics and linear characteristics of GF-NLFSR, which builds a nice link between the lower differential bound and linear bound of such construction, and demonstrate that proving the cipher's resistance against either DC or LC is enough to show its resistance against both DC and LC. We hope that the result in the current paper will be useful when designing ciphers based on GF-NLFSR structure with SPN round function.

**Keywords:** cryptography, block cipher, practical security, differential cryptanalysis, linear cryptanalysis, GF-NLFSR, SPN.

## 1 Introduction

Differential cryptanalysis [1] and linear cryptanalysis [2] are the two most important cryptanalytic methods for evaluating the security of modern block ciphers.

S.S.M. Chow et al. (Eds.): ProvSec 2014, LNCS 8782, pp. 40–54, 2014.

And most block cipher constructions are now provided their resistance against DC and LC. There are two general approaches to achieve this goal, the provable security approach [3,4] and the practical security approach [5]. The first one concentrates on the differential [6] probabilities and linear hull [4] probabilities, while the second one focuses on the differential characteristic and linear characteristic probabilities, which generally can be reduced to the lower bound of the number of active S-boxes when the round function is SPN type [7].

The concept of practical security [5] was first proposed by Knudsen at FSE 1994 on Feistel ciphers. By evaluating the lower bound of the number of active S-boxes in differential/linear characteristic [7], Kanda applied such concept on Feistel ciphers with SPN round function, and his approach is based on the exact proof. Recently, many new methods to evaluate such bound are further proposed, such as the Mixed-Integer Linear Programming [8], searching algorithm [9], *etc.* Given the number of sub-blocks $n$ and the number of round $r$, these approaches can be used to calculate the exact lower bound. However, they cannot provide the lower bound for the general numbers $n$ and $r$, and especially with the growth of $n$ and $r$, obtaining the bound would be very time-consuming.

At ACISP 2009, Choy *et al.* proposed a generalised Feistel nonlinear feedback shift register structure (GF-NLFSR) [10]. GF-NLFSR containing $n$ sub-blocks ($n$-cell GF-NLFSR) can be parallelized for up to $n$ rounds. Thus, it may be suitable for the security algorithms in resource-limited environments such as smart cards, RFID tags, and sensor nodes.

Although the security of GF-NLFSR against other cryptanalytic approaches are evaluated by the authors, its resistance against the integral and impossible differential cryptanalysis is carefully studied in [11,12]. Choy *et al.* provided the provable security bound against DC and LC for any $n + 1$ rounds of an $n$-cell GF-NLFSR [10]. In [13], Yap *et al.* further study the practical security bound when GF-NLFSR is instanced with SPN round function. They provide a lower differential bound for $2nr$ consecutive rounds, while for the linear bound, they can only give some partial results for $n = 2, 4$. As an application, they present two new block ciphers known as p-Camellia and p-SMS4, whose encryption speed is improved greatly compared with Camellia and SMS4. For $n = 2$, GF-NLFSR becomes the MISTY structure [14], and it is Li *et al.* in [15] that prove a unified lower bound of the number of differential/linear active S-boxes of any consecutive $4r$-round. However, there is still no general result for $n \geq 3$.

The contribution of this paper is twofold. On one hand, by adopting the "divide and conquer" strategy and studying the propagation of the mask values for various rounds of GF-NLFSR, we present a lower bound of the number of linear active sboxes that is consistent with the differential bound presented in [13] for a general number $n$, and thus eliminate the discrepancy between the differential and linear bound of GF-NLFSR with SPN round function. On the other hand, we find a relationship between the truncated form of differential and linear characteristics, which allows us to simplify the proof of such construction against DC and LC, in other words, providing either the differential bound or linear bound of GF-NLFSR with SPN is enough to show the cipher's resistance against both DC and LC. This result is useful in the cipher design when adopting the GF-NLFSR structure.

This paper is organized as follows: Section 2 introduces some preliminaries, includes some notations, necessary definitions, and a brief introduction of GF-NLFSR. GF-NLFSR's practical security evaluation against LC is given in Section 3. In Section 4, we study the relationship between the truncated form of differential and linear characteristics, which indicates a nice link between the lower linear bound and differential bound of GF-NLFSR with SPN round function. Finally, Section 5 concludes this paper.

## 2    Preliminary

### 2.1    Notations

Let $X = (x_1, x_2, \ldots, x_m), Y = (y_1, y_2, \ldots, y_m) \in \mathbb{F}_{2^d}^m$, where $d$ and $m$ are some integers, we use the following notations in the rest of this paper.

$\Gamma X$: mask value of $X$;

$\Delta X$: difference of $X$ and $X'$, $\Delta X = X \oplus X'$;

$X \oplus Y$: bitwise exclusive-OR (XOR) of $X$ and $Y$;

$X \cdot \Gamma Y$: parity of bitwise product $X$ and $\Gamma Y$.

### 2.2    Definitions

In this subsection, we give several definitions which will be used in the rest of this paper.

**Definition 1.** *A **differential active s-box** is defined as an s-box whose input difference is non-zero, while a **linear active s-box** is defined as an s-box whose output mask value is non-zero. Note that if the s-box is bijective, then such s-box given a non-zero output difference (resp.input mask value) is also a differential (resp. linear) active s-box.*

**Definition 2.** *Let $X = (x_1, x_2, \ldots, x_m) \in \mathbb{F}_{2^d}^m$, then the **bundle weight** of $X$ is defined by*

$$H_w(X) = \#\{i | x_i \neq 0\}.$$

Given a linear transformation $P : \mathbb{F}_2^{md} \to \mathbb{F}_2^{md}$, we use $P$ to denote its matrix presentation and $P^T$ to denote the transpose of $P$.

**Definition 3.** *The **differential branch number** of $P$ is defined as*

$$\mathcal{B}_d = \min_{\Delta X \neq 0} (H_w(\Delta X) + H_w(P \cdot \Delta X)).$$

**Definition 4.** *The **linear branch number** of $P$ is defined as*

$$\mathcal{B}_l = \min_{\Gamma Y \neq 0} (H_w(\Gamma Y) + H_w(P^T \cdot \Gamma Y)).$$

## 2.3   GF-NLFSR

GF-NLFSR was proposed by Choy *et al.* at ACISP 2009. The $i$-th round of GF-NLFSR is shown in Fig. 1. Let $(X_{i-1}, X_i, \ldots, X_{i+n-2})$ be the input of the $i$-th round, then the output is $(X_i, X_{i+1}, \ldots, X_{i+n-1})$, and it satisfies

$$X_{i+n-1} = F(X_{i-1}, K_i) \oplus X_i \oplus X_{i+1} \oplus \cdots \oplus X_{i+n-2},$$

where $F(\cdot, \cdot)$ is the round function and $K_i$ is the round key.

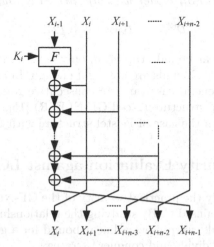

**Fig. 1.** The $i$-th round of $n$-cell GF-NLFSR

In this paper, we only consider SPN-type round function. It contains three layers, *i.e.*, the *round key addition* layer, the *substitution* layer and the *diffusion* layer. The round function can be represented as $F(X, K) = P(S(X \oplus K))$, where,

$$S : \mathbb{F}_{2^d}^m \to \mathbb{F}_{2^d}^m, X = (x_1, x_2, \ldots, x_m) \mapsto Z = S(X) = (s_1(x_1), \ldots, s_m(x_m)),$$
$$P : \mathbb{F}_2^{md} \to \mathbb{F}_2^{md}, Z = (z_1, z_2, \ldots, z_m) \mapsto Y = P(Z) = (y_1, y_2, \ldots, y_m), z_i, y_i \in \mathbb{F}_2^d.$$

Assume that the round-key consists of independent and uniform random bits, and it is XORed with the data, we neglect the effect of the round key addition layer when considering the practical security evaluation of block ciphers. In the rest of this paper, we denote the input (*resp.* output) of the $i$-th round function by $X_{i-1}$ (*resp.* $Y_{i-1}$), and denote the intermediate variable after the substitution layer of the $i$-th round function by $Z_{i-1}$, thus $Y = F(x \oplus K) = F(X) = P(S(X))$, $Z_{i-1} = S(X_{i-1})$ and $Y_{i-1} = P(Z_{i-1})$.

For the $n$-cell GF-NLFSR structure with SPN round function, the **minimum number of linear active S-boxes** over $r$-round is defined by

$$\mathcal{L}^{(r)} = \min_{(\Gamma Y_0, \Gamma Y_1, \ldots, \Gamma Y_{r+1}) \neq (0, 0, \ldots, 0)} \sum_{i=0}^{r-1} H_w(\Gamma Z_i).$$

while the **minimum number of differential active S-boxes** over $r$-round is defined by

$$\mathcal{D}^{(r)} = \min_{(\Delta X_0, \Delta X_1, \ldots, \Delta X_{r+1}) \neq (0,0,\ldots,0)} \sum_{i=0}^{r-1} H_w(\Delta X_i).$$

Yap $et$ $al.$ have presented a result for the minimum number of differential active S-boxes of $n$-cell GF-NLFSR structure.

**Proposition 1.** [1] ([13]) *The minimum number of differential active S-boxes for $2nr$-round $n$-cell GF-NLFSR cipher with bijective SPN round function satisfies*

$$\mathcal{D}^{(2nr)} \geq \mathcal{B}_d \times r + \lfloor r/2 \rfloor.$$

However, for the linear bound, Yap $et$ $al.$ only gave some results for $n = 2, 4$ and $\mathcal{B}_l = 5$ [13], and some bounds are not tight enough. Li $et$ $al.$ presented a new linear bound for the general case (any $4r$ consecutive rounds and no concrete value for $\mathcal{B}_l$) of MISTY structure (2-cell GF-NLFSR) [15], and proved that the bound is consistent with the case of Feistel structure with SPN round function.

# 3   Practical Security Evaluation against LC

In this section, we study the practical security of the GF-NLFSR structure with SPN round function against LC. By studying the relationship of the mask values between different rounds, we present a linear bound for a general number $n$ for GF-NLFSR using the "divide and conquer" strategy.

Similar to the Feistel structure [16,17], there exists a duality between differential characteristic and linear characteristic in GF-NLFSR. Fig. 2 shows the duality of $n$-cell GF-NLFSR. Thus, for a differential characteristic, we have

$$\Delta Y_i = \Delta X_{i+1} \oplus \Delta X_{i+2} \oplus \cdots \oplus \Delta X_{i+n}, i \geq 0. \tag{1}$$

while for a linear characteristic,

$$\Gamma X_{i+n} = \Gamma Y_i \oplus \Gamma Y_{i+1} \oplus \cdots \oplus \Gamma Y_{i+n-1}, i \geq 0. \tag{2}$$

Li $et$ $al.$ have proved the following result:

**Proposition 2.** ( [15]) *Let $\Gamma X_{i-1}$ and $\Gamma Y_{i-1} \neq 0$ be the mask value of the input $X_{i-1}$ and output $Y_{i-1}$ in the $i$-th round, where $i \geq 1$, then*

$$H_w(P^T \cdot \Gamma X_{i-1}) + H_w(P^T \cdot \Gamma Y_{i-1}) \geq \mathcal{B}_l.$$

For convenience, we adopt the following useful definition introduced in [15].

---

[1] This proposition is presented as Theorem 3 in [13] without detail proof.

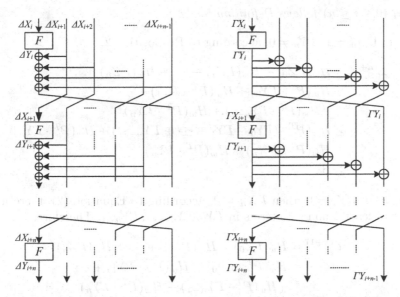

**Fig. 2.** GF-NLFSR structure (Left) and its Dual structure (Right)

**Definition 5.** *For a GF-NLFSR structure with SPN round function, let* $O_r = (Y_i, Y_{i+1}, \ldots, Y_{i+r-1})$ *be the output of the* $(i+1)$*-th,* $(i+2)$*-th, ...,* $(i+r)$*-th round functions, and* $\Gamma O_r = (\Gamma Y_i, \Gamma Y_{i+1}, \ldots, \Gamma Y_{i+r-1})$ *be the corresponding mask value of* $O_r$*, then the truncated form (or pattern) of* $\Gamma O_r$ *is defined by a binary sequence* $(a_i, a_{i+1}, \ldots, a_{i+r-1})$*, where* $a_{i+j} = 0$ *if* $\Gamma Y_{i+j} = 0$ *and* $a_{i+j} = 1$ *if* $\Gamma Y_{i+j} \neq 0$*,* $j = 0, 1, \ldots, r-1$*.*

In this paper, we do not consider the trivial (all zero) case for any $(n+1)$-round linear characteristic, since for the $(i+1)$-th round, if $\Gamma Y_i \neq 0$, we will have $\Gamma X_i \neq 0$, and there exist at least 2 non-zero terms in Equation (2), thus the pattern of any $(n+1)$-round linear characteristic satisfies:

$$\sum_{j=0}^{n} a_{i-j} \geq 2, \quad i \geq n. \tag{3}$$

where $a_{i-j}$ $(0 \leq j \leq n)$ follows Definition 5.

Based on Equation (2) and Proposition 2, we can obtain the following Lemma:

**Lemma 1.** *The minimum number of linear active S-boxes for any consecutive* $n+1$ *rounds ( w.l.o.g., denote from 0 to n) n-cell GF-NLFSR cipher with SPN round function satisfies:*

$$\mathcal{L}^{(n+1)} \geq \begin{cases} \mathcal{B}_l, & \text{if } a_n = 1; \\ 2, & \text{if } a_n = 0. \end{cases}$$

*where $a_i$ $(0 \leq i \leq n)$ follows Definition 5.*

*Proof.* 1. If $a_n = 1$, $\Gamma Y_n \neq 0$, according to Proposition 2,

$$
\begin{aligned}
\mathcal{L}^{(n+1)} &= H_w(\Gamma Z_0) + H_w(\Gamma Z_1) + \cdots + H_w(\Gamma Z_n) \\
&= H_w(P^T \cdot \Gamma Y_0) + H_w(P^T \cdot \Gamma Y_1) + \cdots \\
&\quad + H_w(P^T \cdot \Gamma Y_{n-1}) + H_w(P^T \cdot \Gamma Y_n) \\
&\geq H_w(P^T \cdot (\Gamma Y_0 \oplus \Gamma Y_1 \oplus \cdots \oplus \Gamma Y_{n-1})) + H_w(P^T \cdot \Gamma Y_n) \\
&= H_w(P^T \cdot \Gamma X_n) + H_w(P^T \cdot \Gamma Y_n) \\
&\geq \mathcal{B}_l.
\end{aligned}
$$

2. If $a_n = 0$, $\Gamma Y_n = 0$, then $\Gamma X_n = 0$, according to Equation (2), there must exist at least 2 non-zero terms in $\Gamma Y_0, \Gamma Y_1, \ldots, \Gamma Y_{n-1}$. Therefore,

$$
\begin{aligned}
\mathcal{L}^{(n+1)} &= H_w(\Gamma Z_0) + H_w(\Gamma Z_1) + \cdots + H_w(\Gamma Z_n) \\
&= H_w(P^T \cdot \Gamma Y_0) + H_w(P^T \cdot \Gamma Y_1) + \cdots \\
&\quad + H_w(P^T \cdot \Gamma Y_{n-1}) + H_w(P^T \cdot \Gamma Y_n) \\
&\geq 2.
\end{aligned}
$$

$\square$

**Lemma 2.** *For n-cell GF-NLFSR cipher with SPN round functions, the minimum number of linear active S-boxes in any 2n consecutive rounds (w.l.o.g., denote from 0 to 2n − 1) satisfies*

$$
\mathcal{L}^{(2n)} \geq \begin{cases} \mathcal{B}_l; \\ \mathcal{B}_l + 1, \text{ if } a_{2n-1} = 1. \end{cases}
$$

*Proof.* We consider the first $n+1$ rounds at first, there exist the following 2 cases according to Lemma 1.

1. If $a_n = 1$ (see Fig.3), according to Lemma 1, $\mathcal{L}^{(n+1)} \geq \mathcal{B}_l$, then $\mathcal{L}^{(2n)} \geq \mathcal{L}^{(n+1)} \geq \mathcal{B}_l$. Now if $a_{2n-1} = 1$, $\mathcal{L}^{(2n)} \geq \mathcal{L}^{(n+1)} + 1 \geq \mathcal{B}_l + 1$.

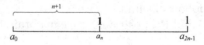

**Fig. 3.** Compute $\mathcal{L}^{(2n)}$ when $a_n = 1$

2. If $a_n = 0$, then there must exist at least 2 nonzero terms in $a_0, a_1, \ldots, a_{n-1}$. Now we denote the last nonzero term by $a_j$ $(1 \leq j \leq n-1)$, i.e., $a_{j+1}, a_{j+2}, \ldots, a_n$ are equal to 0. Then we consider the sequence $(a_j, a_{j+1}, \ldots, a_{j+n})$, there also exist 2 cases:

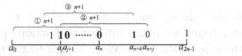

**Fig. 4.** Compute $\mathcal{L}^{(2n)}$ when $a_n = 0$ and $a_{j+n} = 1$

**Fig. 5.** Compute $\mathcal{L}^{(2n)}$ when $a_n = 0$ and $a_{j+n} = 0$

(a) if $a_{j+n} = 1$ (see Fig.4), then according to Lemma 1, for $(a_j, a_{j+1}, \ldots, a_{j+n})$, $\mathcal{L}^{(n+1)} \geq \mathcal{B}_l$. Combined with another nonzero term in $a_0, a_1, \ldots, a_{j-1}$, $\mathcal{L}^{(2n)} \geq 1 + \mathcal{L}^{(n+1)} \geq 1 + \mathcal{B}_l$. Now if $j = n - 1$, then $a_{2n-1} = a_{j+n} = 1$, and $\mathcal{L}^{(2n)} \geq 1 + \mathcal{L}^{(n+1)} \geq 1 + \mathcal{B}_l$; if $j < n - 1$ and $a_{2n-1} = 1$, then $\mathcal{L}^{(2n)} \geq 1 + \mathcal{L}^{(n+1)} + 1 \geq \mathcal{B}_l + 2$.

(b) if $a_{j+n} = 0$ (see Fig.5), according to Equation (2), there exist at least 1 nonzero term in $(a_{n+1}, \ldots, a_{n+j-1})$, denote the last nonzero term by $a_{n+k}, 1 \leq k \leq j-1$, so $(a_k, \ldots, a_{n+k})$ constitute a $(n+1)$-round sequence, and $\mathcal{L}^{(n+1)} \geq \mathcal{B}_l$. Now if $a_{2n-1} = 1$, then we can know that $j < n - 1$, and $\mathcal{L}^{(2n)} \geq \mathcal{L}^{(n+1)} + 1 \geq \mathcal{B}_l + 1$.

To sum up, for any $2n$ consecutive rounds, there exist at least one $(n+1)$-round sequence which can meet the first condition of Lemma 1. So $\mathcal{L}^{(2n)} \geq \mathcal{B}_l$. Furthermore, if $a_{2n-1} = 1$, then $\mathcal{L}^{(2n)} \geq \mathcal{L}^{(n+1)} + 1 \geq \mathcal{B}_l + 1$.     □

**Lemma 3.** *For n-cell GF-NLFSR cipher with SPN round functions, the minimum numbers of linear active S-boxes in any $2n+1$ consecutive rounds satisfies:*

$$\mathcal{L}^{(2n+1)} \geq \mathcal{B}_l + 1.$$

*Proof.* Without loss of generality, we consider the first $2n$ rounds. According to Lemma 2, we can divided it into the following 2 cases:

1. If $a_{2n} = 1$, since for $(a_0, a_1, \ldots, a_{2n-1})$, we have $\mathcal{L}^{(2n)} \geq \mathcal{B}_l$ according to Lemma 2, so $\mathcal{L}^{(2n+1)} \geq \mathcal{B}_l + 1$;
2. If $a_{2n} = 0$, among the $(n+1)$-round sequence $(a_n, a_{n+1}, \ldots, a_{2n})$, there exist at least 2 nonzero terms, denote the first nonzero term by $a_{n+j}, 0 \leq j \leq n-2$, then $(a_j, a_{j+1}, \ldots, a_{n+j})$ is a $(n+1)$-round sequence, which ends with 1, and its minimum number of linear active S-boxes is $\mathcal{L}^{(n+1)} \geq \mathcal{B}_l$. Combined with another nonzero term in $(a_{n+j+1}, a_{n+j+2}, \ldots, a_{2n-1})$, we can deduce that $\mathcal{L}^{(2n+1)} \geq \mathcal{B}_l + 1$, as Fig.6 shows.     □

**Lemma 4.** *For n-cell GF-NLFSR cipher with SPN round functions, the minimum numbers of linear active S-boxes in any 4n consecutive rounds satisfies:*

$$\mathcal{L}^{(4n)} \geq 2\mathcal{B}_l + 1.$$

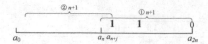

**Fig. 6.** Compute $\mathcal{L}^{(2n+1)}$ when $a_{2n} = 0$

*Proof.* We can use the "divide and conquer" strategy to get the bound. First, we divide the longer-round sequence into small portions properly, make all the lower bounds of these portions are already known to us, then the lower bound can be expressed by the combination of these bounds.

Without loss of generality, let's consider the first $4n$ rounds. Note that $(a_0, a_1, \ldots, a_{4n-1})$ can be split into 2 parts, *i.e.*, $(a_0, a_1, \ldots, a_{2n-1})$ and $(a_{2n}, a_{2n+1}, \ldots, a_{4n-1})$. According to Lemma 2, there exist the following 2 cases:

1. If $a_{2n-1} = 1$ (see Fig.7), then according to Lemma 2, for $(a_0, a_1, \ldots, a_{2n-1})$, $\mathcal{L}^{(2n)} \geq \mathcal{B}_l + 1$, and for the second part $(a_{2n}, a_{2n+1}, \ldots, a_{4n-1})$, $\mathcal{L}^{(2n)} \geq \mathcal{B}_l$. Thus $\mathcal{L}^{(4n)} \geq \mathcal{L}^{(2n)} + \mathcal{L}^{(2n)} \geq 2\mathcal{B}_l + 1$.

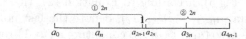

**Fig. 7.** Compute $\mathcal{L}^{(4n)}$ when $a_{2n-1} = 1$

2. If $a_{2n-1} = 0$, we move $a_{2n-1}$ from the first part to the second part, *i.e.*, the $4n$-round sequence is split into $(a_0, a_1, \ldots, a_{2n-2})$ and $(a_{2n-1}, a_{2n}, \ldots, a_{4n-1})$ (as Fig.8 shows). Since $a_{2n-1} = 0$, the minimum number of linear active S-boxes of the first part $(a_0, a_1, \ldots, a_{2n-2})$ is consistent with that of $(a_0, a_1, \ldots, a_{2n-1})$, *i.e.*, $\mathcal{L}^{(2n-1)} = \mathcal{L}^{(2n)} \geq \mathcal{B}_l$. For the second part $(a_{2n-1}, a_{2n}, \ldots, a_{4n-1})$, according to Lemma 3, we have $\mathcal{L}^{(2n+1)} \geq \mathcal{B}_l + 1$. Thus, $\mathcal{L}^{(4n)} \geq \mathcal{L}^{(2n-1)} + \mathcal{L}^{(2n+1)} \geq \mathcal{B}_l + (\mathcal{B}_l + 1) \geq 2\mathcal{B}_l + 1$. □

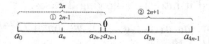

**Fig. 8.** Compute $\mathcal{L}^{(4n)}$ when $a_{2n-1} = 0$

Now the lower bound of the linear active S-boxes for $n + 1$, $2n$, $2n + 1$ and $4n$ consecutive rounds have been obtained, then we can get the lower bound for longer consecutive rounds using a similar approach as in [7,15].

**Theorem 1.** *For $n$-cell GF-NLFSR cipher, the minimum numbers of linear active S-boxes in any $2nr$ consecutive rounds satisfies:*

$$\mathcal{L}^{(2nr)} \geq \mathcal{B}_l \times r + \lfloor r/2 \rfloor.$$

*Proof.* According to Lemma 2 and Lemma 4, $\mathcal{L}^{(2n)} \geq \mathcal{B}_l$ and $\mathcal{L}^{(4n)} \geq 2\mathcal{B}_l + 1$. Let $q = \lfloor r/2 \rfloor$, then $r - 2q \geq 0$, and

$$
\begin{aligned}
\mathcal{L}^{(2nr)} &= \mathcal{L}^{(2nr-4nq+4nq)} \\
&\geq \mathcal{L}^{(2n(r-2q))} + \mathcal{L}^{(4nq)} \\
&\geq \mathcal{B}_l \times (r - 2q) + (2\mathcal{B}_l + 1) \times q \\
&= \mathcal{B}_l \times r + q \\
&= \mathcal{B}_l \times r + \lfloor r/2 \rfloor.
\end{aligned}
$$

$\square$

# 4  Links between the differential and Linear Bounds of GF-NLFSR

In this section, we study the relationship between the lower linear bound and the lower differential bound of GF-NLFSR.

First, we present the following Proposition.

**Proposition 3.** *Let $\Delta X_{i-1} \neq 0$ and $\Delta Y_{i-1}$ be the differences of the input $X_{i-1}$ and output $Y_{i-1}$ in the $i$-th round of GF-NLFSR structure, where $i \geq 1$, then*

$$
H_w(\Delta X_{i-1}) + H_w(\Delta Y_{i-1}) \geq \mathcal{B}_d.
$$

*Proof.* Since $Z_{i-1} = S(X_{i-1})$ and $Y_{i-1} = P \cdot Z_{i-1}$, then

$$
H_w(\Delta X_{i-1}) = H_w(\Delta Z_{i-1}) \text{ and } \Delta Y_{i-1} = P \cdot \Delta Z_{i-1},
$$

thus $H_w(\Delta X_{i-1}) + H_w(\Delta Y_{i-1}) = H_w(\Delta Z_{i-1}) + H_w(P \cdot \Delta Z_{i-1}) \geq \mathcal{B}_d.$  $\square$

For convenience, we define the pattern of differences as follows, which is similar to the pattern of linear mask value defined in Definition 5.

**Definition 6.** *For a GF-NLFSR structure with SPN round function, let $I_r = (X_i, X_{i+1}, \ldots, X_{i+r-1})$ be the input of the $(i+1)$-th, $(i+2)$-th, $\ldots$, $(i+r)$-th round functions, and $\Delta I_r = (\Delta X_i, \Delta X_{i+1}, \ldots, \Delta X_{i+r-1})$ be the corresponding difference of $I_r$, then the pattern of $\Delta I_r$ is defined by a binary sequence $(b_i, b_{i+1}, \ldots, b_{i+r-1})$, where $b_{i+j} = 0$ if $\Delta X_{i+j} = 0$ and $b_{i+j} = 1$ if $\Delta X_{i+j} \neq 0$, $j = 0, 1, \ldots, r-1$.*

Based on Equation (1) and Proposition 3, we can get $\mathcal{D}^{(n+1)}$ as shown in the following lemma.

**Lemma 5.** *The minimum number of differential active S-boxes for any $n + 1$ consecutive rounds (w.l.o.g., denote from 0 to n) n-cell GF-NLFSR cipher with SPN round function satisfies:*

$$
\mathcal{D}^{(n+1)} \geq \begin{cases} \mathcal{B}_d, & \text{if } b_0 = 1; \\ 2, & \text{if } b_0 = 0. \end{cases}
$$

*where $b_i$ $(0 \leq i \leq n)$ follows Definition 6.*

*Proof.* 1. If $b_0 = 1$, $\Gamma X_0 \neq 0$, according to Proposition 3,

$$
\begin{aligned}
\mathcal{D}^{(n+1)} &= H_w(\Delta X_0) + H_w(\Delta X_1) + \cdots + H_w(\Delta X_n) \\
&\geq H_w(\Delta X_0) + H_w(\Delta X_1 \oplus \Delta X_2 \oplus \cdots \oplus \Delta X_n) \\
&= H_w(\Delta X_0) + H_w(\Delta Y_0) \\
&\geq \mathcal{B}_d.
\end{aligned}
$$

2. If $b_0 = 0$, $\Delta X_0 = 0$, then $\Delta Y_0 = 0$, according to Equation (1), there must exist at least two non-zero terms in $\Delta X_1, \Delta X_2, \ldots, \Delta X_n$. Therefore,

$$
\mathcal{D}^{(n+1)} = H_w(\Delta X_0) + H_w(\Delta X_1) + \cdots + H_w(\Delta X_n) \geq 2.
$$

$\square$

Note that for the $(i + 1)$-th round, if $\Delta X_i \neq 0$ we have $\Delta Y_i \neq 0$. For any $(n + 1)$-round differential characteristic (except the all-zero case), since there exist at least 2 non-zero differences according to Equation (1), the pattern of the differences satisfies

$$
\sum_{j=0}^{n} b_{i+j} \geq 2, \quad i \geq 0, \tag{4}
$$

where $b_{i+j}$ follows Definition 6.

If a binary sequence can satisfies Equation (3) (*resp.* Equation (4)), we call it a *possible pattern* of linear mask values (*resp.* differences).

To further facilitate our description, for a given binary sequence $\mathcal{E}^r = (e_0, e_1, \ldots, e_{r-2}, e_{r-1})$, we denote its reverse sequence by $\overleftarrow{\mathcal{E}^r}$, where $\overleftarrow{\mathcal{E}^r} = (e_{r-1}, e_{r-2}, \ldots, e_1, e_0)$, $r \geq n + 1$. If $\mathcal{E}^r$ is a possible pattern of linear mask values, the minimum number of linear active S-boxes corresponding to $\mathcal{E}^r$ is denoted by $\mathcal{L}_{\mathcal{E}^r}$. Respectively, if it is a possible pattern of differences, then the minimum number of differential active S-boxes is denoted by $\mathcal{D}_{\mathcal{E}^r}$.

**Lemma 6.** *Let $\Omega^r$ denote all the $t$ $(\geq 1)$ possible patterns of linear mask values for $r$ $(\geq n+1)$ consecutive rounds of GF-NLFSR with SPN round function, and define $\overleftarrow{\Omega^r} = \{\overleftarrow{\Omega_j^r} \mid \Omega_j^r \in \Omega^r, 0 \leq j \leq t-1\}$, then $\overleftarrow{\Omega^r}$ contains all the possible patterns of differences, and vice versa. Furthermore, for $\Omega_j^r \in \Omega^r$ $(0 \leq j \leq t-1)$,*

$$
\mathcal{L}_{\Omega_j^r} \geq f_j(\mathcal{B}_l) \quad \Longleftrightarrow \quad \mathcal{D}_{\overleftarrow{\Omega_j^r}} \geq f_j(\mathcal{B}_d),
$$

*where $f_j(\cdot)$ denotes a polynomial.*

*Proof.* Assume $\Omega_j^r \in \Omega^r$ $(0 \leq j \leq t-1)$ is a possible pattern of the $r$-round linear characteristic such that it satisfies Equation (3), *i.e.*, $\Omega_j^r = (e_0, e_1, \ldots, e_{r-2}, e_{r-1})$, and

$$
e_{k+n} + e_{k+n-1} + \cdots + e_{k+1} + e_k \geq 2 \quad (r \geq n+1, 0 \leq k \leq r - n - 1).
$$

If $\overleftarrow{\Omega_j^r}$ is not a possible pattern of a differential characteristic, there will exist at least one index $l$ $(0 \le l \le r-n-1)$ such that $e_l + e_{l+1} + \ldots + e_{l+n-1} + e_{l+n} = 1$, thus for the same $l$, we have $e_{l+n} + e_{l+n-1} + \ldots + e_{l+1} + e_l = 1$, which is contradictory to the fact that $\Omega_j^r$ satisfies Equation (3).

Note that $(\overleftarrow{\overleftarrow{\Omega_j^r}}) = \Omega_j^r$, and if $\Omega_j^r$ satisfies Equation (3), $\overleftarrow{\Omega_j^r}$ must satisfy Equation (4) at the same time, and vice versa. That is to say, if a binary sequence is a possible pattern of a linear characteristic, then its reverse sequence must be a possible pattern of a differential characteristic, and vice versa. The relationship is shown in Figure 9.

Furthermore, a long sequence $\Omega_j^r$ $(r > n + 1)$ can be split into several subsequences, assume that $\Omega_j^r = \Omega_j^{r_0} \parallel \Omega_j^{r_1} \parallel \cdots \parallel \Omega_j^{r_{q-1}}$, where $r = r_0 + r_1 + \cdots + r_{q-1}$ and $r_i \le n + 1, 0 \le i \le q - 1$. And for the subsequence $\Omega_j^{r_i}$ $(0 \le i \le q - 1)$, if the corresponding lower linear bound $\mathcal{L}_{\Omega_j^{r_i}} \ge \mathcal{B}_l$, then according to Proposition 2 and Proposition 3, we can get that for its reverse sequence, the corresponding lower differential bound $\mathcal{D}_{\Omega_j^{r_i}} \ge \mathcal{B}_d$; while if the lower linear bound is some positive integer (e.g., when the number of terms is less than $n + 1$, the lower bound is evaluated by the minimum number of non-zero terms), then for its reverse sequence, the lower differential bound is the same value. The lower linear bound of $\Omega_j^{r_i}$ can be denoted by $c_i \mathcal{B}_l + d_i$, where $c_i \in \{0, 1\}$, $0 \le d_i \le n$, $c_i d_i = 0$ and $c_i + d_i \ne 0$. To sum up,

$$\mathcal{L}_{\Omega_j^r} \ge \sum_{i=0}^{q-1} \mathcal{L}_{\Omega_j^{r_i}} \ge \sum_{i=0}^{q-1} (c_i \mathcal{B}_l + d_i) = f_j(\mathcal{B}_l),$$

and

$$\mathcal{D}_{\overleftarrow{\Omega_j^r}} \ge \sum_{i=0}^{q-1} \mathcal{D}_{\overleftarrow{\Omega_j^{r_i}}} \ge \sum_{i=0}^{q-1} (c_i \mathcal{B}_d + d_i) = f_j(\mathcal{B}_d).$$

Thus, the only difference between the corresponding lower linear bound of $\Omega_j^r$ and the corresponding lower differential bound of $\overleftarrow{\Omega_j^r}$ is the difference between $\mathcal{B}_l$ and $\mathcal{B}_d$, which demonstrates that

$$\mathcal{L}_{\Omega_j^r} \ge f_j(\mathcal{B}_l) \iff \mathcal{D}_{\overleftarrow{\Omega_j^r}} \ge f_j(\mathcal{B}_d).$$

□

According to Lemma 6, for a given binary sequence $\Omega_j^r$ $(r \ge n + 1, 0 \le j \le t - 1)$, if we have gotten $\mathcal{L}_{\Omega_j^r}$ (resp. $\mathcal{D}_{\Omega_j^r}$), then we can get $\mathcal{D}_{\overleftarrow{\Omega_j^r}}$ (resp. $\mathcal{L}_{\overleftarrow{\Omega_j^r}}$) just by switching $\mathcal{B}_l$ and $\mathcal{B}_d$.

*Example 1.* In [15], Li *et al.* have given the lower linear bound of 2-cell GF-NLFSR. For instance, given a binary sequence $\Omega_6^6 = (1, 0, 1, 1, 1, 0)$, $\mathcal{L}_{\Omega_6^6} \ge \mathcal{B}_l + 2$. Then, according to Lemma 6, we have $\mathcal{D}_{\overleftarrow{\Omega_6^6}} \ge \mathcal{B}_d + 2$, which can be proved as follows: since $\overleftarrow{\Omega_6^6} = (0, 1, 1, 1, 0, 1)$, by Lemma 5, the lower differential bound of $(0, 1, 1)$ is 2, and for $\overline{(1, 0, 1)}$, the lower differential bound is $\mathcal{B}_d$, so $\mathcal{D}_{\overleftarrow{\Omega_6^6}} \ge 2 + \mathcal{B}_d$.

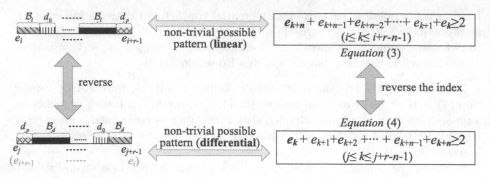

**Fig. 9.** Links between non-trivial possible patterns of difference and linear mask

In general, we have the following result.

**Theorem 2.** *For $r$ $(\geq n+1)$ consecutive rounds of $n$-cell GF-NLFSR cipher with SPN round function, if its lower linear bound $\mathcal{L}^{(r)} \geq f(\mathcal{B}_l)$, then $\mathcal{D}^{(r)} \geq f(\mathcal{B}_d)$, and vice versa.*

*Proof.* Let $\Omega^r$ denote all the $t$ $(\geq 1)$ possible patterns of linear mask values corresponding to $r$ $(\geq n+1)$ consecutive rounds of $n$-cell GF-NLFSR cipher with SPN round function. According to Lemma 6, $\overleftarrow{\Omega^r}$ contains all the possible patterns of the $r$-round differential characteristic.

Let $\mathcal{L}_{\Omega_j^r} \geq f_j(\mathcal{B}_l)$, $f(\mathcal{B}_l) = \min\{f_j(\mathcal{B}_l)\}$, $f(\mathcal{B}_d) = \min\{f_j(\mathcal{B}_d)\}$, $0 \leq j \leq t-1$, then

$$\mathcal{L}^{(r)} \geq f(\mathcal{B}_l) \Longleftrightarrow \mathcal{L}_{\Omega_j^r} \geq f(\mathcal{B}_l), 0 \leq j \leq t-1$$

$$\Longleftrightarrow \mathcal{D}_{\overleftarrow{\Omega_j^r}} \geq f(\mathcal{B}_d), 0 \leq j \leq t-1$$

$$\Longleftrightarrow \mathcal{D}^{(r)} \geq f(\mathcal{B}_d).$$

□

*Example 2.* Lemma 1 and Lemma 5 can be viewed as a valid example for $r = n+1$.

*Remark 1.* Note that the lower linear bound in Theorem 1 is consistent with the lower differential bound as Proposition 1 shows. Furthermore, according to Theorem 2, for any $r$ $(\geq n+1)$ consecutive rounds of $n$-cell GF-NLFSR, if we get the lower linear bound $\mathcal{L}^{(r)} \geq f(\mathcal{B}_l)$, then we can know the lower differential bound is $\mathcal{D}^{(r)} \geq f(\mathcal{B}_d)$, and vice versa. This result demonstrates that, for ciphers adopting GF-NLFSR structure with SPN round function, to evaluate its practical security bounds against DC and LC, it only needs to evaluate one of the two lower bounds, and then the other one can be directly deduced. This result is useful in the cipher designment when using such structure.

# 5    Conclusion

This paper focuses on the practical security evaluation of the GF-NLFSR structure with SPN round function against linear cryptanalysis. By studying the relationship of the mask values between different rounds, we present a lower bound of the number of linear active S-boxes for $n$-cell GF-NLFSR using the "divide and conquer" strategy, and this bound is consistent of its differential lower bound provided by a previous result. Furthermore, we find a relationship between the truncated differential and linear characteristic, which demonstrates that providing either the differential bound or linear bound is enough for GF-NLFSR with SPN round function to show its resistance against both DC and LC. This result is useful in the cipher designment when adopting the GF-NLFSR structure.

**Acknowledgement.** The work in this paper is partially supported by the National Natural Science Foundation of China (No. 61103192, 61402515), the Foundation of Science and Technology on Information Assurance Laboratory (No.KJ-14-003), and the 973 Program (No. 2013CB338002).

# References

1. Biham, E., Shamir, A.: Differential cryptanalysis of DES-like cryptosystems. Journal of Cryptology 4(1), 3–72 (1991)
2. Matsui, M.: Linear cryptanalysis method for DES cipher. In: Helleseth, T. (ed.) EUROCRYPT 1993. LNCS, vol. 765, pp. 386–397. Springer, Heidelberg (1994)
3. Nyberg, K., Knudsen, L.R.: Provable security against a differential attacks. Journal of Cryptology 8(1), 27–37 (1995)
4. Nyberg, K.: Linear approximation of block ciphers. In: De Santis, A. (ed.) EUROCRYPT 1994. LNCS, vol. 950, pp. 439–444. Springer, Heidelberg (1995)
5. Knudsen, L.R.: Practically secure Feistel ciphers. In: Anderson, R. (ed.) FSE 1993. LNCS, vol. 809, pp. 211–221. Springer, Heidelberg (1994)
6. Lai, X., Massey, J.L., Murphy, S.: Markov ciphers and differential cryptanalysis. In: Davies, D.W. (ed.) EUROCRYPT 1991. LNCS, vol. 547, pp. 17–38. Springer, Heidelberg (1991)
7. Kanda, M.: Practical security evaluation against differential and linear cryptanalyses for Feistel ciphers with SPN round function. In: Stinson, D.R., Tavares, S. (eds.) SAC 2000. LNCS, vol. 2012, pp. 324–338. Springer, Heidelberg (2001)
8. Mouha, N., Wang, Q., Gu, D., Preneel, B.: Differential and Linear Cryptanalysis Using Mixed-Integer Linear Programming. In: Wu, C.-K., Yung, M., Lin, D. (eds.) Inscrypt 2011. LNCS, vol. 7537, pp. 57–76. Springer, Heidelberg (2012)
9. Shibutani, K.: On the Diffusion of Generalized Feistel Structures Regarding Differential and Linear Cryptanalysis. In: Biryukov, A., Gong, G., Stinson, D.R. (eds.) SAC 2010. LNCS, vol. 6544, pp. 211–228. Springer, Heidelberg (2011)
10. Choy, J., Chew, G., Khoo, K., Yap, H.: Cryptographic properties and application of a generalized unbalanced Feistel network structure. In: Boyd, C., González Nieto, J. (eds.) ACISP 2009. LNCS, vol. 5594, pp. 73–89. Springer, Heidelberg (2009)

11. Li, R., Sun, B., Li, C., Qu, L.: Cryptanalysis of a generalized unbalanced Feistel network structure. In: Steinfeld, R., Hawkes, P. (eds.) ACISP 2010. LNCS, vol. 6168, pp. 1–18. Springer, Heidelberg (2010)
12. Wu, W., Zhang, L., Zhang, L., Zhang, W.: Security analysis of the GF-NLFSR structure and Four-Cell block cipher. In: Qing, S., Mitchell, C.J., Wang, G. (eds.) ICICS 2009. LNCS, vol. 5927, pp. 17–31. Springer, Heidelberg (2009)
13. Yap, H., Khoo, K., Poschmann, A.: Parallelizing the Camellia and SMS4 block ciphers. In: Bernstein, D.J., Lange, T. (eds.) AFRICACRYPT 2010. LNCS, vol. 6055, pp. 387–406. Springer, Heidelberg (2010)
14. Matsui, M.: New structure of block ciphers with provable security against differenital and linear cyrptanalysis. In: Gollmann, D. (ed.) FSE 1996. LNCS, vol. 1039, pp. 205–218. Springer, Heidelberg (1996)
15. Li, R., Li, C., Su, J., Sun, B.: Security evaluation of MISTY structure with SPN round function. Computers and Mathematics with Applications 65(9), 1264–1279 (2013)
16. Biham, E.: On Matsui's linear cryptanalysis. In: De Santis, A. (ed.) EUROCRYPT 1994. LNCS, vol. 950, pp. 341–355. Springer, Heidelberg (1995)
17. Matsui, M.: On correlation between the order of S-boxes and the strength of DES. In: De Santis, A. (ed.) EUROCRYPT 1994. LNCS, vol. 950, pp. 366–375. Springer, Heidelberg (1995)

# Misuse-Resistant Variants of the OMD Authenticated Encryption Mode

Reza Reyhanitabar, Serge Vaudenay, and Damian Vizár

EPFL, Lausanne, Switzerland

**Abstract.** We present two variants of OMD which are robust against nonce *misuse*. Security of OMD—a CAESAR candidate—relies on the assumption that implementations always ensure *correct* use of nonce (a.k.a. message number); namely that, the nonce never gets repeated. However, in some application environments, this non-repetitiveness requirement on nonce might be compromised or ignored, yielding to full collapse of the security guaranty. We aim to reach maximal possible level of robustness against repeated nonces, as defined by Rogaway and Shrimpton (EUROCRYPT 2006) under the name misuse-resistant AE (MRAE). Our first scheme, called misuse-resistant OMD (MR-OMD), is designed to be substantially similar to OMD while achieving stronger security goals; hence, being able to reuse any existing common code/hardware. Our second scheme, called parallelizable misuse-resistant OMD (PMR-OMD), further deviates from the original OMD design in its encryption process, providing a parallelizable algorithm, in contrast with OMD and MR-OMD which have serial encryption/decryption processes. Both MR-OMD and PMR-OMD are single-key mode of operation. It is known that maximally robust MRAE schemes are necessarily two-pass, a price paid compared to a one-pass scheme such as OMD. Nevertheless, in MR-OMD and PMR-OMD, we combine the two passes in a way that minimizes the incurred additional cost: the overhead incurred by the second pass in our two-pass variants is about 50% of the encryption time for OMD.

**Keywords:** authenticated encryption, misuse-resistance, OMD, CAESAR competition.

## 1 Introduction

An authenticated encryption scheme (AE) is a symmetric-key scheme that guarantees confidentiality (privacy) and authenticity (integrity) of data at the same time. Classical authenticated encryption schemes were based on the *generic composition* paradigm: combining a traditional encryption scheme for privacy with a message authentication code (MAC) for integrity. Generic composition based schemes were formally analysed for the first time in [2], and more recently, further investigated in [17].

The syntax and security notions for authenticated encryption, as a primitive of its own right, were originally formalized in [2,3,14], and further developed to include different variations in [10,20,22,23].

S.S.M. Chow et al. (Eds.): ProvSec 2014, LNCS 8782, pp. 55–70, 2014.
© Springer International Publishing Switzerland 2014

Once the topic started to be investigated more, it became clear that there is a need for *dedicated* authenticated encryption schemes—designs that would provide higher security levels, efficiency or other desired features, in particular, being easier to use and less prone to implementation errors/attacks, compared to the generic composition-based schemes. This is backed by the fact that the generic composition paradigm is neither the most efficient (it requires processing the inputs at least twice) nor the most robust to implementation errors [17, 25].

In this line, one of the most commonly known schemes is the GCM algorithm, which was originally introduced in [16] and standardized by NIST [9] as a blockcipher mode of operation for AE. GCM is a representative example of a nonce-based, one-pass AE scheme which supports "associated data"—data that are logically bound to the plaintext, need to be authenticated, but not to be encrypted. Other prominent standard algorithms in this category include CCM [8], OCB [15, 21, 22], and EAX [4], which are specified in ISO/IEC 19772:2009.

Lately, authenticated encryption has received a lot of attention through the recent CAESAR competition [5]. There were 57 submissions to the first round of CAESAR, from which (at the time of writing this paper) 7 were withdrawn due to major attacks. The proposed CAESAR candidates vary in design and advertise different features, such as, being super efficient, single-pass (online), fully or partially nonce-misuse-resistant; online misuse-resistant, and so on.

One of the CAESAR candidates is the Offset Merkle-Damgård (OMD)—a nonce-based, single-pass mode of operation for authenticated encryption with associated data that uses a compression function as its lower-level primitive. To the best of our knowledge, OMD is the only candidate that uses a compression function (in particular, those of SHA-256 and SHA-512). The majority of other candidates are (AES) blockcipher-based or permutation-based, and some use round functions of AES. OMD has some promising features, among them, are provable security in the standard model based on the well-known PRF assumption on the compression function and high bit-security level (127 bits and 255 bits for OMD-sha256 and OMD-sha512, respectively). Being able to take advantage of the Intel SHA instructions on next-generation processors [26] also seems to be quite interesting.

However, we notice that the security of OMD relies on the assumption that implementations always ensure *correct* use of nonce (a.k.a. message number); namely that, the nonce never gets repeated, otherwise security will fully collapse. While the nonce-based security is sufficient and desirable in many situations, it is not rare that in practice nonces are misused due to poor or erroneous implementations; e.g., a random IV with bad randomness generator might be used instead of the nonce, a counter with a short cycle of repetition can be used as a nonce, or the nonce can even be set to a constant.

Providing robustness against such nonce-misuse scenarios has motivated development of *nonce-misuse-resistant AE* schemes—an AE scheme, that retains most of its security even if the nonces are not used properly. There are two different categories of such schemes with different levels of robustness.

The first is the category of two-pass schemes that can provide maximal security in the presence of nonce reuse. These schemes make a first pass over all data (message and authenticated data) to compute a tag (or IV) and then uses the result (IV) to parametrize a second pass for encryption. The first such (two-pass) scheme is the synthetic-IV (SIV) construction described in [23]; other examples are HBS [13] and BTM [12]. When the nonce is reused, these two-pass schemes only leak minimal additional information compared to semantically secure encryption schemes—the leaked information being the fact that a plaintext together with its associated data are exactly repeated.

The second category are the one-pass (online) AE schemes that promise some limited level of misuse resistance; the first such scheme is McOE [11], followed by several other designs, such as those in [1,7]. Being online is considered as an advantage in many applications, but it must be noted that such online AE schemes will reveal much more information compared to the two-pass scheme; namely, the ciphertext reveals to the adversary whether two messages share a common prefix when the nonce is reused. This is intrinsic to deterministic online encryption.

Aiming to keep the good features of OMD as far as possible and making it robust to nonce reuse, we introduce two variants of OMD, called misuse-resistant OMD (MR-OMD) and parallelizable misuse-resistant OMD (PMR-OMD). We aim to reach maximal possible level of robustness against repeated nonces, as defined by Rogaway and Shrimpton [23] under the name misuse-resistant AE (MRAE), so similar to the previously known schemes in this category (e.g., SIV, HBS and BTM) our constructions are also two-pass. The main motives that influenced design of MR-OMD are the struggle to have a construction that is very similar to OMD (so that common code and hardware can be reused) and to have an efficient, provably secure MRAE scheme at the same time. The design of PMR-OMD further deviates from OMD, providing a fully parallelizable variant, in contrast with OMD and MR-OMD which have serial encryption process.

In MR-OMD and PMR-OMD, the two passes are combined in a way that minimizes the incurred additional cost: using a keyed compression function with $(n + m)$-bit input and $n$-bit output, for processing a message $M$ with associated data $A$, MR-OMD and PMR-OMD only need $|M|/(n + m)$ more calls to the compression function compared to OMD, where $|M|$ is the bit length of $M$. Noticing that the encryption pass in OMD requires $1 + |M|/m$ compression function calls, and considering $m = n$ (as suggested in OMD), the overhead incurred by the second pass in our two-pass variants is about 50% of the encryption time for OMD. We note that the overhead is independent of $A$ as it is processed in the same way in all these algorithms.

Compared with SIV which requires two keys, MR-OMD and PMR-OMD only uses a single key (as is also the case for HBS and BTM). Compared to HBS and BTM which use polynomial-based hashing and need general finite field multiplications in their IV generation part, MR-OMD and PMR-OMD use compression function-based hashing process and only need doubling (multiplication by 2) operation in $GF(2^n)$ which can be easily and efficiently implemented as shown in

Section 2. Avoiding polynomial based hashing seems to be an advisable practice due to the recent attacks and issues of such schemes as recently described in [18, 24]. We note that all these two-pass schemes have the same high-level generic structure (called "Scheme A4" in [17]); what differs is the design of the IV generation and encryption processes.

There is also another subtle difference between the design of our variants of OMD with those of SIV, HBS and BTM; namely, while the latter schemes are designed to be deterministic AE (DAE) and incorporate nonce (if used) and associated data as the header information, our schemes treat the nonce and associated data differently from the beginning. As stated by Rogaway and Shrimpton [23] "the MRAE goal is conceptually different from the DAE goal, the former employing an IV and gaining for this a stronger notion of security. The header and the IV are conceptually different, the one being user-supplied data that the user wants authenticated, the other being a mechanism-supplied value needed to obtain a strong notion of security."

## 2   Preliminaries

NOTATIONS. For a finite set $\mathcal{S}$, by $x \xleftarrow{\$} S$ we denote that $x$ is chosen from $S$ uniformly at random. Any string is a binary string. Let $\{0, 1\}^n$ denote set of all binary strings of length $n$ and let $\{0, 1\}^*$ denote the set of all finite-length strings. For two strings $X$ and $Y$, $X \| Y$ and $XY$ denote the result of concatenating the two strings. For an $n$-bit binary string $X = X[n-1] \cdots X[0]$, let $X[i \cdots j] = X[i] \cdots X[j]$ denote a substring of $X$, for $0 \le j \le i \le m - 1$; let $\mathrm{msb}(X) = X[n-1]$ and $\mathrm{lsb}(X) = X[0]$. Let $1^n 0^m$ denote concatenation of $n$ ones by $m$ zeros. For a non-negative integer $i$ let $\langle i \rangle_m$ denote binary representation of $i$ by an $m$-bit string.

The special symbol $\perp$ means that a variable is undefined and it also signifies an error. Let $|Z|$ denote the cardinality of $Z$ if $Z$ is a set, and the length of $Z$ in bits if $Z$ is a binary string. The empty string is denoted by $\varepsilon$ and we let $|\varepsilon| = 0$. For $X \in \{0, 1\}^*$ let $X_1 \| X_2 \cdots \| X_m \xleftarrow{b} X$ denote partitioning $X$ into blocks $X_i$ such that $|X_i| = b$ for $1 \le i \le m - 1$ and $|X_m| \le b$. Let $|X|_b = \lceil |X|/b \rceil$ denote length of $X$ in $b$-bit blocks and let $\|X\|_b = \max\{1, |X|_b\}$.

For two binary strings $X = X[m - 1] \cdots X[0]$ and $Y = Y[n - 1] \cdots Y[0]$, the notation $X \oplus Y$ denotes bitwise xor of $X[m - 1] \cdots X[m - 1 - \ell]$ and $Y[n - 1] \cdots Y[n - 1 - \ell]$ where $\ell = \min\{m - 1, n - 1\}$. That is, $X \oplus Y$ is the result of xoring first $\ell$ msb bits of $X$ and $Y$ and dropping the rest (if any) for the longer string. When $m = n$, this simply denotes the conventional bitwise xor of two strings. For any string $X$, define $X \oplus \varepsilon = \varepsilon \oplus X = \varepsilon$. The notation $X \oplus_{msb} Y$ stands for bitwise xor $X \| 0^{L-m} \oplus Y \| 0^{L-n}$, where $L = \max\{m, n\}$. In other words, we xor the the shorter string to the longer one, aligning the strings by their leftmost bits.

THE FINITE FIELD WITH $2^n$ POINTS. Let $(GF(2^n), \oplus, .)$ denote the Galois Field with $2^n$ points. When considering a point $\alpha$ in $GF(2^n)$ it can be represented in any of the following equivalent ways: (1) as an integer between 0 and $2^n - 1$, (2) as a binary string $\alpha_{n-1} \cdots \alpha_0 \in \{0,1\}^n$, or (3) as a formal polynomial $\alpha(X) = \alpha_{n-1}X^{n-1} + \cdots + \alpha_1 X + \alpha_0$ with binary coefficients. The addition "$\oplus$" and multiplication "." of two field elements in $GF(2^n)$ are defined as usual (e.g. see [22]). For $GF(2^{256})$, we use $P_{256}(X) = X^{256} + X^{10} + X^5 + X^2 + 1$, and for $GF(2^{512})$ we use $P_{512}(X) = X^{512} + X^8 + X^5 + X^2 + 1$ as the irreducible polynomials used in the field multiplications. We point out that it is easy to multiply an arbitrary field element $\alpha$ by the element 2 (i.e. $X$), as shown in [6].

## 3   Security Definitions

The insecurity of a scheme $\Pi$ is measured using the resource parametrized function $\mathbf{Adv}_{\Pi}^{xxx}(\mathbf{r})$, denoting the maximal value of the adversary's advantage — $\mathbf{Adv}_{\Pi}^{xxx}(\mathbf{r}) = max_A \{\mathbf{Adv}_{\Pi}^{xxx}(A)\}$ — over all adversaries $A$, against the xxx property of a primitive or scheme $\Pi$, that use resources bounded by $\mathbf{r}$. Let $A$ be an adversary that returns a binary value; by $A^{f(\cdot)}(X) \Rightarrow 1$ we refer to the event that $A$ on input $X$ and access to an oracle function $f(.)$ returns 1.

SYNTAX AND SECURITY OF KEYED COMPRESSION FUNCTIONS. We denote a keyed compression function by $F : \mathcal{K} \times (\{0,1\}^n \times \{0,1\}^m) \to \{0,1\}^n$, where $m$ and $n$ are two positive integers, and the keyspace $\mathcal{K}$ is a non-empty set of strings. The notations $F_K(H,M) = F(K; H, M)$ are equivalent. We can alternatively think of $F_K$ as a single argument function whose domain is $\{0,1\}^{n+m}$ and write $F_K(H\|M) = F_K(H,M)$. Given a keyless compression function $F' : \{0,1\}^n \times \{0,1\}^b \to \{0,1\}^n$ (e.g. sha-256 : $\{0,1\}^{256} \times \{0,1\}^{512} \to \{0,1\}^{256}$) we convert it to a keyed compression function $F$ by dedicating $k$ bits of its $b$-bit input block to the secret key; i.e. we define $F_K(H,M) = F'(H, K\|M)$. For example in the case of sha-256 we have $n = 256$ and we will set $k = 256$ which will give us $m = 512 - k = 256$. We assess the security of compression functions in the sense of pseudorandom function security described below.

PSEUDORANDOM FUNCTIONS (PRFS) AND TWEAKABLE PRFS. We denote by $\mathrm{Func}(m,n) = \{f : \{0,1\}^m \to \{0,1\}^n\}$ the set of all functions from $m$-bit strings to $n$-bit strings and by $\mathrm{Func}(\mathcal{M},n) = \{f : \mathcal{M} \to \{0,1\}^n\}$ the set of all functions from a set $\mathcal{M}$ to $n$-bit strings. A random function $R \xleftarrow{\$} \mathrm{Func}(m,n)$ is a function selected uniformly at random from $\mathrm{Func}(m,n)$. We define a random function $R'$ with input from set $\mathcal{M}$ and $n$-bit output in a similar manner.

Let $\mathrm{Func}^{\mathcal{T}}(m,n)$ be the set of all functions $\{\widetilde{f} : \mathcal{T} \times \{0,1\}^m \to \{0,1\}^n\}$, where $\mathcal{T}$ is a set of tweaks. A tweakable random function (RF) with the tweak space $\mathcal{T}$, $m$-bit input and $n$-bit output is a map $\widetilde{R} : \mathcal{T} \times \{0,1\}^m \to \{0,1\}^n$ selected uniformly at random from $\mathrm{Func}^{\mathcal{T}}(m,n)$; i.e. $\widetilde{R} \xleftarrow{\$} \mathrm{Func}^{\mathcal{T}}(m,n)$. We use $\widetilde{R}^{\langle T \rangle}(.)$ and $R(T,.)$ interchangeably, for every $T \in \mathcal{T}$. Notice that each tweak $T$ names a random function $\widetilde{R}^{\langle T \rangle} : \{0,1\}^m \to \{0,1\}^n$ and distinct tweaks name distinct (independent) random functions.

Let $F : \mathcal{K} \times \{0,1\}^m \to \{0,1\}^n$ be a keyed function and let $\widetilde{F} : \mathcal{K} \times \mathcal{T} \times \{0,1\}^m \to \{0,1\}^n$ be a keyed and tweakable function, where the key space $\mathcal{K}$ is some nonempty set. Let $F_K(.) = F(K,.)$ and $\widetilde{F}_K^{\langle T \rangle}(.) = \widetilde{F}(K,T,.)$. Let $A$ be an adversary. Then we define $\mathbf{Adv}_F^{\mathrm{prf}}(A) = \Pr\left[K \xleftarrow{\$} \mathcal{K} : A^{F_K(\cdot)} \Rightarrow 1\right] - \Pr\left[R \xleftarrow{\$} \mathrm{Func}(m,n) : A^{R(\cdot)} \Rightarrow 1\right]$ and $\mathbf{Adv}_{\widetilde{F}}^{\mathrm{prf}}(A) = \Pr\left[K \xleftarrow{\$} \mathcal{K} : A^{\widetilde{F}_K^{\langle \cdot \rangle}(\cdot)} \Rightarrow 1\right] - \Pr\left[\widetilde{R} \xleftarrow{\$} \mathrm{Func}^{\mathcal{T}}(m,n) : A^{\widetilde{R}^{\langle \cdot \rangle}(\cdot)} \Rightarrow 1\right]$. The resource parametrized advantage functions are defined accordingly, considering that the adversarial resources of interest here are the time complexity $(t)$ of the adversary and the total number of queries $(q)$ asked by the adversary (note that we just consider fixed-input-length functions, so the lengths of queries are fixed and known). We say that $F$ is $(t, q; \epsilon)$-PRF if $\mathbf{Adv}_F^{\mathrm{prf}}(t, q) \leq \epsilon$. We say that $\widetilde{F}$ is $(t, q; \epsilon)$-tweakable PRF if $\mathbf{Adv}_{\widetilde{F}}^{\mathrm{prf}}(t, q) \leq \epsilon$. Extending these definitions for variable-input-length functions is straightforward; namely, for a VIL function $G : \mathcal{K} \times \mathcal{D} \to \{0,1\}^n$, with a non-empty key space $\mathcal{K}$ and message space $\mathcal{D} = \{0,1\}^*$, the ideal primitive to which a randomly selected function $G_K$ is compared will be $R \xleftarrow{\$} \mathrm{Func}(\mathcal{D}, n)$. The resource of interest in this case is the total length of all processed queries in $n$-bit blocks $\sigma$ for some positive $n$.

IV-BASED ENCRYPTION SCHEMES. An IV-based encryption scheme is a privacy-only scheme, with a special security notion, as for example the CBC mode. We say that an encryption scheme $\Pi = (\mathcal{K}, \mathcal{E}, \mathcal{D})$ is an IV-based encryption scheme if the encryption function $\mathcal{E}$ takes a tuple $(K, \mathsf{IV}, M)$ as input, such that $K \in \mathcal{K}$, $\mathsf{IV} \in \{0,1\}^\tau$ for some fixed positive $\tau$ and $M \in \{0,1\}^*$. We call $\mathsf{IV}$ the initialization vector. The notations $\mathcal{E}(K, \mathsf{IV}, M)$, $\mathcal{E}_K(\mathsf{IV}, M)$ and $\mathcal{E}_K^{\mathsf{IV}}(M)$ are used interchangeably. We also assume that if $\mathbb{C} = \mathcal{E}_K^{\mathsf{IV}}(M)$, then we have $|\mathbb{C}| = |M| + \tau$ and $\mathbb{C} = \mathsf{IV} \| C$; i.e. the IV is a part of the ciphertext. We define the advantage of an adversary $A$ in breaking the \$-privacy of $\Pi$ as $\mathbf{Adv}_\Pi^{\mathrm{priv\$}}(A) = \Pr\left[K \xleftarrow{\$} \mathcal{K} : A^{\mathcal{E}_K^\$(\cdot)} \Rightarrow 1\right] - \Pr\left[A^{\$(\cdot)} \Rightarrow 1\right]$ with $\$(\cdot)$ being a random string oracle that on input $M$ returns a random string of length $|M| + \tau$ and $\mathcal{E}_K^\$$ returning $\mathcal{E}_K^{\mathsf{IV}}$ with $\mathsf{IV} \xleftarrow{\$} \{0,1\}^\tau$. It is assumed, that the adversary never asks a query outside the proper message space of $\Pi$. Note that in the priv\$ security game, the IV is chosen by the challenger. We remark that we make use of an IV-based scheme as a building block for our misuse-resistant scheme.

SYNTAX OF AN AEAD SCHEME. A nonce-based authenticated encryption with associated data (AEAD) is a symmetric key scheme $\Pi = (\mathcal{K}, \mathcal{E}, \mathcal{D})$. The key space $\mathcal{K}$ is some non-empty finite set. The encryption algorithm $\mathcal{E} : \mathcal{K} \times \mathcal{N} \times \mathcal{A} \times \mathcal{M} \to \mathcal{C} \cup \{\bot\}$ takes four arguments, a secret key $K \in \mathcal{K}$, a nonce $N \in \mathcal{N}$, an associated data (a.k.a. header data) $A \in \mathcal{A}$ and a message $M \in \mathcal{M}$, and returns either a ciphertext $\mathbb{C} \in \mathcal{C}$ or a special symbol $\bot$ indicating an error. The decryption algorithm $\mathcal{D} : \mathcal{K} \times \mathcal{N} \times \mathcal{A} \times \mathcal{C} \to \mathcal{M} \cup \{\bot\}$ takes four arguments $(K, N, A, \mathbb{C})$ and either outputs a message $M \in \mathcal{M}$ or an error indicator $\bot$.

For correctness of the scheme, it is required that $\mathcal{D}(K, N, A, \mathbb{C}) = M$ for any $\mathbb{C}$ such that $\mathbb{C} = \mathcal{E}(K, N, A, M)$. It is assumed that if algorithms $\mathcal{E}$ and $\mathcal{D}$ receive parameter not belonging to their specified domain of arguments they will output $\perp$. We write $\mathcal{E}_K(N, A, M) = \mathcal{E}(K, N, A, M)$ and $\mathcal{D}_K(N, A, \mathbb{C}) = \mathcal{D}(K, N, A, \mathbb{C})$.

In this paper we assume that the message and associated data are binary strings of arbitrary but finite length; i.e. $\mathcal{M} = \{0,1\}^*$ and $\mathcal{A} = \{0,1\}^*$ and the key and nonce are some fixed-length binary strings, i.e. $\mathcal{N} = \{0,1\}^{|N|}$ and $\mathcal{K} = \{0,1\}^k$ for positive integers $|N|$ and $k$ (the nonce length and the key length). We assume that $|\mathcal{E}_K(N, A, M)| = |M| + \tau$ for some positive fixed constant $\tau$. Moreover, we will have $\mathsf{IV}||C = \mathbb{C}$ where $|C| = |M|$ and $|\mathsf{IV}| = \tau$. We call $C$ the core ciphertext and $\mathsf{IV}$ the initialization vector (or IV for short). The IV is not to be confused with the nonce. The IV here is generated by the encryption algorithm and is in fact a form of authentication tag.

NONCE RESPECTING AND NONCE MISUSING ADVERSARIES. We say that an adversary $\boldsymbol{A}$ is nonce-respecting if it never repeats a nonce in its *encryption* queries. That is, if $\boldsymbol{A}$ queries the encryption oracle $\mathcal{E}_K(\cdot, \cdot, \cdot)$ with the queries $(N^1, A^1, M^1) \cdots (N^q, A^q, M^q)$ then $N^1, \cdots, N^q$ must be distinct. If there are at least two queries $(N^i, A^i, M^i)$ and $(N^j, A^j, M^j)$ that share the same nonce, i.e. $N^i = N^j$, then we say that $\boldsymbol{A}$ is a nonce-misusing (or a nonce-reusing) adversary. Note that adversaries of both types may repeat nonces in their decryption queries.

AE SECURITY. To establish the security of MR-OMD scheme, we use the all-in-one MRAE security notion introduced in [23]. As shown in [23], the all-in-one security notion is equivalent to the conventional two-requirement security notion (that combines IND-CPA for privacy and INT-CTXT for integrity), as put forth in [2, 3, 14].

**Definition 1.** *Let $\Pi = (\mathcal{K}, \mathcal{E}, \mathcal{D})$ be a nonce based AEAD scheme. The MRAE-advantage of an adversary $\boldsymbol{A}$ in attacking the scheme $\Pi$ is defined as:*

$$\mathbf{Adv}_\Pi^{mrae}(\boldsymbol{A}) = \Pr\left[K \xleftarrow{\$} \mathcal{K} : \boldsymbol{A}^{\mathcal{E}_K(\cdot,\cdot,\cdot), \mathcal{D}_K(\cdot,\cdot,\cdot)} \Rightarrow 1\right] - \Pr\left[\boldsymbol{A}^{\$(\cdot,\cdot,\cdot), \perp(\cdot,\cdot,\cdot)} \Rightarrow 1\right].$$

*To prevent trivial wins, we forbid $\boldsymbol{A}$ to ask a query $(N, A, \mathbb{C})$ of the decryption oracle, after obtaining result $\mathbb{C}$ upon query $(N, A, M)$ from the encryption oracle; we also assume that $\boldsymbol{A}$ never repeats an encryption query $(N, A, M)$. On query $(N, A, M)$, the random-bit oracle $\$(\cdot, \cdot, \cdot)$ returns a random string of length $|M| + \tau$ if the inputs $N, A$ and $M$ belong to the respective input domains and $\perp$ otherwise. The $\perp(\cdot, \cdot, \cdot)$ oracle returns $\perp$ on every query.*

The resource-based advantage function $\mathbf{Adv}_\Pi^{mrae}(\mathbf{r})$ is parametrized by adversarial resource vector $\mathbf{r} = (t, \sigma_A, \sigma_M, q_e, q_d)$ where $t$ denotes the time complexity, $\sigma_A = (\sum_{i=1}^{q_e} |A^i| + \sum_{j=1}^{q_d} |A^j|)$ is the total length of associated data in all queries, $\sigma_M = (\sum_{i=1}^{q_e} |M^i| + \sum_{j=1}^{q_d} |\mathbb{C}^j| - \tau|)$ is the total length of plaintexts in all queries, $q_e$ denotes the maximal number of encryption queries and $q_d$ the maximal number of decryption queries made by the adversary.

Clearly, the MRAE security notion implies the nonce-respecting security; the latter being a special case of the former, where adversary cannot repeat the nonce and hence no query to the encryption oracle is repeated. We denote the conventional nonce-respecting notion by "nr-ae" and let the related resource-parametrized advantage function be $\mathbf{Adv}_{\Pi}^{nr\text{-}ae}(\mathbf{r})$, measuring the maximal insecurity over all "nonce-respecting" adversaries $\boldsymbol{A}$ with resources bounded by $\mathbf{r}$. We sometimes use simplified notation for adversary's oracles and the choice of the key in a security game. For a scheme $\Pi = (\mathcal{K}, \mathcal{E}, \mathcal{D})$, the notations $K \xleftarrow{\$} \mathcal{K} : \boldsymbol{A}^{\mathcal{E}_K(\cdot,\cdot,\cdot), \mathcal{D}_K(\cdot,\cdot,\cdot)}$ and $\boldsymbol{A}^{\Pi_K(\cdot,\cdot,\cdot), \Pi_K^{-1}(\cdot,\cdot,\cdot)}$ are equivalent.

# 4    Specification of MR-OMD

MR-OMD is a compression function mode of operation for nonce-misuse resistant AEAD. It has the following parameters.

- keyed compression function $F : \mathcal{K} \times (\{0,1\}^n \times \{0,1\}^m) \to \{0,1\}^n$
- IV length $\tau < n$

where the key space $\mathcal{K} = \{0,1\}^k$ and $m \leq n$.

Let MR-OMD-$F$ denote the MR-OMD mode of operation using a keyed compression function $F_K : \{0,1\}^n \times \{0,1\}^m \to \{0,1\}^n$ with $m \leq n$ and an unspecified tag length. We let MR-OMD$[F, \tau]$denote the MR-OMD mode of operation using the keyed compression function $F_K$ and the IV of length $\tau$. The encryption algorithm of MR-OMD$[F, \tau]$ takes four input arguments (secret key $K \in \{0,1\}^k$, nonce $N \in \{0,1\}^{|N|}$, associated data $A \in \{0,1\}^*$, message $M \in \{0,1\}^*$) and outputs $\mathbb{C} = \mathsf{IV}||C \in \{0,1\}^{|M|+\tau}$. The decryption algorithm of MR-OMD$[F, \tau]$ inputs four arguments (secret key $K \in \{0,1\}^k$, nonce $N \in \{0,1\}^{|N|}$, associated data $A \in \{0,1\}^*$, ciphertext $\mathsf{IV}||C \in \{0,1\}^*$) and either outputs the whole $M \in \{0,1\}^{|C|}$ at once or an error message $\perp$.

A schematic representation of the encryption algorithm of MR-OMD$[F, \tau]$ is shown in figure 1. The construction of the decryption algorithm is similar to the encryption except that the ciphertext is first decrypted using $\mathsf{IV}$ from the input and then the $\mathsf{IV}$ from input is compared to $\mathsf{IV}'$ computed over the associated data and decrypted message. Figure 2 shows the algorithmic description of the encryption and decryption algorithms of MR-OMD$[F, \tau]$

COMPUTING THE MASKING VALUES. As seen from the description of MR-OMD in Figure 1, before each call to the underlying keyed compression function, we xor a masking value $\Delta$. Seven different sets of masking values are used:

- masks $\Delta_{N,i,j}$ for $j \in \{0, \ldots, 5\}$ are used in the IV generation process,
- masks $\bar{\Delta}_{\mathsf{IV},i}$ are used in the encrypt/decryption process.

In the following, all multiplications are in $GF(2^n)$, $\mathtt{ntz}(i)$ denotes the number of trailing zeros (i.e. the number of rightmost bits that are zero) in the binary representation of a positive integer $i$.

**Initialization.** Let $L_* = F_K(0^n, 0^m)$; $L(0) = 8 \cdot L_*$, and $L(i) = 2 \cdot L(i-1)$ for $i \geq 1$. The rule to compute $L(i)$ is described as a part of the initialization, because these values can be precomputed and stored in a table. Further on let $\Delta_{N,0,0} = F_K(N \| 10^{n-1-|N|}, 0^m)$; $\Delta_{N,0,1} = F_K(N \| 10^{n-1-|N|}, 0^m) \oplus L_*$.

**Masking sequence for IV generation.** For $i \geq 1$ let $\Delta_{N,i,0} = \Delta_{N,i-1,0} \oplus L(\mathtt{ntz}(i))$; and $\Delta_{N,i,1} = \Delta_{N,i-1,1} \oplus L(\mathtt{ntz}(i))$. For $i \geq 1$ and $j, j' \in \{0, \ldots, 5\}$: $\Delta_{N,i,j} = \Delta_{N,i,j'} \oplus (\langle j \rangle_n \oplus \langle j' \rangle_n) \cdot L_*$.

**Masking sequence for encryption.** Let $\bar{\Delta}_{\mathsf{IV},0} = F_K(\mathsf{IV} \| 10^{n-1-\tau}, 0^m) \oplus 6 \cdot L_*$. We have $\bar{\Delta}_{\mathsf{IV},i} = \bar{\Delta}_{\mathsf{IV},i-1} \oplus L(\mathtt{ntz}(i))$ for $i \geq 1$.

# 5  Security Analysis

We analyse the security of MR-OMD in two cases: (1) as a MRAE, considering adversaries that are nonce-reusing; (2) in the case that adversaries are nonce-respecting. As MR-OMD is designed as a nonce-misuse resistant scheme, we first focus on analysing the security bounds in the nonce-misuse scenario. Clearly, an upper-bound for the MRAE insecurity (i.e. MRAE advantage) also upper-bounds the insecurity in the nonce-respecting case. Intuitively, the latter can be lower than the former.

## 5.1  Security in the Case of Nonce Misuse

Theorem 1 gives the MRAE security of MR-OMD. The high-level structure of the proof is similar to those of previous MRAE schemes following the synthetic-IV (SIV) design paradigm [23], such as HBS [13] and BTM [12], but the details differ. We first prove the security in the information-theoretic setting using tweakable random functions. To obtain the information-theoretic security, we prove security of MR-OMD.HASH as a PRF and that of MR-OMD.$\mathcal{E}$ as a secure IV-based encryption scheme. Consequently, we prove security of MR-OMD in the MR-AE sense using the previous two results. A complexity-theoretic security bound is then determined by instantiating the tweakable random functions using the XE construction from [21].

**Theorem 1.** *Fix $n \geq 1$ and $\tau \in \{0, 1, \cdots, n\}$. Let $F : \mathcal{K} \times (\{0,1\}^n \times \{0,1\}^m) \to \{0,1\}^n$ be a PRF, where the key space $\mathcal{K} = \{0,1\}^k$ for $k \geq 1$ and $1 \leq m \leq n$. Then*

$$\mathbf{Adv}^{\mathrm{mrae}}_{\mathrm{MR\text{-}OMD}[F,\tau]}(t, \sigma, q_e, q_d) \leq \mathbf{Adv}^{\mathrm{prf}}_F(t', 2\sigma) + \frac{3.5\sigma^2}{2^n} + \frac{0.5q_e^2}{2^\tau} + \frac{q_d}{2^\tau}$$

*where $q_e$ and $q_d$ are, respectively, the number of encryption and decryption queries, $t' = t + cn\sigma$ for some constant $c$ and $\sigma$ is the total number of calls made to the underlying compression function $F$.*

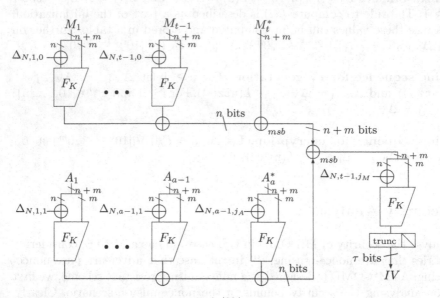

If $|M_t| < n + m$ set $M_t^* = M_t || 10^{n+m-1-|M_t|}$ and $j_M = 4$. Otherwise $M_t^* = M_t$, $j_M = 2$.
If $|A_a| < n + m$ set $A_a^* = A_a || 10^{n+m-1-|A_a|}$ and $j_A = 5$. Otherwise $A_a^* = A_a$, $j_A = 3$.

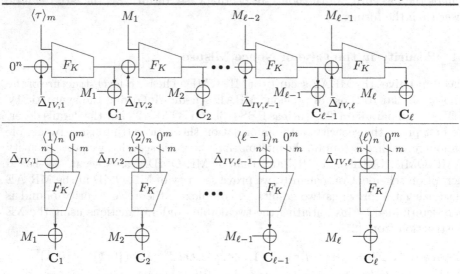

**Fig. 1.** The encryption process of MR-OMD$[F, \tau]$ and PMR-OMD$[F, \tau]$ using a keyed compression function $F_K : (\{0,1\}^n \times \{0,1\}^m) \to \{0,1\}^n$ with $m \leq n$. (**Top**) The process of generating the IV. Both associated data and message are parsed into $n + m$ bit blocks and padded if needed as shown. (**Bottom**) The encryption process (upper part for MR-OMD and lower for PMR-OMD). The output ciphertext is IV$||C$. For operations $\oplus$ and $\oplus_{msb}$ see our convention in Section 2.

```
 1: Algorithm INITIALIZE(K)                   34:    else
 2:    L_* ← F_K(0^n, 0^m)                     35:       Δ_M ← Δ_M ⊕ L_*^{(4)}
 3:    L_*^{(2)} ← 2 · L_*                     36:       M_t^* ← M_t || 10^{b-|M_t|-1}
 4:    L_*^{(4)} ← 2 · L_*^{(2)}               37:       Left ← M_t^*[b-1···m] ⊕ Σ_A
 5:    L_*^{(6)} ← L_*^{(4)} ⊕ L_*^{(2)}       38:       Right ← M_t^*[m-1···0]
 6:    L(0) ← 2 · L_*^{(4)}                    39:       IV ← F_K(Left ⊕ Δ_M, Right)
 7:    for i ← 1, 2, · · · do                  40:    return IV[n-1···n-τ]
 8:       L(i) = 2.L(i-1)
 9:    return
                                                1: Algorithm E_K(N, A, M)
                                                2:    if |N| > n-1 then
 1: Algorithm HASH_K(N, A, M)                   3:       return ⊥
 2:    b ← n + m                                4:       M_1||M_2···M_{ℓ-1}||M_ℓ ←^m M
 3:    A_1||A_2···A_{a-1}||A_a ←^b A            5:    IV ← HASH_K(N, A, M)
 4:    M_1||M_2···M_{t-1}||M_t ←^b M            6:    Δ ← F_K(IV||10^{n-1-τ}, 0^m)
 5:    Σ_A ← 0^n; Σ_M ← 0^n                     7:    Δ ← Δ ⊕ L(0) ⊕ L_*^{(6)}
 6:    Δ_M ← F_K(N||10^{n-1-|N|}, 0^m)          8:    H ← 0^n
 7:    Δ_A ← Δ_M ⊕ L_*                          9:    H ← F_K(H ⊕ Δ, ⟨τ⟩_m)
 8:    for i ← 1 to a-1 do                     10:    for i ← 1 to ℓ-1 do
 9:       Δ_A ← Δ_A ⊕ L(ntz(i))                11:       C_i ← H ⊕ M_i
10:       Left ← A_i[b-1···m]                  12:       Δ ← Δ ⊕ L(ntz(i+1))
11:       Right ← A_i[m-1···0]                 13:       H ← F_K(H ⊕ Δ, M_i)
12:       Σ_A ← Σ_A ⊕ F_K(Left ⊕ Δ_A, Right)   14:    C_ℓ ← H ⊕ M_ℓ
13:    if |A_a| = b then                       15:    C ← IV||C_1||C_2||···||C_ℓ
14:       Δ_A ← Δ_A ⊕ L_*^{(2)}                16:    return C
15:       Left ← A_a[b-1···m]
16:       Right ← A_a[m-1···0]
17:       Σ_A ← Σ_A ⊕ F_K(Left ⊕ Δ, Right)      1: Algorithm D_K(N, A, C)
18:    else if |A| > 0 then                     2:    if |N| > n-1 or |C| < τ then
19:       Δ_A ← Δ_A ⊕ L_*^{(4)}                 3:       return ⊥
20:       A_a^* ← A_a||10^{b-|A_a|-1}           4:       IV||C_1||C_2···C_{ℓ-1}||C_ℓ ←^m C
21:       LeftA_a^*[b-1···m]                    5:    H ← 0^n
22:       Right ← A_a^*[m-1···0]                6:    Δ ← F_K(IV||10^{n-1-τ}, 0^m)
23:       Σ_A ← Σ_A ⊕ F_K(Left ⊕ Δ_A, Right)   7:    Δ ← Δ ⊕ L(0) ⊕ L_*^{(6)}
24:    for i ← 1 to t-1 do                      8:    H ← F_K(H ⊕ Δ, ⟨τ⟩_m)
25:       Δ_M ← Δ_M ⊕ L(ntz(i))                9:    for i ← 1 to ℓ-1 do
26:       Left ← M_i[b-1···m]                  10:       M_i ← H ⊕ C_i
27:       Right ← M_i[m-1···0]                 11:       Δ ← Δ ⊕ L(ntz(i+1))
28:       Σ_M ← Σ_M ⊕ F_K(Left⊕Δ_M, Right)     12:       H ← F_K(H ⊕ Δ, M_i)
29:    if |M_t| = b then                       13:    M_ℓ ← H ⊕ C_ℓ
30:       Δ_M ← Δ_M ⊕ L_*^{(2)}                14:    IV' ← HASH_K(N, A, M)
31:       Left ← M_t[b-1···m] ⊕ Σ_A           15:    if IV' = IV then
32:       Right ← M_t[m-1···0]                 16:       return M ← M_1||M_2||···||M_ℓ
33:       IV ← F_K(Left ⊕ Δ_M, Right)          17:    else
                                               18:       return ⊥
```

**Fig. 2.** Definition of MR-OMD[$F, τ$]. The function $F : \mathcal{K} \times (\{0,1\}^n \times \{0,1\}^m) \rightarrow \{0,1\}^n$ is a keyed compression function with $\mathcal{K} = \{0,1\}^k$ and $m \leq n$. The IV length is $τ \in \{0, 1, \cdots, n\}$. Algorithms $\mathcal{E}$ and $\mathcal{D}$ can be called with arguments $K \in \mathcal{K}$, $N \in \{0,1\}^{\leq n-1}$, and $A, M, \mathbb{C} \in \{0,1\}^*$.

*Remark 1.* We can verify that $\sigma = \lceil \sigma_A/(m+n) \rceil + \lceil \sigma_M/(m+n) \rceil + \lceil \sigma_M/(m) \rceil + \sum_{i=1}^{q_e} 1_{|M^i|=0} + \sum_{j=1}^{q_d} 1_{|C^j|=\tau} + q_e + q_d$.

*Proof.* The proof is obtained by combing Lemma 3, Lemma 1 and Lemma 2 in subsection 5.1.1 with Lemma 4 and Lemma 5 in subsection 5.1.2. □

### 5.1.1 Generalization of MR-OMD Based on Tweakable Random Functions

We define the scheme $\mathbb{MR}\text{-}\mathbb{OMD}[\widetilde{R},\tau]$, a generalization of MR-OMD$[F,\tau]$ that uses a tweakable random function $\widetilde{R} : \mathcal{T} \times (\{0,1\}^n \times \{0,1\}^m) \to \{0,1\}^n$. The tweak space $\mathcal{T}$ consists of seven mutually exclusive sets of tweaks; namely, $\mathcal{T} = \mathcal{N} \times \mathbb{N} \times \{0\} \cup \mathcal{N} \times \mathbb{N} \times \{1\} \cup \mathcal{N} \times \mathbb{N} \times \{2\} \cup \mathcal{N} \times \mathbb{N} \times \{3\} \cup \mathcal{N} \times \mathbb{N} \times \{4\} \cup \mathcal{N} \times \mathbb{N} \times \{5\} \cup \mathcal{IV} \times \mathbb{N}$, where $\mathcal{N} = \{0,1\}^{|N|}$ is the set of nonces, $\mathcal{IV} = \{0,1\}^\tau$ is the set of IV-s and $\mathbb{N}$ is the set of positive integers.

**Lemma 1.** *Let* $\mathbb{MR}\text{-}\mathbb{OMD}\ [\widetilde{R},\tau]$ *be the* MR-OMD *scheme that uses tweakable RF* $\widetilde{R}$*. Then*

$$\mathbf{Adv}^{\mathrm{prf}}_{\mathbb{MR}\text{-}\mathbb{OMD}[\widetilde{R},\tau].HASH}(\sigma) \leq \frac{0.5\sigma^2}{2^n}$$

*where* $\sigma = \sum_{i=1}^q (|A^i|_{m+n} + ||M^i||_{m+n})$ *is the total number of calls to the underlying tweakable RF* $\widetilde{R}$ *in all* $q$ *queries asked by a nonce-misusing adversary.*

The proof of the lemma follows from that of the well-known hash-then-PRF paradigm. A brief outline of the proof is as follows. We first observe that using different nonces makes the outputs of the HASH algorithm completely independent. Among queries with the same nonce, the HASH algorithm behaves as a true RF unless there is a collision on the input to the final tweakable RF. We bound the probability of this collision by an exhaustive case-analysis. The complete proof is provided in the full version of the paper [19].

We introduce a new notation which makes the security analysis better structured. We split the encryption algorithm $\mathbb{MR}\text{-}\mathbb{OMD}[\widetilde{R},\tau].\mathcal{E}_K(N, A, M)$ into two parts. First part computes $\mathsf{IV} = \mathbb{MR}\text{-}\mathbb{OMD}[\widetilde{R},\tau].HASH_K(N, A, M)$. The second part comprises all the steps after computing the IV. We can formalize the second step as $\mathbb{MR}\text{-}\mathbb{OMD}[\widetilde{R},\tau].\bar{\mathcal{E}}_K(\mathsf{IV}, M)$, so that, if we simplify the notation, we have $\mathcal{E}_K(N, A, M) = \bar{\mathcal{E}}_K(HASH_K(N, A, M), M)$. $\mathbb{MR}\text{-}\mathbb{OMD}[\widetilde{R},\tau].\bar{\mathcal{D}}_K(\mathsf{IV}, M)$ is defined in a similar manner.

**Lemma 2.** *Let* $\mathbb{MR}\text{-}\mathbb{OMD}[\widetilde{R},\tau]$ *be the* MR-OMD *scheme that uses tweakable RF* $\widetilde{R}$*. Then*

$$\mathbf{Adv}^{\mathrm{priv\$}}_{\mathbb{MR}\text{-}\mathbb{OMD}[\widetilde{R},\tau].\bar{\mathcal{E}}}(q_e) \leq \frac{0.5q_e^2}{2^\tau}$$

*where* $q_e$ *is the number of all encryption queries asked by the adversary.*

The proof is based on the observation that, unless an IV is used twice, the algorithm $\mathbb{MR}\text{-}\mathbb{OMD}[\widetilde{R},\tau].\bar{\mathcal{E}}$ has the same output distribution as the random bits oracle. We bound the advantage of an adversary by the upper bound of the probability of IV collision. The complete proof is provided in the full version of the paper [19].

**Lemma 3.** *Let* $\mathbb{MR}\text{-}\mathbb{OMD}[\widetilde{R}, \tau]$ *be the MR-OMD scheme that uses tweakable RF* $\widetilde{R}$. *Let* $A$ *be an MR-AE adversary attacking* $\mathbb{MR}\text{-}\mathbb{OMD}[\widetilde{R}, \tau]$. *Let* $q_e$ *be the number of encryption queries and* $q_d$ *the number of decryption queries made by* $A$ *and let* $\sigma$ *be the total number of calls to the underlying tweakable RF* $\widetilde{R}$ *in all* $A$'s *queries. Then there exist adversaries* $E$ *and* $R$, *such that*

$$\mathbf{Adv}^{\mathrm{prf}}_{\mathbb{MR}\text{-}\mathbb{OMD}[\widetilde{R},\tau].HASH}(R) + \mathbf{Adv}^{\mathrm{priv\$}}_{\mathbb{MR}\text{-}\mathbb{OMD}[\widetilde{R},\tau].\bar{\mathcal{E}}}(E) \geq \mathbf{Adv}^{\mathrm{mrae}}_{\mathbb{MR}\text{-}\mathbb{OMD}[\widetilde{R},\tau]}(A) - \frac{q_d}{2^\tau}$$

*where* $E$ *asks at most* $q_e$ *queries and* $R$ *asks at most* $q = q_e + q_d$ *queries in total. Both* $E$ *and* $R$ *are limited to a total number* $\sigma$ *of calls to underlying tweakable RF* $\widetilde{R}$ *in all their queries.*

*Proof.* For the sake of readability, we shall refer to $\mathbb{MR}\text{-}\mathbb{OMD}[\widetilde{R}, \tau]$ by $\Pi$ throughout this proof. The proof proceeds in two steps.

In the first step, we consider the scheme $\bar{\Pi}$, which is the same as $\Pi$, except that we replace the algorithm $\Pi.HASH$ by $Func(\{0,1\}^{|N|} \times \{0,1\}^* \times \{0,1\}^*, \tau)$.
We first bound $\bar{p} = \Pr\left[A^{\bar{\Pi}_{\widetilde{R},\rho}(\cdot,\cdot,\cdot),\bar{\Pi}^{-1}_{\widetilde{R},\rho}(\cdot,\cdot,\cdot)} \Rightarrow 1\right] - \Pr\left[A^{\$(\cdot,\cdot,\cdot),\perp(\cdot,\cdot,\cdot)} \Rightarrow 1\right] =$
$\bar{p}_1 + \bar{p}_2$ with $\bar{p}_1 = \Pr\left[A^{\bar{\Pi}_{\widetilde{R},\rho}(\cdot,\cdot,\cdot),\bar{\Pi}^{-1}_{\widetilde{R},\rho}(\cdot,\cdot,\cdot)} \Rightarrow 1\right] - \Pr\left[A^{\bar{\Pi}_{\widetilde{R},\rho}(\cdot,\cdot,\cdot),\perp(\cdot,\cdot,\cdot)} \Rightarrow 1\right]$
and $\bar{p}_2 = \Pr\left[A^{\bar{\Pi}_{\widetilde{R},\rho}(\cdot,\cdot,\cdot),\perp(\cdot,\cdot,\cdot)} \Rightarrow 1\right] - \Pr\left[A^{\$(\cdot,\cdot,\cdot),\perp(\cdot,\cdot,\cdot)} \Rightarrow 1\right]$. We prove upper bounds for the terms $p_1$ and $\bar{p}_2$. To bound $\bar{p}_2$, we construct an adversary $E$ for attacking the priv\$ security of $\bar{\Pi}.\bar{\mathcal{E}}$ from $A$. The construction of the adversary $E$ and the bound are obtained similarly as in [23]. We deduce $\bar{p}_2 \leq \mathbf{Adv}^{\mathrm{priv\$}}_{\bar{\Pi}.\bar{\mathcal{E}}}(E)$.
The bound of $\bar{p}_1$ is obtained in a similar manner as in [23], however instead of revealing to the adversary $A$ the secret key for the encryption we reveal the tweakable RF $\widetilde{R}$. The adversary $A$ is left to guess the correct IV for the decryption queries. If we consider all queries made by $A$, we have $\bar{p}_1 \leq q_d/2^n$.
We then have $\bar{p} \leq \mathbf{Adv}^{\mathrm{priv\$}}_{\bar{\Pi}.\bar{\mathcal{E}}}(E) + q_d/2^\tau$.

The second step of the proof is based on the observation that $\mathbf{Adv}^{\mathrm{mrae}}_{\Pi}(A) =$
$\bar{p} + \Pr\left[A^{\Pi_{\widetilde{R}}(\cdot,\cdot,\cdot),\Pi^{-1}_{\widetilde{R}}(\cdot,\cdot,\cdot)} \Rightarrow 1\right] - \Pr\left[A^{\bar{\Pi}_{\widetilde{R},\rho}(\cdot,\cdot,\cdot),\bar{\Pi}^{-1}_{\widetilde{R},\rho}(\cdot,\cdot,\cdot)} \Rightarrow 1\right]$. We construct an adversary $R$ for attacking $\Pi.HASH$ as PRF, that uses $A$ as a subroutine similarly as in [23]. The adversary $R$ uses its own oracle (which is either $\Pi.HASH$ or a corresponding random function) to compute IVs and simulates $\Pi.\bar{\mathcal{E}}$ for $A$. We let $R$ choose a tweakable RF $\widetilde{R}$ and point out, that the challenger for $R$ picks its own tweakable RF $\widetilde{R}'$. This way $R$ in fact always simulates $\Pi$ with some $\widetilde{R}^* \in Func^\mathcal{T}(m+n, n)$ for $A$. This is the case because the sets of tweaks used in the algorithms $\Pi.HASH$ and $\Pi.\bar{\mathcal{E}}$ are disjoint. We show that the distribution of the tweakable RF $\widetilde{R}^*$ observed by $A$ is uniform using a counting argument. We

deduce $\mathbf{Adv}_{\Pi}^{\mathrm{mr-ae}}(A) \leq \bar{p} + \mathbf{Adv}_{\Pi.HASH}^{\mathrm{prf}}(R)$. The complete proof is provided in the full version of the paper [19]. $\qquad\square$

### 5.1.2   Instantiating Tweakable RFs with PRFs

The proof of Theorem 1 is completed in the same way as in [6]. First, the tweakable RF $\widetilde{R}$ is replaced by a tweakable PRF $\widetilde{F} : \mathcal{K} \times \mathcal{T} \times (\{0,1\}^n \times \{0,1\}^m) \to \{0,1\}^n$, where $\mathcal{K} = \{0,1\}^k$. This will increase the security bound as shown in Lemma 4.

**Lemma 4.** *Let $\widetilde{R} : \mathcal{T} \times (\{0,1\}^n \times \{0,1\}^m) \to \{0,1\}^n$ be a tweakable RF and $\widetilde{F} : \mathcal{K} \times \mathcal{T} \times (\{0,1\}^n \times \{0,1\}^m) \to \{0,1\}^n$ be a tweakable PRF. Then we have*
$$\mathbf{Adv}_{\mathrm{MR\text{-}OMD}[\widetilde{F},\tau]}^{\mathrm{mrae}}(t, q_e, q_d, \sigma) \leq \mathbf{Adv}_{\mathrm{MR\text{-}OMD}[\widetilde{R},\tau]}^{\mathrm{mrae}}(q_e, q_d, \sigma) + \mathbf{Adv}_{\widetilde{F}}^{\mathrm{prf}}(t', \sigma) \text{ where}$$
*$q_e$ and $q_d$ are, respectively, the number of encryption and decryption queries, $t' = t + cn\sigma$ for some constant $c$ and $\sigma$ is the total number of calls to the underlying tweakable PRF $\widetilde{F}$ in all queries asked by the MR-AE adversary.*

Consequently, we instantiate the tweakable PRF from an ordinary PRF by the means of xoring a mask to (a part of) the input of the PRF, exactly as in [6]. The masking function $\Delta_K(T) = \Delta_K(\alpha, i, j)$ outputs an $n$-bit mask as described in Section 4. The transition from tweakable PRFs to PRFs with xor-masks being exactly the same, we use the result on security bound from [6].

**Lemma 5.** *Let $\widetilde{F} : \mathcal{K} \times (\{0,1\}^n \times \{0,1\}^m) \to \{0,1\}^n$ be a function family with key space $\mathcal{K}$. Let $\widetilde{F} : \mathcal{K} \times \mathcal{T} \times (\{0,1\}^n \times \{0,1\}^m) \to \{0,1\}^n$ be defined by $\widetilde{F}_K^{\langle T \rangle}(X||Y) = F_K((X \oplus \Delta(T))||Y)$ for every $T \in \mathcal{T}, K \in \mathcal{K}, X \in \{0,1\}^n, Y \in \{0,1\}^m$ and $\Delta_K(T)$ is the masking function of MR-OMD as defined in Section 4. If $F$ is PRF then $\widetilde{F}$ is tweakable PRF; more precisely $\mathbf{Adv}_{\widetilde{F}}^{\mathrm{prf}}(t, q) \leq \mathbf{Adv}_F^{\mathrm{prf}}(t', 2q) + \frac{3q^2}{2^n}$.*

For the proofs for both Lemma 4 and Lemma 5, the reader can refer to [6] and [15].

### 5.2   Security in the Nonce-Respecting Case

Intuitively, one would expect that the security bound in the nonce-respecting setting should be somewhat better than the one in the nonce-reuse case. Indeed, we have $\mathbf{Adv}_{\mathrm{MR\text{-}OMD}[F,\tau]}^{\mathrm{nr\text{-}ae}}(t, \sigma, q_e, q_d) \leq \mathbf{Adv}_F^{\mathrm{prf}}(t', 2\sigma) + \frac{3\sigma^2}{2^n} + \frac{0.5q_e^2}{2^\tau} + \frac{q_d}{2^\tau}$, which confirms this intuition. The proof of this bound on adversarial advantage in nonce-respecting scenario can be found in the full version of the paper [19].

## 6   Parallelizable MR-OMD

The MR-OMD scheme described in section 4 is designed to be substantially similar to OMD; hence, being able to share a lot of common code/hardware, while achieving different (stronger) security goals than OMD itself. This similarity also implies that the encryption/decryption process in MR-OMD is serial as it is in OMD. However, we notice that the two-pass construction (in contrast to OMD which is one-pass) also opens up the possibility of having a parallelizable encryption/ decryption process. For this purpose, we propose PMR-OMD. PMR-OMD uses the same algorithms Initialize and HASH as MR-OMD, while the encryption/ decryption algorithm uses counter mode. Schematic visualisation can be found in Figure 1. This replacement will of course get us further from the original OMD, which may be inconvenient in hardware implementations; however, in software implementations, the parallel execution might be exactly what we want, especially in general purpose CPUs with multiple cores. The PMR-OMD is almost fully parallelizable, with a single bottleneck in processing the final message block in its HASH algorithm. The results of security analysis of MR-OMD apply to PMR-OMD as well, since the two schemes are identical to big extent and the security analysis of counter mode and original OMD encryption is essentially the same. For a complete discussion refer to the full version of the paper [19].

**Acknowledgments.** We would like to thank the anonymous reviewers of ProvSec 2014 for their constructive comments. This work was partially supported by Microsoft Research under MRL Contract No. 2014-006 (DP1061305).

# References

1. Andreeva, E., Bogdanov, A., Luykx, A., Mennink, B., Tischhauser, E., Yasuda, K.: Parallelizable and authenticated online ciphers. In: Sako, K., Sarkar, P. (eds.) ASIACRYPT 2013, Part I. LNCS, vol. 8269, pp. 424–443. Springer, Heidelberg (2013)
2. Bellare, M., Namprempre, C.: Authenticated Encryption: Relations among Notions and Analysis of the Generic Composition Paradigm. In: Okamoto, T. (ed.) ASIACRYPT 2000. LNCS, vol. 1976, pp. 531–545. Springer, Heidelberg (2000)
3. Bellare, M., Rogaway, P.: Encode-Then-Encipher Encryption: How to Exploit Nonces or Redundancy in Plaintexts for Efficient Cryptography. In: Okamoto, T. (ed.) ASIACRYPT 2000. LNCS, vol. 1976, pp. 317–330. Springer, Heidelberg (2000)
4. Bellare, M., Rogaway, P., Wagner, D.: The EAX Mode of Operation. In: Roy, B., Meier, W. (eds.) FSE 2004. LNCS, vol. 3017, pp. 389–407. Springer, Heidelberg (2004)
5. Bernstein, D.J.: Cryptographic competitions: CAESAR, http://competitions.cr.yp.to
6. Cogliani, S., Ştefania Maimuţ, D., Naccache, D., do Canto, R.P., Reyhanitabar, R., Vaudenay, S., Vizár, D.: Offset merkle-damgård (omd) version 1.0 a caesar proposal. Proposal in CAESAR competition (March 2014)
7. Datta, N., Nandi, M.: Elmd. CAESAR submission (2013), http://competitions.cr.yp.to/caesar.html
8. Dworkin, M.: Recommendation for block cipher modes of operation: the CCM mode for authentication and confidentiality. NIST Special Publication 800-38C (May 2004)
9. Dworkin, M.: Recommendation for block cipher modes of operation: Galois/Counter Mode (GCM) and GMAC. NIST Special Publication 800-38D (November 2007)
10. Fleischmann, E., Forler, C., Lucks, S.: McOE: A family of almost foolproof online authenticated encryption schemes. In: Canteaut, A. (ed.) FSE 2012. LNCS, vol. 7549, pp. 196–215. Springer, Heidelberg (2012)

11. Fleischmann, E., Forler, C., Lucks, S., Wenzel, J.: McOE: A Foolproof On-Line Authenticated Encryption Scheme. IACR Cryptology ePrint Archive 2011 (2011)
12. Iwata, T., Yasuda, K.: BTM: A Single-Key, Inverse-Cipher-Free Mode for Deterministic Authenticated Encryption. In: Jacobson Jr., M.J., Rijmen, V., Safavi-Naini, R. (eds.) SAC 2009. LNCS, vol. 5867, pp. 313–330. Springer, Heidelberg (2009)
13. Iwata, T., Yasuda, K.: HBS: A Single-Key Mode of Operation for Deterministic Authenticated Encryption. In: Dunkelman, O. (ed.) FSE 2009. LNCS, vol. 5665, pp. 394–415. Springer, Heidelberg (2009)
14. Katz, J., Yung, M.: Unforgeable Encryption and Chosen Ciphertext Secure Modes of Operation. In: Schneier, B. (ed.) FSE 2000. LNCS, vol. 1978, pp. 284–299. Springer, Heidelberg (2001)
15. Krovetz, T., Rogaway, P.: The Software Performance of Authenticated-Encryption Modes. In: Joux, A. (ed.) FSE 2011. LNCS, vol. 6733, pp. 306–327. Springer, Heidelberg (2011)
16. McGrew, D.A., Viega, J.: The Security and Performance of the Galois/Counter Mode (GCM) of Operation. In: Canteaut, A., Viswanathan, K. (eds.) INDOCRYPT 2004. LNCS, vol. 3348, pp. 343–355. Springer, Heidelberg (2004)
17. Namprempre, C., Rogaway, P., Shrimpton, T.: Reconsidering Generic Composition. In: Nguyen, P.Q., Oswald, E. (eds.) EUROCRYPT 2014. LNCS, vol. 8441, pp. 257–274. Springer, Heidelberg (2014)
18. Procter, G., Cid, C.: On Weak Keys and Forgery Attacks against Polynomial-based MAC Schemes. IACR Cryptology ePrint Archive (full version to appear in the Journal of Cryptology. A short version of this paper was presented at Fast Software Encryption 2013) (2013)
19. Reyhanitabar, R., Vaudenay, S., Vizár, D.: Misuse-Resistant Variants of the OMD Authenticated Encryption Mode, https://infoscience.epfl.ch/record/200501
20. Rogaway, P.: Authenticated-encryption with associated-data. In: Atluri, V. (ed.) ACM Conference on Computer and Communications Security, pp. 98–107. ACM (2002)
21. Rogaway, P.: Efficient Instantiations of Tweakable Blockciphers and Refinements to Modes OCB and PMAC. In: Lee, P.J. (ed.) ASIACRYPT 2004. LNCS, vol. 3329, pp. 16–31. Springer, Heidelberg (2004)
22. Rogaway, P., Bellare, M., Black, J., Krovetz, T.: OCB: a block-cipher mode of operation for efficient authenticated encryption. In: Reiter, M.K., Samarati, P. (eds.) ACM Conference on Computer and Communications Security, pp. 196–205. ACM (2001)
23. Rogaway, P., Shrimpton, T.: A provable-security treatment of the key-wrap problem. In: Vaudenay, S. (ed.) EUROCRYPT 2006. LNCS, vol. 4004, pp. 373–390. Springer, Heidelberg (2006)
24. Saarinen, M.-J.O.: Cycling Attacks on GCM, GHASH and Other Polynomial MACs and Hashes. In: Canteaut, A. (ed.) FSE 2012. LNCS, vol. 7549, pp. 216–225. Springer, Heidelberg (2012)
25. Vaudenay, S.: Security Flaws Induced by CBC Padding - Applications to SSL, IPSEC, WTLS ... In: Knudsen, L.R. (ed.) EUROCRYPT 2002. LNCS, vol. 2332, pp. 534–546. Springer, Heidelberg (2002)
26. Whiting, D., Housley, R., Ferguson, N.: Intel®SHA Extensions New Instructions Supporting the Secure Hash Algorithm on Intel®Architecture Processors. Intel White Paper (July 2013), https://software.intel.com/en-us/articles/intel-sha-extensions

# A Block-Cipher-Based Hash Function Using an MMO-Type Double-Block Compression Function

Shoichi Hirose[1] and Hidenori Kuwakado[2]

[1] Graduate School of Engineering, University of Fukui, Japan
[2] Faculty of Informatics, Kansai University, Japan

**Abstract.** Methods to construct a hash function using an existing block cipher recently attract some interests as an approach to implement a hash function on constrained devices. It is often required to construct a hash function whose output length is larger than that of the underlying block cipher to provide sufficient level of collision resistance with the use of an existing block cipher. This article presents a new mode of double-block compression function, which is based on the mode proposed by Jonsson and Robshaw at PKC 2005. The mode can be instantiated with a block cipher whose key-length is larger than its block-length such as AES-192/256, PRESENT-128, etc. This article also provides provable security analyses to an iterated hash function using the proposed mode and the MDP domain extension. The security properties discussed are collision resistance, preimage resistance, pseudorandom-function property of the keyed-via-IV mode, and the indifferentiability from a random oracle.

## 1 Introduction

*Background.* A cryptographic hash function transforms strings of arbitrary length to strings of fixed length. It usually consists of a compression function and domain extension. A compression function is a function from strings of fixed length to strings of fixed smaller length. Domain extension specifies how to process input strings of arbitrary length using a given compression function. A cryptographic hash function of this type is called an iterated hash function.

Most of the iterated hash functions are classified into two types according to their compression-function construction: block-cipher-based and permutation-based. The methods to construct block-cipher-based compression functions are further classified into dedicated and using existing block ciphers. The former includes most of the widely deployed or well-known hash functions such as MD$x$ [25,26], SHA-$x$ [8], Whirlpool [24] and so on. On the other hand, the latter attracts some interests as an approach to implement a hash function on constrained devices [4,27]. This is the topic of this article.

The collision resistance of a hash function producing $n$-bit digests is at most $O(2^{n/2})$ due to the birthday attack. To provide sufficient level of collision resistance with the use of existing block ciphers, it is necessary to construct a compression function whose output length is larger than that of the underlying block ciphers. There have been several proposals for modes to construct double-block

S.S.M. Chow et al. (Eds.): ProvSec 2014, LNCS 8782, pp. 71–86, 2014.

compression functions [6,11,13,15]. One line of research is to present a general model and discuss security properties in a unified way [22]. We are interested in another line of research: identifying modes of practical interest.

*Our Contribution.* We first present a mode of compression function based on the mode proposed by Jonsson and Robshaw [13]. Then, we provide provable security analyses to an iterated hash function using the proposed compression function and the MDP domain extension [12] in terms of collision resistance (CR), preimage resistance (PR), pseudorandomness as a function (PRF), and indifferentiability from a random oracle (IRO).

CR, PR and IRO are discussed in the ideal cipher model, and PRF is discussed in the standard model. Birthday-type lower bounds are given to its CR and IRO. These bounds are optimal up to some constant factors for this kind of iterated hash functions. A lower bound optimal up to a constant factor is also given to its PR. The keyed-via-IV (KIV) mode is shown to be a PRF if the underlying block cipher is a pseudorandom permutation (PRP) under rather mild related-key attacks.

The proposed mode requires an underlying block cipher with its key length larger than its block length, which is similar to that of abreast-/tandem-DM [15] and Hirose mode [11]. The advantage of the proposed mode over them is that the key input of the underlying block cipher only receives the chaining value. It prevents attackers from manipulating the key inputs directly. It also enables the reduction of the PRF property of the hash function to the PRP property of the underlying block cipher. The advantage of the proposed mode over MDC-2/4 [6] is that the security reductions are settled and, in particular, optimal security levels (up to some constants) are achieved for CR, PR and IRO.

*Related Work.* Security properties such as collision resistance and preimage resistance of existing double-block modes have also been analysed in the ideal cipher model. Steinberger gave a lower bound on CR of MDC-2 [28], which is quite lower than the birthday bound. Optimal birthday-type lower bounds were obtained on CR of abreast-DM and Hirose modes [9,11,16]. A nearly optimal lower bound was obtained on CR for tandem-DM [19]. Optimal lower bounds on PR were obtained for abreast-DM, tandem-DM and Hirose modes [1].

Özen and Stam [22] presented a general model of double-block modes using one or two calls to a $2n$-bit-key and $n$-bit-block block cipher, and discussed CR and PR of the modes in this model. Strictly, our analysis of CR is not covered by theirs since our analysis accepts a block cipher with variable-length key. Furthermore, they discussed neither IRO nor PRF.

There are some proposals to construct double-block iterated hash functions using a block cipher. Naito [21] proposed a scheme using a $2n$-bit-key and $n$-bit-block block cipher. He also presented a birthday-type lower bound on IRO of the hash functions in the ideal cipher model. Kuwakado and Hirose [14] proposed a scheme suitable for lightweight block ciphers. They discussed the preimage resistance of the hash function and the PRF property of its keyed mode in the standard model. Lee and Stam [18] recently showed that the iterated hash function using the double-block compression function called MJH [17] has asymptotically optimal collision resistance in the ideal cipher model.

*Organization.* Section 2 gives some notations and definitions of security properties used and discussed in the paper. The proposed double-block mode is presented in Sect. 3. The iterated hash function composed of the compression function with the MDP domain extension is also presented in this section. Collision resistance and preimage resistance are discussed in Sect. 4. Pseudorandomness of the KIV mode is discussed in Sect. 5. IRO is discussed in Sect. 6.

## 2 Preliminaries

### 2.1 Notations

Let $F(\mathcal{X}, \mathcal{Y})$ be the set of all functions with domain $\mathcal{X}$ and range $\mathcal{Y}$. Let $P(\mathcal{X})$ be the set of all permutations on $\mathcal{X}$. Let $\mathcal{BC}(n, \kappa)$ be the set of all $(n, \kappa)$ block ciphers, where $n$ and $\kappa$ represent their block size and key size, respectively.

Let $\Sigma = \{0, 1\}$. Let $\Sigma^* = \bigcup_{i=0}^{\infty} \Sigma^i$, $(\Sigma^n)^+ = \bigcup_{i=1}^{\infty} \Sigma^{ni}$, and $(\Sigma^n)^{\leq i} = \bigcup_{j=0}^{i} \Sigma^{nj}$.

For binary strings $x$ and $y$, let $x\|y$ be their concatenation. For simplicity, for $M_1, M_2, \ldots, M_l \in \Sigma^n$, $M_1\|M_2\| \cdots \|M_l$ will be denoted by $M_{[1,l]}$ or $M_1 M_2 \cdots M_l$.

Let $\phi$ be the permutation on $\Sigma^k$ defined by $\phi(x_L\|x_R) = x_R\|x_L$ for every $x_L$ and $x_R$ in $\Sigma^{k/2}$.

### 2.2 Collision Resistance and Preimage Resistance

Let $H^E$ be a hash function using a block cipher $E$. The collision resistance and preimage resistance of a block-cipher-based hash function are often discussed in the ideal cipher model [3]. We follow this convention.

In the ideal cipher model, the underlying block cipher $E$ is assumed to be uniformly distributed over $\mathcal{BC}(n, \kappa)$. An encryption/decryption operation is an encryption/decryption query to the oracle $E$. Without loss of generality, it is assumed that an adversary does not make any query to which it already knows the answer.

Let $A$ be an adversary trying to find a collision for $H^E$, that is, a pair of distinct inputs mapped to the same output by $H^E$. The col-advantage of $A$ against $H^E$ is given by

$$\mathrm{Adv}_{H^E}^{\mathrm{col}}(A) = \Pr[A^E = (M, M') \wedge H^E(M) = H^E(M') \wedge M \neq M'] ,$$

where $E$ is uniformly distributed over $\mathcal{BC}(n, \kappa)$. It is assumed that $A$ makes all the queries necessary to compute $H^E(M)$ and $H^E(M')$. Let $\mathrm{Adv}_{H^E}^{\mathrm{col}}(q)$ be the maximum col-advantage over all adversaries asking at most $q$ queries.

Let $A$ be an adversary trying to find a preimage of a given output $v$ for $H^E$. The pre-advantage of $A$ against $H^E$ is given by

$$\mathrm{Adv}^{\mathrm{pre}}_{H^E}(A) = \Pr[A^E(v) = M \wedge H^E(M) = v] \ ,$$

where $E$ is uniformly distributed over $\mathcal{BC}(n, \kappa)$. It is assumed that $A$ makes all the queries necessary to compute $H^E(M)$. Let $\mathrm{Adv}^{\mathrm{pre}}_{H^E}(q)$ be the maximum pre-advantage over all adversaries asking at most $q$ queries.

## 2.3  Pseudorandom Function and Permutation (PRF & PRP)

Let $f \in \boldsymbol{F}(\mathcal{K} \times \mathcal{X}, \mathcal{Y})$ be a keyed function from $\mathcal{X}$ to $\mathcal{Y}$ with key space $\mathcal{K}$. Let $A$ be an adversary which has oracle access to a function from $\mathcal{X}$ to $\mathcal{Y}$ and outputs 0 or 1. The prf-advantage of $A$ against $f$ is given by

$$\mathrm{Adv}^{\mathrm{prf}}_{f}(A) = \left| \Pr[A^{f_K} = 1] - \Pr[A^{\rho} = 1] \right| \ ,$$

where $K$ is uniformly distributed over $\mathcal{K}$ and $\rho$ is uniformly distributed over $\boldsymbol{F}(\mathcal{X}, \mathcal{Y})$.

Let $f \in \boldsymbol{F}(\mathcal{K} \times \mathcal{X}, \mathcal{X})$ be a keyed function. Then, the prp-advantage of $A$ against $f$ is given by

$$\mathrm{Adv}^{\mathrm{prp}}_{f}(A) = \left| \Pr[A^{f_K} = 1] - \Pr[A^{\rho} = 1] \right| \ ,$$

where $K$ is uniformly distributed over $\mathcal{K}$ and $\rho$ is uniformly distributed over $\boldsymbol{P}(\mathcal{X})$.

## 2.4  PRF & PRP under Related-Key Attacks

The PRF and PRP under related-key attacks are formalized by Bellare and Kohno [2]. Let $\Phi \subset \boldsymbol{F}(\mathcal{K}, \mathcal{K})$. Let $A$ be an adversary which has oracle access to $g(\mathsf{key}(\cdot, K), \cdot)$, where $g \in \boldsymbol{F}(\mathcal{K} \times \mathcal{X}, \mathcal{Y})$, $K \in \mathcal{K}$ and $\mathsf{key} \in \boldsymbol{F}(\Phi \times \mathcal{K}, \mathcal{K})$ such that $\mathsf{key}(\varphi, K) = \varphi(K)$. $A$ asks a pair of $\varphi \in \Phi$ and $x \in \mathcal{X}$ as a query, and obtains $g(\varphi(K), x)$. For simplicity, $g(\mathsf{key}(\cdot, K), \cdot)$ is denoted by $(g, K)$. The prf-rka-advantage of $A$ against $f \in \boldsymbol{F}(\mathcal{K} \times \mathcal{X}, \mathcal{Y})$ restricted by $\Phi$ is given by

$$\mathrm{Adv}^{\mathrm{prf\text{-}rka}}_{\Phi, f}(A) = \left| \Pr[A^{(f, K)} = 1] - \Pr[A^{(\rho, K)} = 1] \right| \ ,$$

where $K$ is uniformly distributed over $\mathcal{K}$ and $\rho$ is uniformly distributed over $\boldsymbol{F}(\mathcal{K} \times \mathcal{X}, \mathcal{Y})$.

Let $\boldsymbol{P}(\mathcal{K} \times \mathcal{X}, \mathcal{X})$ be the set of all keyed permutations on $\mathcal{X}$ with key space $\mathcal{K}$. The prp-rka-advantage of $A$ against $f \in \boldsymbol{F}(\mathcal{K} \times \mathcal{X}, \mathcal{X})$ restricted by $\Phi$ is given by

$$\mathrm{Adv}^{\mathrm{prp\text{-}rka}}_{\Phi, f}(A) = \left| \Pr[A^{(f, K)} = 1] - \Pr[A^{(\rho, K)} = 1] \right| \ ,$$

where $K$ is uniformly distributed over $\mathcal{K}$ and $\rho$ is uniformly distributed over $\boldsymbol{P}(\mathcal{K} \times \mathcal{X}, \mathcal{X})$.

## 2.5    Indifferentiability from Random Oracle

The notion of indifferentiability is introduced by Maurer et al. [20] as a generalized notion of indistinguishability. It is tailored to security analysis of hash functions by Coron et al. [7].

Let $C$ be an algorithm with oracle access to an ideal primitive $\mathcal{F}$. In the setting of this article, $C$ is an algorithm to construct a hash function using $\mathcal{F}$ with fixed input length. Let $\mathcal{H}$ be a variable-input-length (VIL) random oracle and $S$ be a simulator which has oracle access to $\mathcal{H}$. $S^{\mathcal{H}}$ tries to behave like $\mathcal{F}$ in order to convince an adversary that $\mathcal{H}$ is $C^{\mathcal{F}}$. Let $A$ be an adversary with access to two oracles. The indiff-advantage of $A$ against $C$ with respect to $S$ is given by

$$\mathrm{Adv}_{C,S}^{\mathrm{indiff}}(A) = \left| \Pr[A^{C^{\mathcal{F}},\mathcal{F}} = 1] - \Pr[A^{\mathcal{H},S^{\mathcal{H}}} = 1] \right| .$$

# 3    Construction

Let $E \in \mathcal{BC}(n, k)$, where $k$ is an even integer such that $n \leq k \leq 2n$. We consider constructions of an iterated hash function with the following compression function $F : \Sigma^k \times \Sigma^n \to \Sigma^k$ based on $E$:

$$F(h_i, M_i) = \mathrm{tr}_{k/2}(E_{h_i}(M_i) \oplus M_i) \| \mathrm{tr}_{k/2}(E_{h_i}(\sigma(M_i)) \oplus \sigma(M_i)) .$$

$\sigma : \Sigma^n \to \Sigma^n$ is an involution with no fixed points, that is, $\sigma = \sigma^{-1}$ and $\sigma(M_i) \neq M_i$ for any $M_i \in \Sigma^n$. $\mathrm{tr}_{k/2} : \Sigma^n \to \Sigma^{k/2}$ outputs $k/2$ least significant bits of the input. $F$ is depicted in Fig. 1. It is based on the mode proposed by Jonsson and Robshaw [13], and its upper or right half has the structure of the Matyas-Meyer-Oseas (MMO) mode. It can be instantiated with AES with 256-bit or 192-bit key.

MDP [12] is adopted for domain extension. Let $\pi$ be a permutation on $\Sigma^k$ with at most few fixed points. For $1 \leq i \leq N$, let $M_i \in \Sigma^n$. $F_\pi^\circ : \Sigma^k \times (\Sigma^n)^+ \to \Sigma^k$ is an iterated hash function such that $F_\pi^\circ(IV, M_1 \| \cdots \| M_N) = h_N$, where $h_0 = IV$ is a fixed initial value, $h_i = F(h_{i-1}, M_i)$ for $1 \leq i \leq N-1$, and $h_N = F(\pi(h_{N-1}), M_N)$. Notice that $h_1 = F(\pi(IV), M_1)$ if $N = 1$. For $M \in \Sigma^*$, an unambiguous padding function $\mathrm{pad} : \Sigma^* \to (\Sigma^n)^+$ is necessary to apply $F_\pi^\circ$ to $M$. $F_\pi^\circ$ is illustrated in Fig. 2.

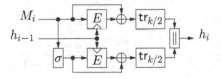

**Fig. 1.** Compression function $F$

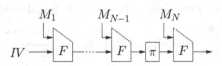

**Fig. 2.** Hash function $F_\pi^\circ$

## 4   Collision Resistance and Preimage Resistance

In this section, the collision resistance and preimage resistance of $F_\pi^\circ$ is evaluated in the ideal cipher model. The followings are assumed here:

- When adversary $A$ makes an encryption query $(K, X)$, $A$ receives $Y$ such that $E_K(X) = Y$ and also gets for free $Y' = E_K(\sigma(X))$.
- When $A$ makes a decryption query $(K, Y)$, $A$ receives $X$ such that $E_K(X) = Y$ and also gets for free $Y' = E_K(\sigma(X))$.

### 4.1   Collision Resistance

The theorem given below implies that the collision resistance of $F_\pi^\circ$ is optimal up to some constant factor.

**Theorem 1.** *For $1 \leq q < 2^{n-1}$,*

$$\mathrm{Adv}_{F_\pi^\circ}^{\mathrm{col}}(q) \leq \frac{q}{2^{k/2}(1 - q/2^{n-1})} + \frac{q^2 + 2q}{2^k(1 - q/2^{n-1})^2} .$$

*Example 1.* The upper bound of Theorem 1 is 0.5 if $q = 2^{125.7}$ for $(n, k) = (128, 256)$ and if $q = 2^{94.5}$ for $(n, k) = (128, 192)$.

It is easy to see that $\mathrm{Adv}_{F_\pi^\circ}^{\mathrm{col}}(q) \leq \mathrm{Adv}_F^{\mathrm{col}}(q) + \mathrm{Adv}_F^{\mathrm{pre}}(q)$. Upper bounds on $\mathrm{Adv}_F^{\mathrm{col}}(q)$ and $\mathrm{Adv}_F^{\mathrm{pre}}(q)$ are given in Lemmas 1 and 2, respectively. The upper bound on $\mathrm{Adv}_F^{\mathrm{pre}}(q)$ is not so tight but suffices for our purpose.

**Lemma 1.** *For $1 \leq q < 2^{n-1}$,*

$$\mathrm{Adv}_F^{\mathrm{col}}(q) \leq \frac{q}{2^{k/2}(1 - q/2^{n-1})} + \left( \frac{q}{2^{k/2}(1 - q/2^{n-1})} \right)^2 .$$

*Proof.* Let $A$ be any collision-finding adversary against $F$ asking at most $q$ queries to $E$. For $1 \leq i \leq q$, making the $i$-th query, adversary $A$ obtains some $(K_i, X_i, Y_i)$ and $(K_i, \sigma(X_i), Y_i')$ such that $E_{K_i}(X_i) = Y_i$ and $E_{K_i}(\sigma(X_i)) = Y_i'$. Let $W_i = \mathrm{tr}_{k/2}(Y_i \oplus X_i) \| \mathrm{tr}_{k/2}(Y_i' \oplus \sigma(X_i))$.

Let $\mathsf{Col}_{1,i}$ be the event that $W_i = \phi(W_i)$. Let $\mathsf{Col}_{2,i}$ be the event that $W_i \in \bigcup_{j=1}^{i-1}\{W_j, \phi(W_j)\}$. If $A$ succeeds in finding a collision for $F$ just after the $i$-th query, then either $\mathsf{Col}_{1,i}$ or $\mathsf{Col}_{2,i}$ occurs. For the two events,

$$\Pr[\mathsf{Col}_{1,i}] \leq \frac{2^{n-k/2}}{2^n - (2i - 1)} \quad \text{and} \quad \Pr[\mathsf{Col}_{2,i}] \leq \frac{(2^{n-k/2})^2 2(i - 1)}{(2^n - (2i - 2))(2^n - (2i - 1))} .$$

The probability that $A$ finds a collision for $F$ is bounded above by

$$\sum_{i=1}^{q} (\Pr[\mathsf{Col}_{1,i}] + \Pr[\mathsf{Col}_{2,i}]) \leq \frac{2^{n-k/2}q}{2^n - (2q - 1)} + \frac{(2^{n-k/2})^2 q(q - 1)}{(2^n - (2q - 2))(2^n - (2q - 1))}$$

$$\leq \frac{2^{n-k/2}q}{2^n - 2q} + \left( \frac{2^{n-k/2}q}{2^n - 2q} \right)^2 .$$

□

**Lemma 2.** *For* $1 \leq q < 2^{n-1}$,

$$\mathrm{Adv}_F^{\mathrm{pre}}(q) \leq \frac{2q}{2^k(1 - q/2^{n-1})^2} .$$

*Proof.* Let $A$ be any preimage-finding adversary against $F$ asking at most $q$ queries to $E$. For $1 \leq i \leq q$, making the $i$-th query, adversary $A$ obtains some $(K_i, X_i, Y_i)$ and $(K_i, \sigma(X_i), Y_i')$ such that $E_{K_i}(X_i) = Y_i$ and $E_{K_i}(\sigma(X_i)) = Y_i'$. Let $W_i = \mathrm{tr}_{k/2}(Y_i \oplus X_i) \| \mathrm{tr}_{k/2}(Y_i' \oplus \sigma(X_i)))$.

Let $T$ be the given digest. Let $\mathsf{Pre}_i$ be the event that $W_i = T$ or $\phi(W_i) = T$. Then,

$$\Pr[\mathsf{Pre}_i] \leq \frac{(2^{n-k/2})^2 \cdot 2}{(2^n - (2i-2))(2^n - (2i-1))} .$$

The probability that $A$ finds a preimage of $T$ for $F$ is bounded above by

$$\sum_{i=1}^{q} \Pr[\mathsf{Pre}_i] \leq \frac{(2^{n-k/2})^2 \cdot 2q}{(2^n - (2q-2))(2^n - (2q-1))} \leq \frac{(2^{n-k/2})^2 \cdot 2q}{(2^n - 2q)^2} .$$

$\square$

### 4.2 Preimage Resistance

With the technique of "super query" introduced by [19], it can also be proved that the preimage resistance of $F_\pi^\circ$ is optimal up to a constant factor in the ideal cipher model.

**Theorem 2.**

$$\mathrm{Adv}_{F_\pi^\circ}^{\mathrm{pre}}(q) \leq \frac{q}{2^{k-4}(1 - 2^{1-n})} .$$

*Proof.* Let $A$ be any preimage-finding adversary against $F$ asking at most $q$ queries to $E$. Here, we call the queries normal queries. It is assumed that, if $A$ makes $2^{n-2}$ normal queries with respect to a key, then it is given for free the remaining $2^{n-1}$ pairs of plaintexts and ciphertexts with respect to the same key. This event is called a super query.

Let $\mathsf{PreN}$ be the event that a preimage is obtained by some normal query. Let $\mathsf{PreS}$ be the event that a preimage is obtained by some super query. Then,

$$\mathrm{Adv}_{F_\pi^\circ}^{\mathrm{pre}}(q) \leq \Pr[\mathsf{PreN}] + \Pr[\mathsf{PreS}] .$$

For $\mathsf{PreN}$, the probability that a preimage is obtained by a normal query is at most $(2^{n-k/2}/2^{n-1})^2 \cdot 2 = 1/2^{k-3}$. Since $A$ makes at most $q$ normal queries, $\Pr[\mathsf{PreN}] \leq q/2^{k-3}$.

On the other hand, for $\mathsf{PreS}$, the probability that a preimage is obtained by a super query is at most

$$\frac{2^{n-k/2}}{2^{n-1}} \cdot \frac{2^{n-k/2}}{2^{n-1} - 1} \cdot 2 \cdot 2^{n-2} \leq \frac{2^{n+1}}{2^k(1 - 2^{1-n})} .$$

Since $A$ makes at most $q/2^{n-2}$ super queries, $\Pr[\mathsf{PreS}] \leq q/(2^{k-3}(1 - 2^{1-n}))$. $\square$

# 5   Keyed Hashing Mode

We consider a keyed hashing mode of $F_\pi^\circ$: keyed-via-IV (KIV) mode. It is obtained simply by replacing the initial value $IV$ with secret key $K$, that is, $F_\pi^\circ(K, \cdot)$, where $K \in \Sigma^k$.

For this mode, it is assumed that the inputs satisfy the following property. Let $\mathcal{M} \subset (\Sigma^n)^+$ be the domain of the KIV mode of $F_\pi^\circ$. For any positive integer $l$, for any $M_{[1,l]}$ and $M'_{[1,l]}$ in $\mathcal{M} \cap \Sigma^{nl}$, $M_l \neq \sigma(M'_l)$ if $M_{[1,l-1]} = M'_{[1,l-1]}$. Let us call this property $\sigma$-free. It is easy to see that the KIV mode of $F_\pi^\circ$ cannot be a PRF if its domain is not $\sigma$-free.

The following theorem implies that the KIV mode of $F_\pi^\circ$ is a PRF if $E$ is a PRP under related-key attacks with respect to $\mathsf{Rel} = \{id, \phi, \pi, \pi \circ \phi\}$, where $id$ is the identity permutation on $\Sigma^k$. Let $P_{\pi,\phi} = \{x \in \Sigma^k \mid \pi(x) = x \vee \pi(x) = \phi(x)\}$.

**Theorem 3.** *Let $A$ be a prf-adversary against the KIV mode of $F_\pi^\circ$. Suppose that the domain of the KIV mode of $F_\pi^\circ$ is $\sigma$-free. Suppose that $A$ runs in time at most $\tau$, and makes at most $q$ queries, and each query has at most $\ell$ message blocks. Suppose that $q \leq \lambda 2^n / \mathrm{e}$ for some positive constant $\lambda < 1$, where $\mathrm{e}$ is the base of the natural logarithm. Then, there exists a prp-rka-adversary $B$ against $E$ such that*

$$\mathrm{Adv}_{F_\pi^\circ}^{\mathrm{prf}}(A) \leq \ell q \cdot \mathrm{Adv}_{\mathsf{Rel},E}^{\mathrm{prp\text{-}rka}}(B) + \ell q \left( \frac{|P_{\pi,\phi}|}{2^k} + \frac{1}{2^{k/2}} \right) + \frac{\ell \, 2^{k/2}}{1-\lambda} \left( \frac{\mathrm{e}\, q}{2^n} \right)^{2^{n-k/2}+1} .$$

*$B$ makes at most $q$ queries restricted by $\mathsf{Rel}$ and runs in time at most $\tau + O(\ell q T_E)$, where $T_E$ represents the time required to compute $E$.*

It is easy to make $P_{\pi,\phi}$ small. For example, $P_{\pi,\phi}$ is empty if $\pi(x_\mathrm{L}\|x_\mathrm{R}) = (x_\mathrm{L} \oplus c_\mathrm{L})\|(x_\mathrm{R} \oplus c_\mathrm{R})$, where $x_\mathrm{L}, x_\mathrm{R}, c_\mathrm{L}, c_\mathrm{R} \in \Sigma^{k/2}$ and $c_\mathrm{L}$ and $c_\mathrm{R}$ are distinct constants.

The last term of the upper bound in Theorem 3 is $\Omega(1)$ for $\sqrt{\ell} q = \Omega(2^{n/2})$ if $k = 2n$. If $k = 2n - 2c$ for some constant $c$, then it is $\Omega(1)$ for $\ell^{1/(2^c+1)} q = \Omega(2^{n/(1+2^{-c})})$.

Theorem 3 directly follows from the succeeding three lemmas.

Let $A$ be an adversary with access to $m$ oracles $(u_1, K_1)$, $(u_2, K_2)$, ..., $(u_m, K_m)$, where $u_i \in \mathbf{F}(\mathcal{K} \times \mathcal{X}, \mathcal{Y})$ and $K_i \in \mathcal{K}$ for $1 \leq i \leq m$. Each query by $A$ is directed to just one of the $m$ oracles. Let us define the following notation: $\langle (u_j, K_j) \rangle_{j=1}^m = (u_1, K_1), (u_2, K_2), \ldots, (u_m, K_m)$. The $m$-prf-rka-advantage of $A$ against $h$ under $\Phi$-related-key attacks is defined as follows:

$$\mathrm{Adv}_{\Phi,h}^{m\text{-prf-rka}}(A) = \left| \Pr[A^{\langle (h, K_j) \rangle_{j=1}^m} = 1] - \Pr[A^{\langle (\rho_j, K_j) \rangle_{j=1}^m} = 1] \right| ,$$

where $K_j$'s are independent random variables uniformly distributed over $\mathcal{K}$, and $\rho_j$'s are independent random keyed functions uniformly distributed over $\mathbf{F}(\mathcal{K} \times \mathcal{X}, \mathcal{Y})$.

**Lemma 3.** *Suppose that there are $q$ balls and $t$ bins. Each ball is placed in a bin chosen independently and uniformly at random. Let $m$ be a positive integer* and $\lambda$ be a real such that $0 < \frac{eq}{mt} \leq \lambda < 1$. Then, some bin contains $m$ or more balls with probability at most

$$\frac{t}{1-\lambda}\left(\frac{eq}{mt}\right)^m .$$

*Proof.* Omitted due to the page limit. □

**Lemma 4.** *Let* $f(K,x) = \mathrm{tr}_{k/2}(E_K(x) \oplus x)$. *Let* $A$ *be a prf-adversary against the KIV mode of* $F_\pi^\circ$. *Suppose that the domain of the KIV mode of* $F_\pi^\circ$ *is* $\sigma$-*free. Suppose that* $A$ *runs in time at most* $\tau$, *and makes at most* $q$ *queries, and each query has at most* $\ell$ *message blocks. Then, there exists a prf-rka-adversary* $B$ *against* $f$ *with access to* $q$ *oracles such that*

$$\mathrm{Adv}^{\mathrm{prf}}_{F_\pi^\circ}(A) \leq \ell \cdot \mathrm{Adv}^{q\text{-}\mathrm{prf}\text{-}\mathrm{rka}}_{\mathrm{Rel},f}(B) + \ell q \left(\frac{|P_{\pi,\phi}|}{2^k} + \frac{1}{2^{k/2}}\right) .$$

$B$ *makes at most* $q$ *queries restricted by* Rel *and runs in time at most* $\tau + O(\ell q T_E)$, *where* $T_E$ *represents the time required to compute* $E$.

*Proof.* For $i \in \{0, 1, \dots, \ell\}$ ($\ell \geq 1$), let $I_i : (\Sigma^n)^{\leq \ell} \to \Sigma^k$ be a random function such that

$$I_i(M_{[1,l]}) = \begin{cases} \alpha_0(M_{[1,l]}) & \text{if } 1 \leq l \leq i, \\ F_\pi^\circ(\alpha_1(M_{[1,i]}), M_{[i+1,l]}) & \text{if } i+1 \leq l \leq \ell , \end{cases}$$

where $\alpha_0$ and $\alpha_1$ are independent and random functions; $\alpha_0$ is uniformly distributed over $\boldsymbol{F}((\Sigma^n)^{\leq i}, \Sigma^k)$, and $\alpha_1$ is uniformly distributed over

$$\{\alpha \,|\, \alpha \in \boldsymbol{F}((\Sigma^n)^i, \Sigma^k) \text{ and } \alpha(M_{[1,i-1]}\|\sigma(M_i)) = \phi(\alpha(M_{[1,i]}))\} .$$

Notice that $\alpha_0$ and $\alpha_1$ are independent and random elements uniformly distributed over $\Sigma^k$ if $i = 0$. Then,

$$\mathrm{Adv}^{\mathrm{prf}}_{F_\pi^\circ}(A) = \left|\Pr[A^{I_0} = 1] - \Pr[A^{I_\ell} = 1]\right| .$$

A prf-rka-adversary $B$ with $q$ oracles $\langle(u_j, K_j)\rangle_{j=1}^q$ is constructed using $A$ as a subroutine. $B$ first selects $i \in \{1, \dots, \ell\}$ uniformly at random. Then, $B$ runs $A$. $B$ simulates a random function $\beta$ uniformly distributed over $\boldsymbol{F}((\Sigma^n)^{\leq i-1}, \Sigma^k)$ via lazy sampling. $B$ answers to the $t$-th query of $A$, $M^{(t)} = M^{(t)}_{[1,l]}$, as follows:

1. If $1 \leq l \leq i - 1$, then $B$ returns $\beta(M^{(t)})$.
2. Suppose that $i \leq l \leq \ell$. Let

$$p = \min\left\{t' \,|\, t' < t \wedge \left(M^{(t')}_{[1,i-1]} = M^{(t)}_{[1,i-1]} \vee M^{(t')}_{[1,i-1]} = M^{(t)}_{[1,i-2]}\|\sigma(M^{(t)}_{i-1})\right)\right\} .$$

(a) Suppose that $l = i$. If $p \neq \bot$, then $B$ returns
   $-\ u_p(\pi(K_p), M^{(t)}_i)\|u_p(\pi(K_p), \sigma(M^{(t)}_i))$ if $M^{(t)}_{[1,i-1]} = M^{(t)}_{[1,i-1]}$, and

      – $u_p(\pi(\phi(K_p)), M_i^{(t)})\|u_p(\pi(\phi(K_p)), \sigma(M_i^{(t)}))$ if $M_{[1,i-1]}^{(p)} = M_{[1,i-2]}^{(t)}\|\sigma(M_{i-1}^{(t)})$.

Otherwise, $B$ returns $u_t(\pi(K_t), M_i^{(t)})\|u_t(\pi(K_t), \sigma(M_i^{(t)}))$.

(b) Suppose that $i + 1 \leq l \leq \ell$. If $p \neq \bot$, then $B$ returns

      – $F_\pi^\circ(u_p(K_p, M_i^{(t)})\|u_p(K_p, \sigma(M_i^{(t)})), M_{[i+1,l]}^{(t)})$ if $M_{[1,i-1]}^{(p)} = M_{[1,i-1]}^{(t)}$, and

      – $F_\pi^\circ(u_p(\phi(K_p), M_i^{(t)})\|u_p(\phi(K_p), \sigma(M_i^{(t)})), M_{[i+1,l]}^{(t)})$ if $M_{[1,i-1]}^{(p)} = M_{[1,i-2]}^{(t)}\|\sigma(M_{i-1}^{(t)})$.

Otherwise, $B$ returns $F_\pi^\circ(u_t(K_t, M_i^{(t)})\|u_t(K_t, \sigma(M_i^{(t)})), M_{[i+1,l]}^{(t)})$.

Now, suppose that $B$ is given oracles $\langle (f, K_j) \rangle_{j=1}^q$, where $K_j$'s are independent random variables uniformly distributed over $\Sigma^k$. Then,

$$u_p(\pi(K_p), M_i^{(t)})\|u_p(\pi(K_p), \sigma(M_i^{(t)})) = F_\pi^\circ(K_p, M_i^{(t)})$$
$$u_p(\pi(\phi(K_p)), M_i^{(t)})\|u_p(\pi(\phi(K_p)), \sigma(M_i^{(t)})) = F_\pi^\circ(\phi(K_p), M_i^{(t)})$$

and

$$F_\pi^\circ(u_p(K_p, M_i^{(t)})\|u_p(K_p, \sigma(M_i^{(t)})), M_{[i+1,l]}^{(t)}) = F_\pi^\circ(K_p, M_{[i,l]}^{(t)})$$
$$F_\pi^\circ(u_p(\phi(K_p), M_i^{(t)})\|u_p(\phi(K_p), \sigma(M_i^{(t)})), M_{[i+1,l]}^{(t)}) = F_\pi^\circ(\phi(K_p), M_{[i,l]}^{(t)}) .$$

Therefore, we can say that $A$ has oracle access to $I_{i-1}$, and

$$\Pr\left[ B^{\langle (f, K_j) \rangle_{j=1}^q} = 1 \right] = \frac{1}{\ell} \sum_{i=1}^\ell \Pr[A^{I_{i-1}} = 1] .$$

Next, suppose that $B$ has oracle access to $\langle (\rho_j, K_j) \rangle_{j=1}^q$, where $\rho_j$'s are independent random functions uniformly distributed over $F(\Sigma^k \times \Sigma^n, \Sigma^{k/2})$, and $K_j$'s are independent random variables uniformly distributed over $\Sigma^k$. Since the domain of $F_\pi^\circ$ is $\sigma$-free, $B$ can successfully simulate $I_i$ to $A$ if $\phi(K_j) \neq K_j$ and $\{\pi(K_j), \pi(\phi(K_j))\} \cap \{K_j, \phi(K_j)\}$ is empty for every $1 \leq j \leq q$. Let Bad be the event that $\phi(K_j) = K_j$ or $\{\pi(K_j), \pi(\phi(K_j))\} \cap \{K_j, \phi(K_j)\}$ is not empty for some $j$. Then,

$$\Pr\left[ B^{\langle (\rho_j, K_j) \rangle_{j=1}^q} = 1 \right]$$
$$= \Pr[\neg\mathsf{Bad}] \Pr\left[ B^{\langle (\rho_j, K_j) \rangle_{j=1}^q} = 1 \,\middle|\, \neg\mathsf{Bad} \right] + \Pr\left[ \mathsf{Bad} \wedge B^{\langle (\rho_j, K_j) \rangle_{j=1}^q} = 1 \right]$$
$$= \frac{\Pr[\neg\mathsf{Bad}]}{\ell} \sum_{i=1}^\ell \Pr[A^{I_i} = 1] + \Pr\left[ \mathsf{Bad} \wedge B^{\langle (\rho_j, K_j) \rangle_{j=1}^q} = 1 \right]$$
$$= \frac{1}{\ell} \sum_{i=1}^\ell \Pr[A^{I_i} = 1] - \frac{\Pr[\mathsf{Bad}]}{\ell} \sum_{i=1}^\ell \Pr[A^{I_i} = 1] + \Pr\left[ \mathsf{Bad} \wedge B^{\langle (\rho_j, K_j) \rangle_{j=1}^q} = 1 \right] .$$

From the discussions above,

$$\mathrm{Adv}_{\mathsf{Rel},f}^{q\text{-}\mathrm{prf}\text{-}\mathrm{rka}}(B) = \left| \Pr\left[ B^{\langle\langle (f,K_j)\rangle\rangle_{j=1}^{q}} = 1 \right] - \Pr\left[ B^{\langle\langle (\rho_j,K_j)\rangle\rangle_{j=1}^{q}} = 1 \right] \right|$$

$$\geq \frac{1}{\ell} \left| \Pr[A^{I_0} = 1] - \Pr[A^{I_\ell} = 1] \right| - \Pr[\mathrm{Bad}]$$

$$= \frac{1}{\ell} \mathrm{Adv}_{F_\pi^\circ}^{\mathrm{prf}}(A) - \Pr[\mathrm{Bad}] \ .$$

Thus,

$$\mathrm{Adv}_{F_\pi^\circ}^{\mathrm{prf}}(A) \leq \ell \cdot \mathrm{Adv}_{\mathsf{Rel},f}^{q\text{-}\mathrm{prf}\text{-}\mathrm{rka}}(B) + \ell \cdot \Pr[\mathrm{Bad}]$$

$$\leq \ell \cdot \mathrm{Adv}_{\mathsf{Rel},f}^{q\text{-}\mathrm{prf}\text{-}\mathrm{rka}}(B) + \ell\, q \left( \frac{|P_{\pi,\phi}|}{2^k} + \frac{1}{2^{k/2}} \right) \ .$$

$B$ makes at most $q$ queries and runs in time at most $\tau + O(\ell q T_E)$. $\qquad\square$

**Lemma 5.** *Let $f(K,x) = \mathrm{tr}_{k/2}(E_K(x)\oplus x)$. Let $A$ be a prf-rka-adversary against $f$ with $m$ oracles. Suppose that $A$ runs in time at most $\tau$ and makes at most $q$ queries restricted by $\mathsf{Rel}$. Suppose that $q \leq \lambda 2^n/e$ for some positive constant $\lambda < 1$. Then, there exists a prp-rka-adversary $B$ against $E$ such that*

$$\mathrm{Adv}_{\mathsf{Rel},f}^{m\text{-}\mathrm{prf}\text{-}\mathrm{rka}}(A) \leq m \cdot \mathrm{Adv}_{\mathsf{Rel},E}^{\mathrm{prp}\text{-}\mathrm{rka}}(B) + \frac{2^{k/2}}{1-\lambda}\left(\frac{e\,q}{2^n}\right)^{2^{n-k/2}+1} .$$

*$B$ makes at most $q$ queries restricted by $\mathsf{Rel}$ and runs in time at most $\tau + O(q\,T_E)$, where $T_E$ represents the time required to compute $E$.*

*Proof.* Let $K_1,\ldots,K_m$ be independent random variables uniformly distributed over $\Sigma^k$. Let $\rho_1,\ldots,\rho_m$ be independent and random keyed functions uniformly distributed over $\boldsymbol{F}(\Sigma^k \times \Sigma^n, \Sigma^{k/2})$. Let $\varpi_1,\ldots,\varpi_m$ be independent random keyed permutations uniformly distributed over $\boldsymbol{P}(\Sigma^k \times \Sigma^n, \Sigma^n)$, and let $\tilde{\varpi}_j(\cdot,x) = \mathrm{tr}_{k/2}(\varpi_j(\cdot,x) \oplus x)$ for $1 \leq j \leq m$. Then,

$$\mathrm{Adv}_{\mathsf{Rel},f}^{m\text{-}\mathrm{prf}\text{-}\mathrm{rka}}(A) \leq \left| \Pr\left[ A^{\langle\langle (f,K_j)\rangle\rangle_{j=1}^{m}} = 1 \right] - \Pr\left[ A^{\langle\langle (\tilde{\varpi}_j,K_j)\rangle\rangle_{j=1}^{m}} = 1 \right] \right| +$$
$$\left| \Pr\left[ A^{\langle\langle (\tilde{\varpi}_j,K_j)\rangle\rangle_{j=1}^{m}} = 1 \right] - \Pr\left[ A^{\langle\langle (\rho_j,K_j)\rangle\rangle_{j=1}^{m}} = 1 \right] \right| .$$

Let $\mathcal{O}_i$ be $m$ oracles such that $(f,K_1),\ldots,(f,K_i),(\tilde{\varpi}_{i+1},K_{i+1}),\ldots,(\tilde{\varpi}_m,K_m)$ for $0 \leq i \leq m$. Notice that $\mathcal{O}_0 = \langle\langle (\tilde{\varpi}_j,K_j)\rangle\rangle_{j=1}^{m}$ and $\mathcal{O}_m = \langle\langle (f,K_j)\rangle\rangle_{j=1}^{m}$.

A prp-rka-adversary $B$ is constructed using $A$ as a subroutine. The algorithm of $B$ with an oracle $(u,K)$ is given below, where $u$ is either $E$ or $\varpi$. $\varpi$ is a random keyed permutation uniformly distributed over $\boldsymbol{P}(\Sigma^k \times \Sigma^n, \Sigma^n)$, and $K$ is a random variable uniformly distributed over $\Sigma^k$.

1. selects $i$ from $\{1,2,\ldots,m\}$ uniformly at random.
2. runs $A$ with oracles $(f,K_1),\ldots,(f,K_{i-1})$, $(\tilde{u},K)$, $(\tilde{\varpi}_{i+1},K_{i+1}),\ldots,$ $(\tilde{\varpi}_m,K_m)$ by simulating $(f,K_1),\ldots,(f,K_{i-1})$, and $(\tilde{\varpi}_{i+1},K_{i+1}),\ldots,$ $(\tilde{\varpi}_m,K_m)$, where $\tilde{u}(\cdot,x) = \mathrm{tr}_{k/2}(u(\cdot,x) \oplus x)$.

3. outputs $A$'s output.

Then,

$$\Pr\left[B^{(E,K)} = 1\right] = \frac{1}{m}\sum_{i=1}^{m}\Pr\left[A^{\mathcal{O}_i} = 1\right]$$

and

$$\Pr\left[B^{(\varpi,K)} = 1\right] = \frac{1}{m}\sum_{i=0}^{m-1}\Pr\left[A^{\mathcal{O}_i} = 1\right] \ .$$

Thus,

$$\mathrm{Adv}_{\mathrm{Rel},E}^{\mathrm{prp\text{-}rka}}(B) = \frac{1}{m}\left|\Pr\left[A^{\mathcal{O}_m} = 1\right] - \Pr\left[A^{\mathcal{O}_0} = 1\right]\right| \ .$$

$B$ makes at most $q$ queries and runs in time at most $\tau + O(q\,T_E)$.

It is possible to distinguish $\tilde{\varpi}_j$ and $\rho_j$ only by the fact that there may be $(2^{n-k/2} + 1)$-collision for $\rho_j(\cdot, x) \oplus x$. Thus, since $A$ makes at most $q$ queries,

$$\left|\Pr\left[A^{\langle(\tilde{\varpi}_j,K_j)\rangle_{j=1}^{m}} = 1\right] - \Pr\left[A^{\langle(\rho_j,K_j)\rangle_{j=1}^{m}} = 1\right]\right| \leq \frac{2^{k/2}}{1 - \lambda}\left(\frac{e\,q}{2^n}\right)^{2^{n-k/2}+1} ,$$

which follows from Lemma 3.                                                                 $\square$

## 5.1   An Example of Padding for $\sigma$-Free Inputs

In this subsection, $\sigma$ is assumed to be a permutation on $\varSigma^n$ such that $\sigma(x) = x \oplus c$ for some non-zero constant $c$. The permutation is denoted by $\sigma_c$.

Let pad be a padding function such that

$$\mathsf{pad}(M) = M\|10^{d+n/2}\|\mathsf{len}_{n/2}(M) \ ,$$

where $d$ is a minimum non-zero integer such that $|M| + d \equiv n - 1 \pmod{n}$, and $\mathsf{len}_{n/2}(M)$ is the $n/2$-bit binary representation of $|M|$. It is easy to see that pad is $\sigma_c$-free if, for example, $c = 1^{n/2}\|0^{n/2}$.

# 6   Indifferentiability from Random Oracle

We show that $F_\pi^\circ$ is indifferentiable from a VIL random oracle in the ideal cipher model with pad and $\sigma_c$ given in the previous section.

**Theorem 4.** *Let $E \in \mathcal{BC}(n,k)$. Let $P_\pi$ be the set of fixed points of $\pi$. Let $A$ be an adversary that asks at most $q_\mathrm{V}$ queries to the VIL oracle, $q_\mathrm{e}$ queries to the encryption oracle and $q_\mathrm{d}$ queries to the decryption oracle. Let $\ell$ be the maximum number of message blocks in a VIL query. Suppose that $q = \ell q_\mathrm{V} + q_\mathrm{e} + q_\mathrm{d} < 2^{n-1}/3$. Then, in the ideal cipher model, $\mathrm{Adv}_{F_\pi^\circ,S}^{\mathrm{indiff}}(A)$ is bounded from above by*

$$\frac{q}{2^{k/2}(1 - 3q/2^{n-1})} + \frac{9q^2 + 2(|P_\pi| - 1)q}{2^k(1 - 3q/2^{n-1})^2} + \frac{q^2}{4(2^k - 2^{k/2} - 6q - |P_\pi| + 4)} + \frac{q}{2^{n-1}} ,$$

*where the simulator $S$ is given in Figure 3. $S$ makes at most $2(q_\mathrm{e} + q_\mathrm{d})$ queries and runs in time $O((q_\mathrm{e} + q_\mathrm{d})^2)$.*

*Proof.* Omitted due to the page limit. □

Theorem 4 implies that the query complexity to differentiate $F_\pi^\circ$ from a VIL random oracle is $\Omega(\min\{2^{k/2}, 2^n\})$, which is optimal up to a constant factor.

*Example 2.* The upper bound of Theorem 4 is 0.5 if $q = 2^{124.3}$ for $k = 256$ and if $q = 2^{93.5}$ for $k = 192$. Though IRO implies CR, Theorem 1 gives a slightly better bound for CR than Theorem 4.

The simulator $S$ given in Figure 3 simulates the ideal cipher by lazy evaluation. $\mathcal{P}(s)$ ($\mathcal{C}(s)$) is the set of plaintexts (ciphertexts) which are available for the reply to the current query with the key $s$. $\mathsf{E}_s(x)$ and $\mathsf{D}_s(x)$ are $\perp$ for any $s \in \Sigma^k$ and $x \in \Sigma^n$ initially. They get defined by the queries of the adversary and the corresponding oracle replies. $\mathcal{V}$ is the set of the keys in the queries so far.

The simulator keeps a tree, which initially consists of the root $IV$. $\mathcal{T}$ is the set of the nodes in the tree so far. During the simulation, for example, new nodes $F(s, x) = t_0\|t_1$ and $F(s, \sigma(x)) = t_1\|t_0$ are created by an encryption query $(s, x)$ if $s \in \mathcal{T}$, and they augment the tree together with the edges $s \xrightarrow{x} t_0\|t_1$ and $s \xrightarrow{\sigma(x)} t_1\|t_0$.

The procedure $\mathsf{extend}(s)$ uses the VIL random oracle $\mathsf{H}$ and evaluates $F_\pi^\circ(IV, \cdot)$ for the message, if any, corresponding to the path in the tree from the root $IV$ to $s$ such that $s$ is the chaining value fed into final $F$ through $\pi$. Owing to the padding $\mathsf{pad}$, the message is unique if it exists. The procedure $\mathsf{path}(s)$ returns the message. $\mathsf{lb}(\tilde{M})$ is the last block of $\mathsf{pad}(\tilde{M})$. $\mathsf{fhalf}$ and $\mathsf{shalf}$ give the first half and the second half of the input string, respectively.

## 7    Implementation

We implemented the proposed compression function by instantiating the ideal cipher $E$ with AES-192 or AES-256. The involution $\sigma$ was defined with the bitwise complement of the first byte of $M_i$. The throughput of the compression function was measured on the Intel Core i7-2600S, the Intel Core i7-2600, and the Intel Core i7-2720QM, which support the AES instruction set (AES-NI). The GNU Compiler Collection version 4.4.5 or 4.4.6 was used for code compilation. The result is shown in Table 1. In the *serial* implementation, after the topside encryption is finished, the downside encryption is performed. In the *pipelined* implementation, each round of two encryption functions is interleaved. In both of implementations, the key schedule is performed only once. The throughput of our hash function will approach asymptotically to these values for sufficiently large data.

The result showed that the pipelined implementation was better. The Intel manual [10] recommends to process 4 or 8 blocks in parallel for optimized throughput since the hardware that supports the four AES round instructions is pipelined. Bos et al. [5] pointed out that constructions such as the DM construction gave an advantage on exploiting such a hardware feature. Our hash function can also gain the benefit of the hardware feature by interleaving each round of two encryption functions.

Initialize:

  1: $\mathcal{V} \leftarrow \emptyset$; $\mathcal{T} \leftarrow \{IV\}$; $\mathcal{P}(s) \leftarrow \Sigma^n$; $\mathcal{C}(s) \leftarrow \Sigma^n$;

Interface $\mathcal{E}(s, x)$:

300: **if** $\mathrm{E}_s(x) = \perp$ **then**
310:     **if** $s \in \mathcal{T}$ **then**
320:         $\mathrm{E}_s(x) \xleftarrow{\$} \mathcal{C}(s)$; $\mathrm{E}_s(\sigma(x)) \xleftarrow{\$} \mathcal{C}(s) \setminus \{\mathrm{E}_s(x)\}$;
330:         $t_0 \leftarrow \mathrm{tr}_{k/2}(\mathrm{E}_s(x) \oplus x)$; $t_1 \leftarrow \mathrm{tr}_{k/2}(\mathrm{E}_s(\sigma(x)) \oplus \sigma(x))$;
331:         **if** $t_0 = t_1 \vee \{t_0 \| t_1, t_1 \| t_0\} \cap \boldsymbol{B} \neq \emptyset$ **then abort**;
340:         $\mathcal{T} \leftarrow \mathcal{T} \cup \{t_0 \| t_1, t_1 \| t_0\}$;
341:         $\mathrm{extend}(t_0 \| t_1)$; $\mathrm{extend}(t_1 \| t_0)$;
350:     **else**
360:         $\mathrm{E}_s(x) \xleftarrow{\$} \mathcal{C}(s)$; $\mathrm{E}_s(\sigma(x)) \xleftarrow{\$} \mathcal{C}(s) \setminus \{\mathrm{E}_s(x)\}$;
370:     $\mathcal{V} \leftarrow \mathcal{V} \cup \{s\}$; $\mathcal{P}(s) \leftarrow \mathcal{P}(s) \setminus \{x, \sigma(x)\}$; $\mathcal{C}(s) \leftarrow \mathcal{C}(s) \setminus \{\mathrm{E}_s(x), \mathrm{E}_s(\sigma(x))\}$;
380: **return** $\mathrm{E}_s(x)$;

Interface $\mathcal{D}(s, x)$:

500: **if** $\mathrm{D}_s(x) = \perp$ **then**
510:     **if** $s \in \mathcal{T}$ **then**
520:         $\mathrm{D}_s(x) \xleftarrow{\$} \mathcal{P}(s)$; $\mathrm{E}_s(\sigma(\mathrm{D}_s(x))) \xleftarrow{\$} \mathcal{C}(s) \setminus \{x\}$;
530:         $t_0 \leftarrow \mathrm{tr}_{k/2}(\mathrm{D}_s(x) \oplus x)$; $t_1 \leftarrow \mathrm{tr}_{k/2}(\sigma(\mathrm{D}_s(x)) \oplus \mathrm{E}_s(\sigma(\mathrm{D}_s(x))))$;
531:         **if** $t_0 = t_1 \vee \{t_0 \| t_1, t_1 \| t_0\} \cap \boldsymbol{B} \neq \emptyset$ **then abort**;
540:         $\mathcal{T} \leftarrow \mathcal{T} \cup \{t_0 \| t_1, t_1 \| t_0\}$;
541:         $\mathrm{extend}(t_0 \| t_1)$; $\mathrm{extend}(t_1 \| t_0)$;
550:     **else**
560:         $\mathrm{D}_s(x) \xleftarrow{\$} \mathcal{P}(s)$; $\mathrm{E}_s(\sigma(\mathrm{D}_s(x))) \xleftarrow{\$} \mathcal{C}(s) \setminus \{x\}$;
570:     $\mathcal{V} \leftarrow \mathcal{V} \cup \{s\}$; $\mathcal{P}(s) \leftarrow \mathcal{P}(s) \setminus \{\mathrm{D}_s(x), \sigma(\mathrm{D}_s(x))\}$; $\mathcal{C}(s) \leftarrow \mathcal{C}(s) \setminus \{x, \mathrm{E}_s(\sigma(\mathrm{D}_s(x)))\}$;
580: **return** $\mathrm{D}_s(x)$;

Subroutine $\mathrm{extend}(s)$:

700: $\tilde{s} \leftarrow \pi(s)$; $\tilde{M} \leftarrow \mathrm{path}(\tilde{s})$; $x \leftarrow \mathrm{lb}(\tilde{M})$;
710: **if** $x \neq \perp \wedge \mathrm{E}_{\tilde{s}}(x) = \perp$ **then**                                   $\triangleright$ if $\tilde{M}$ exists
720:     $t_0' \xleftarrow{\$} \Sigma^{n-k/2}$; $t_1' \xleftarrow{\$} \Sigma^{n-k/2}$;
721:     $t_0 \leftarrow t_0' \| \mathrm{fhalf}(\mathrm{H}(\tilde{M}))$; $t_1 \leftarrow t_1' \| \mathrm{shalf}(\mathrm{H}(\tilde{M}))$;
722:     $\mathrm{E}_{\tilde{s}}(x) \leftarrow t_0 \oplus x$; $\mathrm{E}_{\tilde{s}}(\sigma(x)) \leftarrow t_1 \oplus \sigma(x)$;
723:     **if** $\mathrm{E}_{\tilde{s}}(x) = \mathrm{E}_{\tilde{s}}(\sigma(x)) \vee \{\mathrm{E}_{\tilde{s}}(x), \mathrm{E}_{\tilde{s}}(\sigma(x))\} \not\subset \mathcal{C}(\tilde{s})$ **then abort**;
730:     $\mathcal{V} \leftarrow \mathcal{V} \cup \{\tilde{s}\}$; $\mathcal{P}(\tilde{s}) \leftarrow \mathcal{P}(\tilde{s}) \setminus \{x, \sigma(x)\}$; $\mathcal{C}(\tilde{s}) \leftarrow \mathcal{C}(\tilde{s}) \setminus \{\mathrm{E}_{\tilde{s}}(x), \mathrm{E}_{\tilde{s}}(\sigma(x))\}$;

**Fig. 3.** Pseudocode for the simulator $S$. $\boldsymbol{B} = \mathcal{V} \cup \mathcal{T} \cup \pi^{-1}(\mathcal{V} \cup \mathcal{T}) \cup \pi(\mathcal{T}) \cup P_\pi$.

**Table 1.** Throughput [cycles/byte]

| $k$ | 192 | | | 256 | | |
|---|---|---|---|---|---|---|
| Core i7 | 2600S | 2600 | 2720QM | 2600S | 2600 | 2720QM |
| serial | 7.07 | 8.43 | 6.44 | 9.07 | 11.09 | 8.21 |
| pipelined | 6.44 | 8.06 | 5.84 | 8.00 | 9.80 | 7.26 |

# References

1. Armknecht, F., Fleischmann, E., Krause, M., Lee, J., Stam, M., Steinberger, J.: The preimage security of double-block-length compression functions. In: Lee, D.H., Wang, X. (eds.) ASIACRYPT 2011. LNCS, vol. 7073, pp. 233–251. Springer, Heidelberg (2011)
2. Bellare, M., Kohno, T.: A theoretical treatment of related-key attacks: RKA-PRPs, RKA-PRFs, and applications. In: Biham, E. (ed.) EUROCRYPT 2003. LNCS, vol. 2656, pp. 491–506. Springer, Heidelberg (2003)
3. Black, J., Rogaway, P., Shrimpton, T., Stam, M.: An analysis of the blockcipher-based hash functions from PGV. Journal of Cryptology 23(4), 519–545 (2010)
4. Bogdanov, A., Leander, G., Paar, C., Poschmann, A., Robshaw, M.J.B., Seurin, Y.: Hash functions and RFID tags: Mind the gap. In: Oswald, E., Rohatgi, P. (eds.) CHES 2008. LNCS, vol. 5154, pp. 283–299. Springer, Heidelberg (2008)
5. Bos, J.W., Özen, O., Stam, M.: Efficient hashing using the AES instruction set. In: Preneel, B., Takagi, T. (eds.) CHES 2011. LNCS, vol. 6917, pp. 507–522. Springer, Heidelberg (2011)
6. Brachtl, B.O., Coppersmith, D., Hyden, M.M., Matyas Jr., S.M., Meyer, C.H.W., Oseas, J., Pilpel, S., Schilling, M.: Data authentication using modification detection codes based on a public one-way encryption function. U. S. Patent # 4,908,861 (March 1990)
7. Coron, J.-S., Dodis, Y., Malinaud, C., Puniya, P.: Merkle-Damgård revisited: How to construct a hash function. In: Shoup, V. (ed.) CRYPTO 2005. LNCS, vol. 3621, pp. 430–448. Springer, Heidelberg (2005)
8. FIPS PUB 180-4. Secure hash standard (SHS) (March 2012)
9. Fleischmann, E., Gorski, M., Lucks, S.: Security of cyclic double block length hash functions. In: Parker (ed.) [23], pp. 153–175
10. Gueron, S.: Intel advanced encryption standard (AES) instructions set (2010), http://software.intel.com/en-us/articles/intel-advanced-encryption-standard-aes-instructions-set/
11. Hirose, S.: Some plausible constructions of double-block-length hash functions. In: Robshaw, M.J.B. (ed.) FSE 2006. LNCS, vol. 4047, pp. 210–225. Springer, Heidelberg (2006)
12. Hirose, S., Park, J.H., Yun, A.: A simple variant of the Merkle-Damgård scheme with a permutation. In: Kurosawa, K. (ed.) ASIACRYPT 2007. LNCS, vol. 4833, pp. 113–129. Springer, Heidelberg (2007)
13. Jonsson, J., Robshaw, M.J.B.: Securing RSA-KEM via the AES. In: Vaudenay, S. (ed.) PKC 2005. LNCS, vol. 3386, pp. 29–46. Springer, Heidelberg (2005)
14. Kuwakado, H., Hirose, S.: Hashing mode using a lightweight blockcipher. In: Stam, M. (ed.) IMACC 2013. LNCS, vol. 8308, pp. 213–231. Springer, Heidelberg (2013)
15. Lai, X., Massey, J.L.: Hash functions based on block ciphers. In: Rueppel, R.A. (ed.) EUROCRYPT 1992. LNCS, vol. 658, pp. 55–70. Springer, Heidelberg (1993)

16. Lee, J., Kwon, D.: The security of Abreast-DM in the ideal cipher model. IEICE Transactions 94-A(1), 104–109 (2011)
17. Lee, J., Stam, M.: MJH: A faster alternative to MDC-2. In: Kiayias, A. (ed.) CT-RSA 2011. LNCS, vol. 6558, pp. 213–236. Springer, Heidelberg (2011)
18. Lee, J., Stam, M.: MJH: A faster alternative to MDC-2. Cryptology ePrint Archive, Report 2014/108 (2014), http://eprint.iacr.org/
19. Lee, J., Stam, M., Steinberger, J.: The collision security of Tandem-DM in the ideal cipher model. In: Rogaway, P. (ed.) CRYPTO 2011. LNCS, vol. 6841, pp. 561–577. Springer, Heidelberg (2011)
20. Maurer, U.M., Renner, R., Holenstein, C.: Indifferentiability, impossibility results on reductions, and applications to the random oracle methodology. In: Naor, M. (ed.) TCC 2004. LNCS, vol. 2951, pp. 21–39. Springer, Heidelberg (2004)
21. Naito, Y.: Blockcipher-based double-length hash functions for pseudorandom oracles. In: Miri, A., Vaudenay, S. (eds.) SAC 2011. LNCS, vol. 7118, pp. 338–355. Springer, Heidelberg (2012)
22. Özen, O., Stam, M.: Another glance at double-length hashing. In: Parker (ed.) [23], pp. 176–201
23. Parker, M.G. (ed.): Cryptography and Coding 2009. LNCS, vol. 5921. Springer, Heidelberg (2009)
24. Rijmen, V., Barreto, P.S.L.M.: The Whirlpool hash function (2000), http://www.larc.usp.br/~pbarreto/WhirlpoolPage.html
25. Rivest, R.: The MD4 message-digest algorithm. Request for Comments 1320 (RFC 1320), The Internet Engineering Task Force (1992)
26. Rivest, R.: The MD5 message-digest algorithm. Request for Comments 1321 (RFC 1321), The Internet Engineering Task Force (1992)
27. Rohde, S., Eisenbarth, T., Dahmen, E., Buchmann, J., Paar, C.: Fast hash-based signatures on constrained devices. In: Grimaud, G., Standaert, F.-X. (eds.) CARDIS 2008. LNCS, vol. 5189, pp. 104–117. Springer, Heidelberg (2008)
28. Steinberger, J.P.: The collision intractability of MDC-2 in the ideal-cipher model. In: Naor, M. (ed.) EUROCRYPT 2007. LNCS, vol. 4515, pp. 34–51. Springer, Heidelberg (2007)

# Forward-Secure Sequential Aggregate Message Authentication Revisited

Shoichi Hirose[1] and Hidenori Kuwakado[2]

[1] Graduate School of Engineering, University of Fukui, Japan
[2] Faculty of Informatics, Kansai University, Japan

**Abstract.** The notion of forward-secure sequential aggregate message authentication was introduced by Ma and Tsudik in 2007. It is suitable for applications such as audit logging systems and wireless sensor networks. Ma and Tsudik also constructed a scheme with a MAC function and a collision resistant hash function. However, the notion has not been fully formalized and the security of the scheme has not been confirmed. In this paper, forward-secure sequential aggregate message authentication schemes and their security are formalized. Then, a generic construction with a MAC function and a pseudorandom generator is presented. It is also shown that the construction is secure if the underlying primitives are secure.

## 1 Introduction

*Background.* Message authentication is one of the most basic and important roles of cryptography. The cryptographic functions such as HMAC [8] and CMAC [17] are widely used for this purpose in various applications.

Some applications may require additional properties of message authentication schemes. One of the typical examples is to secure audit logging systems [4]. For audit logging systems, it is not sufficient only to detect forgeries of log entries. It is also necessary to detect deletions and reorderings of log entries. Aggregation of authenticators called tags is useful for reducing memory consumption. Another important property is forward security. It is achieved by updating secret keys. With this mechanism, leakage of current secret keys by intrusion does not compromise the security of past secret keys. These properties also seem useful for wireless sensor netwoks.

The notion of forward-secure sequential aggregate message authentication (FS SAMA) was presented by Ma and Tsudik [14]. Ma and Tsudik also proposed an FS SAMA scheme in the same paper. Unfortunately, the notion of FS SAMA has not been fully formalized, and the security of the Ma-Tsudik scheme has not been discussed in detail.

The Ma-Tsudik scheme is composed of a MAC function and a cryptographic hash function. The cryptographic hash function is required to be collision resistant. Cryptanalytic results on hash functions [21,22] suggest that collision resistance is difficult to be achieved. It is also shown that there exists a large gap between collision resistance and onewayness (preimage resistance) in terms

S.S.M. Chow et al. (Eds.): ProvSec 2014, LNCS 8782, pp. 87–102, 2014.

of computational complexity theory [19]. Thus, it is preferable if a provably secure FS SAMA scheme is constructed without collision resistance.

*Our Contribution.* Forward-secure sequential aggregate message authentication schemes (FS SAMASes) and their security are formalized in this paper. In this formalization, we assume, as Bellare and Yee did [4], that each secret key is used to authenticate multiple messages during some time interval.

A simple generic construction with a MAC function and a pseudorandom bit generator (PRG) is also proposed. The proposed scheme is a kind of linking scheme. A new message is tagged together with the current tag for previous messages, which makes it possible to detect deletions and reorderings. The forward secure PRG [5] is used for updating secret keys to achieve forward security.

Finally, it is shown that the generic construction is provably secure. More precisely, the generic construction is shown to be secure if the underlying MAC function is unforgeable and the underlying PRG is secure. It is also shown to be secure if the underlying MAC function is a secure pseudorandom function (PRF) and the underlying PRG is secure. Notice that the MAC functions such as HMAC and CMAC are shown to be secure as a PRF [1,11].

*Related Work.* Forward security was first considered for key exchange protocols [10]. It was then discussed in the context of public key schemes [3].

Bellare and Yee formalized forward secure symmetric key primitives and their security notions [5]. Among them, they presented a generic construction of a forward-secure message authentication scheme provably secure under its security definition. Their scheme does not intend aggregation.

Ma and Tsudik presented the notion of forward-secure sequential aggregate signature as well as forward-secure sequential message authentication [14].

Some forward-secure message authentication schemes were proposed with application to audit logging systems. They are classified into two classes. Some may be called numbering schemes and others may be called linking schemes.

A numbering scheme was proposed by Bellare and Yee [4]. Their scheme produces a tag for each message accompanied with a sequence number. Sequence numbers are used to detect deletions or reorderings of messages. Prior to updating the logging system to a new stage, their scheme produces a tag for a special message with a sequence number. It works as a marker of the end of the stage, and is used to detect log truncation. Their scheme does not allow aggregation.

A linking scheme of Ma and Tsudik [15] is based on the scheme in their previous paper [14]. Their scheme sequentially hashes tags of messages using a collision-resistant hash function. Another linking scheme was proposed by Schneier and Kelsey [18]. Their scheme sequentially hashes messages using a collision-resistant hash function, and produces tags for the resultant digests. These linking schemes allow aggregation but use a collision-resistant hash function.

The notion of aggregate message authentication codes was proposed by Katz and Lindell [12]. They assume aggregation of multiple tags from different senders. Deletions and reorderings of messages are out of scope.

Eikemeier et al. [7] introduced the notion of history-free message authentication. They also presented two schemes for history-free sequential message authentication. Their schemes sequentially aggregate multiple tags from different senders. They can detect deletions and reorderings. Their schemes cover more general settings than ours. Our scheme provides a simpler and more efficient solution than their scheme for limited but still significant scenarios. Actually, both of their schemes need a pseudorandom permutation: one scheme uses CMAC [17] and the other scheme is composed of a MAC function and a pseudorandom permutation. Thus, instantiation of their schemes always requires a block cipher. On the other hand, our scheme is able to be instantiated only with a hash function.

Wang and Hong also proposed a sequential aggregate message authentication scheme [20]. It uses pairing operations and its security is based on number-theoretic assumptions.

A sequential aggregate signature scheme was proposed by Lysyanskaya et al. [13]. It combines multiple signatures from different signers and the signers are ordered.

*Organization.* Section 2 gives notations and definitions of some cryptographic primitives. Section 3 presents definitions of an FS SAMAS and its security. It also describes a generic construction of an FS SAMAS. Section 4 shows that the generic construction is secure if the underlying primitives are secure.

# 2 Preliminaries

## 2.1 Notation

For a pair of elements $e_1$ and $e_2$ of a totally ordered set, let $[e_1, e_2]$ denote the set of elements $e$ in the set such that $e_1 \leq e \leq e_2$. In particular, for integers $n_1$ and $n_2$, let $[n_1, n_2]$ denote the set of integers $n$ such that $n_1 \leq n \leq n_2$. For variable $s$ and set $S$, let $s \leftarrow S$ denote that an element chosen uniformly at random from $S$ is assigned to $s$. For sequences $x$ and $y$, $x\|y$ represents their concatenation. An empty sequence is denoted by $\varepsilon$. Let $F(\mathcal{X}, \mathcal{Y})$ be the set of all functions with domain $\mathcal{X}$ and range $\mathcal{Y}$. A function $F : \mathcal{K} \times \mathcal{X} \to \mathcal{Y}$ is called a keyed function with key space $\mathcal{K}$. $F(K, \cdot)$ is often denoted by $F_K(\cdot)$.

## 2.2 Pseudorandom Function

A pseudorandom function (PRF) [9] is a keyed function $F : \mathcal{K} \times \mathcal{X} \to \mathcal{Y}$. The PRF $F$ is called secure if it is intractable to distinguish $F_K$ with secret $K$ chosen uniformly at random and a function with domain $\mathcal{X}$ and range $\mathcal{Y}$ chosen uniformly at random.

Let $\mathcal{A}$ be an adversary against $F$. $\mathcal{A}$ is given a function with domain $\mathcal{X}$ and range $\mathcal{Y}$ as an oracle. $\mathcal{A}$ makes queries to the oracle one by one adaptively. A query is an element in $\mathcal{X}$ and the reply is a corresponding image in $\mathcal{Y}$. Finally,

$\mathcal{A}$ outputs 0 or 1. The security of $F$ is quantified by the advantage of $\mathcal{A}$ against $F$, which is defined as

$$\mathrm{Adv}_F^{\mathrm{prf}}(\mathcal{A}) = \left| \Pr[\mathcal{A}^{F_K} \Rightarrow 1] - \Pr[\mathcal{A}^\rho \Rightarrow 1] \right| \ ,$$

where $K \leftarrow \mathcal{K}$ and $\rho \leftarrow F(\mathcal{X}, \mathcal{Y})$.

We often deal with adversaries against a PRF with independent multiple oracles. Let

$$\mathrm{Adv}_F^{n\text{-}\mathrm{prf}}(\mathcal{A}) = \left| \Pr[\mathcal{A}^{F_{K_1}, \dots, F_{K_n}} \Rightarrow 1] - \Pr[\mathcal{A}^{\rho_1, \dots, \rho_n} \Rightarrow 1] \right| \ ,$$

where $(K_1, K_2, \dots, K_n) \leftarrow \mathcal{K}^n$ and $(\rho_1, \rho_2, \dots, \rho_n) \leftarrow F(\mathcal{X}, \mathcal{Y})^n$. The following lemma is a paraphrase of Lemma 3.3 in [2]:

**Lemma 1.** *Let $\mathcal{A}$ be an adversary against $F$ with access to $n$ oracles. Then, an adversary $\mathcal{A}'$ against $F$ can be constructed with $\mathcal{A}$ as a subroutine such that*

$$\mathrm{Adv}_F^{n\text{-}\mathrm{prf}}(\mathcal{A}) = n \cdot \mathrm{Adv}_F^{\mathrm{prf}}(\mathcal{A}') \ .$$

*The running time of $\mathcal{A}'$ is approximately the sum of the running time of $\mathcal{A}$ and the time required to compute $F$ to answer to the queries made by $\mathcal{A}$. $\mathcal{A}'$ makes at most $\max\{q_i \,|\, 1 \le i \le n\}$ queries to its oracle, where $q_i$ is the number of the queries made by $\mathcal{A}$ to its $i$-th oracle.*

## 2.3   MAC Function

A MAC function (MAF) [9] is a keyed function $F : \mathcal{K} \times \mathcal{X} \to \mathcal{Y}$. The MAF $F$ is called secure if it is intractable to find a pair of message $M$ and tag $\tau$ such that $\tau = F_K(M)$ with secret $K$ chosen uniformly at random.

Let $\mathcal{A}$ be an adversary against $F$. $\mathcal{A}$ is given $F_K$ as an oracle. $\mathcal{A}$ makes queries to the oracle one by one adaptively. A query is an element in $\mathcal{X}$ and the reply is a corresponding image in $\mathcal{Y}$. Finally, $\mathcal{A}$ outputs a pair $(M, \tau) \in \mathcal{X} \times \mathcal{Y}$. $\mathcal{A}$ is successful in forgery if $\tau = F_K(M)$ and $\mathcal{A}$ has not asked $M$ as a query. The security of $F$ is quantified by the advantage of $\mathcal{A}$ against $F$, which is defined as

$$\mathrm{Adv}_F^{\mathrm{mac}}(\mathcal{A}) = \Pr[\mathcal{A}^{F_K} \text{ is successful}] \ ,$$

where $K \leftarrow \mathcal{K}$.

We also deal with adversaries against a MAF with independent multiple oracles. Let

$$\mathrm{Adv}_F^{n\text{-}\mathrm{mac}}(\mathcal{A}) = \Pr[\mathcal{A}^{F_{K_1}, \dots, F_{K_n}} \text{ is successful}] \ ,$$

where $(K_1, K_2, \dots, K_n) \leftarrow \mathcal{K}^n$. $\mathcal{A}$ is successful in forgery if there exists some $i \in [1, n]$ such that $\tau = F_{K_i}(M)$ and $\mathcal{A}$ has not asked $M$ as a query to $F_{K_i}$. The following lemma is similar to Lemma 1:

**Lemma 2.** *Let $\mathcal{A}$ be an adversary against $F$ with access to $n$ oracles. Then, an adversary $\mathcal{A}'$ against $F$ can be constructed with $\mathcal{A}$ as a subroutine such that*

$$\mathrm{Adv}_F^{n\text{-}\mathrm{mac}}(\mathcal{A}) = n \cdot \mathrm{Adv}_F^{\mathrm{mac}}(\mathcal{A}') \ .$$

*The running time of $\mathcal{A}'$ is approximately the sum of the running time of $\mathcal{A}$ and the time required to compute $F$ to answer to the queries made by $\mathcal{A}$. $\mathcal{A}'$ makes at most $\max\{q_i \mid 1 \le i \le n\}$ queries to its oracle, where $q_i$ is the number of the queries made by $\mathcal{A}$ to its $i$-th oracle.*

## 2.4  Forward-Secure Pseudorandom Bit Generator

**Pseudorandom Bit Generator.** A pseudorandom bit generator (PRG) [6] is a length-expanding function $G : \{0,1\}^\ell \to \{0,1\}^{\ell+l}$. The PRG $G$ is called secure if it is intractable to distinguish $G(K)$ with $K$ chosen uniformly at random and a binary sequence of length $(\ell + l)$ chosen uniformly at random.

Let $\mathcal{A}$ be an adversary against $G$. $\mathcal{A}$ takes a binary string of length $(\ell + l)$ and outputs 0 or 1. The security of $G$ is quantified by the advantage of $\mathcal{A}$ against $G$, which is defined as

$$\mathrm{Adv}_G^{\mathrm{prg}}(\mathcal{A}) = |\Pr[\mathcal{A}(G(K)) \Rightarrow 1] - \Pr[\mathcal{A}(s) \Rightarrow 1]| \ ,$$

where $K \leftarrow \{0,1\}^\ell$ and $s \leftarrow \{0,1\}^{\ell+l}$.

**Forward-Secure Pseudorandom Bit Generator.** A forward-secure pseudorandom bit generator (FS PRG) was formalized by Bellare and Yee [5]. It is a stateful bit generator $\mathsf{SGen} = (\mathsf{seed}, \mathsf{gen}, l, n)$. The algorithm $\mathsf{seed}$ generates an initial secret key $K_1$ for a given security parameter $\ell$. The algorithm $\mathsf{gen}$ takes a current secret key as input and produces a binary sequence of length $l$ and a new secret key. $n$ is the number of calls to $\mathsf{gen}$. Namely, $(s_i, K_{i+1}) \leftarrow \mathsf{gen}(K_i)$ for $1 \le i \le n$, where $s_i \in \{0,1\}^l$.

The security of an FS PRG is indistinguishability against adaptive attacks. Let $\mathrm{Exp}_{\mathsf{SGen},\mathcal{A}}^{\mathrm{fsprg}\text{-}b}$ be an experiment given in Algorithm 1. An adversary $\mathcal{A}$ against $\mathsf{SGen}$ works in two phases. The first phase is the query phase. In this phase, $\mathcal{A}$ gets $s_1, s_2, \ldots, s_{i'}$ for some $i' \le n$. $\mathcal{A}$ is allowed to choose $i'$ arbitrarily. $s_1, s_2, \ldots, s_{i'}$ are generated by $\mathsf{gen}$ or chosen uniformly at random. In the next phase, which we call the try phase, $\mathcal{A}$ receives the secret key $K_{i'+1}$ and tries to tell whether $s_1, s_2, \ldots, s_{i'}$ are generated by $\mathsf{gen}$ or chosen uniformly at random. The advantage of $\mathcal{A}$ against $\mathsf{SGen}$ is defined by

$$\mathrm{Adv}_{\mathsf{SGen}}^{\mathrm{fsprg}}(\mathcal{A}) = \left| \Pr\left[ \mathrm{Exp}_{\mathsf{SGen},\mathcal{A}}^{\mathrm{fsprg}\text{-}0} \Rightarrow 1 \right] - \Pr\left[ \mathrm{Exp}_{\mathsf{SGen},\mathcal{A}}^{\mathrm{fsprg}\text{-}1} \Rightarrow 1 \right] \right| \ .$$

Bellare and Yee also presented a generic construction of an FS PRG with a PRG. Let $G : \{0,1\}^\ell \to \{0,1\}^{\ell+l}$ be a PRG. Let $\mathsf{SGen}[G, n]$ be an FS PRG defined as follows:

- $\mathsf{seed}$ simply chooses $K_1 \in \{0,1\}^\ell$ uniformly at random.
- $(s_i, K_{i+1}) \leftarrow \mathsf{gen}(K_i)$ is simply defined by $(s_i, K_{i+1}) \leftarrow G(K_i)$ for $1 \le i \le n$.

$\mathsf{SGen}[G, n]$ is depicted in Figure 1.

The following theorem states that $\mathsf{SGen}[G, n]$ is a secure FS PRG if $G$ is a secure PRG:

---

**Algorithm 1.** Experiment $\mathrm{Exp}_{\mathsf{SGen},\mathcal{A}}^{\mathsf{fsprg}\text{-}b}$, where $b \in \{0, 1\}$

---

$i \leftarrow 1$; $note \leftarrow \varepsilon$
$K_1 \leftarrow \mathsf{seed}(1^\ell)$
**repeat**
    $(s_i, K_{i+1}) \leftarrow \mathsf{gen}(K_i)$
    **if** $b = 1$ **then**
        $s_i \leftarrow \{0,1\}^l$
    **end if**
    $(phase, note) \leftarrow \mathcal{A}(\mathsf{query}, s_i, note)$
    $i \leftarrow i + 1$
**until** $(phase = \mathsf{try}) \vee (i > n)$
$b' \leftarrow \mathcal{A}(\mathsf{try}, K_i, note)$
**return** $b'$

---

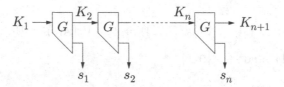

**Fig. 1.** SGen$[G, n]$

**Theorem 1 ([5]).** *Let $\mathcal{A}$ be an adversary against* SGen$[G, n]$. *Then, there exists an adversary $\mathcal{B}$ against $G$ such that*

$$\mathrm{Adv}_{\mathsf{SGen}[G,n]}^{\mathsf{fsprg}}(\mathcal{A}) \leq 2n \cdot \mathrm{Adv}_G^{\mathsf{prg}}(\mathcal{B}) ,$$

*where the running time of $\mathcal{B}$ is the sum of the running time of $\mathcal{A}$ and $O(n(\ell + l))$.*

## 3 Forward-Secure Sequential Aggregate MA Scheme

### 3.1 Definition

**Scheme.** A forward-secure sequential aggregate message authentication scheme (FS SAMAS) is a stateful scheme SAM $=$ (kgen, tag, verif, update, $n$). The algorithms kgen, tag, verif and update are described below. $n$ is the number of the stages.

**Key Generation.** $K_1 \leftarrow \mathsf{kgen}(1^\ell)$.
    For a given security parameter $\ell$, the algorithm kgen produces the master secret key $K_1$ for the first stage.
**Update.** $(S_i, K_{i+1}) \leftarrow \mathsf{update}(K_i)$ for $1 \leq i \leq n$.
    The algorithm update takes $K_i$ as input. It produces the secret tagging key $S_i$ for the current stage and updates the master secret key to $K_{i+1}$ for the next stage.

**Tagging.** $(\langle \tau_{i,j}, i \rangle, T_{i,j}) \leftarrow \mathsf{tag}(S_i, T_{i,j-1}, M_{i,j})$ for $1 \le i \le n$.
The algorithm $\mathsf{tag}$ takes tagging key $S_i$, state $T_{i,j-1}$ and message $M_{i,j}$ as input. $T_{i,0}$ is an initial state. $\mathsf{tag}$ admits messages in $\mathcal{M} \cup \{M_{\mathtt{fin}}\}$ as inputs, where $\mathcal{M}$ is a message space and $M_{\mathtt{fin}} \notin \mathcal{M}$. $M_{\mathtt{fin}}$ is a special message tagged only at the end of the current stage.

**Verification.** Let $\boldsymbol{M} = (\boldsymbol{M}_1, \boldsymbol{M}_2, \dots, \boldsymbol{M}_n)$ be the ordered sequence of the tagged messages, where $\boldsymbol{M}_i = (M_{i,1}, M_{i,2}, \dots, M_{i,\sigma_i})$ and $\sigma_i$ is the number of the messages tagged in the $i$-th stage for $1 \le i \le n$. $M_{i,j} \in \mathcal{M}$ for $1 \le j \le \sigma_i - 1$ and $M_{i,\sigma_i} = M_{\mathtt{fin}}$. Let $(i,j)$ be a pair of integers such that $1 \le i \le n$ and $1 \le j \le \sigma_i$. We define $(i,j) \le (i',j')$ if and only if $i < i'$, or $i = i'$ and $j \le j'$. The algorithm $\mathsf{verif}$ is defined as follows:

$$\alpha \leftarrow \mathsf{verif}(\boldsymbol{S}_{[i_1,i_2]}, T_{i_1,j_1-1}, \boldsymbol{M}_{[(i_1,j_1),(i_2,j_2)]}, \langle \tau_{i_2,j_2}, i_2 \rangle),$$

where
- $\boldsymbol{S}_{[i_1,i_2]} = (S_{i_1}, S_{i_1+1}, \dots, S_{i_2})$,
- $\boldsymbol{M}_{[(i_1,j_1),(i_2,j_2)]} = (M_{i_1,j_1}, \dots, M_{i_2,j_2})$

for $1 \le i_1 \le i_2 \le n$, $1 \le j_1 \le \sigma_1$, $1 \le j_2 \le \sigma_2$ and $j_1 \le j_2$ if $i_1 = i_2$. For $(T_{i_1,j_1-1}, \boldsymbol{M}_{[(i_1,j_1),(i_2,j_2)]}, \langle \tau_{i_2,j_2}, i_2 \rangle)$, the algorithm $\mathsf{verif}$ outputs **valid** if
- $\mathsf{tag}(S_i, \tilde{T}_{i,j-1}, M_{i,j})$ returns $(\langle \tilde{\tau}_{i,j}, i \rangle, \tilde{T}_{i,j})$ for $(i_1,j_1) \le (i,j) \le (i_2,j_2)$, where $\tilde{T}_{i_1,j_1-1} = T_{i_1,j_1-1}$ and $\tilde{T}_{i+1,0} = \tilde{T}_{i,\sigma_i}$ for $i_1 \le i \le i_2 - 1$, and
- $\tilde{\tau}_{i_2,j_2} = \tau_{i_2,j_2}$.

Otherwise, it outputs **invalid**.

Tagging $M_{\mathtt{fin}}$ at the end of the stages is a countermeasure against truncation attacks [4,15]. A truncation attack is an attack simply deleting the tail of a sequence of tagged messages and the corresponding tags. It cannot be detected without any kind of end marker.

**Aggregation.** The aggregation is fairly straightforward and already implicit in the description of the verification algorithm:

$$(T_{i_1,j_1-1}, \boldsymbol{M}_{[(i_1,j_1),(i_2,j_2)]}, \langle \tau_{i_2,j_2}, i_2 \rangle)$$
$$\leftarrow \mathsf{aggre}(T_{i_1,j_1-1}, \boldsymbol{M}_{[(i_1,j_1),(i_2,j_2)]}, \boldsymbol{\tau}_{[(i_1,j_1),(i_2,j_2)]}) ,$$

where $\boldsymbol{\tau}_{[(i_1,j_1),(i_2,j_2)]} = (\langle \tau_{i_1,j_1}, i_1 \rangle, \dots, \langle \tau_{i_2,j_2}, i_2 \rangle)$ is the sequence of the tags to the messages of $\boldsymbol{M}_{[(i_1,j_1),(i_2,j_2)]}$.

**Security.** The security of an FS SAMAS $\mathsf{SAM} = (\mathsf{kgen}, \mathsf{tag}, \mathsf{verif}, \mathsf{update}, n)$ is existential unforgeability against adaptive attacks. Let $\mathrm{Exp}_{\mathsf{SAM},\mathcal{A}}^{\mathsf{fs\text{-}samac}}$ be the experiment given in Algorithm 2. An adversary $\mathcal{A}$ against SAM works in two phases. The first phase is the query phase. In this phase, $\mathcal{A}$ makes queries to $\mathsf{tag}(S_i, \cdot, \cdot)$ adaptively. $\mathcal{A}$ should respect the state: $\mathcal{A}$ should ask a new message along with the current state returned by $\mathsf{tag}$ as a reply to the previous message. On the other hand, $\mathcal{A}$ is allowed to repeat same messages. $\mathcal{A}$ is also allowed to control when to proceed to the next stages and when to break into the system. If $\mathcal{A}$ decides to break into the system during the $a$-th stage, then $\mathcal{A}$ receives the secret key $K_{a+1}$ of the next stage and enters into the second phase. This phase is the try phase. In this phase, $\mathcal{A}$ tries to forge a pair of a sequence of messages and a tag for some (consecutive) stage(s) prior to the break-in.

Let $\boldsymbol{M} = (\boldsymbol{M}_1, \boldsymbol{M}_2, \ldots, \boldsymbol{M}_a)$ be the sequence of the messages made by $\mathcal{A}$ as queries. For $1 \leq i_1 \leq i_2 \leq a$, let

$$\boldsymbol{V}(\boldsymbol{M}, i_1, i_2) =$$
$$\begin{cases} \{(T_{i_1, u_1 - 1}, \boldsymbol{M}_{[(i_1, u_1), (i_2, u_2)]}) \mid 1 \leq u_1 \leq \sigma_{i_1},\ 1 \leq u_2 \leq \sigma_{i_2}\} & \text{if } i_1 < i_2, \\ \{(T_{i_1, u_1 - 1}, \boldsymbol{M}_{[(i_1, u_1), (i_2, u_2)]}) \mid 1 \leq u_1 \leq u_2 \leq \sigma_{i_1}\} & \text{if } i_1 = i_2. \end{cases}$$

The forgery $(T'_{i_1, j_1 - 1}, \boldsymbol{M}'_{[(i_1, j_1), (i_2, j_2)]}, \langle \tau'_{i_2, j_2}, i_2 \rangle)$ is successful if

- $1 \leq i_1 \leq i_2 \leq a$,
- $\mathsf{verif}(\boldsymbol{S}_{[i_1, i_2]}, T'_{i_1, j_1 - 1}, \boldsymbol{M}'_{[(i_1, j_1), (i_2, j_2)]}, \langle \tau'_{i_2, j_2}, i_2 \rangle) = \mathsf{valid}$, and
- $(T'_{i_1, j_1 - 1}, \boldsymbol{M}'_{[(i_1, j_1), (i_2, j_2)]}) \notin \boldsymbol{V}(\boldsymbol{M}, i_1, i_2)$.

The security of FS SAMAS SAM is quantified by the probability that an adversary $\mathcal{A}$ against SAM succeeds in forgery. The advantage of $\mathcal{A}$ against SAM is defined by

$$\mathrm{Adv}_{\mathsf{SAM}}^{\mathsf{fs\text{-}samac}}(\mathcal{A}) = \Pr\left[\mathrm{Exp}_{\mathsf{SAM}, \mathcal{A}}^{\mathsf{fs\text{-}samac}} \Rightarrow 1\right] .$$

---

**Algorithm 2.** Experiment $\mathrm{Exp}_{\mathsf{SAM}, \mathcal{A}}^{\mathsf{fs\text{-}samac}}$. $\boldsymbol{M}$ represents the sequence of all messages in the queries made by $\mathcal{A}$.

---
$i \leftarrow 1;\ note \leftarrow \varepsilon$
$K_1 \leftarrow \mathsf{kgen}(1^\ell)$
**repeat**
$\quad (S_i, K_{i+1}) \leftarrow \mathsf{update}(K_i)$
$\quad (phase, note) \leftarrow \mathcal{A}^{\mathsf{tag}(S_i, \cdot, \cdot)}(\mathbf{query}, note)$
$\quad i \leftarrow i + 1$
**until** $(phase = \mathbf{try}) \vee (i > n)$
$(T'_{i_1, j_1 - 1}, \boldsymbol{M}'_{[(i_1, j_1), (i_2, j_2)]}, \langle \tau'_{i_2, j_2}, i_2 \rangle) \leftarrow \mathcal{A}(\mathbf{try}, K_i, note)$
**if** $(T'_{i_1, j_1 - 1}, \boldsymbol{M}'_{[(i_1, j_1), (i_2, j_2)]}, \langle \tau'_{i_2, j_2}, i_2 \rangle)$ is a successful forgery **then**
$\quad$ **return** 1
**else**
$\quad$ **return** 0
**end if**

---

## 3.2   Generic Construction

Let $F : \{0, 1\}^l \times \{0, 1\}^* \to \{0, 1\}^t$ and $G : \{0, 1\}^\ell \to \{0, 1\}^{l+\ell}$. An FS SAMAS using $F$ and $G$ is presented below.

The message space $\mathcal{M}$ and the special message $M_{\mathtt{fin}}$ are defined as $\mathcal{M} = \{0 \| M \mid M \in \{0, 1\}^*\}$ and $M_{\mathtt{fin}} = 1$, respectively.

**Key Generation** For a given security parameter $\ell$, the key generation algorithm simply selects $K_1 \in \{0,1\}^{\ell}$ uniformly at random.

**Update** $(S_i, K_{i+1}) \leftarrow G(K_i)$ for $1 \le i \le n$.

**Tagging** $(\langle \tau_{i,j}, i \rangle, \tau_{i,j}) \leftarrow \mathsf{tag}(S_i, \tau_{i,j-1}, M_{i,j})$ for $1 \le i \le n$ and $1 \le j \le \sigma_i$, where

- $\sigma_i$ is the total number of the messages tagged in the $i$-th stage,
- $\tau_{i,j} = F_{S_i}(\tau_{i,j-1} \| M_{i,j})$,
- $\tau_{1,0} = 0^t$,
- $\tau_{i,0} = \tau_{i-1,\sigma_{i-1}}$ for $i \ge 2$,
- $M_{i,\sigma_i} = M_{\mathtt{fin}}$, and $M_{i,j} \in \mathcal{M}$ for $1 \le j \le \sigma_i - 1$.

The descriptions of the verification algorithm and the aggregation algorithm are omitted since they are apparent from the definiton and the descriptions of the other algorithms given above. The FS PRG with $G$ is used for the key generation and the update procedures.

Figure 2 depicts the tagging procedure for a sequence of messages.

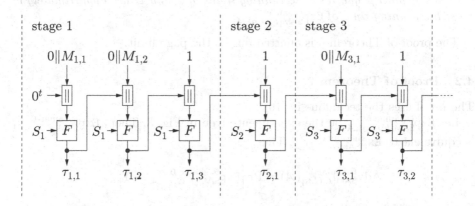

**Fig. 2.** An example of the tagging procedure for a sequence of messages

## 4    Provable Security of Generic Construction

### 4.1    Summary

Let $\mathsf{SAM}[F, G, n]$ be the FS SAMAS using $F$ and $G$ proposed in the previous section. The following theorem shows that $\mathsf{SAM}[F, G, n]$ is secure if $F$ is a secure MAF and $G$ is a secure PRG.

**Theorem 2 (Reduction to MAC and PRG).** *Let $\mathcal{A}$ be an adversary against $\mathsf{SAM}[F, G, n]$. Let $\mu$ be the sum of the maximum number of the queries made by $\mathcal{A}$ and the maximum number of the messages in the output of $\mathcal{A}$. Then, there exist an adversary $\mathcal{B}$ against $F$ and an adversary $\mathcal{D}$ against $G$ such that*

$$\mathrm{Adv}^{\mathsf{fs\text{-}samac}}_{\mathsf{SAM}[F,G,n]}(\mathcal{A}) \le \frac{n\mu(\mu+3)}{2} \mathrm{Adv}^{\mathrm{mac}}_{F}(\mathcal{B}) + 2n \cdot \mathrm{Adv}^{\mathrm{prg}}_{G}(\mathcal{D}) .$$

*$\mathcal{B}$ makes at most $\mu$ queries. The running times of $\mathcal{B}$ and $\mathcal{D}$ are approximately at most the running time of $\mathrm{Exp}^{\mathsf{fs\text{-}samac}}_{\mathsf{SAM}[F,G,n],\mathcal{A}}$.*

It is easy to see that a secure PRF is a secure MAF. Thus, Theorem 2 also implies that $\mathsf{SAM}[F, G, n]$ is secure if $F$ is a secure PRF and $G$ is a secure PRG. However, the direct reduction of the theorem presented below is much tighter than the reduction following from Theorem 2. In general, distinction is expected to be much easier than forgery. Thus, the advantage of an adversary against $F$ regarding the PRF property is expected to be much larger than the advantage of another adversary regarding the MAC property if their resources are comparable.

**Theorem 3 (Reduction to PRF and PRG).** *Let $\mathcal{A}$ be an adversary against* $\mathsf{SAM}[F, G, n]$. *Let $\mu$ be the sum of the maximum number of the queries made by $\mathcal{A}$ and the maximum number of the messages in the output of $\mathcal{A}$. Then, there exist an adversary $\mathcal{C}$ against $F$ and an adversary $\mathcal{D}$ against $G$ such that*

$$\mathrm{Adv}_{\mathsf{SAM}[F,G,n]}^{\mathrm{fs\text{-}samac}}(\mathcal{A}) \leq n \cdot \mathrm{Adv}_F^{\mathrm{prf}}(\mathcal{C}) + 2n \cdot \mathrm{Adv}_G^{\mathrm{prg}}(\mathcal{D}) + \frac{\mu^2 + \mu + 2}{2^{t+1}} .$$

*$\mathcal{C}$ makes at most $\mu$ queries. The running times of $\mathcal{C}$ and $\mathcal{D}$ are approximately at most the running time of* $\mathrm{Exp}_{\mathsf{SAM}[F,G,n],\mathcal{A}}^{\mathrm{fs\text{-}samac}}$.

The proof of Theorem 3 is omitted due to the page limit.

## 4.2 Proof of Theorem 2

The proof uses the technique in [16].

Let $\mathrm{Exp}_{\mathsf{SAM}[F,G,n],\mathcal{A}}^{\mathrm{fs\text{-}samac}\text{-}b}$ be the experiment given in Fig. 3. Then, $\mathrm{Exp}_{\mathsf{SAM}[F,G,n],\mathcal{A}}^{\mathrm{fs\text{-}samac}\text{-}0}$ is equivalent to $\mathrm{Exp}_{\mathsf{SAM}[F,G,n],\mathcal{A}}^{\mathrm{fs\text{-}samac}}$. Thus,

$$\mathrm{Adv}_{\mathsf{SAM}[F,G,n]}^{\mathrm{fs\text{-}samac}}(\mathcal{A}) = \Pr\left[\mathrm{Exp}_{\mathsf{SAM}[F,G,n],\mathcal{A}}^{\mathrm{fs\text{-}samac}\text{-}0} \Rightarrow 1\right] .$$

Let $\mathrm{Exp}_{\mathsf{SGen}[G,n],\mathcal{D}_1}^{\mathrm{fsprg}\text{-}b}$ be the experiment given in Fig. 4. $\mathcal{D}_1(\mathbf{query}, S_i, note)$ runs $\mathcal{A}^{\mathsf{tag}(S_i,\cdot,\cdot)}(\mathbf{query}, note)$ and simulates $\mathsf{tag}(S_i, \cdot, \cdot)$ to answer to the queries made by $\mathcal{A}$. $\mathcal{D}_1(\mathbf{try}, K_i, note)$ works as follows:

1. Runs $\mathcal{A}(\mathbf{try}, K_i, note)$ and gets $(T'_{i_1,j_1-1}, \boldsymbol{M}'_{[(i_1,j_1),(i_2,j_2)]}, \langle \tau'_{i_2,j_2}, i_2 \rangle)$.
2. If $(T'_{i_1,j_1-1}, \boldsymbol{M}'_{[(i_1,j_1),(i_2,j_2)]}, \langle \tau'_{i_2,j_2}, i_2 \rangle)$ is a successful forgery, then return 1. Otherwise, return 0.

Then,

$$\Pr\left[\mathrm{Exp}_{\mathsf{SAM}[F,G,n],\mathcal{A}}^{\mathrm{fs\text{-}samac}\text{-}b} \Rightarrow 1\right] = \Pr\left[\mathrm{Exp}_{\mathsf{SGen}[G,n],\mathcal{D}_1}^{\mathrm{fsprg}\text{-}b} \Rightarrow 1\right] ,$$

which implies

$$\left|\Pr\left[\mathrm{Exp}_{\mathsf{SAM}[F,G,n],\mathcal{A}}^{\mathrm{fs\text{-}samac}\text{-}0} \Rightarrow 1\right] - \Pr\left[\mathrm{Exp}_{\mathsf{SAM}[F,G,n],\mathcal{A}}^{\mathrm{fs\text{-}samac}\text{-}1} \Rightarrow 1\right]\right| = \mathrm{Adv}_{\mathsf{SGen}[G,n]}^{\mathrm{fsprg}}(\mathcal{D}_1) .$$

Thus,

$$\mathrm{Adv}_{\mathsf{SAM}[F,G,n]}^{\mathrm{fs\text{-}samac}}(\mathcal{A}) \leq \Pr\left[\mathrm{Exp}_{\mathsf{SAM}[F,G,n],\mathcal{A}}^{\mathrm{fs\text{-}samac}\text{-}1} \Rightarrow 1\right] + \mathrm{Adv}_{\mathsf{SGen}[G,n]}^{\mathrm{fsprg}}(\mathcal{D}_1) .$$

$i \leftarrow 1;\ note \leftarrow \varepsilon$
$K_1 \leftarrow \{0,1\}^\ell$
**repeat**
    $(S_i, K_{i+1}) \leftarrow G(K_i)$
    **if** $b = 1$ **then**
        $S_i \leftarrow \{0,1\}^l$
    **end if**
    $(phase, note) \leftarrow \mathcal{A}^{\mathsf{tag}(S_i,\cdot,\cdot)}(\mathsf{query}, note)$
    $i \leftarrow i + 1$
**until** $(phase = \mathsf{try}) \vee (i > n)$
$(T'_{i_1,j_1-1}, \boldsymbol{M}'_{[(i_1,j_1),(i_2,j_2)]}, \langle \tau'_{i_2,j_2}, i_2 \rangle) \leftarrow \mathcal{A}(\mathsf{try}, K_i, note)$
**if** $(T'_{i_1,j_1-1}, \boldsymbol{M}'_{[(i_1,j_1),(i_2,j_2)]}, \langle \tau'_{i_2,j_2}, i_2 \rangle)$ is a successful forgery **then**
    **return** 1
**else**
    **return** 0
**end if**

**Fig. 3.** $\mathrm{Exp}^{\text{fs-samac-}b}_{\mathrm{SAM}[F,G,n],\mathcal{A}}$

The running time of $\mathcal{D}_1$ is approximately the sum of the running time of $\mathcal{A}$ and time to simulate $\mathsf{tag}(S_i, \cdot, \cdot)$ and verify whether $(T'_{i_1,j_1-1}, \boldsymbol{M}'_{[(i_1,j_1),(i_2,j_2)]}, \langle \tau'_{i_2,j_2}, i_2 \rangle)$ is a successful forgery or not with respect to $\boldsymbol{S}_{[i_1,i_2]}$. It is at most the running time of $\mathrm{Exp}^{\text{fs-samac}}_{\mathrm{SAM}[F,G,n],\mathcal{A}}$. From Theorem 1, there exists an adversasry $\mathcal{D}$ such that

$$\mathrm{Adv}^{\text{fsprg}}_{\mathrm{SGen}[G,n]}(\mathcal{D}_1) \leq 2n \cdot \mathrm{Adv}^{\text{prg}}_G(\mathcal{D})\ ,$$

where the running time of $\mathcal{D}$ is also approximately at most the running time of $\mathrm{Exp}^{\text{fs-samac}}_{\mathrm{SAM}[F,G,n],\mathcal{A}}$.

$i \leftarrow 1;\ note \leftarrow \varepsilon$
$K_1 \leftarrow \{0,1\}^\ell$
**repeat**
    $(S_i, K_{i+1}) \leftarrow G(K_i)$
    **if** $b = 1$ **then**
        $S_i \leftarrow \{0,1\}^l$
    **end if**
    $(phase, note) \leftarrow \mathcal{D}_1(\mathsf{query}, S_i, note)$
    $i \leftarrow i + 1$
**until** $(phase = \mathsf{try}) \vee (i > n)$
$b' \leftarrow \mathcal{D}_1(\mathsf{try}, K_i, note)$
**return** $b'$

**Fig. 4.** $\mathrm{Exp}^{\text{fsprg-}b}_{\mathrm{SGen}[G,n],\mathcal{D}_1}$

Let $\mathcal{B}_1$ be the algorithm given in Fig. 5. $\mathcal{B}_1$ has oracle access to $F_{\tilde{S}_i}$ such that $\tilde{S}_i$ is chosen uniformly at random from $\{0,1\}^l$ for $1 \le i \le n$. Then,

$$\Pr\left[\mathcal{B}_1 \Rightarrow 1\right] = \Pr\left[\mathrm{Exp}^{\text{fs-samac-1}}_{\mathrm{SAM}[F,G,n],\mathcal{A}} \Rightarrow 1\right] \ .$$

```
i ← 1; note ← ε
K₁ ← {0,1}^ℓ
repeat
    (Sᵢ, Kᵢ₊₁) ← G(Kᵢ)
    (phase, note) ← A^tag(S̃ᵢ,·,·)(query, note)
    i ← i + 1
until (phase = try) ∨ (i > n)
(T'_{i₁,j₁−1}, M'_{[(i₁,j₁),(i₂,j₂)]}, ⟨τ'_{i₂,j₂}, i₂⟩) ← A(try, Kᵢ, note)
if (T'_{i₁,j₁−1}, M'_{[(i₁,j₁),(i₂,j₂)]}, ⟨τ'_{i₂,j₂}, i₂⟩) is a successful forgery then
    b' ← 1
else
    b' ← 0
end if
return b'
```

**Fig. 5.** The algorithm $\mathcal{B}_1$ with oracle access to $F_{\tilde{S}_1}, F_{\tilde{S}_2}, \ldots, F_{\tilde{S}_n}$. $\mathcal{B}_1$ can simulate $\mathrm{tag}(\tilde{S}_i, \cdot, \cdot)$ by using $F_{\tilde{S}_i}$.

Suppose that $\mathcal{A}$ outputs $(T'_{i_1,j_1-1}, M'_{[(i_1,j_1),(i_2,j_2)]}, \langle \tau'_{i_2,j_2}, i_2 \rangle)$ as a forgery in the try phase, where $M'_{[(i_1,j_1),(i_2,j_2)]}$ is

$$\begin{cases} (M'_{i_1,j_1}, \ldots, M'_{i_1,\sigma'_{i_1}}, M'_{i_1+1,1}, \ldots, M'_{i_1+1,\sigma'_{i_1+1}}, \ldots, M'_{i_2,1}, \ldots, M'_{i_2,j_2}) & \text{if } i_1 < i_2, \\ (M'_{i_1,j_1}, \ldots, M'_{i_1,j_2}) & \text{if } i_1 = i_2. \end{cases}$$

Then, during the verification of the forgery, $\mathcal{B}_1$ asks $\tau'_{i,j-1} \| M'_{i,j}$ to $F_{\tilde{S}_i}$ and gets the corresponding tag $\tau'_{i,j} = F_{\tilde{S}_i}(\tau'_{i,j-1} \| M'_{i,j})$ for $(i,j)$ such that $(i_1, j_1) \le (i,j) \le (i_2, j_2)$. If the forgery is successful, then

$$\tau'_{i_2,j_2} = F_{\tilde{S}_{i_2}}(\tau'_{i_2,j_2-1} \| M'_{i_2,j_2}) \wedge (T'_{i_1,j_1-1}, M'_{[(i_1,j_1),(i_2,j_2)]}) \notin V(M, i_1, i_2) \ .$$

Suppose that the forgery $(T'_{i_1,j_1-1}, M'_{[(i_1,j_1),(i_2,j_2)]}, \langle \tau'_{i_2,j_2}, i_2 \rangle)$ is successful. For $(i,j)$ such that $(i_1, 1) \le (i,j) \le (i_2, \sigma_{i_2})$, let $\tau_{i,j-1} \| M_{i,j}$ be the queries made by $\mathcal{B}_1$ to the oracle $F_{\tilde{S}_i}$ during the execution of $\mathcal{A}$ in the query phase, where $1 \le j \le \sigma_i$.

If $\tau'_{i_2,j_2-1} \| M'_{i_2,j_2}$ is new, that is, it does not appear as a query during the execution of $\mathcal{A}$ in the query phase, then $(\tau'_{i_2,j_2-1} \| M'_{i_2,j_2}, \tau'_{i_2,j_2})$ is a successful forgery for $F_{\tilde{S}_{i_2}}$. Notice that there may exist some $1 \le j'_2 < j_2$ such that $\tau'_{i_2,j'_2-1} \| M'_{i_2,j'_2} = \tau'_{i_2,j_2-1} \| M'_{i_2,j_2}$.

Suppose that $\tau'_{i_2,j_2-1}\|M'_{i_2,j_2}$ is not new. Two cases are considered: $i_1 < i_2$ and $i_1 = i_2$.

First, suppose that $i_1 < i_2$. Suppose that $\tau_{i_2,j-1}\|M_{i_2,j} = \tau'_{i_2,j_2-1}\|M'_{i_2,j_2}$ for some $j \in [1,\sigma_{i_2}]$. Let $d = \min\{j \mid \tau_{i_2,j-1}\|M_{i_2,j} = \tau'_{i_2,j_2-1}\|M'_{i_2,j_2}\}$. There are three cases:

1. there exists a collision for $F_{\tilde{S}_{i_2}}$:

$$F_{\tilde{S}_{i_2}}(\tau_{i_2,d-j-1}\|M_{i_2,d-j}) = F_{\tilde{S}_{i_2}}(\tau'_{i_2,j_2-j-1}\|M'_{i_2,j_2-j})$$

and $\tau_{i_2,d-j-1}\|M_{i_2,d-j} \neq \tau'_{i_2,j_2-j-1}\|M'_{i_2,j_2-j}$ for some $j \in [1,\min\{j_2,d\}-1]$,
2. there exists a collision for $F_{\tilde{S}_{i_2-1}}$ and $F_{\tilde{S}_{i_2}}$:
   (a) $\tau_{i_2,d-j_2} = \tau'_{i_2,0} = \tau'_{i_2-1,\sigma'_{i_2-1}}$ if $d > j_2$, that is,

$$F_{\tilde{S}_{i_2}}(\tau_{i_2,d-j_2-1}\|M_{i_2,d-j_2}) = F_{\tilde{S}_{i_2-1}}(\tau'_{i_2-1,\sigma'_{i_2-1}-1}\|M'_{i_2-1,\sigma'_{i_2-1}}) ,$$

   and
   (b) $\tau_{i_2-1,\sigma_{i_2-1}} = \tau_{i_2,0} = \tau'_{i_2,j_2-d}$ if $d < j_2$, that is,

$$F_{\tilde{S}_{i_2-1}}(\tau_{i_2-1,\sigma_{i_2-1}-1}\|M_{i_2-1,\sigma_{i_2-1}}) = F_{\tilde{S}_{i_2}}(\tau'_{i_2,j_2-d-1}\|M'_{i_2,j_2-d}) ,$$

   or
3. $d = j_2$ and $\tau_{i_2,d-j-1}\|M_{i_2,d-j} = \tau'_{i_2,j_2-j-1}\|M'_{i_2,j_2-j}$ for all $j \in [0,d-1]$.

For the case 3 above, cases for the $i$-th stage are considered for $i_1 < i < i_2$. Without loss of generality, it is assumed that $\tau_{i,\sigma_i} = \tau'_{i,\sigma'_i}$. There are also three cases:

4. there exists a collision for $F_{\tilde{S}_i}$: $F_{\tilde{S}_i}(\tau_{i,\sigma_i-j-1}\|M_{i,\sigma_i-j}) = F_{\tilde{S}_i}(\tau'_{i,\sigma'_i-j-1}\|M'_{i,\sigma'_i-j})$
   and $\tau_{i,\sigma_i-j-1}\|M_{i,\sigma_i-j} \neq \tau'_{i,\sigma'_i-j-1}\|M'_{i,\sigma'_i-j}$ for some $j \in [1,\min\{\sigma_i,\sigma'_i\}-1]$,
5. there exists a collision for $F_{\tilde{S}_{i-1}}$ and $F_{\tilde{S}_i}$:
   (a) $\tau_{i,\sigma_i-\sigma'_i} = \tau'_{i,0} = \tau'_{i-1,\sigma'_{i-1}}$ if $\sigma_i > \sigma'_i$, that is, $F_{\tilde{S}_i}(\tau_{i,\sigma_i-\sigma'_i-1}\|M_{i,\sigma_i-\sigma'_i}) = F_{\tilde{S}_{i-1}}(\tau'_{i-1,\sigma'_{i-1}-1}\|M'_{i-1,\sigma'_{i-1}})$, and
   (b) $\tau_{i-1,\sigma_{i-1}} = \tau_{i,0} = \tau'_{i,\sigma'_i-\sigma_i}$ if $\sigma_i < \sigma'_i$, that is, $F_{\tilde{S}_{i-1}}(\tau_{i-1,\sigma_{i-1}-1}\|M_{i-1,\sigma_{i-1}}) = F_{\tilde{S}_i}(\tau'_{i,\sigma'_i-\sigma_i-1}\|M'_{i,\sigma'_i-\sigma_i})$,
   or
6. $\sigma_i = \sigma'_i$ and $\tau_{i,\sigma_i-j-1}\|M_{i,\sigma_i-j} = \tau'_{i,\sigma'_i-j-1}\|M'_{i,\sigma'_i-j}$ for all $j \in [0,\sigma_i-1]$.

Suppose that the case 3 is encountered for $i_2$ and that the case 6 is encountered for every $i$ such that $i_1 < i < i_2$. Then, cases for the $i_1$-th stage are considered. Without loss of generality, it is assumed that $\tau_{i_1,\sigma_{i_1}} = \tau'_{i_1,\sigma'_{i_1}}$. There are four cases:

7. there exists a collision for $F_{\tilde{S}_{i_1}}$:

$$F_{\tilde{S}_{i_1}}(\tau_{i_1,\sigma_{i_1}-j-1}\|M_{i_1,\sigma_{i_1}-j}) = F_{\tilde{S}_{i_1}}(\tau'_{i_1,\sigma'_{i_1}-j-1}\|M'_{i,\sigma'_{i_1}-j})$$

and $\tau_{i_1,\sigma_{i_1}-j-1}\|M_{i_1,\sigma_{i_1}-j} \neq \tau'_{i_1,\sigma'_{i_1}-j-1}\|M'_{i,\sigma'_{i_1}-j}$ for some $j \in [0,\min\{\sigma_{i_1}-1,\sigma'_{i_1}-j_1\}]$,

8. $i_1 \geq 2$, $\sigma'_{i_1} - j_1 + 1 > \sigma_{i_1}$ and there exists a collision for $F_{\tilde{S}_{i_1-1}}$ and $F_{\tilde{S}_{i_1}}$, that is, $F_{\tilde{S}_{i_1-1}}(\tau_{i_1-1,\sigma_{i_1-1}-1}\|M_{i_1-1,\sigma_{i_1-1}}) = F_{\tilde{S}_{i_1}}(\tau'_{i_1,\sigma'_{i_1}-\sigma_{i_1}-1}\|M'_{i_1,\sigma'_{i_1}-\sigma_{i_1}})$,

9. $i_1 = 1$, $\sigma'_{i_1} - j_1 + 1 > \sigma_{i_1}$ and $F_{\tilde{S}_{i_1}}(\tau'_{i_1,\sigma'_{i_1}-\sigma_{i_1}-1}\|M'_{i_1,\sigma'_{i_1}-\sigma_{i_1}}) = \tau_{i_1,0} = 0^t$, or

10. $\sigma'_{i_1} - j_1 + 1 \leq \sigma_{i_1}$ and $\tau_{i_1,\sigma_{i_1}-j-1}\|M_{i_1,\sigma_{i_1}-j} = \tau'_{i_1,\sigma'_{i_1}-j-1}\|M'_{i_1,\sigma'_{i_1}-j}$ for all $j \in [0, \sigma'_{i_1} - j_1]$.

The case 10 contradicts the assumption that $(T'_{i_1,j_1-1}, M'_{[(i_1,j_1),(i_2,j_2)]}) \notin V(M, i_1, i_2)$.

Second, suppose that $i_1 = i_2$. Then, $j_1 \leq j_2$. Suppose that $\tau_{i_1,d-1}\|M_{i_1,d} = \tau'_{i_1,j_2-1}\|M'_{i_1,j_2}$ for some $d \in [1, \sigma_{i_1}]$. Then, there are three cases:

1. there exists a collision for $F_{\tilde{S}_{i_1}}$:

$$F_{\tilde{S}_{i_1}}(\tau_{i_1,d-j-1}\|M_{i_1,d-j}) = F_{\tilde{S}_{i_1}}(\tau'_{i_1,j_2-j-1}\|M'_{i_1,j_2-j})$$

and $\tau_{i_1,d-j-1}\|M_{i_1,d-j} \neq \tau'_{i_1,j_2-j-1}\|M'_{i_1,j_2-j}$ for some $j \in [1, \min\{d, j_2\} - 1]$,

2. $i_1 \geq 2$ and there exists a collision for $F_{\tilde{S}_{i_1-1}}$ and $F_{\tilde{S}_{i_1}}$:

$$F_{\tilde{S}_{i_1-1}}(\tau_{i_1-1,\sigma_{i_1-1}-1}\|M_{i_1-1,\sigma_{i_1-1}}) = F_{\tilde{S}_{i_1}}(\tau'_{i_1,j_2-d-1}\|M'_{i_1,j_2-d}) \ ,$$

or

3. $i_1 = 1$ and $F_{\tilde{S}_{i_1}}(\tau'_{i_1,j_2-d-1}\|M'_{i_1,j_2-d}) = \tau_{i_1,0} = 0^t$.

Let $\mathcal{B}_2$ be an adversary with oracle access to $F_{\tilde{S}_1}, F_{\tilde{S}_2}, \ldots, F_{\tilde{S}_n}$. $\mathcal{B}_2$ first selects one of the following strategies uniformly at random, and then runs $\mathcal{B}_1$ under the strategy. Let $\mu_1$ be the total number of the queries made by $\mathcal{B}_1$ to the oracles during the execution of $\mathcal{A}$ during the query phase. Let $\mu_2$ be the total number of the queries made by $\mathcal{B}_1$ to the oracles during the verification of the forgery by $\mathcal{A}$.

- Stops just before the $j$-th query $u_j$ and returns $(u_j, \tau'_{i_2,j_2})$, where $\mu_1 + 1 \leq j \leq \mu_2$.
- Stops just before the $j$-th query $u_j$ and returns $(u_j, 0^t)$, where $1 \leq j \leq \mu_1 + \mu_2$.
- Stops just before the $j$-th query $u_j$ and returns $(u_j, \tau_{j'})$, where $1 \leq j' < j \leq \mu_1 + \mu_2$.

If $\mathcal{B}_1$ is successful, then at least one of the strategies listed above gives $\mathcal{B}_2$ a successful forgery for $F_{\tilde{S}_i}$ for some $i \in [1, n]$. The number of the queries made by $\mathcal{B}_2$ is $\mu \geq \mu_1 + \mu_2$. Thus, the number of the strategies are at most

$$\mu + \mu + \mu(\mu - 1)/2 = \mu(\mu + 3)/2 \ .$$

Since $\mathcal{B}_2$ selects a strategy uniformly at random,

$$\mathrm{Adv}_F^{n\text{-mac}}(\mathcal{B}_2) = \frac{2}{\mu(\mu + 3)} \Pr\left[\mathcal{B}_1^{F_{\tilde{S}_1}, \ldots, F_{\tilde{S}_n}} \Rightarrow 1\right] \ .$$

The running time of $\mathcal{B}_2$ is approximately at most the running time of $\mathrm{Exp}_{\mathrm{SAM}[F,G,n],\mathcal{A}}^{\text{fs-samac}}$ without computation of $F_{\tilde{S}_1}, \ldots, F_{\tilde{S}_n}$. This completes the proof with Lemma 2. $\qed$

**Acknowledgments.** The authors would like to thank the anonymous reviewers for their valuable comments. This work is partially supported by JSPS KAK-ENHI Grant Number 25330150.

# References

1. Bellare, M.: New proofs for NMAC and HMAC: Security without collision-resistance. In: Dwork, C. (ed.) CRYPTO 2006. LNCS, vol. 4117, pp. 602–619. Springer, Heidelberg (2006), The full version is "Cryptology ePrint Archive: Report 2006/043" at http://eprint.iacr.org/
2. Bellare, M., Canetti, R., Krawczyk, H.: Pseudorandom functions revisited: The cascade construction and its concrete security. In: Proceedings of the 37th IEEE Symposium on Foundations of Computer Science, pp. 514–523 (1996)
3. Bellare, M., Miner, S.K.: A forward-secure digital signature scheme. In: Wiener, M. (ed.) CRYPTO 1999. LNCS, vol. 1666, pp. 431–448. Springer, Heidelberg (1999)
4. Bellare, M., Yee, B.S.: Forward integrity for secure audit logs. Technical report, University of California, San Diego (1997)
5. Bellare, M., Yee, B.S.: Forward-security in private-key cryptography. In: Joye, M. (ed.) CT-RSA 2003. LNCS, vol. 2612, pp. 1–18. Springer, Heidelberg (2003), The full version is IACR Cryptology ePrint Archive: Report 2001/035 at http://eprint.iacr.org/
6. Blum, M., Micali, S.: How to generate cryptographically strong sequences of pseudo-random bits. SIAM Journal of Computing 13(4), 850–864 (1984)
7. Eikemeier, O., Fischlin, M., Götzmann, J.-F., Lehmann, A., Schröder, D., Schröder, P., Wagner, D.: History-free aggregate message authentication codes. In: Garay, J.A., De Prisco, R. (eds.) SCN 2010. LNCS, vol. 6280, pp. 309–328. Springer, Heidelberg (2010)
8. FIPS PUB 198-1. The keyed-hash message authentication code, HMAC (2008)
9. Goldreich, O., Goldwasser, S., Micali, S.: How to construct random functions. Journal of the ACM 33(4), 792–807 (1986)
10. Günther, C.G.: An identity-based key-exchange protocol. In: Quisquater, J.-J., Vandewalle, J. (eds.) EUROCRYPT 1989. LNCS, vol. 434, pp. 29–37. Springer, Heidelberg (1990)
11. Iwata, T., Kurosawa, K.: OMAC: One-key CBC MAC. In: Johansson, T. (ed.) FSE 2003. LNCS, vol. 2887, pp. 129–153. Springer, Heidelberg (2003), An updated version is "Cryptology ePrint Archive: Report 2002/180" at http://eprint.iacr.org/
12. Katz, J., Lindell, A.Y.: Aggregate message authentication codes. In: Malkin, T. (ed.) CT-RSA 2008. LNCS, vol. 4964, pp. 155–169. Springer, Heidelberg (2008)
13. Lysyanskaya, A., Micali, S., Reyzin, L., Shacham, H.: Sequential aggregate signatures from trapdoor permutations. In: Cachin, C., Camenisch, J. (eds.) EUROCRYPT 2004. LNCS, vol. 3027, pp. 74–90. Springer, Heidelberg (2004)
14. Ma, D., Tsudik, G.: Extended abstract: Forward-secure sequential aggregate authentication. In: IEEE Symposium on Security and Privacy, pp. 86–91. IEEE Computer Society (2007), Also published as IACR Cryptology ePrint Archive: Report 2007/052 at http://eprint.iacr.org/
15. Ma, D., Tsudik, G.: A new approach to secure logging. ACM Transactions on Storage 5(1), 2:1–2:21 (2009)

16. Maurer, U.M., Sjödin, J.: Single-key AIL-MACs from any FIL-MAC. In: Caires, L., Italiano, G.F., Monteiro, L., Palamidessi, C., Yung, M. (eds.) ICALP 2005. LNCS, vol. 3580, pp. 472–484. Springer, Heidelberg (2005)
17. NIST Special Publication 800-38B. Recommendation for block cipher modes of operation: The CMAC mode for authentication (2005)
18. Schneier, B., Kelsey, J.: Secure audit logs to support computer forensics. ACM Transactions on Information and System Security 2(2), 159–176 (1999)
19. Simon, D.R.: Findings collisions on a one-way street: Can secure hash functions be based on general assumptions? In: Nyberg, K. (ed.) EUROCRYPT 1998. LNCS, vol. 1403, pp. 334–345. Springer, Heidelberg (1998)
20. Wang, B., Hong, X.: Sequential message authentication code without random oracles. Cryptology ePrint Archive, Report 2013/444 (2013), http://eprint.iacr.org/
21. Wang, X., Feng, D., Lai, X., Yu, H.: Collisions for hash functions MD4, MD5, HAVAL-128 and RIPEMD. In: Cryptology ePrint Archive, Report 2004/199 (2004), http://eprint.iacr.org/
22. Wang, X., Yin, Y.L., Yu, H.: Finding collisions in the full SHA-1. In: Shoup, V. (ed.) CRYPTO 2005. LNCS, vol. 3621, pp. 17–36. Springer, Heidelberg (2005)

# A Provable Secure Batch Authentication Scheme for EPCGen2 Tags

Jiageng Chen, Atsuko Miyaji, and Chunhua Su

School of Information Science,
Japan Advanced Institute of Science and Technology, Japan
{jg-chen,miyaji,su}@jaist.ac.jp

**Abstract.** EPC Class1 Gen2 (EPCGen2) is an international industrial standards for low cost RFID system used in many applications such as supply chain and consumer service. While RFID technology offers convenience and being employed in various applications in our society, security and privacy issues are still the number one concern of most RFID applications today. In this paper, we study the problems occurring where a reader wants to authenticate and identify legitimate RFID EPCGen2 tags in a batch to guarantee the integrity of the products. Most of the EPCGen2 tags are passive and have limited computational ability to compute cryptographic functions. For this reason, to design a mechanism to protect low-cost EPCGen2 tags from security and privacy risks is a challenging task. We propose a provable secure batch authentication scheme for EPCGen2 tags using the pseudo-random number generator (PRNG) and cyclic redundancy check (CRC) code. Our ultra-lightweight scheme which integrates the operations of EPCGen2 and only relies on build-in CRC-16 and PRNG function with secret keys inside the tags. We formally analyze security and privacy of the proposed scheme by using mathematical modeling and proof. Our analysis shows that our scheme provides strong ability to prevent existing possible attacks.

**Keywords:** RFID, batch authentication, pseudo-random number generators, security protocol.

## 1 Introduction

RFID system is widely applied in counterfeiting products and RFID-enable supply chain in recent years. An RFID system consists of RFID tags, an RFID reader, and sometimes a back-end server. The communication channel between the reader and the backend server is (usually) assumed to be secure while the (wireless) channel between the reader and the tag is insecure. As the RFID reader communicates with the tags using RF signals, RFID protocols may face various security threats such as location privacy, authentication, and re-synchronization between read and tags. EPCGen2 standardization which covers the whole RFID architecture, from tag data structure to network communication specifications. EPC tags are not provided of on-board batteries, but are passively powered

S.S.M. Chow et al. (Eds.): ProvSec 2014, LNCS 8782, pp. 103–116, 2014.

through radio-frequency waves. The problem of authenticating tags in large-scale RFID systems can be easily reduced to verifying each tag one by one. However, this is not efficient enough for the practical usage for the extremely busy supply chain. A number of different authentication protocols have been proposed to address supply chain application.

There is scope for securing low cost devices. It is obviously that the level of security may not be sufficient for sensitive applications. However there are many low cost applications where there is no alternative in the practical industrial applications. It is difficult for them to adapt the existing authentication protocols using cryptographic primitives which require a lot of computation cost and storage space. Thus, we need to find a novel way to guarantee the security and privacy of such low-cost EPCGen2 tags.

*The scenario of our scheme:* We recognize that there are situations in which one has to design security into systems with restricted capability so as to promote low-cost widespread usage. In this paper, we concern with the security of universal EPCGen2 application. We focus on such a supply chain scenario in which a batch of products are transported from one place to another. The receivers who can be retailers or transportation service providers want to confirm that the products are the original ones and none of them is lost during the outsourcing supply chain procedures such as Third party logistics which is one of the most dominating kind of supply chains that has been widely adopted by many companies.

## 1.1   Related Works

To execute the authentication while maintaining the security and privacy-preserving features in RFID system have been research for years. For the lightweight tags, there are also many proposals such as using one-way hash functions by Song et al. [16], performing authentication by hashing random challenges, tag identity, and/or secret key into one message [14], etc. However, hardware implementations of hash functions such as SHA-1 and MD5 are generally considered too expensive to be implemented on low-cost EPCGen2 RFID tags. For this reason, lightweight solutions are needed for low-cost RFID tags such as EPCGen2. Lightweight authentication protocols aim to achieve fast and cost-efficient authentication through simple operations like bitwise XOR and binary addition. In 2006, Juels and Weis proposed a multi-round lightweight authentication protocol called HB+ [9], after that many improvements of the HB+ protocol such as Peinado in 2007 [12] and Gilbert et al. in 2008 [8].

In 2009, Sun and Ting presented the EPCGen2 protocol [17] for EPCGen2 standard in which each tag stores a string and shared with a back-end server. Burmester et al. demonstrated an attack to break this protocol in 2009 [2]. Until recent years, it still remains a challenging task to design a reasonable secure and efficient solution for EPCGen2 application. Recently, there are some practical works focusing on the security of lightweight solutions for EPCGen2 tags, such as pseudo-random number generator for EPCGen2 [11] and CRC-based solutions [7]. In recent years, there are some batch authentication methods for RFID being proposed, Yang *et al.* [18] and Guo *et al.* [6] study the RFID batch authentication issue and propose the first probabilistic approach to meet the requirement of prompt and reliable batch authentications in large scale RFID applications. However, their solutions are not light-weight to be used for EPC-Gen2 tags authentication. In 2014, Qi *et al.* [19] proposed a batch recall protocol for RFID-enable supply chain and industry manufacturers, there is a so-called collector to recall the products based on public key technologies. In practical implementation, the public key cryptography-based solutions are still too expensive to be broadly applied to low-cost RFID tags.

### 1.2  Our Contributions and Organization

The security level of EPCGen2 heavily depends only on 16-bits PRNG which makes RFID protocol potentially vulnerable up to a certain point, for example, adversary can perform ciphertext-only attacks to exhaust the 16-bit range of the components of protocol flows. Due to such a reason, we have to revisit the security and privacy issues for EPCGen2 tags and find a way to do better based on the limited computation resource of EPCGen2 tags.

- We first propose a provable secure scheme for batch authentication of EPC-Gen2 RFID. The main contribution of our paper is that our scheme can apply to EPCGen2 tags without modifying steps or components of the standard.
- Besides the efficiency for RFID authentication, our scheme uses very little computational and memory resource which includes one PRNG and one CRC along with a few conditional xors computation. The seed to be input to the PRNG can be considered as if it is a key for the blocks cipher; in particular, we forgo the need for key-separation for each tag.
- Different from related works of RFID authentication, we provide security property between reader and back-end server. Our scheme can prevent unauthorized reader to attack against RFID system.
- We provide security and privacy proof and analysis to show the limits of the adversary who tries to compromise our scheme.

The rest of the paper is organized as follows: Section 2 provides some preliminaries to understand the technical details in our proposal. We propose our provable secure batch authentication scheme in Section 3. We also provide the security and privacy analysis and proof of our proposed scheme in Section 4. We draw conclusions in Section 5.

## 2  Preliminaries

In this section, we give brief introduction of RFID system and EPCGen2 tags, providing syntax definitions and security primitives such as pseudo-random number generator and cyclic redundancy check code.

## 2.1   Brief Description RFID System and of EPCGen2 Tags

Our batch authentication relies on tag's internal PRNG and cyclic redundancy check.

- Passive Tag: RFID tags can be classified into two types, active or passive depending on powering technique. While an active tag can generate power by itself, a passive tag is not able to supply a power by itself. Therefore the passive tag obtains power from the reading devices when it is within range of some reading devices.
- Reader: A reader can read and re-write the data in a tag. A reader can also obtain the tags contents through queries. After the reader queries to a tag and receives some information from the tag, the reader forwards the information to a back-end server.
- Back-end server : A back-end server is a computer which manages and stores various information for authenticating of each tag, so as to determine a tags identity from the information of a tag sent by an authenticated reader. But if the reader can have enough memories and computational ability, the back-end server is not a must in a RFID system.

EPCGen2 was adopted as 18000-6 international Standard by ISO/IEC. As a result, RFID system will be able to be recognized without confusion. EPCGen2 tag has properties as follows [4]: Tag is passive and communication range is 2-10m and it has on-chip Pseudo-Random Number Generator (PRNG) and Cyclic Redundancy Code (CRC). It also has two 32-bit PIN for kill command for disable the tag and access command to write into the tag or to read something in password fields.

## 2.2   Security and Privacy Requirement for RFID Batch Authentication

*Security for Tag authentication:* Theoretically, RFID authentication is insecure if there exists a polynomial-time adversary such that one tag session on a legitimate tag output OK but had no matching conversation with any reader session, with non-negligible probability. That means the adversary can forge the tags and pass the authentication processing. RFID tags may contain sensitive information about the carrier in which the information should not be revealed to anyone, especially to an attacker. In other words, tags should first authenticate the reader validation before sending private data. Meanwhile, readers should also be able to authenticate tags to prevent counterfeit tags.

*Tag Privacy:* In a typical RFID system, when an RFID reader queries an RFID tag, it responds by sending its identifier to the reader; the reader can then request further details by sending this identifier to a server. If unauthorized readers can also get a tag identifier, then they may be able to determine the additional information related to the tag. For example, if the information associated with a tag attached to a passport, ID-card or medical record could be obtained by any reader, then the damage would be very serious. To protect against such information leakage, RFID systems need to be controlled so that only authorized readers are able to access the information associated with a tag.

## 2.3   Mathematical Definitions

*Binary Fields:* All the communication executed between reader and tags can be represented as an element of $GF(2^n)$ as a polynomial over the field $GF(2)$ of degree less than $n$. The set $\{0,1\}^n$ of bit strings can be considered as the finite field $GF(2^n)$ consisting of $2^n$ elements. A string $a_{n-1}a_{n-2}\cdots a_1a_0 \in \{0,1\}^n$ corresponds to the polynomial $a_{n-1}x^{n-1} + a_{n-2}x^{n-2} + \cdots + a_1x + a_0 \in GF(2^n)$. The addition in the field is just the addition of polynomials over $GF(2)$ (that is, bitwise XOR, denoted by $\oplus$. To define multiplication in the field, we fix an irreducible polynomial f(x) of degree n over the field $GF(2)$. Given two elements $a(x), b(x) \in GF(2^n)$, their product is defined as $a(x)b(x)$ mod $f(x)$-polynomial multiplication over the field $GF(2)$ reduced modulo $f(x)$. We simply write $a(x)b(x)$ and $a(x) \cdot b(x)$ to mean the product in the field $GF(2^n)$. We use the Arabic number to represent the polynomials. For example. "2" means $x$, "3" means $x + 1$, and "7" means $x^2 + x + 1$. When we write multiplications such as $2 \cdot 3$ and $7^2$, we mean those in the field $GF(2^n)$.

*Pseudo-random Number Generator:* A pseudo-random number generator (PRNG) can be defined as an function for generating a sequence of numbers that approximates the properties of random numbers. A deterministic function $G : \{0,1\}^d \rightarrow \{0,1\}^m$ is a $(t, \epsilon)$ is a pseudo-random number generator (PRNG) if $d < m$, $G(x)$ and $U_m$ ($U_m$ is a $m$-bit truly random string) are $(t, \epsilon)$ indistinguishable. In this paper, we model the PRNG as a deterministic function $G() : \mathcal{K} \times \{0,1\}^m \rightarrow \{0,1\}^g$.

*CRC code* Cyclic Redundancy Check code (CRC) is a kind of calibration method that checks the correctness of data communication. In original usage of CRC, the sender sents $m$-bit information data represented as a polynomial $T(x)$, and the receiver receives the data as $D(x)$. For a given $n$, CRC code use a polynomial $g(x)$ as a generator, the sender moves $T(x)$ left to $k$ bits, and then makes XOR operation with $g(x)$. The remainder is the check number $r(x)$. A CRC is called an $n$-bit CRC when its check value is $n$-bits. Such a polynomial has highest degree $n$, and hence $n + 1$ terms (the polynomial has a length of $n + 1$). The remainder has length $n$. The CRC has a name of the form $CRC - n$.

## 3   Our Batch Authentication Scheme

There are some essential requirements of a good batch authentication scheme for large-scale RFID systems. First, the authentication scheme should be efficient. Second, the authentication result should be informative to support various application demands. Knowing that whether there exist counterfeits in a batch of tags or not is far from adequate, since the administrator of RFID systems may still resort to per-tag authentication to count how many counterfeits in a number of tags. Our protocol is designed for EPCGen2 RFID tags; therefore, the requirement for implementing our protocol will not overload the capabilities of the tags.

Our Proposal is inspired by the parallelized message authentication code [3] and online cipher design [1] in which a cipher taking input of arbitrary length and it can output ciphertext blocks as it is receiving the plaintext blocks. Specifically, the $i$-th ciphertext block should only depend on the key and the first $i$ plaintext blocks. The system we built consists of EPCGen2 compliant RFID tags and an EPCGen2 compliant RFID reader. Our protocol are limited to computing an XOR sum of the RIFD internal processed data and using two extra CRC computation calls. The sketch of our batch authentication scheme can be referred to Fig 1.

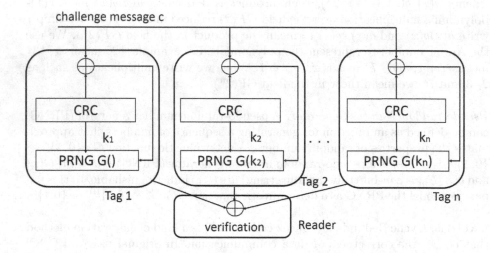

**Fig. 1.** Parallelized computation for the responds of tags

## 3.1    Initialization

The back-end server storages tags' identification information for the batch authentication, such as EPC for each tag. So that it can identify a tag from the information sent to an authenticated reader for tag. Reader generates different random challenge message and sends tags during each different session. We provide a table of notions which are used in our scheme as follows:

We consider an RFID system comprising of a single legitimate reader and a set of $n$ tags $T = \{t_1, \cdots, t_n\}$, with some polynomials as security parameters. We assume that reader and each tag share a secret string for the authentication, here we denote it as $k_i$. Our scheme is based the parallelizable computation for each tag and allows reader to gather all the responds from tags for the batch

**Table 1.** Notions used in our scheme

| Notions | Descriptions |
|---|---|
| $t_i$ | $i$-th tag in a set of tags $T$ |
| $k_i$ | the secret key shared between reader and $i$-th tag |
| $\oplus$ | exclusive-or operation |
| $\|$ | concatenation of two inputs |
| $\Pr[A\|B]$ | the probability of event A given B |
| $G()$ | 16-bit pseudo-random number generator |
| CRC() | cyclic redundancy check computation |

authentication. We use the framework of XE and XEX constructions in [1,13], which makes our constructions and secure proofs simple and easy to be analyzed. For the secure communication and between reader and back-end server, we apply a block cipher $E()$ with shared key between server and reader as $kr$.

Typically, each tag is a passive transponder identified by a unique ID and has only limited memory which can be used to store only several keys and/or state information. The reader is composed of one or more transceivers and a backend processing subsystem. In this paper, we assume that the reader is secure, which means that an adversary cannot obtain any information about the RFID system from the legitimate reader except the information obtained from RFID communications and tags (in other words, the legitimate reader is a "black-boxh to an adversary).

### 3.2 Tag's Internal Processing

The internal processing of tag involves two function calls, one is for pseudo-random number generator and the other is for CRC computation.

For a particular construction PRNG $G()$ which consists of three major algorithms (setup, next, refresh)for the pseudo-random number generation and internal state update, we let $Pr[A(m, H)^{I(G)} = 1]$ denote the probability that adversary $\mathcal{A}$ outputs the bit 1 after interacting as above with the system. Here I(G) stands for the ideal random process and note that we only use G in this game to answer queries that are made while the compromised flag is set to true. The details of the our PRNG are given as follows.

- setup: it is a probabilistic algorithm that outputs some parameters related to the secret key $k_i$ of tag $T_i$ for the generator.
- refresh: it is a deterministic algorithm that, given $k_i$ of tag $T_i$, a state $ST \in \{0,1\}^n$ and an input $I \in \{0,1\}^p$, outputs a new state $ST' = \mathsf{refresh}(ST, I) = refresh(k_i, ST, I) \in \{0,1\}^n$
- next: it is a deterministic algorithm that, given $k_i$ and a state $ST \in \{0,1\}^n$, outputs a pair $(ST'; R) == (k_i, ST)$ where $ST' \in \{0,1\}^n$ is the new state and a pseudo-random number $r \in \{0,1\}^g$ is the output.

According to EPCGen2 standard [4], the CRC-16 algorithm maps arbitrary length inputs onto 16-bit outputs as follows: an $n$-bit input $p$ is first replaced by a binary polynomial $p(x)$ of degree $n - 1$, and then reduced modulo a specific polynomial $g(x)$ of degree 16 to a polynomial remainder $r(x) : p(x) = q(x)g(x) + r(x)$. The remainder has degree less than 16 and corresponds to a 16-bit number. For EPCGen2, the polynomial $g(x)$ is the irreducible polynomial: $x^{16} + x^{12} + x^5 + 1$ (over the finite field GF(2) of two elements). CRC-16 will detect burst errors of 16-bits or less, any odd number of errors less than 16, and error patterns of length 2. For the $CRC()$ function, we use it to generate the dummy mask for individual tag. $CRC()$ is an efficient checksum algorithm and the input to $CRC()$ is divided into groups, each has 16 bits. Each 16-bit group will be encoded one by one. The output of each is a 16-bit encoded data. Each output will be combined together to generate the mask.

We assume a fixed, polynomial-size tag set $T = \{t_1, \cdots, t_n\}$ and a reader $RD$ as the elements for an RFID system: $S = \{RD, T\}$. As to model the communication between tags and reader, we assume that the update process of new internal state and secret-key, by an uncorrupted tag in a session run, automatically overwrites (i.e., erases) its old internal state and secret-key to the PRNG. Each uncorrupted tag and reader use fresh and independent random coins (generated on the fly) in each session, in case it is an randomized algorithm enhanced by their internal PRNG. We assume that the random coins used in each session are erased once the session is completed (whether successfully finished or aborted).

### 3.3  Batch Authentication

Formally, we consider an RFID system comprising of a single legitimate reader and a set of $n$ tags $T = \{t_1, \cdots, t_n\}$, where $l$ is a polynomial in a security parameter $p$. The reader and the tags can be modeled as probabilistic polynomial time interactive Turing machines. The RFID system (RD, T) is setup by a procedure, denoted Setup$(p, l)$. This setup procedure generates the system parameter such internal keys for PRNG and the key for encryption. It may also setup an initial backend database DB for R to store necessary information for identifying and authenticating tags. We use $para = (w, k_1, ..., k_n)$ to denote the RFID system parameters. We assume that in the RFID system, the reader is secure; in other words, the legitimate reader is a "black-boxh to an adversary.

The reader collects all the responding massage from all tags and make aggregative computation to generate a authenticated massage and send it back to back-end server for further processing. The supply chain service providers and product manufacturers write a fix batch identification value $w$ into each tag and using it to compute $CRC(w)$. In every tag, the value of $w$ is different from each other. We use $CRC(w)$ to generate different mask value to avoid the collision in the batch authentication. The sketch our scheme is illustrated in Fig. 2. At each new single session between reader and tags, let $S = G(0^{16})$ and the PRNG and CRC will be resumed to initial state.

---

### Batch Authentication Protocol for RFID EPCGen2 Tags

- Reader $\rightarrow$ tags : The reader sends a challenge message $c$ to all tag to initiate a session.
- Tags $t_i \rightarrow$ reader : Let $V[0] \leftarrow CRC(w) \oplus S)$, and $\Delta_0 \leftarrow 3 \cdot CRC(w)$ $\Delta_1 \leftarrow 2 \cdot CRC(w)$.
  After receiving the challenge message, for each tag $t_i \in T$ parse $k_i$ with $c$ runs its internal PRNG $a_i = G_i(c \oplus k_i)$.
  $V[i] \leftarrow G(a_i \oplus \Delta_0) \oplus V[i-1]$
  $R[i] \leftarrow G(V[i]) \oplus \Delta_1$
  $\Delta_0 \leftarrow 2\Delta_0, \Delta_1 \leftarrow 2\Delta_1$
  The tag $t_i$ sends $R[i]$ to the reader.
- Reader $\rightarrow$ back-end server: The reader gathers all the message from the tags and computes $M = E_k(E_k(\Sigma \oplus 2^{d-1}3^2S) \oplus R) \oplus 2^{d-1}7S$ and sends $M$ to the back-end server.
  Here, $R = R[1] \oplus R[2] \oplus \cdots \oplus R[n]$ and $\Sigma \overset{def}{=} k_1 \oplus k_2 \oplus \cdots \oplus k_n$.
- Server processing: The back-end server receives $M$ from the reader who gathers all the response from tags. The server perform verification by checking if $R \oplus E_{kr}(\Sigma \oplus 2^{d-1}3^2S) = E_{kr}^{-1}(M \oplus 2^{d-1}7S)$, where the tag is rejected if the equality is not true. After that, it can recover the further information of the authenticated tags.

**Fig. 2.** Batch Authentication Scheme

The masking method in [3,13] enables us to produce many different values of the mask $\Delta$ from just one secret value $\Delta = CRC(w)$. Namely, the masks are produced as $\Delta = 2\alpha3\beta7\gamma \cdot R$ for varying indices of $\alpha, \beta$ and $\gamma$. To do this, we need to choose our irreducible polynomial $f(x)$ carefully. First, $f(x)$ needs to be primitive for the implementation of $CRC()$ inside of tags, and is able to generate the whole multiplicative group. Second, we make sure that $\log 2 \cdot 3$ and $\log 2 \cdot 7$ are both lager enough. Third, we check if $\log 2 \cdot 3$ and $\log 2 \cdot 7$ are defer enough (modulo $2^{n-1}$). We impose these conditions to ensure that values $2\alpha3\beta7\gamma$ do not collide or become equal to 1. Combining CRC-16 with pseudo-random number generator can prevent the batch collision and tampering attacks effectively, it avoids occupying the resource of back-end server, and reduce the time complexity.

### 3.4 Post-Authentication Processing

By reconsidering the solution of batch authentication in another perspective, we find it is not always necessary to ensure the genuineness of every single product in a batch. It is acceptable if we guarantee the percentage of deactivated is sufficiently small.

Typically, the reader and the tag would exchange data after completing the authentication process. These data are sometimes considered private; for example, the tag used in a hospital would contain the records of its carrier. The threat of eavesdropping attacks makes the tag carriers feel insecure about transmitting sensitive data. To address this problem, we construct a mechanism to establish a session key and use it to encrypt the sensitive data. We suggest that reader and tags use the key stream generated by PRNG to encrypt the messages. Without the secret key the adversary cannot decrypt the message break the encrypted messages.

## 4  Security and Privacy Proofs of Tags Authentication

In this section, we provide the security and privacy proof for our batch authentication scheme. For the security analysis, we show the security bound for an adversary to forge the batch security. For the privacy analysis, we show that the adversary has limited advantage to distinguishable two communication session between reader and tags. This implicates that the adversary cannot do malicious tracing against the tags. Here, we model the adversary as a polynomial probabilistic Turing machine which tries to break the security and privacy of our batch authentication scheme.

The core security element is the PRNG which provides the minimum security property as follows which is shown in the existing result in [2,10]:

1. Probability of PRNG: The probability that a 16 bits pseudo-random number drawn from the PRNG has value $r$ is bounded by: $0.8/2^{16} < \Pr(G(k_i) = r) < 1.25/2^{16}$.
2. Drawing identical sequences: For a tag population of up to 10,000 tags, the probability that any two or more tags simultaneously draw the same sequence of 16-bit pseudo-random number is $< 0.1\%$, regardless of when the tags are energized.
3. Next random number prediction: A random number which is generated by a tag PRNG is not predictable with probability better than $0.025\%$, given the outcomes of all prior draws.

There is an important point here is that the adversary cannot attack our scheme using the similar forging attack in message authentication codes using the arbitrary length of messages to get a collision. The number of the tags are determined pre-authentication. We prove our security and privacy as follows. The interaction between an adversary $\mathcal{A}$ and the protocol participants occurs only via oracle, which model the adversary capabilities in a real attack. During the execution, the adversary may create several instances of a participant. Let $U_i$ denote the instance $i$ of a participant $U \in \{RD, T\}$

Adversary runs a $\mathtt{Setup}(t_i, k_i)$ is a setup procedure which generates key $k_i$ for a tag $T_i$ and sets the tagfs initial internal state $st_0$. It also associates the tag $T_i$ with its unique ID as well as other necessary information such as tag key and/or tag state information as a record in the database of reader.

## 4.1    The Security of our Scheme

In our analysis, we modify the security definition of our scheme from Rogaway
et al. [3,15]. The security notions also can be found in [5]. For our batch authentication, the security refers to unforgablity of the aggregated tags which can
pass the authentication. Let $\{0,1\}^n$ denote the set of strings whose length is a
positive multiple of $n$ bits. Here, we model the pseudo-random number generator
as $G : \mathcal{K} \times \{0,1\}^* \to \{0,1\}^g$ is a function such that it is a permutation on every
tag's $n$ bits output, we can replace our PRNG calls with random permutations.
Second, we show that the batch authentication behaves exactly the same as the
ideal functionality for the security, as long as certain successful attacks from
adversary do not occur. The successful attack here means collisions of tag state
values, and the proof amounts to evaluating the probabilities of these attacks.

Let $\mathcal{A}$ be an adversary trying to distinguish $G()$ from the family all tweakable
permutations with the same tweak space. Say that A runs in time $t$ and makes
exactly $q$ queries. Without loss of generality assume that $\mathcal{A}$ is deterministic.
Here, we define key space for PRNG as $K$, the adversary can make random
sample from the key space $\mathcal{K}$ to attack the PRNG and forge tags response.

**Definition 1.** *We define the security using the advantage of an adversary $\mathcal{A}$.*

$$\mathbf{Adv}_G(\mathcal{A}) = \Pr\left[k \xleftarrow{\mathcal{R}} \mathcal{K} : \mathcal{A}^{G(k)} = 1\right] - \Pr\left[\pi \xleftarrow{\mathcal{R}} Perm(n) : \mathcal{A}^{\pi(\cdot)} = 1\right] \quad (1)$$

The above is the probability that adversary A outputs 1 when given an oracle
for $G(k,\cdot)$, minus the probability that A outputs 1 when given an oracle for $\pi()$,
where $k$ is selected at random from $K$ and $\pi$ is selected at random from $Perm(n)$.

If the adversary knows no additional information, the success probability is
surely $1/2^g$. If the adversary acquires function for $CRC()$ by compromising a
tag or a reader, it will have some advantages in constructing the codewords.

The adversary will try to generate the collision to get the same value of $V[j]$
coming from different secret value inside RFID tags $k_1, k_2, ..., k_n$ and $k'_1, k'_2, ..., k'_n$.
At the beginning, the adversary chooses $k'_1, k'_2, ..., k'_n$ from the key space $\mathcal{K}$, and
uses the PRNG oracle to generate the collision to pass the batch authentication.
We can see that the outputs may be the same for a common mask for CRC-
16. So an PRNG $G(k_i)$ yields a pseudo-random generator of $i - th$ tags, where
the permutation is determined by the input (i.e. the secret key of tag $k_i$). Let
$Perm(n)$ be the set of all such permutations to be distinguished from PRNG
$G()$. We notice that unless the collision occurs, the adversary cannot distinguish
an output of $G$ from an output of Perm(n).

We want to model adversary's behavior to forge tags. Adversary show find
some collisions in order to forge the targets tags without knowing their internal secret keys. Tagcoll(n) measures the probability of getting a collision when
the adversary sends challenge message to $n$ tags. The tag collision means a collision among the values $R[1], R[2], \cdots, R[n]$, where $R[0] = 0^n$ and each $k_i$ is
the PRNG input associated to tag $i$. Informally, CollisionM(n) measures the
probability of finding collision at the finalized computation for readeracross two

different batches of tags, $T$ and $T'$, each having $n$ tags. This can be a "non-trivial" collision. That is, consider the $2n$ points at which the PRNG is applied in processing the finalized $M$ and $M'$.

The adversary also can choose $n$ elements at random key $k_i'$ and $w'$ and then there is the point to get the same output as the legal tags (the PRNG is applied at this point). There are $n$ responses from original tags $R[1], \cdots, R[n]$, other responses from other faked tags $R'[1], \cdots, R'[n]$, Adversary can get some pairs of the collision of finalized tag could coincide for a "trivialh reason: namely, we know that $R[i] = R'[j]$ if $k_i' = k_j'$ and $M = M'$. We say that there is a nontrivial collision between $T$ and $T'$ if some other $R[i]$ and $R[j]$ happened to coincide. Note that M-collisions include collisions with $0^n$, while CollisionM(n)s do not. Also, both collisions do not include collisions within a single tag (or collisions with all zero input) because both of these possibilities are taken care of by way of $n$-collisions.

We can further to apply the PMAC security proof for our scheme. We can make use of the theorem for parallel MAC construction in [3] and claim that for aggregated $M$ from $n$ tags, the adversary queries all $n$ tags and then the advantage $\mathbf{Adv}_G(\mathcal{A})$ is less than $n^2/2^g$, here $g$ is the output length of PRNG. For EPCGen2 tags, the advantage is less than $n^2/2^{16}$.

## 4.2    The Privacy of our Scheme

Adversary who try to beak the privacy of tags should execute as the following three phrases. The attack intentionally desynchronizes the tag from the reader by sending the tag some messages.

1. Learning: An adversary sends $m$ number of queries $Q_i$ for $1 \leq i \leq m$ to a batch@of targeting tags, and records the tagfs response $R[i] for 1 \leq i \leq m$. Since the adversary is impersonating the reader, thus each time it will not pass the check by the tag, and so each time the tag would update its stored secret as $k_i = G(k_i)$, from which ti will be derived in the next session.
2. Challenge: Query $m$ times to random tags in $\{t_1, \cdots t_n\}$ and obtain their response $R$ and $M$
3. Guess: Check if $t = t_i$. If so, then the adversary knows this was the tag it queried during the learning phase i.e. $T_b = T$. Else, it knows that $T_b = T'$.

Intuitively, an adversary can trace location of tags if response of tag is always the same or similar pattern for each session. We can see that dummy masks generated by $CRC$ is similar to the all XE an XEX construction can be modeled using the techniques in. For each query from reader, tags' response are different even the challenge message $c$ is the same. This property guarantees the privacy of our scheme. It is easy to prove that for individual tag, the privacy is well preserved.

More formally, we discuss the batch privacy which preserve the privacy for the whole batch of tags. We use $\mathbf{Adv}_G^{\mathcal{A}}(t, q, n, l)$ we denote the maximum advantage taken over all distinguishers that run in time $t$ and make $q$ queries, each of at most $l$ out of totally $n$ tags. Based on the security proof of [13], we can claim that for two pseudo-random function $f_1 : \{0,1\}^* \to \{0,1\}^g$ and $f_2 : \{0,1\}^* \to \{0,1\}^g$, the distinguishing advantage is at most $n^2/2^g$.

For the batch of RFID tags, adversary cannot distinguish from two queries if the collision does not occur. As same in the security analysis, adversary can access a PRNG oracle and use it to distinguish the queries. After get some priori knowledge by sending the query, the advantage of adversary can be bounded as $\mathbf{Adv}_G^{\mathcal{A}}(t,q,n,l) \leq \frac{39(n+q)^2}{2^g} + \mathbf{Adv}_{\mathrm{Perm}()}^{\mathcal{A}}(t, 4(n+q)) + \frac{(l+2)(q-1)^2}{2^g}$ according to the proof of [1].

## 5   Conclusion and Future Works

The EPCGen2 standardized tags focuses on reliability and efficiency while proving only a very basic security level, which is at risk of security and privacy breach. To overcome such risks is particularly challenging because the only security tool that is available in this standard is a 16-bit PRNG. In this paper, we proposed a scheme for EPCGen2 tags batch authentication which are provably secure. In this paper we have studied the recently proposed EPCGen2 related schemes and made some arguments on how to achieve maximum security and privacy levels supported by this standard. We proposed a batch authentication RFID protocol that provides strong anonymity and that complies with the EPCGen2 standard. Finally, we examine the successful probability for an adversary to forge a batch of tags and distinguish every responses in different session between reader and tags. In the future work, we want to extend our scheme to more sophisticated and practical scenarios, such as reader corruption, tag cloning (or more feasibly, protocols to prevent swapping attacks, tag group authentication, anonymizer-enabled RFID systems, and tag ownership transfer.

## References

1. Andreeva, E., Bogdanov, A., Luykx, A., Mennink, B., Tischhauser, E., Yasuda, K.: Parallelizable and Authenticated Online Ciphers. In: Sako, K., Sarkar, P. (eds.) ASIACRYPT 2013, Part I. LNCS, vol. 8269, pp. 424–443. Springer, Heidelberg (2013)
2. Burmester, M., de Medeiros, B., Munilla, J., Peinado, A.: Secure EPC Gen2 compliant radio frequency identification. In: Ruiz, P.M., Garcia-Luna-Aceves, J.J. (eds.) ADHOC-NOW 2009. LNCS, vol. 5793, pp. 227–240. Springer, Heidelberg (2009)
3. Black, J., Rogaway, P.: A Block-Cipher Mode of Operation for Parallelizable Message Authentication. In: Knudsen, L.R. (ed.) EUROCRYPT 2002. LNCS, vol. 2332, pp. 384–397. Springer, Heidelberg (2002)
4. EPCglobal Inc., Class 1 Generation 2 UHF RFID protocol for communication at 860Mhz-960Mhz version 1.2.0 (2008)
5. Fleischmann, E., Forler, C., Lucks, S.: McOE: A Family of Almost Foolproof On-Line Authenticated Encryption Schemes. In: Canteaut, A. (ed.) FSE 2012. LNCS, vol. 7549, pp. 196–215. Springer, Heidelberg (2012)

6. Gong, W., Liu, K., Miao, X., Ma, Q., Yang, Z., Liu, Y.: Informative counting: Fine-grained batch authentication for large-scale rfid systems. In: ACM MobiHoc (2013)
7. Gao, L., Ma, M., Shu, Y., Wei, Y.: An ultralightweight RFID authentication protocol with CRC and permutation. Journal of Network and Computer Applications (2013)
8. Gilbert, H., Robshaw, M.J.B., Seurin, Y.: HB#: Increasing the security and efficiency of HB+. In: Smart, N.P. (ed.) EUROCRYPT 2008. LNCS, vol. 4965, pp. 361–378. Springer, Heidelberg (2008)
9. Juels, A., Weis, S.A.: Authenticating pervasive devices with human protocols. In: Shoup, V. (ed.) CRYPTO 2005. LNCS, vol. 3621, pp. 293–308. Springer, Heidelberg (2005)
10. Melia-Segui, J., Garcia-Alfaro, J., Herrera-Joancomarti, J.: Analysis and improvement of a pseudorandom number generator for EPC Gen2 tags. In: Sion, R., Curtmola, R., Dietrich, S., Kiayias, A., Miret, J.M., Sako, K., Sebé, F. (eds.) FC 2010 Workshops. LNCS, vol. 6054, pp. 34–46. Springer, Heidelberg (2010)
11. Mandal, K., Fan, X., Gong, G.: Warbler. A Lightweight Pseudorandom Number Generator for EPC C1 Gen2 Passive RFID Tags. International Journal of RFID Security and Cryptography (IJRFIDSC) 2(1-4), 82–91 (2013)
12. Munilla, J., Peinado, A.: HB-MP: a further step in the HB-family of lightweight authentication protocols. Computer Networks 51(9), 2262–2267 (2007)
13. Rogaway, P.: Efficient Instantiations of Tweakable Blockciphers and Refinements to Modes OCB and PMAC. In: Lee, P.J. (ed.) ASIACRYPT 2004. LNCS, vol. 3329, pp. 16–31. Springer, Heidelberg (2004)
14. Ranasinghe, D., Engels, D., Cole, P.: Low-cost RFID systems: confronting security and privacy. In: Proceedings of the Auto-ID Labs Research Workshop, pp. 54–77 (2004)
15. Rogaway, P., Zhang, H.: Online Ciphers from Tweakable Blockciphers. In: Kiayias, A. (ed.) CT-RSA 2011. LNCS, vol. 6558, pp. 237–249. Springer, Heidelberg (2011)
16. Song, B., Mitchell, C.J.: RFID authentication protocol for low-cost tags. In: Proceedings of the 1st ACM Conference on Wireless Network Security, pp. 140–147 (April 2008)
17. Sun, H.M., Ting, W.C.: Gen2-based RFID authentication protocol for security and privacy. IEEE Transactions on Mobile Computing 8(8), 1052–1062 (2009)
18. Yang, L., Han, J., Qi, Y., Liu, Y.: Identification-free batch authentication for RFID tags. In: Proceedings of the 18th IEEE International Conference on Network Protocols, pp. 154–163 (October 2010)
19. Qi, S., Zheng, Y., Li, M., Lu, L., Liu, Y.: COLLECTOR: A Secure RFID-Enabled Batch Recall Protocol. In: IEEE INFOCOM, Canada (April 2014)

# Generic Transformation to Strongly Existentially Unforgeable Signature Schemes with Leakage Resiliency*

Yuyu Wang and Keisuke Tanaka

Tokyo Institute of Technology, Japan

**Abstract.** This paper presents an efficient transformation method that converts fully leakage resilient signature schemes which are weakly existentially unforgeable into ones which are strongly existentially unforgeable. To achieve our goal, we give a definition of leakage resilient chameleon hash function and present a construction based on the leakage resilient hard relation. Then we combine leakage resilient chameleon hash function with the technique presented by Steinfeld, Pieprzyk, and Wang to obtain a generic transformation that works well in the bounded leakage model.

**Keywords:** generic transformation, signature, strong existential unforgeability, leakage resiliency, chameleon hash function.

## 1 Introduction

### 1.1 Background

Signature schemes are said to be weakly existentially unforgeable (wEUF) if it is hard to forge signatures on messages not signed before. But for some applications, a stronger security called strong existential unforgeability (sEUF) is required which also prevents forgery of new signatures on messages signed before.

If a signature scheme is existentially unforgeable (EUF) while the information of signing keys and randomness may be leaked and the amount of leaked bits is bounded, then it is said to be fully leakage resilient (FLR) in the bounded leakage model. If only the information of the signing key is leaked, then the scheme is said to be leakage resilient (LR).

The bounded leakage model was suggested by Akavia, Goldwasser, and Vaikuntanathan [1]. In this model, the adversary is allowed to learn some bounded leakage on the secret information during the lifetime of the system. There has

---

* Department of Mathematical and Computing Sciences, Graduate School of Information Science and Engineering, Tokyo Institute of Technology, W8-55, 2-12-1 Ookayama, Meguro-ku, Tokyo 152-8552, Japan. Supported by the Ministry of Education, Science, Sports and Culture, Grant-in-Aid for Scientific Research (A) No.24240001 and (C) No.23500010, a grant of I-System Co. Ltd., and NTT Secure Platform Laboratories.

S.S.M. Chow et al. (Eds.): ProvSec 2014, LNCS 8782, pp. 117–129, 2014.

already been a great deal of research proposed for cryptographic primitives in the bounded leakage model (c.f., [17,14,3,2,16,8,10]). However, most of the previously presented FLR signature schemes in this model just satisfies the wEUF property. The only one that satisfies the sEUF property was proposed by Wang and Tanaka [22]. We hope there may be a technique that can transfer wEUF-FLR signature schemes to sEUF-FLR ones in the bounded leakage model.

Boneh, Shen, and Waters [6] presented a transformation that converts wEUF signature schemes into sEUF ones based on chameleon hash function. However, this transformation applies to a class of signature schemes called partitioned signature schemes. Later works [21,20,5] proposed transformations that can convert any signature scheme into an sEUF one. Another work by Huang, Wong, and Zhao [13] presented such a transformation that keeps key pairs unchanged by making use of strong one-time signature schemes. Note that all the transformations mentioned above need to change the key pairs or generate additional randomness in the signing process. If we consider the leakage on signing keys or randomness, the security of the signature schemes will not hold after being converted by these methods.

## 1.2    Our Results

First, in this paper, we propose a new definition of LR chameleon hash function. For the standard chameleon hash functions [15,19], collisions can be found efficiently by making use of the secret key, and it is hard to find any collisions without knowing the secret key. In the case of LR chameleon hash function, it is hard to find collisions even when a part of the information of the secret key is leaked. To obtain the construction of LR chameleon hash function, we exploit the representation assumption [9,4] and the Okamoto-style second preimage resistant (SPR) relation [18] which satisfies the LR hard relation defined by Dodis et al. [10]. Our construction of LR chameleon hash function inherits the properties of this instantiation of LR hard relation, and can tolerate any leakage of length $\ell = (1 - o(1))L$ bits where $L$ is the length of the secret key.

Then, we present a generic transformation from wEUF-FLR signature schemes into sEUF-FLR ones based on the Generalized Boneh-Shen-Waters (GBSW) transformation by Steinfeld, Pieprzyk, and Wang [20]. By substituting the standard chameleon hash functions in the GBSW transformation for the LR chameleon hash functions, we obtain a generic transformation from wEUF-FLR signature schemes to sEUF-FLR ones and prove the security of the resulting schemes. If the wEUF-FLR signature scheme with signing key of length $L$ can tolerate leakage of $\ell_w$ bits, then the converted signature scheme is resilient to any leakage of $min\{\ell, \ell_w\}$ bits. Assume that $\ell_w = (1 - o(1))L$ (e.g., the signature scheme in [7]), then we can obtain a signature scheme with signing key of length $L' = 2L$ which can tolerate leakage of $(\frac{1}{2} - o(1))L'$ bits.

Furthermore, by applying our technique to the wEUF-FLR signature scheme in [12], we can obtain an $\ell_s$-sEUF-FLR signature scheme with signing key of length $L''$ where $\ell_s = (1 - o(1))L''$.

As far as we know, this is the first generic transformation to sEUF(-FLR) signature schemes in the bounded leakage model.

## 2 Preliminaries

Now we recall the definitions of LR hard relation and SPR relation [10].

As the same as in [10], we define a leakage oracle as $\mathcal{O}_x^{k,\ell}(\cdot)$, where $x$ is a secret value, $\ell$ is the leakage parameter, and $k$ is the security parameter. The adversary can adaptively access to learn leakage on the secret value. Every time the adversary makes an efficient computable leakage query $f_i : \{0,1\}^* \to \{0,1\}^{\ell_i}$ to the leakage oracle, the oracle answers with $f_i(x)$. It is required that the total number of bits leaked is not more than $\ell$.

**Definition 1.** *(LR Hard Relation [10]). A relation $\mathcal{R}$ with a probabilistic polynomial time (PPT) sampling algorithm KeyGen$(\cdot)$ is an $\ell$-LR hard relation if the following three properties hold.*

- *For any $(y,x) \leftarrow$ KeyGen$(1^k)$, we have $(y,x) \in \mathcal{R}$.*
- *There is a polynomial-time algorithm that decides if $(y,x) \in \mathcal{R}$.*
- *For all PPT adversaries $\mathcal{A}^{\mathcal{O}_x^{k,\ell}(\cdot)}$ with access to the leakage oracle $\mathcal{O}_x^{k,\ell}(\cdot)$, we have that*

$$\Pr[\mathcal{R}(y,x^*) = 1 \mid (y,x) \leftarrow \text{KeyGen}(1^k); x^* \leftarrow \mathcal{A}^{\mathcal{O}_x^{k,\ell}(\cdot)}(y)] \leq \text{negl}(k).$$

Before recalling the notion of SPR relation, we introduce the notion of average-conditional min-entropy [11].

**Definition 2.** *(Average-Conditional Min-Entropy [11]). The average-conditional min-entropy of a random variable $X$ conditioned on $Y$, denoted as $\tilde{\mathbf{H}}_\infty(X \mid Y)$ is*

$$\tilde{\mathbf{H}}_\infty(X \mid Y) = -\log(\mathbb{E}_{y \leftarrow Y}[\max_x \Pr[X = x \mid Y = y]]).$$

**Definition 3.** *(Second-Preimage Resistant Relation [10]). A relation $\mathcal{R}$ with a PPT sampling algorithm KeyGen$(\cdot)$ is second-preimage resistant if the following three properties hold.*

- *For any $(y,x) \leftarrow$ KeyGen$(1^k)$, we have $(y,x) \in \mathcal{R}$.*
- *There is a polynomial-time algorithm that decides if $(y,x) \in \mathcal{R}$.*
- *For all PPT adversaries $\mathcal{A}$, we have that*

$$\Pr[\mathcal{R}(y,x^*) = 1 \wedge x^* \neq x \mid (y,x) \leftarrow \text{KeyGen}(1^k); x^* \leftarrow \mathcal{A}(y,x)] \leq \text{negl}(k).$$

The average-case pre-image entropy of the SPR relation is defined to be $\mathbf{H}_{avg}(\mathcal{R}) = \tilde{\mathbf{H}}_\infty(X \mid Y)$, where the random variables $(X, Y)$ are distributed according to KeyGen$(1^k)$. In [10], the following theorem was shown.

**Theorem 1.** *If $\mathcal{R}$ is SPR relation, then it is also an $\ell$-LR hard relation for $\ell = \mathbf{H}_{avg}(\mathcal{R}) - \omega(\log k)$, where $k$ is the security parameter.*

We now recall the definition of FLR signature schemes in the bounded leakage model from [12,7,14].

A signature scheme consists of three PPT algorithms. KG is a randomized algorithm that takes as input $1^k$ and outputs a public/secret key pair $(pk, sk)$. Sign is a randomized algorithm that takes as input a signing key $sk$ and a message $m$ and returns a signature $\sigma$. Verify is a deterministic algorithm that takes as input a verification key $pk$, a message $m$, and a signature $\sigma$ and returns 1 (accept) or 0 (reject). In addition to the correctness, we require the following property.

**Definition 4.** *(wEUF-FLR Signature schemes [12,7,14]). A signature scheme* (KG, Sign, Verify) *is said to be* wEUF *and* $\ell$-FLR *in the bounded leakage model if for any PPT adversary* $\mathcal{A}$, *we have that* $\Pr[\mathcal{A}$ *wins*$] \leq negl(k)$ *in the following game:*

1. *Compute* $(pk, sk) \leftarrow$ KG$(1^k, \ell)$, *set state* $= sk$.
2. *Run the adversary* $\mathcal{A}$ *on input tuple* $(1^k, pk, \ell)$. *The adversary may make adaptive queries to the signing oracle and the leakage oracle, defined as follows:*
   - *Signing oracle: On receiving a query* $m_i$, *the signing oracle samples* $r_i \leftarrow \{0, 1\}^*$, *and computes* $\sigma_i \leftarrow$ Sign$_{sk}(m_i; r_i)$. *It updates state* $=$ *state*$\|r_i$ *and outputs* $\sigma_i$.
   - *Leakage oracle: On receiving a polynomial-time computable function* $f_j :$ $\{0, 1\}^* \rightarrow \{0, 1\}^{\ell_j}$, *the leakage oracle outputs* $f_j(state)$.
3. $\mathcal{A}$ *outputs* $(m^*, \sigma^*)$ *and wins if :* (a) Verify$_{pk}(m^*, \sigma^*) = 1$, (b) $m^*$ *was not queried to the signing oracle, and* (c) $\sum_j \ell_j \leq \ell$.

The definition of *sEUF-FLR signature schemes* is the same as the above one, except the winning condition (b) being set as follows.

- the pair $(m^*, \sigma^*)$ is new, that is, either $m^*$ was not queried to the signing oracle, or it was and $\sigma^*$ is not the one(s) generated as a signature of $m^*$ by the signing oracle.

Without loss of generality, we can assume that the adversary makes a leakage query every time after making a signing query.

## 3    LR Chameleon Hash Functions

### 3.1    Our Definition

In this section we define *LR chameleon hash function*. This definition is an extension of the notion of chameleon hash function [15,19].

LR chameleon hash function consists of three PPT algorithms (KG$_F$, TC$_F$, F).

KG$_F$ is a *key generation* algorithm that takes as input $(1^k, \ell)$, and outputs $(pk_F, sk_F)$, where $pk_F$ is the public key and $sk_F$ is the secret key. F is a *hash function evaluation* algorithm that takes as input $pk_F$, a message $m$, and a randomizer $r$, and outputs a hash value $h = F_{pk_F}(m; r)$. TC is a *trapdoor collision finder* algorithm that takes as input $sk_F$, a message/randomizer pair $(m, r)$ and a second message $m'$, and outputs $r' = \mathsf{TC}_F(sk_F, (m, r), m')$ such that $F_{pk_F}(m; r) = F_{pk_F}(m'; r')$.

$\ell$-LR chameleon hash function must satisfy three properties, which are *reversibility, random trapdoor collision*, and *LR collision-resistance*.

The reversibility property is satisfied if $r' = \mathsf{TC}_F(sk_F, (m, r), m')$ is equivalent to $r = \mathsf{TC}_F(sk_F, (m', r'), m)$.

The random trapdoor collision property is satisfied if for a secret key $sk_F$, an arbitrary message pair $(m, m')$, and a randomizer $r$, $r' = \mathsf{TC}_F(sk_F, (m, r), m')$ has uniform probability distribution on the randomness space.

The LR collision-resistance property is satisfied if for any PPT adversary $\mathcal{A}$, we have

$$\Pr[(pk_F, sk_F) \leftarrow \mathsf{KG}_F(1^k), ((m, r), (m', r')) \leftarrow \mathcal{A}^{\mathcal{O}^{k,\ell}_{sk_F}(\cdot)}(pk_F):$$
$$(m, r) \neq (m', r') \wedge F_{pk_F}(m, r) = F_{pk_F}(m', r')] \leq negl(k),$$

where $\mathcal{O}^{k,\ell}_{sk_F}$ is the leakage oracle as described in Section 2, to which $\mathcal{A}$ can adaptively make queries to and learn leakage on $sk_F$. The total bits leaked cannot be more than $\ell$.

## 3.2 SPR Construction

Before presenting our construction of LR chameleon hash function, we recall the $n$-representation assumption [9,4] and the construction of the Okamoto-style SPR relation [18], which was used by [3] and mentioned by many previous works on leakage resiliency (e.g., [10,7]).

*n-Representation Assumption.* For any PPT adversary $\mathcal{A}$, given $h_1, h_2, ..., h_n$ which are random elements in $\mathbb{G}$ (cyclic group of order $q$), the probability that $\mathcal{A}$ finds $\boldsymbol{x} = (x_1, ..., x_n) \in \mathbb{Z}^n_q$ and $\boldsymbol{x}^* = (x_1^*, ..., x_n^*) \in \mathbb{Z}^n_q$ such that $\boldsymbol{x} \neq \boldsymbol{x}^*$ and $\prod_{i=1}^n h_i^{x_i} = \prod_{i=1}^n h_i^{x_i^*}$ is negligible.

**Lemma 1 ([9,4]).** *The n-representation assumption holds under the hardness of the discrete logarithm problem in $\mathbb{G}$.*

*SPR Construction.* Let $\mathbb{G}$ be a cyclic group of prime order $q$, $n \geq 2$ and $h_1, h_2, ..., h_n$ random elements in $\mathbb{G}$, the construction of Okamoto-style SPR relation is given in Figure 1.

**Lemma 2 ([18,3,10,7]).** *Under the discrete logarithm assumption, the relation $\mathcal{R}$ described in Figure 1 is SPR with average-case preimage entropy $\mathbf{H}_{avg}(\mathcal{R}) = (n-1)\log(q)$.*

Since $\mathcal{R}$ is SPR relation, we have the following lemma according to Theorem 1.

**Lemma 3 ([10]).** *The SPR relation $\mathcal{R}$ described in Figure 1 is an $\ell$-LR hard relation for $\ell = (n-1)\log(q) - \omega(\log k)$, where $k$ is the security parameter.*

---

- KeyGen($1^k$) : Output $x = (x_1, ..., x_n)$ and $y$ where $x_1, ..., x_n \leftarrow \mathbb{Z}_q$, $y = \prod_{i=1}^{n} h_i^{x_i} \in \mathbb{G}$.
- $\mathcal{R}(y, x)$ : Output 1 if $y = \prod_{i=1}^{n} h_i^{x_i}$. Otherwise output 0.

---

**Fig. 1.** SPR Relation

## 3.3 Our Scheme

We present our construction of LR chameleon hash function in Figure 2.

---

- Key generation algorithm $\mathsf{KG}_F(1^k)$ outputs $pk_F = (y, \boldsymbol{h} = (h_1, ..., h_n))$ and $sk_F = \boldsymbol{x} = (x_1, ..., x_n)$ where $\mathbb{G}$ is a cyclic group of prime order $q$, $n \geq 2$, $h_1, ..., h_n \leftarrow \mathbb{G}$, $x_1, ..., x_n \leftarrow \mathbb{Z}_q$ and $y = \prod_{i=1}^{n} h_i^{x_i} \in \mathbb{G}$.
- Hash function evaluation algorithm $F_{pk_F}(m, \boldsymbol{r}) = (y \prod_{i=1}^{n} h_i^{r_i})^{J(m)} \in \mathbb{G}$ where $\boldsymbol{r} = (r_1, ..., r_n) \leftarrow \mathbb{Z}_q^n$ and $J$ denotes a strongly collision-resistant hash function from $\{0, 1\}^*$ to $\mathbb{Z}_q / \{0\}$.
- Trapdoor collision finder algorithm $\mathsf{TC}_F(sk_F, (m, \boldsymbol{r}), m')$ outputs $\boldsymbol{r}'$ where $\boldsymbol{r}' = (r'_1, ..., r'_n)$ and $r'_i \equiv J(m)(x_i + r_i)/J(m') - x_i \pmod{q}$ for $i = 1, ..., n$.

---

**Fig. 2.** LR Chameleon Hash Function

*Claim.* The scheme described in Figure 2 is $\ell$-LR chameleon hash function for $\ell = (n - 1) \log(q) - \omega(\log k)$ if the discrete logarithm assumption holds.

*Proof.* First we argue that the collision found by $\mathsf{TC}_F$ is correct (i.e, $F_{pk_F}(m, \boldsymbol{r}) = F_{pk_F}(m', \boldsymbol{r}')$ if $\boldsymbol{r}' = \mathsf{TC}_F(sk_F, (m, \boldsymbol{r}), m')$). According to the trapdoor collision finder algorithm described above, we have $J(m')(r'_i + x_i) \equiv J(m)(r_i + x_i) \pmod{q}$ for $i = 1, ..., n$, which means that we have $\prod_{i=1}^{n} h_i^{J(m')(x_i+r'_i)} = \prod_{i=1}^{n} h_i^{J(m)(x_i+r_i)}$, equivalently, $F_{pk_F}(m', \boldsymbol{r}') = F_{pk_F}(m, \boldsymbol{r})$.

Since $r'_i \equiv J(m)(x_i + r_i)/J(m') - x_i \pmod{q}$ is equivalent to $r_i \equiv J(m')(x_i + r'_i)/J(m) - x_i \pmod{q}$, if $\boldsymbol{r}' = \mathsf{TC}_F(sk_F, (m, \boldsymbol{r}), m')$ holds, $\boldsymbol{r} = \mathsf{TC}_F(sk_F, (m', \boldsymbol{r}'), m)$ holds as well, which means that the reversibility property is satisfied. Furthermore, since $\boldsymbol{r}$ has uniform probability distribution on $\mathbb{Z}_q^n$, it is not hard to see that $\boldsymbol{r}'$ has uniform probability distribution on $\mathbb{Z}_q^n$. So our scheme satisfies the random trapdoor collision property.

What we are left to do is to prove that our scheme satisfies the LR strong collision-resistance property.

It is clear that the public key and private key of our scheme satisfies the $\ell$-LR hard relation $\mathcal{R}$ stated in Section 3.2. We argue that given access to the leakage oracle $L_{sk_F}^{k,\ell}(\cdot)$ and the public key, if there exists a PPT adversary $\mathcal{B}$

that can find two pairs $(m, r)$ and $(m', r')$ such that $(m, r) \neq (m', r')$ and $F_{pk_F}(m, r) = F_{pk_F}(m', r')$, then there exists a PPT adversary denoted by $\mathcal{A}$ that can either break the $\ell$-leakage resiliency of $\mathcal{R}$ or $n$-representation assumption.

Consider that given access to $L_{sk_F}^{k,\ell}(\cdot)$ and public key $pk_F$, $\mathcal{B}$ can find $(m, r)$ and $(m', r')$ where $m \neq m'$ and $F_{pk_F}(m, r) = F_{pk_F}(m', r')$ with non-negligible probability $\epsilon$. We construct $\mathcal{A}$ that breaks the $\ell$-leakage resiliency of $\mathcal{R}$.

Given $h_1, ..., h_n, y$ (described in Section 3.2), $\mathcal{A}$ gives $(h_1, ..., h_n, y)$ to $\mathcal{B}$ as a public key. Every time getting the query $f_i(\cdot)$ from $\mathcal{B}$, $\mathcal{A}$ simulates the leakage oracle of $\mathcal{B}$, i.e, it sends the query to its leakage oracle $L_x^{k,\ell}(\cdot)$ and gives the answer back to $\mathcal{B}$. Since the number of leakage bits obtained by $\mathcal{B}$ should be less than $\ell$, all of the queries from $\mathcal{B}$ can be answered. After getting the output of $\mathcal{B}$ denoted by $(m, r)$ and $(m', r')$, $\mathcal{A}$ computes $x_i^* \equiv (J(m)r_i - J(m')r_i')/(J(m') - J(m))$ (mod $q$) for $i = 1, ..., n$ (As $m' \neq m$ and $J(\cdot)$ is a strongly collision-resistant hash function, we know the probability that $(J(m') - J(m))$ mod $q = 0$ is negligible). $\mathcal{A}$ outputs $x^*$ where $x^* = (x_1^*, ..., x_n^*)$.

If $\mathcal{B}$ has found the collision successfully, we have

$$\prod_{i=1}^{n} h_i^{J(m)x_i + J(m)r_i} \equiv \prod_{i=1}^{n} h_i^{J(m')x_i + J(m')r_i'}.$$

Let $g$ be a generator of $\mathbb{G}$ and $h_i = g^{F_i} \in \mathbb{G}$ ($F_i \in \mathbb{Z}_q$) for $i = 1, ..., n$, we have

$$g^{\sum_{i=1}^{n} F_i J(m)(x_i + r_i)} = g^{\sum_{i=1}^{n} F_i J(m')(x_i + r_i')}.$$

Furthermore, we have

$$g^{\sum_{i=1}^{n} F_i J(m)(x_i^* + r_i)} = g^{\sum_{i=1}^{n} F_i J(m')(x_i^* + r_i')}.$$

As a consequence, we have

$$\sum_{i=1}^{n} F_i x_i \equiv \sum_{i=1}^{n} F_i x_i^* \equiv \sum_{i=1}^{n} F_i (J(m')r_i' - J(m)r_i)/(J(m) - J(m')) \pmod{q},$$

which means that $\prod_{i=1}^{n} h_i^{x_i^*} = \prod_{i=1}^{n} h_i^{x_i} = y$. So if $\mathcal{B}$ can find a collision successfully with probability $\epsilon$ in polynomial time $t$, $\mathcal{A}$ can break the leakage hard relation with the same probability in the same running time.

Now we consider another situation when messages are the same, i.e., $\mathcal{B}$ can find $(m, r)$ and $(m, r')$ where $r \neq r'$ and $F_{pk_F}(m, r) = F_{pk_F}(m, r')$ with non-negligible probability $\epsilon$. We can construct an adversary $\mathcal{A}'$ that breaks the $n$-representation assumption.

Given $h_1, ..., h_n$, $\mathcal{A}'$ samples $(x, y)$ where $y = \prod_{i=1}^{n} h_i^{x_i}$ and give $y$ to $\mathcal{B}$. Since $\mathcal{A}'$ owns $x$ as the secret key, $\mathcal{A}'$ can answer all the leakage queries from $\mathcal{B}$ correctly. With probability $\epsilon$, $\mathcal{B}$ outputs two pairs $(m, r)$ and $(m, r')$ such that $r \neq r'$ and $(y \prod_{i=1}^{n} h_i^{r_i})^{J(m)} = (y \prod_{i=1}^{n} h_i^{r_i'})^{J(m)}$. Since $J(m)$ mod $q \neq 0$, we have $\prod_{i=1}^{n} h_i^{r_i} = \prod_{i=1}^{n} h_i^{r_i'}$. $\mathcal{A}'$ outputs $(r, r')$ such that breaks the $n$-representation assumption successfully with non-negligible probability $\epsilon$, completing the proof.

Since the length of the secret key is $L = n \log q$, we have that $\ell = (1 - o(1))L$.

## 4   Generic Transformationation

Let $\Sigma = (\mathsf{KG}, \mathsf{Sign}, \mathsf{Verify})$ (with randomness space $\Omega_\Sigma$) be $\ell_w$-FLR signature that satisfies the wEUF property. $\mathcal{F} = (\mathsf{KG}_F, F, \mathsf{TC}_F)$ (with randomness space $\mathcal{R}_F$) denotes the $\ell$-LR chameleon hash function described in Section 3.

We make use of the GBSW transformation [20] to convert $\Sigma$ into another signature scheme $\Sigma'$. The resulting signature scheme is shown in Figure 3. What we do here is just substituting the standard chameleon hash functions used in [20] for our $\ell$-LR chameleon hash functions. We will prove that the resulting signature scheme satisfies the $\ell_s$-sEUF-FLR property. Some parts of the proof are similar to [20].

---

- $\mathsf{KG}'(1^k)$:
  1. Run $(pk, sk) \leftarrow \mathsf{KG}(1^k)$.
  2. Run $(pk_F, sk_F) \leftarrow \mathsf{KG}_F(1^k)$.
  3. Run $(pk_H, sk_H) \leftarrow \mathsf{KG}_F(1^k)$.
  4. Output verification key $pk_s = (pk, pk_F, pk_H, m', \sigma')$ and signing key $sk_s = (sk, sk_F)$, where $m'$ and $\sigma'$ are arbitrary fixed strings.
- $\mathsf{Sign}'_{sk_s}(m)$:
  1. Parse $sk_s = (sk, sk_F)$.
  2. Randomly choose $\omega \leftarrow \Omega_\Sigma$, $s \leftarrow \mathcal{R}_F$, and $r' \leftarrow \mathcal{R}_F$.
  3. Compute $h = F_{pk_F}(m'||\sigma'; r')$.
  4. Compute $\bar{m} = F_{pk_H}(h; s)$.
  5. Compute $\sigma = \mathsf{Sign}_{sk}(\bar{m}; \omega)$.
  6. Compute $r = \mathsf{TC}_F(sk_F, (m'||\sigma', r'), m||\sigma)$.
  7. Output $\sigma' = (\sigma, r, s)$.
- $\mathsf{Verify}'(pk_s, m, \sigma')$:
  1. Parse $pk_s = (pk, pk_F, pk_H, m', \sigma')$, and $\sigma' = (\sigma, r, s)$.
  2. Compute $h = F_{pk_F}(m||\sigma; r)$.
  3. Compute $\bar{m} = F_{pk_H}(h; s)$.
  4. Output 1 if $\mathsf{Verify}(pk, \bar{m}, \sigma) = 1$ and output 0 otherwise.

---

**Fig. 3.** GBSW Transformation in the Bounded Leakage Model

*Claim.* The scheme described in Figure 3 is $\ell_s$-sEUF-FLR signature for $\ell_s = \min\{\ell, \ell_w\}$.

*Proof.* For $i = 1, ..., q$, let $m_i$ be the $i$th signing query, $\sigma'_i = (\sigma_i, r_i, s_i)$ be the answer to the $i$th signing query, $h_i = F_{pk_H}(m_i||\sigma_i; r_i)$, and $\bar{m}_i = F_{pk_F}(h_i; s_i)$. We denote $f_i$ as the $i$th leakage query of $\mathcal{A}$. At some point, $\mathcal{A}$ outputs $(m^*, (\sigma^*, r^*, s^*))$ as the forgery. In the same way, $h^* = F_{pk_H}(m^*||\sigma^*; r^*)$ and $\bar{m}^* = F_{pk_F}(h^*; s^*)$.

If $\mathcal{A}$ wins the sEUF-FLR experiment with non-negligible probability $\epsilon$, then $\mathcal{A}$ outputs a forgery, which is one of the following three types with probability $\epsilon/3$ in the sEUF-FLR experiment.

- **type I** forgery: $\bar{m}^* \notin \{\bar{m}_1, ..., \bar{m}_q\}$,
- **type II** forgery: there exists $i^* \in \{1, ..., q\}$ such that $\bar{m}^* = \bar{m}_{i^*}$, but $(h^*, s^*) \neq (h_{i^*}, s_{i^*})$,
- **type III** forgery: there exists $i^* \in \{1, ..., q\}$ such that $\bar{m}^* = \bar{m}_{i^*}$ and $(h^*, s^*) = (h_{i^*}, s_{i^*})$, but $(m^*, \sigma^*, r^*) \neq (m_{i^*}, \sigma_{i^*}, r_{i^*})$.

We now show how to construct PPT adversary $\mathcal{A}_I$ against the $\ell_w$-wEUF-FLR property of $\Sigma$, and adversary $\mathcal{A}_{II}$ and $\mathcal{A}_{III}$ against the $\ell$-LR collision-resistance property of $\mathcal{F}$, by making use of $\mathcal{A}$. Each of the adversaries $\mathcal{A}_I$, $\mathcal{A}_{II}$, and $\mathcal{A}_{III}$ succeeds if $\mathcal{A}$ outputs a **type I**, **type II**, and **type III** forgery, respectively.

*Adversary $\mathcal{A}_I$.* The challenger runs $(pk, sk) \leftarrow \mathsf{KG}(1^k)$, sets $state = sk$, and gives $pk$ to $\mathcal{A}_I$.

*Setup.* $\mathcal{A}_I$ runs $(pk_F, sk_F) \leftarrow \mathsf{KG}_F(1^k)$, $(pk_H, sk_H) \leftarrow \mathsf{KG}_F$, and sends $pk_s = (pk, pk_F, pk_H, m', \sigma')$ to $\mathcal{A}$. $m'$ and $\sigma'$ are some arbitrary fixed strings.

*Signing Queries.* When $\mathcal{A}$ sends the $i$th signing query message $m_i$ to $\mathcal{A}_I$, $\mathcal{A}_I$ responds as follows:

1. Randomly choose $s_i \leftarrow \mathcal{R}_F$, $r_i' \leftarrow \mathcal{R}_F$.
2. Compute $h_i = F_{pk_F}(m' \| \sigma'; r_i')$.
3. Compute $\bar{m}_i = F_{pk_H}(h_i; s_i)$.
4. Send $\bar{m}_i$ to the signing oracle and obtain the signature $\sigma_i = \mathsf{Sign}_{sk}(\bar{m}_i; \omega_i)$, where $\omega_i \leftarrow \Omega_\Sigma$. The signing oracle updates $state = state \| \omega_i$.
5. Compute $r_i = \mathsf{TC}_F(sk_F, (m' \| \sigma', r_i'), (m_i \| \sigma_i))$.
6. Store $(m', \sigma_i' = (\sigma_i, r_i, s_i))$ and return $\sigma_i'$ to $\mathcal{A}$.

*Leakage Queries.* When $\mathcal{A}$ makes its $i$th leakage query $f_i(\cdot)$ to $\mathcal{A}_I$, $\mathcal{A}_I$ sends $f_i(\cdot \| sk_F \| (r_1', ..., r_i'))$ to the leakage oracle and obtains the answer $f_i(state \| sk_F \| (r_1', ..., r_i'))$ (although the order of $state, sk_F, r_1', ..., r_i'$ is different from the definition, but it does not affect the correctness of our proof). Then $\mathcal{A}_I$ returns the answer back to $\mathcal{A}$.

*Output.* At some point, $\mathcal{A}$ outputs $(m^*, (\sigma^*, r^*, s^*))$. Then $\mathcal{A}_I$ computes $h^* = F_{pk_H}(m^* \| \sigma^*; r^*)$ and $\bar{m}^* = F_{pk_F}(h^*; s^*)$, and outputs $(\bar{m}^*, \sigma^*)$.

Since the number of leaked bits obtained by $\mathcal{A}$ in each round is at most $\ell_s$ and the leakage parameter of $\mathcal{A}_I$'s leakage oracle is $\ell_w$ (which is larger than $\ell_s$), $\mathcal{A}_I$ perfectly simulates the leakage oracle of $\mathcal{A}$. What is more, since $\mathcal{A}_I$ simply follows the real signing procedure, it also perfectly simulates the real signing oracle $\mathsf{Sign}$ of $\mathcal{A}$.

As a result, if $\mathcal{A}$ outputs a **type I** forgery successfully, $(\bar{m}^*, \sigma^*)$ is valid and $\bar{m}^* \notin \{\bar{m}_1, ..., \bar{m}_q\}$, which means $\mathcal{A}_I$ breaks the $\ell_w$-wEUF-FLR of $\Sigma$ successfully.

*Adversary $\mathcal{A}_{II}$.* The challenger runs $(pk_H, sk_H) \leftarrow \mathsf{KG}_F(1^k)$ and sends $pk_H$ to $\mathcal{A}_{II}$.

*Setup.* $\mathcal{A}_I$ runs $(pk, sk) \leftarrow \mathsf{KG}(1^k)$, $(pk_F, sk_F) \leftarrow \mathsf{KG}_F(1^k)$, sets $state = sk$, and sends $pk_s = (pk, pk_F, pk_H)$ to $\mathcal{A}$. $m'$ and $\sigma'$ are some arbitrary fixed strings.

*Signing Queries.* When $\mathcal{A}$ sends the $i$th signing query message $m_i$ to $\mathcal{A}_{II}$, $\mathcal{A}_{II}$ chooses $\omega_i \leftarrow \Omega_\Sigma$, $s_i \leftarrow \mathcal{R}_F$, and $r'_i \leftarrow \mathcal{R}_F$. Then it stores $(m_i, \sigma_i, r_i, s_i)$ and returns $\Sigma' = \mathsf{Sign}_{sk_s}(m_i; \omega_i, s_i, r'_i)$ back to $\mathcal{A}$ where $sk_s = (sk, sk_F)$. $\mathcal{A}_{II}$ updates $state = state||\omega_i$.

*Leakage Queries.* When $\mathcal{A}$ sends the $i$th leakage query $f_i(\cdot)$ to $\mathcal{A}_{II}$, $\mathcal{A}_{II}$ returns $f_i(state||sk_F||(r'_1, ..., r'_i)))$ to $\mathcal{A}$.

*Output.* At some point, $\mathcal{A}$ outputs $(m^*, (\sigma^*, r^*, s^*))$. Then $\mathcal{A}_{II}$ computes $h^* = F_{pk_H}(m^*||\sigma^*; r^*)$ and $\bar{m}^* = F_{pk_F}(h^*; s^*)$. $\mathcal{A}_{II}$ finds entry $i^*$ such that $i^* \in \{1, ..., q\}$, $\bar{m}^* = \bar{m}_{i^*}$, and $(h^*, s^*) \neq (h_{i^*}, s_{i^*})$, and outputs $(h^*, s^*)$ and $(h_{i^*}, s_{i^*})$. If such an entry does not exist, $\mathcal{A}_{II}$ aborts.

Since $\mathcal{A}_{II}$ owns the signing key $sk_s$ and generates the randomness itself, it perfectly simulates the real signing oracle and leakage oracle of $\mathcal{A}$. If $\mathcal{A}$ outputs a **type II** forgery, then $\mathcal{A}_{II}$ breaks the collision-resistance property of $\mathcal{F}$ successfully.

*Adversary $\mathcal{A}_{III}$.* The challenger runs $(pk_F, sk_F) \leftarrow \mathsf{KG}_F(1^k)$, and sends $pk_F$ to $\mathcal{A}_{III}$.

*Setup.* $\mathcal{A}_{III}$ runs $(pk, sk) \leftarrow \mathsf{KG}(1^k)$, $(pk_H, sk_H) \leftarrow \mathsf{KG}_F(1^k)$, sets $state = sk$, and sends $pk_s = (pk, pk_F, pk_H, m', \sigma')$ to $\mathcal{A}$. $m'$ and $\sigma'$ are some arbitrary fixed strings.

*Signing Queries.* When $\mathcal{A}$ sends the $i$th signing query message $m_i$ to $\mathcal{A}_{III}$, $\mathcal{A}_{III}$ responds as follows:

1. Randomly choose $\omega_i \leftarrow \Omega_\Sigma$, $s'_i \leftarrow \mathcal{R}_F$, and $r_i \leftarrow \mathcal{R}_F$.
2. Compute $\bar{m}_i = F_{pk_H}(h'_i; s'_i)$, where $h'_i$ is some arbitrary string.
3. Compute $\sigma_i = \mathsf{Sign}_{sk}(\bar{m}_i; \omega_i)$, and update $state = state||\omega_i$.
4. Compute $h_i = F_{pk_F}(m_i||\sigma_i; r_i)$.
5. Compute $s_i = \mathsf{TC}_F(sk_H, (h'_i, s'_i), h_i)$.
6. Store $(m', \sigma'_i = (\sigma_i, r_i, s_i))$ and return $\sigma'_i$ to $\mathcal{A}$.

*Leakage Queries.* When adversary $\mathcal{A}$ makes its $i$th leakage query which is $f_i(\cdot)$, $\mathcal{A}_I$ sends $f'_i(state||\cdot)$ to the leakage oracle, where

$$f'_i(state||\cdot) = f_i(state|| \cdot ||\{TC_F(\cdot, (m_j||\sigma_j, r_j), m'||\sigma')\}_{j=1,...,i}).$$

So we have that

$$f'_i(state||sk_F) = f_i(state||sk_F||\{TC_F(sk_F, (m_j||\sigma_j, r_j), m'||\sigma')\}_{j=1,...,i})$$
$$= f_i(state||sk_F||\{r'_j\}_{j=1,...,i}).$$

Then $\mathcal{A}_{III}$ returns the answer to $\mathcal{A}$.

*Output.* At some point, $\mathcal{A}$ outputs $(m^*, (\sigma^*, r^*, s^*))$. Then $\mathcal{A}_{III}$ computes $h^* = F_{pk_F}(m^*||\sigma^*; r^*)$, and finds entry $i^*$ such that $i^* \in \{1, ..., q\}$, $h^* = h_{i^*}$, and $(m^*||\sigma^*, r^*) \neq (m_{i^*}||\sigma_{i^*}, r_{i^*})$. Then $\mathcal{A}_{III}$ outputs $(m^*||\sigma^*, r^*)$ and $(m_{i^*}||\sigma_{i^*}, r_{i^*})$. If such an entry does not exist, $\mathcal{A}_{III}$ aborts.

Since the number of leaked bits obtained by $\mathcal{A}$ in each leakage round is at most $\ell_s$ and the leakage parameter of $\mathcal{A}_{III}$'s leakage oracle is $\ell_w$ (which is larger than $\ell_s$), all the leakage queries of $\mathcal{A}$ can be answered. What is more, according to the reversibility property and trapdoor collision property, it is impossible for $\mathcal{A}$ to distinguish the signatures and leakage given by $\mathcal{A}_{III}$ with those given by the real signing oracle and the real leakage oracle. As a result, $\mathcal{A}_{III}$ perfectly simulates the leakage oracle of $\mathcal{A}$.

If $\mathcal{A}$ outputs a **type III** forgery successfully, $\mathcal{A}_{III}$ breaks the $\ell_w$-CLR collision-resistance property of $\mathcal{F}$ successfully.

*Remark 1.* We set the leakage parameter as $\min\{\ell, \ell_w\}$. In fact, the number of bits allowed to be leaked can be more than that. The signature schemes will remain sEUF if the leaked bits of $sk$ and $\omega_1, ...\omega_q$ is less than $\ell_w$, and the leaked bits of $sk_F$ and $r'_1, ..., r'_q$ is less than $\ell$.

*Remark 2.* We also argue that if the original signature scheme can tolerate leakage during the key generation, the sEUF-signature scheme converted by our technique can also tolerate leakage during the key generation, i.e, the *state* of Definition 4 can be initially set as the randomness used by the key generation algorithm instead of $sk$ (we refer the reader to the definition of [7]).

In fact, the randomness used to generate the key pairs of the LR chameleon hash function (Figure 2) contains $(h_1, ..., h_n)$ sampled from $\mathbb{G}^n$ and $x$ sampled from $\mathbb{Z}_q^n$. Since $h_1, ..., h_n$ are public information and $x$ is the secret key, all the leakage queries on the randomness of $KG_F$ can be treated as the leakage queries on the secret keys, which means that the security does not change while the leakage during the key generation is allowed. Furthermore, we do not have to consider the leakage on $sk_H$ since $pk_H$ can be sampled directly without learning knowledge of $sk_H$.

*Remark 3.* If we apply our technique to the $(1 - o(1))L$-wEUF-FLR signature scheme proposed in [12] where $L$ is the length of the secret key, we can obtain a $(1 - o(1))L$-sEUF-FLR signature scheme by setting $sk_F = sk$.

For the signature scheme in [12], a signature is generated as $\pi \leftarrow P(crs, y, m, x; \omega)$, where $P$ is a prover of LR non-interactive proof system (NIZK), $crs$ is the common reference string, $(y, x)$ is sampled by KeyGen (c.f., Figure 1), $m$ is the message, and $\omega$ is the randomizer. $(crs, y)$ is the verification key and $x$ is the secret key. If we set $(pk, sk) = ((crs, y), x)$ and $(pk_F, sk_F) = (y, x)$ in our scheme, the resulting signature scheme is still sEUF-FLR. To prove this, we have to face two problems. The first one is how $\mathcal{A}_I$ can simulate the signing oracle and leakage oracle without $sk_F$, and the second one is how $\mathcal{A}_{III}$ can simulate the signing oracle and leakage oracle without $sk$.

When it comes to the first problem, $A_I$ can simulate the signing oracle and leakage oracle in the same way as $A_{III}$ as we described in the proof before. When it comes to the second problem, $A_{III}$ can generate $crs$ with a trapdoor information $\tau$, and it can use the simulator of the LR-NIZK proof system to generate a proof by using $\tau$ instead of $sk$. Furthermore, since the simulator of the LR-NIZK proof system can reduce leakage on both $sk$ and $w$ to leakage only on $sk$, $A_{III}$ can also simulate the leakage oracle.

We refer the reader to [12] for details of the definition of LR-NIZK and the construction of the signature scheme.

# References

1. Akavia, A., Goldwasser, S., Vaikuntanathan, V.: Simultaneous hardcore bits and cryptography against memory attacks. In: Reingold, O. (ed.) TCC 2009. LNCS, vol. 5444, pp. 474–495. Springer, Heidelberg (2009)
2. Alwen, J., Dodis, Y., Naor, M., Segev, G., Walfish, S., Wichs, D.: Public-key encryption in the bounded-retrieval model. In: Gilbert, H. (ed.) EUROCRYPT 2010. LNCS, vol. 6110, pp. 113–134. Springer, Heidelberg (2010)
3. Alwen, J., Dodis, Y., Wichs, D.: Leakage-resilient public-key cryptography in the bounded-retrieval model. In: Halevi, S. (ed.) CRYPTO 2009. LNCS, vol. 5677, pp. 36–54. Springer, Heidelberg (2009)
4. Bellare, M., Goldreich, O., Goldwasser, S.: Incremental cryptography: The case of hashing and signing. In: Desmedt, Y.G. (ed.) CRYPTO 1994. LNCS, vol. 839, pp. 216–233. Springer, Heidelberg (1994)
5. Bellare, M., Shoup, S.: Two-tier signatures, strongly unforgeable signatures, and fiat-shamir without random oracles. In: Okamoto, T., Wang, X. (eds.) PKC 2007. LNCS, vol. 4450, pp. 201–216. Springer, Heidelberg (2007)
6. Boneh, D., Shen, E., Waters, B.: Strongly unforgeable signatures based on computational diffie-hellman. In: Yung, M., Dodis, Y., Kiayias, A., Malkin, T. (eds.) PKC 2006. LNCS, vol. 3958, pp. 229–240. Springer, Heidelberg (2006)
7. Boyle, E., Segev, G., Wichs, D.: Fully leakage-resilient signatures. In: Paterson, K.G. (ed.) EUROCRYPT 2011. LNCS, vol. 6632, pp. 89–108. Springer, Heidelberg (2011)
8. Brakerski, Z., Goldwasser, S.: Circular and leakage resilient public-key encryption under subgroup indistinguishability. In: Rabin, T. (ed.) CRYPTO 2010. LNCS, vol. 6223, pp. 1–20. Springer, Heidelberg (2010)
9. Brands, S.A.: An efficient off-line electronic cash system based on the representation problem. Technical report, Amsterdam, The Netherlands (1993)
10. Dodis, Y., Haralambiev, K., López-Alt, A., Wichs, D.: Efficient public-key cryptography in the presence of key leakage. In: Abe, M. (ed.) ASIACRYPT 2010. LNCS, vol. 6477, pp. 613–631. Springer, Heidelberg (2010)
11. Dodis, Y., Ostrovsky, R., Reyzin, L., Smith, A.: Fuzzy extractors: How to generate strong keys from biometrics and other noisy data. SIAM J. Comput. 38(1), 97–139 (2008)
12. Garg, S., Jain, A., Sahai, A.: Leakage-resilient zero knowledge. In: Rogaway, P. (ed.) CRYPTO 2011. LNCS, vol. 6841, pp. 297–315. Springer, Heidelberg (2011)
13. Huang, Q., Wong, D.S., Zhao, Y.: Generic transformation to strongly unforgeable signatures. In: Katz, J., Yung, M. (eds.) ACNS 2007. LNCS, vol. 4521, pp. 1–17. Springer, Heidelberg (2007)

14. Katz, J., Vaikuntanathan, V.: Signature schemes with bounded leakage resilience. In: Matsui, M. (ed.) ASIACRYPT 2009. LNCS, vol. 5912, pp. 703–720. Springer, Heidelberg (2009)
15. Krawczyk, H., Rabin, T.: Chameleon signatures. In: NDSS. The Internet Society (2000)
16. Lyubashevsky, V., Palacio, A., Segev, G.: Public-key cryptographic primitives provably as secure as subset sum. In: Micciancio, D. (ed.) TCC 2010. LNCS, vol. 5978, pp. 382–400. Springer, Heidelberg (2010)
17. Naor, M., Segev, G.: Public-key cryptosystems resilient to key leakage. In: Halevi, S. (ed.) CRYPTO 2009. LNCS, vol. 5677, pp. 18–35. Springer, Heidelberg (2009)
18. Okamoto, T.: Provably secure and practical identification schemes and corresponding signature schemes. In: Brickell, E.F. (ed.) CRYPTO 1992. LNCS, vol. 740, pp. 31–53. Springer, Heidelberg (1993)
19. Shamir, A., Tauman, Y.: Improved online/offline signature schemes. In: Kilian, J. (ed.) CRYPTO 2001. LNCS, vol. 2139, pp. 355–367. Springer, Heidelberg (2001)
20. Steinfeld, R., Pieprzyk, J., Wang, H.: How to strengthen any weakly unforgeable signature into a strongly unforgeable signature. In: Abe, M. (ed.) CT-RSA 2007. LNCS, vol. 4377, pp. 357–371. Springer, Heidelberg (2006)
21. Teranishi, I., Oyama, T., Ogata, W.: General conversion for obtaining strongly existentially unforgeable signatures. In: Barua, R., Lange, T. (eds.) INDOCRYPT 2006. LNCS, vol. 4329, pp. 191–205. Springer, Heidelberg (2006)
22. Wang, Y., Tanaka, K.: Strongly simulation-extractable leakage-resilient NIZK. In: Susilo, W., Mu, Y. (eds.) ACISP 2014. LNCS, vol. 8544, pp. 66–81. Springer, Heidelberg (2014)

# Bounded Pre-image Awareness and the Security of Hash-Tree Keyless Signatures

Ahto Buldas[1,2,], Risto Laanoja[1,2], Peeter Laud[3], and Ahto Truu[1,*]

[1] GuardTime AS, Tammsaare tee 60, 11316 Tallinn, Estonia
[2] Tallinn University of Technology, Raja 15, 12618 Tallinn, Estonia
[3] Cybernetica AS, Mäealuse 2/1, 12618 Tallinn, Estonia

**Abstract.** We present a new tighter security proof for unbounded hash tree keyless signature (time-stamping) schemes that use Merkle-Damgård (MD) hash functions with Preimage Aware (PrA) compression functions. It is known that the PrA assumption alone is insufficient for proving the security of unbounded hash tree schemes against back-dating attacks. We show that many known PrA constructions satisfy a stronger *Bounded Pre-Image Awareness (BPrA)* condition that assumes the existence of an extractor $\mathcal{E}$ that is bounded in the sense that for any efficiently computable query string $\alpha$, the number of outputs $y$ for which $\mathcal{E}(y, \alpha)$ succeeds does not exceed the number of queries in $\alpha$. We show that block-cipher based MD-hash functions with rate-1 compression functions (such as Davies-Meyer and Miyaguchi-Preneel) of both type I and type II are BPrA. We also show that the compression function of Shrimpton-Stam that uses non-compressing components is BPrA. The security proof for unbounded hash-tree schemes is very tight under the BPrA assumption. In order to have $2^s$-security against back-dating, the hash function must have $n = 2s + 4$ output bits, assuming that the security of the hash function is close to the birthday barrier, i.e. that there are no structural weaknesses in the hash function itself. Note that the previous proofs that assume PrA gave the estimation $n = 2s + 2\log_2 C + 2$, where $C$ is the maximum allowed size of the hash tree. For example, if $s = 100$ ($2^{100}$-security) and $C = 2^{60}$, the previous proofs require $n = 322$ output bits, while the new proof requires $n = 204$ output bits.

## 1 Introduction

Keyless time-stamping [10] was proposed by Haber *et al* in order to avoid key-based cryptography and trusted third parties so that time stamps become irrefutable proofs of time. A collection of $C$ documents is hashed down to a single digest of a few dozen bytes that is then published in widely available media such as newspapers. Merkle hash trees [12] enable creations of compact "keyless signatures" of size $O(\log C)$ for each of the $C$ documents. Every such signature

---

* This work has been supported by Estonian Research Council through grant IUT27-1 and by Eestonian Research and Development Foundation (ERDF) through the Centre of Excellence in Computer Science (EXCS).

S.S.M. Chow et al. (Eds.): ProvSec 2014, LNCS 8782, pp. 130–145, 2014.

consists of all sibling hash values in the path from a document (a leaf of the tree) to the root of the tree. After the root hash value is published, it will be impossible for anyone to *back-date* a new document in terms of creating a hash chain from a new document to the already published hash value. In [1], a global-scale hash-tree scheme was drafted where during every unit of time a large hash tree is created co-operatively by numerous servers all over the globe and the root value is published in newspapers.

The security of hash-tree schemes against back-dating can be reduced to collision-resistance of the hash function. The first correct security proof was published in 2004 [6], but this proof assumes that the size $C$ of the global hash tree (the *capacity* of the scheme) is limited and the number $n$ of the output bits of the hash function needed for $2^s$-security was $n = 4s + 2\log_2 C + 2$, i.e. $n$ depends on $C$ (Tab. 1). This means that if the maximum hash tree size is $2^{60}$, then for $2^{100}$-security against back-dating one has to use 522-bit hash functions. The practical hash functions in such schemes might be 256-bit and twice larger output size will double the amount of data in the system.

The tightest possible proof of security [5] against back-dating under the collision-resistance assumption requires the output size $n = 3s + \log_2 C + 8$, which in case $C = 2^{60}$ and $s = 100$ gives $n = 368$ (Tab. 1), which is still too large if one desires to use 256-bit hash functions in a global hash tree scheme. The proof in [5] has been shown to be asymptotically optimally tight if the collision-resistance property is used as the security assumption. So, the only way to obtain tighter security proofs is to use stronger (or incomparable) security assumptions for hash functions.

In [4], a tighter security proof was presented that used a stronger assumption called Pre-Image Awareness (PrA) (first proposed in [9]) instead of collision-resistance. The PrA condition makes sense if the hash function uses ideal components (ideal ciphers, random permutations, etc.). The proof under PrA required hash size $n = 2s + 2\log_2 C + 2$. This might be valuable for high security requirements, but for the case of $C = 2^{60}$ and $s = 100$ gives $n = 322$, which is still too large for using 256-bit hash functions, for example.

Therefore, in [4], a new non-standard and seemingly just slightly stronger than PrA security assumption—Strong Pre-Image Awareness (SPrA)—was used to obtain a tighter security proof with required hash size $n = 2s + 2\log_2 \log_2 C + 2$, which in case $C = 2^{60}$ and $s = 100$ gives $n = 214$. However, the SPrA is a new assumption and not sufficiently studied. In contrast to the PrA condition, which is known to hold for many cryptographic constructions of hash functions [9], there are no similar proofs of SPrA. Considering the formal definition of SPrA, such proofs might be hard to construct, mostly because the SPrA condition involves arbitrary "parsing" functions.

In this work, we define another strenghtening of the PrA condition, the so-called *Bounded Pre-Image Awareness (BPrA)* that assumes the existence of an extractor $\mathcal{E}$ that is bounded in the sense that for any efficiently computable query string $\alpha$, the number of outputs $y$ for which $\mathcal{E}(y, \alpha)$ succeeds does not exceed the number of queries in $\alpha$. We show that many known PrA constructions actually are BPrA. For example, we show that blockcipher based MD-hash functions with rate-1 compression functions (such as Davies-Meyer and Miyaguchi-Preneel) of both type I and type II are BPrA. We also show that some compression functions with uncompressing components (such as Shrimpton-Stam) are BPrA. Therefore, the BPrA assumption is (at least for now) more justified in practice than the SPrA assumption.

The security proof for unbounded hash-tree schemes is very tight under the BPrA assumption, even tighter than under the SPrA assumption. In order to have $2^s$-security against back-dating, the hash function must have $n = 2s + 4$ output bits (Tab. 1), assuming that the security of the hash function is close to the birthday barrier, i.e. that there are no structural weaknesses in the hash function itself. In the case of $s = 100$ this gives $n = 204$.

**Table 1.** Efficiency of security proofs, where $n(C, T, s)$ is the required output size of the hash function, assuming that the scheme uses hash trees of size $C$, is intended for a time period of $T$ units, and needs to be $2^s$-secure. The results of this work are presented in bold.

| Assumption | Formula | Required Output Size $n$ | $n(2^{60}, 2^{32}, 100)$ |
|---|---|---|---|
| CR [6] | $\frac{t'}{\delta'} \approx 2C\left(\frac{t}{\delta}\right)^2$ | $n = 2\log_2 C + 4s + 2$ | 522 |
| CR [5] | $\frac{t'}{\delta'} \approx 14\sqrt{C}\left(\frac{t}{\delta}\right)^{1.5}$ | $n = \log_2 C + 3s + 8$ | 368 |
| PrA [4] | $\frac{t'}{\delta'} \approx 2C\frac{t}{\delta}$ | $n = 2(\log_2 C + s + 1)$ | 322 |
| SPrA [4] | $\frac{t'}{\delta'} \approx 4\log_2 C\frac{t}{\delta}$ | $n = 2(\log_2 \log_2 C + s + 2)$ | 216 |
| **BPrA** | $\frac{t'}{\delta'} \approx 4\frac{t}{\delta}$ | $n = 2s + 4$ | **204** |
| **RO (bounded)** | $\frac{t}{\delta} \geq \frac{2^{n-1}}{CT}$ | $n = s + \log_2 C + \log_2 T + 1$ | **193** |
| RO (unbounded) [4] | $\frac{t}{\delta} \geq 2^{\frac{n-1}{2}}$ | $n = 2s + 1$ | 201 |

Tab. 1 summarizes the efficiency of the existing security reductions, in which a $t$-time backdating adversary with success probability $\delta$ is converted to a $t'$-time collision-finding adversary with success probability $\delta'$. An $n$-bit hash function is assumed to be $2^{n/2}$-secure, i.e. near to the birthday barrier. The third column of Tab. 1 presents a formula for the required output size $n$ of the hash function for the time-stamping scheme to be $2^s$-secure. The last column presents the output size in a particular case, where $C = 2^{60}$, $T = 2^{32}$, and $s = 100$. In addition to the new security proof under the BPrA assumption, we also show in this work that in the RO model bounded schemes are secure beyond the birthday barrier.

The paper is organized as follows. In Sec. 2, we provide readers with necessary preliminary concepts and the state of the art in the security proofs of hash tree schemes. In Sec. 3, we study the security proofs in the random oracle model and present the motivation behind the new BPrA security condition. In Sec. 4, we show that many of the block cipher based hash function constructions (and also some constructions with non-compressing ideal components, e.g. Shrimpton-Stam [14]) that have been proved to be PrA are actually BPrA and hence these hash functions are much more secure for hash-tree time-stamping than the previously known security proofs suggest.

# 2  Preliminaries

## 2.1  Tightness of Security Proofs

The security of cryptographic schemes is measured by the amount of resources needed for an adversary to break the primitive. Considering that the running time $t$ and the success probability $\delta$ of attacks against a scheme may vary, Luby [11] proposed the *time-success ratio* $\frac{t}{\delta}$ as a measure for attacking resources. A scheme is said to be $S$-secure, if the success probability $\delta$ of any $t$-time adversary does not exceed $\frac{t}{S}$.

In a typical security proof for a scheme $\mathcal{P}$ built from a primitive $\mathcal{Q}$, it is shown that if $\mathcal{Q}$ is $S_q$-secure, then $\mathcal{P}$ is $S_p$-secure. Bellare and Rogaway [2,3] first emphasized the importance of the *tightness* $S_p/S_q$ of security proofs in practical applications. Informally, tightness shows how much security of the primitive is retained by the scheme. Security proofs are mostly *reductions*: an adversary for $\mathcal{P}$ with running time $t$ and success probability $\delta$ is transformed to an adversary for $\mathcal{Q}$ with running time $t'$ and success probability $\delta'$. This means that for having $\frac{t}{\delta}$-secure $\mathcal{P}$, it is sufficient to use a $\frac{t'}{\delta'}$-secure $\mathcal{Q}$.

## 2.2  Security Properties of Hash Functions

In this paper, we study the security properties of hash functions $H^P$ that use some kind of ideal functionality $P$ (random permutations, random functions, ideal ciphers, etc.) as an oracle. For example, in case of the Merkle-Damgård hash functions, the compression function and the output transform are often assumed to be ideal objects. In this section, we describe some of the properties of hash functions, starting from the strongest ones.

**Random Oracles.** By a *random oracle* $\mathcal{R}$, we mean a function that is chosen randomly from the set of all functions of type $\{0,1\}^m \to \{0,1\}^n$. By the *random oracle heuristic* we mean a security argument when an application of a hash function (e.g. a time-stamping scheme, a signature scheme) is proved to be secure in the so-called *random oracle model*, where the hash function is replaced with a random oracle. The random oracle heuristic was first introduced by Bellare and Rogaway [2]. Although it was proved later by Canetti et al [7] that the random oracle heuristic fails in certain theoretical cases, proofs in the random oracle model are still considered valuable security arguments, especially if no better security proofs are known.

**Pre-image Awareness.** Pre-Image Awareness (PrA) of a (hash) function $H$ means, that if we first commit an output $y$ and later come up with an input $x$, such that $y = H(x)$, then it is safe to conclude that we knew $x$ before committing $y$. This notion was first formalized by Dodis et al. [9] for hash functions $H^P$ that are built using an ideal primitive $P$ as a black box. For $H^P$ being PrA, there has to be an efficient deterministic extractor $\mathcal{E}$ which when given $y$ and the list $\alpha$ of all previously made $P$-calls, outputs an input $x$, such that $H^P(x) = y$, or $\perp$ if $\mathcal{E}$ was unable to find such an $x$. The adversary tries to find $x$ and $y$ so that

$x \neq \mathcal{E}(\alpha, y)$ and $y = H^P(x)$. A weaker form of PrA (so-called WPrA) allows $\mathcal{E}$ output a set $\mathcal{L}$ of inputs $x$, and the adversary tries to find $x$, such that the query $\mathcal{L} \leftarrow \mathcal{E}(\alpha, y)$ was made, $y = H^P(x)$, but $x \notin \mathcal{L}$. Obviously, WPrA becomes PrA if the number of elements in $\mathcal{L}$ is limited to one, i.e. $|\mathcal{L}| \leq 1$. To define pre-image

| $\mathbf{Exp}^{\mathrm{pra}}_{H,P,\mathcal{E},B}$: | **oracle** P($m$): | **oracle** Ex($y$): |
|---|---|---|
| $x \leftarrow B^{\mathsf{P},\mathsf{Ex}}$ | $c \leftarrow P(m)$ | $\mathsf{Q}[y] \leftarrow 1$ |
| $y \leftarrow H^P(x)$ | $\alpha \leftarrow \alpha\|\|(m,c)$ | $\mathsf{V}[y] \leftarrow \mathcal{E}(y,\alpha)$ |
| If $\mathsf{Q}[y] = 1$ and $\mathsf{V}[y] \neq x$ **return** 1, | **return** $c$ | **return** $\mathsf{V}[y]$ |
| else **return** 0 | | |

Fig. 1. Preimage awareness experiment with the oracles P and Ex

awareness of $H^P$ in a precise way, we set up an experiment **Exp** (see Fig. 1), specified as a game which an attacker $B$ is trying to win. $B$ is constrained to oracle access to $P$, via a wrapper oracle P, which records all $P$-calls made by $B$ as an advise string $\alpha$. Likely, the extractor $\mathcal{E}$ is also accessible through another wrapper oracle Ex, which uses global arrays Q (initially $\perp$ everywhere) and V (initially blank). Q is used to record all input parameters to $\mathcal{E}$; V is used to store all successfully extracted values corresponding to $\mathcal{E}$'s inputs. The adversary $B$ tries to output a value $x$ such that $H^P(x) = y$, $\mathsf{Q}[y] = 1$ and $\mathsf{V}[y] \neq x$, i.e. $\mathcal{E}$ tried to invert $y$, but was unsuccessful. As P- and Ex-calls are unit cost, the running time of $B$ does not depend on the running time of $\mathcal{E}$. Note that PrA implies collision-resistance [9], but WPrA does not.

**Definition 1 (Pre-image Awareness).** *A function $H^P$ is S-secure pre-image aware (PrA) if there is an efficient extractor $\mathcal{E}$, so that for every $t$-time $B$:*

$$\mathbf{Adv}^{\mathrm{pra}}_{H,P,\mathcal{E}}(B) = \mathsf{Pr}\left[1 \leftarrow \mathbf{Exp}^{\mathrm{pra}}_{H,P,\mathcal{E},B}\right] \leq \frac{t}{S} . \tag{1}$$

In [4], a stronger notion of *Strong Pre-Image Awareness* (SPrA) was presented in which the Ex-oracle is allowed to use the "oldest" possible $\alpha$. For example, if we obtain $x \leftarrow \mathsf{Ext}(y)$ (where $x = x_1 x_2$ and $x_1, x_2 \in \{0,1\}^n$) for which the oracle uses $\alpha$, and later we call $\mathsf{Ext}(x_1)$, the same $\alpha$ is used for extraction, because the oracle remembers that $x_1$ was created by just "parsing" $x$ and it is thereby as old as $x$ and the use of $\alpha$ is justified. This new notion allows one to establish more tight security proofs for hash-tree time-stamping than the PrA would allow.

**Collision Resistance.** Informally, the collision resistance of a hash function $H^P$ means that it is infeasible for adversaries to find two different inputs $x$ and $x'$ that have the same hash value, i.e. $H^P(x) = H^P(x')$. This definition makes sense only if the ideal primitive $P$ contains some randomness, as the collisions of fixed functions can always be "wired" into the adversary.

**Definition 2 (Collision Resistance).** *A function $H^P$ is S-secure collision resistant (CR) if for every adversary $B$ with running time $t$:*

$$\mathbf{Adv}^{\mathrm{cr}}_{H,P}(B) = \mathsf{Pr}\left[x, x' \leftarrow B^P : x \neq x', H^P(x) = H^P(x')\right] \leq \frac{t}{S} . \tag{2}$$

Due to the so-called birthday bound, functions with $n$-bit output can only be up to $2^{n/2}$-secure collision resistant.

## 2.3   Merkle-Damgård Hash Functions

Merkle-Damgård (or iterated) hash functions use a compression function $F(m, v)$ to iteratively compute a hash of an arbitrary size message $m$ divided into equal blocks $m_1, \ldots, m_\ell$ of suitable size. The hash $h = H(m)$ is computed as follows: (1) $h \leftarrow IV$; (2) for $i \in \{1, \ldots, \ell\}$ do: $h \leftarrow F(m_i, h)$; (3) and output $H(m) = h$. Here, $IV$ is a public and standard initial value. It has been proved [9] that if $F$ is PrA, then so is $H$.

## 2.4   Blockcipher-Based Hash Functions

Many hash functions are constructed from secure blockciphers. The most common approach for creating a $2n \to n$ hash function is to use a blockcipher with $n$-bit block and $n$-bit key and make a compression function that makes only a single call to the blockcipher. Such constructions were first analyzed by Preneel et al. [13] and are called *rate-1 schemes*. The most general approach is that of Stam [15], where the compression function is defined by the following three steps:

1. Prepare key and plaintext: $(k, x) \leftarrow C_{\mathrm{pre}}(m, v)$;
2. Use the blockcipher: $y \leftarrow E_k(x)$;
3. Output the digest: $w \leftarrow C_{\mathrm{post}}(m, v, y)$.

There are two types of rate-1 compression functions.

**Definition 3.** *A blockcipher-based rate-1 compression function $F^E$ is called Type-I iff: (1) $C_{\mathrm{pre}}$ is bijective; (2) $C_{\mathrm{post}}(m, v, \cdot)$ is bijective for all $m, v$; and (3) $C_{\mathrm{aux}}(\cdot) = C_{\mathrm{post}}(C_{\mathrm{pre}}^{-1}(k, \cdot), y)$ is bijective for all $k, y$.*

**Definition 4.** *A blockcipher-based rate-1 compression function $F^E$ is called Type-II iff: (1) $C_{\mathrm{pre}}$ is bijective; (2) $C_{\mathrm{post}}(m, v, \cdot)$ is bijective for all $m, v$; and (3) $C_{\mathrm{pre}}^{-1}(k, \cdot)$ (restricted to its second output $v$) is bijective for all $k$.*

Type-I functions are preimage aware [9] and thus also collision-resistant. Type-II functions become preimage-aware (and collision-resistant) when iterated as Merkle-Damgård hash functions [9].

## 2.5   Hash-Tree Schemes and Their Security Against Back-Dating

Hash trees were introduced by Merkle [12]. Let $h: \{0, 1\}^{2n} \to \{0, 1\}^n$ be a hash function. By a *hash-tree* we mean a tree-shaped data structure that consists of nodes labeled with $n$-bit hash values. Each node is either a *leaf* which means it has no children, or an *internal node* with two child nodes (the left and the right child). The hash value $y$ of an internal node is computed as a hash $y = h(y_0, y_1)$, where $y_0$ and $y_1$ are the hash values of the left and right child, respectively.

There is one *root node* that is not a child of any node. By $r = \mathcal{T}(x_1, \ldots, x_m)$ we mean that $r$ is the root label of a hash tree $\mathcal{T}$ with leaves labeled with hash values $x_1, \ldots, x_m$.

**Encoding the Leaves of a Hash Tree.** Nodes of a hash tree can be named in a natural way with finite bit-strings. The root node is named by the empty string $\sqcup$. If a node is named by $\ell$, then its left and right child nodes are named by $\ell 0$ and $\ell 1$, respectively. The name $\ell$ of a node is also an "address" of the node, considering that one starts searching from the root node, and then step by step, chooses one of the children depending on the corresponding bit in $\ell$.

**Shape of a Hash Tree.** Hash tree has a particular *shape* by which we mean the set of all names of the leaf-nodes. For example, a balanced complete tree with four nodes (Fig. 2, left) has the shape $\{00, 01, 10, 11\}$. If the root hash value is denoted by $r$ (instead of $r_\sqcup$) and $r_\ell$ denotes the hash value of a node with name $\ell$, then in this example, the relations between the nodes are the following: $r = h(r_0, r_1)$, $r_0 = h(r_{00}, r_{01})$, and $r_1 = h(r_{10}, r_{11})$. The shape $\{000, 001, 01, 1\}$ represents a tree with four leaves (Fig. 2, right) with the hash values being in the following relations: $r = h(r_0, r_1)$, $r_0 = h(r_{00}, r_{01})$, and $r_{00} = h(r_{000}, r_{001})$. Note also that any shape is a *prefix-free code*.

**Fig. 2.** Trees with shape $\{00, 01, 10, 11\}$ (left) and $\{000, 001, 01, 1\}$ (right)

**Hash Chains.** In order to prove that a hash value $r_\ell$ (where $\ell_1 \ell_2 \ldots \ell_m$ is the binary code of $\ell$) participated in the computation of the root hash $r$, it is sufficient to present all the sibling hashes of the nodes on the unique path from $r_\ell$ to the root $r$. For example, in the left tree of Fig. 2, to prove that $r_{01}$ belongs to the tree, one has to present the hashes $r_{00}$ and $r_1$ that enable us to compute $r_0 = h(\underline{r_{00}}, r_{01})$ and $r = h(r_0, \underline{r_1})$. Hash chains are defined as follows [4]:

**Definition 5 (Hash-Chain).** *A hash-link from $x$ to $r$ (where $x, r \in \{0,1\}^n$) is a pair $(s, b)$, where $s \in \{0,1\}^n$ and $b \in \{0,1\}$, such that either $b = 0$ and $r = h(x\|s)$, or $b = 1$ and $r = h(s\|x)$. A hash-chain from $x$ to $r$ is a (possibly empty) list $c = ((s_1, b_1), \ldots, (s_m, b_m))$, such that either $c = ()$ and $x = r$; or there is a sequence $x_0, x_1, \ldots, x_m$ of hash values, such that $x = x_0$, $r = x_m$, and $(s_i, b_i)$ is a hash-link from $x_{i-1}$ to $x_i$ for every $i \in \{1, \ldots, m\}$. We denote by $x \overset{c}{\rightsquigarrow} r$ the proposition that $c$ is a hash chain from $x$ to $r$. Note that $x \overset{()}{\rightsquigarrow} x$ for every $x \in \{0,1\}^n$. By the shape $\ell(c)$ of $c$ we mean the $m$-bit string $b_m b_{m-1} \ldots b_2 b_1$.*

**Hash-Tree Keyless Signature Schemes.** The signing (time-stamping) procedure runs as follows. During every time unit $t$ (e.g. one second) the server receives a list $\mathfrak{X}_t = (x_1, \ldots, x_m)$ of requests ($n$-bit hash values) from clients, computes the root hash value $r_{(t)} = \mathfrak{T}(x_1, \ldots, x_m)$ of a hash tree $\mathfrak{T}$ and publishes $r_{(t)}$ in a public repository $\mathcal{R} = (r_{(1)}, r_{(2)}, \ldots, r_{(t)})$ organized as an append-only list. Each request $x_i$ is then provided with a hash chain $c_i$ (the *signature* for $x_i$) that proves the participation of $x_i$ in the computation of the root hash value $r_{(t)}$. A request $x \in \mathfrak{X}_t$ is said to *precede* another request $x' \in \mathfrak{X}_{t'}$ if $t < t'$. The requests of the same batch are considered simultaneous. In order to verify the hash chain $c_i$ (the signature) of a request $x_i$, one computes the output hash value of $c_i$ (the last hash value $x_m$ in the sequence) and checks whether $x_m = r$.

**Bounded and Unbounded Schemes.** A hash-tree keyless signature (time-stamping) scheme is said to be $C$-bounded, if the shape $\mathcal{S}$ of the hash tree is assumed to be upper-bounded: $|\mathcal{S}| \leq C$ and while verifying a hash chain $c$ it is checked if $\ell(c) \in \mathcal{S}$. A hash-tree keyless signature scheme is $(C, T)$-strongly bounded if it is $C$-bounded and also $|\mathcal{R}| \leq T$.

**Security Against Back-Dating.** Informally, we want that no efficient adversary can *back-date* any request $x$, i.e. first publishing a hash value $r$, and only after that generating a new "fresh" $x$ (not pre-computed by the adversary), and a hash chain $c$, so that $x \overset{c}{\rightsquigarrow} r$. We use the formal security condition from [4] that involves a two-stage back-dating adversary $A = (A_1, A_2)$. The first stage $A_1$ creates a public repository $\mathcal{R}$ of hash values that may be created in an arbitrary way, not necessary by using hash trees. The second stage $A_2$ of $A$ presents a high-entropy $x$ and a hash chain $x \overset{c}{\rightsquigarrow} r$ with $r \in \mathcal{R}$. The high entropy of $x$ is crucial because otherwise $x$ could have been pre-computed or guessed by $A_1$ before $r$ is published and hence $x$ could be in fact older than $r$ and thereby not really back-dated by $A_2$. Therefore, only *unpredictable* adversaries (that produce high-entropy $x$) are considered, i.e. $x$ must be hard to guess for $A_2$ even if the contents of $\mathcal{R}$ and all the internal computations of $A_1$ are known. There are many ways to define unpredictability. We use the so-called *strong unpredictability* [4]:

**Definition 6 ($k$-Strong Unpredictability).** *A back-dating adversary $(A_1, A_2)$ is $k$-strongly unpredictable if the conditional min-entropy $H_\infty[x \mid \mathcal{R}, a]$ of $x$ (back-dated by $A_2$) is at least $k$ bits, i.e. for every input of $A_2$ and for any possible value $x_0$ of $x$, the probability of $x = x_0$ is upper bounded by $\frac{1}{2^k}$.*

**Definition 7 (Security against Back-Dating).** *A hash-tree keyless signature (time-stamping) scheme is $S$-secure against back-dating if for every $t$-time $k$-strongly unpredictable adversary $(A_1, A_2)$ :*

$$\delta = \Pr\left[(\mathcal{R}, a) \leftarrow A_1, (x, c) \leftarrow A_2(\mathcal{R}, a): \ x \overset{c}{\rightsquigarrow} \mathcal{R}, \ \ell(c) \in \mathcal{S}\right] \leq \frac{t}{S} , \qquad (3)$$

*where by $x \overset{c}{\rightsquigarrow} \mathcal{R}$ we mean that $x \overset{c}{\rightsquigarrow} r$ for some $r \in \mathcal{R}$, and $a$ is an advice string that contains possibly useful information that $A_1$ stores for $A_2$.*

In the rest of this paper, we will restrict our back-dating adversaries to be $(n-1)$-strongly unpredictable. This restriction is in practice justified by (i) the time-stamped values $x$ being hashes of much longer documents, containing significant

amounts of new information, and (ii) the cryptographic hash functions suppos-
edly being good entropy extractors [4].

**Existing Security Proofs and Their Tightness.** The tightness of the existing security proofs is summarized in Tab. 1. The proofs of [6,5] use the collision-
resistance assumption and apply only to bounded time-stamping schemes. Their
tightness depends on the capacity $C$. Both proofs are in the form of a reduction:
a $t$-time backdating adversary with success probability $\delta$ is converted to a $t'$-time
collision-finding adversary with success probability $\delta'$. An $n$-bit hash function is
assumed to be $2^{n/2}$-secure, i.e. near to the birthday barrier. The third column of
Tab. 1 presents a formula for the required output size $n$ of the hash function for
the time-stamping scheme to be $2^s$-secure. The last column presents the output
size in a particular case, where $C = 2^{60}$, $T = 2^{32}$, and $s = 100$. Note that $2^{32}$
seconds is about one hundred years. The proof under PrA assumption is from [4].
We see that even though PrA seems to be much stronger than CR, the required
output length is not much smaller. This is because the security loss is linear in
$C$ and not in $\sqrt{C}$ as in the case of the CR assumption. SPrA [4] allows much
more tight security reductions but has not been sufficiently studied yet. We also
see that the random oracle (RO) assumption makes proofs very tight and also
to hold for unbounded schemes. The RO proof for unbounded schemes is from
[4]. The bounded version is proved in this work.

**Security Proofs for Unbounded Schemes.** It is known that neither collision-
resistance [6] nor PrA [4] is sufficient for proving the security of *unbounded* time-
stamping schemes. The only known proof for unbounded schemes [4] uses the
random oracle assumption. In order to move forward in this direction, we first
examine the main ideas of the proofs in the random oracle model and see how
to generalize them for the assumptions weaker than RO.

## 3    Security in the Random Oracle Model

We first show that for bounded schemes the random oracle model enables security
beyond the birthday barrier, i.e. even when using a hash function with $n$ output
bits, the security (against back-dating) we achieve is far beyond $2^{n/2}$.

**Theorem 1.** *If $h : \{0,1\}^{2n} \to \{0,1\}^n$ is a random oracle, then the corresponding $(C,T)$-strongly bounded hash-tree time-stamping schemes are $\frac{2^{n-1}}{CT}$-secure
against $(n-1)$-strongly unpredictable back-dating adversaries.*

*Proof.* Let $A = (A_1, A_2)$ be a $t$-time $(n-1)$-strongly unpredictable adversary
(Def. 6) and with success $\delta$ as defined in (3). Let $t_1$ and $t_2$ be the running times of
$A_1$ and $A_2$, respectively. Considering that $(\mathcal{R}, a) \leftarrow A_1$, and $r \in \mathcal{R}$ is an arbitrary
element of $\mathcal{R}$, let $R_1^r \subseteq \{0,1\}^n$ be the set of all $x$-s so that the $h$-calls performed
by $A_1$ induce a proper shape hash-chain from $x$ to an $r$. Let $R_1 = \cup_{r \in \mathcal{R}} R_1^r$. Note
that $\mathcal{R} \subseteq R_1$, as an empty hash-chain is always induced by any set of $h$-calls.
Note also that $|R_1| \le CT$, because $|\mathcal{R}| \le T$ and $|R_1^r| \le C$ for any $r \in \mathcal{R}$.

Now let $x$ denote the hash-value back-dated by $A_2$. The probability that $x \in R_1$ is upper-bounded by $\frac{|R_1|}{2^{n-1}}$ because $A$ is $(n-1)$-strongly unpredictable. In case of $x \notin R_1$, in order to be successful, $A_2$ has to make additional $h$-calls so that a chain from $x$ to $r \in \mathcal{R}$ is induced. A necessary condition that $A_2$ has to satisfy is that it has to find $x' = x_1' \| x_2'$ such that $x_1' \notin R_1$ or $x_2' \notin R_1$ (this means that $A_1$ did not make $h$-calls with input $x'$), but $h(x') \in R_1$. The probability of this condition does not exceed $t_2 \frac{|R_1|}{2^n}$, hence, considering that $|R_1| \leq CT$, and $t_1 \geq 1$, the overall success probability of $A$ is:

$$\delta \leq \frac{|R_1|}{2^{n-1}} + \left(1 - \frac{|R_1|}{2^{n-1}}\right) t_2 \frac{|R_1|}{2^n} \leq \frac{CT}{2^{n-1}} + t_2 \frac{CT}{2^{n-1}} \leq (1+t_2)\frac{CT}{2^{n-1}} \leq t\frac{CT}{2^{n-1}} .$$

Hence, $\frac{t}{\delta} \geq \frac{2^{n-1}}{CT}$. $\qquad\square$

The next theorem is from [4]. We repeat their proof in order to draw conclusions about why it holds in the RO model but does not in the PrA-environment.

**Theorem 2.** *If $h : \{0,1\}^{2n} \to \{0,1\}^n$ is a random oracle, then the corresponding unbounded hash-tree schemes are $2^{\frac{n-1}{2}}$-secure against $(n-1)$-strongly unpredictable back-dating adversaries.*

*Proof.* Let $A = (A_1, A_2)$ be a $t$-time $(n-1)$-strongly unpredictable adversary (Def. 6). Let $t_1$ and $t_2$ denote the running times of $A_1$ and $A_2$, respectively. Assuming that $(\mathcal{R}, a) \leftarrow A_1$, let $R_1 \subseteq \{0,1\}^n$ be the set of all values of $x$ such that the $h$-calls performed by $A_1$ induce a hash-chain $x \overset{c}{\leadsto} r$ with $r \in \mathcal{R}$. Note that $\mathcal{R} \subseteq R_1$ and we assume without loss of generality that the advice $a$ contains $R_1$.

Let $x$ denote the (back-dated) hash value produced by $A_2$. Due to the strong unpredictability of $A$, we have $\Pr[x \in R_1] \leq \frac{|R_1|}{2^{n-1}}$. If $x \notin R_1$ then $A_2$ has to make $h$-calls that induce a chain $x \leadsto r \in \mathcal{R}$. For that, $A_2$ has to find $x' = x_1' \| x_2'$ such that $x_1' \notin R_1$ or $x_2' \notin R_1$ (i.e. $A_1$ did not make $h$-calls with $x'$), but $h(x') \in R_1$. This happens with probability that does not exceed $t_2 \frac{|R_1|}{2^n}$. Hence, as $|R_1| \leq 2t_1$ and $t_1, t_2 \geq 1$, the success probability of $A$ is $\delta \leq \frac{|R_1|}{2^{n-1}} + \left(1 - \frac{|R_1|}{2^{n-1}}\right)t_2 \frac{|R_1|}{2^n} \leq \frac{2t_1}{2^{n-1}} + \frac{t_1 t_2}{2^{n-1}} \leq \frac{(t_1+t_2)^2}{2^{n-1}} = \frac{t^2}{2^{n-1}}$, and as $\delta^2 \leq \delta \leq \frac{t^2}{2^{n-1}}$, we have $\frac{t}{\delta} \geq 2^{\frac{n-1}{2}}$. $\qquad\square$

The key factor of success of this proof is the ability to define the set $R_1$ and to estimate its size by $|R_1| \leq 2t_1$. In the PrA-type environment where the hash function $H^P$ is not a random oracle, the computable (given the query-sequence $\alpha$) hash chains that lead to the hash values in $\mathcal{R}$ can be constructed via the extractor $\mathcal{E}$. We start applying $\mathcal{E}$ to the elements of $\mathcal{R}$ and after each try $x \leftarrow \mathcal{E}(\alpha, y)$ apply $\mathcal{E}$ also to the right and the left halves of $x$, until we reach $\perp$ in every branch. The problem is that the standard PrA assumption does not guarantee that this iterative procedure will end. The new security condition presented in the next section is motivated by the need to make this iterative extraction-tree generation procedure to end eventually. This means that $\mathcal{E}(\alpha, y) \neq \perp$ is allowed to hold only for a limited number of outputs $y$. This leads to the following new variation of the Pre-Image Awareness security condition.

# 4     Bounded Pre-image Awareness

We show that many known PrA constructions actually satisfy a new stronger security condition called *Bounded Pre-Image Awareness* (BPrA) that assumes the existence of a PrA-extractor $\mathcal{E}$ that is bounded in the sense that for efficiently computable query strings $\alpha$, the number of outputs $y$ for which $\mathcal{E}(y, \alpha) \neq \bot$ does not exceed the number of queries in $\alpha$.

The security proof for unbounded hash-tree schemes turns out to be very tight under BPrA. In order to have $2^s$-security against back-dating, the hash function must have $k = 2s + 4$ output bits, assuming that the security of the hash function is close to the birthday barrier, i.e. that there are no structural weaknesses in the hash function itself. In the case of $s = 100$, this gives $k = 204$.

## 4.1     Formal Security Condition

The BPrA security condition can be formalized as follows. We have to consider the case where the output size of $H^P$ is larger than the input size of $P$. Thus, in the extreme case where $\alpha$ contains all possible $P$-queries, it might be the case that $\mathcal{E}$ is able to determine the inputs of more than $|\alpha|$ of outputs. Hence, instead of requiring the condition $|\{y \colon \mathcal{E}(y, \alpha) \neq \bot\}| \leq |\alpha|$ unconditionally, we require this condition to hold for efficiently computable query-strings $\alpha$.

**Definition 8.** *A function* $H^P \colon \{0,1\}^{2n} \to \{0,1\}^n$ *is S-secure Bounded Pre-Image Aware (BPrA) if it is S-secure PrA, and for any t-time adversary* $\alpha \leftarrow A^P$ *that produces a P-query list* $\alpha$ *the probability that* $|\{y \colon \mathcal{E}(y, \alpha) \neq \bot\}| > |\alpha|$ *does not exceed* $\frac{t^2}{2^n}$, *where* $\mathcal{E}$ *is the extractor from the PrA condition.*

This means that efficient adversaries with oracle access to $P$ can only produce query strings $\alpha$ such that the number of outputs $y$ for which $\mathcal{E}(y, \alpha) \neq \bot$ is bounded by the number of $P$-queries in $\alpha$.

The bound $\frac{t^2}{2^n}$ may seem ad hoc, but this is actually the natural birthday bound, because in case of output collisions that may occur with probability $\frac{t^2}{2^n}$, a single $P$-query in $\alpha$ may contribute to computing several different output values.

## 4.2     Security Proof under BPrA

In order to establish a security proof with measurable tightness, we have to assume a concrete BPrA-security of $H^P$. As BPrA implies PrA and PrA implies Collision Resistance, by using the birthday bound, no hash function with $n$-bit output can be more than $2^{n/2}$-secure BPrA. Therefore, in the next proof, we assume that the security of $H^P$ lies between $2^{n/3}$ and $2^{n/2}$.

**Theorem 3.** *For unbounded time-stamping schemes with* $H^P \colon \{0,1\}^{2n} \to \{0,1\}^n$ *to be S-secure* $(S \leq 2^{\frac{n-1}{2}} - 2)$ *against* $(n-1)$-*strongly unpredictable back-dating adversaries, it is sufficient that the hash function* $H^P$ *is 4S-secure BPrA.*

Procedure ExForest$^{\mathsf{Ex}}$():
$\mathcal{T} := \emptyset$
$N := 2 \times$ "a time bound for $A_1$"
**For all** $r \in \mathcal{R}$ **do**
ExTree$^{\mathsf{Ex}}(r)$ .

Procedure ExTree$^{\mathsf{Ex}}(y)$:
**If** $y \notin \mathcal{T}$ **and** $N > 0$, **then**
$\mathcal{T} := \mathcal{T} \cup \{y\}$
$N := N - 1$
**If** $\bot \neq \mathrm{Ex}(y) = (y_0, y_1)$ **then**
Define $y_0, y_1$ as children of $y$
ExTree$^{\mathsf{Ex}}(y_0)$
ExTree$^{\mathsf{Ex}}(y_1)$ .
**endif**
**endif**

**Fig. 3.** Procedures for extracting the set $\mathcal{T}$ from the published hash database $\mathcal{R}$

*Proof.* Due to the BPrA assumption there exists an efficient bounded extractor $\mathcal{E}$. Let $A^P = (A_1^P, A_2^P)$ be a $(n-1)$-strongly unpredictable back-dating adversary with running time $t$ and success probability $\delta$, such that $\frac{t}{\delta} \leq 2^{\frac{n-1}{2}} - 2$. We construct a PrA-adversary $B^{P,\mathsf{Ex}}$ that first simulates $(\mathcal{R}, a) \leftarrow A_1^P$ so that all its $P$-calls are executed through the P-oracle. Let $\alpha$ be the query string after such simulation.

After that, the adversary builds a hash-forest $\mathcal{T}$ by using the ExForest procedure described in Fig. 3 using the bound $N = 2t$. Due to the boundedness, with probability $1 - \frac{t^2}{2^n}$ the number of non-leaf vertices of $\mathcal{T}$ is bounded by $|\alpha| \leq t_1$ and hence, $|\mathcal{T}| \leq 2t_1 + 1 \leq 2t = N$ and hence, such bound is never applied during the procedure, which means that for all $y \in \mathcal{T}$, the extraction call $\mathcal{E}(y)$ has indeed been performed.

Finally, $B$ simulates $A_2^P$ so that all its $P$ calls are executed through the P-oracle. With probability $\delta$ we obtain a hash value $x$ and a hash chain $c$ such that $x \overset{c}{\leadsto} r$ for some $r \in \mathcal{R}$. Due to the strong unpredictability of $A$, the probability that $x$ coincides with some of the extracted hash values $r_\ell$ is upper bounded by $\frac{2t}{2^{n-1}} = \frac{4t}{2^n}$. Hence, with probability at least $\delta - \frac{t^2}{2^n} - \frac{4t}{2^n}$ we have a hash value $x \notin \mathcal{T}$ and a hash chain $c = \{(c_1, b_1), (c_2, b_2), \ldots, (c_m, b_m)\}$ with output hash value $r \in \mathcal{R} \subseteq \mathcal{T}$. Let $x_0, x_1, \ldots, x_m$ be the intermediate hash values (outputs of hash links) as described in Def. 5. Let $k$ be the smallest index such that $x_{k-1} \notin \mathcal{T}$ but $x_k \in \mathcal{T}$. For such $k$,

$$\begin{cases} \mathsf{H}^P(c_k \| x_{k-1}) = x_k \text{ and } \mathsf{Ex}(x_k) \neq (c_k \| x_{k-1}) \text{ if } b_k = 0 \; ; \\ \mathsf{H}^P(x_{k-1} \| c_k) = x_k \text{ and } \mathsf{Ex}(x_k) \neq (x_{k-1} \| c_k) \text{ if } b_k = 1 \; . \end{cases}$$

The output of $B$ is $(c_k \| x_{k-1})$ if $b_k = 0$ or $(x_{k-1} \| c_k)$ if $b_k = 1$. Hence, $B$ with time $t' \leq 2t$ has success $\delta' \geq \delta - \frac{t^2}{2^n} - \frac{4t}{2^n} = \frac{\delta}{2}\left(2 - \frac{1}{2^{n-1}}\frac{t^2+4t}{\delta}\right)$. Hence,

$$\frac{t'}{\delta'} \leq 4\frac{t}{\delta} \cdot \frac{1}{2 - \frac{1}{2^{n-1}}\frac{t^2+4t}{\delta}} \leq 4\frac{t}{\delta} \cdot \frac{1}{2 - \frac{1}{2^{n-1}}\left(\frac{t}{\delta}+2\right)^2} \leq 4\frac{t}{\delta} \cdot \frac{1}{2 - \frac{1}{2^{n-1}}\left(2^{\frac{n-1}{2}}\right)^2} = 4\frac{t}{\delta} \; .$$

Hence, if $H^P$ is $4S$-secure BPrA, then $\frac{t'}{\delta'} \geq 4S$ and $\frac{t}{\delta} \geq S$, which means that $H^P$ is $S$-secure against strongly unpredictable back-dating adversaries.     □

**Corollary 1.** *Unbounded hash-tree schemes are $2^s$-secure against back-dating if one uses $2^{s+2}$-secure BPrA hash functions with $2s + 4$ output bits.*

This is close to the tightness achieved in the random oracle model. In our example with $s = 100$, we conclude that 204 output bits are sufficient.

# 5  Existing PrA Constructions Are BPrA

We show that blockcipher based MD-hash functions with rate-1 compression functions (such as Davies-Meyer and Miyaguchi-Preneel) of both type I and type II are BPrA. We also show that some compression functions with uncompressing components (such as Shrimpton-Stam [14]) are BPrA.

It is unknown whether a BPrA compression function is sufficient for the Merkle-Damgård construction to be BPrA. We define a new *Unique P-query (UPQ)* property for $H^P$, which as we show, the MD-construction preserves.

## 5.1  Unique P-Query Property (UPQ)

We model the compression function $F^P$ as a boolean (or arithmetic) circuit with $P$-gates. The Merkle-Damgård structure is modeled as a cascade of such circuits. For every input $x$, we define $\alpha_x$ as the set of $P$-queries that the cascade of $F^P$ circuits makes in case of input $x$.

Fox every set $\alpha$ of $P$-queries, we define $H^\alpha$ as a function that is computed exactly like $H^P$, but instead of making $P$-queries, the answers are taken from $\alpha$. Obviously, $H^\alpha$ is only defined for those inputs $x$, for which $\alpha_x \subseteq \alpha$. We denote by $D_\alpha$ the set of all such inputs $x$. This is called the domain of $H^\alpha$. The range $R_\alpha$ is defined as $H^\alpha(D_\alpha)$. Hence, $H^\alpha$ is a function of type $D_\alpha \to R_\alpha$.

**Definition 9.** *A hash function $H^P$ has the unique P-query property (UPQ), if for every set $\alpha$, there is a function $\varphi_\alpha: R_\alpha \to \alpha$, such that for any efficient adversary $\alpha \leftarrow A^P$, the function $\varphi_\alpha$ is injective with overwhelming probability.*

## 5.2  Merkle-Damgård is UPQ-Preserving

We show that if the compression function used in the Merkle-Damgård construction has the UPQ property, then so does the iterated hash function.

**Theorem 4.** *The Merkle-Damgård transform is UPQ-preserving.*

*Proof.* We use the property of the MD-transform that for every input $x \in \{0,1\}^*$ and $\alpha_x \subseteq \alpha$ there is an input $x'$ of the last compression round such that $H^\alpha(x) = F^\alpha(x')$. Hence, $R_\alpha = R_\alpha^H \subseteq R_\alpha^F$. As $F$ is UPQ, there is a (computably injective) function $\varphi_\alpha^F: R_\alpha^F \to \alpha$. We simply define $\varphi_\alpha$ as the restriction of $\varphi_\alpha^F$ to $R_\alpha$. Obviously, $\varphi_\alpha$ is injective if $\varphi_\alpha^F$ is injective.     □

## 5.3  UPQ and PrA Imply BPrA for Honest Extractors

We show that practical PrA constructions that are UPQ are also BPrA, but for this we have to assume that the PrA-extractor for $H^P$ is *honest*:

**Definition 10.** *An extractor $\mathcal{E}$ for $H^P$ is said to be* honest *if for every $y$ and for every query string $\alpha$, it holds that $\mathcal{E}(y, \alpha) \neq \perp$ only if $y \in R_\alpha$, i.e. if there is $x$ such that $H^\alpha(x) = y$. We say that a function $H^P$ is* honest preimage aware *(HPrA) if it is PrA with a honest extractor.*

It is easy to verify that most extractors that have been constructed in the PrA framework (like those in [9]) are honest in this sense. This is because given the output value $y$ and the $P$-query string $\alpha$, the extractors (e.g. in [9]) mostly traverse $\alpha$ in order to find suitable $P$-queries that together lead to $y$, and only in that case, output the corresponding input $x$. The practical extractors never try to just guess $x$ and hope for being lucky. Note that the notion of honesty defined in [9] is somewhat weaker than in Def. 10 and requires $H^P(x) = y$ instead of $H^\alpha(x) = y$, but it is easy to see that the extractors in [9] satisfy the stronger version too.

Formally we can construct functions $H^P$ that may be PrA in the general sense but not PrA when the extractor is required to be honest by Def. 10. For example, in constructions like $H^P(x) = P(x) \oplus P(x+1) \oplus P(x+1)$ if $(x, P(x)) \in \alpha$ but $(x+1, P(x+1)) \notin \alpha$ then honest extractors on input $y = P(x)$ are forced to output $\perp \leftarrow \mathcal{E}(y, \alpha)$ because $y \notin R_\alpha$. To avoid such dummy oracle queries, we may assume that the constructions $H^P$ have the property that once $y \notin R_\alpha$, for every $x$ the probability $\mathsf{Pr}_{P \leftarrow \Omega|\alpha}[H^P(x) = y]$ is negligible, where $\Omega \mid \alpha$ denotes the probability space of all $P$-oracles consistent with $\alpha$. This means that whenever $y$ is not an output that can (formally) be computed from an input $x$ with the query string $\alpha$ then there are no inputs $x$ that will lead to $y$ with high probability and hence cannot be guessed by dishonest extractors.

**Theorem 5.** *If $H^P$ is UPQ and HPrA then it is BPrA.*

*Proof.* If $H^P$ is HPrA then there is a honest PrA-extractor $\mathcal{E}$. Hence, for every $\alpha$ that is produced by an efficient adversary, $\{y : \mathcal{E}(y, \alpha) \neq \perp\} \subseteq R_\alpha$. Hence, by the UPQ property as $R_\alpha \hookrightarrow \alpha$, we have $|\{y : \mathcal{E}(y, \alpha) \neq \perp\}| \leq |R_\alpha| \leq |\alpha|$.  □

Hence, to show that a Merkle-Damgård hash function is BPrA, it is sufficient to show that its compression function satisfies UPQ. In the following, we show that many hash functions that have been proved to be PrA are actually BPrA.

## 5.4  The Type-I and Type-II Compression Functions Are BPrA

We prove that the rate-1 blockcipher-based hash functions that have been proved to be PrA [9] are UPQ, which by Thm. 5 means that they are also BPrA.

**Theorem 6.** *The rate-1 block-cipher based Type-I and Type-II compression functions are UPQ.*

*Proof.* Assume that $H^P$ is a rate-1 block-cipher based compression function that is either of Type-I or Type-II. In both cases, the function $C_{\text{pre}}$ is bijective and has an inverse-function $C_{\text{pre}}^{-1}$ that transforms a pair $(x, k)$ (as input of an $E$-query) to the input $(m, v)$ of the compression function $H^P$.

Let $\alpha$ be any $P$-query string that consists of ideal cipher calls in the form $(x_i, k_i, y_i)$, where $y_i = E_{k_i}(x_i)$, or equivalently $x_i = E_{k_i}^{-1}(y_i)$. We define a function $\varphi_\alpha$ as follows. For any given output $w \in R_\alpha$, the function $\varphi_\alpha(w)$ returns the first query $(x_i, k_i, y_i)$ in $\alpha$, such that $C_{\text{post}}(C_{\text{pre}}^{-1}(x_i, k_i), y_i) = w$. Such a query must exist because of $w \in R_\alpha$. Therefore, $\varphi_\alpha$ is correctly defined.

If $\varphi_\alpha(w) = (x, k, y) = \varphi_\alpha(w')$ for some $w, w' \in R_\alpha$, then by the definition of $\varphi_\alpha$, we have $w' = C_{\text{post}}(C_{\text{pre}}^{-1}(x_i, k_i), y_i) = w$, which means $\varphi_\alpha$ is injective.     $\square$

Consequently, the Davies-Meyer, the Matyas-Meyer-Oseas, and the Miyaguchi-Preneel compression functions as well as many others are UPQ. Due to the fact that these constructions are HPrA, we conclude based on Thm. 5 that all Type-I and iterated Type-II constructions are BPrA.

## 5.5   Shrimpton-Stam Is BPrA

The Shrimpton-Stam [14] compression function $F^P \colon \{0,1\}^n \times \{0,1\}^n \to \{0,1\}^n$ involves independent random oracles $f_1$, $f_2$ and $f_3$ of type $\{0,1\}^n \to \{0,1\}^n$:

$$F^P(c, x) = f_3(f_1(x) \oplus f_2(c)) \oplus f_1(x) \ .$$

**Theorem 7.** *The Shrimpton-Stam compression function is BPrA.*

*Proof.* We define the mapping $\varphi$ as follows to show that Shrimpton-Stam compression function is UPQ. For any query string $\alpha$ and any input $y \in R_\alpha = F^\alpha(D_\alpha)$ we search from $\alpha$ an $f_3$-query $(z_3; y_3) \in \alpha$ for which there exists an $f_1$-query $(x_1; y_1) \in \alpha$ such that $y = y_3 \oplus y_1$ and an $f_2$-query $(c; y_2)$ such that $y_1 \oplus y_2 = z_3$. There must be such a query because of $y \in R_\alpha$. We define $\varphi(y)$ as the first such $f_3$-query in $\alpha$. Now, if $\varphi(y) = (z_3; y_3) = \varphi(y')$, then there are $f_1$-queries $(x_1; y_1)$ and $(x_1'; y_1')$ such that $y = y_3 \oplus y_1$ and $y' = y_3 \oplus y_1'$, and $f_2$-queries $(c; y_2)$ and $(c'; y_2')$ such that $y_1 \oplus y_2 = z_3$ and $y_1' \oplus y_2' = z_3$. But then

$$f_1(x_1) \oplus f_2(c) = f_1(x_1') \oplus f_2(c') \ , \tag{4}$$

which is hard to satisfy for efficient adversaries, because this is equivalent of finding collisions for the Dodis-Pietrzak-Punyia (DPP) compression function $H^{f_1,f_2}(m, v) = f_1(m) \oplus f_2(v)$ [8] which is about $2^{n/4}$-secure collision-free.     $\square$

Note that the DPP compression function itself is not UPQ, because knowing only five $P$-queries, say $y_1 = f_1(m_1)$, $y_2 = f_1(m_2)$, $y_3 = f_1(m_3)$, $y_1' = f_2(v_1)$, and $y_2' = f_2(v_2)$ allows one to compute six different outputs of $H^{f_1,f_2}$.

# References

1. Bayer, D., Haber, S., Stornetta, W.-S.: Improving the efficiency and reliability of digital timestamping. In: Sequences II: Methods in Communication, Security, and Computer Sci., pp. 329–334. Springer, Heidelberg (1993)
2. Bellare, M., Rogaway, P.: Random oracles are practical: a paradigm for designing efficient protocols. In: The 1st ACM Conference on Computer and Communications Security: CCS 1993, pp. 62–73. ACM (1993)
3. Bellare, M., Rogaway, P.: The exact security of digital signatures - How to sign with RSA and Rabin. In: Maurer, U.M. (ed.) EUROCRYPT 1996. LNCS, vol. 1070, pp. 399–416. Springer, Heidelberg (1996)
4. Buldas, A., Laanoja, R.: Security proofs for hash tree time-stamping using hash functions with small output size. In: Boyd, C., Simpson, L. (eds.) ACISP 2013. LNCS, vol. 7959, pp. 235–250. Springer, Heidelberg (2013)
5. Buldas, A., Niitsoo, M.: Optimally tight security proofs for hash-then-publish time-stamping. In: Steinfeld, R., Hawkes, P. (eds.) ACISP 2010. LNCS, vol. 6168, pp. 318–335. Springer, Heidelberg (2010)
6. Buldas, A., Saarepera, M.: On provably secure time-stamping schemes. In: Lee, P.J. (ed.) ASIACRYPT 2004. LNCS, vol. 3329, pp. 500–514. Springer, Heidelberg (2004)
7. Canetti, R., Goldreich, O., Halevi, S.: The random oracle methodology, revisited. JACM 51(4), 557–594 (2004)
8. Dodis, Y., Pietrzak, K., Puniya, P.: A new mode of operation for block ciphers and length-preserving MACs. In: Smart, N. (ed.) EUROCRYPT 2008. LNCS, vol. 4965, pp. 198–219. Springer, Heidelberg (2008)
9. Dodis, Y., Ristenpart, T., Shrimpton, T.: Salvaging Merkle-Damgård for practical applications. In: Joux, A. (ed.) EUROCRYPT 2009. LNCS, vol. 5479, pp. 371–388. Springer, Heidelberg (2009)
10. Haber, S., Stornetta, W.-S.: How to time-stamp a digital document. Journal of Cryptology 3(2), 99–111 (1991)
11. Luby, M.: Pseudorandomness and Cryptographic Applications. Princeton University Press, Princeton (1996)
12. Merkle, R.C.: Protocols for public-key cryptosystems. In: Proceedings of the 1980 IEEE Symposium on Security and Privacy, pp. 122–134 (1980)
13. Preneel, B., Govaerts, R., Vandewalle, J.: Hash functions based on block ciphers: A synthetic approach. In: Stinson, D.R. (ed.) CRYPTO 1993. LNCS, vol. 773, pp. 368–378. Springer, Heidelberg (1994)
14. Shrimpton, T., Stam, M.: Building a collision-resistant compression function from non-compressing primitives. In: Aceto, L., Damgård, I., Goldberg, L.A., Halldórsson, M.M., Ingólfsdóttir, A., Walukiewicz, I. (eds.) ICALP 2008, Part II. LNCS, vol. 5126, pp. 643–654. Springer, Heidelberg (2008)
15. Stam, M.: Blockcipher-based hashing revisited. In: Dunkelman, O. (ed.) FSE 2009. LNCS, vol. 5665, pp. 67–83. Springer, Heidelberg (2009)

# Verifiable Computation in Multiparty Protocols with Honest Majority

Peeter Laud[1] and Alisa Pankova[1,2,3]

[1] Cybernetica AS, Estonia
[2] Software Technologies and Applications Competence Centre (STACC), Estonia
[3] University of Tartu, Estonia

**Abstract.** We present a generic method for turning passively secure protocols into protocols secure against covert attacks. The method adds a post-execution verification phase to the protocol that allows a misbehaving party to escape detection only with negligible probability. The execution phase, after which the computed protocol result is already available for parties, has only negligible overhead added by our method. The checks, based on linear probabilistically checkable proofs, are done in zero-knowledge, thereby preserving the privacy guarantees of the original protocol. Our method is inspired by recent results in verifiable computation, adapting them to multiparty setting and significantly lowering their computational costs for the provers.

**Keywords:** Secure multiparty computation, Verifiable computation, Linear PCP.

## 1 Introduction

Any multiparty computation can be performed in a manner that the participants only learn their own outputs and nothing else [24]. While the generic construction is expensive in computation and communication, the result has sparked research activities in secure multiparty computation (SMC), with results that are impressive both performance-wise [9, 11, 17, 20], as well as in the variety of concrete problems that have been tackled [10, 14, 16, 21]. From the start, two kinds of adversaries — passive and active — have been considered in the construction of SMC protocols, with highest performance and the greatest variety achieved for protocol sets secure only against passive adversaries.

Verifiable computation (VC) [22] allows a weak client to outsource a computation to a more powerful server that accompanies the computed result with a proof of correct computation, the verification of which by the client is cheaper than performing the computation itself. VC could be used to strengthen protocols secure against passive adversaries — after executing the protocol, the parties could prove to each other that they have correctly followed the protocol. If the majority of the parties are honest (an assumption which is made also by the most efficient SMC protocol sets secure against passive adversaries), then the resulting protocol would satisfy a strong version of *covert security* [2], where any

S.S.M. Chow et al. (Eds.): ProvSec 2014, LNCS 8782, pp. 146–161, 2014.
© Springer International Publishing Switzerland 2014

deviations from the protocol are guaranteed to be discovered and reported. Unfortunately, existing approaches to VC have a large computational overhead for the server/prover. Typically, if the computation is represented as an arithmetic circuit $C$, the prover has to perform $\Omega(|C|)$ public-key operations in order to ensure its good behaviour, as well as to protect its privacy.

In this paper we show that in the multiparty context, with an honest majority, these public-key operations are not necessary. Instead, the verifications can be done in distributed manner, in a way that provides the same security properties. For this, we apply the ideas of existing VC approaches based on linear probabilistically checkable proofs (PCPs) [25], and combine them with linear secret sharing, which we use also for commitments. We end up with a protocol transformation that makes the executions of any protocol (and not just SMC protocols) verifiable afterwards. Our transformation commits the randomness (this takes place offline), inputs, and the communication of the participants. The commitments are cheap, being based on digital signatures and not adding a significant overhead to the execution phase. The results of the protocol are available after the execution. The verification can take place at any time after the execution; dedicated high-bandwidth high-latency communication channels can be potentially used for it. The verification itself is succinct. The proof is generated in $O(|C| \log |C|)$ field operations, but the computation is local. The generation of challenges costs $O(1)$ in communication and $O(|C|)$ in local computation.

We present our protocol transformation as a functionality in the universal composability (UC) framework. After reviewing related work in Sec. 2, we describe the ideal functionality in Sec. 3 and its implementation in Sec. 5. Before the latter, we give an overview of the existing building blocks we use in Sec. 4. The computational overhead of our transformation is estimated in Sec. 6.

Besides increasing the security of SMC protocols, our transformation can be used to add verifiability to other protocols. In Sec. 7 we demonstrate how a verifiable secret sharing (VSS) scheme can be constructed. We compare it with state-of-the-art VSS schemes and find that despite much higher genericity, our construction enjoys similar complexity.

## 2    Related Work

The property brought by our protocol transformation is similar to security against *covert* adversaries [2] that are prevented from deviating from the prescribed protocol by a non-negligible chance of getting caught. A similar transformation, applicable to protocols of certain structure, was introduced by Damgård et al. [18]. Compared to their transformation, ours is more general, has lower overhead in the execution phase, and is guaranteed to catch the deviating parties. Our transformation can handle protocols, where some of the results are made available to the computing parties already before the end of the protocol; this may significantly lower the protocol's complexity [10]. A good property of their construction is its black-box nature, which our transformation does not have. Hence different transformations may be preferable in different situations.

There have been many works dedicated to short verifications of solutions to NP-complete problems. Probabilistically checkable proofs [1] allow to verify a possibly long proof by querying a small number of its bits. Micali [31] has presented *computationally sound proofs*, where the verification is not perfect, and the proof can be forged, but it is computationally hard to do. Kilian [26] proposed interactive probabilistically checkable proofs using bit commitments. A certain class of *linear* probabilistically checkable proofs [25], allows to make argument systems much simpler and more general.

In computation verification, the prover has to prove that, given valuations of certain wires of a circuit, there exists a correct valuation of all the other wires such that the computation is correct with respect to the given circuit. Verifiable computation can in general be based not only on the PCP theorem. In [22], Yao's garbled circuits [37] are executed using fully homomorphic encryption. Quadratic span programs for boolean circuits and quadratic arithmetic programs for arithmetic circuits without PCP have first been proposed in [23], later extended to PCP by [6], and further optimized and improved in [5,29,32]. Particular implementations of verifiable computations have been done for example in [5,32,35].

The goal of our transformation is to provide security against a certain form of active attackers. SMC protocols secure against active attackers have been known for a long time [15,24]. SPDZ [19,20] is probably the SMC protocol set secure against active adversaries with currently the best online performance, achieved through extensive offline precomputations. Similarly to several other protocol sets, SPDZ provides only a minimum amount of protocols to cooperatively evaluate an arithmetic circuit. We note that very recently, a form of post-execution verifiability has been proposed for SPDZ [4].

# 3   Ideal Functionality

We use the universal composability (UC) framework [13] to specify our verifiable execution functionality. We have $n$ parties (indexed by $[n] = \{1, \ldots, n\}$), where $\mathcal{C} \subseteq [n]$ are corrupted for $|\mathcal{C}| = t < n/2$ (we denote $\mathcal{H} = [n] \backslash \mathcal{C}$). The protocol has $r$ rounds, where the computations of the party $P_i$ on the $\ell$-th round are given by an arithmetic circuit $C_{ij}^{\ell}$ over a field $\mathbb{F}$, computing the $\ell$-th round messages $m_{ij}^{\ell}$ to all parties $j \in [n]$ from the input $x_i$, randomness $r_i$ and the messages $P_i$ has received before (all values $x_i, r_i, m_{ij}^{\ell}$ are vectors over $\mathbb{F}$). We define that the messages received during the $r$-th round comprise the *output of the protocol*. The ideal functionality $\mathcal{F}_{vmpc}$, running in parallel with the environment $\mathcal{Z}$ and the adversary $\mathcal{A}_S$, is given in Fig. 1.

We see that $\mathcal{M}$ is the set of parties actually deviating from the protocol. Our verifiability property is very strong — they *all* will be reported to *all* honest parties. Even if only *some* rounds of the protocol are computed, all the parties that deviated from the protocol in completed rounds will be detected. Also, no honest parties (in $\mathcal{H}$) can be falsely blamed. We also note that if $\mathcal{M} = \emptyset$, then $\mathcal{A}_S$ does not learn anything that a semi-honest adversary could not learn.

---

**In the beginning,** $\mathcal{F}_{vmpc}$ gets from $\mathcal{Z}$ for each party $P_i$ the message (circuits, $i, (C_{ij}^{\ell})_{i,j,\ell=1,1,1}^{n,n,r}$) and forwards them all to $\mathcal{A}_S$. For each $i \in \mathcal{H}$ [resp $i \in \mathcal{C}$], $\mathcal{F}_{vmpc}$ gets (input, $\boldsymbol{x}_i$) from $\mathcal{Z}$ [resp. $\mathcal{A}_S$]. For each $i \in [n]$, $\mathcal{F}_{vmpc}$ randomly generates $r_i$. For each $i \in \mathcal{C}$, it sends (randomness, $i, r_i$) to $\mathcal{A}_S$.
**For each round** $\ell \in [r]$, $i \in \mathcal{H}$ and $j \in [n]$, $\mathcal{F}_{vmpc}$ uses $C_{ij}^{\ell}$ to compute the message $\boldsymbol{m}_{ij}^{\ell}$. For all $j \in \mathcal{C}$, it sends $\boldsymbol{m}_{ij}^{\ell}$ to $\mathcal{A}_S$. For each $j \in \mathcal{C}$ and $i \in \mathcal{H}$, it receives $\boldsymbol{m}_{ji}^{\ell}$ from $\mathcal{A}_S$.
**After $r$ rounds,** $\mathcal{F}_{vmpc}$ sends (output, $\boldsymbol{m}_{1i}^{r}, \ldots, \boldsymbol{m}_{ni}^{r}$) to each party $P_i$ with $i \in \mathcal{H}$. Let $r' = r$ and $\mathcal{B}_0 = \emptyset$.
**Alternatively, at any time** before outputs are delivered to parties, $\mathcal{A}_S$ may send (stop, $\mathcal{B}_0$) to $\mathcal{F}_{vmpc}$, with $\mathcal{B}_0 \subseteq \mathcal{C}$. In this case the outputs are not sent. Let $r' \in \{0, \ldots, r-1\}$ be the last completed round.
**After $r'$ rounds,** $\mathcal{A}_S$ sends to $\mathcal{F}_{vmpc}$ the messages $\boldsymbol{m}_{ij}^{\ell}$ for $\ell \in [r']$ and $i, j \in \mathcal{C}$. $\mathcal{F}_{vmpc}$ defines $\mathcal{M} = \mathcal{B}_0 \cup \{i \in \mathcal{C} \mid \exists j \in [n], \ell \in [r'] : \boldsymbol{m}_{ij}^{\ell} \neq C_{ij}^{\ell}(\boldsymbol{x}_i, r_i, \boldsymbol{m}_{1i}^{1}, \ldots, \boldsymbol{m}_{ni}^{\ell-1})\}$.
**Finally,** for each $i \in \mathcal{H}$, $\mathcal{A}_S$ sends (blame, $i, \mathcal{B}_i$) to $\mathcal{F}_{vmpc}$, with $\mathcal{M} \subseteq \mathcal{B}_i \subseteq \mathcal{C}$. $\mathcal{F}_{vmpc}$ forwards this message to $P_i$.

---

**Fig. 1.** The ideal functionality for verifiable computations

# 4   Building Blocks

Throughout this paper, bold letters $\boldsymbol{x}$ denote vectors, where $x_i$ denotes the $i$-th coordinate of $\boldsymbol{x}$. Concatenation of $\boldsymbol{x}$ and $\boldsymbol{y}$ is denoted by $(\boldsymbol{x}\|\boldsymbol{y})$, and their scalar product by $\langle \boldsymbol{x}, \boldsymbol{y} \rangle$, which is defined (only if $|\boldsymbol{x}| = |\boldsymbol{y}|$) as $\langle \boldsymbol{x}, \boldsymbol{y} \rangle = \sum_{i=1}^{|\boldsymbol{x}|} x_i y_i$.

Our implementation uses a number of previously defined subprotocols and algorithm sets.

**Message Transmission.** For message transmission between parties, we use functionality $\mathcal{F}_{tr}$ [18], which allows one to prove to third parties which messages one received during the protocol, and to further transfer such revealed messages. Our definition of $\mathcal{F}_{tr}$ differs from Damgård et al.'s [18] $\mathcal{F}_{transmit}$ by supporting the forwarding of received messages, as well as broadcasting as a part of the outer protocol. The definition of the ideal functionality of $\mathcal{F}_{tr}$ is shown in Fig. 2. The real implementation of the transmission functionality is built on top of signatures. This makes the implementation very efficient, as hash trees allow several messages (sent in the same round) to be signed with almost the same computation effort as a single one [30], and signatures can be verified in batches [12]. An implementation of $\mathcal{F}_{tr}$ is given in the full version of this paper [28].

**Shamir's Secret Sharing.** For commitments, we use $(n,t)$ Shamir secret sharing [36], where any $t$ parties are able to recover the secret, but less than $t$ are not. By sharing a *vector* $\boldsymbol{x}$ over $\mathbb{F}$ into vectors $\boldsymbol{x}^1, \ldots, \boldsymbol{x}^n$ we mean that each $i$-th entry $x_i \in \mathbb{F}$ of $\boldsymbol{x}$ is shared into the $i$-th entries $x_i^1 \in \mathbb{F}, \ldots, x_i^n \in \mathbb{F}$ of $\boldsymbol{x}^1, \ldots, \boldsymbol{x}^n$. In this way, for each $T = \{i_1, \ldots, i_t\} \subseteq [n]$, the entries can be restored as $x_i = \sum_{j=1}^{t} b_{Tj} x_i^{i_j}$ for certain constants $b_{Tj}$, and hence $\boldsymbol{x} = \sum_{j=1}^{t} b_{Tj} \boldsymbol{x}^{i_j}$. The linearity extends to scalar products: if a vector $\boldsymbol{\pi}$ is shared to $\boldsymbol{\pi}^1, \ldots, \boldsymbol{\pi}^n$, then for any vector $\boldsymbol{q}$ and $T = \{i_1, \ldots, i_t\}$, we have $\sum_{j=1}^{t} b_{Tj} \langle \boldsymbol{\pi}^{i_j}, \boldsymbol{q} \rangle = \langle \boldsymbol{\pi}, \boldsymbol{q} \rangle$.

$\mathcal{F}_{tr}$ works with unique message identifiers $mid$, encoding a sender $s(mid) \in [n]$, a receiver $r(mid) \in [n]$, and a party $f(mid) \in [n]$ to whom the message should be forwarded by the receiver (if no forwarding is foreseen then $f(mid) = r(mid)$).

**Secure transmit:** Receiving (transmit, $mid$, $m$) from $P_{s(mid)}$ and (transmit, $mid$) from all (other) honest parties, store $(mid, m, r(mid))$, mark it as undelivered, and output $(mid, |m|)$ to the adversary. If the input of $P_{s(mid)}$ is invalid (or there is no input), and $P_{r(mid)}$ is honest, then output (corrupt, $s(mid)$) to all parties.

**Secure broadcast:** Receiving (broadcast, $mid$, $m$) from $P_{s(mid)}$ and (broadcast, $mid$) from all honest parties, store $(mid, m, \mathsf{bc})$, mark it as undelivered, output $(mid, |m|)$ to the adversary. If the input of $P_{s(mid)}$ is invalid, output (corrupt, $s(mid)$) to all parties.

**Synchronous delivery:** At the end of each round, for each undelivered $(mid, m, r)$ send $(mid, m)$ to $P_r$; mark $(mid, m, r)$ as delivered. For each undelivered $(mid, m, \mathsf{bc})$, send $(mid, m)$ to each party and the adversary; mark $(mid, m, \mathsf{bc})$ as delivered.

**Forward received message:** On input (forward, $mid$) from $P_{r(mid)}$ after $(mid, m)$ has been delivered to $P_{r(mid)}$, and receiving (forward, $mid$) from all honest parties, store $(mid, m, f(mid))$, mark as undelivered, output $(mid, |m|)$ to the adversary. If the input of $P_{r(mid)}$ is invalid, and $P_{f(mid)}$ is honest, output (corrupt, $r(mid)$) to all parties.

**Publish received message:** On input (publish, $mid$) from the party $P_{f(mid)}$ which at any point received $(mid, m)$, output $(mid, m)$ to each party, and also to the adversary.

**Do not commit corrupt to corrupt:** If for some $mid$ both $P_{s(mid)}$, $P_{r(mid)}$ are corrupt, then on input (forward, $mid$) the adversary can ask $\mathcal{F}_{tr}$ to output $(mid, m')$ to $P_{f(mid)}$ for any $m'$. If additionally $P_{f(mid)}$ is corrupt, then the adversary can ask $\mathcal{F}_{tr}$ to output $(mid, m')$ to all honest parties.

**Fig. 2.** Ideal functionality $\mathcal{F}_{tr}$

We note that sharing a value $x$ as $x^1 = \cdots = x^k = x$ is valid, i.e. $x$ can be restored from $x^{i_1}, \ldots, x^{i_t}$ by forming the same linear combination. In our implementation of the verifiable computation functionality, we use such "sharing" for values that end up public due to the adversary's actions.

**Linear PCP** This primitive forms the basis of our verification. Before giving its definition, let us formally state when a protocol is statistically privacy-preserving.

**Definition 1 ($\delta$-private protocol [8]).** *Let $\Pi$ be a multiparty protocol that takes input $\boldsymbol{x}$ from honest parties and $\boldsymbol{y}$ from adversarially controlled parties. The protocol $\Pi$ is $\delta$-private against a class of adversaries $\mathcal{A}$ if there exists a simulator* Sim, *such that for all adversaries $A \in \mathcal{A}$ and inputs $\boldsymbol{x}, \boldsymbol{y}$, $\left| \mathbf{Pr}\left[ A^{\Pi(\boldsymbol{x}, \boldsymbol{y})}(\boldsymbol{y}) = 1 \right] - \mathbf{Pr}\left[ A^{\mathsf{Sim}(\boldsymbol{y})}(\boldsymbol{y}) = 1 \right] \right| \leq \delta$.*

**Definition 2 (Linear Probabilistically Checkable Proof (LPCP) [6]).** *Let $\mathbb{F}$ be a finite field, $\upsilon, \omega \in \mathbb{N}$, $R \subseteq \mathbb{F}^\upsilon \times \mathbb{F}^\omega$. Let $P$ and $Q$ be probabilistic algorithms, and $D$ a deterministic algorithm. The pair $(P, V)$, where $V = (Q, D)$ is a $d$-query $\delta$-statistical HVZK linear PCP for $R$ with knowledge error $\varepsilon$ and query length $m$, if the following holds.*

**Syntax.** *On input $\boldsymbol{v} \in \mathbb{F}^\upsilon$ and $\boldsymbol{w} \in \mathbb{F}^\omega$, algorithm $P$ computes $\boldsymbol{\pi} \in \mathbb{F}^m$. The algorithm $Q$ randomly generates $d$ vectors $\boldsymbol{q}_1, \ldots \boldsymbol{q}_d \in \mathbb{F}^m$ and some state* information $\boldsymbol{u}$. On input $\boldsymbol{v}$, $\boldsymbol{u}$, as well as $a_1, \ldots, a_d \in \mathbb{F}$, the algorithm $D$ accepts or rejects. Let $V^{\pi}(\boldsymbol{v})$ denote the execution of $Q$ followed by the execution of $V$ on $\boldsymbol{v}$, the output $\boldsymbol{u}$ of $Q$, and $a_1, \ldots, a_d$, where $a_i = \langle \pi, \boldsymbol{q}_i \rangle$.

**Completeness.** For every $(\boldsymbol{v}, \boldsymbol{w}) \in R$, the output of $P(\boldsymbol{v}, \boldsymbol{w})$ is a vector $\pi \in \mathbb{F}^m$ such that $V^{\pi}(\boldsymbol{v})$ accepts with probability 1.

**Knowledge.** There exists a knowledge extractor $E$ such that for every vector $\pi^* \in \mathbb{F}^m$, if

$\Pr\left[V^{\pi^*}(\boldsymbol{v}) \text{ accepts}\right] \geq \varepsilon$ then $E(\pi^*, \boldsymbol{v})$ outputs $\boldsymbol{w}$ such that $(\boldsymbol{v}, \boldsymbol{w}) \in R$.

**Honest Verifier Zero Knowledge.** The protocol between an honest prover executing $\pi \leftarrow P(\boldsymbol{v}, \boldsymbol{w})$ and adversarial verifier executing $V^{\pi}(\boldsymbol{v})$ with common input $\boldsymbol{v}$ and prover's input $\boldsymbol{w}$ is $\delta$-private for the class of passive adversaries.

Similarly to different approaches to verifiable computation [5, 6, 23, 29, 32], in our work we let the relation $R$ to correspond to the circuit $C$ executed by the party whose observance of the protocol is being verified. In this correspondence, $\boldsymbol{v}$ is the tuple of all inputs, outputs, and used random values of that party. The vector $\boldsymbol{w}$ extends $\boldsymbol{v}$ with the results of all intermediate computations by that party. Differently from existing approaches, $\boldsymbol{v}$ itself is private. Hence it is unclear how the decision algorithm $D$ can be executed on it. Hence we do not use $D$ as a black box, but build our solution on top of a particular LPCP [5].

The LPCP algorithms used by Ben-Sasson et al. [5] are statistical HVZK. Namely, the values $\langle \pi, \boldsymbol{q}_i \rangle$ do not reveal any private information about $\pi$, unless the random seed $\tau \in \mathbb{F}$ for $Q$ is chosen in a bad way, which happens with negligible probability for a sufficiently large field. In [5], $Q$ generates 5 challenges $\boldsymbol{q}_1, \ldots, \boldsymbol{q}_5$ and the state information $\boldsymbol{u}$ with length $|\boldsymbol{v}| + 2$. Given the query results $a_i = \langle \pi, \boldsymbol{q}_i \rangle$ for $i \in \{1, \ldots, 5\}$ and the state information $\boldsymbol{u} = (u_0, u_1, \ldots, u_{|\boldsymbol{v}|+1})$, the following two checks have to pass:

$$a_1 a_2 - a_3 - a_4 u_{|\boldsymbol{v}|+1} = 0, \tag{$*$}$$
$$a_5 - \langle (1 \| \boldsymbol{v}), (u_0, u_1, \ldots, u_{|\boldsymbol{v}|}) \rangle = 0. \tag{$**$}$$

Here $(*)$ is used to show the existence of $\boldsymbol{w}$, and $(**)$ shows that a certain segment of $\pi$ equals $(1 \| \boldsymbol{v})$ [5]. Throughout this work, we reorder the entries of $\pi$ compared to [5] and write $\pi = (\boldsymbol{p} \| 1 \| \boldsymbol{v})$ where $\boldsymbol{p}$ represents all the other entries of $\pi$, as defined in [5]. The challenges $\boldsymbol{q}_1, \ldots, \boldsymbol{q}_5$ are reordered in the same way.

This linear interactive proof can be converted to a zero-knowledge succinct non-interactive argument of knowledge [6]. Unfortunately, it requires homomorphic encryption, and the number of encryptions is linear in the size of the circuit. We show that the availability of honest majority allows the proof to be completed without public-key encryptions.

The multiparty setting introduces a further difference from [5]: the vector $\boldsymbol{v}$ can no longer be considered public, as it contains a party's private values. We thus have to strengthen the HVZK requirement in Def. 2, making $\boldsymbol{v}$ private to the prover. The LPCP constructions of [5] do not satisfy this strengthened HVZK requirement, but their authors show that this requirement would be satisfied if $a_5$ were not present. In the following, we propose a construction where just the first check $(*)$ is sufficient, so only $a_1, \ldots, a_4$ have to be published. We prove that the second check $(**)$ will be passed implicitly. We show the following.

**Theorem 1.** *Given a $\delta$-statistical HVZK instance of the LPCP of Ben-Sasson et al. [5] with knowledge error $\varepsilon$, any n-party r-round protocol $\Pi$ can be transformed into an n-party $(r + 8)$-round protocol $\Xi$ in the $\mathcal{F}_{tr}$-hybrid model, which computes the same functionality as $\Pi$ and achieves covert security against adversaries statically corrupting at most $t < n/2$ parties, where the cheating of any party is detected with probability at least $(1 - \varepsilon)$. If $\Pi$ is $\delta'$-private against passive adversaries statically corrupting at most $t$ parties, then $\Xi$ is $(\delta' + \delta)$-private against cover adversaries. Under active attacks by at most $t$ parties, the number of rounds of the protocol may at most double.*

Theorem 1 is proved by the construction of the real functionality in the next section, as well as the simulator presented in [28]. In the construction, we use the following algorithms implicitly defined by Ben-Sasson et al. [5]:

- $witness(C, \boldsymbol{v})$: if $\boldsymbol{v}$ corresponds to a valid computation of $C$, returns a witness $\boldsymbol{w}$ such that $(\boldsymbol{v}, \boldsymbol{w}) \in \mathcal{R}_C$.
- $proof(C, \boldsymbol{v}, \boldsymbol{w})$: if $(\boldsymbol{v}, \boldsymbol{w}) \in \mathcal{R}_C$, it constructs a corresponding proof $\boldsymbol{p}$.
- $challenge(C, \tau)$: returns $\boldsymbol{q}_1, \ldots, \boldsymbol{q}_5, \boldsymbol{u}$ that correspond to $\tau$, such that:
  - for any valid proof $\boldsymbol{\pi} = (\boldsymbol{p}\|1\|\boldsymbol{v})$, where $\boldsymbol{p}$ is generated by $proof(C, \boldsymbol{v}, \boldsymbol{w})$ for $(\boldsymbol{v}, \boldsymbol{w}) \in \mathcal{R}_C$, the checks $(*)$ and $(**)$ succeed with probability 1;
  - for any proof $\boldsymbol{\pi}^*$ generated without knowing $\tau$, or such $\boldsymbol{w}$ that $(\boldsymbol{v}, \boldsymbol{w}) \in \mathcal{R}_C$, either $(*)$ or $(**)$ fails, except with negligible probability $\varepsilon$.

## 5   Real Functionality

The protocol $\Pi_{vmpc}$ implementing $\mathcal{F}_{vmpc}$ consists of $n$ machines $M_1, \ldots, M_n$ doing the work of parties $P_1, \ldots, P_n$, and the functionality $\mathcal{F}_{tr}$. The internal state of each $M_i$ contains a bit-vector $mlc_i$ of length $n$ where $M_i$ marks which other parties are acting maliciously. The protocol $\Pi_{vmpc}$ runs in five phases: initialization, execution, message commitment, verification, and accusation.

In the initialization phase, the inputs $\boldsymbol{x}_i$ and the randomness $\boldsymbol{r}_i$ are committed. It is ensured that the randomness indeed comes from uniform distribution. This phase is given in Fig.3. If at any time $(\mathsf{corrupt}, j)$ comes from $\mathcal{F}_{tr}$, each (uncorrupted) $M_i$ writes $mlc_i[j] := 1$ (for each message $(\mathsf{corrupt}, j)$) and goes to the accusation phase.

In the execution phase, the parties run the original protocol as before, just using $\mathcal{F}_{tr}$ to exchange the messages. This is given in Fig.4. If at any time at some round $\ell$ the message $(\mathsf{corrupt}, j)$ comes from $\mathcal{F}_{tr}$ (all uncorrupted machines receive it at the same time), the execution is cut short, no outputs are produced and the protocol continues with the commitment phase.

In the message commitment phase, all the $n$ parties finally commit their sent messages $\boldsymbol{c}_{ij}^\ell$ for each round $\ell \in [r']$ by sharing them to $\boldsymbol{c}_{ij}^{\ell 1}, \ldots, \boldsymbol{c}_{ij}^{\ell n}$ according to $(n, t + 1)$ Shamir scheme. This phase is given in Fig. 5. Let $\boldsymbol{v}_{ij}^\ell = (\boldsymbol{x}_i\|\boldsymbol{r}_i\|\boldsymbol{c}_{1i}^1\| \cdots \|\boldsymbol{c}_{ni}^{\ell-1}\|\boldsymbol{c}_{ij}^\ell)$ be the vector of inputs and outputs to the circuit $C_{ij}^\ell$ that $M_i$ uses to compute the $\ell$-th message to $M_j$. If the check performed by $M_j$ fails, then $M_j$ has received from $M_i$ enough messages to prove its corruptness

---

**Circuits:** $M_i$ gets from $\mathcal{Z}$ the message (circuits, $i$, $(C_{ij}^\ell)_{i,j,\ell=1,1,1}^{n,n,r}$) and sends it to $\mathcal{A}$.
**Randomness generation and commitment:** Let $\mathcal{R} = [t+1]$. For all $i \in \mathcal{R}$, $j \in [n]$, $M_i$ generates $r_{ij}$ for $M_j$. $M_i$ shares $r_{ij}$ to $n$ vectors $r_{ij}^1, \dots, r_{ij}^n$ according to $(n, t+1)$ Shamir scheme. For $j \in [n]$, $M_i$ sends (transmit, (r_share, $i, j, k$), $r_{ij}^k$) to $\mathcal{F}_{tr}$ for $M_k$.
**Randomness approval:** For each $j \in [n] \setminus \{k\}$, $i \in \mathcal{R}$, $M_k$ sends (forward, (r_share, $i$, $j, k$)) to $\mathcal{F}_{tr}$ for $M_j$. Upon receiving ((r_share, $i, j, k$), $r_{ij}^k$) for all $k \in [n]$, $i \in \mathcal{R}$, $M_j$ checks if the shares comprise a valid $(n, t+1)$ Shamir sharing. $M_j$ sets $r_i = \sum_{i \in \mathcal{R}} r_{ij}$.
**Input commitments:** $M_i$ with $i \in \mathcal{H}$ [resp. $i \in \mathcal{C}$] gets from $\mathcal{Z}$ [resp. $\mathcal{A}$] the input $x_i$ and shares it to $n$ vectors $x_i^1, \dots, x_i^n$ according to $(n, t+1)$ Shamir scheme. For each $k \in [n] \setminus \{i\}$, $M_i$ sends to $\mathcal{F}_{tr}$ (transmit, (x_share, $i, k$), $x_i^k$) for $M_k$.
**At any time:** if (corrupt, $j$) comes from $\mathcal{F}_{tr}$, $M_i$ writes $mlc_i[j] := 1$ and goes to the accusation phase.

**Fig. 3.** The real functionality: initialization phase

---

**For each round** $\ell$ the machine $M_i$ computes $c_{ij}^\ell = C_{ij}^\ell(x_i, r_i, c_{1i}^1, \dots, c_{ni}^{\ell-1})$ for each $j \in [n]$ and sends to $\mathcal{F}_{tr}$ the message (transmit, (message, $\ell, i, j$), $c_{ij}^\ell$) for $M_j$.
**After** $r$ **rounds,** uncorrupted $M_i$ sends (output, $c_{1i}^r, \dots, c_{ni}^r$) to $\mathcal{Z}$ and sets $r' := r$.
**At any time:** if (corrupt, $j$) comes from $\mathcal{F}_{tr}$, each (uncorrupted) $M_i$ writes $mlc_i[j] := 1$, sets $r' := \ell - 1$ and goes to the message commitment phase.

**Fig. 4.** The real functionality: execution phase

to others (but Fig. 5 presents an alternative, by publicly agreeing on $c_{ij}^\ell$). After this phase, $M_i$ has shared $v_{ij}^\ell$ among all $n$ parties. Let $v_{ij}^{\ell k}$ be the share of $v_{ij}^\ell$ given to machine $M_k$.

Each $M_i$ generates $w_{ij}^\ell = witness(C_{ij}^\ell, v_{ij}^\ell)$, a proof $p_{ij}^\ell = proof(C_{ij}^\ell, v_{ij}^\ell, w_{ij}^\ell)$, and $\pi_{ij}^\ell = (p_{ij}^\ell \| 1 \| v_{ij}^\ell)$ in the verification phase, as explained in Sec. 4. The vector $p_{ij}^\ell$ is shared to $p_{ij}^{\ell 1}, \dots, p_{ij}^{\ell n}$ according to $(n, t+1)$ Shamir scheme.

All parties agree on a random $\tau$, with $M_i$ broadcasting $\tau_i$ and $\tau$ being their sum. A party refusing to participate is ignored. The communication must be synchronous, with no party $P_i$ learning the values $\tau_j$ from others before he has sent his own $\tau_i$. Note that $\mathcal{F}_{tr}$ already provides this synchronicity. If it were not available, then standard tools (commitments) could be used to achieve fairness.

---

**Message sharing:** As a sender, $M_i$ shares $c_{ij}^\ell$ to $c_{ij}^{\ell 1}, \dots, c_{ij}^{\ell n}$ according to $(n, t + 1)$ Shamir scheme. For each $k \in [n] \setminus \{i\}$, $M_i$ sends to $\mathcal{F}_{tr}$ the messages (transmit, (c_share, $\ell, i, j, k$), $c_{ij}^{\ell k}$) for $M_j$.
**Message commitment:** upon receiving ((c_share, $\ell, i, j, k$), $c_{ij}^{\ell k}$) from $\mathcal{F}_{tr}$ for all $k \in [n]$, the machine $M_j$ checks if the shares correspond to $c_{ij}^\ell$ it has already received. If they do not, $M_j$ sends (publish, (message, $\ell, i, j$)) to $\mathcal{F}_{tr}$, so now everyone sees the values that it has actually received from $M_i$, and each (uncorrupted) $M_k$ should now use $c_{ij}^{\ell k} := c_{ij}^\ell$. If the check succeeds, then $M_i$ sends to $\mathcal{F}_{tr}$ (forward, (c_share, $\ell, i, j, k$)) for $M_k$ for all $k \in [n] \setminus \{i\}$,.

**Fig. 5.** The real functionality: message commitment phase

All (honest) parties generate $q_{1ij}^{\ell}, \ldots, q_{4ij}^{\ell}, q_{5ij}^{\ell}, u_{ij}^{\ell} = challenge(C_{ij}^{\ell}, \tau)$ for $\ell \in [r']$, $i \in [n]$, $j \in [n]$. In the rest of the protocol, only $q_{1ij}^{\ell}, \ldots, q_{4ij}^{\ell}$, and $(u_{ij}^{\ell})_{|v|+1}$ will be actually used.

As a verifier, each $M_k$ computes $\pi_{ij}^{\ell k} = (p_{ij}^{\ell k} \| 1 \| v_{ij}^{\ell k}) = (p_{ij}^{\ell k} \| 1 \| x_i^k \| \sum_{j \in \mathcal{R}} r_{ji}^k \| c_{1i}^{1k} \| \cdots \| c_{ni}^{\ell-1,k} \| c_{ij}^{\ell k})$, and then computes and publishes the values $\langle \pi_{ij}^{\ell k}, q_{1ij}^{\ell} \rangle$, $\ldots, \langle \pi_{ij}^{\ell k}, q_{4ij}^{\ell} \rangle$. $M_i$ checks these values and complains about $M_k$ that has incorrectly computed them. An uncorrupted $M_k$ may disprove the complaint by publishing the proof and message shares that it received. Due to the linearity of scalar product and the fact that all the vectors have been shared according to the same $(n, t+1)$ Shamir sharing, if the $n$ scalar product shares correspond to a valid $(n, t+1)$ Shamir sharing, the shared value is uniquely defined by any $t+1$ shares, and hence by the shares of some $t+1$ parties that are all from $\mathcal{H}$. Hence $M_i$ is obliged to use the values it has committed before. The verification phase for $C_{ij}^{\ell}$ for fixed $\ell \in [r']$, $i \in [n]$, $j \in [n]$ is given in Fig.6. For different $C_{ij}^{\ell}$, all the verifications can be done in parallel.

As described, the probability of cheating successfully in our scheme is proportional to $1/|\mathbb{F}|$. In order to exponentially decrease it, we may run $s$ instances of the verification phase in parallel, since by that time $v_{ij}^{\ell}$ are already committed. This will not break HVZK assumption if fresh randomness is used in $p_{ij}^{\ell}$.

During the message commitment and the verification phases, if at any time $(\mathsf{corrupt}, j)$ comes from $\mathcal{F}_{tr}$, the proof for $P_j$ ends with failure, and all uncorrupted machines $M_i$ write $mlc_i[j] := 1$.

Finally, each party outputs the set of parties that it considers malicious. This short phase is given in Fig. 7.

## 6    Efficiency

In this section we estimate the overheads caused by our protocol transformation. The numbers are based on the dominating complexities of the algorithms of linear PCP of [5]. We omit local addition and concatenation of vectors since it is cheap. The preprocessing phase of [5] is done offline, and can be re-used, so we do not estimate the complexity here. It can be done with practical overhead [5].

Let $n$ be the number of parties, $t < n/2$ the number of corrupt parties, $r$ the number of rounds, $N_g$ the number of gates, $N_w$ the number of wires, $N_x$ the number of inputs (elements of $\mathbb{F}$), $N_r$ the number of random elements of $\mathbb{F}$, $N_c$ the number of communicated elements of $\mathbb{F}$, and $N_i = N_w - N_x - N_r - N_c$ the number of intermediate wires in the circuit; then $|v| = N_x + N_r + N_c$.

Let $\overline{S}(n, k)$ denote the number of field operations used in sharing one field element according to Shamir scheme with threshold $k$, which is at most $nk$ multiplications. We use $\overline{S}^{-1}(n, k)$ to denote the complexity of verifying if the shares comprise a valid sharing and recovering the secret, which is also at most $nk$ multiplications. Compared to the original protocol, for each $M_i$ the proposed solution has the following computation/communication overheads.

**Initialization:** Do Shamir sharing of one vector of length $N_x$ in $N_x \cdot \overline{S}(n, t+1)$ field operations. Transmit $t+1$ vectors of length $N_r$ and one vector of length $N_x$

**Remaining proof commitment:** As the prover, $M_i$ obtains $\boldsymbol{w}_{ij}^\ell$ and $\boldsymbol{\pi}_{ij}^\ell = (\boldsymbol{p}_{ij}^\ell \| 1 \| \boldsymbol{v}_{ij}^\ell)$ using the algorithms *witness* and *proof*. $M_i$ shares $\boldsymbol{p}_{ij}^\ell$ to $\boldsymbol{p}_{ij}^{\ell 1}, \ldots, \boldsymbol{p}_{ij}^{\ell n}$ according to $(n, t+1)$ Shamir scheme. For each $k \in [n] \setminus \{i\}$, it sends to $\mathcal{F}_{tr}$ (transmit, $(\mathsf{p\_share}, \ell, i, j, k), \boldsymbol{p}_{ij}^{\ell k})$ for $M_k$.

**Challenge generation:** Each $M_k$ generates random $\tau_k \leftarrow \mathbb{F}$ and sends to $\mathcal{F}_{tr}$ the message (broadcast, $(\mathsf{challenge\_share}, \ell, i, j, k), \tau_k)$. If some party refuses to participate, its share will just be omitted. The challenge randomness is $\tau = \tau_1 + \ldots + \tau_n$. Machine $M_k$ generates $\boldsymbol{q}_{1ij}^\ell, \ldots, \boldsymbol{q}_{4ij}^\ell, \boldsymbol{q}_{5ij}^\ell, \boldsymbol{u}_{ij}^\ell = challenge(C_{ij}^\ell, \tau)$, then computes $\boldsymbol{\pi}_{ij}^{\ell k} = (\boldsymbol{p}_{ij}^{\ell k} \| 1 \| \boldsymbol{v}_{ij}^{\ell k}) = (\boldsymbol{p}_{ij}^{\ell k} \| 1 \| \boldsymbol{x}_i^k \| \sum_{j \in \mathcal{R}} r_{ji}^k \| c_{1i}^{1k} \| \cdots \| c_{ni}^{\ell-1,k} \| c_{ij}^{\ell k})$, and finally computes and broadcasts $\langle \boldsymbol{\pi}_{ij}^{\ell k}, \boldsymbol{q}_{1ij}^\ell \rangle, \ldots, \langle \boldsymbol{\pi}_{ij}^{\ell k}, \boldsymbol{q}_{4ij}^\ell \rangle$.

**Scalar product verification:** Each $M_i$ verifies the published $\langle \boldsymbol{\pi}_{ij}^{\ell k}, \boldsymbol{q}_{sij}^\ell \rangle$ for $s \in \{1, \ldots, 4\}$. If $M_i$ finds that $M_k$ has computed the scalar products correctly, it sends to $\mathcal{F}_{tr}$ the message (broadcast, $(\mathsf{complain}, \ell, i, j, k), 0)$. If some $M_k$ has provided a wrong value, $M_i$ sends to $\mathcal{F}_{tr}$ (broadcast, $(\mathsf{complain}, \ell, i, j, k), (1, sh_{sij}^{\ell k}))$, where $sh_{sij}^{\ell k}$ is $M_i$'s own version of $\langle \boldsymbol{\pi}_{ij}^{\ell k}, \boldsymbol{q}_{sij}^\ell \rangle$. Everyone waits for a disproof from $M_k$. An uncorrupted $M_k$ sends to $\mathcal{F}_{tr}$ the messages (publish, $mid$) for $mid \in \{(\mathsf{x\_share}, i, k), (\mathsf{r\_share}, 1, i, k), \ldots, (\mathsf{r\_share}, |\mathcal{R}|, i, k), (\mathsf{p\_share}, \ell, i, j, k), (\mathsf{c\_share}, 1, 1, i, k), \ldots, (\mathsf{c\_share}, r', n, i, k), (\mathsf{c\_share}, \ell, i, j, k)\}$. Now everyone may construct $\boldsymbol{\pi}_{ij}^{\ell k}$ and verify whether the version provided by $M_i$ or $M_k$ is correct.

**Final verification:** Given $\langle \boldsymbol{\pi}_{ij}^{\ell k}, \boldsymbol{q}_{sij}^\ell \rangle$ for all $k \in [n]$, $s \in \{1, \ldots, 4\}$, each machine $M_v$ checks if they indeed correspond to valid $(n, t+1)$ Shamir sharing, and then locally restores $a_{sij}^\ell = \langle \boldsymbol{\pi}_{ij}^\ell, \boldsymbol{q}_{sij}^\ell \rangle$ for $s \in \{1, \ldots, 4\}$, and checks $(*)$. If the check succeeds, then $M_v$ accepts the proof of $M_i$ for $C_{ij}^\ell$. Otherwise it immediately sets $mlc_v[i] := 1$.

**Fig. 6.** The real functionality: verification phase

**Finally,** each party $M_i$ sends to $\mathcal{Z}$ the message (blame, $i, \{j \mid mlc_i[j] = 1\}$).

**Fig. 7.** The real functionality: accusation phase

to each other party. Do $t+1$ recoverings in $(t+1) \cdot N_r \cdot \overline{S}^{-1}(n, t+1)$. The parties that generate randomness do $n \cdot N_r \cdot \overline{S}(n, t+1)$ more field operations to compute $n$ more sharings and transmit $n$ more vectors of length $N_r$ to each other party.

**Execution:** No computation/communication overheads, except those caused by the use of the message transmission functionality.

**Message Commitment:** Share all the communication in $rn(n-1) \cdot N_c \cdot \overline{S}(n, t+1)$ operations. Send to each other party $rn$ vectors of length $N_c$. Do $r(n-1)$ recoverings in $r(n-1) \cdot N_c \cdot \overline{S}^{-1}(n, t+1)$ operations.

**Verification:** Compute the proof $\boldsymbol{p}$ of length $(4 + N_g + N_i)$ in $18 N_g + 3 \cdot \overline{FFT}(N_g) + \log N_g + 1$ field operations [5], where $\overline{FFT}(N)$ denotes the complexity of the Fast Fourier Transform which is $c \cdot N \cdot \log N$ for a small constant $c$. Share $\boldsymbol{p}$ in $(4 + N_g + N_i) \cdot \overline{S}(n, t+1)$ operations. Send a vector of length $(4 + N_g + N_i)$ to every other party. Broadcast one field element (the $\tau$). Generate the 4 challenges and the state information in $14 \cdot N_g + \log(N_g)$ field operations [5]. Compute and broadcast 4 scalar products of vectors of length $(5 + N_w + N_g)$

(the shares of $\langle(\boldsymbol{p}\|1\|\boldsymbol{v}), \boldsymbol{q}_s\rangle$). Compute 4 certain linear combinations of $t$ scalar products and do 2 multiplications in $\mathbb{F}$ (the products in $a_1a_2 - a_3 - a_4u$).

Assuming $N_w \approx 2 \cdot N_g$, for the whole verification phase, this adds up to $\approx rn(2 \cdot \overline{S}(n, t+1)N_g + 3\overline{FFT}(2N_g) + 26nN_g)$ field operations, the transmission of $\approx 4rn^2N_g$ elements of $\mathbb{F}$, and the broadcast of $4rn^2$ elements of $\mathbb{F}$ per party.

If there are complaints, then at most $rn$ vectors of length $N_c$ should be published in the message commitment phase, and at most $rn$ vectors of length $(4 + N_g + N_i)$ ($\boldsymbol{p}$ shares), $rn^2$ vectors of length $N_c$ (communication shares), $n \cdot (t + 1)$ vectors of length $N_r$ (randomness shares) and $n$ vectors of length $N_x$ (input shares) in the verification phase (per complaining party).

As long as there are no complaints, the only overheads that $\mathcal{F}_{tr}$ causes is that each message is signed, and each signature is verified.

The knowledge error of the linear PCP of [5] is $\varepsilon = 2N_g/\mathbb{F}$, and the zero knowledge is $\delta$-statistical for $\delta = N_g/\mathbb{F}$. Hence desired error and the circuit size define the field size. If we do not want to use too large fields, then the proof can be parallelized as proposed in the end of Sec. 5.

# 7   Example: Verifiable Shamir Secret Sharing

In this section we show how our solution can be applied to [36], yielding a verifiable secret sharing (VSS) protocol. Any secret sharing scheme has two phases — sharing and reconstruction — to which the construction presented in this paper adds the verification phase.

To apply our construction, we have to define the arithmetic circuits used in [36]. For $i \in \{1, \ldots, n\}$ let $C_i$ be a circuit taking $s, r_1, \ldots, r_t \in \mathbb{F}$ as inputs and returning $s + \sum_{j=1}^{t} r_j i^j$. If $s$ is the secret to be shared, then $C_i$ is the circuit used by the dealer (who is one of the parties $P_1, \ldots, P_n$) to generate the share for the $i$-th party using the randomness $(r_1, \ldots, r_t)$. It computes a linear function, and has no multiplication gates. According to the LPCP construction that we use, each circuit should end with a multiplication. Hence we append a multiplication gate to it, the other argument of which is 1. Let $C$ be the union of all $C_i$, it is a circuit with $1 + t$ inputs and $n$ outputs.

In the reconstruction phase, the parties just send the shares they've received to each other. A circuit computing the messages of this phase is trivial — it just copies its input to output. We note that $\mathcal{F}_{tr}$ already provides the necessary publishing functionality for that. Hence we're not going to blindly follow our VMPC construction, but use this opportunity to optimize the protocol. In effect, this amounts to only verifying the sharing phase of the VSS protocol, and relying on $\mathcal{F}_{tr}$ to guarantee the proper behaviour of parties during the reconstruction. The whole protocol is depicted in Fig. 8.

A couple of points are noteworthy there. First, the reconstruction and verification phases can take place in any order. In particular, verification could be seen as a part of the sharing, making a 3-round protocol (in optimistic case). Second, the activities of the dealer in the sharing phase have a dual role in terms of the VMPC construction. They form both the *input commitment* step in Fig. 3, as well as the execution step for actual sharing.

---

**Preprocessing.** Parties run the *Randomness generation and commitment* and *Randomness approval* steps of Fig. 3, causing the dealer to learn $r_1, \ldots, r_t$. Each $r_i$ is shared as $r_{i1}, \ldots, r_{in}$ between $P_1, \ldots, P_n$.

**Sharing.** Dealer computes the shares $s_1, \ldots, s_n$ of the secret $s$, using the randomness $r_1, \ldots, r_t$ [36], and uses $\mathcal{F}_{tr}$ to send them to parties $P_1, \ldots, P_n$.

**Reconstruction.** All parties use the publish-functionality of $\mathcal{F}_{tr}$ to make their shares known to all parties. The parties reconstruct $s$ as in [36].

**Verification.** The dealer shares each $s_i$, obtaining $s_{i1}, \ldots, s_{in}$. It transmits them all to $P_i$, which verifies that they are a valid sharing of $s_i$ and then forwards each $s_{ij}$ to $P_j$. *[Message commitment]*

The dealer computes $\boldsymbol{w} = witness(C, s, r_1, \ldots, r_t)$ and $\boldsymbol{p} = proof(C, (s, r_1, \ldots, r_t), \boldsymbol{w})$. It shares $\boldsymbol{p}$ as $\boldsymbol{p}_1, \ldots, \boldsymbol{p}_n$ and transmits $\boldsymbol{p}_j$ to $P_j$. *[Proof commitment]*

Each party $P_i$ generates a random $\tau_i \in \mathbb{F}$ and broadcasts it. Let $\tau = \tau_1 + \cdots + \tau_n$. Each party constructs $\boldsymbol{q}_1, \ldots, \boldsymbol{q}_4, \boldsymbol{q}_5, \boldsymbol{u} = challenge(C, \tau)$. *[Challenge generation]*

Each party $P_i$ computes $a_{ji} = \langle (\boldsymbol{p}_i \| 1 \| s_i \| r_{1i} \| \cdots \| r_{ti} \| s_{1i} \| \cdots \| s_{ni}), \boldsymbol{q}_j \rangle$ for $j \in \{1, 2, 3, 4\}$ and broadcasts them. The dealer may complain, in which case $\boldsymbol{p}_i, s_i, r_{1i}, \ldots, r_{ti}, s_{1i}, \ldots, s_{ni}$ are made public and all parties repeat the computation of $a_{ji}$. *[Scalar product verification]*

Each party reconstructs $a_1, \ldots, a_4$ and verifies the LPCP equation $(*)$.

**Fig. 8.** LPCP-based VSS

Ignoring the randomness generation phase (which takes place offline), the communication complexity of our VSS protocol is the following. In sharing phase, $(n-1)$ values (elements of $\mathbb{F}$) are transmitted by the dealer and in the reconstruction phase, each party broadcasts a value. These coincide with the complexity numbers for non-verified secret sharing. In the verification phase, in order to commit to the messages, the dealer transmits a total of $n(n-1)$ values to different parties. The same number of values are forwarded. According to Sec. 6, the proof $\boldsymbol{p}$ contains $t + n + 4$ elements of $\mathbb{F}$. The proof is shared between parties, causing $(n-1)(t+n+4)$ elements of $\mathbb{F}$ to be transmitted. The rest of the verification phase takes place over the broadcast channel. In the optimistic case, each party broadcasts a value in the challenge generation and four values in the challenge verification phase. Hence the total cost of the verification phase is $(n-1)(3n+t+4)$ point-to-point transmissions and $5n$ broadcasts of $\mathbb{F}$ elements.

We have evaluated the communication costs in terms of $\mathcal{F}_{tr}$ invocations, and have avoided estimating the cost of implementing $\mathcal{F}_{tr}$. This allows us to have more meaningful comparisons with other VSS protocols. We will compare our solution to the 4-round statistical VSS of [27], the 3-round VSS of [33], and the 2-round VSS of [3] (see Table 1). These protocols have different security models and different optimization goals, therefore also selecting different methods for securing communication between parties. The number of field elements thus communicated is likely the best indicator of complexity.

**The 4-Round Statistical VSS of [27].** This information-theoretically secure protocol uses an *information checking protocol* (*ICP*) for transmission, which is a modified version of *ICP* introduced in [34]. The broadcast channel is also used.

**Table 1.** Comparing the Efficiency of VSS Protocols ($tr$ transmissions, $bc$ broadcasts)

|          | Rounds | Sharing | Reconstruction | Verification |
|----------|--------|---------|----------------|--------------|
| Ours     | 7      | $(n-1) \cdot tr$ | $n \cdot bc$ | $(3n + t + 4)(n-1) \cdot tr + 5n \cdot bc$ |
| [27]     | 4      | $3n^2 \cdot tr$ | $O(n^2) \cdot tr$ | 0 |
| [33]     | 3      | $2n \cdot tr + (n+1) \cdot bc$ | $2n \cdot bc$ | 0 |
| [3]      | 2      | $4n^2 \cdot tr + 5n^2 \cdot bc$ | $n^2 \cdot bc$ | 0 |

In the protocol, the dealer constructs a symmetric bivariate polynomial $F(x, y)$ with $F(0,0) = s$, and gives $f_i(x) = F(i, x)$ to party $P_i$. Conflicts are then resolved, leaving the honest parties with a polynomial $F^H(x, y)$ that allows the reconstruction of $s$. The distribution takes $3n^2$ transmissions of field elements using the $ICP$ functionality, while the conflict resolution requires $4n^2$ broadcasts (in the optimistic case). The reconstruction phase requires each honest party $P_i$ to send its polynomial $f_i$ to all other parties using the $ICP$ functionality, which again takes $O(n^2)$ transmissions.

**The 3-Round VSS of [33].** Pedersen's VSS is an example of a computationally secure VSS. The transmission functionality of this protocol is based on homomorphic commitments. Although the goal of commitments is also to ensure message delivery and make further revealing possible, they are much more powerful than $\mathcal{F}_{tr}$ and $ICP$, so direct comparison is impossible. In the following, let $Comm(m, d)$ denote the commitment of the message $m$ with the witness $d$. We note that the existence of a suitable $Comm$ is a much stronger computational assumption than the existence of a signature scheme sufficient to implement $\mathcal{F}_{tr}$.

To share $s$, the dealer broadcasts a commitment $Comm(s, r)$ for a random $r$. It shares both $s$ and $r$, using Shamir's secret sharing with polynomials $f$ and $g$, respectively. It also broadcasts commitments to the coefficients of $f$, using the coefficients of $g$ as witnesses. This takes $2n$ transmissions of field elements, and $(n + 1)$ broadcasts (in the optimistic case). Due to the homomorphic properties of $Comm$, the correctness of any share can be verified without further communication. The reconstruction requires the shares of $s$ and $r$ to be broadcast; i.e. there are 2 broadcasts from each party.

**The 2-Round VSS of [3].** This protocol also uses commitments that do not have to be homomorphic. This is still different from $\mathcal{F}_{tr}$ and $ICP$: commitments can ensure that the same message has been transmitted to distinct parties.

The protocol is again based on the use of a symmetric bivariate polynomial $F(x, y)$ with $F(0,0) = s$ by the dealer. The dealer commits to all values $F(x, y)$, where $1 \leq x, y \leq n$ and opens the polynomial $F(i, x)$ for the $i$-th party. The reduction in rounds has been achieved through extra messages committed and sent to the dealer by the receiving parties. These messages can help in conflict resolution. In the optimistic case, the sharing protocol requires $4n^2$ transmissions of field elements and $5n^2$ broadcasts. The reconstruction protocol is similar to [27], with each value of $F(x, y)$ having to be broadcast by one of the parties.

We see that the LPCP-based approach performs reasonably well in verifiable Shamir sharing. The protocols from the related works have less rounds, and the 3-round protocol of [33] has also clearly less communication. However, for a full comparison we would also have to take into account the local computation, since operations on homomorphic commitments are more expensive. Also, the commitments may be based on more stringent computational assumptions than the signature-based communication primitives we are using. We have shown that the LPCP-based approach is at least comparable to similar VSS schemes. Its low usage of the broadcast functionality is definitely of interest.

# 8  Conclusions and Further Work

We have proposed a scheme transforming passively secure protocols to covertly secure ones, where a malicious party can skip detection only with negligible probability. The protocol transformation proposed here is particularly attractive to be implemented on top of some existing, highly efficient, passively secure SMC framework. The framework would retain its efficiency, as the time from starting a computation to obtaining the result at the end of the execution phase would not increase. Also, the overheads of verification, proportional to the number of parties, would be rather small due to the small number of *computing parties* in all typical SMC deployments (the number of *input* and *result parties* [7] may be large, but they can be handled separately).

The implementation would allow us to study certain trade-offs. Sec. 6 shows that the proof generation is still slightly superlinear in the size of circuits, due to the complexity of FFT. Shamir's secret sharing would allow the parties to commit to some intermediate values in their circuits, thereby replacing a single circuit with several smaller ones, and decreasing the computation time at the expense of communication. The usefulness of such modifications, and the best choice of intermediate values to be committed, would probably depend to large extent on the actual circuits.

Note that the verifications could be done after each round. This would give us security against active adversaries in a quite cheap manner, but would incur the overhead of the verification phase during the runtime of the actual protocol. The implementation will allow us to evaluate the usefulness of such transformation.

**Acknowlegements.**  This work has been supported by Estonian Research Council through grant IUT27-1, ERDF through EXCS and STACC, ESF through the ICT doctoral school, and EU FP7 through grant no. 284731 (UaESMC).

# References

1. Arora, S., Safra, S.: Probabilistic Checking of Proofs: A New Characterization of NP. J. ACM 45(1), 70–122 (1998)
2. Aumann, Y., Lindell, Y.: Security against covert adversaries: Efficient protocols for realistic adversaries. J. Cryptology 23(2), 281–343 (2010)
3. Backes, M., Kate, A., Patra, A.: Computational verifiable secret sharing revisited. In: Lee, D.H., Wang, X. (eds.) ASIACRYPT 2011. LNCS, vol. 7073, pp. 590–609. Springer, Heidelberg (2011)

4. Baum, C., Damgård, I., Orlandi, C.: Publicly Auditable Secure Multi-Party Computation. In: Abdalla, M., De Prisco, R. (eds.) SCN 2014. LNCS, vol. 8642, pp. 175–196. Springer, Heidelberg (2014)

5. Ben-Sasson, E., Chiesa, A., Genkin, D., Tromer, E., Virza, M.: SNARKs for C: Verifying Program Executions Succinctly and in Zero Knowledge. In: Canetti, R., Garay, J.A. (eds.) CRYPTO 2013, Part II. LNCS, vol. 8043, pp. 90–108. Springer, Heidelberg (2013)

6. Bitansky, N., Chiesa, A., Ishai, Y., Ostrovsky, R., Paneth, O.: Succinct non-interactive arguments via linear interactive proofs. In: Sahai, A. (ed.) TCC 2013. LNCS, vol. 7785, pp. 315–333. Springer, Heidelberg (2013)

7. Bogdanov, D., Kamm, L., Laur, S., Pruulmann-Vengerfeldt, P.: Secure multi-party data analysis: end user validation and practical experiments. Cryptology ePrint Archive, Report 2013/826 (2013)

8. Bogdanov, D., Laud, P., Laur, S., Pullonen, P.: From Input Private to Universally Composable Secure Multi-party Computation Primitives. In: Proceedings of the 27th IEEE Computer Security Foundations Symposium, pp. 184–198. IEEE (2014)

9. Bogdanov, D., Niitsoo, M., Toft, T., Willemson, J.: High-performance secure multi-party computation for data mining applications. Int. J. Inf. Sec. 11(6), 403–418 (2012)

10. Brickell, J., Shmatikov, V.: Privacy-preserving graph algorithms in the semi-honest model. In: Roy, B. (ed.) ASIACRYPT 2005. LNCS, vol. 3788, pp. 236–252. Springer, Heidelberg (2005)

11. Burkhart, M., Strasser, M., Many, D., Dimitropoulos, X.: SEPIA: Privacy-preserving aggregation of multi-domain network events and statistics. In: USENIX Security Symposium, Washington, DC, USA, pp. 223–239 (2010)

12. Camenisch, J., Hohenberger, S., Pedersen, M.Ø.: Batch verification of short signatures. In: Naor, M. (ed.) EUROCRYPT 2007. LNCS, vol. 4515, pp. 246–263. Springer, Heidelberg (2007)

13. Canetti, R.: Universally composable security: A new paradigm for cryptographic protocols. In: FOCS, pp. 136–145. IEEE Computer Society (2001)

14. Catrina, O., de Hoogh, S.: Secure multiparty linear programming using fixed-point arithmetic. In: Gritzalis, D., Preneel, B., Theoharidou, M. (eds.) ESORICS 2010. LNCS, vol. 6345, pp. 134–150. Springer, Heidelberg (2010)

15. Cramer, R., Damgård, I., Nielsen, J.B.: Multiparty computation from threshold homomorphic encryption. In: Pfitzmann, B. (ed.) EUROCRYPT 2001. LNCS, vol. 2045, pp. 280–299. Springer, Heidelberg (2001)

16. Damgård, I., Fitzi, M., Kiltz, E., Nielsen, J.B., Toft, T.: Unconditionally secure constant-rounds multi-party computation for equality, comparison, bits and exponentiation. In: Halevi, S., Rabin, T. (eds.) TCC 2006. LNCS, vol. 3876, pp. 285–304. Springer, Heidelberg (2006)

17. Damgård, I., Geisler, M., Krøigaard, M., Nielsen, J.B.: Asynchronous Multiparty Computation: Theory and Implementation. In: Jarecki, S., Tsudik, G. (eds.) PKC 2009. LNCS, vol. 5443, pp. 160–179. Springer, Heidelberg (2009)

18. Damgård, I., Geisler, M., Nielsen, J.B.: From passive to covert security at low cost. In: Micciancio, D. (ed.) TCC 2010. LNCS, vol. 5978, pp. 128–145. Springer, Heidelberg (2010)

19. Damgård, I., Keller, M., Larraia, E., Pastro, V., Scholl, P., Smart, N.P.: Practical Covertly Secure MPC for Dishonest Majority – Or: Breaking the SPDZ Limits. In: Crampton, J., Jajodia, S., Mayes, K. (eds.) ESORICS 2013. LNCS, vol. 8134, pp. 1–18. Springer, Heidelberg (2013)

20. Damgård, I., Pastro, V., Smart, N., Zakarias, S.: Multiparty computation from somewhat homomorphic encryption. In: Safavi-Naini, R., Canetti, R. (eds.) CRYPTO 2012. LNCS, vol. 7417, pp. 643–662. Springer, Heidelberg (2012)
21. Franklin, M., Gondree, M., Mohassel, P.: Communication-efficient private protocols for longest common subsequence. In: Fischlin, M. (ed.) CT-RSA 2009. LNCS, vol. 5473, pp. 265–278. Springer, Heidelberg (2009)
22. Gennaro, R., Gentry, C., Parno, B.: Non-interactive verifiable computing: Outsourcing computation to untrusted workers. In: Rabin, T. (ed.) CRYPTO 2010. LNCS, vol. 6223, pp. 465–482. Springer, Heidelberg (2010)
23. Gennaro, R., Gentry, C., Parno, B., Raykova, M.: Quadratic Span Programs and Succinct NIZKs without PCPs. In: Johansson, T., Nguyen, P.Q. (eds.) EUROCRYPT 2013. LNCS, vol. 7881, pp. 626–645. Springer, Heidelberg (2013)
24. Goldreich, O., Micali, S., Wigderson, A.: How to Play any Mental Game or A Completeness Theorem for Protocols with Honest Majority. In: STOC, pp. 218–229. ACM (1987)
25. Ishai, Y., Kushilevitz, E., Ostrovsky, R.: Efficient arguments without short PCPs. In: Twenty-Second Annual IEEE Conference on Computational Complexity, CCC 2007, pp. 278–291. IEEE (2007)
26. Kilian, J.: A note on efficient zero-knowledge proofs and arguments (extended abstract). In: Proceedings of the Twenty-fourth Annual ACM Symposium on Theory of Computing, STOC 1992, pp. 723–732. ACM, New York (1992), http://doi.acm.org/10.1145/129712.129782
27. Kumaresan, R., Patra, A., Rangan, C.P.: The round complexity of verifiable secret sharing: The statistical case. In: Abe, M. (ed.) ASIACRYPT 2010. LNCS, vol. 6477, pp. 431–447. Springer, Heidelberg (2010)
28. Laud, P., Pankova, A.: Verifiable Computation in Multiparty Protocols with Honest Majority. Cryptology ePrint Archive, report 2014/060 (2014)
29. Lipmaa, H.: Succinct non-interactive zero knowledge arguments from span programs and linear error-correcting codes. Cryptology ePrint Archive, report 2013/121 (2013)
30. Merkle, R.C.: Secrecy, authentication, and public key systems. Ph.D. thesis, Stanford University (1979)
31. Micali, S.: CS Proofs (Extended Abstract). In: FOCS, pp. 436–453. IEEE Computer Society (1994)
32. Parno, B., Howell, J., Gentry, C., Raykova, M.: Pinocchio: Nearly practical verifiable computation. In: IEEE Symposium on Security and Privacy, pp. 238–252. IEEE Computer Society (2013)
33. Pedersen, T.P.: Non-interactive and information-theoretic secure verifiable secret sharing. In: Feigenbaum, J. (ed.) CRYPTO 1991. LNCS, vol. 576, pp. 129–140. Springer, Heidelberg (1992)
34. Rabin, T., Ben-Or, M.: Verifiable secret sharing and multiparty protocols with honest majority (extended abstract). In: Johnson, D.S. (ed.) STOC, pp. 73–85. ACM (1989)
35. Setty, S.T.V., Vu, V., Panpalia, N., Braun, B., Blumberg, A.J., Walfish, M.: Taking proof-based verified computation a few steps closer to practicality. In: USENIX Security Symposium (2012)
36. Shamir, A.: How to share a secret. Commun. ACM 22(11), 612–613 (1979)
37. Yao, A.: Protocols for secure computations. In: Proceedings of the 23rd Annual Symposium on Foundations of Computer Science, pp. 160–164 (1982)

# Lossy Trapdoor Relation
# and Its Applications to Lossy Encryption
# and Adaptive Trapdoor Relation*

Haiyang Xue[1,2,3], Xianhui Lu[1,2], Bao Li[1,2], and Yamin Liu[1,2]

[1] Data Assurance and Communication Security Research Center,
Chinese Academy of Sciences, Beijing, China
[2] State Key Laboratory of Information Security, Institute of Information Engineering,
Chinese Academy of Sciences, Beijing, China
[3] University of Chinese Academy of Sciences, Beijing, China
{hyxue12,xhlu,lb,ymliu}@is.ac.cn

**Abstract.** Peikert and Waters proposed the notion of lossy trapdoor function in STOC 2008. In this paper, we propose a relaxation of lossy trapdoor function, called lossy trapdoor relation. Unlike the lossy trapdoor function, lossy trapdoor relation does not require completely recovering the input but a public computable injective map of it. Interestingly, the lossy trapdoor relation maintains the application of lossy trapdoor function on the lossy encryption. Moreover, motivated by the construction of adaptive trapdoor relation proposed by Wee (Crypto 2010), we introduce all-but-one verifiable lossy trapdoor relation which is in fact a relaxation of all-but-one lossy trapdoor function.
  – The lossy trapdoor relation can be constructed from discrete logarithm related assumptions and subgroup membership assumptions efficiently. We also give an efficient construction of all-but-one verifiable lossy trapdoor relation from DLDH assumption over pairing group. As a byproduct, we propose an all-but-one lossy trapdoor function directly based on DLDH assumption which partially solve the open problem of Freeman *et al.* (PKC 2010).
  – The lossy trapdoor relation has a direct application to the lossy encryption and we propose new lossy encryptions based on three subgroup membership assumptions. The all-but-one verifiable lossy trapdoor relation can be used to construct adaptive trapdoor relation, which derives chosen ciphertext secure encryption.

**Keywords:** Lossy trapdoor relation, Lossy trapdoor functions, Lossy encryption, Adaptive trapdoor relation.

# 1 Introduction

Peikert and Waters [20] proposed the notion of lossy trapdoor function (LTDF) in STOC 2008. LTDF implies cryptographic primitives such as one-way trapdoor

* Supported by the National Basic Research Program of China (973 project)(No.2013CB338002), the National Nature Science Foundation of China (No.61070171, No.61272534).

S.S.M. Chow et al. (Eds.): ProvSec 2014, LNCS 8782, pp. 162–177, 2014.

function [4], collision resistant hash function [8], oblivious transfer protocol [9], chosen ciphertext secure public key encryption scheme[20], deterministic public key encryption scheme [2], OAEP based public key encryption scheme [13], and selective opening secure public key encryption scheme [11]. LTDFs can be constructed based on many assumptions[20] [5] [13] [24] [21], especially lattice-based assumption [20].

Peikert and Waters [20] proposed a construction of LTDF, based on the Decisional Diffie-Hellman (DDH) assumption over a group of prime order $p$. But the construction is inefficient since it requires a function index of size $\mathcal{O}(n^2)$ where $n$ is greater than $\log p$. Boyen et al. [3] shrank the function index of the DDH-based construction from $\mathcal{O}(n^2)$ to $\mathcal{O}(n)$ with common reference string and pairing. But their method can only be applied to bilinear groups and their algorithm requires computing pairing, which is an expensive operation. Freeman et al. [5], [6] proposed a construction based on the $d$-linear assumption which is a generalization of the DDH assumption. This construction is inefficient either since the size of the function index is $\mathcal{O}(n^2)$ where $n$ is greater than $d \log p$. Both constructions use the ElGamal encryption variant, and the input are embedded into the exponents of group elements. In order to recover the input, only one bit (or a few bits) can be embedded into one group element. And $n$ should be large enough in order to make lossiness.

Freeman et al. [5], [6] proposed an efficient LTDF based on the decisional composite residuosity (DCR) assumption over $Z_{N^s}^*$, for $s \geq 3$. The underlying technique is that, given the factorization of $N$, the subgroup discrete logarithm (SDL) problem (given $(1+N)^x y^{N^{s-1}} \bmod N^s$ to compute $x$) is easy. Xue et al. [24] shown a generic framework of DCR-based LTDF based on subgroup membership assumption with two special requirements. Let $G = KL$ and $(G, L)$ be the instance of subgroup membership assumption. The first requirement is that $K$'s order must be significantly larger than $L$'s order in order to make lossiness. The second requirement is that the subgroup discrete logarithm problem is solvable with a trapdoor. The second requirement is too strong such that only DCR [18] and Higher Residue [15] assumptions have this property.

But some cryptographic primitives do not require the recovering of the input, such as the key encapsulation mechanism. We consider the relaxation of LTDF, lossy trapdoor relation, which does not require the recovering of the input but a public computable injective map of it. We also investigate whether the lossy trapdoor relation maintains the applications of LTDF, such as lossy encryption and adaptive trapdoor relation.

## 1.1  Our Contribution

In this paper, we propose a relaxation of lossy trapdoor function, called lossy trapdoor relation (LR). Our institution is that the decapsulation algorithm of key encapsulation mechanism dose not require completely recovering the random string but the encapsulated key which is a function of the random string. The lossy trapdoor relation, unlike the lossy trapdoor function, does not require completely recovering the input but a public computable injective map of it.

Interestingly, the lossy trapdoor relation maintains the application of lossy trapdoor function on the lossy encryption. Moreover, motivated by the construction of adaptive trapdoor relation, we introduce all-but-one (ABO) verifiable lossy trapdoor relation (VLR) which is a relaxation of all-but-one LTDF. In the following, we explain our result in details.

**Lossy Trapdoor Relation and Verifiable Lossy Trapdoor Relation.** LTDFs require that, in the injective model, on input the trapdoor $t$ and $F(x)$, there is an inverse algorithm to compute $x$. Lossy trapdoor relations relax this requirement: on input the trapdoor $t$ and $F(x)$, there is an inverse algorithm to compute $H(x)$, where $H$ is a public computable injective function. $(H(x), F(x))$ is the binary relation here. In the key encapsulation mechanism, we only need to encapsulate an random string, but not to recover the it. This relaxation fulfills the functionality requirement of the key encapsulation mechanism.

Wee [22] proposed the notion of adaptive trapdoor relation $(H(x), f(x))$. An adaptive trapdoor relation is one that, given challenge $f^*(x^*)$, it remains difficult to compute $H^*(x^*)$ even if the adversary is given access to an inverse algorithm to compute $H(x)$, except that the adversary cannot query the oracle on the challenge. Motivated by the construction of adaptive trapdoor relation, we introduce all-but-one verifiable lossy trapdoor relation. Given an all-but-one lossy trapdoor relation $G_{lr}(x)$, the inverse algorithm needs only to compute $H(x)$ instead of the input $x$. Given the trapdoor $t, H(x)$ and $G_{lr}(y)$, there is an efficient algorithm $Ver$ to check that if $G_{lr}(x) = G_{lr}(y)$ or not.

**Efficient Constructions of LR and VLR.** There are efficient constructions of LRs based on the DDH and $d$-linear assumptions. Since there is no requirement to compute discrete logarithm over prime order group $G$, $\log |G|$ bits can be embedded into the exponent of one group element. The LRs based on DDH and $d$-linear assumptions contain only constant number of group elements. We also propose a generic construction of LR based on subgroup membership assumption without the requirement of subgroup discrete logarithm property. But we require that the generators of subgroups must be public.

We propose efficient all-but-one VLR based on DLDH assumption over pairing group. Although there is generic construction of all-but-one LTDF from LTDF in [20], and thus all-but-one LTDF from $d$-linear assumption, the direct construction of all-but-one LTDF from $d$-linear assumption ($d > 1$) is unknown. Freeman et al. [5] pointed out that it is not easy to construct all-but-one LTDF from $d$-linear assumption directly for $d \geq 2$, and left this as an open problem. The main obstacle is the reduction of hidden lossy branch property to the discrete logarithm assumption. In our construction, we apply the lossy tag to submatrix, and it is feasible to reduce the hidden lossy branch property to the discrete logarithm assumption. As a byproduct, we give an all-but-one LTDF directly based on DLDH assumption and partially solve the open problem.

**Lossy Encryption and Adaptive Trapdoor Relation.** The lossy trapdoor relation maintains the lossy encryption application of LTDF. These LRs above derives efficient constructions of lossy encryptions based on discrete logarithm related assumptions and subgroup membership assumption. The lossy encryption based on DDH assumption is less efficient than that proposed by [1]. The main difference is that, in our construction, we extract lost randomness by hash function and then encrypt message, while the one in [1] use the lossiness directly. By instantiating the subgroup membership assumption, our generic construction derives three new efficient lossy encryptions.

We also give the construction of adaptive trapdoor relation from verifiable LR and all-but-one VLR. One example of adaptive trapdoor relation is given based on DLDH assumption over pairing group. Our result gives new insight of the adaptive trapdoor relation.

## 1.2 Outline

This paper is organized as follows. In Sect. 2, we introduce the notations and recall two definitions. In Sect. 3, we present the concept of lossy trapdoor relation. In Sect. 4, we present concrete constructions of lossy trapdoor relation and all-but-one verifiable lossy trapdoor relation based on the number theory assumptions. In Sect. 5, we show lossy encryption based on lossy trapdoor relation. In Sect. 6, we give the adaptive trapdoor relation from all-but-one verifiable lossy trapdoor relation. In Sect. 7, we conclude this paper.

## 2  Preliminaries

### 2.1  Definitions

**Definition 1 (Lossy Encryption).** *A lossy encryption scheme is a tuple of probability polynomial time (PPT) algorithms* $(Gen_{inj}, Gen_{loss}, Enc, Dec)$.

$Gen_{inj}$ *Output injective keys* $(pk, sk)$. *The private key space is* $\mathcal{K}$.
$Gen_{loss}$ *Output lossy keys* $(pk_{loss}, \bot)$.
**Enc** $\mathcal{M} \times \mathcal{R} \to \mathcal{C}$. *The message space is* $\mathcal{M}$. *The random string space is* $\mathcal{R}$ *and the ciphertext space is* $\mathcal{C}$.
**Dec** $\mathcal{K} \times \mathcal{C} \to \mathcal{M}$.

*These algorithms satisfy the following properties:*

1. *Correctness. For all* $m \in \mathcal{M}$ *and* $r \in \mathcal{R}$, $Dec(sk, Enc(pk, m, r)) = m$.
2. *Indistinguishability of injective keys from lossy keys. The injective and lossy public keys are computationally indistinguishable.*

$$\{pk|(pk, sk) \leftarrow Gen_{inj}\} =_c \{pk|(pk, \bot) \leftarrow Gen_{loss}\}$$

3. *Lossiness of encryption with lossy keys. For any lossy public key* $pk_{loss}$, *and any pair of message* $m_0, m_1 \in \mathcal{M}$, *there is*

$$\{Enc(pk_{loss}, m_0, r))|r \in \mathcal{R}\} =_s \{Enc(pk_{loss}, m_1, r))|r \in \mathcal{R}\}$$

We recall the definition of adaptive trapdoor relation given by Wee [22] here.

**Definition 2 (Adaptive Trapdoor Relations).** *A family of tag based adaptive trapdoor relations is a family of algorithms $(TDG, F_{ID}, F_{ID}^{-1})$ that satisfies the following properties:*

**Trapdoor Generation** $TDG$. *It outputs a random $(ID, Td, H)$, where $ID$ is the function index, $Td$ is the trapdoor and $H$ is an injective map.*

**Public Evaluation** $F_{ID}$. *On input $(ID, H)$, $TAG$ and a random number $r$, it computes $(H(r), f_{ID}(TAG, r))$, where $(H(r), f_{ID}(TAG, r))$ is the so called relation.*

**Inversion** $F_{ID}^{-1}$. *For all $(ID, Td, H)$, $TAG$ and $y = F_{ID}(TAG, r)$, it computes $F_{ID}^{-1}(Td, TAG, F_{ID}(TAG, r))) = H(r)$*

*The above algorithms should satisfy the adaptive one-way property, i.e., for all PPT adversary $A$ the following probability is negligible:*

$$Pr\left[s = s' : \begin{array}{l} TAG^* \leftarrow A(1^k); (ID, Td) \leftarrow TDG(1^k); \\ (s, y) \leftarrow F_{ID}(TAG^*, r, H)); s' \leftarrow A^{F_{ID}^{-1}(Td, \cdot, \cdot)} \end{array}\right],$$

*where $A$ is allowed to query $F_{ID}^{-1}(Td, \cdot, \cdot)$ on any tag except $TAG^*$.*

## 3　Lossy Trapdoor Relation

In this section, we propose the definition of lossy trapdoor relation and all-but-one verifiable lossy trapdoor relation.

**Informal Description.** A collection of lossy trapdoor relations consists of two families of functions. Functions in the first mode are injective, while functions in the second are lossy, meaning that the size of their image is significantly smaller than the size of their preimage. Functions $\{F_{lr}\}$ in two modes are indexed by function index $\{\sigma\}$. The main relaxation is that: in both modes the evaluation algorithm, on input $x$, compute the function $F_{lr}(\sigma, x)$ and the injective map $H(x)$; in the injective mode, given the trapdoor, the inverse algorithm computes $H(x)$ instead of $x$. In fact, the evaluation algorithm is a sample algorithm for binary relation $(H(x), F_{lr}(\sigma, x))$ here.

**Definition 3 (Lossy Trapdoor Relation).** *A collection of $(m, l)$-lossy trapdoor relations is a 4-tuple of PPT algorithms $(S_{inj}, S_{loss}, F_{lr}, F_{lr}^{-1})$ such that:*

1. Sample injective mode $S_{inj}(1^n)$. *On input security parameters, it outputs a triple $(\sigma, \tau, H) \in \{0,1\}^* \times \{0,1\}^* \times \{0,1\}^*$ where $\sigma$ is a function index, $\tau$ is a trapdoor, and $H$ is a public computable injective map.*
2. Sample lossy mode $S_{loss}(1^n)$. *On input security parameters, it outputs a function index $\sigma \in \{0,1\}^*$ and a public computable injective map $H$.*
3. Evaluation algorithm $F_{lr}$. *For every function index $\sigma$ produced by either $S_{loss}$ or $S_{inj}$, the algorithm $F_{lr}(\sigma, \cdot)$ computes a function $f_\sigma : \{0,1\}^m \to \{0,1\}^*$ and a public computable injective map $H : \{0,1\}^m \to D$ with one of the two following modes:*

– *Lossy: If $\sigma$ is produced by $S_{loss}$, then the size of the image of $f_\sigma$ is at most $2^{m-l}$.*
– *Injective: If $\sigma$ is produced by $S_{inj}$, then the function $f_\sigma$ is injective.*
4. Decapsulation algorithm $F_{lr}^{-1}$. *For every pair $(\sigma, \tau)$ produced by $S_{inj}$ and every $f = f_\sigma(x)$ for some $x \in \{0,1\}^m$, it computes $F_{lr}^{-1}(\tau, f) = H(x)$.*

*In the above algorithms, the two ensembles $\{\sigma, \sigma \leftarrow S_{loss}(1^n)\}$ and $\{\sigma, (\sigma, \tau) \leftarrow S_{inj}(1^n)\}$ are computationally indistinguishable.*

*Remark 1.* We do not require that the injective map $H(\cdot)$ here is invertible even given the trapdoor. It is actually the lossy trapdoor function if $H(\cdot)$ is invertible given the trapdoor. The lossy trapdoor function is a lossy trapdoor relation associated with $H(\cdot)$ being the identity map.

Motivated by the construction of the adaptive trapdoor relation, we propose the definition of all-but-one verifiable lossy trapdoor relation. In the adaptive trapdoor relation, the challenger should provide the decryption oracle and should check the *well-formedness* of the queried ciphertext. We add the all-but-one and verifiable property in the lossy trapdoor relation in order to provide the functionality of verification.

**Definition 4 (All-but-one Verifiable Lossy Trapdoor Relation).** *A collection of $(m, l)$-all-but-one lossy trapdoor functions is a 5-tuple of PPT algorithms $(ABOB, ABOGen, G_{lr}, G_{lr}^{-1}, Ver)$ such that:*

1. Sample a branch $ABOB$. *On input $1^n$, it outputs a value $b^* \in \{0,1\}^*$.*
2. Sample a function $ABOGen$. *For every value $b^*$ produced by $ABOB$, the algorithm outputs a tuple $(\sigma, \tau, \beta, H) \in \{0,1\}^* \times \{0,1\}^* \times \{0,1\}^* \times \{0,1\}^*$ where $\sigma$ is a function index, $\tau$ is a trapdoor, $\beta$ is a set of lossy branch, and $H$ is a public computable injective map.*
3. Evaluation algorithm $G_{lr}$. *For any $b$ and $b^*$ produced by $ABOB$, every $\sigma$ produced by $ABOGen$, it computes a function $f_{\sigma,b} : \{0,1\}^m \rightarrow \{0,1\}^*$ and an injective map $H : \{0,1\}^m \rightarrow D$ with one of the two following modes:*
   – *Lossy: If $b = b^*$, then the size of the image of $f_{\sigma,b}$ is at most $2^{m-l}$.*
   – *Injective: If $b \notin \beta$, then the function $f_{\sigma,b}$ is injective.*
4. Decapsulation algorithm $G_{lr}^{-1}$. *For any $b$ and $b^*$ produced by $ABOB$, trapdoor $\tau$ and $f_{\sigma,b}(x)$, it extracts $H(x)$. For every $x \in \{0,1\}^m$, it holds that,*

$$G_{lr}^{-1}(\tau, b, f_{\sigma,b}(x)) = H(x).$$

5. Verification algorithm $Ver$. *For any $(H(x), f_{\sigma,b}(y)) \in D \times \{0,1\}^*$, it output 1 if $f_{\sigma,b}(y) = f_{\sigma,b}(x)$ and 0 otherwise. This is a public verification of the binary relation $(H(x), f_{\sigma,b}(x))$.*

– *In the above algorithms, the two ensembles $\{\sigma, (\sigma, \tau, \beta) \leftarrow ABOGen(1^n, b)\}$ and $\{\sigma, (\sigma, \tau, \beta) \leftarrow ABOGen(1^n, b^*)\}$ are computationally indistinguishable.*
– *Any PPT algorithm $A$ that receives an input $(\sigma, b^*)$, where $b^* \leftarrow ABOB(1^n)$ and $(\sigma, \tau, \beta) \leftarrow G(1^n, b^*)$, has only a negligible probability of outputting an element $b \in \beta \setminus \{b^*\}$. We call this the hidden lossy branch property.*

*Remark 2.* The all-but-one lossy trapdoor function is an all-but-one verifiable lossy trapdoor relation.

# 4    Instantiation of LR and All-But-One VLR

In this section, we first propose the lossy trapdoor relations from the DDH, $d$-linear and subgroup membership assumptions and then give an all-but-one verifiable lossy trapdoor relation from DLDH assumption over pairing group.

## 4.1    Instantiation of LR

### DDH Based Lossy Trapdoor Relation

We use the "matrix encryption" mechanism proposed by Peikert and Waters in [20]. We just use the simple version of the $2 \times 2$ matrix encryption. In the lossy model, the first column and second column compose a DDH tuple, first and third column compose another DDH tuple. The image of function is decide by $r_1 x_1 + r_2 x_2 \mod p$, which is at most $p$. In the injective model, the first column and second column compose an ElGamal like encryption, first and third column compose another ElGamal like encryption.

**Definition 5 (DDH Assumption).** *Let $g$ be the generator of $G$, $g_1, g_2, g_3$ are chosen randomly in $G$. $g_1 = g^{r_1}, g_2 = g^{r_2}$ and $g_3 = g^{r_3}$. The problem of deciding whether $r_3 = r_1 r_2$ or not is the DDH problem and the DDH assumption asserts that the DDH problem is hard.*

We define $LR_{DDH}$ as 4-tuple of PPT algorithms $(S_{inj}, S_{loss}, F_{lr}, F_{lr}^{-1})$.

1. *Sample injective mode $S_{inj}$.* On input $1^n$, it chooses a cyclic group $G = <g>$ with order $p$. It samples random $r_1, r_2, s_1, s_2 \in Z_p$. The function index is

$$c = \begin{pmatrix} g^{r_1}, & g^{r_1 s_1} g, & g^{r_1 s_2} \\ g^{r_2}, & g^{r_2 s_1}, & g^{r_2 s_2} g \end{pmatrix}.$$

   The trapdoor is $t = (s_1, s_2)$. The injective map is $H : (x_1, x_2) \in Z_p^2 \mapsto (g^{x_1}, g^{x_2})$.

2. *Sample lossy mode $S_{loss}$.* On input $1^n$, it chooses a cyclic group $G = <g>$ with order $p$. It samples random $r_1, r_2, s_1, s_2 \in Z_p$. The function index is

$$c = \begin{pmatrix} g^{r_1}, & g^{r_1 s_1}, & g^{r_1 s_2} \\ g^{r_2}, & g^{r_2 s_1}, & g^{r_2 s_2} \end{pmatrix}.$$

   The injective map is $H : (x_1, x_2) \in Z_p^2 \mapsto (g^{x_1}, g^{x_2})$.

3. *Evaluation algorithm $F_{lr}$.* Given a function index $c = (c_{ij})_{2 \times 3}$ and the input $x = (x_1, x_2) \in Z_p^2$ the algorithm outputs the function $f(x) = (c_{11}^{x_1} c_{21}^{x_2}, c_{12}^{x_1} c_{22}^{x_2}, c_{13}^{x_1} c_{23}^{x_2})$ and $H(x) = (g^{x_1}, g^{x_2})$.

4. *Decapsulation algorithm $F_{lr}^{-1}$.* Given the trapdoor $t = (s_1, s_2)$ and the vector $f = (f_1, f_2, f_3)$, it computes $h = (f_2/f_1^{s_1}, f_3/f_1^{s_2})$.

**Theorem 1.** *Under the DDH assumption, $LR_{DDH}$ is a $(2 \log p, \log p)$-lossy trapdoor relation.*

*Proof.* By Lemma 3.1 in [20], the matrix encryption of $I_{2\times 2}$ and $0_{2\times 2}$ are computationally indistinguishable under DDH assumption. Thus, the function indexes in two modes are computationally indistinguishable under DDH assumption. The decapsulation algorithm computes $f_2/f_1^{s_1} = g^{x_1+r_1s_1x_1+r_2s_1x_2}/g^{s_1(r_1x_1+r_2x_2)} = g^{x_1}$ and $f_3/f_1^{s_2} = g^{x_2+r_1s_2x_1+r_2s_2x_2}/g^{s_2(r_1x_1+r_2x_2)} = g^{x_2}$. The correctness of decapsulation algorithm holds. In the lossy mode, the function image is decided by $x_1r_1 + x_2r_2 \mod p$, the image size is at most $p$.    □

**$d$-Linear Based Lossy Trapdoor Relation.** In the following, we generalize the construction above to the LR based on $d$-linear assumption. We will use the notation and method in [5]. We denote the finite field of $p$ elements by $F_p$ and the set of $n \times n$ matrices of rank $k$ by $Rk_k(F_p^{n\times n})$ $(1 \leq k \leq n)$. For a group $G$ of order $p$, an element $g \in G$ and a vector $\vec{x} = (x_1, \cdots, x_n) \in F_p^{n\times n}$, let $g^{\vec{x}} = (g^{x_1}, \cdots, g^{x_n})$. For an $n\times n$ matrix $M = (m_{ij})$ over $F_p^{n\times n}$, let $g^M = (g^{m_{ij}})$, and $(g_1, \cdots, g_n)^M = (\prod_{j=1}^n g_j^{m_{1j}}, \cdots, \prod_{j=1}^n g_j^{m_{nj}})$. For a matrix $S = (g_{ij}) \in G^{n\times n}$ and a vector $\vec{x} = (x_1, \cdots, x_n) \in F_p^{n\times n}$, let $S^{\vec{x}} = (\prod_{j=1}^n g_{1j}^{x_j}, \cdots, g_{nj}^{x_j})$. It satisfies that

$$(g^M)^{\vec{x}} = g^{M\vec{x}} = (g^{\vec{x}})^M.$$

We recall the $d$-linear assumption here. And the 2-linear assumption is also known as the Decision Linear assumption (DLDH).

**Definition 6 ($d$-linear Assumption).** *Let $g$ be the generator of $G$ with order $p$ and $d \geq 2$ be an integer. We say that the $d$-linear assumption holds in $G$ if the distributions*

$$\{(g_1, \cdots, g_d, g_1^{r_1}, \cdots, g_d^{r_d}, g^{r_1+\cdots+r_d}) : g_1 \cdots, g_d \leftarrow G, r_1 \cdots, r_d \leftarrow Z_p\},$$

$$\{(g_1, \cdots, g_d, g_1^{r_1}, \cdots, g_d^{r_d}, g^s) : g_1 \cdots, g_d \leftarrow G, r_1 \cdots, r_d, s \leftarrow Z_p\},$$

*are computationally indistinguishable.*

We define $LR_{d\text{-linear}}$ as 4-tuple of PPT algorithms $(S_{inj}, S_{loss}, F_{lr}, F_{lr}^{-1})$.

1. *Sample injective mode $S_{inj}$.* On input $1^n$, it chooses a cyclic group $G = <g>$ with order $p$. It samples a random matrix $M \in Rk_n(F_p^{n\times n})$. The function index is $S = g^M$. The trapdoor is $t = M^{-1}$. The injective map is $H : F_P^n \to G^n$.
2. *Sample lossy mode $S_{loss}$.* On input $1^n$, it chooses a cyclic group $G = <g>$ with order $p$. It samples a random matrix $M \in Rk_d(F_p^{n\times n})$. The function index is $S = g^M$. The injective map is $H : F_P^n \to G^n$.
3. *Evaluation algorithm $F_{lr}$.* Given a function index $\sigma = c$ and the input $\vec{x} \in F_p^n$, the algorithm outputs the function $f(x) = S^{\vec{x}}$ and $H(x) = g^{\vec{x}}$.
4. *Decapsulation algorithm $F_{lr}^{-1}$.* Given the trapdoor $t = M^{-1}$ and the vector $f = (f_1, \cdots, f_n)$, it computes $h = f^t$.

**Theorem 2.** *Under the $d$-linear assumption, $LR_{d\text{-linear}}$ is an $(n\log p, (n-d)\log p)$-lossy trapdoor relation for $n > d$.*

## Subgroup Membership Assumption (SMA) Based LR

**Definition 7 (Subgroup Membership Assumption [7]).** *Let $G$ be a finite cyclic group with subgroup $K$ and $L$, such that $G = KL$ and $K \cap L = \{1\}$. The subgroup membership problem $SM_{(G,L)}$ asserts that, for any PPT distinguisher $D$, the advantage*

$$Adv_D^{SM_{(G,L)}} = |\Pr[A(G, L, x) = 1|x \leftarrow L] - \Pr[A(G, L, x) = 1|x \leftarrow G \setminus L]|.$$

*is negligible, where the probability is taken over coin tosses.*

Xue et al. [24] proposed generic constructions of LTDFs based on SMA with two special requirements. The first requirement is that $K$'s order must be significantly larger than $L$'s order. The second requirement is that the subgroup discrete logarithm problem is solvable with a trapdoor. The second requirement is so strong that only DCR [18] and Higher Residue [15] assumptions have this property.

In order to construct lossy trapdoor relation, we do not require subgroup discrete logarithm property, but we require that generators for both subgroup $K$ and $L$ must be public. Let $k$(resp. $l$) be a generator of group $K$ (resp. $L$). The lossy trapdoor relation based on subgroup membership assumption follows. We define $LR_{SMA}$ as 4-tuple of PPT algorithms $(S_{inj}, S_{loss}, F_{lr}, F_{lr}^{-1})$.

1. *Sample injective mode $S_{inj}$.* On input $1^n$, it chooses a random $r \in Z_{|L|}$ and computes $c := kl^r$. The function index is $\sigma = (G, k, l, c)$. The trapdoor is $t = (|L|, |K|)$ and the injective map is $H : x \in Z_{|K|} \mapsto k^x$.
2. *Sample lossy mode $S_{loss}$.* On input $1^n$, it chooses a random $r \in Z_{|L|}$ and computes $c := l^r$. The function index is $\sigma = (G, k, l, c)$, and the injective map is $H : x \in Z_{|K|} \mapsto k^x$.
3. *Evaluation algorithm $F_{lr}$.* Given a function index $\sigma = (N, k, l, c)$ and input $x \in Z_{|K|}$, the algorithm outputs $z = c^x$ and injective map $H(x) = k^x$.
4. *Decapsulation algorithm $F_{lr}^{-1}$.* Given a function index $(N, k, l, c)$, the trapdoor $t = (t_1, t_2)$ and a message $z$, the algorithm computes and outputs $(z^{t_1})^{t_2}$.

**Theorem 3.** *Under the subgroup membership assumption with generators being public, $LR_{SMA}$ is an $(\log|K|, \log|K| - \log|L|)$-lossy trapdoor relation for $n \geq d$.*

### 4.2   VLR from DLDH over Pairing Group

Freeman et al. [5] noted that it is not easy to construct all-but-one LTDF from $d$-linear assumption for $d \geq 2$ and left it as an open problem. The main obstacle is the reduction of hidden lossy branch property to the discrete logarithm assumption. In our construction, we apply the lossy tag to submatrix, and it is feasible to reduce the hidden lossy branch property to the discrete logarithm assumption. The all-but-one verifiable lossy trapdoor relation $ABOLR_{DLDH} = (ABOB, ABOGen, G_{lr}, G_{lr}^{-1}, Ver)$ is constructed below:

1. *Sample a branch ABOB.* On input $1^n$, it outputs a uniformly distributed $b^* \in F_p$.
2. *Sample a function ABOGen.* On input a lossy branch $b^*$, it chooses a cyclic pairing group $G = <g>$ with order $p$. It samples random matrix $M \in Rk_2(F_p^{3\times3})$. Denote $\begin{bmatrix} 0 & 0 \\ 0 & I_{2\times2} \end{bmatrix}$ by $I^*$, where $I_{2\times2}$ is the identity matrix. Let $A = (a_{ij}) = M - b^*I^*$ The function index is

$$S = (s_{ij}) = \begin{pmatrix} g^{a_{11}}, g^{a_{12}}, g^{a_{13}} \\ g^{a_{21}}, g^{a_{22}}, g^{a_{23}} \\ g^{a_{31}}, g^{a_{32}}, g^{a_{33}} \end{pmatrix}.$$

The trapdoor is $t = A$. The injective map is $H : Z_p^3 \rightarrow G^3$.
3. *Evaluation algorithm $G_{lr}$.* Given a function index $\sigma = S$ and the input $x \in Z_p^3$, the algorithm outputs the function $f(x) = S^x(g^{bI^*})^x$ and $H(x) = (g^{x_1}, g^{x_2}, g^{x_3})$.
4. *Decapsulation algorithm $G_{lr}^{-1}$.* Given the trapdoor $t = A$ and the vector $f = (f_1, f_2, f_3)$, it computes $H = f^{(A+bI^*)^{-1}}$.
5. *Verification algorithm $Ver(S, b, h, f)$.* Given input $S = (s_{ij})$, $h = (h_1, h_2, h_3)$, $b \in F_p$, and $f = (f_1, f_2, f_3)$, the algorithm checks that

$$e(f_1, g) \overset{?}{=} e(s_{11}, h_1)e(s_{21}, h_2)e(s_{31}, h_3);$$

$$e(f_2, g) \overset{?}{=} e(s_{12}, h_1)e(s_{22}g^b, h_2)e(s_{32}, h_3);$$

$$e(f_3, g) \overset{?}{=} e(s_{13}, h_1)e(s_{23}, h_2)e(s_{33}g^b, h_3).$$

It outputs 1 if all the tests are passed, 0 otherwise.

**Theorem 4.** *Under the DLDH assumption, $ABOLR_{DLDH}$ is a $(3\log p, \log p)$-all-but-one verifiable lossy trapdoor relation.*

*Proof.* The lossy property and indistinguishability of two modes are guaranteed by the DLDH assumption. We need to prove the verifiability property. Assume that $h = H(x)$ for some $x \in Z_p^3$ and $f = (f_1, f_2, f_3) = f(y)$ for some $y \in Z_p^3$. The verification algorithm computes

$$e(f_i, g) = e(g^{a_{1i}y_1}g^{a_{2i}y_2}g^{a_{3i}y_3}, g)$$
$$= e(g^{a_{1i}}, g^{y_1})e(g^{a_{2i}}, g^{y_2})e(g^{a_{3i}}, g^{y_3}).$$

If $f(x) = f(y)$, all the tests are passed, otherwise the tests are not passed.

Now, we need only to prove the hidden lossy branch property. For a random chosen matrix $M = (m_{ij}) \in F_p^{3\times3}$, $m_{11} \neq 0$ with probability $1 - \frac{1}{p}$. Assume that $m_{11} \neq 0$ in the following. Apply Gaussian elimination algorithm on the first column of $M$ and get $\begin{pmatrix} m_{11}, & m_{12}, & m_{13} \\ 0, & m_{22} - \frac{m_{21}m_{12}}{m_{11}}, & m_{23} - \frac{m_{21}m_{13}}{m_{11}} \\ 0, & m_{32} - \frac{m_{21}m_{12}}{m_{11}}, & m_{33} - \frac{m_{31}m_{13}}{m_{11}} \end{pmatrix}$. Denote the submatrix $\begin{pmatrix} m_{22} - \frac{m_{21}m_{12}}{m_{11}}, & m_{23} - \frac{m_{21}m_{13}}{m_{11}} \\ m_{32} - \frac{m_{21}m_{12}}{m_{11}}, & m_{33} - \frac{m_{31}m_{13}}{m_{11}} \end{pmatrix}$ by $\overline{M}$. Since $Rank(M) = 2$ and $m_{11} \neq 0$, the rank of matrix $\overline{M}$ is 1. The eigenvalues of $\overline{M}$ is 0 and $Tr(\overline{M})$. The condition that $M - (b^* - b)I^*$ is not invertible is equivalent to $(b^* - b)$ being an eigenvalue of $\overline{M}$. Thus, the lossy branch space is $\{b^*, b^* - Tr(\overline{M})\}$.

We show that any adversary $A$ that produces a different element of lossy branch given $S$ and a lossy branch $b^*$, can be used to compute the discrete logarithm in $G$, contradicting the $d$-linear assumption. For a $3 \times 3$ matrix $M = (m_{ij})$ of rank 2 and any $t \in Z_p$, let $M(t)$ be the matrix of $M$ with the last two columns multiplied by $t$, $M(t)$ is a uniform matrix of rank 2. Let $(g, g^t)$ be the discrete logarithm challenge for $G$. Choose $b^*$ and compute $S = g^{M(t)-b^*I^*}$ and send $S, b^*$ to adversary $A$. If the adversary outputs lossy branch $b$ with $b \neq b^*$, then $b^* - b$ is $Tr(\overline{M(t)})$, and we have, $(m_{22} - \frac{m_{21}m_{12}}{m_{11}})t + (m_{33} - \frac{m_{31}m_{14}}{m_{11}})t = b + b^*$. Since $m_{11} = 0$ with probability $\frac{1}{p}$ and $m_{22} - \frac{m_{21}m_{12}}{m_{11}} + m_{33} - \frac{m_{31}m_{14}}{m_{11}} = 0$ with probability $\frac{1}{p}$, we can solve $t$ with non-negligible probability.     $\square$

*Remark 3.*

1. It is easy to generalize the above construction to the $n \times n$ matrix case for $n \geq 3$. Then we will get an $(n \log p, (n - 2) \log p)$ all-but-one verifiable lossy trapdoor relation. The proof just needs a trivial extension.
2. If $M$ is an $n \times n$ matrix for $n > 2 \log p$ and the input is $x \in \{0, 1\}^n$, then the resulting lossy trapdoor relation is an $(n, n - 2 \log p)$-all-but-one LTDF based on the DLDH assumption. Although there is generic construction of all-but-one LTDF from LTDF in [20], and thus all-but-one LTDF from $d$-linear assumption, the direct construction of all-but-one LTDF from $d$-linear assumption $(d > 1)$ is unknown. Freeman *et al.* [5] left the problem of constructing all-but-one LTDF based on the $d$-linear assumption *directly* as an open problem. We partially solve this open problem as a byproduct.
3. It is not easy to extend to the $d$-linear case for $d \geq 3$. If $d = 2$, we have that the rank of $2 \times 2$ submatrix $\overline{M}$ is 1 when $Rank(M) = 2$ and $m_{ii} \neq 0$. If $d \geq 3$, it is not easy to decide which $(n - d + 1) \times (n - d + 1)$ submatrix has rank 1 when $Rank(M) = d$.

## 5   Lossy Encryption

In [19], Peikert *et al.* defined dual-mode encryption with two modes. In the normal mode, the cryptosystem behaves normally, and in the *lossy* mode, the system loses information of the message. In [1], Bellare *et al.* they defined the lossy encryption, extending the definition of dual-mode encryption in [19] and meaningful/meaningless encryption in [14]. Hemenway *et al.* [10] proposed construction of lossy encryption based on statistically-hiding 2-round Oblivious Transfer and derived lossy encryption schemes based on DDH, DCR and QR assumptions.

We now describe an instantiation of lossy encryption based on the lossy trapdoor relation and three concrete intances based on subgroup membership assumption. Let $LR = (S_{inj}, S_{loss}, F_{lr}, F_{lr}^{-1})$ be a collection of $(n, l)$-lossy trapdoor relation associated with $H : \{0,1\}^n \rightarrow D$. Let $\mathcal{H}$ be a universal family of hash functions from $\{0,1\}^n$ to $\{0,1\}^k$ where $k \leq l - 2\log(1/\varepsilon)$ for some negligible $\epsilon = \text{negl}(n)$. The lossy encryption $LE$ is constructed below:

**KeyGen:** It generates an injective trapdoor relation $(\sigma, \tau, H) \leftarrow S_{inj}$, and chooses a hash function $h$ from $\mathcal{H}$. $pk = (\sigma, H, h), sk = \tau$.

**KeyGen$_{loss}$:** It generates a lossy trapdoor relation $(\sigma, H) \leftarrow S_{loss}$, and chooses a hash function $h$ from $\mathcal{H}$. $pk_{loss} = (\sigma, H, h)$.

**Enc:** On input a message $m \in \{0,1\}^k$, it chooses $r \in \{0,1\}^n$ uniformly at random and computes: $c_1 = F_{lr}(\sigma, r), c_2 = m \oplus h(H(r))$. The ciphertext is $C = (c_1, c_2)$.

**Dec:** On input $sk = \tau$, and a ciphertext $C = (c_1, c_2)$, it computes $T = F_{lr}^{-1}(\tau, c_1)$ and outputs $c_2 \oplus h(T)$.

**Theorem 5.** *Under the assumption that $LR$ is an $(n, l)$-lossy trapdoor relation, the encryption scheme $LE$ is a lossy encryption.*

We need a generalized Leftover Hash lemma in order to prove the lossy property.

**Lemma 1 (Lemma A.1 in [16]).** *Let $X, Y$ be random variables such that $X \in \{0,1\}^n$ and the average min-entropy [16] $\tilde{H}_\alpha(X|Y) \geq k$. $H : \{0,1\}^n \rightarrow D$ is the one to one injective map. Let $\mathcal{H}$ be a family of universal hash family from $D$ to $\{0,1\}^l$, where $l \leq k - 2\log(1/\varepsilon)$. It holds that for $h \leftarrow \mathcal{H}$ and $r \leftarrow \{0,1\}^l$,*

$$\Delta((h, h(H(X)), Y)), (h, r, Y)) \leq \varepsilon.$$

*Proof of Theorem 8.* We show that the above scheme $LE$ satisfies three properties of lossy encryption.

1. Correctness on real keys. For all $m \in \mathcal{M}$ and $r \in \mathcal{R}$

$$Dec(sk, Enc(pk, m, r)) = h(F_{lr}^{-1}(\tau, F_{lr}(\sigma, r))) \oplus (m \oplus h(H(r))$$
$$= h(H(r)) \oplus (m \oplus h(H(r)) = m.$$

2. Indistinguishability of injective keys from lossy keys. The computational indistinguishability is guaranteed by the indistinguishability of the two modes of lossy trapdoor relation.

3. Lossiness of encryption with lossy keys. For any $pk_{loss}$ and any pair of messages $m_0, m_1 \in \mathcal{M}$, we have that $\{Enc(pk_{loss}, m_0, r))|r \in \mathcal{R}\} =_s \{Enc(pk_{loss}, m_1, r))|r \in \mathcal{R}\}$. Since $H$ is a one-to-one map, the average min-entropy $\tilde{H}_\alpha(\mathcal{R}|F_{lr}(s, \mathcal{R})) \geq n - (n - l) = l$ in the lossy mode. Since $k \leq l - 2\log(1/\varepsilon)$, $m_b \oplus h(H(\mathcal{R}))$ will be $\varepsilon$-close to uniform distribution by Lemma 1. The statistical distance between $\{Enc(pk_{loss}, m_0, r))|r \in \mathcal{R}\}$ and $\{Enc(pk_{loss}, m_0, r))|r \in \mathcal{R}\}$ will be $2\varepsilon$. $\square$

This derives efficient lossy encryption schemes from the DDH, $d$-linear and subgroup membership assumptions list in Section 4.1. Let $LR_{SMA} = (S_{inj}, S_{loss}, F_{lr}, F_{lr}^{-1})$ be the generic lossy trapdoor relation and $(G = KL, L)$ be the subgroup membership instance proposed in Section 4.1. The following $LE_{SMA}$ is a lossy encryption based on the SMA assumption.

**KeyGen:** On the output of $S_{inj} = (\sigma, t, H) = (G, k, l, c, t, H)$, it chooses a hash function $h$ from $\mathcal{H} : G \to \{0,1\}^{\log |K| - \log |L|}$. The trapdoor is $t$. The injective map is $H : Z_{|K|} \to K$. $pk = (\sigma, H, h)$, $sk = t$.

**KeyGen$_{loss}$:** On the output of $S_{loss} = (\sigma, H) = (G, k, l, c, H)$, it chooses a hash function $h$ from $\mathcal{H} : G \to \{0,1\}^{\log |K| - \log |L|}$. The injective map is $H : Z_{|K|} \to K$. $pk_{loss} = (\sigma, H, h)$.

**Enc:** On input a message $m \in \{0,1\}^{\log |K| - \log |L|}$, it chooses $x \in Z_{|K|}$ uniformly at random and computes: $c_1 = F_{lr}(\sigma, x) = c^x$, $c_2 = m \oplus h(H(x))$. The ciphertext is $C = (c_1, c_2)$.

**Dec:** On input $sk = t$, and a ciphertext $C = (c_1, c_2)$, it computes $T = F_{lr}^{-1}(t, c)$ and outputs $c_2 \oplus h(T)$.

The $LR_{SMA}$ above derives new efficient lossy encryption schemes by instantiating the subgroup membership assumption. We list three interesting instances of subgroup membership assumptions here.

1. Let $p = 2n + 1$, where $n = q_0 q_1$ and $p, q_0, q_1$ are distinct primes. The multiplication group $Z_p^*$ has order $2n$. We denote the subgroups of order $q_0$, $q_1$ and $n$ by $G_{q_0}$, $G_{q_1}$ and $G_n$. The subgroup assumptions $SM_{(G_n, G_{q_0})}$ and $SM_{(G_n, G_{q_1})}$ were suggested in [17]. If the length of $q_0$ and $q_1$ are not equal, either $SM_{(G_n, G_{q_0})}$ or $SM_{(G_n, G_{q_1})}$ can be used to construct lossy trapdoor relation.

2. Let $n$ be a composite number with two primes factors $p, q$ and $p > q$. Let $p'$ be a prime and $E$ be a elliptic curve defined over $F_{p'}$ such that $\#E(F_{p'}) = n$. We denote $G_p$ and $G_q$ the subgroup of $E(F_p')$ with order $p$ and $q$. If the length of $p$ and $q$ are not equal, either $SM_{(E(F_{p'}), G_p)}$ or $SM_{(E(F_{p'}), G_q)}$ can be used to construct lossy trapdoor relation.

3. Let $a, b, c, d, p = 2ab + 1$ and $q = 2cd + 1$ be primes, let $n = pq$, and let $G$ be the subgroup of $Z_n^*$ with Jacobin symbol 1. Let $K$ be the subgroup of order $bd$ and $L$ be the subgroup of order $ac$. The subgroup assumptions $SM_{(G,L)}$ was suggested in [7]. Note also that $ac$ can be made much smaller than $bd$.

## 6   Adaptive Trapdoor Relation

In this section, we show an construction of adaptive trapdoor relation from verifiable lossy trapdoor relation and all-but-one verifiable lossy trapdoor relation. Let $LR = (LR_{inj}, LR_{loss}, F_{lr}, F_{lr}^{-1}, Ver_1)$ be an $(n, k_1)$-verifiable lossy trapdoor relation and $ABO = (ABOB, ABOGen, G_{lr}, G_{lr}^{-1}, Ver_2)$ be an $(n, k_2)$-all-but-one verifiable lossy trapdoor relation. We require that the two lossy trapdoor relations has the same public computable injective map $H$. We also require that the residual leakage of the lossy and all-but-one lossy trapdoor relation is $(n - k_1) + (n - k_2) \leq n - \log(1/\varepsilon))$, for some negligible $\varepsilon = \text{negl}(n)$. The tag space $\{0,1\}^v$ of the resulting adaptive trapdoor relation is the same with the branch space of $ABO$.

**Trapdoor Generation.** On input $1^n$, it makes query to $LR_{inj}(1^n)$, $ABOGen$ $(1^n, 0^v)$ and gets $(\sigma_1, td_{lr}, H)$ and $(\sigma_2, td_{abo}, H)$, then returns $ID = (\sigma_1, \sigma_2)$, $Td = (td_{lr}, td_{abo})$, $H$.

**Public Evaluation.** On input $ID = (\sigma_1, \sigma_2)$, $TAG \in \{0,1\}^v$ and $x \in \{0,1\}^n$, it makes query to $F_{lr}$ and $G_{lr}$ and gets $(H(x), c_1) \leftarrow F_{lr}(\sigma_1, x)$, $(H(x), c_2) \leftarrow G_{lr}(\sigma_2, TAG, x)$. Return $(H(x), TAG, c_1, c_2)$.

**Inversion.** On input $(td_{lr}, td_{abo})$ and $(TAG, c_1, c_2)$, computes $h = F_{lr}^{-1}(td_{lr}, c_1)$. If $Ver_1(\sigma_1, h, c_1) = 1$ and $Ver_2(\sigma_2, TAG, h, c_2) = 1$, returns $h$, else returns $\perp$.

**Theorem 6.** *If $k_1 + k_2 \geq n + \log(1/\varepsilon))$, $LR$ is an $(n, k_1)$-verifiable lossy trapdoor relation and ABO is an $(n, k_2)$-all-but-one verifiable lossy trapdoor relation, the construction above is an adaptive trapdoor relation.*

*Proof.* The correctness of the inverse algorithm is guaranteed by the correctness of the decapsulation algorithm in lossy trapdoor relation. In the following, we prove the adaptive one-ways property by describing a sequence of experiments **Game 0**, **Game 1**, **Game 2**, and **Game 3**. We denote the challenge tag by $TAG^*$, the challenge relation by $(H^*(x), TAG^*, c_1^*, c_2^*)$ in these games.

**Game 0.** This game is identical to that in the original adaptive one-ways property. That is, the trapdoor generation algorithm $TDG$ outputs the function indexes $\sigma_1$ and $\sigma_2$ with lossy branch $0^v$, and the corresponding trapdoor$(td_{lr}, td_{abo})$. On input a query $(TAG, c_1, c_2)$ from $A$, the inverse algorithm outputs the corresponding relation $H(x)$ or $\perp$. The challenge algorithm outputs challenge relation $(c_1^*, c_2^*)$ on tag $TAG^*$.

**Game 1.** The only difference with Game 0 is that the lossy branch is changed. The all-but-one lossy trapdoor relation is chosen to have lossy branch $TAG^*$ rather than $0^v$. That is $(\sigma_2, td_{abo}) \leftarrow ABOGen(1^n, TAG^*)$.

**Game 2.** The only difference with Game 1 is that the inversion oracle is changed. The inverse algorithm is now done by using the all-but-one relation trapdoor $td_{abo}$ rather than $td_{lr}$. The full description of inversion oracle is here: if $TAG = TAG^*$, output $\perp$. Compute $h = G^{-1}(td_{abo}, TAG, c_1, c_2)$ and check that if $Ver_1(\sigma_1, h, c_1) = 1$ and $Ver_1(\sigma_2, TAG, h, c_2) = 1$; if so, output $h$, otherwise output $\perp$.

**Game 3.** The only change is the lossy trapdoor relation $LR$, in which we replace the injective relation $LR_{inj}$ with a lossy one $LR_{loss}$.

The adversary's view is computationally indistinguishable in **Game 0** and **Game 1** with the replacement of lossy branch. This is guaranteed by the the indistinguishability of function indexes generated by different lossy branches. In **Game 1** the adversary cannot find another lossy branch. This is guaranteed by the hidden lossy branch property of the all-but-one verifiable lossy trapdoor relation.

The only difference between **Game 1** and **Game 2** is the inverse algorithm. They produce identical outputs. Since the inverse algorithm always outputs $\perp$ in both games if $TAG = TAG^*$, we may assume that $TAG \neq TAG^*$. Additionally, both implementations check that $(h, c_1)$ and $(h, c_2)$ satisfy binary relations, and output $\perp$ if not. It suffices to show that this $h$ is unique. In both games, $LR$ is in the injective mode and $ABO$ is injective on input branch $TAG = TAG^*$. Since $H$ is an injective map, $h$ is unique.

The only difference between **Game 2** and **Game 3** is that the injective mode of $LR$ is replaced by lossy model. Since the injective and lossy modes of the lossy trapdoor relation are computationally indistinguishable, the adversary's view in **Game 2** and **Game 3** are indistinguishable.

In **Game 3**, the image size of both relations are at most $2^{n-k_1}$ and $2^{n-k_2}$. The random variable $(TAG^*, c_1^*, c_2^*)$ takes at most $2^{2n-k_1-k_2}$ values and $n - (2n - k_1 - k_2) = k_1 + k_2 - n \geq \log(1/\varepsilon))$ bits information of $H^*(x)$ is uncertain. We have that the advantage of $A$ in **Game 3** is at most $\varepsilon$.

By the combination of the sequence of results, this theorem holds.     □

**Adaptive Trapdoor Relation from DLDH.** Using the result in Section 4.2, we get an adaptive trapdoor relation based on DLDH assumption. Since 50 group elements are needed in the function index, the derived adaptive trapdoor relation is inefficient. But our result gives new insight of the relation between lossy trapdoor relation and adaptive trapdoor relation.

# 7   Conclusion

In this paper, we introduce the notion of lossy trapdoor relations and provides several constructions from this primitive. Unlike the lossy trapdoor function, lossy trapdoor relation does not require completely recovering the input but a public computable injective map of it. The lossy trapdoor relation maintains the application of lossy trapdoor function on the lossy encryption. We gave several constructions based on DDH, DLDH and SMA assumptions. We also introduce the all-but-one verifiable lossy trapdoor relation and an construction of adaptive trapdoor relation from it.

# References

1. Bellare, M., Hofheinz, D., Yilek, S.: Possibility and impossibility results for encryption and commitment secure under selective opening. In: Joux, A. (ed.) EUROCRYPT 2009. LNCS, vol. 5479, pp. 1–35. Springer, Heidelberg (2009)
2. Boldyreva, A., Fehr, S., O'Neill, A.: On notions of security for deterministic encryption, and efficient constructions without random oracles. In: Wagner, D. (ed.) CRYPTO 2008. LNCS, vol. 5157, pp. 335–359. Springer, Heidelberg (2008)
3. Boyen, X., Waters, B.: Shrinking the keys of discrete-log-type lossy trapdoor functions. In: Zhou, J., Yung, M. (eds.) ACNS 2010. LNCS, vol. 6123, pp. 35–52. Springer, Heidelberg (2010)
4. Diffie, W., Hellman, M.E.: New directions in cryptography. IEEE Trans. on Information Theory 22(6), 644–654 (1976)
5. Freeman, D.M., Goldreich, O., Kiltz, E., Rosen, A., Segev, G.: More constructions of lossy and correlation-secure trapdoor functions. In: Nguyen, P.Q., Pointcheval, D. (eds.) PKC 2010. LNCS, vol. 6056, pp. 279–295. Springer, Heidelberg (2010)
6. Freeman, D.M., Goldreich, O., Kiltz, E., Rosen, A., Segev, G.: More constructions of lossy and correlation-secure trapdoor functions. J. Cryptology 26(1), 39–74 (2013)

7. Gjøsteen, K.: Symmetric subgroup membership problems. In: Vaudenay, S. (ed.) PKC 2005. LNCS, vol. 3386, pp. 104–119. Springer, Heidelberg (2005)
8. Goldreich, O.: The Foundations of Cryptography. Basic Techniques, vol. 1. Cambridge University Press (2001)
9. Goldreich, O.: The Foundations of Cryptography. Basic Applications, vol. 2. Cambridge University Press (2004)
10. Hemenway, B., Libert, B., Ostrovsky, R., Vergnaud, D.: Lossy encryption: Constructions from general assumptions and efficient selective opening chosen ciphertext security. In: Lee, D.H., Wang, X. (eds.) ASIACRYPT 2011. LNCS, vol. 7073, pp. 70–88. Springer, Heidelberg (2011)
11. Hofheinz, D.: Possibility and impossibility results for selective decommitments. J. Cryptology 24(3), 470–516 (2011)
12. Kiltz, E., Mohassel, P., O'Neill, A.: Adaptive trapdoor functions and chosen-ciphertext security. In: Gilbert, H. (ed.) EUROCRYPT 2010. LNCS, vol. 6110, pp. 673–692. Springer, Heidelberg (2010)
13. Kiltz, E., O'Neill, A., Smith, A.: Instantiability of RSA-OAEP under chosen-plaintext attack. In: Rabin, T. (ed.) CRYPTO 2010. LNCS, vol. 6223, pp. 295–313. Springer, Heidelberg (2010)
14. Kol, G., Naor, M.: Cryptography and game theory: Designing protocols for exchanging information. In: Canetti, R. (ed.) TCC 2008. LNCS, vol. 4948, pp. 320–339. Springer, Heidelberg (2008)
15. Naccache, D., Stern, J.: A new public key cryptosystem based on higher residues. In: ACM Conference on Computer and Communications Security, pp. 59–66 (1998)
16. Naor, M., Segev, G.: Public-key cryptosystems resilient to key leakage. In: Halevi, S. (ed.) CRYPTO 2009. LNCS, vol. 5677, pp. 18–35. Springer, Heidelberg (2009)
17. González Nieto, J.M., Boyd, C., Dawson, E.: A public key cryptosystem based on the subgroup membership problem. In: Qing, S., Okamoto, T., Zhou, J. (eds.) ICICS 2001. LNCS, vol. 2229, pp. 352–363. Springer, Heidelberg (2001)
18. Paillier, P.: Public-key cryptosystems based on composite degree residuosity classes. In: Stern, J. (ed.) EUROCRYPT 1999. LNCS, vol. 1592, pp. 223–238. Springer, Heidelberg (1999)
19. Peikert, C., Vaikuntanathan, V., Waters, B.: A framework for efficient and composable oblivious transfer. In: Wagner, D. (ed.) CRYPTO 2008. LNCS, vol. 5157, pp. 554–571. Springer, Heidelberg (2008)
20. Peikert, C., Waters, B.: Lossy trapdoor functions and their applications. In: STOC, pp. 187–196 (2008)
21. Seurin, Y.: On the lossiness of the rabin trapdoor function. In: Krawczyk, H. (ed.) PKC 2014. LNCS, vol. 8383, pp. 380–398. Springer, Heidelberg (2014)
22. Wee, H.: Efficient chosen-ciphertext security via extractable hash proofs. In: Rabin, T. (ed.) CRYPTO 2010. LNCS, vol. 6223, pp. 314–332. Springer, Heidelberg (2010)
23. Wee, H.: Public key encryption against related key attacks. In: Fischlin, M., Buchmann, J., Manulis, M. (eds.) PKC 2012. LNCS, vol. 7293, pp. 262–279. Springer, Heidelberg (2012)
24. Xue, H., Li, B., Lu, X., Jia, D., Liu, Y.: Efficient lossy trapdoor functions based on subgroup membership assumptions. In: Abdalla, M., Nita-Rotaru, C., Dahab, R. (eds.) CANS 2013. LNCS, vol. 8257, pp. 235–250. Springer, Heidelberg (2013)

# Compact Public Key Encryption
# with Minimum Ideal Property of Hash Functions

Kazuki Yoneyama[1] and Goichiro Hanaoka[2]

[1] NTT Secure Platform Laboratories
3-9-11 Midori-cho Musashino-shi Tokyo 180-8585, Japan
yoneyama.kazuki@lab.ntt.co.jp
[2] National Institute of Advanced Industrial Science and Technology
1-1-1 Umezono Tsukuba-shi Ibaraki 305-8568, Japan

**Abstract.** Achieving shorter ciphertext length under weaker assumptions in chosen-ciphertext (CCA) secure public-key encryption (PKE) is one of the most important research topics in cryptography. However, it is also known that it is hard to construct a CCA-secure PKE whose ciphertext overhead is less than two group elements in the underlying prime-order group under non-interactive assumption. A naive approach for achieving more compactness than the above bound is to use random oracles (ROs), but the full RO has various ideal properties like programmability. In this paper, we pursue how to achieve compact PKE only with a minimum ideal property of ROs. Specifically, only with observability, we can give three CCA-secure PKE schemes whose ciphertext overhead is less than two group elements. Our schemes are provably secure under standard assumptions such as the CDH and DDH assumptions. This study shows that ideal properties other than observability are not necessary to construct compact PKE beyond the bound.

**Keywords:** random oracle, observability, public key encryption, chosen ciphertext security, ciphertext overhead.

## 1 Introduction

The aim of this paper is to clarify how small a ciphertext overhead can be achieved with a minimum ideal property of random oracles (ROs). Ciphertext overhead means the size of the ciphertext minus the size of the message. We find that if a hash function has just one ideal property, *observability* [1, 2], there exist chosen-ciphertext (CCA) secure public-key encryption (PKE) schemes whose ciphertext overhead is *less than two group elements* in the underlying prime-order group under a non-interactive standard assumption such as the decisional Diffie-Hellman (DDH) assumption and the computational Diffie-Hellman (CDH) assumption. Up to the present, there exists no such a compact PKE scheme in the standard model (StdM), and it is hard to achieve without any ideal property due to an impossibility result [3].

S.S.M. Chow et al. (Eds.): ProvSec 2014, LNCS 8782, pp. 178–193, 2014.

## 1.1   Background

From the seminal work by Cramer and Shoup [4], many practical PKE schemes without ROs have been proposed (e.g., [5–8]). However, all of these schemes need at least two group elements ciphertext overhead. Also, Hanaoka et al. [3] show a strong negative result that there is no algebraic black-box reduction from the CCA security of PKEs which ciphertext overhead is one group element in prime order groups and a string (i.e., less than $2|g|$ where $|g|$ is the length of a group element) to any non-interactive assumption. This result clarifies that to achieve more compact ciphertext overhead than two group elements is very difficult with known techniques.

On the other hand, ECIES [9] achieves one group element ($|g|$) ciphertext overhead with the random oracle model (ROM) [10] and an interactive assumption. The ROM is well studied as a useful approach to reduce ciphertext overhead with the help of various ideal properties like programmability [1, 11] and observability [1, 2]. Indeed, we have CCA-secure PKE schemes with extremely compact ciphertexts relying on ROs (e.g., [12–14]). However, the ROM has a well known problem; ROs do not exist, and is not always instantiatable by real hash functions. Canetti et al. [15, 16] show that there are digital signature schemes and PKE schemes which are secure in the ROM but insecure if ROs are instantiated by real hash functions. Thus, ROs are not implementable in reality, and relying on such a strongly ideal primitive is undesirable.

Recently, Bellare et al. [17] try to solve the problem of ROs. They propose a notion of hash functions, called universal computational extractor (UCE), and provide secure instantiations of ROs in several cryptographic schemes with UCEs. The notion of UCEs is a standard-model security attribute; and thus, instantiated schemes are secure without ROs if UCE exists. Naturally, UCEs are easily implemented by ROs. Also, an implementation of UCEs based on the HMAC construction where the compression function is ideal is roughly discussed. Though existing implementations need ideal primitives, this does not mean that there is no hope to implement UCEs without ideal primitives. Hence, the assumption of UCEs does not conflict with the Canetti et al.'s impossibility result [15, 16], and to assume a given family of hash functions as a UCE is hardly impractical. They show that several PKE schemes (e.g., OAEP [18]) are secure with UCEs, and Matsuda and Hanaoka [19] proposed a CCA-secure PKE scheme with UCEs. However, a compact CCA-secure PKE scheme is not known, even with UCEs. Also, it is shown that some of known variants of UCEs do not exist if indistinguishability obfuscation exists [20].

## 1.2   Our Contribution

We pursue a similar research goal to Bellare et al.; that is, to construct practical and secure schemes with a family of hash functions which is different from ROs (like UCEs) without conflicting the Canetti et al.'s impossibility result. Especially, we focus on constructing CCA-secure PKE which ciphertext overhead is less than two group elements.

Our approach is different from UCEs; that is, we achieve our goal with another resource. Specifically, we use a class of hash functions which satisfies observability and target collision-resistance (TCR). Observability [1, 2] guarantees that hash values cannot be locally computed for any entity. It is usually represented as any entity obtain hash values through an oracle access. It means that all of input and output values of a hash function are visible for a simulator in the security proof but not the adversary. It has been considered as one of ideal properties of ROs.

We try to modify known secure PKE schemes in the StdM. In general, PKE schemes secure in the StdM need large ciphertext overhead, especially in order to obtain the CCA security. The most compact ciphertext overhead of known CCA PKE schemes in the StdM is two group elements. We introduce first PKE schemes with hash functions satisfying only observablity and TCR, which are CCA-secure and achieve less than two group elements ciphertext overhead.

## 1.3　Our Technique

First, as a warm up to construct specific schemes, we show a design principle of secure and compact PKE schemes. We propose two tricks to get compact ciphertext overhead using observability of hash functions: *base unification* and *hashing verification-tag*.

- The base unification trick means that when public parameter contains two random group elements as $g_1$ and $g_2$ and the ciphertext contains two group elements as $g_1^r$ and $g_2^r$ for randomness $r$, we can unite bases as $g_1$ and $g_2 = g_1^w$ for an exponent $w$ and remove $g_2^r$ from the ciphertext. Then, the receiver can reconstruct $g_2^r$ from $g_1^r$ and $w$ by adding $w$ to the secret key. Hence, the ciphertext can be reduced by deleting $g_2^r$. On the other hand, in the security proof, though the simulator has to obtain $g_2^r$ without knowing $w$, it can be done by the help of observability.
- The hashing verification-tag trick means that the sender applies a hash to a component (called verification-tag) in order to verify the validity of the ciphertext in the case that the verification can be done from the hashed verification-tag and the secret key. Generally, a verification-tag needs to be at least $|g|$. But, this technique can reduce it to just $|TCR|$ where $|TCR|$ is the length of an output of a TCR hash function (i.e., it can be $\kappa$-bits for the security parameter $\kappa$). Thus, ciphertext overhead is getting more compact. For example, if we modify the Cramer-Shoup (CS) PKE [4] by this trick, the modified scheme is also secure. Moreover, the hashing verification-tag trick is more effective for PKE schemes using the twinning trick [21], such as the Cash-Kiltz-Shoup PKE [21] and the Haralambiev-Jager-Kiltz-Shoup (HJKS) KEM [8, 22].[1]

Next, we obtain new CCA-secure PKE schemes and KEM by assuming observability as follows:

---

[1] [8] and [22] gave almost the same scheme based on the computational Diffie-Hellman (CDH) assumption, independently.

**Compact PKE from the DDH Assumption.** Our first scheme is based on the CS PKE [4], applying both the hashing verification-tag trick and the base unification trick. While the CS PKE has ciphertext overhead consisting of $3|g|$, our scheme has only that consisting of $|g| + |TCR|$. This scheme has an advantage that it is proved to be secure by assuming observability and the standard DDH assumption.

**Optimally Compact KEM.** Our second scheme is based on the Okamoto KEM [23], applying the base unification trick. This scheme achieves more compact ciphertext overhead than that of the first scheme. Ciphertext overhead consists of only $|g|$, which is the same as the ElGamal PKE [24].[2] We remark that ciphertext overhead consisting of one group element is conjectured as optimal length under the DDH assumption due to the generic attacks on the discrete logarithm problem in the group. Moreover, the computational complexity of encryption and decryption operations is very light, which is comparable to the Kiltz KEM [7]. CCA-security is proved by assuming observability, the DDH assumption, and the existence of a pseudorandom function with pairwise-independent random sources ($\pi$PRF). $\pi$PRF is a stronger primitive than the ordinary PRF, which was introduced in [23].

**Compact KEM from the CDH Assumption.** Our third scheme is based on the HJKS KEM [8, 22], applying the hashing verification-tag trick. While security can be proved by assuming observability and the CDH assumption, ciphertext overhead consists of $|g| + |TCR|$ as the first scheme. Thus, we can construct PKE schemes from the CDH assumption, where ciphertext overhead is the same as the scheme from the DDH assumption.

The comparison of previous CCA-secure PKE schemes and our schemes is found in Table 1.

## 1.4   Instantiability of Observable Hash Functions

It is clear that, like UCEs, observable hash functions can be instantiated from (full) ROs because ROs naturally satisfy observability and TCR. Moreover, we show theoretical instantiatiability of such functions *without ROs*. If hash functions satisfy an additional property, it is (impractically) implementable in the real world without any idealized building block. Specifically, though standard observability requires that adversaries cannot see input-output pairs of hash functions, we consider a stronger observability that adversaries also can see input-output pairs of hash functions. We call this property *public observability*. Public observability of ROs is previously discussed in [26, 27].

An example of implementation of publicly observable hash functions is with an on-line hash server and a keyed hash function as follows: The hash server maintains a hashing key of the hash function, and returns a hash value corresponding to an input value by evaluating the specified hash function. Since

---

[2]   The original Okamoto KEM has ciphertext overhead consisting of $2|g|$.

**Table 1.** Comparison of previous CCA-secure PKE schemes and our schemes

| | Requirement for Hash | Assumption | Ciphertext overhead | |
|---|---|---|---|---|
| [4] | TCR | DDH | $3\|g\|$ | 768 |
| [6] | injection | DBDH | $2\|g\|$ | 512 |
| [7] | GHDH or RO$^3$ | GHDH (GDH) | $2\|g\|$ | 512 |
| [8] | TCR | CDH | $2\|g\| + \|MAC\|$ | 640 |
| [23] | TCR | DDH & $\pi$PRF | $2\|g\|$ | 512 |
| [14] | RO | CDH | $\|g\|$ | 256 |
| **Ours** §4.1 | Observability & TCR | DDH | $\|g\| + \|TCR\|$ | 384 |
| **Ours** §4.2 | Observability & TCR | DDH & $\pi$PRF | $\|g\|$ | 256 |
| **Ours** §4.3 | Observability & TCR | CDH | $\|g\| + \|TCR\|$ | 384 |

Part of this table is borrowed from [7] and [25]. $|MAC|$ is the length of a tag of a message authentication code. DBDH means the Decisional Bilinear Diffie-Hellman assumption. For concreteness expected ciphertext overhead for a 128-bit implementation is also given.

entities except the server do not know the hashing key, the hash evaluation is not locally computed. Also, if the hash function satisfies TCR, both observability and TCR are guaranteed. Note that a channel between users and the server is *not necessarily confidential*, and an authenticated channel is enough because input and output values are public.

We compare instantiability of observable hash functions with that of full ROs and that of UCEs. Firstly, full ROs can be also instantiated by an on-line hash server who maintains a universal table of input/output pairs and chooses a random element for a new input. While, for observable hash functions, the server just evaluates the underlying specific hash function and must not maintain any table, the server must maintain a large table for full ROs. Thus, the instantiation of observable hash functions is more efficient than full ROs. Next, it is shown that UCEs can be constructed from indistinguishable obfuscation (iO) [28]. Though UCEs are achievable in the StdM without an on-line hash server, known iO candidates are impractical in efficiency such as [29–31]. Thus, the instantiation of observable hash functions is also more efficient than UCEs, though there is a disadvantage that communications between users and the server is necessary for each hash evaluation.

Our CCA-secure PKE schemes and KEM are still secure if hash functions are publicly observable because input-output pairs do not contain any secret information in these schemes. Therefore, our schemes can (theoretically) enjoy the standard model security while implementations are not practical due to the on-line hash server.

---

[3] The Kiltz KEM is secure in the StdM under the Gap Hashed Diffie-Hellman (GHDH) assumption, and also secure in the ROM under the Gap Diffie-Hellman (GDH) assumption.

# 2    Preliminaries

In this section, we show the definition of observability, and some basic notions of building blocks. Throughout this paper we use the following notations. If Set is a set, then by $m \in_R$ Set we denote that $m$ is sampled uniformly from Set. If $\mathcal{ALG}$ is an algorithm, then by $y \leftarrow \mathcal{ALG}(x; r)$ we denote that $y$ is output by $\mathcal{ALG}$ on input $x$ and randomness $r$ (if $\mathcal{ALG}$ is deterministic, $r$ is empty). "$|V|$" means the bit length of a value $V$. We say a function $f(\kappa)$ is negligible ($negl(\kappa)$) in $\kappa$ if for any $c \in \mathbb{N}$ there exists $\kappa_0 \in \mathbb{N}$ such that for all $\kappa > \kappa_0$ $f(\kappa) < \kappa^{-c}$.

## 2.1    Observability and Target-Collision Resistance of Hash Functions

The difference between ordinary hash functions and observable hash functions is whether hash values can be locally evaluated or not. Thus, evaluations of observable hash functions are represented as an oracle access. Since the adversary must pose inputs to the oracle in order to obtain hash values, input-output pairs of functions are observed by the simulator in security proofs. How to evaluate hash values depends on the hashing algorithm of the underlying hash function. The following is the definition of observability.

**Definition 1 (Observability).** *We say that a function $H$ with a domain* **Dom** *and a range* **Rng** *is observable if any entity obtains $H(x)$ for $x \in$ **Dom** through an oracle $\mathcal{O}_H$ who evaluates and outputs $y = H(x)$, and for any probabilistic polynomial-time (PPT) adversary $\mathcal{A}$, $\Pr[(x \in$ **Dom**$, y \in$ **Rng**$) \leftarrow \mathcal{A}^{\mathcal{O}_H}; H(x) = y] \leq negl(\kappa)$, where $\mathcal{A}$ must not pose $x$ to $\mathcal{O}_H$.*

We note that observability is an ideal property. Thus, we can suppose that there exists $\mathcal{O}_H$ like full ROs. An instantiation of observable hash functions using a keyed hash function can be found in Section 1.4.

**Definition 2 (Target-Collision Resistance).** *We say that a family of functions $\mathcal{H}$ with a family of domains $\{$**Dom**$_\kappa\}_{\kappa \in \mathbb{N}}$ and a family of ranges $\{$**Rng**$_\kappa\}_{\kappa \in \mathbb{N}}$ is target-collision resistant if the following condition holds for a security parameter $\kappa$: For any PPT adversary $\mathcal{A}$, $\Pr[H \in_R \mathcal{H}; x \in_R$ **Dom**$_\kappa; x' \leftarrow \mathcal{A}(x, H); x \neq x'; H(x) = H(x')] \leq negl(\kappa)$.*

## 2.2    Public Key Encryption

**Definition 3 (Syntax for Public Key Encryption Schemes).** *A PKE scheme consists of the following 3-tuple* (**Gen, Enc, Dec**):

**Gen** :    *a key generation algorithm which on input $1^\kappa$, where $\kappa$ is the security parameter, outputs a pair of public and secret keys $(pk, sk)$.*

**Enc** :    *an encryption algorithm which takes as input public key $pk$ and plaintext $m$, outputs ciphertext $CT$.*

**Dec** :    *a decryption algorithm which takes as input secret key $sk$ and ciphertext $CT$, outputs plaintext $m$ or reject symbol $\bot$.*

**Definition 4 (CCA-security).** *A PKE scheme is CCA-secure if the following property holds for security parameter $\kappa$; For any adversary $\mathcal{A} = (\mathcal{A}_1, \mathcal{A}_2)$, $|\Pr[(pk, sk) \leftarrow \mathbf{Gen}(1^\kappa); (m_0, m_1, state) \leftarrow \mathcal{A}_1^{\mathcal{DO}(sk, \cdot)}(pk); b \in_R \{0, 1\}; CT^* \leftarrow \mathbf{Enc}(pk, m_b); b' \leftarrow \mathcal{A}_2^{\mathcal{DO}(sk, \cdot)}(pk, CT^*, state); b' = b] - 1/2| \leq negl(\kappa)$, where $\mathcal{DO}$ is the decryption oracle which outputs $m$ or $\perp$ on receiving $CT$, state is state information (possibly including $pk$, $m_0$ and $m_1$) which $\mathcal{A}$ wants to preserve. $\mathcal{A}$ cannot submit the ciphertext $CT = CT^*$ to $\mathcal{DO}$.*

# 3    Our Strategy

In this section, we show our strategy in order to construct compact PKE or KEM beyond the HMS bound.

Most of PKE (or KEM) schemes in the ROM heavily depend on various ideal properties of ROs such as programmability and perfect one-wayness. It is hard to improve such schemes to rely only observability. Thus, we start from schemes in the StdM, and consider a method to reduce the ciphertext length by using observability. Specifically, we try to reduce ciphertext overhead into less than $2|g|$. In this section, we propose two tricks.

**Base Unification Trick.** The CS PKE [4] (shown in Section 4.1), the Kurosawa-Desmedt (KD) PKE [5] and the Okamoto KEM [23] (shown in Section 4.2) have a common structure in the ciphertext; that is, for a randomness $r$ the ciphertext contains $g_1^r$ and $g_2^r$ where $g_1$ and $g_2$ are random group elements included in the public key. To reduce ciphertext overhead, a simple idea is to modify the derivation of $g_2$ in the key generation as follows: $w$ is chosen from $\mathbb{Z}_p$, $g_2$ is computed as $g_1^w$ and $w$ is added to the secret key. By this modification, the receiver can reconstruct $g_2^r$ with $w$ as $g_2^r = (g_1^r)^w$. Hence, it seems that the ciphertext can be reduced by deleting $g_2^r$. These modifications can be understood as the methods to reduce the ciphertext while retaining the validity of the decryption. However, for the security proof, we cannot use $w$ to simulate the decryption oracle in the StdM because $(g_2)^r$ the part of the DDH tuple and so the discrete logarithm of it cannot be known. Thus, this idea does not work in the StdM.

Right then, how does it work by using observability? Our answer is positive. Thanks to observability, the simulator can make use of the hash table. If the encryption procedure contains the application of $(g_2)^r$ to a hash function, the simulator can obtain $(g_2)^r$ by referring the hash table without knowing $w$. Hence, one can directly obtain $(g_2)^r$ by knowledge of the hash function (for the simulator) or can compute $g_2^r = (g_1^r)^w$ by a known discrete log $w$ (for a receiver in the scheme). The CS PKE, the KD PKE and the Okamoto KEM can be modified like above by using observability.

**Hashing Verification-Tag Trick.** First, let's observe the CS PKE. The ciphertext of the CS PKE contains $v = (g_1^{x_1} g_2^{x_2})^r \cdot (g_1^{y_1} g_2^{y_2})^{r\alpha}$ to verify the validity of the decryption, we call such a content as a verification-tag. Then, we can change the derivation of $v$ into $v' = H'((g_1^{x_1}g_2^{x_2})^r \cdot (g_1^{y_1}g_2^{y_2})^{r\alpha})$ where $H'$ is a hash function. By this modification, the receiver can also verify $g_1^r$ and $e$ as checking whether $v' = H'((g_1^r)^{x_1+y_1\alpha}(g_2^r)^{x_2+y_2\alpha})$. Note that, the length of such $v'$ ($|TCR|$) needs only $\kappa$-bits for a security parameter $\kappa$ while $v$ (without hashing) consists of a group element. Specifically, when $\kappa = 128$, $|v'|$ is 128-bit and $|v|$ is 256-bit. Hence, the ciphertext can be reduced. If we modify the CS PKE as the derivation of $v$ into $v' = H'((g_1^{x_1}g_2^{x_2})^r(g_1^{y_1}g_2^{y_2})^{r\alpha})$ where $H'$ is observable, the modified scheme is also secure, and then, the ciphertext is reduced to $|TCR|$.

Next, let's observe the HJKS KEM (shown in Section 4.3). It contains verification-tags $v_1 = ((g^{x_1})^\alpha g^{x_2})^r$ and $v_2 = ((g^{y_1})^\alpha g^{y_2})^r$ where $\alpha$ is derived from the ciphertext. With the twinning trick, the simulator can check the validity of $v_1$ and $v_2$ without knowing $x_1$ or $r$. We can compress verification-tags into one hash value as $v = H(v_1, v_2)$. If $H$ is observable, the simulator can find $v_1$ and $v_2$ from the hash table with $v$ posed for a decryption query. Thus, the simulator can check validity of the compressed verification-tag with the twinning trick. Though the size of verification-tags in the original scheme is $2|g|$, the size of the compressed verification-tag is only $|TCR|$.

# 4    Our Constructions

In this section, we show three new PKE or KEM schemes. All of our proposed schemes use observability to beat the HMS bound on ciphertext overhead. Each scheme has different advantages. The CS PKE is the best example to show an effect of our tricks. Ciphertext overhead can be get more compact to $|g| + |TCR|$ from $3|g|$ with the base unification trick (reducing $|g|$) and the hashing verification-tag trick (reducing $|g| - |TCR|$). We can achieve optimal length ($|g|$) ciphertext overhead from the Okamoto KEM with the base unification trick. Moreover, we give a CDH-based KEM schemes with same ciphertext overhead ($|g| + |TCR|$) as the modified CS PKE, which is obtained from the HJKS KEM with the hashing verification-tag trick.

## 4.1    Compact CCA-secure PKE from the DDH Assumption

In this section, we firstly present a CCA-secure PKE scheme by applying the hashing verification-tag trick and the base unification trick to the CS PKE. This scheme achieves $|g| + |TCR|$ ciphertext overhead and the CCA security based on the DDH assumption, which is one of most standard number theoretic assumptions.

**Original Cramer-Shoup PKE.** Firstly, we review the original CS PKE.

Let $p$ be a prime and $G$ be a finite cyclic group of order $p$. $H : G^3 \to \mathbb{Z}_p$ is a TCR hash function.

*Key generation* : For input $\kappa$, output a public key $pk = (g_1, g_2, g_1^{x_1} g_2^{x_2}, g_1^{y_1} g_2^{y_2}, g_1^z,$
$H)$ and a secret key $sk = (x_1, x_2, y_1, y_2, z)$ such that $(g_1, g_2) \in_R G^2$ and $(x_1,$
$x_2, y_1, y_2, z) \in_R \mathbb{Z}_p^5$.

*Encryption* :  For input a plaintext $m \in G$, generate randomness $r \in_R \mathbb{Z}_p$,
compute $u_1 = g_1^r$, $u_2 = g_2^r$, $e = m \cdot (g_1^z)^r$, $\alpha = H(u_1, u_2, e)$ and $v = (g_1^{x_1} g_2^{x_2})^r \cdot$
$(g_1^{y_1} g_2^{y_2})^{r\alpha}$, and output the ciphertext $CT = (u_1, u_2, e, v)$.

*Decryption* : For input a ciphertext $CT = (u_1, u_2, e, v)$, compute $\alpha = H(u_1, u_2,$
$e)$. If $u_1^{x_1+y_1\alpha} \cdot u_2^{x_2+y_2\alpha} \neq v$, reject the decryption as an invalid ciphertext.
Otherwise, output the plaintext $m = e \cdot u_1^{-z}$.

For the validity check of ciphertexts, the receiver needs both $u_1$ and $u_2$ because
he does not know $r$. Thus, the sender has to include both $u_1$ and $u_2$ in the
ciphertext. The CS PKE is CCA-secure under the DDH assumption and the
TCR hash function. For the definition of the DDH assumption, please refer to
[4].

**Compact Cramer-Shoup PKE.**  We show our first scheme by applying the
hashing verification-tag trick and the base unification trick to the CS PKE.

Let $p$ be a prime and let $g$ be a generator of a finite cyclic group $G$ of order
$p$. $H : G^3 \rightarrow \mathbb{Z}_p$ and $H' : G \rightarrow \{0,1\}^k$ are TCR hash functions. To represent
observability, evaluations of $H$ and $H'$ are done through oracles $\mathcal{O}_H$ and $\mathcal{O}_{H'}$
respectively.

*Key generation* : For input $\kappa$, output a public key $pk = (g, g^w, g^{x_1} g^{wx_2}, g^{y_1} g^{wy_2},$
$g^z, \mathcal{O}_H, \mathcal{O}_{H'})$ and a secret key $sk = (w, x_1, x_2, y_1, y_2, z)$ such that $(w, x_1, x_2,$
$y_1, y_2, z) \in_R \mathbb{Z}_p^6$, where $\mathcal{O}_H$ and $\mathcal{O}_{H'}$ means that oracle accesses to $\mathcal{O}_H$ and
$\mathcal{O}_{H'}$ are given. (After that, we describe the oracle access to $\mathcal{O}_H$ (or $\mathcal{O}_{H'}$) as
"compute $H$ (or $H'$)" for simplicity.)

*Encryption* :  For input a plaintext $m \in G$, generate randomness $r \in_R \mathbb{Z}_p$,
compute $u_1 = g^r$, $u_2 = (g^w)^r$, $e = m \cdot (g^z)^r$, $\alpha = H(u_1, u_2, e)$, $v = (g^{x_1} g^{wx_2})^r \cdot$
$(g^{y_1} g^{wy_2})^{r\alpha}$ and $v' = H'(v)$, and output the ciphertext $CT = (u_1, e, v')$.

*Decryption* : For inputs a ciphertext $CT = (u_1, e, v')$, compute $\alpha = H(u_1, u_1^w, e)$
and $H'(u_1^{x_1+y_1\alpha+w(x_2+y_2\alpha)})$. If $v' \neq H'(u_1^{x_1+y_1\alpha+w(x_2+y_2\alpha)})$, reject the decryption as an invalid ciphertext. Otherwise, output the plaintext $m = e \cdot u_1^{-z}$.

**Security.**  In this section, we show the security of the above scheme.

**Theorem 1.** *If the original CS scheme is CCA-secure where H is TCR, then
the compact CS PKE is CCA-secure where H and H' are observable and TCR.*

First, we give an intuition of the proof. We construct an adversary of the original CS scheme from an adversary of the compact CS scheme. The simulation of
queries is almost the same manner as the original CS PKE. There is a difference
between the real CCA game and the simulation environment in the simulation
of the decryption oracle. The adversary of the original CS scheme decides the
result of the decryption by using the hash tables due to observability. In this

case, the adversary may accept an invalid ciphertext, or rejects a valid ciphertext. The first case occurs with a negligible probability because of TCR, and the other case also occurs with a negligible probability because of observability.

*Proof.* By assuming a CCA adversary $\mathcal{A}$ for our compact CS scheme, we construct a CCA adversary $\mathcal{B}$ for the original CS scheme. The construction of $\mathcal{B}$ is as follows:

The input is $pk = (g_1, g_2, X = g_1^{x_1} g_2^{x_2}, Y = g_1^{y_1} g_2^{y_2}, Z = g_1^z, H)$. Let $\mathcal{L}_H$ be the hash table for $H$. $\mathcal{L}_H$ contains tuples of $(u_{1_i}, u_{2_i}, e_i, H(u_{1_i}, u_{2_i}, e_i))$ $(0 \leq i \leq q_H)$ where $q_H$ is the number of queries to $H$. Let $\mathcal{L}_{H'}$ be the hash table for $H'$. $\mathcal{L}_{H'}$ contains tuples of $(v_i, H'(v_i))$ $(0 \leq i \leq q_{H'})$ where $q_{H'}$ is the number of queries to $H'$.

**Setting of public key :** Choose a hash function $H' : G \to \{0,1\}^k$ from the family of TCR hash functions $\mathcal{H}$. Set the public key $pk = (g_1, g_2, X, Y, Z, \mathcal{O}_H, \mathcal{O}_{H'})$ where oracles $\mathcal{O}_H$ and $\mathcal{O}_{H'}$ are simulated by $\mathcal{B}$. Give $pk$ to $\mathcal{A}$.

**Simulation of $\mathcal{O}_H$ :** For a query $(u_1, u_2, e)$ to $H$, evaluate $\alpha = H(u_1, u_2, e)$, add $(u_1, u_2, e, \alpha)$ to $\mathcal{L}_H$, and output $\alpha$ as the answer to the query.

**Simulation of $\mathcal{O}_{H'}$ :** For a query $v$ to $H'$, evaluate $v' = H'(v)$, add $(v, v')$ to $\mathcal{L}_{H'}$ and output $v'$ as the answer to the query.

**Simulation of the decryption oracle :** For a decryption query $CT = (u_1, e, v')$ from $\mathcal{A}$, check if there are tuples $(u_1, *, e, *) \in \mathcal{L}_H$ and $(*, v') \in \mathcal{L}_{H'}$ where $*$ means the wild-card. If not, reject $CT$ as an invalid ciphertext. Otherwise, find $u_2$, $\alpha$ and $v$ corresponding to $(u_1, u_2, e, \alpha)$ from $\mathcal{L}_H$ and $(v, v')$ from $\mathcal{L}_{H'}$. Note that $u_2$, $\alpha$ and $v$ may be plurally found. Then, pose decryption queries $(u_1, u_2, e, v)$ for all combinations of $u_2$ and $v$ to $\mathcal{DO}$ of the original CS scheme. If $\mathcal{DO}$ rejects all decryption queries, also reject $CT$ as an invalid ciphertext. Otherwise, receive $m$ for one of decryption queries, and output $m$ to $\mathcal{A}$.

**Simulation of the challenge ciphertext :** For an encryption query $(m_0, m_1)$ from $\mathcal{A}$, pose the encryption query $(m_0, m_1)$, and receive the challenge ciphertext $CT^* = (u_1^*, u_2^*, e^*, v^*)$. Compute $v'^* = H'(v^*)$, and add $(v^*, v'^*)$ to $\mathcal{L}_{H'}$. Output $(u_1^*, e^*, v'^*)$ to $\mathcal{A}$.

**Final output :** On receiving the guessed bit $b$ from $\mathcal{A}$, output $b$.

We show the validity of the simulation.

The simulation of $\mathcal{O}_H$, $\mathcal{O}_{H'}$ and the challenge ciphertext is perfectly same as the compact CS scheme. Thus, $\mathcal{A}$ cannot distinguish the real CCA game from the simulation by these queries.

The simulation of the decryption oracle may be distinguished from the real CCA game if either of the following cases occurs.

**Case 1.** $\mathcal{A}$ poses an invalid ciphertext, but $\mathcal{B}$ does not reject the decryption.

**Case 2.** $\mathcal{A}$ poses a valid ciphertext, but $\mathcal{B}$ rejects the decryption.

Firstly, Case 1 occurs if $\mathcal{A}$ poses $CT = (u_1, e, v')$ such that

- $((u_1, u_2, e, \alpha) \in \mathcal{L}_H) \wedge ((v, v') \in \mathcal{L}_{H'}) \wedge (v \neq u_1^{x_1+y_1\alpha} u_2^{x_2+y_2\alpha}) \wedge (H'(v) = H'(u_1^{x_1+y_1\alpha} u_2^{x_2+y_2\alpha}))$, and
- $((u_1, u_2, e, \alpha) \in \mathcal{L}_H) \wedge ((v, v') \in \mathcal{L}_{H'}) \wedge (\log_{g_1} u_1 \neq \log_{g_2} u_2) \wedge (v = u_1^{x_1+y_1\alpha} u_2^{x_2+y_2\alpha})$.

In the first event, $\mathcal{A}$ must pose $v$ such that $H'(v) = H'(u_1^{x_1+y_1\alpha} u_2^{x_2+y_2\alpha})$. By TCR of $H'$, $\mathcal{A}$ cannot find $v$ except the negligible probability. Next, the situation of the second event is same as the proof of CCA-security of the original CS scheme. By the similar information-theoretic analysis, this event also occurs with negligible probability.

Secondly, Case 2 occurs if $\mathcal{A}$ poses $CT = (u_1, e, v')$ such that

- $(H(u_1, u_2, e) = \alpha) \wedge ((u_1, u_2, e, \alpha) \notin \mathcal{L}_H) \wedge ((v, v') \in \mathcal{L}_{H'}) \wedge (v = u_1^{x_1+y_1\alpha} u_2^{x_2+y_2\alpha})$, and
- $((u_1, u_2, e, \alpha) \in \mathcal{L}_H) \wedge (H'(v) = v') \wedge ((v, v') \notin \mathcal{L}_{H'}) \wedge (v = u_1^{x_1+y_1\alpha} u_2^{x_2+y_2\alpha})$.

In the first event, $\mathcal{A}$ must find $\alpha$ without posing $(u_1, u_2, e)$ to $\mathcal{O}_H$. Similarly, in the second event, $\mathcal{A}$ must find $v'$ without posing $v$ to $\mathcal{O}_{H'}$. By observability of $H$ and $H'$, these events occur with negligible probability.

Therefore, $\mathcal{A}$ cannot distinguish the real CCA game and the simulation except negligible probability. If $\mathcal{A}$ wins with non-negligible probability, then $\mathcal{B}$ wins with non-negligible probability. □

## 4.2 Optimally Compact CCA-secure KEM

In this section, we present another CCA-secure (KEM) scheme by applying the base unification trick to the Okamoto KEM. The main advantage of the scheme is its very compact ciphertext, that is, only $|g|$ ciphertext overhead. Hence, this scheme achieves most compact (and optimal) ciphertext overhead. Moreover, computational complexity for the encryption and decryption operation is lower than the PKE scheme proposed in Section 4.1. This scheme needs an additional assumption, $\pi$PRF, besides the DDH assumption.

**Original Okamoto KEM.**  Firstly, we review the original Okamoto KEM.

Let $p$ be a prime and $G$ be a finite cyclic group of order $p$. $H : G^4 \to \mathbb{Z}_p$ is a TCR hash function. $F$ is a $\pi$PRF with index $(I_G, f_G)$ where $I_G \leftarrow \{(V, W, d)|(V, W, d) \in G^2 \times \mathbb{Z}_p\}$ and $f_G : (V, W, d) \mapsto V^{\gamma_1 + d\gamma_2} W$ with $(\gamma_1, \gamma_2) \in_R \mathbb{Z}_p^2$.

*Key generation* : For input $\kappa$, output a public key $pk = (g_1, g_2, g_1^{x_1} g_2^{x_2}, g_1^{y_1} g_2^{y_2}, H, F)$ and a secret key $sk = (x_1, x_2, y_1, y_2)$ such that $(g_1, g_2) \in_R G^2$ and $(x_1, x_2, y_1, y_2) \in_R \mathbb{Z}_p^4$.

*Encryption* :  Generate randomness $r \in_R \mathbb{Z}_p$, compute $u_1 = g_1^r$, $u_2 = g_2^r$, $\alpha = H(g_1^{x_1} g_2^{x_2}, g_1^{y_1} g_2^{y_2}, u_1, u_2)$, $v = (g_1^{x_1} g_2^{x_2})^r \cdot (g_1^{y_1} g_2^{y_2})^{r\alpha}$ and $K = F_v(pk, u_1, u_2)$, and output the ciphertext $CT = (u_1, u_2)$ and the session key $K$.

*Decryption* :  For input a ciphertext $CT = (u_1, u_2)$ and the part of public key $(g_1^{x_1} g_2^{x_2}, g_1^{y_1} g_2^{y_2})$, if $(g_1^{x_1} g_2^{x_2}, g_1^{y_1} g_2^{y_2}, u_1, u_2) \notin G^4$, reject the decryption as an invalid ciphertext. Otherwise, compute $\alpha = H(g_1^{x_1} g_2^{x_2}, g_1^{y_1} g_2^{y_2}, u_1, u_2)$, $v = u_1^{x_1 + \alpha y_1} u_2^{x_2 + \alpha y_2}$ and $K = F_v(pk, u_1, u_2)$, and output the session key $K$.

For the derivation of session keys, the receiver needs both $u_1$ and $u_2$ because he does not know $r$. Thus, the sender has to include both $u_1$ and $u_2$ in the ciphertext.

**Compact Okamoto KEM.**   Next, we show our second scheme by applying the base unification trick to the Okamoto KEM.

Let $p$ be a prime and $G$ be a finite cyclic group of order $p$. $H : G^4 \to \mathbb{Z}_p$ is a TCR hash function. To represent observability, evaluations of $H$ are done through oracles $\mathcal{O}_H$. $F$ is a $\pi$PRF with index $(I_G, f_G)$ where $I_G \leftarrow \{(V, W, d) | (V, W, d) \in G^2 \times \mathbb{Z}_p\}$ and $f_G : (V, W, d) \mapsto V^{\gamma_1 + d\gamma_2} W$ with $(\gamma_1, \gamma_2) \in_R \mathbb{Z}_p^2$.

*Key generation* :  For input $\kappa$, output a public key $pk = (g, g^w, g^{x_1} g^{wx_2}, g^{y_1} g^{wy_2}, \mathcal{O}_H, F)$ and a secret key $sk = (w, x_1, x_2, y_1, y_2)$ such that $g \in_R G$ and $(w, x_1, x_2, y_1, y_2) \in_R \mathbb{Z}_p^5$.

*Encryption* :  Generate randomness $r \in_R \mathbb{Z}_p$, compute $u_1 = g^r$, $u_2 = (g^w)^r$, $\alpha = H(g^{x_1} g^{wx_2}, g^{y_1} g^{wy_2}, u_1, u_2)$, $v = (g^{x_1} g^{wx_2})^r \cdot (g^{y_1} g^{wy_2})^{r\alpha}$ and $K = F_v(pk, u_1, u_2)$, and output the ciphertext $CT = u_1$ and the session key $K$.

*Decryption* :  For input a ciphertext $CT = u_1$ and the part of public key $(g^{x_1} g^{wx_2}, g^{y_1} g^{wy_2})$, compute $\alpha = H(g^{x_1} g^{wx_2}, g^{y_1} g^{wy_2}, u_1, u_1^w)$. If $(g^{x_1} g^{wx_2}, g^{y_1} g^{wy_2}, u_1, u_1^w) \notin G^4$, reject the decryption as an invalid ciphertext. Otherwise, compute $v = u_1^{x_1 + \alpha y_1 + w(x_2 + \alpha y_2)}$ and $K = F_v(pk, u_1, u_1^w)$, and output the session key $K$.

**Security.**   In this section, we show the security of the above scheme.

**Theorem 2.** *If the DDH assumption on $G$ holds, and $F$ is a $\pi$PRF with index $(I_G, f_G)$ where $I_G \leftarrow \{(V, W, d) | (V, W, d) \in G^2 \times \mathbb{Z}_p\}$ and $f_G : (V, W, d) \mapsto V^{\gamma_1 + d\gamma_2} W$ with $(\gamma_1, \gamma_2) \in_R \mathbb{Z}_p^2$, then the compact Okamoto KEM is CCA-secure where $H$ is observable and TCR.*

The proof of Theorem 2 will be given in the full paper. The difference from the proof of the original Okamoto KEM is in the base unification, and can be solved as the proof of Theorem 1 similarly.

## 4.3   Compact CCA-secure PKE from the CDH Assumption

In this section, we present a CCA-secure PKE scheme by applying the hashing verification-tag trick to the HJKS KEM. This scheme achieves the same length of ciphertext as the transformed CS PKE (i.e., under the DDH assumption) though the scheme relies on the CDH assumption which is weaker than the DDH assumption.

**Original Haralambiev-Jager-Kiltz-Shoup KEM.**   Firstly, we review the original HJKS KEM. The HJKS KEM uses the twinning trick.

Let $p$ be a prime and $G$ be a finite cyclic group of order $p$. $H : G \to \mathbb{Z}_p$ is a TCR hash function. $f : G \to \{0,1\}$ is a hardcore bit function for Diffie-Hellman key in $G$.

*Key generation* : For input $\kappa$, output a public key $pk = (g, g^{x_1}, g^{x_2}, g^{y_1}, g^{y_2}, g^{z_1}, \ldots, g^{z_k}, H, f)$ and a secret key $sk = (x_1, x_2, y_1, y_2, z_1, \ldots, z_k)$ such that $g \in_R G$ and $(x_1, x_2, y_1, y_2, z_1, \ldots, z_k) \in_R \mathbb{Z}_p^{k+4}$.

*Encryption* :   Generate randomness $r \in_R \mathbb{Z}_p$, compute $u = g^r$, $\alpha = H(u)$, $v_1 = ((g^{x_1})^{\alpha} g^{x_2})^r$, $v_2 = ((g^{y_1})^{\alpha} g^{y_2})^r$, and $K = (f((g^{z_1})^r), \ldots, f((g^{z_k})^r))$, and output the ciphertext $CT = (u, v_1, v_2)$ and the session key $K$.

*Decryption* :   For input a ciphertext $CT = (u, v_1, v_2)$, compute $\alpha = H(u)$. If $v_1 \neq u^{x_1 \alpha + x_2}$ or $v_2 \neq u^{y_1 \alpha + y_2}$, reject the decryption as an invalid ciphertext. Otherwise, output the session key $K = (f(u^{z_1}), \ldots, f(u^{z_k}))$.

For the twinning trick, $v_1$ and $v_2$ are doubly verified. For definitions of the CDH assumption and the S2DH assumption, please refer to [8].

**Compact Haralambiev-Jager-Kiltz-Shoup KEM.**   Next, we show our third scheme which is applied the hashing verification-tag trick to the HJKS KEM.

Let $p$ be a prime and let $g$ be a generator of a finite cyclic group $G$ of order $p$. $H : G \to \mathbb{Z}_p$ and $H' : G^2 \to \{0,1\}^k$ are O-TCRHFs. To represent observability, evaluations of $H$ and $H'$ are done through oracles $\mathcal{O}_H$ and $\mathcal{O}_{H'}$ respectively. $f : G \to \{0,1\}$ is a hardcore bit function for Diffie-Hellman key in $G$.

*Key generation* : For input $\kappa$, output a public key $pk = (g, g^{x_1}, g^{x_2}, g^{y_1}, g^{y_2}, g^{z_1}, \ldots, g^{z_k}, \mathcal{O}_H, \mathcal{O}_{H'}, f)$ and a secret key $sk = (x_1, x_2, y_1, y_2, z_1, \ldots, z_k)$ such that $g \in_R G$ and $(x_1, x_2, y_1, y_2, z_1, \ldots, z_k) \in_R \mathbb{Z}_p^{k+4}$.

*Encryption* :   Generate randomness $r \in_R \mathbb{Z}_p$, compute $u = g^r$, $\alpha = H(u)$, $v_1 = ((g^{x_1})^{\alpha} g^{x_2})^r$, $v_2 = ((g^{y_1})^{\alpha} g^{y_2})^r$, $v = H'(v_1, v_2)$ and $K = (f((g^{z_1})^r), \ldots, f((g^{z_k})^r))$, and output the ciphertext $CT = (u, v)$ and the session key $K$.

*Decryption* :   For input a ciphertext $CT = (u, v)$, compute $\alpha = H(u)$ and $H'(u^{x_1 \alpha + x_2}, u^{y_1 \alpha + y_2})$. If $v \neq H'(u^{x_1 \alpha + x_2}, u^{y_1 \alpha + y_2})$, reject the decryption as an invalid ciphertext. Otherwise, output the session key $K = (f(u^{z_1}), \ldots, f(u^{z_k}))$.

**Security.**   In this section, we show the security of the above scheme.

**Theorem 3.** *If the CDH assumption on $G$ holds, then the compact HJKS KEM is CCA-secure where $H$ and $H'$ are observable and TCR.*

The proof of Theorem 3 will be given in the full paper. The difference from the proof of the original HJKS KEM is in the hashing verification-tag, and can be solved as the proof of Theorem 1 similarly.

# 5    Comparison

In this section, we give the efficiency comparison of our schemes and previous CCA-secure PKE and KEM schemes (i.e., the CS PKE, the Boyen-Mei-Waters (BMW) PKE, the Kiltz KEM, the HJKS PKE, the Okamoto KEM, and the Abe-Kiltz-Okamoto PKE).

Our first scheme is based on the CS PKE. It has mainly two advantages compared with the CS PKE. Firstly, this scheme needs one less regular exponentiation for the decryption operation than that of the CS PKE. This benefit comes from that all exponentiations in the decryption are computed on the base $u_1$. By using Pippenger's algorithm [32], these computations can be batched as one multi-exponentiation. Secondly, ciphertext overhead of this scheme is $|g| + |TCR|$. The BMW PKE achieves both the HMS bound $(2|g|)$ and the CCA-security. However, our scheme achieves more compact ciphertext overhead than this bound. Also, the BMW PKE needs a pairing computation for the decryption operation. Thus, even assuming a bilinear pairing takes three times as long as a regular exponentiation, this scheme has the advantage of computational complexity for the decryption operation. The first scheme can be proved only under the DDH assumption.

Our second scheme is based on the Okamoto KEM. Though the scheme needs the assumption of $\pi$PRF as the Okamoto KEM, it achieves less ciphertext overhead than the first scheme, which equals ciphertext overhead of the ElGamal PKE and optimal ciphertext length. Also, computational complexity for both the encryption and the decryption operation is same as the lowest complexity of previous schemes. Such an optimally compact ciphertext is due to the assumption of $\pi$PRF. However, since there is no previous study about how $\pi$PRF is stronger than PRF explicitly, the assumption of $\pi$PRF may be too strong.

Our third scheme is based on the HJKS KEM. The most attractive point of the scheme is that it relies on just the CDH assumption which is weaker than the DDH assumption. Also, though previous secure schemes with O-TCRHFs under the CDH assumption (such as the HJKS PKE) needs ciphertext overhead consisting of $3|g|$ or $2|g| + |MAC|$, this scheme needs just $|g| + |TCR|$. It is same ciphertext overhead as the first scheme which is proved under the DDH assumption though the key size is very large.

# References

1. Nielsen, J.D.: Separating Random Oracle Proofs from Complexity Theoretic Proofs: The Non-committing Encryption Case. In: Yung, M. (ed.) CRYPTO 2002. LNCS, vol. 2442, pp. 111–126. Springer, Heidelberg (2002)

2. Ananth, P., Bhaskar, R.: Non Observability in the Random Oracle Model. In: Susilo, W., Reyhanitabar, R. (eds.) ProvSec 2013. LNCS, vol. 8209, pp. 86–103. Springer, Heidelberg (2013)
3. Hanaoka, G., Matsuda, T., Schuldt, J.C.N.: On the Impossibility of Constructing Efficient Key Encapsulation and Programmable Hash Functions in Prime Order Groups. In: Safavi-Naini, R., Canetti, R. (eds.) CRYPTO 2012. LNCS, vol. 7417, pp. 812–831. Springer, Heidelberg (2012)
4. Cramer, R., Shoup, V.: A Practical Public Key Cryptosystem Provably Secure against Adaptive Chosen Ciphertext Attack. In: Krawczyk, H. (ed.) CRYPTO 1998. LNCS, vol. 1462, pp. 13–25. Springer, Heidelberg (1998)
5. Kurosawa, K., Desmedt, Y.: A New Paradigm of Hybrid Encryption Scheme. In: Franklin, M. (ed.) CRYPTO 2004. LNCS, vol. 3152, pp. 426–442. Springer, Heidelberg (2004)
6. Boyen, X., Mei, Q., Waters, B.: Direct chosen ciphertext security from identity-based techniques. In: ACM Conference on Computer and Communications Security 2005, pp. 320–329. ACM Press (2005)
7. Kiltz, E.: Chosen-Ciphertext Secure Key-Encapsulation Based on Gap Hashed Diffie-Hellman. In: Okamoto, T., Wang, X. (eds.) PKC 2007. LNCS, vol. 4450, pp. 282–297. Springer, Heidelberg (2007)
8. Haralambiev, K., Jager, T., Kiltz, E., Shoup, V.: Simple and Efficient Public-Key Encryption from Computational Diffie-Hellman in the Standard Model. In: Nguyen, P.Q., Pointcheval, D. (eds.) PKC 2010. LNCS, vol. 6056, pp. 1–18. Springer, Heidelberg (2010)
9. Abdalla, M., Bellare, M., Rogaway, P.: The Oracle Diffie-Hellman Assumptions and an Analysis of DHIES. In: Naccache, D. (ed.) CT-RSA 2001. LNCS, vol. 2020, pp. 143–158. Springer, Heidelberg (2001)
10. Bellare, M., Rogaway, P.: Random Oracles are Practical: A Paradigm for Designing Efficient Protocols. In: ACM Conference on Computer and Communications Security 1993, pp. 62–73. ACM Press (1993)
11. Fischlin, M., Lehmann, A., Ristenpart, T., Shrimpton, T., Stam, M., Tessaro, S.: Random Oracles with(out) Programmability. In: Abe, M. (ed.) ASIACRYPT 2010. LNCS, vol. 6477, pp. 303–320. Springer, Heidelberg (2010)
12. Boyen, X.: Miniature CCA2 PK Encryption: Tight Security Without Redundancy. In: Kurosawa, K. (ed.) ASIACRYPT 2007. LNCS, vol. 4833, pp. 485–501. Springer, Heidelberg (2007)
13. Abe, M., Kiltz, E., Okamoto, T.: Chosen Ciphertext Security with Optimal Ciphertext Overhead. In: Pieprzyk, J. (ed.) ASIACRYPT 2008. LNCS, vol. 5350, pp. 355–371. Springer, Heidelberg (2008)
14. Abe, M., Kiltz, E., Okamoto, T.: Compact CCA-Secure Encryption for Messages of Arbitrary Length. In: Jarecki, S., Tsudik, G. (eds.) PKC 2009. LNCS, vol. 5443, pp. 377–392. Springer, Heidelberg (2009)
15. Canetti, R., Goldreich, O., Halevi, S.: The Random Oracle Methodology, Revisited (Preliminary Version). In: STOC 1998, pp. 131–140. ACM Press (1998)
16. Canetti, R., Goldreich, O., Halevi, S.: The Random Oracle Methodology, Revisited. J. ACM 51(4), 557–594 (2004)
17. Bellare, M., Hoang, V.T., Keelveedhi, S.: Instantiating Random Oracles via UCEs. In: Canetti, R., Garay, J.A. (eds.) CRYPTO 2013, Part II. LNCS, vol. 8043, pp. 398–415. Springer, Heidelberg (2013)
18. Bellare, M., Rogaway, P.: Optimal Asymmetric Encryption. In: De Santis, A. (ed.) EUROCRYPT 1994. LNCS, vol. 950, pp. 92–111. Springer, Heidelberg (1995)

19. Matsuda, T., Hanaoka, G.: Chosen Ciphertext Security via UCE. In: Krawczyk, H. (ed.) PKC 2014. LNCS, vol. 8383, pp. 56–76. Springer, Heidelberg (2014)
20. Brzuska, C., Farshim, P., Mittelbach, A.: Indistinguishability Obfuscation and UCEs: The Case of Computationally Unpredictable Sources. Cryptology ePrint Archive: 2014/099 (2014)
21. Cash, D., Kiltz, E., Shoup, V.: The Twin Diffie-Hellman Problem and Applications. J. Cryptology 22(4), 470–504 (2009)
22. Yamada, S., Kawai, Y., Hanaoka, G., Kunihiro, N.: Public Key Encryption Schemes from the (B)CDH Assumption with Better Efficiency. IEICE Transactions 93-A(11), 1984–1993 (2010)
23. Okamoto, T.: Authenticated Key Exchange and Key Encapsulation in the Standard Model. In: Kurosawa, K. (ed.) ASIACRYPT 2007. LNCS, vol. 4833, pp. 474–484. Springer, Heidelberg (2007), http://eprint.iacr.org/2007/473/
24. Elgamal, T.: A public key cryptosystem and a signature scheme based on discrete logarithms. IEEE Transactions on Information Theory 31(4), 469–472 (1985)
25. Hanaoka, G., Kurosawa, K.: Efficient Chosen Ciphertext Secure Public Key Encryption under the Computational Diffie-Hellman Assumption. In: Pieprzyk, J. (ed.) ASIACRYPT 2008. LNCS, vol. 5350, pp. 308–325. Springer, Heidelberg (2008)
26. Dodis, Y., Ristenpart, T., Shrimpton, T.: Salvaging Merkle-Damgård for Practical Applications. In: Joux, A. (ed.) EUROCRYPT 2009. LNCS, vol. 5479, pp. 371–388. Springer, Heidelberg (2009)
27. Yoneyama, K., Miyagawa, S., Ohta, K.: Leaky Random Oracle (Extended Abstract). In: Baek, J., Bao, F., Chen, K., Lai, X. (eds.) ProvSec 2008. LNCS, vol. 5324, pp. 226–240. Springer, Heidelberg (2008)
28. Brzuska, C., Mittelbach, A.: Using Indistinguishability Obfuscation via UCEs. Cryptology ePrint Archive: 2014/381 (2014)
29. Garg, S., Gentry, C., Halevi, S., Raykova, M., Sahai, A., Waters, B.: Candidate Indistinguishability Obfuscation and Functional Encryption for all Circuits. In: FOCS 2013, pp. 40–49. IEEE (2013)
30. Pass, R., Seth, K., Telang, S.: Indistinguishability Obfuscation from Semantically-Secure Multilinear Encodings. In: Garay, J.A., Gennaro, R. (eds.) CRYPTO 2014, Part I. LNCS, vol. 8616, pp. 500–517. Springer, Heidelberg (2014)
31. Gentry, C., Lewko, A.B., Sahai, A., Waters, B.: Indistinguishability Obfuscation from the Multilinear Subgroup Elimination Assumption. Cryptology ePrint Archive: 2014/309 (2014)
32. Bernstein, D.J.: Pippenger's exponentiation algorithm (2001), http://cr.yp.to/papers.html

# RCCA-Secure Multi-use Bidirectional Proxy Re-encryption with Master Secret Security

Rongxing Lu[1], Xiaodong Lin[2], Jun Shao[3], and Kaitai Liang[4]

[1] School of Electrical and Electronic Engineering, Nanyang Technological University,
50 Nanyang Avenue, Singapore 639798
[2] Faculty of Business and Information Technology,
University of Ontario Institute of Technology, Ontario, Canada
[3] School of Computer and Information Engineering, Zhejiang Gongshang University,
Hangzhou, Zhejiang, P.R. China
[4] Department of Computer Science, City University of Hong Kong,
Tat Chee Avenue, Kowloon, Hong Kong
rxlu@ntu.edu.sg, xiaodong.lin@uoit.ca, chn.junshao@gmail.com,
kliang4-c@my.cityu.edu.hk

**Abstract.** Bidirectional proxy re-encryption allows ciphertext transformation between Alice and Bob via a semi-trusted proxy, who however cannot obtain the corresponding plaintext. Due to this special property, bidirectional proxy re-encryption has become a flexible tool in many dynamic environments, such as publish subscribe systems, group communication, and cloud computing. Nonetheless, how to design a secure and efficient bidirectional proxy re-encryption is still challenging. In this paper, we propose a novel bidirectional proxy re-encryption scheme that holds the following nice properties: 1) constant ciphertext size no matter how many times the transformation performed; 2) master secret security in the random oracle model, i.e., Alice (resp. Bob) colluding with the proxy cannot obtain Bob's (resp. Alice's) private key; 3) Replayable chosen ciphertext (RCCA) security in the random oracle model. To the best of our knowledge, our proposal is the first bidirectional proxy re-encryption scheme that holds the above three properties simultaneously.

**Keywords:** bidirectional proxy re-encryption, replayable chosen-ciphertext attack, random oracle model, multi-use.

## 1 Introduction

*Proxy re-encryption* (PRE) [2] allows a secure ciphertext transformation in a way that a semi-trusted proxy can use a re-encryption key delegated from Alice (and Bob) to re-encrypt a ciphertext under Alice's public key into a new ciphertext that Bob can decrypt by using his own private key. However, the proxy cannot do any decryption on the ciphertexts of either Alice or Bob. If the re-encryption key can be used to do the re-encryption in both directions, the PRE scheme is called bidirectional; otherwise, it is called unidirectional. Both types of PRE have their own interesting applications. In this work, we shall focus on bidirectional

S.S.M. Chow et al. (Eds.): ProvSec 2014, LNCS 8782, pp. 194–205, 2014.

proxy re-encryption (BPRE), as it still encounters many research challenges when applied to practical scenarios.

The applications of BPRE mainly include publish/subscribe systems [9], vehicular communications [14], group communications [12,7], and cloud computing [17,15,10,8]. All these applications work in a dynamic environment which requires the PRE scheme to hold multi-usability and constant ciphertext size. In other words, it demands that the transformed ciphertext can be further transformed while the ciphertext size keeps the same.

To the best of our knowledge, there are only few BPRE schemes [2,5,11,16] satisfying the above requirements. However, those previously reported schemes in [2,5,11] suffer from the so-called collusion attack, i.e., Alice (resp. Bob) colluding with the proxy can obtain Bob's (resp. Alice's) private key. In practice, collusion resistance is crucial, especially when Alice (resp. Bob) uses the same private key to perform decrypting and signing, and she (resp. he) wants to delegate the decryption rights while keeping the signing rights. In general, the security notion dealing with the collusion attack is called master secret security proposed by Ateniese et al. [1]. Recently, Weng and Zhao [16] proposed two BPRE schemes based on pairings. One is multi-use but with only CPA secure, the other is CCA secure but not multi-use. Meanwhile, it has been showed that replayable chosen ciphertext (RCCA) security is also crucial in the applications of distributed storage [5]. Therefore, in this paper, to address the above challenges, we would like to propose the first scheme with multi-useability, constant ciphertext size, and RCCA security.

## 1.1  Related Work

At EUROCRYPT 1998, Blaze, Bleumer and Strauss [2] proposed the first BPRE scheme (named BBS98) base on ElGamal encryption [6]. Later on, Canetti and Hohenberger [5] proposed the first (R)CCA-secure BPRE scheme (named CH07) by using pairings. At PKC 2011, Matsuda, Nishimaki and Tanaka [11] proposed a new pairing-free CPA-secure bidirectional scheme (named MNT10). All of the above schemes hold multi-usability and constant ciphertext size, but they all suffer from the collusion attack. The main reason that the collusion attack works is that the re-encryption key is computed by $sk_A/sk_B$, where $sk_A$ and $sk_B$ are the private keys of Alice and Bob, respectively. It is easy to see that once $sk_A$ (resp. $sk_B$) and $sk_A/sk_B$ are put together, $sk_B$ (resp. $sk_A$) would be revealed.

Recently, Weng and Zhao [16] proposed two new BPRE schemes by using pairings. The first one (named WZ11a) is multi-use, CPA-secure and master secret secure, and the second one (named WZ11b) is multi-use, CCA-secure, and master secret secure. To obtain master secret security, the re-encryption key is computed by $sk_A'/sk_B'$, where $sk_A'$ and $sk_B'$ are not the private keys but the decryption keys of Alice and Bob, respectively. The analogous relations between $sk_A$ and $sk_A'$ can be found in the identity-based encryption [13,3], where the private key generator's master secret key and the user's private key can be considered as the analogies $sk_A$ and $sk_A'$, respectively. Clearly, knowing $sk_A'$ does not hurt the secrecy of $sk_A$.

In Table 1, we summarize the existing BPRE schemes in terms of secrecy of message, master secret security, multi useability and their complexity assumptions. From this table, we can see that our proposal would be the only one that can hold the desired properties at the same time.

Table 1. Summary of bidirectional proxy re-encryption schemes

|  | BBS98[2] | CH07[5] | MNT10[11] | WZ11a[16] | WZ11b[16] | Our proposal |
|---|---|---|---|---|---|---|
| **RCCA** | ✗ | ✓ | ✗ | ✗ | ✓ | ✓ |
| **CA**[a] | DDH | DBDH | re-applicable LTDFs | DBDH | 1-AwDBDHI | mDBDH |
| **MSS**[b] | ✗ | ✗ | ✗ | ✓ | ✓ | ✓ |
| **CA** | — | — | — | DL | DL | DL |
| **MU**[c] | ✓ | ✓ | ✓ | ✓ | ✗ | ✓ |

[a] CA denotes "Complexity Assumption".
[b] MSS denotes "Master Secret Security".
[c] MU denotes "Multi-Useability".

The rest of this paper is organized as follows. In Section 2, we give the definitions, security models of BPRE. Then, we present our proposal in Section 3, including the description, security analysis and computation comparison. Finally, we draw our conclusions in Section 4.

## 2  Definitions

### 2.1  Definition of Bidirectional Proxy Re-encryption

**Definition 1 (Bidirectional Proxy Re-Encryption).** *A Bidirectional proxy re-encryption scheme is a tuple of probabilistic polynomial time (PPT) algorithms (KeyGen, ReKeyGen, Enc, ReEnc, Dec):*

- KeyGen($1^\kappa$) → ($pk, sk$). *On input of the security parameter $1^\kappa$, the key generation algorithm* KeyGen *outputs a public key and private key pair ($pk, sk$).*
- ReKeyGen($sk_1, sk_2$) → $rk_{1,2}$. *On input of two private keys $sk_1$ and $sk_2$, the re-encryption key generation algorithm* ReKeyGen *outputs a bidirectional re-encryption key $rk_{1,2}$. Since it is bidirectional,* ReKeyGen($sk_2, sk_1$) *can be easily computed from* ReKeyGen($sk_1, sk_2$) *via a public function $\mathcal{F}$. For instance, $\mathcal{F}$ is the inversion of* ReKeyGen($sk_1, sk_2$) *in [2,5,16].*
  *In general speaking, this algorithm is interactive, involving the delegator, delegatee and proxy.*
- Enc($pk, m$) → $C$. *On input of a message $m$ from the message space and a public key $pk$, the encryption algorithm* Enc *outputs a ciphertext $C$.*

- $\text{ReEnc}(rk_{1,2}, C_1) \rightarrow C_2$. *On input of a re-encryption key $rk_{1,2}$ and a cipher-text $C_1$, the re-encryption algorithm* $\text{ReEnc}$ *outputs a re-encrypted ciphertext $C_2$ or a special symbol* reject.
- $\text{Dec}(sk, C) \rightarrow m$. *On input of a private key $sk$, and a ciphertext $C$, the decryption algorithm* $\text{Dec}$ *outputs a message $m$ or a special symbol* reject.

**Correctness.** For any message $m$ in the message space and any key pairs $(pk, sk), (pk', sk') \leftarrow \text{KeyGen}(1^\kappa)$, the following two conditions must hold:

$$\text{Dec}(sk, \text{Enc}(pk, m)) = m \text{ and } \text{Dec}(sk', \text{ReEnc}(rk, C)) = m,$$

where $rk$ is generated by $\text{ReKeyGen}(sk, sk')$ or $\mathcal{F}(\text{ReKeyGen}(sk', sk))$, and $C$ is the ciphertext for message $m$ under $pk$ from algorithm $\text{Enc}$ or $\text{ReEnc}$ if the bidirectional proxy re-encryption scheme is multi-use.

## 2.2 Replayable Chosen Ciphertext Security for Multi-use Bidirectional Proxy Re-encryption

The replayable chosen ciphertext security for multi-use BPRE is defined by the following RCCA game played between a challenger $\mathcal{C}$ and an adversary $\mathcal{A}$. As usual, the challenger $\mathcal{C}$ does not answer any queries which the adversary $\mathcal{A}$ can answer by itself using the secret it has been supplied, and returns only one answer for the same query. Moreover, the adversary $\mathcal{A}$ should decide which party will be corrupted before the game starts. In other words, our RCCA security is defined in the static model.

*Setup:* The challenger $\mathcal{C}$ sets up the system parameters, and initializes one empty table $\mathbb{T}_k$ which will be used to record all key pairs.
*Phase 1:* The adversary $\mathcal{A}$ can issue the following queries adaptively.
  - *Public key generation oracle $\mathcal{O}_{pk}$:* $\mathcal{C}$ takes a security parameter $1^\kappa$, runs $\text{KeyGen}(1^\kappa)$ to generate a key pair $(pk_i, sk_i)$, gives $pk_i$ to $\mathcal{A}$ and records $(pk_i, sk_i)$ in the table $\mathbb{T}_k$. In the following, $sk_i$ is the corresponding private key of $pk_i$.
  - *Private key generation oracle $\mathcal{O}_{sk}$:* On input of $pk_i$ by $\mathcal{A}$, $\mathcal{C}$ searches for $pk_i$ in the table $\mathbb{T}_k$, and returns $sk_i$.
  - *Re-encryption key generation oracle $\mathcal{O}_{rk}$:* On input of two different public keys $(pk_i, pk_j)$ by $\mathcal{A}$, $\mathcal{C}$ returns the re-encryption key $rk_{i,j} = \text{ReKeyGen}(sk_i, sk_j)$. It is required that both $pk_i$ and $pk_j$ are corrupted or uncorrupted.
  - *Re-encryption oracle $\mathcal{O}_{re}$:* On input of $(pk_i, pk_j, C)$ by $\mathcal{A}$, $\mathcal{C}$ returns the re-encrypted ciphertext $C' = \text{ReEnc}(\text{ReKeyGen}(sk_i, sk_j), C)$.
  - *Decryption oracle $\mathcal{O}_{dec}$:* On input $(pk_i, C_i)$, $\mathcal{C}$ returns $\text{Dec}(sk_i, C_i)$.
*Challenge:* Once $\mathcal{A}$ decides that Phase 1 is over, it outputs two equal length plaintexts $m_0^*, m_1^*$ from the message space, and an uncorrupted public key $pk^*$ on which it wishes to challenge. $\mathcal{C}$ picks a random bit $\mathbf{b} \in \{0, 1\}$ and sets $C^* = \text{Enc}(pk^*, m_{\mathbf{b}}^*)$. It sends $C^*$ as the challenge to $\mathcal{A}$.

**Phase 2:** This phase is almost the same as Phase 1 but with the following restrictions.

- $\mathcal{O}_{re}$: On input of $(pk_1, pk_2, C_1)$ by $\mathcal{A}$, if $(pk_1, C_1)$ is a derivative of $(pk^*, C^*)$, and $pk_2$ is corrupted, $\mathcal{C}$ outputs reject. We say $(pk_1, C_1)$ is a derivative of $(pk^*, C^*)$ if one of the following conditions holds.
  - $(pk_1, C_1) = (pk^*, C^*)$.
  - $(pk, C)$ is a derivative of $(pk^*, C^*)$, and $(pk_1, C_1)$ is a derivative of $(pk, C)$.
  - $(pk_1, C_1) \leftarrow \mathcal{O}_{re}(pk, pk_1, C)$, where $(pk, C)$ is a derivative of $(pk^*, C^*)$.
  - The adversary $A$ can use the re-encryption keys from $\mathcal{O}_{rk}$ to transform ciphertexts under $pk^*$ to that under $pk$ by running ReEnc, and $\mathcal{O}_{dec}(pk_1, C_1) \in \{m_0^*, m_1^*\}$.
- $\mathcal{O}_{dec}$: On input of $(pk_i, C_i)$, if the output is $m_0^*$ or $m_1^*$, $\mathcal{C}$ returns reject.

**Guess:** Finally, the adversary $\mathcal{A}$ outputs a guess $\mathbf{b}' \in \{0, 1\}$ and wins the game if $\mathbf{b} = \mathbf{b}'$.

We refer to such an adversary $\mathcal{A}$ as an RCCA adversary. We define adversary $\mathcal{A}$'s advantage in attacking multi-use BPRE as the following function of the security parameter $\kappa$: $\mathbf{Adv}_{\text{MBPRE}}^{\text{RCCA}}(1^\kappa) = |\Pr[\mathbf{b} = \mathbf{b}'] - 1/2|$. Using the RCCA game, we can define RCCA security of multi-use BPRE.

**Definition 2 (RCCA Security).** *If for any PPT RCCA adversary $\mathcal{A}$ the function $\mathbf{Adv}_{\text{MBPRE}}^{\text{RCCA}}(1^\kappa)$ is negligible, the multi-use bidirectional proxy re-encryption scheme is RCCA-secure.*

### 2.3 Master Secret Security for Multi-use Bidirectional Proxy Re-encryption.

The master secret security for multi-use BPRE is defined by the following MSS game played between a challenger $\mathcal{C}$ and an adversary $\mathcal{A}$. As usual, the challenger $\mathcal{C}$ does not answer any queries which the adversary $\mathcal{A}$ can answer by itself using the secret it has been supplied, and returns only one answer for the same query. Moreover, all the public keys involved in the following oracles (except $\mathcal{O}_{pk}$) are from $\mathcal{O}_{pk}$. It is worth mentioning that in the MSS game, the adversary does not need to decide the corrupted user before the game starts. In other words, our master secret security is defined in the adaptive model.

**Find:** The adversary $\mathcal{A}$ can issue the following queries adaptively.

- *Public key generation oracle* $\mathcal{O}_{pk}$: $\mathcal{C}$ takes a security parameter $1^\kappa$, runs KeyGen($1^\kappa$) to generate a key pair $(pk_i, sk_i)$, gives $pk_i$ to $\mathcal{A}$ and records $(pk_i, sk_i)$ in the table $\mathbb{T}_k$. In the following, $sk_i$ is the corresponding private key of $pk_i$.
- *Private key generation oracle* $\mathcal{O}_{sk}$: On input of $pk_i$ by $\mathcal{A}$, $\mathcal{C}$ searches for $pk_i$ in the table $\mathbb{T}_k$, and returns $sk_i$.
- *Re-encryption key generation oracle* $\mathcal{O}_{rk}$: On input of $(pk_i, pk_j)$ by $\mathcal{A}$, $\mathcal{C}$ returns the re-encryption key $rk_{i,j} = \text{ReKeyGen}(sk_i, sk_j)$.

- *Re-encryption oracle* $\mathcal{O}_{re}$: On input of $(pk_i, pk_j, C)$ by $\mathcal{A}$, $\mathcal{C}$ returns the re-encrypted ciphertext $C' = \text{ReEnc}(\text{ReKeyGen}(sk_i, sk_j), C)$.
- *Decryption oracle* $\mathcal{O}_{dec}$: On input of $(pk_i, C_i)$, $\mathcal{C}$ returns $\text{Dec}(sk_i, C_i)$.

**Output:** If $\mathcal{A}$ outputs a private key of a public key that has not been queried to $\mathcal{O}_{sk}$, $\mathcal{A}$ wins the game.

We also define $\text{Adv}_{\text{MBPRE}}^{\text{MSS}}(1^\kappa) = \Pr[\mathcal{A} \text{ Wins}]$ for the security parameter $\kappa$ as that in RCCA security.

**Definition 3 (Master Secret Security).** *If for any PPT MSS adversary $\mathcal{A}$ the function $\text{Adv}_{\text{MBPRE}}^{\text{MSS}}(1^\kappa)$ is negligible, the multi-use bidirectional proxy re-encryption scheme is MS-secure.*

## 2.4  Bilinear Groups

In this subsection, we briefly review the definitions about bilinear maps and bilinear map groups, which follow those in [3,4].

1. $\mathbb{G}$ and $\mathbb{G}_T$ are two (multiplicative) cyclic groups of prime order $q$;
2. $g$ is a generator of $\mathbb{G}$;
3. $e$ is a bilinear map $e : \mathbb{G} \times \mathbb{G} \to \mathbb{G}_T$.

Let $\mathbb{G}$ and $\mathbb{G}_T$ be two groups as above. An *admissible bilinear map* is a map $e : \mathbb{G} \times \mathbb{G} \to \mathbb{G}_T$ with the following properties:

1. *Bilinearity*: For all $P, Q, R \in \mathbb{G}$, $e(P \cdot Q, R) = e(P, R) \cdot e(Q, R)$ and $e(P, Q \cdot R) = e(P, Q) \cdot e(P, R)$.
2. *Non-degeneracy*: If $e(P, Q) = 1$ for all $Q \in \mathbb{G}$, then $P = \mathcal{O}$, where $\mathcal{O}$ is a point at infinity.

We say that $\mathbb{G}$ is a bilinear group if the group action in $\mathbb{G}$ can be computed efficiently and there exists a group $\mathbb{G}_T$ and an efficiently computable bilinear map as above. We denote BSetup as an algorithm that, on input the security parameter $1^\kappa$, outputs the parameters for a bilinear map as $(q, g, \mathbb{G}, \mathbb{G}_T, e)$, where $q \in \Theta(2^\kappa)$.

## 2.5  Complexity Assumptions

The security of our proposal is based on the modified decisional bilinear Diffie-Hellman assumption and discrete logarithm assumption. Since the latter assumption is quite well-known, we only give the definition of the former assumption in this paper.

**Definition 4 (Modified   Decisional   Bilinear   Diffie-Hellman Assumption).** *Let $(q, g, \mathbb{G}, \mathbb{G}_T, e) \leftarrow \text{BSetup}(1^k)$. The modified decisional bilinear Diffie-Hellman problem (mDBDH) in $(\mathbb{G}, \mathbb{G}_T)$ is defined as follows: given tuple $(g, g^a, g^{1/a}, g^b, g^c, T) \in \mathbb{G}^5 \times \mathbb{G}_T$ as input, decide whether $S = e(g,g)^{abc}$. An algorithm $\mathcal{A}$ has advantage $\varepsilon$ in solving the mDBDH problem in $(\mathbb{G}, \mathbb{G}_T)$ if*

$$|\Pr[\mathcal{A}(g, g^a, g^{1/a}, g^b, g^c, e(g,g)^{abc}) = 0] - \Pr[\mathcal{A}(g, g^a, g^{1/a}, g^b, g^c, T) = 0]| \geq \epsilon,$$

*where the probability is taken over the random choices of $a, b, c \in \mathbb{Z}_q$, $S \in \mathbb{G}$ and the random bits of $\mathcal{A}$.*

*We say that the $(t, \epsilon)$-modified decisional Bilinear Diffie-Hellman assumption holds in $(\mathbb{G}, \mathbb{G}_T)$ if no $t$-time algorithm has advantage $\epsilon$ at least in solving the mDBDH problem in $(\mathbb{G}, \mathbb{G}_T)$.*

# 3  Our Proposal

## 3.1  Description

The system parameters are $(q, g, h, e, \mathbb{G}, \mathbb{G}_T)$, where $(q, g, e, \mathbb{G}, \mathbb{G}_T)$ are from BSetup, and $h$ is a random element from $\mathbb{G}$. Furthermore, it requires two secure cryptographic hash functions $H_1 : \{0,1\}^* \to \{0,1\}^\kappa$ and $H_2 : \{0,1\}^* \to \{0,1\}^\kappa$, where $\kappa$ is a security parameter.

- KeyGen: Select random $x_1, x_2, z_1 \in \mathbb{Z}_q$, Next, compute $X_{1,g} = e(g,g)^{x_1}$, $X_{1,h} = e(g,h)^{x_1}$, $X_2 = g^{x_2}$, $Z_1 = g^{z_1}$, $z_2 = (x_1 - z_1)/x_2 \bmod q$, and $Z_2 = g^{z_2}$. The public key is

$$pk = (X_{1,g}, X_{1,h}, X_2, Z_1, Z_2),$$

  and the private key is

$$sk = (x_1, x_2, z_1, z_2).$$

- ReKeyGen: On input two private keys $sk = (x_1, x_2, z_1, z_2)$ and $sk' = (x'_1, x'_2, z'_1, z'_2)$, it outputs the re-encryption key

$$rk = (rk_1, rk_2) = (z_1/z'_1 \bmod q, z_2/z'_2 \bmod q).$$

  The re-encryption key can be computed efficiently by the method in [2,5].
- Enc: On input $pk = (X_{1,g}, X_{1,h}, X_2, Z_1, Z_2)$ and $m \in \mathbb{G}_T$, do the following steps.
    • Choose random $r$ from $\mathbb{Z}_q$.
    • Compute

$$u_1 = g^r, \quad u_2 = X_2^r, \quad v = X_{1,h}^r \cdot m, \quad u_3 = X_{1,g}^r,$$

$$u_4 = H_1(v \| u_3)^r, \quad u_5 = H_2(v \| u_3)^r$$

  Note that the item $u_5$ is only useful in the security proof.
    • Output $C = (u_1, u_2, v, u_3, u_4, u_5)$ as the ciphertext.
- ReEnc: On input a re-encryption key $rk = (rk_1, rk_2) = (z_1/z'_1 \bmod q, z_2/z'_2 \bmod q)$ and a ciphertext $C = (u_1, u_2, v, u_3, u_4, u_5)$ under key $pk = (X_{1,g}, X_{1,h}, X_2, Z_1, Z_2)$, the proxy performs as follows.
    • Check whether

$$e(u_1, H_1(v \| u_3)) = e(g, u_4) \tag{1}$$

$$e(u_2, H_2(v \| u_3)) = e(g, u_5) \tag{2}$$

$$e(u_1, Z_1) \cdot e(u_2, Z_2) = u_3 \tag{3}$$

all hold. If not, abort; otherwise, do the next steps.

- Compute $u_1' = u_1^{rk_1}$, $u_2' = u_2^{rk_2}$, $u_4' = u_4^{rk_1}$, and $u_5' = u_5^{rk_1}$.
- Output $(u_1', u_2', v, u_3, u_4', u_5')$ as the re-encrypted ciphertext.

Note that

$$u_1' = u_1^{rk_1} = g^{rz_1/z_1'}, \quad u_2' = u_2^{rk_2} = g^{rx_2z_2/z_2'}$$

$$u_4' = u_4^{rk_1} = H_1(v\|u_3)^{rz_1/z_1'}, \quad u_5' = u_5^{rk_2} = H_2(v\|u_3)^{rz_1/z_1'}$$

- Dec: On input a private key $(x_1, x_2, z_1, z_2)$ and any ciphertext $C = (u_1, u_2, v, u_3, u_4, u_5)$, the decryptor performs as follows.
  - Check whether Equalities (1), (2), (3) all hold. If not, abort; otherwise, do the next steps.
  - Compute $m = v/(e(u_1^{z_1}, h) \cdot e(u_2^{z_2}, h))$. Note that if the ciphertext $C$ is from Enc, we have that

$$v/(e(u_1^{z_1}, h) \cdot e(u_2^{z_2}, h)) = e(h, g^{x_1 r}) \cdot m/(e(h, g^{z_1 r}) \cdot e(h, g^{z_2 x_2 r})) = m;$$

  if the ciphertext $C$ is from ReEnc, we have that

$$v/(e(u_1^{z_1}, h) \cdot e(u_2^{z_2}, h)) = e(h, g^{x_1' r}) \cdot m/(e(h, g^{z_1' r}) \cdot e(h, g^{z_2' x_2' r})) = m.$$

  - Output the message $m$.

## 3.2 Security Analysis

**Theorem 1.** *If the mDBDH assumption holds in $\mathbb{G}$, our proposal is RCCA-secure in the random oracle model. In particular, we have*

$$\mathbf{Adv}_{MBPRE}^{RCCA}(1^\kappa) \leq \mathbf{Adv}_{mDBDH}^{\mathcal{A}}(1^\kappa),$$

*where $\mathbf{Adv}_{mDBDH}^{\mathcal{A}}(1^\kappa)$ is the advantage of that $\mathcal{A}$ breaks the mDBDH assumption under the security parameter $\kappa$.*

*Proof.* Assume there exists a RCCA adversary $\mathcal{A}$ that can break the RCCA security of our proposal. Then we can build another algorithm $\mathcal{B}$ that can break the mDBDH assumption (i.e., given $g, g^a, g^{1/a}, g^b, g^c, T$, it is hard to decide $T = e(g, g)^{abc}$) by playing the RCCA game with $\mathcal{A}$. The details are as follows. Before the game starts, $\mathcal{B}$ sets $h = g^b$.

$H_1$ **Oracle:** On input of $(v, u_3)$, check whether the tuple $(v, u_3, \alpha_1)$ exists in the list $L_{H_1}$. If yes, return $(g^a)^{\alpha_1}$; otherwise, it chooses a random $\alpha_1$ from $\mathbb{Z}_q$, and then records $(v, u_3, \alpha_1)$ in the list $L_{H_1}$, and return $(g^a)^{\alpha_1}$. Note that if the input $(v, u_3)$ is a part of the challenge ciphertext, then $\mathcal{B}$ just returns $g^{\alpha_1}$.

$H_2$ **Oracle:** On input of $(v, u_3)$, check whether the tuple $(v, u_3, \alpha_2)$ exists in the list $L_{H_2}$. If yes, return $(g^{1/a})^{\alpha_2}$; otherwise, it chooses a random $\alpha_2$ from $\mathbb{Z}_q$, and then records $(v, u_3, \alpha_2)$ in the list $L_{H_2}$, and return $(g^{1/a})^{\alpha_2}$. Note that if the input $(v, u_3)$ is a part of the challenge ciphertext, then $\mathcal{B}$ just returns $g^{\alpha_2}$.

**Phase 1:** $\mathcal{B}$ builds the oracles as follows.

– $\mathcal{O}_{pk}$: $\mathcal{B}$ chooses random elements $z_1, z_2, x_2$ from $\mathbb{Z}_q$. If the public key is uncorrupted, then $\mathcal{B}$ computes $X_1 = g^{z_1}((g^a)^{x_2})^{z_2}$ and returns

$$pk = (X_{1,g}, X_{1,h}, X_2, Z_1, Z_2)$$
$$= (e(g, X_1), e(h, X_1), g^{x_2}, g^{z_1}, (g^a)^{z_2});$$

if the public key is corrupted, then $\mathcal{B}$ computes $X_1 = g^{z_1}(g^{x_2})^{z_2}$ and returns

$$pk = (X_{1,g}, X_{1,h}, X_2, Z_1, Z_2)$$
$$= (e(g, X_1), e(h, X_1), g^{x_2}, g^{z_1}, g^{z_2}).$$

At last, $\mathcal{B}$ records $(pk, X_1, z_1, z_2, x_2)$ in $\mathbb{T}_k$.

– $\mathcal{O}_{sk}$: On input of a corrupted public key $pk$ by $\mathcal{A}$, $\mathcal{B}$ gets $(pk, z_1, z_2, x_2)$ from $\mathbb{T}_k$. $\mathcal{B}$ returns $sk = (z_1 + x_2 \cdot z_2 \bmod q, x_2, z_1, z_2)$.

– $\mathcal{O}_{rk}$: On input of $(pk, pk')$ by $\mathcal{A}$, $\mathcal{B}$ gets $(pk, z_1, z_2, x_2)$ and $(pk', z_1', z_2', x_2')$ from $\mathbb{T}_k$, and then returns

$$rk = (rk_1, rk_2) = (z_1/z_1' \bmod q, z_2/z_2' \bmod q).$$

Note that we have the following for the correctness.

• If the two public keys are both uncorrupted,

$$sk = (z_1 + x_2 \cdot a \cdot z_2 \bmod q, x_2, z_1, z_2 \cdot a \bmod q)$$

and

$$sk' = (z_1' + x_2' \cdot a \cdot z_2' \bmod q, a \cdot x_2', z_1', z_2' \cdot a \bmod q),$$

hence, $rk = (rk_1, rk_2) = (z_1/z_1' \bmod q, z_2/z_2' \bmod q)$.

• If the two public keys are both corrupted,

$$sk = (z_1 + x_2 \cdot z_2 \bmod q, x_2, z_1, z_2)$$

and

$$sk' = (z_1' + x_2' \cdot z_2' \bmod q, x_2', z_1', z_2'),$$

hence, $rk = (rk_1, rk_2) = (z_1/z_1' \bmod q, z_2/z_2' \bmod q)$.

– $\mathcal{O}_{re}$: On input of $C = (u_1, u_2, v, u_3, u_4, u_5)$ and two public keys $pk$ and $pk'$, $\mathcal{B}$ first checks the well-formness as the real execution. If it does not pass, abort; otherwise, do the followings.

• If the two public keys are both uncorrupted or corrupted, then $\mathcal{B}$ gets the re-encryption key from $\mathcal{O}_{rk}$, and returns the result of ReEnc.

• Otherwise, do the followings.

  * Find the items $(pk, X_1, z_1, z_2, x_2)$ and $(pk', X_1', z_1', z_2', x_2')$ in $\mathbb{T}_k$.
  * Compute $u_1' = u_1^{z_1/z_2}$, $u_4' = u_4^{z_1/z_2}$, and $u_5' = u_5^{z_1/z_2}$.
  * Find the original decryptor $pk_o$ of the ciphertext $C$ by checking $e(u_1, X_1) = u_3$ for all items in $\mathbb{T}_k$. Assume that the found item is $(pk_o, X_{o1}, z_{o1}, z_{o2}, x_{o2})$.

* Compute $g^r = u_1^{z_1/z_{o1}}$, $(g^a)^r = (u_4^{z_1/z_{o1}})^{1/\alpha_1}$ and $(g^{1/a})^r = (u_5^{z_1/z_{o1}})^{1/\alpha_2}$, where $\alpha_1, \alpha_2$ are the values in $L_{H_1}$ and $L_{H_2}$ corresponding to $(v, u_3)$, respectively.

* If $pk_o$ and $pk'$ are both corrupted or uncorrupted, then compute $u'_2 = (g^r)^{x_{o2} \cdot z_{o2}/z_2}$. If $pk_o$ is corrupted and $pk'$ is uncorrupted, then compute $u'_2 = ((g^{1/a})^r)^{x_{o2} \cdot z_{o2}/z_2}$. If $pk_o$ is uncorrupted and $pk'$ is corrupted, then compute $u'_2 = ((g^a)^r)^{x_{o2} \cdot z_{o2}/z_2}$.

* Output $(u'_1, u'_2, v, u_3, u'_4, u'_5)$ as the resultant ciphertext.

- $\mathcal{O}_{dec}$: On input of $C = (u_1, u_2, v, u_3, u_4)$ under $pk$, $\mathcal{B}$ first checks the well-formness as the real execution. If it does not pass, output $\perp$; otherwise, re-encrypt the ciphertext to the one under a corrupted public key by querying $\mathcal{O}_{re}$, then decrypt the resultant ciphertext by using the corresponding private key.

**Challenge:** $\mathcal{A}$ sends $\mathcal{C}$ two messages $m_0, m_1$ from $\mathbb{G}$ and an uncorrupted public key

$$pk^* = (X^*_{1,g}, X^*_{1,h}, X^*_2, Z^*_1, Z^*_2)$$
$$= (e(g, g^{z^*_1}(g^a)^{z^*_2}), e(h, g^{z^*_1}(g^a)^{z^*_2}), g^{x^*_2}, g^{z^*_1}, (g^a)^{z^*_2}),$$

$\mathcal{B}$ chooses a random number $\mathbf{b} \in \{0,1\}$, and returns $(u^*_1, u^*_2, v^*, u^*_3, u^*_4, u^*_5)$ as the challenge ciphertext.

$$u^*_1 = g^c, \quad u^*_2 = (g^b)^{x^*_2}, \quad v^* = e(g^b, g^c)^{z^*_1} \cdot T^{x^*_2 \cdot z^*_2} \cdot m_{\mathbf{b}},$$
$$u^*_3 = e(X^*_1, g^c), \quad u_4 = (g^b)^{\alpha^*_1}, \quad u_4 = (g^b)^{\alpha^*_2},$$

where $(X^*_1, z^*_1, z^*_2, x^*_2)$, $\alpha^*_1$ and $\alpha^*_2$ are from $\mathbb{T}_k$, $L_{H_1}$ and $L_{H_2}$, respectively. Note that if $T = g^{abc}$, we have that $v^* = e(g^b, g^c)^{z^*_1} \cdot T^{x^*_2 \cdot z^*_2} \cdot m_{\mathbf{b}} = e(g^b, X^*_1)^c \cdot m_{\mathbf{b}}$.

**Phase 2:** Almost the same as that in Phase 1, except the restrictions in the RCCA game.

**Guess:** $\mathcal{A}$ outputs the guess $\mathbf{b}'$. If $\mathbf{b}' = \mathbf{b}$, $\mathcal{B}$ decides $T = e(g,g)^{abc}$; otherwise, $T \neq e(g,g)^{abc}$.

It is easy to see that in the random oracle, the above simulation is perfect. Hence, we obtain this theorem. □

**Theorem 2.** *If the DL assumption holds in $\mathbb{G}$, our proposal is MS-secure in the random oracle model. In particular, we have*

$$\mathbf{Adv}^{\mathrm{MSS}}_{\mathrm{MBPRE}}(1^\kappa) \leq \frac{\mathbf{Adv}^{\mathcal{A}}_{\mathrm{DL}}(1^\kappa)}{e(1 + q_{sk})},$$

*where $\mathbf{Adv}^{\mathcal{A}}_{\mathrm{DL}}(1^\kappa)$ is the advantage of that $\mathcal{A}$ breaks the DL assumption under the security parameter $\kappa$, and $q_{sk}$ is the number of private key generation queries.*

*Proof.* Assume there exists an MSS adversary $\mathcal{A}$ that can break the MS security of our proposal. Then we can build another algorithm $\mathcal{B}$ that can break the DL assumption (i.e., given $g, g^a$, it is hard to compute $a$) by playing the MSS game with $\mathcal{A}$. The details are as follows.

**Find:** $\mathcal{B}$ builds the oracles as follows.
- Hash oracles: Identical to the proof of Theorem 1.
- $\mathcal{O}_{pk}$: $\mathcal{B}$ chooses random elements $z_1, z_2, x_2$ from $\mathbb{Z}_q$ and decides $\theta \in \{0, 1\}$ under $\Pr[\theta = 1] = \delta$. If $\theta = 0$, then $\mathcal{B}$ returns

$$pk = (X_{1,g}, X_{1,h}, X_1, Z_1, Z_2)$$
$$= (e(g, g^{z_1}((g^a)^{x_2})^{z_2}), e(h, g^{z_1}((g^a)^{x_2})^{z_2}), (g^a)^{x_2}, g^{z_1}, g^{z_2});$$

  if $\theta = 1$, then $\mathcal{B}$ returns

$$pk = (X_{1,g}, X_{1,h}, X_1, Z_1, Z_2)$$
$$= (e(g, g^{z_1}(g^{x_2})^{z_2}), e(h, g^{z_1}(g^{x_2})^{z_2}), g^{x_2}, g^{z_1}, g^{z_2})$$

  At last, $\mathcal{B}$ records $(pk, z_1, z_2, x_2, \theta)$ in $\mathbb{T}_k$.
- $\mathcal{O}_{sk}$: On input of a public key $pk$ by $\mathcal{A}$, $\mathcal{B}$ gets $(pk, z_1, z_2, x_2, \theta)$ from $\mathbb{T}_k$. If $\theta = 1$, then $\mathcal{B}$ returns $sk = (z_1 + x_2 \cdot z_2 \bmod q, x_2, z_1, z_2)$; otherwise, $\mathcal{B}$ outputs `failure`.
- $\mathcal{O}_{rk}$: On input of $(pk, pk')$ by $\mathcal{A}$, $\mathcal{B}$ gets $(pk, z_1, z_2, x_2, \theta)$ and $(pk', z_1', z_2', x_2', \theta')$ from $\mathbb{T}_k$, and then returns $rk = (rk_1, rk_2) = (z_1/z_1' \bmod q, z_2/z_2' \bmod q)$.
- $\mathcal{O}_{re}$: $\mathcal{B}$ can use the re-encryption keys from $\mathcal{O}_{rk}$ to reply the queries.
- $\mathcal{O}_{dec}$: Identical to the proof of Theorem 1.

**Output:** $\mathcal{A}$ outputs a private key $sk^* = (x_1, x_2, z_1, z_2)$ of public key $pk^*$ that has not been queried to $\mathcal{O}_{sk}$. $\mathcal{B}$ searches $(pk^*, z_1^*, z_2^*, x_2^*, \theta^*)$ in $\mathbb{T}_k$, if $\theta^* = 1$, then $\mathcal{B}$ outputs `failure`; otherwise, $\mathcal{B}$ outputs $a = x_2/x_2^*$.

If $\mathcal{B}$ has not output `failure`, then the above simulation is perfect. On the other hand, the probability of that $\mathcal{B}$ has not output `failure` is $\delta^{q_{sk}}(1 - \delta)$. The maximize value of $\delta^{q_{sk}}(1 - \delta)$ is $1/(e(1 + q_{sk}))$ when $\delta = 1 - 1/(q_{sk} + 1)$. Hence, we obtain this theorem. $\qquad\square$

# 4    Conclusion

In this paper, we have proposed a novel multi-use, bidirectional proxy re-encryption with constant ciphertext size, master secret security and RCCA security. To the best of our knowledge, it is the first BPRE scheme holding the above properties at the same time. There are still various future works left, e.g., how to design a pairing-free, multi-use BPRE scheme with constant ciphertext size, master secret security, and RCCA security is still unknown.

**Acknowledgements.** The authors thank the anonymous reviewers for their insightful comments and helpful suggestions. The first author would also like to thank the support of Nanyang Technological University under Grant NTU-SUG (M4081196) and MOE Tier 1 (M4011177). In addition, this work was also supported by NSFZJ (No. LR13F02003), Program for Zhejiang Leading Team of Science and Technology Innovation, the Science and Technology Project of Zhejiang Province (No. 2012C33070).

# References

1. Ateniese, G., Fu, K., Green, M., Hohenberger, S.: Improved proxy re-encryption schemes with applications to secure distributed storage. In: NDSS. The Internet Society (2005)
2. Blaze, M., Bleumer, G., Strauss, M.: Divertible protocols and atomic proxy cryptography. In: Nyberg, K. (ed.) EUROCRYPT 1998. LNCS, vol. 1403, pp. 127–144. Springer, Heidelberg (1998)
3. Boneh, D., Franklin, M.: Identity-based encryption from the weil pairing. In: Kilian, J. (ed.) CRYPTO 2001. LNCS, vol. 2139, pp. 213–229. Springer, Heidelberg (2001)
4. Boneh, D., Franklin, M.: Identity-based encryption from the weil pairing. SIAM Journal of Computing 32(3), 586–615 (2003)
5. Canetti, R., Hohenberger, S.: Chosen-ciphertext secure proxy re-encryption. In: Ning, P., De Capitani di Vimercati, S., Syverson, P.F. (eds.) ACM Conference on Computer and Communications Security, pp. 185–194. ACM (2007)
6. ElGamal, T.: A public key cryptosystem and a signature scheme based on discrete logarithms. IEEE Transactions on Information Theory 31(4), 469–472 (1985)
7. Huang, C.-Y., Chiu, Y.-P., Chen, K.-T., Lei, C.-L.: Secure multicast in dynamic environments. Computer Networks (Amsterdam, Netherlands: 1999) 51(10), 2805–2817 (2007)
8. Hur, J.: Improving Security and Efficiency in Attribute-Based Data Sharing. IEEE Transactions on Knowledge and Data Engineering (2012)
9. Kapadia, A., Tsang, P.P., Smith, S.W.: Attribute-based publishing with hidden credentials and hidden policies. In: NDSS. The Internet Society (2007)
10. Lin, H.-Y., Tzeng, W.-G.: A secure erasure code-based cloud storage system with secure data forwarding. IEEE Trans. Parallel Distrib. Syst. 23(6), 995–1003 (2012)
11. Matsuda, T., Nishimaki, R., Tanaka, K.: CCA proxy re-encryption without bilinear maps in the standard model. In: Nguyen, P.Q., Pointcheval, D. (eds.) PKC 2010. LNCS, vol. 6056, pp. 261–278. Springer, Heidelberg (2010)
12. Mukherjee, R., William Atwood, J.: Scalable solutions for secure group communications. Computer Networks (Amsterdam, Netherlands: 1999) 51(12), 3525–3548 (2007)
13. Shamir, A.: Identity-based cryptosystems and signature schemes. In: Blakely, G.R., Chaum, D. (eds.) CRYPTO 1984. LNCS, vol. 196, pp. 47–53. Springer, Heidelberg (1985)
14. Sun, Y., Lu, R., Lin, X., Shen, X., Su, J.: An Efficient Pseudonymous Authentication Scheme With Strong Privacy Preservation for Vehicular Communications. IEEE Transactions on Vehicular Technology 59(7), 3589–3603 (2010)
15. Wang, G., Liu, Q., Wu, J., Guo, M.: Hierarchical attribute-based encryption and scalable user revocation for sharing data in cloud servers. Computers & Security 30(5) (2011)
16. Weng, J., Zhao, Y.: Direct constructions of bidirectional proxy re-encryption with alleviated trust in proxy. IACR Cryptology ePrint Archive, 2011:208 (2011)
17. Yu, S., Wang, C., Ren, K., Lou, W.: Achieving secure, scalable, and fine-grained data access control in cloud computing. In: INFOCOM, pp. 534–542. IEEE (2010)

# Fine-Grained Conditional Proxy Re-Encryption and Application

Yanjiang Yang[1], Haibing Lu[2], Jian Weng[3,5],
Youcheng Zhang[4], and Kouichi Sakurai[5]

[1] Institute for Infocomm Research, Singapore
[2] The Leavey School of Business, Santa Clara University, USA
[3] Department of Computer Science, Jinan University, China
[4] Nanjing Unary Information Technology Co., Ltd, China
[5] Department of Informatics, Kyushu University, Japan
yyang@i2r.a-star.edu.sg, hlu@scu.edu, cryptjweng@gmail.com,
zyc@unary.com.cn

**Abstract.** Conditional proxy re-encryption (CPRE) enables delegation of decryption rights, and is useful in many applications. In this paper, we present a ciphertext-policy attribute based CPRE scheme, together with a formalization of the primitive and its security proof. We further propose applying the scheme for fine-grained encryption of cloud data. This application well implements the idea of cloud-enabled user revocation, offering an alternative yet more feasible solution to the user revocation issue when using attribute based encryption over cloud data. Features of the application include little cost in case of user revocation, and high user-side efficiency when users access cloud data.

**Keywords:** Conditional proxy re-encryption, Attribute-based encryption, User revocation, Cloud data.

## 1 Introduction

The notion of proxy re-encryption (PRE) was first introduced by Blaze, Bleumer and Strauss [4]. In a PRE scheme, a semi-trusted proxy is given a re-encryption key, thus able to translate ciphertexts under Alice's public key into ciphertexts under Bob's public key. The proxy, however, cannot learn anything about the messages encrypted under either key. This re-encryption procedure can be intuitively depicted as $E(pk_A, m) \xrightarrow{rk_{A \to B}} E(pk_B, m)$, where $rk_{A \to B}$ denotes the re-encryption key from Alice to Bob. In this setting, Alice is delegator and Bob is delegatee, and PRE enables Alice to delegate her decryption right to Bob.

A weakness of traditional PRE is that the proxy can transform *all* of Alice's ciphertexts, without any discrimination. This is not satisfactory in many applications where fine-grained delegation of decryption rights is to be desired. As a result, the concept of *conditional* proxy re-encryption (CPRE) [30,34] emerged, which strengthens PRE such that transformation of ciphertexts by the proxy is conditional: a ciphertext under Alice's public key is generated with a value $w$,

S.S.M. Chow et al. (Eds.): ProvSec 2014, LNCS 8782, pp. 206–222, 2014.
© Springer International Publishing Switzerland 2014

and the re-encryption key from Alice to Bob is associated with another value $w'$; the ciphertext can be transferred to a ciphertext for Bob if and only if $w = w'$. Intuitively, the procedure is depicted as $E(pk_A, m, w) \xrightarrow{\ rk_{A} \xrightarrow{w'} B\ } E(pk_B, m)$. CPRE turns out to be a useful primitive, and can find many applications. In this paper, we show one such example: applying CPRE to achieve *revocable* fine-grained encryption of data outsourced to cloud storage.

Indeed, it is commonly agreed that data entrusted to a cloud storage should be encrypted in order to safeguard their secrecy against the cloud provider [10,11,13], which may not be trusted by the data owner. However, encryption of cloud data poses challenges. First of all, cloud storage services promise a powerful platform for sharing of data among a number of stakeholders. In practice data sharing is often obliged to enforce fine-grained access control policies such that different users have different access privileges. This leads to the first challenge that encryption of cloud data must support fine-grained encryption competencies such that users with different privileges possess different decryption rights. Secondly, user revocation is another challenge arising from data sharing, where some users should be deprived of their access rights in certain circumstances, e.g., they resign from their duty. The usual solution to user revocation requires to invalidate the existing key (used in data encryption) by re-generating the encrypted data with a new key, which is then re-distributed to the remaining valid users. This is a prohibitively costly task, especially in the case of encryption of cloud data where normally a large number of data are involved.

We are aimed to get over these challenges by encryption of cloud data with CPRE and implementing cloud-enabled user revocation: the cloud server is exploited to act as the proxy, and thus is given a set of re-encryption keys, each being from the data owner (who is the delegator) to an authorized user. When a user requests some data from the cloud storage, the cloud server transforms the data using the corresponding re-encryption key if the user is authorized. User revocation is attained by simply erasing the revoked user's re-encryption key from the cloud server, requiring neither update of the encryption key and re-distribution of the key, nor re-generation of cloud data.

While the above idea is promising, there remains an issue to be solved that the majority of existing CPRE schemes such as [30,34,36] can only cope with simple, keyword-based conditions, i.e., both $w$ and $w'$ are a keyword or an "AND" concatenation of keywords. This is far from satisfactory in terms of fine-grainedness required for encryption of cloud data. We are thus motivated to propose a new CPRE scheme that is capable of handling more fine-grained conditions. In particular, our CPRE scheme can be denoted as $E(pk_A, m, \mathbb{P}) \xrightarrow{\ rk_{A} \xrightarrow{\mathbb{A}} B\ } E(pk_B, m)$, where $\mathbb{P}$ is an access policy and $\mathbb{A}$ is a set of attributes, and transformation of ciphertext can be accomplished only if $\mathbb{P}$ is satisfied by $\mathbb{A}$. Access policies $\mathbb{P}$ in our scheme are expressive and can be any monotonic access structures, comparable to those considered in attribute-based encryption (ABE) [6,16]. Following the naming convention of ABE [6,16], our proposal is actually a ciphertext-policy attribute based CPRE scheme, the first of its kind as far as we know.

**Organization.** In Section 2, we review related work on PRE/CPRE. Formulation of ciphertext-policy attribute based CPRE is presented in Section 3, and a concrete scheme is given in Section 4, together with security analysis. In Section 5 we apply the scheme for encryption of cloud data, so as to realize cloud-enabled user revocation. Section 6 concludes the paper.

## 2    Related Work

In this section, we review related work on PRE/CPRE, and defer the background information as to encryption of cloud data to Section 5.2.

Mambo and Okamoto [26] firstly introduced the concept of delegation of decryption right, as an alternative to the trivial decrypting-then-encrypting approach but with better performance. Blaze, Bleumer and Strauss [4] formalized the concept of proxy re-encryption (PRE), and proposed the first bidirectional PRE scheme (in which the delegation from Alice to Bob also allows for re-encryption from Bob to Alice). The first unidirectional PRE schemes are due to Ateniese et al. [1,2], and these schemes are based on bilinear pairing.

The schemes in [1,2,4] are only secure against chosen-plaintext attacks (CPA). Canetti and Hohenberger [8] presented the first CCA-secure PRE scheme from bilinear pairing, which is a bidirectional scheme. Later, Libert and Vergnaud [24,25] presented a unidirectional PRE scheme with a weaker form of CCA security, namely, security under replayable chosen-ciphertext attacks (RCCA) [9].

Earlier PRE schemes rely on bilinear pairings, which are costly operations. This motivates a different line of research, to construct PRE schemes without the reliance on bilinear pairings. Deng et al. [14] probably was the first to come up with a PRE scheme with this feature, which is CCA-secure bidirectional scheme. The first unidirectional PRE scheme without bilinear pairings was due to Shao and Cao [28], which was immediately succeeded by Weng et al. [35,36].

Conditional proxy re-encryption (CPRE) aims at restricting the transformation capability of the proxy, such that a transformation by the proxy can succeed only if the prescribed conditions are met. Earlier CPRE schemes [30,34,36] can only accommodate simple, keyword-based conditions, where both the values embedded with the delegator's ciphertext and with the re-encryption keys are a keyword or a "AND" concatenation of several keywords. As a result, these CPRE schemes are not capable in enforcing finer-grained delegation of decryption rights.

Recently, Zhao et al. [38] proposed an attribute-based CPRE scheme, which supports fine-grained conditions beyond keyword. Their scheme can be described as $E(pk_A, m, \mathbb{A}) \xrightarrow[A \xrightarrow{\mathbb{P}} B]{rk} E(pk_B, m)$, where $\mathbb{A}$ is a set of attributes and $\mathbb{P}$ is an access policy. Following the naming convention of key-policy ABE [16] and ciphertext-policy ABE [6], their scheme is precisely key-policy attribute based CPRE (as opposed to our ciphertext-policy attribute based CPRE). A subsequent scheme by Wang [31] is also key-policy attribute based CPRE, but with enhanced expressiveness on access policy $\mathbb{P}$ such that it can be a non-monotonic access structure.

However, the key-policy attribute based schemes in [31,38] suffer from two weaknesses. (1) Both schemes require to pre-define the total number $N$ of attributes admitted by the system, and the size of the system's public key is linear to $N$. In contrast, our scheme does not have this restriction, and any update of $N$ over the time does not affect the system setting at all. (2) Inheriting the advantages of ciphertext-policy ABE (over key-policy ABE), ciphertext-policy attribute based CPRE is more natural and flexible than its key-policy counterpart in encryption of cloud data, as the former allows the data owner to directly specify the access control policy associated with a ciphertext, under which the ciphertext can be decrypted. It deserves noting that while it is possible to transform ciphertext-policy ABE into key-policy ABE and vice versa [17], it is not clear whether the transformation techniques are applicable to key-policy/ciphertext-policy attribute based CPRE schemes in [31,38]; our proposal is certainly not a direct transformation of those two schemes, though we have drawn on inspiration from [38].

We notice that the attribute based PRE constructions in [20,21,22] seem not fully conforming to the usual notion of PRE, as they implement attribute-set to attribute-set transformation, rather than individual to individual transformation. They can be viewed as an extension to the conventional PRE, with each of the delegator and the delegatee is represented by a set of attributes. For more information on PRE/CPRE, interested readers are referred to [39]. As a final note, the proposal of dynamic credentials and ciphertext delegation for ABE [29] also implements attribute-set to attribute-set transformation.

## 3   Model of Ciphertext-Policy Attribute Based CPRE

In this section, we formalize a model of ciphertext-policy attribute based conditional proxy re-encryption and its security notions. We achieve the same expressiveness of access policies as in ABE schemes [6,16], and thus we use the same notations of "policy" and "attribute" as theirs.

### 3.1   Preliminaries

**Access Tree.** In ciphertext-policy attribute based CPRE, a re-encryption key is generated with a set of *descriptive attributes* $\mathbb{A}$. An encryptor wishing to encrypt a message specifies an *access policy* $\mathbb{P}$ and generates the ciphertext under $\mathbb{P}$. For a re-encryption key to be able to transform the ciphertext, its associated attributes $\mathbb{A}$ must satisfy the access policy $\mathbb{P}$. An access policy is expressed by an *access tree*, where each leaf node represents an attribute and we use $\mathsf{att}(\ell)$ to denote the attribute associated with leaf node $\ell$. Each non-leaf node of the tree represents a threshold gate, described by its children and a threshold value. Let $num_n$ be the number of children of a non-leaf node $n$, and $t_n$ be its threshold value, then $1 \leq t_n \leq num_n$. When $t_n = 1$, the threshold gate is an OR gate and when $t_n = num_n$, it is an AND gate. The parent of a node $n$ in the tree is denoted by $\mathsf{parent}(n)$. The tree also defines an ordering among the children of a node, i.e., the child nodes of a node $n$ are numbered from 1 to $num_n$. The function index($n$) calculates such a unique number associated with a node $n$. Access tree can express any access policy in the form of monotonic formulae.

**Satisfying an Access Tree.** Let $\mathcal{T}$ be an access tree with root $rt$. Denote by $\mathcal{T}_n$ the subtree of $\mathcal{T}$ rooted at node $n$. Hence $\mathcal{T} = \mathcal{T}_{rt}$. When a set $\mathbb{A}$ of attributes satisfy the access tree $\mathcal{T}_n$, it is denoted as $\mathcal{T}_n(\mathbb{A}) = 1$. $\mathcal{T}_n(\mathbb{A})$ is computed in a recursive way as follows: if $n$ is a non-leaf node, compute $\mathcal{T}_{n'}(\mathbb{A})$ for all child nodes $n'$; $\mathcal{T}_n(\mathbb{A})$ returns 1 if and only if at least $t_n$ children return 1; if $n$ is a leaf node, then $\mathcal{T}_n(\mathbb{A})$ returns 1 if and only if att($n$) $\in \mathbb{A}$.

## 3.2  Model

A ciphertext-policy attribute based CPRE scheme consists of the following algorithms.

**Setup**$(1^\kappa) \to params$: On input a security parameter $1^\kappa$, the setup algorithm outputs public parameter $params$. For conciseness, below we assume that $params$ is implicit in the input of the rest algorithms.

**KeyGen**$(u) \to (pk_u, sk_u)$: On input a user identity $U$, the key generation algorithm outputs a public/private key pair $pk_u/sk_u$ for user $u$.

**ReKeyGen**$(sk_A, \mathbb{A}, pk_B) \to rk_{A \xrightarrow{\mathbb{A}} B}$: On input the private key $sk_A$ of the delegator, a set of attributes $\mathbb{A}$ and the public key $pk_B$ of a delegatee, the re-encryption key generation algorithm outputs a re-encryption key $rk_{A \xrightarrow{\mathbb{A}} B}$ from $A$ to $B$ issued upon $\mathbb{A}$.

**Enc$_1$**$(pk, m) \to c$: On input a public key $pk$ and a plaintext $m \in \mathcal{M}$ ($\mathcal{M}$ is an appropriate message space), the first-level encryption algorithm outputs a first-level ciphertext $c$.

**Enc$_2$**$(pk, m, \mathbb{P}) \to \tilde{c}$: On input a public key $pk$, a message $m \in \mathcal{M}$ and an access policy $\mathbb{P}$, the second-level encryption algorithm outputs a second-level ciphertext $\tilde{c}$. Note that in the setting of PRE, it distinguishes between first-level encryption and second-level encryption, and only second-level ciphertexts could be transformed (into first-level ciphertexts).

**ReEnc**$(rk_{A \xrightarrow{\mathbb{A}} B}, \tilde{c}_A) \to c_B$: On input a re-encryption key $rk_{A \xrightarrow{\mathbb{A}} B}$ from $A$ to $B$ associated with $\mathbb{A}$, and a second-level ciphertext $\tilde{c}_A$ under public key $pk_A$ and an access policy $\mathbb{P}$, the re-encryption algorithm outputs a first-level ciphertext $c_B$ under public key $pk_B$ if $\mathbb{A}$ satisfies $\mathbb{P}$; otherwise, it outputs $\bot$.

**Dec$_1$**$(sk, c) \to m$: On input a private key $sk$ and a first-level ciphertext $c$ under $pk$, the first-level decryption algorithm outputs a plaintext $m$ if $pk/sk$ is a valid key pair.

**Dec$_2$**$(sk, \tilde{c}) \to m$: On input a private key $sk$ and a second-level ciphertext $\tilde{c}$ under $pk$ and a certain access policy, the second-level decryption algorithm outputs a plaintext $m$ if $pk/sk$ is a valid key pair.

*Correctness.* The correctness of a cipher-text attribute based CPRE scheme asserts that, for any $m \in \mathcal{M}$, any $\mathbb{P}, \mathbb{A}$, any key pairs $pk_A/sk_A$ and $pk_B/sk_B$, the following holds if $\mathbb{A}$ satisfies $\mathbb{P}$

$$\mathsf{Dec}_1(sk_A, \mathsf{Enc}_1(pk_A, m))) = m$$
$$\mathsf{Dec}_2(sk_A, \mathsf{Enc}_2(pk_A, m, \mathbb{P}))) = m$$
$$\mathsf{Dec}_1(sk_B, \mathsf{ReEnc}(\mathsf{ReKenGen}(sk_A, \mathbb{A}, pk_B), \mathsf{Enc}_2(pk_A, m, \mathbb{P})))$$
$$= m$$

### 3.3 Security Notion

Security of ciphertext-policy attribute based CPRE is defined through the following security game between a challenger and an adversary $\mathcal{A}$.

**Setup.** The challenger runs the Setup algorithm to generate public parameter *params*, and then executes KeyGen with a random user identity $O$ to get a key pair $pk_O/sk_O$. Finally, the challenger passes *params* and $pk_O$ to the adversary $\mathcal{A}$.

**Phase 1.** The adversary $\mathcal{A}$ makes a number of re-encryption key generation queries on sets of attributes $\mathbb{A}_1, \mathbb{A}_2, \cdots, \mathbb{A}_{q_1}$ to the challenger. For each query (which is on $\mathbb{A}_j$), the challenger responds as follows. First, execute the KenGen algorithm with a random user identity to obtain a public/private key pair $pk_j/sk_j$. Then execute $\mathsf{ReKeyGen}(sk_O, \mathbb{A}_j, pk_j) = rk_{O \xrightarrow{\mathbb{A}_j} j}$. Finally, return $pk_j/sk_j$ and $rk_{O \xrightarrow{\mathbb{A}_j} j}$ to $\mathcal{A}$.

**Challenge.** The adversary $\mathcal{A}$ submits two equal length messages $m_0$ and $m_1$, together with a challenge access policy $\mathbb{P}^*$ such that none of $\mathbb{A}_1, \mathbb{A}_2, \cdots, \mathbb{A}_{q_1}$ from Phase 1 satisfies $\mathbb{P}^*$. The challenger flips a random coin $b$, executes $\mathsf{Enc}_2(pk_O, m_b, \mathbb{P}^*) = \tilde{c}^*$, and returns the ciphertext $\tilde{c}^*$ to $\mathcal{A}$.

**Phase 2.** $\mathcal{A}$ again makes a number of re-encryption key generation queries on sets of attributes $\mathbb{A}_{q_1+1}, \mathbb{A}_{q_1+2}$, $\cdots, \mathbb{A}_{q_2}$ to the challenger. For each query on $\mathbb{A}_j$, the challenger responds as follows. First, execute the KenGen algorithm with a random user identity to obtain a public/private key pair $pk_j/sk_j$. Then execute $\mathsf{ReKeyGen}(sk_O, \mathbb{A}_j, pk_j) = rk_{O \xrightarrow{\mathbb{A}_j} j}$. Finally, if $\mathbb{A}_j$ satisfies $\mathbb{P}^*$, then return $pk_j$ and $rk_{O \xrightarrow{\mathbb{A}_j} j}$ to the adversary; otherwise, return $pk_j/sk_j$ and $rk_{O \xrightarrow{\mathbb{A}_j} j}$ to $\mathcal{A}$.

**Guess.** The adversary $\mathcal{A}$ outputs a bit $b'$, which is a guess on $b$.

**Definition 1.** *[CPA Security] A ciphertext-policy attribute based CPRE scheme is CPA (chosen plaintext attack) secure if for any PPT adversary $\mathcal{A}$, it holds that $\Pr[b' = b] = 1/2 + \epsilon(\kappa)$, where $\epsilon$ is a negligible function.*

It is often to separately define first-level encryption security and second-level encryption security in existing PRE/CPRE literature, e.g., [1,2,34,36]. Our formalization simultaneously captures both notions. On one hand, the challenge ciphertext $\tilde{c}^*$ is a second-level ciphertext, thus second-level encryption security is apparently captured. On the other hand, the adversary is allowed to obtain re-encryption keys whose associated attributes satisfy the challenge access policy $\mathbb{P}^*$ (in which case, $\mathcal{A}$ does not get the private keys of delegatees); thus the adversary itself can transform the challenge ciphertext into first-level ciphertexts using these re-encryption keys, and this captures first-level encryption security.

Remark. CPA security suffices to meet the needs for encryption of cloud data - the intended application of CPRE in this paper. Thus, we make our scheme achieve CPA security only, but extending it to achieve CCA security should not be a hard issue, given the generic techniques in the literature for constructing CCA secure schemes, e.g., [12,18].

# 4   Our Scheme

In this section, we present our construction of a ciphertext-policy attribute based CPRE scheme, as well as its security analysis.

## 4.1   The Construction

Our construction is based on the ciphertext-policy ABE scheme [6], but there remains a big gap between the ABE scheme itself and our ciphertext-policy attribute based CPRE scheme, considering the gap between public key encryption and PRE. Let $s \in_R S$ denote an element $s$ randomly drawn from a set $S$. The details of our scheme are as follows.

**Setup**$(1^\kappa)$: Determine a bilinear map $e : G_0 \times G_0 \to G_T$, where $G_0$ and $G_T$ are cyclic groups of $\kappa$-bit prime order $p$; select $g, h$, which are generators of $G_0$, a cryptographic hash function $H : \{0,1\}^* \to G_0$. Then set $params = (g, h, e(g,g), H)$.

**KeyGen**$(u)$: Pick $x_u \in_R Z_p$, and set $(pk_u = g^{x_u}, sk_u = x_u)$.

**ReKeyGen**$(sk_A, \mathbb{A}, pk_B)$: Let $sk_A = x_A$ and $pk_B = g^{x_B}$. Pick $r, r_i \in_R Z_p, \forall i \in \mathbb{A}$, and set the re-encryption key as

$$rk_{A \xrightarrow{\mathbb{A}} B} = (k = g^{\frac{x_B}{x_A}} h^r, \forall i \in \mathbb{A} : \{k_{i1} = g^{x_A \cdot r} H(i)^{r_i}, k_{i2} = h^{r_i}\})$$

**Enc**$_1(pk, m)$: Pick $s \in_R Z_p$, and compute

$$c = (m \cdot e(g,g)^s, e(g, pk)^s)$$

**Enc**$_2(pk, m, \mathbb{P})$: Let $pk = g^x$ and $\mathbb{P}$ be an access tree $\mathcal{T}$. The second-level encryption algorithm proceeds as follows. It first selects a polynomial $q_n$ for each node $n$ (including the leaf nodes) in $\mathcal{T}$. These polynomials are chosen in a top-down manner, starting from the root node $rt$: for each node $n$, set the degree $d_n$ of the polynomial $q_n$ to be $d_n = t_n - 1$, where $t_n$ is the threshold value of node $n$. Starting with the root node $rt$ the algorithm selects a random $s \in_R Z_p$ and sets $q_{rt}(0) = s$. Then it selects $d_{rt}$ other random points to define $q_{rt}$ completely. For any other node $n$, it sets $q_n(0) = q_{\mathsf{parent}(n)}(\mathsf{index}(n))$ and chooses $d_n$ other points to completely define $q_n$.

Let $L$ be the set of leaf nodes in $\mathcal{T}$. Sets the ciphertext $\tilde{c}$ as

$$\tilde{c} = (\mathcal{T}, C = m \cdot e(g,g)^s, \forall l \in L : \{C_{l1} = g^{x \cdot q_l(0)}, C_{l2} = h^{q_l(0)}, C_{l3} = H(\mathsf{att}(l))^{q_l(0)}\})$$

**ReEnc**$(rk_{A\xrightarrow{\mathbb{A}}B}, \tilde{c}_A)$: Let $\tilde{c}_A = (\mathcal{T}, C, \forall l \in L : \{C_{l1}, C_{l2}, C_{l3}\})$ and $rk_{A\xrightarrow{\mathbb{A}}B} = (k, \forall i \in \mathbb{A} : \{k_{i1}, k_{i2}\})$. The re-encryption algorithm is a recursive procedure. We first define an algorithm $\mathsf{ReEncNd}_n(\tilde{c}_A, rk_{A\xrightarrow{\mathbb{A}}B})$ on a node $n$ of $\mathcal{T}$. If node $n$ is a leaf node then we let $z = \mathsf{att}(n)$ and define as follows: $z \notin \mathbb{A}$, then $\mathsf{ReEncNd}_n(\tilde{c}_A, rk_{A\xrightarrow{\mathbb{A}}B}) = \bot$; otherwise $\mathsf{ReEncNd}_n(\tilde{c}_A, rk_{A\xrightarrow{\mathbb{A}}B}) = F_n$, where

$$F_n = \frac{e(k, C_{n1}) \cdot e(k_{z2}, C_{n3})}{e(k_{z1}, C_{n2})}$$

$$= \frac{e(g^{\frac{x_B}{x_A}} h^r, g^{x_A \cdot q_n(0)}) \cdot e(h^{r_z}, H(z)^{q_n(0)})}{e(g^{x_A \cdot r} H(z)^{r_z}, h^{q_n(0)})}$$

$$= e(g, g)^{x_B \cdot q_n(0)}$$

Let us now consider the recursive case when $n$ is a non-leaf node. The algorithm $\mathsf{ReEncNd}_n(\tilde{c}_A, rk_{A\xrightarrow{\mathbb{A}}B})$ then proceeds as follows. For each child node $v$ of $n$, it calls $\mathsf{ReEncNd}_v(\tilde{c}_A, rk_{A\xrightarrow{\mathbb{A}}B})$ and stores the output as $F_v$. Let $S_n$ be an arbitrary $t_n$-sized set of child nodes $v$ such that $F_v \neq \bot$. If no such a set exists then the node was not satisfied and $\mathsf{ReEncNd}_n(\tilde{c}_A, rk_{A\xrightarrow{\mathbb{A}}B}) = F_n = \bot$. Otherwise, let the Lagrange coefficient $\triangle_{i,S}$ for $i \in Z_p$ and a set $S$ of elements in $Z_p$ be $\triangle_{i,S}(x) = \prod_{j \in S, j \neq i} \frac{x-j}{i-j}$, and we compute

$$F_n = \prod_{v \in S_n} F_v^{\triangle_{i,S'_n}(0)}, \text{where} \begin{array}{l} i = \mathsf{index}(v), \\ S'_n = \{\mathsf{index}(v) : v \in S_n\} \end{array}$$

$$= \prod_{v \in S_n} (e(g, g)^{x_B \cdot q_v(0)})^{\triangle_{i,S'_n}(0)}$$

$$= \prod_{v \in S_n} (e(g, g)^{x_B \cdot q_{\mathsf{parent}(v)}(\mathsf{index}(v))})^{\triangle_{i,S'_n}(0)}$$

$$= \prod_{v \in S_n} (e(g, g)^{x_B \cdot q_n(i)})^{\triangle_{i,S'_n}(0)}$$

$$= e(g, g)^{x_B \cdot q_n(0)}$$

In this way, $\mathsf{ReEncNd}_{rt}(\tilde{c}_A, rk_{A\xrightarrow{\mathbb{A}}B})$ for the root node $rt$ can be computed. If $\mathcal{T}_{rt}(\mathbb{A}) = 1$, then we get $\mathsf{ReEncNd}_{rt}(\tilde{c}_A, rk_{A\xrightarrow{\mathbb{A}}B}) = e(g, g)^{x_B \cdot q_{rt}(0)} = e(g, g)^{x_B \cdot s} = F_{rt}$. As such, sets $c_B = (C, F_{rt}) = (m \cdot e(g, g)^s, e(g, g)^{x_B \cdot s})$.

**Dec**$_1(sk, c)$: Decryption of the first level ciphertext is straightforward, and we omit the details.

**Dec**$_2(sk, \tilde{c})$: Let $\breve{c} = (\mathcal{T}, m.e(g, g)^s, \forall l \in L : \{pk^{q_l(0)}, h^{q_l(0)}, H(\mathsf{att}(l))^{q_l(0)}\})$. First compute $pk^s$ from $\{pk^{q_l(0)}\}_{l \in L}$ following the access tree $\mathcal{T}$, and then gets $m = m \cdot e(g, g)^s / e((pk^s)^{sk^{-1}}, g)$.

## 4.2 Security Analysis

For security of the above scheme, we have the following theorem and the proof will be provided in the full version due to limited space.

**Theorem 1.** *The above scheme is CPA secure (as specified in Definition 1) in the generic group model assuming H is a random oracle and E is CPA secure.*

## 5  Application: Encryption of Cloud Data

We present an application of our scheme: encryption of cloud data. We begin with a discussion of the application scenario.

### 5.1  Application Scenario

We consider the following application scenario. To enjoy the advantages of cloud storage services, a Data Owner (DO) establishes a cloud-based data sharing platform, where the DO outsources her data to the cloud storage, and authorizes a group of users to access the data. In particular, users are distinguished by their functional roles (a functional role can be defined by a set of attributes), and are granted access right according to their respective roles. The DO enforces fine-grained access control over the cloud data, such that data are accessed by roles based on the need-to-know basis (i.e., different roles have different access rights).

However, the DO does not fully trust the cloud, and wants to keep data privacy against the cloud. Thus, the data uploaded to the cloud are encrypted by the DO. Each authorized user is granted appropriate decryption right by the DO as per her role. The system must support user revocation, such that once an authorized user is revoked, her decryption capability is nullified immediately.

**An Example.** An example of DO and authorized users are a company and its employees, respectively. The company moves its corporate data to the cloud for management due to reduced cost, and allows employees to access data on the need-to-know basis. In such a context, the company often needs to specify data access control policies based on the roles that employees assume (rather than on the identities of the employees). For example, an access control policy would be "this data can only be accessed by executive manager from the purchasing department". As a result, the employees are distinguished by their roles, i.e., each user should be issued a *role certificate*, rather than *identity certificate*. The need for user revocation occurs, when, e.g., an employee leaves the company. In such a case, the role of that employee remains and will be taken by a substitute, but the employee himself is revoked. Thus, we concern about user revocation, rather than role (or attributes) revocation.

### 5.2  Encryption of Cloud Data with ABE, and User Revocation

To meet the need of enforcing fine-grained encryption of cloud data in the above application scenario, attribute-based encryption (ABE), e.g., [6,16,32], is a primitive having the potential to fulfil the objective. Indeed, a number of proposals in the literature have suggested applying ABE to protect cloud data. Compared to conventional public-key encryption, where a message encrypted under a public key can only be decrypted by a single corresponding private key, ABE is peculiar in offering much finer-grained encryption/decryption capabilities: ABE is a one-to-many encryption primitive, whereby data are encrypted with a system-wide public key under certain access policy/attributes and each decryption key is attached to certain attributes/access policy, such that the ciphertext can be decrypted only if the attributes satisfy the access policy.

Even though ABE appears promising for encryption of cloud data, user revocation poses a challenge. The difficulty is due to the fact that ABE is essentially "group encryption", and thus does not differentiate individual users. The ABE schemes in [6,16,32] propose to include an "expiry time" attribute in the attribute set, such that a decryption key can work only up to its associated expiry time. However, such a mechanism cannot implement immediate revocation of decryption capability. The ABE scheme in [27] supports *negative* constrains in the access policy, which actually provides a means for attribute revocation by negating the attributes to be revoked. Such a "negation" mechanism is not scalable for user revocation in encryption of cloud data, as each revoked user must be explicitly treated as a distinct attribute and included in the ciphertext, making it impractical when the number of revoked users grows large. Other variants of ABE, such as predicate encryption (e.g., [19]) and functional encryption (e.g., [7,23]) are also restricted to these two revocation mechanisms.

There also exist "stateful" user revocation mechanisms which involve update of the decryption keys, e.g., [3,33,37], which would entail re-generation of cloud data and key re-distribution. Take [37] for example, it proposed applying KP-ABE [16] for encryption of cloud data, and adopting the specific technique of PRE scheme [4] to update users' decryption keys in case of user revocation. The advantage of such a user revocation approach is that the cloud is entrusted to take up the majority of the workload for re-generation of cloud data and re-distribution of new keys. Even though this has improved considerably over the trivial solution whereby the encryptor is fully responsible for data re-generation and key re-distribution, it is always preferable to avoid such a burden, as cloud resources do not come free of charge to the customers. The user revocation method in [29] works in a similar way, where the cloud has to re-generate the encrypted cloud data in case of user revocation.

## 5.3 Cloud-Enabled User Revocation

From the above discussions, we can see that it is not yet practical to deploy ABE for encryption of cloud data before a more satisfactory user revocation mechanism is found. Based on our ciphertext-policy attribute based CPRE scheme, we propose a cloud-enabled user revocation approach, with the basic idea as follows. The cloud is enlisted as the proxy in CPRE, and holds the re-encryption keys of all authorized users. As such, the cloud is empowered to transform encrypted data records into ciphertexts under a user's public key, if the user is authorized and thus has a re-encryption key hold by the cloud. To revoke a user, the cloud simply erases the user's re-encryption key and thus cannot transform encrypted data for the user any more. User revocation in this way incurs little cost, requiring no key update, no re-generation of cloud data, and no re-distribution of keys. For clarity, Table 1 summarizes a comparison between our approach and other user revocation approaches mentioned in Section 5.2.

**Table 1.** Comparison Results

| | Immediate Revocation | No Key update & data re-gen. | Scalability |
|---|---|---|---|
| Expiry time | × | ✓ | ✓ |
| Negation | ✓ | ✓ | × |
| [3,33,37] | ✓ | × | ✓ |
| Our approach | ✓ | ✓ | ✓ |

✓ : can achieve; × : cannot achieve

## 5.4   Application Details

We show details on applying our proposed CPRE scheme for encryption of cloud data in the above application scenario. Specifically, the application has the following procedures.

*System Setup.* The DO runs CPRE.Setup to establishes and publishes the public parameter of the CPRE scheme.

The DO runs CPRE.KeyGen to generate a key pair $pk_O/sk_O$ for herself; likewise, each user $u$ also generates a key pair $pk_u/sk_u$ for himself. All public keys are part of the public system parameters.

*User Authorization.* To authorize a user $u$, the DO decides a set of attributes $\mathbb{A}$ according to $u$'s role; then executes $rk_{O\xrightarrow{\mathbb{A}}u} = \mathsf{CPRE.ReKeyGen}(sk_O, \mathbb{A}, pk_u)$, and sends $rk_{O\xrightarrow{\mathbb{A}}u}$ to the cloud in a secret way. Note that $rk_{O\xrightarrow{\mathbb{A}}u}$ can be understood to be the role certificate for $u$. The cloud maintains a Re-encryption Key Table (RKT) with each entry being a user identity along with his re-encryption key, as shown below. As a result, the cloud adds a new entry $(u, rk_{O\xrightarrow{\mathbb{A}}u})$ to this re-encryption key table.

| User Identity | Re-encryption Key |
|---|---|
| Alice | $rk_{O\xrightarrow{\mathbb{A}_A}A}$ |
| Bob | $rk_{O\xrightarrow{\mathbb{A}_B}B}$ |
| John | $rk_{O\xrightarrow{\mathbb{A}_J}J}$ |
| Mary | $rk_{O\xrightarrow{\mathbb{A}_M}M}$ |
| ... | ... |

The cloud manages a RKT, which contains the re-encryption keys of all authorized users.

***Data Outsourcing.*** To outsource a data record $m$ to the cloud, the DO determines the access policy $\mathbb{P}$ of the record, and then computes $\tilde{c} = \mathsf{CPRE.Enc}_2(pk_O, m, \mathbb{P})$. Finally, the DO uploads $\tilde{c}$ to the cloud.

***Data Access.*** Suppose a user $u$ wants to retrieve an encrypted data record $\tilde{c}$ from the cloud, the cloud first gets $u$'s re-encryption key $rk_{O \xrightarrow{A_u} u}$ from the RKT (Re-encryption Key Table), and then computes $c_u = \mathsf{CPRE.ReEnc}(rk_{O \xrightarrow{A_u} u}, \tilde{c})$, and sends it to user $u$. At the user side, $u$ gets $m$ by computing $m = \mathsf{CPRE.Dec}_1(sk_u, c_u)$.

***User Revocation.*** To revoke an authorized user $u$, the re-encryption key of $u$ is simply erased from the re-encryption key table at the cloud side. Depending on applications, either the cloud updates the re-encryption key table instructed by the DO, or a management interface is provided to the DO so that she does the deletion by herself.

It can easily see that the DO encrypts cloud data by the $\mathsf{Enc}_2$ algorithm and decryption at the user side is by $\mathsf{Dec}_1$ algorithm. $\mathsf{Enc}_1$ and $\mathsf{Dec}_2$ are not used in the application.

<u>Remarks</u>. We have the following remarks as to the above application. (1) We assume that the cloud is semi-trusted in that it is considered an adversary mainly to the secrecy of cloud data, but honest in managing cloud data, processing user access requests, and other administrative activities. (2) When a user requests data from the cloud, he needs to include his identity with the request, facilitating the cloud to determine the corresponding re-encryption key to use from the Re-encryption Key Table. However, the cloud is not required to check the authenticity of the request, namely, the cloud does not concern about one user impersonating another. This is because each user's re-encryption key is unique and only pairs up with his own private key. (3) It should not be a surprise if there are proposals in the literature suggesting to apply PRE/CPRE for encryption of cloud data. The novelty of our proposal is that we actually utilize PRE/CPRE for user revocation, and the CPRE scheme we proposed attains fine-grained-ness comparable to ABE.

## 5.5   Security Considerations

The primary security concern in the above application is to protect data privacy against the cloud, which is the motivation for encryption of cloud data (see Section 1). This apparently achieved, because the cloud plays the role of proxy in the CPRE scheme. As we have proved, the proxy in our CPRE scheme learns nothing about the plaintext message. Hence, the application is secure, in terms of keeping data privacy against the cloud.

## 5.6   Advantageous Features

One prominent feature of the application of our CPRE scheme for encryption of cloud data is user-side efficiency. Recall that our CPRE scheme is based on bilinear map and achieves fine-grained encryption comparable to ABE. However, at the user side, a user only needs to receive and decrypt a first-level ciphertext. This results in high user-side efficiency in terms of both communication and computation.

Specifically, let $|G_T|$ denote the bit length of an element in $G_T$. Then the size of a first-level ciphertext is $2|G_T|$, and $\mathsf{Dec}_1$ involves mainly 1 exponentiations in $G_T$, both are constant. Note that $G_T$ is an ordinary multiplicative group. This means that the user-side computation is quite light-weight, and does not involve paring operation, even though our scheme itself is built upon bilinear map. This stands in contrast with all other proposals that apply ABE for encryption of cloud data, which have to perform pairing operations at the user side. The high efficiency and none-requirement of pairing support at the user side make it possible to access cloud data using resource-constrained devices, e.g., mobile phones, tablets.

The second feature is the efficiency of cloud-enabled user revocation. In case of user revocation, all that is needed is to remove the revoked user's re-encryption key from the cloud, and none of key update, re-generation of cloud data, and re-distribution of keys is incurred.

Thirdly, we view our way of realizing cloud-enabled user revocation by CPRE as *split of decryption capability*, where decryption of a ciphertext requires the cooperation between the cloud and a delegatee. We distinguish decryption capability split from *decryption key split* such as in [5]. The distinction between the two is that the entity performing decryption capability split (i.e., the DO in our application) does not necessarily know the secret of a delegatee, while the entity for decryption key split must know the delegatee's secret. Thus, the decryption capability split mechanism in our application is advantageous in keeping the delegatee's secret for himself only. We realize that the method (for delegating the workload of ABE decryption) in [15] is also possible to be applied to realize cloud-enabled user revocation, but will result in decryption key split.

## 5.7  Disadvantages

We stress that our application of CPRE for implementing cloud-enabled user revocation does not come at no cost. This approach requires the cloud to perform the ReEnc operation upon every data access request, which is expensive (although it can be viewed as offloading the workload to the cloud). Indeed, such online computation at the cloud side is inevitable in this application, but could be greatly mitigated due to the following.

The actual deployment of the CPRE scheme should follow the common practice for public-key encryption, namely, the payload data is encrypted with a random key under symmetric encryption, and the encryption key is encapsulated with the public-key encryption (i.e., the $\mathsf{Enc}_2$ algorithm in our case). This allows to amortize the overhead incurred by the key encapsulation. Specifically, all data sharing the same access policy are encrypted by a common symmetric encryption key; as a result, a ReEnc operation by the cloud may allow a user to access many data records (rather than a ReEnc operation per data record).

We stress that this does not necessarily require the data owner to manage the symmetric encryption keys. Instead, she can obtain the encryption key corresponding to an access policy by retrieving and decrypting (i.e., $Enc_2$) the related key encapsulation ciphertext from the cloud, if the access policy in question has already been used.

The overhead-amortization mechanism must support user revocation. To this end, once a user is revoked, the data owner will use a new key for every access policy when encrypting new data records (but leave the old encrypted data records intact). This guarantees that the newly generated cloud records cannot be decrypted by the revoked user. In principle, it is not a concern that a revoked user can decrypt the data he had been entitled to before his revocation.

Caveat. It may seem that the schemes in [3,33,37] implementing "stateful" user revocation mechanisms are advantageous over our application, from the perspective of online computation by cloud. In those schemes, little online computation is required upon the cloud in responding to users' data accesses. While it seems that the high workload entrusted to the cloud due to user revocation in those schemes could be performed offline, in practice it would be hard to arrange the re-generation of cloud data offline so that it does not affect users' online data requests (consider that a user requests data while re-generation of cloud data is in progress).

More importantly, the disadvantage of online computation in our application can be understood to be a tradeoff for the unique feature of user-side efficiency and the none-requirement of pairing support at the user side.

## 6   Conclusion

Encryption of cloud data is now commonly accepted as necessary to achieve data privacy against the cloud. ABE well suits this task in terms of the fine-grained encryption capability it can render, but without a satisfactory solution to the user revocation issue. To solve this problem, we proposed a ciphertext-policy attribute based CPRE scheme, and applied it to instantiate the cloud-enabled user revocation approach. This application achieves access control over cloud data with granularity comparable to ABE, yet incurring virtually no cost for user revocation. This is advantageous over all existing solutions. Another feature of our application is the high user-side efficiency in terms of both computation and communication at the user side. There may be other proposals in the literature using PRE/CPRE for encryption of cloud data, ours is probably the first to apply it for user revocation purposes.

**Acknowledgement.** This work was supported by by A*STAR funded project SecDC-112172014 (Singapore). Jian Weng was supported by National Science Foundation of China under Grant No 61272413 and the Invitation Programs for Foreign-based Researchers provided by NICT.

# References

1. Ateniese, G., Fu, K., Green, M., Hohenberger, S.: Improved Proxy Re-encryption Schemes with Applications to Secure Distributed Storage. In: Proc. of NDSS 2005, pp. 29–43 (2005)
2. Ateniese, G., Fu, K., Green, M., Hohenberger, S.: Improved Proxy Re-encryption Schemes with Applications to Secure Distributed Storage. ACM Transactions on Information and System Security (TISSEC) 9(1), 1–30 (2006)
3. Attrapadung, N., Imai, H.: Attribute-Based Encryption Supporting Direct/Indirect Revocation Modes. In: Parker, M.G. (ed.) Cryptography and Coding 2009. LNCS, vol. 5921, pp. 278–300. Springer, Heidelberg (2009)
4. Blaze, M., Bleumer, G., Strauss, M.J.: Divertible Protocols and Atomic Proxy Cryptography. In: Nyberg, K. (ed.) EUROCRYPT 1998. LNCS, vol. 1403, pp. 127–144. Springer, Heidelberg (1998)
5. Boneh, D., Ding, X., Tsudik, G., Wong, C.M.: A Method for Fast Revocation of Public Key Certificates and Security Capabilities. In: Proc. USENIX Security 2001 (2001)
6. Bethencourt, J., Sahai, A., Waters, B.: Ciphertext-Policy Attribute-Based Encryption. In: Proc. IEEE Symposium on Security & Privacy, S&P 2007 (2007)
7. Boneh, D., Sahai, A., Waters, B.: Functional Encryption: Definitions and Challenges. In: Ishai, Y. (ed.) TCC 2011. LNCS, vol. 6597, pp. 253–273. Springer, Heidelberg (2011)
8. Canetti, R., Hohenberger, S.: Chosen-Ciphertext Secure Proxy Re-Encryption. In: Proc. ACM CCS 2007 (2007)
9. Canetti, R., Krawczyk, H., Nielsen, J.B.: Relaxing Chosen-Ciphertext Security. In: Boneh, D. (ed.) CRYPTO 2003. LNCS, vol. 2729, pp. 565–582. Springer, Heidelberg (2003)
10. Cloud Security Alliance: Security Guidance for Critical Areas of Focus in Cloud Computing (2009), http://www.cloudsecurityalliance.org
11. European Network and Information Security Agency: Cloud computing risk assessment (November 2009), http://www.enisa.europa.eu/act/rm/_les/deliverables/cloud-computing-risk-assessment
12. Fujisaki, E., Okamoto, T.: Secure Integration of Asymmetric and Symmetric Encryption Schemes. In: Wiener, M. (ed.) CRYPTO 1999. LNCS, vol. 1666, pp. 537–554. Springer, Heidelberg (1999)
13. Gartner: Don't Trust Cloud Provider to Protect Your Corporate Assets, May 28 (2012), http://www.mis-asia.com/resource/cloud-computing/gartner-dont-trust-cloud-provider-to-protect-your-corporate-assets
14. Deng, R.H., Weng, J., Liu, S., Chen, K.: Chosen-Ciphertext Secure Proxy Re-encryption without Pairings. In: Franklin, M.K., Hui, L.C.K., Wong, D.S. (eds.) CANS 2008. LNCS, vol. 5339, pp. 1–17. Springer, Heidelberg (2008)
15. Green, M., Hohenberger, S., Waters, B.: Outsourcing the Decryption of ABE Ciphertexts. In: Proc. USENIX Security 2011 (2011)
16. Goyal, V., Pandy, O., Sahai, A., Waters, B.: Attribute-Based Encryption for Fine-Grained Access Control of Encrypted Data. In: Proc. ACM Computer and Communications Security Conference, CCS 2006 (2006)
17. Goyal, V., Jain, A., Pandey, O., Sahai, A.: Bounded Ciphertext Policy Attribute Based Encryption. In: Aceto, L., Damgård, I., Goldberg, L.A., Halldórsson, M.M., Ingólfsdóttir, A., Walukiewicz, I. (eds.) ICALP 2008, Part II. LNCS, vol. 5126, pp. 579–591. Springer, Heidelberg (2008)

18. Hanaoka, G., Kawai, Y., Kunihiro, N., Matsuda, T., Weng, J., Zhang, R., Zhao, Y.: Generic Construction of Chosen Ciphertext Secure Proxy Re-Encryption. In: Dunkelman, O. (ed.) CT-RSA 2012. LNCS, vol. 7178, pp. 349–364. Springer, Heidelberg (2012)

19. Katz, J., Sahai, A., Waters, B.: Predicate Encryption Supporting Disjunctions, Polynomial Equations, and Inner Products. In: Smart, N.P. (ed.) EUROCRYPT 2008. LNCS, vol. 4965, pp. 146–162. Springer, Heidelberg (2008)

20. Liang, X., Cao, Z., Lin, H., Shao, J.: Attribute-Based Proxy Ee-encrytpion with Delegating Capabilities. In: Proc. ACM ASIACCS 2009, pp. 276–286 (2009)

21. Luo, S., Hu, J., Chen, Z.: Ciphertext Policy Attribute-Based Proxy Re-encryption. In: Soriano, M., Qing, S., López, J. (eds.) ICICS 2010. LNCS, vol. 6476, pp. 401–415. Springer, Heidelberg (2010)

22. Liang, K., Fang, L., Wong, D.S., Susilo, W.: A Ciphertext-Policy Attribute-Based Proxy Re-Encryption with Chosen-Ciphertext Security, IACR Cryptology ePrint Archive (2013)

23. Lewko, A., Okamoto, T., Sahai, A., Takashima, K., Waters, B.: Fully Secure Functional Encryption: Attribute-Based Encryption and (Hierarchical) Inner Product Encryption. In: Gilbert, H. (ed.) EUROCRYPT 2010. LNCS, vol. 6110, pp. 62–91. Springer, Heidelberg (2010)

24. Libert, B., Vergnaud, D.: Unidirectional Chosen-Ciphertext Secure Proxy Re-encryption. In: Cramer, R. (ed.) PKC 2008. LNCS, vol. 4939, pp. 360–379. Springer, Heidelberg (2008)

25. Libert, B., Vergnaud, D.: Unidirectional Chosen-Ciphertext Secure Proxy Re-encryption, http://hal.inria.fr/inria-00339530/

26. Mambo, M., Okamoto, E.: Proxy Cryptosystems: Delegation of the Power to Decrypt Ciphertexts. IEICE Trans. Fund. Electronics Communications and Computer Science E80-A(1), 54–63 (1997)

27. Ostrovsky, R., Sahai, A., Waters, B.: Attribute-Based Encryption with Non-monotonic Access Structures. In: Proc. ACM CCS 2007, pp. 195–203 (2007)

28. Shao, J., Cao, Z.: CCA-Secure Proxy Re-encryption without Pairings. In: Jarecki, S., Tsudik, G. (eds.) PKC 2009. LNCS, vol. 5443, pp. 357–376. Springer, Heidelberg (2009)

29. Sahai, A., Seyalioglu, H., Waters, B.: Dynamic Credentials and Ciphertext Delegation for Attribute-Based Encryption. In: Safavi-Naini, R., Canetti, R. (eds.) CRYPTO 2012. LNCS, vol. 7417, pp. 199–217. Springer, Heidelberg (2012)

30. Tang, Q.: Type-Based Proxy Re-encryption and Its Construction. In: Chowdhury, D.R., Rijmen, V., Das, A. (eds.) INDOCRYPT 2008. LNCS, vol. 5365, pp. 130–144. Springer, Heidelberg (2008)

31. Wang, B.: A Unidirectional Conditional Proxy Re-encryption Scheme Based on Non-Monotonic Access Structure. IACR Eprint: eprint.iacr.org/2012/641.pdf (2012)

32. Waters, B.: Ciphertext-Policy Attribute-Based Encryption: An Expressive, Efficient, and Provably Secure Realization. In: Catalano, D., Fazio, N., Gennaro, R., Nicolosi, A. (eds.) PKC 2011. LNCS, vol. 6571, pp. 53–70. Springer, Heidelberg (2011)

33. Wang, G., Liu, Q., Wu, J.: Hierarhical Attribute-Based Encryption for Fine-Grained Access Control in Cloud Storage Services. In: Proc. ACM CCS 2010 (2010)

34. Weng, J., Deng, R.H., Ding, X., Chu, C.-K., Lai, J.: Conditional Proxy Re-encryption Secure Against Chosen-Ciphertext Attack. In: Proc. of ASIACCS 2009 (2009)

35. Weng, J., Chow, S.S.M., Yang, Y., Deng, R.H.: Efficient Unidirectional Proxy Re-Encryption. IACR Eprint: eprint.iacr.org/2009/189.pdf (2009)
36. Weng, J., Yang, Y., Tang, Q., Deng, R.H., Bao, F.: Efficient Conditional Proxy Re-encryption with Chosen-Ciphertext Security. In: Samarati, P., Yung, M., Martinelli, F., Ardagna, C.A. (eds.) ISC 2009. LNCS, vol. 5735, pp. 151–166. Springer, Heidelberg (2009)
37. Yu, S., Wang, C., Ren, K., Lou, W.: Achieving Secure, Scalable, and Fine-Grained Data Access Control in Cloud Computing. In: Proc. IEEE INFOCOM 2010 (2010)
38. Zhao, J., Feng, D., Zhang, Z.: Attribute-Based Conditional Proxy Re-Encryption with Chosen-Ciphertext Security. In: Proc. GLOBECOM 2010, pp. 1–6 (2010)
39. Bibliography on Proxy Re-Cryptography:
    http://ndc.zjgsu.edu.cn/~jshao/prcbib.htm

# Constructing Subspace Membership Encryption through Inner Product Encryption

Shuichi Katsumata and Noboru Kunihiro

The University of Tokyo, Japan
shuichi_katsumata@mist.i.u-tokyo.ac.jp, kunihiro@k.u-tokyo.ac.jp

**Abstract.** Subspace membership encryption is a generalization of inner product encryptions, which was recently formalized by Boneh, Raghunathan, and Segev in Asiacrypt 2013. The construction of this new predicate encryption was motivated by the fact that traditional predicate encryptions did not yield function privacy, a security notion introduced by Boneh et al. in Crypto 2013. This newly defined security notion requires that no information on the predicate associated to a given secret key is revealed, beyond the absolute minimum necessary. Boneh et al. gave a generic construction of the subspace membership encryption based on any inner product encryption. However, our research shows that their construction for subspace membership encryptions when the attribute space is small was incorrect, and that it does not yield the attribute hiding security, which is the baseline notion of security for predicate encryptions. In this paper, we will first show why the construction does not possess the attribute hiding security, and see that this can not be altered through simple reconstruction. Then, we will formulate a generalized construction of subspace membership encryptions by introducing probability distributions over the attribute and predicate space, and prove that the attribute hiding security can not be satisfied even in the generalized setting. We will consider the requirements for subspace membership encryptions to yield the attribute hiding security, and evaluate them probabilistically. Finally, we will present an extension of our generalized construction, and show that it holds the attribute hiding security even in small attribute spaces. However, in our extended generalized construction, function privacy was deprived, which was precisely the motivation of formalizing subspace member encryptions in the first place. Although, we did not succeed in constructing a subspace membership encryption which both yields the attribute hiding security and function privacy, we formalized a richer framework of construction of subspace membership encryptions, and discovered a trade-off like relationship between the two security notions, which presents possibility for a construction inbetween ours and Boneh et al.'s. Furthermore, our extended generalized construction cuts open new perspectives in the construction of subspace membership encryptions and enables us to make various choices on the underlying inner product encryptions.

**Keywords:** predicate encryption, subspace membership encryption, function privacy.

S.S.M. Chow et al. (Eds.): ProvSec 2014, LNCS 8782, pp. 223–242, 2014.
© Springer International Publishing Switzerland 2014

# 1  Introduction

Predicate encryption is a new framework of the traditional public-key encryption which offers wider possibilities in sharing encrypted messages. In traditional public-key encryptions, a message encrypted with respect to a public key is only decrypted by a particular individual who possessed a unique secret key associated with the public key. However, in predicate encryptions, a message can be decrypted by any individual who possesses a secret key that satisfies a certain policy determined by the encryptor. This allows for more flexibility in sharing encrypted messages, and provides many appealing applications.

Predicate encryption was first handled in [4,9], and many previous works can be casted in this framework, e.g. IBE [6,7,14,15], ABE [8,10,13]. However, due to the fact that they are more expressive than former public-key encryptions, providing meaningful security notions are difficult. Beyond the trivial security notion of payload hiding, which guarantees that no information on the message is obtained from the associating ciphertext, an extension of the payload hiding called the attribute hiding security was presented in [1,9]. This guarantees in addition that no essential information on the attribute associated with a ciphertext can be obtained.

Recently, Boneh, Raghunathan, and Segev [2] presented a new security notion called function privacy, which takes a step forward by requiring the secret key to reveal no information on the corresponding predicate, beyond the absolute minimum. This security notion was motivated by the need in providing predicate privacy in public key searchable encryptions. Many existing predicate encryptions do not yield function privacy, and formalizing such a security notion tends to be difficult, owing to the fact that the formalization of function privacy varies according to the family of predicates being used.

One of the most expressive and secured predicate encryption is the inner product encryption, which supports the family of predicates corresponding to the inner products of vectors in $\mathbb{Z}_q^l$. This was first presented by Katz, Sahai, and Waters [9], and since then many researches have been made, e.g. [5,11,12]. However, inner product encryption does not yield function privacy due to its functionality. In light of this, Boneh, Raghunathan, and Segev [3] formalized a generalization of inner product encryptions called subspace membership encryption, and succeeded in a generic construction of function private predicate encryptions. Their method of construction is efficient in that it can easily be constructed based on any underlying inner product encryption, and preserves the security properties of the underlying scheme. Furthermore, since the predicates used in subspace membership encryptions are of a wider class than that of inner product encryptions, it allows for richer applications.

## 1.1  Our Contribution

On looking over at the construction of subspace membership encryptions appeared in the proceeding version of Asiacrypt2013 [3] by Boneh, Raghunathan, and Segev, a fatal mistake was discovered in the proof of the attribute hiding security for the construction in the *small attribute space*, and to our extent, it seems difficult to correct it through simple modification[1]. Therefore, in this paper, we first generalize the framework of their construction by introducing a probability distribution over the attribute and predicate space, and prove that even in the generalized setting the attribute hiding security can not be yielded. More specifically, we will provide essential requirements for the baseline security notion to hold, and evaluate them probabilistically.

Then, we will give an extension of our generalized construction of subspace membership encryptions, and present a generic construction where the attribute hiding property holds even in small attribute spaces. We will point out that our construction does not yield function privacy, which was the primal motivation of Boneh et al. for formalizing subspace membership encryptions. However, through the extended framework, we have discovered a trade-off like relationship between the attribute hiding security and function privacy (and the size of the underlying inner product encryption). This presents a possibility for an existence of a construction method between that of ours and Boneh et al.'s. Furthermore, our extended generalized construction of subspace membership encryptions offers a new perspective in the construction method, and enables us to make wider choices on the underlying inner product encryption.

## 1.2 Outline of the Paper

In Section 2 we will introduce the subspace membership encryption following the works of [3]. In more detail, we will first provide the standard notions and definitions of predicate encryptions. Then, we will show the construction method of subspace membership encryptions given in [3], and point out the mistake in the proof of the attribute hiding security. In Section 3, we will give a generalized construction of subspace membership encryptions and show that the attribute security does not hold even in the generalized setting. In Section 4, we will extend the construction method given in Section 3 and compare it with other constructions of subspace membership encryptions. In Section 5, we will discuss the problem of our construction and see several open questions derived from this work.

## 2 Subspace Membership Encryption and Its Construction

### 2.1 Notation

For an integer $n \in \mathbb{N}$, $[n]$ denotes the set $\{1, 2, \ldots, n\}$. For an element $d$ in a probability distribution $D$, $d \leftarrow D$ denotes the process of sampling $d$ according to the distribution in $D$. Similarly, for a set $S$ and an element $x$ in the set $S$, $x \xleftarrow{\$} S$ denotes the process of sampling $x$ according to the uniform distribution over $S$. A function $f(x) : \mathbb{N} \to \mathbb{R}$ is negligible, when for any positive polynomial $\mathrm{poly}(x)$ there exists an integer $x_{\mathrm{poly}} > 0$ such that for all $x > x_{\mathrm{poly}}$, $|f(x)| < 1/\mathrm{poly}(x)$.

---

[1] Their scheme for the large attribute space is still secure.

A function $g(x) : \mathbb{N} \to \mathbb{R}$ is super polynomial, when for any integer $c > 0$ there exists an integer $x_{const}$ such that for all $x > x_{const}$, $g(x) > x^c$.

## 2.2  Predicate Encryption

We use the definition of Boneh et al. [3] with minor alterations.

**Definition 1 (Predicate Encryption).** A predicate encryption scheme for the class of predicates $\mathcal{F}$ over the set of attributes $\Sigma$ with message space $\mathcal{M}$ consists of four randomized PPT algorithms **Setup, KeyGen, Enc**, and **Dec** defined as follows:

1. **Setup**: Setup takes as input the security parameter $1^\lambda$ and outputs public key **pp** and a master key **msk**.
2. **Key Generation**: KeyGen takes as input the master secret key **msk** and a predicate $f \in \mathcal{F}$ and outputs a secret key $\text{sk}_f$.
3. **Encryption**: Enc takes as input the public key **pp**, an attribute $I \in \Sigma$, and a message $\mathsf{M} \in \mathcal{M}$ and returns a ciphertext $c$.
4. **Decryption**: Dec takes as input a secret key $\text{sk}_f$ and ciphertext $c$, and outputs either $\mathsf{M}$ or $\bot$.

Correctness requires the following conditions to hold with all but negligible probability in $\lambda$ for all $\lambda \in \mathbb{N}$, for all $(\mathbf{pp}, \mathbf{msk})$ generated by $\text{Setup}(1^\lambda)$, for all $f \in \mathcal{F}$, for all secret keys $\text{sk}_f \leftarrow \text{KeyGen}(\mathbf{msk}, f)$, for all $I \in \Sigma$.

**(1)** If $f(I) = 1$, then $\text{Dec}(\text{sk}_f, \text{Enc}(\mathbf{pp}, I, \mathsf{M})) = \mathsf{M}$.
**(2)** If $f(I) = 0$, then $\text{Dec}(\text{sk}_f, \text{Enc}(\mathbf{pp}, I, \mathsf{M})) = \bot$.

Beyond the standard notion of *payload hiding*, which guarantees that no efficient adversary obtains information on the encrypted message, it is often necessary to guarantee *attribute hiding* as well. This is a stronger notion than payload hiding, which guarantees in addition that no efficient adversary obtains information on the attribute associated with the ciphertext. We will follow the definition of (weak) attribute hiding given by Boneh et al. [3].

**Definition 2 (Attribute Hiding).** A predicate encryption scheme $\Pi$ for the class of predicates $\mathcal{F}$ over the set of attribute $\Sigma$ with message space $\mathcal{M}$ is attribute hiding if for all PPT adversaries $\mathcal{A}$, the advantage of $\mathcal{A}$ is negligible in the security parameter $\lambda$. The advantage of adversary $\mathcal{A}$ is defined via a game between an adversary and a challenger:

1. $\mathcal{A}(1^\lambda)$ outputs a pair $(I_0, I_1) \in \Sigma$, and gives these to the challenger.
2. The challenger computes $(\mathbf{pp}, \mathbf{msk}) \leftarrow \text{Setup}(1^\lambda)$ and gives **pp** to the adversary.
3. $\mathcal{A}$ requests keys for predicate $f_i \in \mathcal{F}(i = 1, 2, \ldots, Q)$ subject to the restriction $f_i(I_0) = f_i(I_1) = 0$ to the challenger. For each query the challenger sends back $\text{sk}_{f_i} \leftarrow \text{KeyGen}(\mathbf{msk}, f_i)$ to the adversary.
4. $\mathcal{A}$ submits two equal-length messages $\mathsf{M}_0, \mathsf{M}_1 \in \mathcal{M}$ to the challenger and receives $c \leftarrow \text{Enc}(\mathbf{pp}, I_b, \mathsf{M}_b)$.
5. $\mathcal{A}$ requests additional keys subject to the same restriction as before.

6. $\mathcal{A}$ outputs $b'$.

The advantage of the adversary $\mathcal{A}$ is defined as $|\Pr[b = b'] - 1/2|$.

In predicate encryption, further notion of security called function privacy is introduced by Boneh et al. [2]. Function privacy requires that no efficient adversary obtains information, beyond the absolute minimum necessary, on the identity of predicate $f$ associated with the secret key $\text{sk}_f$. However, we will not be handling this security notion in depth in this paper, so those who are interested should refer to [3] for further detail.

### 2.3 Subspace Membership Encryption

Subspace Membership Encryption (SME) is a predicate encryption formalized by Boneh et al. [3], which generalizes the framework of inner product encryptions (IPE). It supports the class of predicates $\mathcal{F}$ over an attribute space $\Sigma = \mathbb{S}^l$, defined as follows:

$$\mathcal{F} = \{f_{\mathbf{W}} : \mathbf{W} \in \mathbb{S}^{m \times l}\} \text{ , where } f_{\mathbf{W}}(\mathbf{x}) = \begin{cases} 1 & \text{if } \mathbf{W}\mathbf{x} = \mathbf{0} \in \mathbb{S}^m \\ 0 & \text{otherwise} \end{cases}.$$

Here $m, l \in \mathbb{N}$ are integers, $\mathbb{S}$ an additive group of order prime $q$, and $x \in \mathbb{S}^l$ an attribute. $m, l$ and $q$ are functions of $\lambda$ where $m$ and $l$ are traditionally polynomials in $\lambda$. In addition, IPE can be seen as a special case of SME when $m = 1$.

Boneh et al. [3] give a generic construction based on any IPE scheme in the cases of large and small attribute spaces, and gives proofs for each of their attribute hiding and function private properties. However, our research shows that the proof given for the attribute hiding property for SME in the small attribute space is incorrect, and a counterexample can be easily given. In this section we will see how the attribute hiding property does not hold for small attribute spaces.

**Construction in Large Attribute Space** First, we will take a look at the construction of SME for a large attribute space (LA.SME) given by Boneh et al. [3]. We note that a large attribute space is an attribute space $\mathbb{S}^l$ where the size of order $q$ of the additive group $\mathbb{S}$ is super polynomial in the security parameter $\lambda$. In contrast, a small attribute space is an attribute space $\mathbb{S}^l$ where the size of order $q$ of the additive group $\mathbb{S}$ is polynomial in $\lambda$. We will follow the definition of LA.SME given by Boneh et al. [3].

**Definition 3 (LA.SME Algorithm).** Let $\mathcal{IP}$= (IP.Setup, IP.KeyGen, IP.Enc, IP.Dec) be an IPE scheme with attribute set $\Sigma = \mathbb{S}^l$ and message space $\mathcal{M}$. Then a subspace membership encryption scheme $\mathcal{SM}$= (SM.Setup, SM.KeyGen, SM.Enc, SM.Dec) is constructed as follows:

1. **Setup:** SM.Setup takes the security parameter $1^\lambda$ as input and outputs public key **pp** and master key **msk** by running IP.Setup($1^\lambda$).

2. **Key Generation:** SM.KeyGen takes master key $\mathbf{msk}$ and predicate $f_{\mathbf{W}}(\mathbf{W} \in \mathbb{S}^{m \times l})$ as inputs. First, it samples $\mathbf{s} \xleftarrow{\$} \mathbb{S}^m$ and computes $\mathbf{v} = \mathbf{W}^T\mathbf{s} \in \mathbb{S}^l$. Then, it computes $\mathrm{sk}_{\mathbf{v}} \leftarrow$ IP.KeyGen $(\mathbf{msk}, \mathbf{v})$ and outputs $\mathrm{sk}_{\mathbf{W}}(= \mathrm{sk}_{\mathbf{v}})$.

3. **Encryption:** SM.Enc takes public key $\mathbf{pp}$, an attribute $\mathbf{x} \in \mathbb{S}^l$, and a message $\mathsf{M} \in \mathcal{M}$ as inputs, and outputs a ciphertext $c \leftarrow$ IP.Enc$(\mathbf{pp}, \mathbf{x}, \mathsf{M})$.

4. **Decryption:** SM.Dec takes public key $\mathbf{pp}$, a secret key $\mathrm{sk}_{\mathbf{W}}$, and a ciphertext $c$ as inputs, and outputs $\mathsf{M} \leftarrow$ IP.Dec $(\mathbf{pp}, \mathrm{sk}_{\mathbf{v}}, c)$.

The correctness of this construction is proven via the correctness of the underlying IPE scheme. It suffices to show that the following conditions holds for every $\mathbf{W} \in \mathbb{S}^{m \times l}$ and every $\mathbf{x} \in \mathbb{S}^l$.

(1) If $f_{\mathbf{W}}(\mathbf{x}) = 1$, then it holds that $\mathbf{Wx} = \mathbf{0}$. Hence, $\mathbf{x}^T\mathbf{v} = \mathbf{x}^T(\mathbf{W}^T\mathbf{s}) = 0$. Due to the correctness of the underlying IPE, IP.Dec decrypts $c$ correctly. Therefore SM.Dec will correctly output $\mathsf{M}$ as required, which implies that ciphertexts that should be correctly decrypted will always be correctly decrypted by SM.Dec.

(2) If $f_{\mathbf{W}}(\mathbf{x}) = 0$, then it holds that $\mathbf{Wx} = \mathbf{e} \neq \mathbf{0}$. Then, $\mathbf{x}^T\mathbf{v} = \mathbf{x}^T(\mathbf{W}^T\mathbf{s}) = \mathbf{e}^T\mathbf{s}$. Since $\mathbf{s}$ is a random vector chosen from an additive group $\mathbb{S}^l$ with order prime $q$, the quantity $\mathbf{x}^T\mathbf{v}$ equals zero with probability $1/q$. As $q$ is super polynomial in $\lambda$, $1/q$ is negligible in $\lambda$. Hence, ciphertexts that should not be correctly decrypted will not be decrypted correctly by SM.Dec, with all but negligible probability.

LA.SME is proven to be attribute hiding and function private, but we will not get into great detail as readers may inform [3] for detailed explanation. Here we will maintain ourselves to giving only an abstract of the proof.

Firstly, the attribute hiding property of LA.SME can be proven easily via the attribute hiding property of the underlying IPE. This is easily understandable, since the four PPT algorithms used in the SME scheme highly manipulates that of IPE. Secondly, the function private property is proven from the fact that a vector $\mathbf{v}$ corresponding to a predicate in IPE is a product of a random vector $\mathbf{s}$ and a matrix $\mathbf{W}$ corresponding to a predicate in LA.SME. We will remind the readers that function privacy requires no efficient adversary to obtain information, beyond the absolute minimum, on the identity of the predicate associated with the secret key. The intuition behind this is that even if some information on predicate $f_{\mathbf{v}}$ is revealed from the secret key $\mathrm{sk}_{\mathbf{W}} = \mathrm{sk}_{\mathbf{v}}$, as long as $\mathbf{W}$ is masked by a random vector $\mathbf{s}$, it reveals no information on predicate $f_{\mathbf{W}}$, consequently meaning that the secret key $\mathrm{sk}_{\mathbf{W}}$ reveals no information on the predicate $f_{\mathbf{W}}$.

**Construction in Small Attribute Space.** Looking at the proof of the correctness of LA.SME, we can see that correctness requires $1/q$ to be negligible in $\lambda$. In addition, when $1/q$ is not negligible in $\lambda$, it can also be seen that the proof for the attribute hiding property does not hold either. To overcome this difficulty, Boneh et al. refined LA.SME by introducing a new parameter $\tau(\lambda) \in \mathbb{N}$, and gave a construction of SME in a small attribute space (SA.SME) in the proceeding version[2] of Asiacrypt2013 [3]. A proof of the correctness and the attribute hiding property was given, but our research shows that the proof given for the latter is mistaken. Furthermore, it can be easily shown that in fact, SA.SME is not attribute hiding.

The detailed construction of SA.SME is as follows. Here, we use the definition of Boneh et al. [3].

**Definition 4 (SA.SME Algorithm).** Let $\mathcal{IP}$ =(IP.Setup, IP.KeyGen, IP.Enc, IP.Dec) be an IPE scheme with attribute set $\Sigma = \mathbb{S}^l$ and message space $\mathcal{M}$. Then a subspace membership encryption scheme $\mathcal{SM}_\tau$ = (SM.Setup, SM.KeyGen, SM.Enc, SM.Dec) parameterized by a parameter $\tau = \tau(\lambda) \in \mathbb{N}$ is constructed as follows:

1. **Setup:** SM.Setup takes the security parameter $1^\lambda$ as input and runs algorithm IP.Setup($1^\lambda$) $\tau$ times. It outputs public key $\mathbf{pp} = (\mathrm{pp}_1, \ldots, \mathrm{pp}_\tau)$ and master key $\mathbf{msk} = (\mathrm{msk}_1, \ldots, \mathrm{msk}_\tau)$.
2. **Key Generation:** SM.KeyGen takes master key $\mathbf{msk}$ and predicate $f_{\mathbf{W}}(\mathbf{W} \in \mathbb{S}^{m \times l})$ as inputs. First, it samples $\mathbf{s}_i \xleftarrow{\$} \mathbb{S}^m (i \in [\tau])$ independently $\tau$ times and computes $\mathbf{v}_i = \mathbf{W}^T \mathbf{s}_i \in \mathbb{S}^l$ for each $i$. Then, it computes $\mathrm{sk}_{\mathbf{v}_i} \leftarrow$ IP.KeyGen $(\mathrm{msk}_i, \mathbf{v}_i)$ and outputs secret key $\mathrm{sk}_{\mathbf{W}}=(\mathrm{sk}_{\mathbf{v}_1}, \ldots, \mathrm{sk}_{\mathbf{v}_\tau})$.
3. **Encryption:** SM.Enc takes public key $\mathbf{pp}$, an attribute $\mathbf{x} \in \mathbb{S}^l$, and a message $\mathsf{M} \in \mathcal{M}$ as inputs, and samples $\mathsf{M}_1, \ldots, \mathsf{M}_\tau \xleftarrow{\$} \mathcal{M}$ subject to $\mathsf{M} = \mathsf{M}_1 \oplus \cdots \oplus \mathsf{M}_\tau$. Then, it computes $c_i \leftarrow$ IP.Enc($\mathrm{pp}_i, \mathbf{x}, \mathsf{M}_i$) and outputs ciphertext $\mathbf{c} = (c_1, \ldots, c_\tau)$.
4. **Decryption:** SM.Dec takes public key $\mathbf{pp}$, a secret key $\mathrm{sk}_{\mathbf{W}}=(\mathrm{sk}_{\mathbf{v}_1}, \ldots, \mathrm{sk}_{\mathbf{v}_\tau})$, and a ciphertext $\mathbf{c} = (c_1, \ldots, c_\tau)$ as inputs, and computes $\mathsf{M}_i \leftarrow$ IP.Dec $(\mathrm{pp}_i, \mathrm{sk}_{\mathbf{v}_i}, c_i)$. If $\mathsf{M}_i =\perp$ for any $i \in [\tau]$, then SM.Dec outputs $\perp$. Otherwise, it outputs $\mathsf{M} = \mathsf{M}_1 \oplus \cdots \oplus \mathsf{M}_\tau$.

The correctness of this construction is proven the same way as the correctness of LA.SME. It suffices to show that the following conditions holds for every $\mathbf{W} \in \mathbb{S}^{m \times l}$ and every $\mathbf{x} \in \mathbb{S}^l$.

(1) If $f_{\mathbf{W}}(\mathbf{x}) = 1$, then it holds that $\mathbf{W}\mathbf{x} = \mathbf{0}$. Consequently, for every $i \in [\tau]$, $\mathbf{x}^T \mathbf{v}_i = \mathbf{x}^T(\mathbf{W}^T \mathbf{s}_i) = 0$. Due to the correctness of the underlying IPE, IP.Dec decrypts each ciphertexts $c_i$ correctly. Thus, SM.Dec will correctly output $\mathsf{M}$ as required, which implies that ciphertexts that should be correctly decrypted will always be correctly decrypted by SM.Dec.
(2) If $f_{\mathbf{W}}(\mathbf{x}) = 0$, then it holds that $\mathbf{W}\mathbf{x} = \mathbf{e} \neq \mathbf{0}$. Then, $\mathbf{x}^T \mathbf{v}_i = \mathbf{x}^T(\mathbf{W}^T \mathbf{s}_i) = \mathbf{e}^T \mathbf{s}_i$. Since $\mathbf{s}_i$ is a random vector chosen from an additive group $\mathbb{S}^l$ with order prime $q$, the quantity of $\mathbf{x}^T \mathbf{v}_i$ equals zero with probability $1/q$. SM.Dec fails to output $\perp$ if and only if $\mathbf{x}^T \mathbf{v}_i = 0$ for every $i \in [\tau]$. Therefore, the probability for correctly decrypting the ciphertext by mistake is $1/q^\tau$, which is negligible in the choice of parameters. Hence, ciphertexts that should not be correctly decrypted will not be correctly decrypted by SM.Dec, with all but negligible probability.

---

[2] In its full version, the constriction has been cut off.

As shown above, SA.SME yields correctness. It is also proven that SA.SME is function private [3]. However, as we will see in the next section, our research shows that the proof for the attribute hiding property for SA.SME was incorrect, and we will give proof of SA.SME not yielding the attribute hiding property. This is a crucial problem for SA.SME, since the attribute hiding property is the most fundamental security notion for predicate encryptions, i.e., even if it is function private, it can not be called secure unless it is not attribute hiding.

## 2.4  Problem of SA.SME

Boneh et al. [3] gave proof for the attribute hiding property of SA.SME. The proof considered a hybrid argument that basically followed the outline of the proof of LA.SME, however, our research shows that the proof was incorrect. In this section, we will devise an adversary where the advantage of the adversary is 1, and show that SA.SME does not yield the attribute hiding property.

Before explaining how the adversary queries the challenger to disprove SM.SME's attribute hiding property, we will review some properties of SA.SME. Since in SA.SME, the ciphertexts $c$ and the secret keys $sk_W$ are of the form $c = (c_1, \ldots, c_\tau)$ and $sk_W = (sk_{v_1}, \ldots, sk_{v_\tau})$, following from the previous argument, each secret key $sk_{v_i}$ will correctly decrypt ciphertext $c_i$ associated with attribute $x$ by mistake with probability $1/q$ when $f_{v_i}(x) = 0$. Hence, even when the adversary asks for a secret key $sk_W$ associated with the predicate $f_W$ satisfying $f_W(x_0) = f_W(x_1) = 0$ to the challenger, looking at each secret keys individually, the adversary will obtain a secret key $sk_{v_i}$ that correctly decrypts $c_i$ with probability $1/q$.

Saying there exists an adversary with advantage 1, is equivalent to showing there exists an adversary that can correctly decrypt the ciphertext $c$ given by the challenger while only querying predicates $f_W$ that suffices $f_W(x_0) = f_W(x_1) = 0$. In other words, it suffices to show that an adversary can obtain all the secret keys $sk_{v_i}$ which correctly decrypts $c_i$, i.e., the secret key $sk_W$ that correctly decrypts $c$, by only querying predicates $f_W$ with the above property.

To do so, the adversary will ask for a secret key $sk_W$ associated with the predicate $f_W$ satisfying $f_W(x_0) = f_W(x_1) = 0$ to the challenger, and if he receives a secret key $sk_{v_i}$ that successfully decrypts $c_i$, he will keep hold of it, and if not, he will discard of it and ask for a new secret key. We note that when the adversary asks for a new secret key $sk_W$, the associating predicate $f_W$ can be the same as the previous predicate he queried, since each secret keys $sk_{v_i}$ constituting $sk_W$ are constructed via products of a random vector $s_i$ and the matrix $W$ corresponding to the predicate $f_W$.

Since the adversary obtains a secret key $sk_{v_i}$ which correctly decrypts $c_i$ with probability $1/q$ for each $i \in [\tau]$ by making one query, following from the coupon collector's argument, the adversary will be able to collect all the secret keys $sk_{v_i}$ that correctly decrypts $c_i$ by querying no more than a polynomial in $q$ number of times. The mean of the number of queries needed to be made can be exactly evaluated, however, the fact that the mean is polynomial in $q$ is of importance right now. When $q$ is polynomial in the security parameter $\lambda$, a polynomial of $q$

is a polynomial of $\lambda$. Therefore, when the attribute space is small, the adversary will obtain the secret key $sk_W$ that correctly decrypts $c$ given by the challenger through querying only a polynomial in $\lambda$ number of times. Thus proving that SA.SME is not attribute hiding.

The above argument holds for any size of $\tau$, the number of shares of messages, as long as $\tau$ is polynomial in $\lambda$, since its size will only effect the number of queries needed to be made insignificantly. This presents the difficulty of modifying SA.SME to yield the attribute hiding property. It can be seen that the method of segmentation is not causing the problem, but the fact that SA.SME inherits the properties of LA.SME is causing the problem. More specifically, it is because each of the secret keys $sk_{v_i}$ constituting $sk_W$ can be accidentally obtained with probability $1/q$ through one query. When the attribute space is large $1/q$ is negligible, but when it is small $1/q$ is no longer negligible, which consequently deprives the attribute hiding property of SA.SME.

# 3  Generalized Construction of SME

As seen in the previous section, SA.SME does not yield the attribute hiding property, and this can not be fixed through simple reconstruction. The problem is not induced by the method of segmentation of SA.SME, but instead lies within the construction of the secret keys, which can not be altered easily. As long as each ciphertext $c_i$ associated with attribute $x$ can be decrypted by a secret key $sk_{v_i}$ associated with a predicate $f_W$ satisfying $f_W(x) = 0$ with probability $1/q$, SA.SME will not yield the attribute hiding property no matter how we split the messages, due to the fact that there exists an efficient attack to recover the secret key $sk_W$. This essentially means that the problem is caused by the underlying properties of LA.SME. Therefore, we need to rethink the Key Generation algorithm (and the Encryption algorithm) of LA.SME. In other words, we need to argue whether there is a way to construct secret keys $sk_W$ based on an underlying IPE scheme, where the secret keys $sk_W$ that are not intended to decrypt a specific ciphertext $c$, will not decrypt the ciphertext, with all but negligible probability in the security parameter $\lambda$.

In this section, we will give a generalized construction of LA.SME, and prove that such a construction of secret keys $sk_W$ is in fact impossible even in the generalized setting.

## 3.1  Preliminaries

We will introduce a probability distribution over the attribute and predicate space, and denote the new attribute space as $D_{\mathcal{G}}$ and the new predicate space as $D_{\mathcal{F}}$, where each notations are defined as follows.

1. $\mathcal{G}$ : A set of all functions from $\mathbb{S}^l$ to $\mathbb{S}^l$
2. $D_{\mathcal{G}}$ : Some probability distribution over $\mathcal{G}$
3. $\mathcal{F}$ : A set of all functions from $\mathbb{S}^{m \times l}$ to $\mathbb{S}^l$
4. $D_{\mathcal{F}}$ : Some probability distribution over $\mathcal{F}$

We note that the set $\mathcal{G}$ and $\mathcal{F}$ are finite sets.

If we use these newly defined notations, the attribute space $D_{\mathcal{G}_{BRS}}$ considered in [3] can be interpreted as an probability distribution where an identity function $g_{id} : \mathbf{x} \to \mathbf{x}$ is chosen with probability 1. Furthermore, the predicate space $D_{\mathcal{F}_{BRS}}$ can be interpreted as a probability distribution where a function $f_s : \mathbf{W} \to \mathbf{W}^{\mathrm{T}}s$ defined for every $s \in \mathbb{S}^l$ is chosen with probability $1/q^l$.

When $D$ is a probability distribution, $\Pr_{d \leftarrow D}(\text{“condition on } d\text{”})$ denotes the probability of choosing $d$ satisfying the given condition.

When $\mathbf{U}$ is a subset of a vector space $V$, $\mathbf{U}^{\perp}$ denotes the vector space of all vectors that are orthogonal to the elements in $\mathbf{U}$. When $\mathbf{v} \in V$, $\langle \mathbf{v} \rangle \subseteq V$ denotes the vector space spanned by $\mathbf{v}$.

Lastly, since we are handling linear algebra in finite fields, we will introduce some properties of linear algebra in $\mathbb{Z}_q^l$ which we will be using latter on in our proof. For further detail, refer to Appendix A and the full version.

**Lemma 1.** When $\mathrm{rank}(\mathbf{W}) = n$ for $\mathbf{W} \in \mathbb{Z}_q^{m \times l}$, the vector space $\mathbf{W}^{\perp}$ orthogonal to $\mathbf{W}$ is spanned by $l - n$ linearly independent vectors. In other words, $\dim(\mathbf{W}^{\perp}) = l - n$.

**Lemma 2.** When $\mathbf{a}_1, \ldots, \mathbf{a}_n$ are $n$ linearly independent vectors in $\mathbb{Z}_q^l$, there exists a vector $\mathbf{v} \in \mathbb{Z}_q^l$ satisfying the following condition.

$$\begin{cases} \mathbf{a}_i^{\mathrm{T}} \mathbf{v} = 0, & (i = 1, 2, \ldots, k) \\ \mathbf{a}_i^{\mathrm{T}} \mathbf{v} \neq 0, & (i = k+1, \ldots, n). \end{cases}$$

**Lemma 3.** There exists $N_q (= \frac{q^l - 1}{q - 1}) + 1$ vectors $\mathbf{v}_0, \mathbf{v}_1, \ldots \mathbf{v}_{N_q}$ satisfying the following condition, where $\mathbf{v}_0$ denotes the zero vector.

$$\begin{cases} \langle \mathbf{v}_0 \rangle \cup \langle \mathbf{v}_1 \rangle \cup \cdots \cup \langle \mathbf{v}_{N_q} \rangle = \mathbb{Z}_q^l, \\ \langle \mathbf{v}_i \rangle \cap \langle \mathbf{v}_j \rangle = 0, & (\forall i \neq j). \end{cases}$$

## 3.2    Generalized SME

LA.SME can be expressed using the newly defined probability distribution $D_{\mathcal{G}_{BRS}}$ and $D_{\mathcal{F}_{BRS}}$. However, as we saw in the previous section, SA.SME does not yield the attribute hiding property, since the probability of the incorrect secret key correctly decrypting the ciphertext could not be negligible. To state this mathematically, for all $\mathbf{W}$ and $\mathbf{x}$ satisfying $\mathbf{W}\mathbf{x} \neq 0$ the following equation holds in the LA.SME scheme.

$$\Pr_{f \leftarrow D_{\mathcal{F}_{BRS}}, g \leftarrow D_{\mathcal{G}_{BRS}}} (f(\mathbf{W})^{\mathrm{T}} g(\mathbf{x}) = 0) = 1/q.$$

This property holds for SA.SME too, when we look at each of the secret keys $\mathrm{sk}_{\mathbf{v}_i}$ constituting $\mathrm{sk}_{\mathbf{W}}$ individually. Therefore, although SA.SME holds correctness, since $1/q$ is not negligible in the security parameter $\lambda$ when the attribute space is small, it was not attribute hiding.

We will define a more generalized construction of LA.SME called Generalized SME (G.SME), and prove that we can not extend it to an attribute hiding counterpart of SA.SME even in the generalized setting. Consequentially proving that the above equation can not be fined to a degree where the right hand side becomes negligible in $\lambda$. To state this more explicitly, we will begin by giving the definition of G.SME.

**Definition 5 (Generalized SME).** Let $\mathcal{IP} = $ (IP.Setup, IP.KeyGen, IP.Enc, IP.Dec) be an IPE scheme with attribute set $\Sigma = \mathbb{S}^l$, message space $\mathcal{M}$, and $D_{\mathcal{G}}, D_{\mathcal{F}}$ be some probability distribution over sets $\mathcal{G}$ and $\mathcal{F}$. Then a subspace membership encryption scheme $\mathcal{SM} = $ (SM.Setup, SM.KeyGen, SM.Enc, SM.Dec) is constructed as follows:

1. **Setup:** SM.Setup takes the security parameter $1^\lambda$ as input and outputs public key **pp** and master key **msk** by running IP.Setup($1^\lambda$).
2. **Key Generation:** SM.KeyGen takes master key **msk** and predicate $f_{\mathbf{W}}$ ($\mathbf{W} \in \mathbb{S}^{m \times l}$) as inputs. First, it samples a function $f \leftarrow D_{\mathcal{F}}$ and computes $\mathbf{v} = f(\mathbf{W}) \in \mathbb{S}^l$. Then, it computes $\mathrm{sk}_{\mathbf{v}} \leftarrow$ IP.KeyGen(**msk**, $\mathbf{v}$) and outputs $\mathrm{sk}_{\mathbf{W}} (= \mathrm{sk}_{\mathbf{v}})$.
3. **Encryption:** SM.Enc takes public key **pp**, an attribute $\mathbf{x} \in \mathbb{S}^l$, and a message $\mathsf{M} \in \mathcal{M}$ as inputs. First, it samples a function $g \leftarrow D_{\mathcal{G}}$ and computes $\mathbf{y} = g(\mathbf{x}) \in \mathbb{S}^l$. Then it outputs a ciphertext $c \leftarrow$ IP.Enc(**pp**, $\mathbf{y}$, $\mathsf{M}$).
4. **Decryption:** SM.Dec takes public key **pp**, a secret key $\mathrm{sk}_{\mathbf{W}}$, and a ciphertext $c$ as inputs, and outputs $\mathsf{M} \leftarrow$ IP.Dec(**pp**, $\mathrm{sk}_{\mathbf{v}}$, $c$).

We note that if we let $D_{\mathcal{G}} = D_{\mathcal{G}_{BRS}}$ and $D_{\mathcal{F}} = D_{\mathcal{F}_{BRS}}$, we obtain LA.SME. We now need to further inspect the requirements for the probability distributions $D_{\mathcal{G}}$ and $D_{\mathcal{F}}$, in order for G.SME to hold correctness and the attribute hiding property.

### 3.3   Requirements in Constructing G.SME

The problem of LA.SME was that when the attribute space was small, the probability of the incorrect secret key correctly decrypting the ciphertext was not negligible. Hence, in order for G.SME to yield correctness and the attribute hiding property, the following two requirements must hold for large and small attribute spaces.

**Requirement 1 (Correct secret keys correctly decrypt ciphertexts).** For all pairs $\mathbf{W}$ and $\mathbf{x}$ satisfying $\mathbf{W}\mathbf{x} = \mathbf{0}$, the following inequalities holds.

$$\Pr_{f \leftarrow D_{\mathcal{F}}, g \leftarrow D_{\mathcal{G}}} (f(\mathbf{W})^{\mathrm{T}} g(\mathbf{x}) = 0) \geq 1 - \delta,$$

where $\delta$ is a negligible function in the security parameter $\lambda$.

**Requirement 2 (Incorrect secret keys do not decrypt ciphertexts).** For all pairs $\mathbf{W}$ and $\mathbf{x}$ satisfying $\mathbf{W}\mathbf{x} \neq \mathbf{0}$, the following inequalities holds.

$$\Pr_{f \leftarrow D_{\mathcal{F}}, g \leftarrow D_{\mathcal{G}}} (f(\mathbf{W})^{\mathrm{T}} g(\mathbf{x}) = 0) \leq \epsilon,$$

where $\epsilon$ is a negligible function in the security parameter $\lambda$.

Requirement 1 can be seen as a requirement for the correctness of G.SME to follow. Requirement 2 can also be seen as a requirement for the correctness to follow, but we point out that it has a more important relevance than that. To hold correctness, $\epsilon$ does not necessarily have to be negligible in $\lambda$, since as we saw with SA.SME, we can segment the messages in order to preserve the correctness for small attribute spaces. However, since the attribute hiding property can not be attained through changing the method of segmentation, $\epsilon$ needs to be negligible in $\lambda$ for the attribute hiding property to hold even in small attribute spaces.

We note that in LA.SME, the following equations holds.

$$\Pr_{f \leftarrow D_{\mathcal{F}_{\mathrm{BRS}}}, g \leftarrow D_{\mathcal{G}_{\mathrm{BRS}}}} (f(\mathbf{W})^{\mathrm{T}} g(\mathbf{x}) = 0) = 1 \quad \text{for all } \mathbf{W} \text{ and } \mathbf{x} \text{ satisfying } \mathbf{W}\mathbf{x} = 0,$$

$$\Pr_{f \leftarrow D_{\mathcal{F}_{\mathrm{BRS}}}, g \leftarrow D_{\mathcal{G}_{\mathrm{BRS}}}} (f(\mathbf{W})^{\mathrm{T}} g(\mathbf{x}) = 0) = 1/q \quad \text{for all } \mathbf{W} \text{ and } \mathbf{x} \text{ satisfying } \mathbf{W}\mathbf{x} \neq 0.$$

We can see that Requirement 1 holds, but Requirement 2 does not, since $1/q$ will not be negligible in the security parameter $\lambda$ when the attribute space is small.

### 3.4  Properties of Functions in $D_{\mathcal{G}}$ and $D_{\mathcal{F}}$

When the attribute space $D_{\mathcal{G}}$ and predicate space $D_{\mathcal{F}}$ of G.SME meets the Requirement 1 and 2, there are several strong properties we can state. We will introduce them and give the intuition behind each properties. We will only give proofs for the first two lemmas, and for the other lemmas it will be given in the full version.

The following lemma informs that for linearly independent attributes of G.SME, they maintain to be linearly independent with high probability after being mapped to attributes of IPE by a function in $D_{\mathcal{G}}$.

**Lemma 4.** Let $\mathrm{rank}(\mathbf{W}) = n$. From Lemma 1, the vector space $\mathbf{W}^{\perp}$ orthogonal to $\mathbf{W}$ is spanned by $l - n$ linearly independent vectors. Denoting the $l - n$ vectors as $\mathbf{u}_1, \mathbf{u}_2, \ldots, \mathbf{u}_{l-n} \in \mathbb{S}^l$, if $l < \frac{1}{\epsilon + \delta}$, then the following inequality holds for all $\tau \geq \epsilon + \delta$.

$$\Pr_{g_i \leftarrow D_{\mathcal{G}}} (g_1(\mathbf{u}_1), \ldots, g_{l-n}(\mathbf{u}_{l-n}) \text{ are linearly independent}) \geq 1 - \tau.$$

**Proof.**  Let us assume that there exists a $\tau_0 \geq \epsilon + \delta$ satisfying,

$$\Pr_{g_i \leftarrow D_{\mathcal{G}}} (g_1(\mathbf{u}_1), \ldots, g_{l-n}(\mathbf{u}_{l-n}) \text{ are linearly dependent}) \geq \tau_0.$$

This inequality can be rewritten as

$$\Pr_{g_i \leftarrow D_{\mathcal{G}}} \left(g_1(\mathbf{u}_1) = \sum_{i=2}^{l-n} a_i g_i(\mathbf{u}_i) \text{ for some } a_i \in \mathbb{Z}_q (i = 2, \ldots, l - n)\right) \geq \tau_0. \quad (1)$$

Since $\mathbf{u}_1, \mathbf{u}_2, \ldots, \mathbf{u}_{l-n}$ are linearly independent, substituting $k = n - 1$ in Lemma 2, there exists a vector $\mathbf{v}$ satisfying,

$$\begin{cases} \mathbf{u}_1^T \mathbf{v} \neq 0, \\ \mathbf{u}_i^T \mathbf{v} = 0, \quad (i = 2, \ldots, l - n). \end{cases}$$

Hence, if we consider a matrix $\mathbf{W}' \in \mathbb{S}^{m \times l}$ whose rows are $\mathbf{v}^T$, we obtain

$$\begin{cases} \mathbf{W}' \mathbf{u}_1 \neq \mathbf{0}, \\ \mathbf{W}' \mathbf{u}_i = \mathbf{0}, \quad (i = 2, \ldots, l - n). \end{cases}$$

Since from Requirement 1,

$$\Pr_{f \leftarrow D_{\mathcal{F}}, g_i \leftarrow D_{\mathcal{G}}} (f(\mathbf{W}')^T g_i(\mathbf{u}_i) = 0) \geq 1 - \delta$$

holds for all $i = 2, \ldots, l - n$, the following inequality holds.

$$\Pr_{f \leftarrow D_{\mathcal{F}}, g_i \leftarrow D_{\mathcal{G}}} (f(\mathbf{W}')^T g_i(\mathbf{u}_i) = 0 \ (i = 2, .., l - n)) \geq (1 - \delta)^{l-n-1}. \qquad (2)$$

Using (2), we obtain

$$\Pr_{f \leftarrow D_{\mathcal{F}}, g_i \leftarrow D_{\mathcal{G}}} \left( f(\mathbf{W}')^T \sum_{i=2}^{l-n} a_i g_i(\mathbf{u}_i) = 0 \right) \geq (1 - \delta)^{l-n-1}$$

for any $a_i \in \mathbb{Z}_q$ $(i = 2, \ldots, l - n)$. Combining this with (1), we have

$$\Pr_{f \leftarrow D_{\mathcal{F}}, g_1 \leftarrow D_{\mathcal{G}}} (f(\mathbf{W}')^T g_1(\mathbf{u}_1) = 0) \geq \tau_0 (1 - \delta)^{l-n-1}.$$

Since $\delta \ll 1, n \geq 1, \tau_0 \geq \epsilon + \delta, l < \frac{1}{\epsilon + \delta}$,

$$\tau_0 (1 - \delta)^{l-n-1} > \tau_0 \left( 1 - (l - 2)\delta \right) \geq (\epsilon + \delta) \left( 1 - (l - 2)\delta \right)$$
$$= \epsilon + \left( 1 - (l - 2)(\epsilon + \delta) \right) \delta > \epsilon.$$

Therefore,

$$\Pr_{f \leftarrow D_{\mathcal{F}}, g_1 \leftarrow D_{\mathcal{G}}} (f(\mathbf{W}')^T g_1(\mathbf{u}_1) = 0) > \epsilon. \qquad (3)$$

On the other hand, since $\mathbf{W}' \mathbf{u}_1 \neq \mathbf{0}$, the following inequality given by Requirement 2 must hold.

$$\Pr_{f \leftarrow D_{\mathcal{F}}, g_1 \leftarrow D_{\mathcal{G}}} (f(\mathbf{W}')^T g_1(\mathbf{u}_1) = 0) < \epsilon.$$

However, this contradicts (3). Hence the proof is complete.  ∎

The next lemma shows that, if the matrix $\mathbf{W}$ associated with the predicate of SME satisfies $\mathrm{rank}(\mathbf{W}) = n$, then the vector mapped by a function from $D_{\mathcal{F}}$ belongs in a vector space spanned by $n$ basis with high probability.

**Lemma 5.** Let $\text{rank}(\mathbf{W}) = n$. If $l < \frac{1}{\epsilon+\delta}$, then for some linearly independent vectors $\mathbf{v}_1, \ldots, \mathbf{v}_n \in \mathbb{S}^l$, the following inequality holds for all $\mu \geq \frac{\delta}{(\epsilon+\delta)(1-(\epsilon+\delta))}$.

$$\Pr_{f \leftarrow D_{\mathcal{F}}} (f(\mathbf{W}) \text{ is a linear combination of } \mathbf{v}_1, \ldots, \mathbf{v}_n) \geq 1 - \mu.$$

**Proof.**   Let us assume there exists $\mu_0 \geq \frac{\delta}{(\epsilon+\delta)(1-(\epsilon+\delta))}$ satisfying,

$$\Pr_{f \leftarrow D_{\mathcal{F}}} (f(\mathbf{W}) \text{ is not a linear combination of } \mathbf{v}_1, \ldots, \mathbf{v}_n) \geq \mu_0, \qquad (4)$$

for any linearly independent $\mathbf{v}_1, \ldots, \mathbf{v}_n$.

If we denote $\mathbf{u}_1, \ldots, \mathbf{u}_{l-n}$ as the basis for the vector space $\mathbf{W}^\perp$ orthogonal to $\mathbf{W}$, from Lemma 1 and Lemma 4, we obtain

$$\Pr_{g_i \leftarrow D_{\mathcal{G}}} (\text{A vector space orthogonal to } g_1(\mathbf{u}_1), \ldots, g_{l-n}(\mathbf{u}_{l-n})$$

$$\text{is spanned by } n \text{ linearly independent vectors}) \geq 1 - \tau \qquad (5)$$

for all $\tau \geq \epsilon + \delta$.

Therefore, from (4) and (5), we obtain

$$\Pr_{f \leftarrow D_{\mathcal{F}}, g_i \leftarrow D_{\mathcal{G}}} (f(\mathbf{W}) \text{ is not a linear combination of the } n \text{ vectors forming}$$

$$\text{the basis of the vector space orthogonal to } g_1(\mathbf{u}_1), \ldots, g_{l-n}(\mathbf{u}_{l-n})) \geq \mu_0(1-\tau)$$

$$\Longleftrightarrow \Pr_{f \leftarrow D_{\mathcal{F}}, g_i \leftarrow D_{\mathcal{G}}} (f(\mathbf{W})^{\mathrm{T}} g_i(\mathbf{u}_i) \neq 0 \text{ for some } i \in [l-n]) \geq \mu_0(1-\tau).$$

Since this suffices for all $\tau \geq \epsilon + \delta$, we get

$$\Pr_{f \leftarrow D_{\mathcal{F}}, g_i \leftarrow D_{\mathcal{G}}} (f(\mathbf{W})^{\mathrm{T}} g_i(\mathbf{u}_i) \neq 0 \text{ for some } i \in [l-n]) \geq \mu_0(1-(\epsilon+\delta)).$$

Furthermore, since $\mu_0 \geq \frac{\delta}{(\epsilon+\delta)(1-(\epsilon+\delta))}$,

$$\Pr_{f \leftarrow D_{\mathcal{F}}, g_i \leftarrow D_{\mathcal{G}}} (f(\mathbf{W})^{\mathrm{T}} g_i(\mathbf{u}_i) \neq 0 \text{ for some } i \in [l-n]) \geq \frac{\delta}{\epsilon+\delta}. \qquad (6)$$

On the other hand, since $\mathbf{u}_i$ is orthogonal to $\mathbf{W}$, following from Requirement 1,

$$\Pr_{f \leftarrow D_{\mathcal{F}}, g_i \leftarrow D_{\mathcal{G}}} (f(\mathbf{W})^{\mathrm{T}} g_i(\mathbf{u}_i) = 0) \geq 1 - \delta$$

must hold for every $i$.

Therefore,

$$\Pr_{f \leftarrow D_{\mathcal{F}}, g_i \leftarrow D_{\mathcal{G}}} (f(\mathbf{W})^{\mathrm{T}} g_i(\mathbf{u}_i) \neq 0 \text{ for some } i \in [l-n]) < 1 - (1-\delta)^{l-n}.$$

Since $l < \frac{1}{\epsilon+\delta}$, $n \geq 1$, and $\delta \ll 1$, $1 - (1-\delta)^{l-n} < 1 - (1-(l-n)\delta) < l\delta \leq \frac{\delta}{\epsilon+\delta}$. Combining this with the above inequality gives us,

$$\Pr_{f \leftarrow D_{\mathcal{F}}, g_i \leftarrow D_{\mathcal{G}}} (f(\mathbf{W})^{\mathrm{T}} g_i(\mathbf{u}_i) \neq 0 \text{ for some } i \in [l-n]) < \frac{\delta}{\epsilon+\delta}.$$

However, this contradicts (6). Thus completing the proof.   ■

The following lemma presents that, if the matrix $\mathbf{W}$ associated with the predicate of SME satisfies $\text{rank}(\mathbf{W}) = 1$, then a stronger property than lemma 5 can be attained. It says that, if we do not distinguish between $\mathbf{W}$ and $\mathbf{W}'$ satisfying $\mathbf{W}^\perp = \mathbf{W}'^\perp$, then each vector mapped by a function in $D_{\mathcal{F}}$ will belong to a different vector space with high probability.

**Lemma 6.** For every $\mathbf{v} \in \mathbb{S}_q^l$, if $l < \frac{1}{\epsilon+\delta}$, then the following inequality holds for all $\mu \geq \frac{\delta}{(\epsilon+\delta)(1-(\epsilon+\delta))}$ for some $\mathbf{W}$ satisfying $\text{rank}(\mathbf{W}) = 1$.

$$\Pr_{f \leftarrow D_{\mathcal{F}}} (f(\mathbf{W}) \in \langle \mathbf{v} \rangle) \geq 1 - \mu.$$

Furthermore, if we do not distinguish between $\mathbf{W}$ and $\mathbf{W}'$ satisfying $\mathbf{W}^\perp = \mathbf{W}'^\perp$, then such a $\mathbf{W}$ is unique.

Finally, we will show an generalization of lemma 6. This lemma suggests that predicates $\mathbf{W}$ and $\mathbf{W}'$ of SME satisfying $\mathbf{W}^\perp = \mathbf{W}'^\perp$, will belong to a different vector space when mapped by a function in $D_{\mathcal{F}}$ with high probability. This is the main lemma for proving that G.SME can not yield the attribute hiding property.

**Lemma 7.** Let $c$ be a constant satisfying $\delta^c = \epsilon + \delta$. If $l < \frac{1}{\epsilon+\delta}$, then the following inequality holds for all $\nu \geq \frac{\epsilon+\delta^{1-c}}{1-(\epsilon+3\delta^{1-c})}$ and for all $\mathbf{W}_0, \mathbf{W}_1 \in \mathbb{S}^{m \times l}$ satisfying $\mathbf{W}_0^\perp \neq \mathbf{W}_1^\perp$.

$$\max_{\mathbf{v} \in \mathbb{S}^l} \min\{ \Pr_{f_0 \leftarrow D_{\mathcal{F}}} (f_0(\mathbf{W}_0) \in \langle \mathbf{v} \rangle), \Pr_{f_1 \leftarrow D_{\mathcal{F}}} (f_1(\mathbf{W}_1) \in \langle \mathbf{v} \rangle)\} \leq \nu.$$

### 3.5   Proof of G.SME Not Yielding the Attribute Hiding Property

In order for G.SME to be applicable in small attribute spaces, Requirement 1 and 2 must hold when $q$ is polynomial in the security parameter $\lambda$. Here we will prove that no such G.SME exists. In other words, we will prove the following proposition.

**Proposition 1.** Considering arbitrary probability distribution $D_{\mathcal{G}}$ and $D_{\mathcal{F}}$, if $l < \frac{1}{\epsilon+\delta}$, then we can not construct a G.SME that both satisfies Requirement 1 and 2.

We note the condition $l < \frac{1}{\epsilon+\delta}$ is not of great importance due to the fact that $l$ is traditionally arranged as a polynomial in $\lambda$ in real life applications. Hence, proving Proposition 1 under such condition on $l$ is sufficient enough to conclude that G.SME does not yield the attribute hiding property.

**Proof.**   Let us consider a matrix $\mathbf{W}$ with $\text{rank}(\mathbf{W}) = 2$. Then, from Lemma 5, for some linearly independent vector $\mathbf{v}_1$ and $\mathbf{v}_2$, the following inequality holds for every $\mu \geq \frac{\delta}{(\epsilon+\delta)(1-(\epsilon+\delta))}$.

$$\Pr_{f \leftarrow D_{\mathcal{F}}} (f(\mathbf{W}) \in \langle \mathbf{v}_1, \mathbf{v}_2 \rangle) \geq 1 - \mu.$$

Also, from Lemma 6, for each element $\mathbf{u}_i$ in $\langle \mathbf{v}_1, \mathbf{v}_2 \rangle$, there exists a matrix $\mathbf{W}_i$ that is $\mathrm{rank}(\mathbf{W}_i) = 1$ satisfying,

$$\Pr_{f \leftarrow D_{\mathcal{F}}} (f(\mathbf{W}_i) \in \langle \mathbf{u}_i \rangle) \geq 1 - \mu. \tag{7}$$

On the other hand, since $\langle \mathbf{v}_1, \mathbf{v}_2 \rangle$ consists of $q^2$ elements, the following inequality holds.

$$\max_{\mathbf{u} \in \langle \mathbf{v}_1, \mathbf{v}_2 \rangle} \Pr_{f \leftarrow D_{\mathcal{F}}} (f(\mathbf{W}) = \mathbf{u}) \geq \frac{1 - \mu}{q^2}. \tag{8}$$

Let $\mathbf{u}_{\max}$ denote the $\mathbf{u}$ that attains the maximum value, and $\mathbf{W}_{\max}$ denote the $\mathbf{W}_i$ of (7) when $\mathbf{u}_i = \mathbf{u}_{\max}$. Then, from (8),

$$\min\{\Pr(f(\mathbf{W}_{\max}) \in \langle \mathbf{u}_{\max} \rangle),\ \Pr(f(\mathbf{W}) \in \langle \mathbf{u}_{\max} \rangle)\} \geq \frac{1 - \mu}{q^2}.$$

Hence,

$$\max_{\mathbf{u} \in \mathbb{S}^l} \min\{\Pr(f(\mathbf{W}_{\max}) \in \langle \mathbf{u} \rangle), \Pr(f(\mathbf{W}) \in \langle \mathbf{u} \rangle)\} \geq \frac{1 - \mu}{q^2}.$$

Observe that $\mathbf{W}_{\max}^{\perp} \neq \mathbf{W}^{\perp}$ since $\mathrm{rank}(\mathbf{W}_{\max}) = 1$ and $\mathrm{rank}(\mathbf{W}) = 2$. In addition, when $q$ is polynomial in $\lambda$, we can make $\frac{1-\mu}{q^2}$ sufficiently large, i.e., none negligible in $\lambda$, by making $\mu$ adequately small. This contradicts Lemma 7.

Therefore, for arbitrary probability distribution $D_{\mathcal{G}}$ and $D_{\mathcal{F}}$, it is impossible for Requirement 1 and 2 to both satisfy, hence proving Proposition 1. ∎

## 4    Extended Construction of Generalized SME

We see that we can not yield the attribute hiding property when the attribute space is small for SME whose attributes and predicates were simply constructed through those of IPE, e.g., LA.SME and G.SME. Furthermore, this difficulty could not be overcome by segmenting the encryption and decryption process, e.g., SA.SME, due to the fact that it underlines the properties of LA.SME and G.SME.

This can be understood as a consequence of SME using the same sets of attributes as the underlying IPE. To be more specific, the problem was induced because the attributes $\mathbf{x}$ of SME and the attributes $\mathbf{y}$ of IPE were of the same size, i.e., the rows of the matrix $\mathbf{W}$ corresponding to the predicates of SME and the columns of the vectors $\mathbf{v}$ corresponding to the predicates of IPE were of the same size. Therefore, when converting a predicate $f_{\mathbf{W}}$ of SME to the predicate $f_{\mathbf{v}}$ of IPE, since $\mathbf{W}$ was of a much larger class than $\mathbf{v}$, information on $\mathbf{W}$ was inevitably lost. Thus, $\mathbf{W}\mathbf{x} = \mathbf{0} \Leftrightarrow \mathbf{v}^{\mathrm{T}}\mathbf{y} = 0$ could not been satisfied, leading to the loss in correctness and the attribute hiding property.

In this section, we will extend the idea of G.SME, by introducing a construction of a SME who has a different attribute and predicate space than the underlying IPE, and show that it can yield the attribute hiding property.

## 4.1   Extended G.SME

Although in previous constructions of SME, the size of attributes used in SME and IPE were of the same size, this restriction was no means necessary. In this section, we will remove this restriction and extend our method of construction.

We will particularly choose attributes $\mathbf{x}$ for SME from the set $\mathbb{S}^l$, and attributes $\mathbf{y}$ for IPE from the set $\mathbb{S}^{q^{(m+1)l}}$. Furthermore, we prepare a function $f_{EG}$ and $g_{EG}$ defined as,

$$f_{EG}(\mathbf{W}_i) = (0, \cdots, 0, u_{i,1}, \ldots, u_{i,j}, \cdots, u_{i,q^l}, 0, \ldots, 0)^{\mathrm{T}} \in \mathbb{S}^{q^{(m+1)l}},$$

$$g_{EG}(\mathbf{x}_j) = (0, \ldots, v_{1,j}, \ldots, 0, v_{i,j}, 0, \ldots, v_{q^{ml},j}, \ldots, 0)^{\mathrm{T}} \in \mathbb{S}^{q^{(m+1)l}},$$

where $\mathbf{W}_i$ is the $i$-th matrix with some given order in $\mathbb{S}^{m \times l}$, and $\mathbf{x}_j$ is the $j$-th vector with some given order in $\mathbb{S}^l$. We note that the order in $\mathbb{S}^{m \times l}$ and $\mathbb{S}^l$ is arbitrary. Furthermore, $u_{i,j}$ and $v_{i,j}$ represents the $(i-1)q^l + j$-th element in $f_{EG}$ and $g_{EG}$ respectively, and is defined as follows.

$$u_{i,j} = \begin{cases} 0 & \text{if } \mathbf{W}_i\mathbf{x}_j = \mathbf{0} \\ 1 & \text{otherwise} \end{cases}, \qquad v_{i,j} = \begin{cases} 0 & \text{if } \mathbf{W}_i\mathbf{x}_j = \mathbf{0} \\ 1 & \text{otherwise} \end{cases}.$$

Now we will introduce an extended construction of G.SME, and call it Extended Generalized SME (EG.SME). We note that the definition of the set of functions $\mathcal{G}_{EG}$ and $\mathcal{F}_{EG}$ slightly differs from the previous section's in order to meet the definition of EG.SME.

**Definition 6 (Extended   Generalized   SME).** Let $\mathcal{IP} = $ (IP.Setup, IP.KeyGen, IP.Enc, IP.Dec) be an IPE scheme with attribute set $\Sigma = \mathbb{S}^{q^{(m+1)l}}$, message space $\mathcal{M}$, and $D_{\mathcal{G}_{EG}}, D_{\mathcal{F}_{EG}}$ be a probability distribution where the functions $g_{EG}$ and $f_{EG}$ are chosen with probability 1 respectively. Then a subspace membership encryption scheme $\mathcal{SM}$=(SM.Setup, SM.KeyGen, SM.Enc, SM.Dec) is constructed as follows:

1. **Setup:** SM.Setup takes the security parameter $1^\lambda$ as input and outputs public key $\mathbf{pp}$ and master key $\mathbf{msk}$ by running IP.Setup($1^\lambda$).
2. **Key Generation:** SM.KeyGen takes master key $\mathbf{msk}$ and predicate $f_{\mathbf{W}}$($\mathbf{W}$ $\in \mathbb{S}^{m \times l}$) as inputs. First, it samples a function $f_{EG} \leftarrow D_{\mathcal{F}_{EG}}$ and computes $\mathbf{v} = f_{EG}(\mathbf{W}) \in \mathbb{S}^{q^{(m+1)l}}$. Then, it computes $\mathrm{sk}_{\mathbf{v}} \leftarrow$ IP.KeyGen($\mathbf{msk}, \mathbf{v}$) and outputs $\mathrm{sk}_{\mathbf{W}}(= \mathrm{sk}_{\mathbf{v}})$.
3. **Encryption:** SM.Enc takes public key $\mathbf{pp}$, an attribute $\mathbf{x} \in \mathbb{S}^l$, and a message $\mathsf{M} \in \mathcal{M}$ as inputs. First, it samples a function $g_{EG} \leftarrow D_{\mathcal{G}_{EG}}$ and computes $\mathbf{y} = g_{EG}(\mathbf{x}) \in \mathbb{S}^{q^{(m+1)l}}$. Then it outputs a ciphertext $c \leftarrow$ IP.Enc($\mathbf{pp}, \mathbf{y}, \mathsf{M}$).
4. **Decryption:** SM.Dec takes public key $\mathbf{pp}$, a secret key $\mathrm{sk}_{\mathbf{W}}$, and a ciphertext $c$ as inputs, and outputs $\mathsf{M} \leftarrow$ IP.Dec($\mathbf{pp}, \mathrm{sk}_{\mathbf{v}}, c$).

The correctness and the attribute hiding property of EG.SME can be easily shown. From definition, $f_{EG}(\mathbf{W}_i)^{\mathrm{T}} g_{EG}(\mathbf{x}_j) = u_{i,j}v_{i,j}$, and $u_{i,j}v_{i,j}$ equals 0 if and only if $\mathbf{W}_i \mathbf{x}_j = \mathbf{0}$. Therefore, $\mathbf{W}_i \mathbf{x}_j = \mathbf{0} \Leftrightarrow f_{EG}(\mathbf{W}_i)^{\mathrm{T}} g_{EG}(\mathbf{x}_j) = 0$ holds for every $\mathbf{W}_i$ and $\mathbf{x}_j$, thus proving correctness. Furthermore, since correctness always holds, the attribute hiding property can be proven by following a similar argument in [3]. We point out the important fact that the size of $q$ is irrelevant to the correctness and the attribute hiding property of EG.SME.

## 4.2    Comparing with Other Schemes in Small Attribute Space

We successfully assigned the attribute hiding property to EG.SME. Table 1 lists the type of schemes which we handled in this paper, and illustrates each of their properties when the attribute space is small, i.e., when the size of $q$ is polynomial in the security parameter $\lambda$.

Table 1. Each scheme's properties in small attribute spaces

| Type of Scheme | Correctness | Attribute Hiding Security | Function Privacy | Size of Underlying IPE |
|---|---|---|---|---|
| LA.SME[3] | × | × | √ | polynomial in $\lambda$ |
| SA.SME | √ | × | √ | polynomial in $\lambda$ |
| G.SME | depends on construction | × | depends on construction | polynomial in $\lambda$ |
| EG.SME | √ | √ | × | exponential in $\lambda$ |

As we can see, LA.SME (Sec.2.3.1), SA.SME (Sec.2.3.2), and G.SME (Sec.3.2) does not yield the attribute hiding security, the baseline security notion for predicate encryptions. Its security is vital to the scheme and can not be overlooked, even if they possess function privacy. On the other hand, EG.SME successfully yields the attribute hiding security, however, function privacy is deprived. This can be understood as a consequence of $\mathbf{W}_i \mathbf{x}_j = \mathbf{0} \Leftrightarrow f_{EG}(\mathbf{W}_i)^{\mathrm{T}} g_{EG}(\mathbf{x}_j) = 0$ for all $\mathbf{W}_i$ and $\mathbf{x}_i$. Since the projection of the matrix $\mathbf{W}_i$ corresponding to the predicate $f_{\mathbf{W}}$ of SME to the vector $\mathbf{v}_i = f_{EG}(\mathbf{W}_i)$ corresponding to the predicate $f_{\mathbf{v}_i}$ of IPE is injective, if the underlying IPE is not function private, then SME can not be function private. Furthermore, we point out that every type of scheme expect EG.SME has a underlying IPE the size of a polynomial in $q$.

Compared with the other three schemes, because they do not possess the attribute hiding security, one can say that EG.SME is more applicable in small attribute spaces. However, taking in account the lack of function privacy and the exponential size of the underlying IPE, we can not say that EG.SME is better altogether.

## 5    Conclusion and Open Questions

As we saw with G.SME and EG.SME, a trade-off between the "Attribute Hiding Security" and the "Function Privacy & Size of Underlying IPE" can be observed.

---

[3] We note that LA.SME holds correctness and the attribute hiding security in large attribute spaces.

The intuition behind this is that function privacy requires the relationship of SME predicates and IPE predicates to be ambiguous, but the attribute hiding security requires the relationship of SME predicates and IPE predicates to yield similar qualities, e.g., Requirement 1 and 2. Since the size of the predicates of SME is much larger than those of IPE, in order to fulfill the function privacy's requirements, the size of the underlying IPE will inevitably becomes larger.

The methodology of EG.SME brings new perspective in the construction of SME in small attribute spaces. In this paper we only considered attribute $\mathbf{y}$ for IPE from the set $\mathbb{S}^{q^{(m+1)l}}$, which is exponential in the parameter $q$. In addition the probability distribution $\mathcal{D}_G$ and $\mathcal{D}_F$ essentially consisted of one function each, $f_{EG}$ and $g_{EG}$. This can be improved, by considering polynomial sized IPE and introducing new varieties of functions into the probability distribution.

The remaining question is whether there is an in-between construction of G.SME (or SA.SME) and EG.SME which both yields the attribute hiding security and function privacy, while the size of the underlying IPE is polynomial in $q$. In addition, it will be helpful if we could mathematically state the assumption of the trade-off like relationship between the attribute hiding security and function privacy, because this will guide us to assess the necessary size of the underlying IPE for SME to yield function privacy.

**Acknowledgement.** We thank to anonymous reviewers of SCN2014. We thank to Dr. Shota Yamada for helpful discussions. This research was supported by JST, CREST.

# References

1. Agrawal, S., Freeman, D.M., Vaikuntanathan, V.: Functional encryption for inner product predicates from learning with errors. In: Lee, D.H., Wang, X. (eds.) ASIACRYPT 2011. LNCS, vol. 7073, pp. 21–40. Springer, Heidelberg (2011)
2. Boneh, D., Raghunathan, A., Segev, G.: Function-private identity-based encryption: Hiding the function in functional encryption. In: Canetti, R., Garay, J.A. (eds.) CRYPTO 2013, Part II. LNCS, vol. 8043, pp. 461–478. Springer, Heidelberg (2013)
3. Boneh, D., Raghunathan, A., Segev, G.: Function-private subspace-membership encryption and its applications. In: Sako, K., Sarkar, P. (eds.) ASIACRYPT 2013, Part I. LNCS, vol. 8269, pp. 255–275. Springer, Heidelberg (2013)
4. Boneh, D., Waters, B.: Conjunctive, subset, and range queries on encrypted data. In: Vadhan, S.P. (ed.) TCC 2007. LNCS, vol. 4392, pp. 535–554. Springer, Heidelberg (2007)
5. Freeman, D.M.: Converting pairing-based cryptosystems from composite-order groups to prime-order groups. In: Gilbert, H. (ed.) EUROCRYPT 2010. LNCS, vol. 6110, pp. 44–61. Springer, Heidelberg (2010)
6. Gentry, C.: Practical identity-based encryption without random oracles. In: Vaudenay, S. (ed.) EUROCRYPT 2006. LNCS, vol. 4004, pp. 445–464. Springer, Heidelberg (2006)
7. Gentry, C., Peikert, C., Vaikuntanathan, V.: Trapdoors for hard lattices and new cryptographic constructions. In: Dwork, C. (ed.) STOC, pp. 197–206. ACM (2008)

8. Goyal, V., Pandey, O., Sahai, A., Waters, B.: Attribute-based encryption for fine-grained access control of encrypted data. In: Juels, A., Wright, R.N., De Capitani di Vimercati, S. (eds.) ACM Conference on Computer and Communications Security, pp. 89–98. ACM (2006)

9. Katz, J., Sahai, A., Waters, B.: Predicate encryption supporting disjunctions, polynomial equations, and inner products. In: Smart, N.P. (ed.) EUROCRYPT 2008. LNCS, vol. 4965, pp. 146–162. Springer, Heidelberg (2008)

10. Lewko, A., Okamoto, T., Sahai, A., Takashima, K., Waters, B.: Fully secure functional encryption: Attribute-based encryption and (hierarchical) inner product encryption. In: Gilbert, H. (ed.) EUROCRYPT 2010. LNCS, vol. 6110, pp. 62–91. Springer, Heidelberg (2010)

11. Okamoto, T., Takashima, K.: Hierarchical predicate encryption for inner-products. In: Matsui, M. (ed.) ASIACRYPT 2009. LNCS, vol. 5912, pp. 214–231. Springer, Heidelberg (2009)

12. Okamoto, T., Takashima, K.: Adaptively attribute-hiding (hierarchical) inner product encryption. In: Pointcheval, D., Johansson, T. (eds.) EUROCRYPT 2012. LNCS, vol. 7237, pp. 591–608. Springer, Heidelberg (2012)

13. Sahai, A., Waters, B.: Fuzzy identity-based encryption. In: Cramer, R. (ed.) EUROCRYPT 2005. LNCS, vol. 3494, pp. 457–473. Springer, Heidelberg (2005)

14. Shamir, A.: Identity-based cryptosystems and signature schemes. In: Blakely, G.R., Chaum, D. (eds.) CRYPTO 1984. LNCS, vol. 196, pp. 47–53. Springer, Heidelberg (1985)

15. Waters, B.: Efficient identity-based encryption without random oracles. In: Cramer, R. (ed.) EUROCRYPT 2005. LNCS, vol. 3494, pp. 114–127. Springer, Heidelberg (2005)

# A    Qualities of Linear Algebra in a Finite Field $\mathbb{Z}_q^l$

We use linear algebra in the finite field $\mathbb{Z}_q^l$ when constructing SME. However, since the finite field $\mathbb{Z}_q^l$ is not a metric space, we can not define inner products in the usual sense, hence making it difficult to capture the property of linear algebra in $\mathbb{Z}_q^l$. For an example, in $\mathbb{Z}_2^3$, if we take the inner product of vector $(1, 1, 0)^{\mathrm{T}}$, it will equal 0. This violates the inner product property in the metric space, i.e., $\mathbf{x}^{\mathrm{T}}\mathbf{x} = 0$ if and only if $\mathbf{x} = \mathbf{0}$. Another example is, in $\mathbb{Z}_3^3$, a vector space $\mathbf{V}^\perp$ orthogonal to a vector space $\mathbf{V}$ spanned by the vectors $(1, 2, 1)^{\mathrm{T}}$ and $(1, 1, 0)^{\mathrm{T}}$ is spanned by vector $(1, 2, 1)^{\mathrm{T}}$. This violates the property $V \oplus V^\perp = \mathbb{Z}_3^3$, which always holds in the metric space. Furthermore, since in the finite field $\mathbb{Z}_q^l$, $V \oplus V^\perp = \mathbb{Z}_q^l$ does not necessarily hold, we can not conclude $\dim(V) + \dim(V^\perp) = \dim(\mathbb{Z}_q^l)$ without deliberation. Therefore, we will have to carefully prove each of the seemingly obvious properties introduced in section 3.1. Proofs of Lemma 1, 2, and 3 are given in the full paper.

# Efficient (Anonymous) Compact HIBE
# from Standard Assumptions

Somindu C. Ramanna and Palash Sarkar

Applied Statistics Unit
Indian Statistical Institute
203, B.T. Road
Kolkata, India
{somindu_r,palash}@isical.ac.in

**Abstract.** We present two hierarchical identity-based encryption (HIBE) schemes, denoted as $\mathcal{H}_1$ and $\mathcal{H}_2$, from Type-3 pairings with constant sized ciphertexts. Scheme $\mathcal{H}_1$ achieves anonymity while $\mathcal{H}_2$ is non-anonymous. The constructions are obtained by extending the IBE scheme recently proposed by Jutla and Roy (Asiacrypt 2013). Security is based on the standard decisional Symmetric eXternal Diffie-Hellman (SXDH) assumption. In terms of provable security properties, previous direct constructions of constant-size ciphertext HIBE had one or more of the following drawbacks: security in the weaker model of selective-identity attacks; exponential security degradation in the depth of the HIBE; and use of non-standard assumptions. The security arguments for $\mathcal{H}_1$ and $\mathcal{H}_2$ avoid all of these drawbacks. Based on the current state-of-the-art, $\mathcal{H}_1$ and $\mathcal{H}_2$ are the schemes of choice for efficient implementation of (anonymous) HIBE constructions.

**Keywords:** constant-size ciphertext HIBE, asymmetric pairings, standard assumptions, dual-system encryption.

## 1 Introduction

Identity-based encryption (IBE) is a form of public key encryption where a recipient's identity itself is her public key. The corresponding decryption key is generated and securely transmitted by a trusted authority called private key generator (PKG). The concept of IBE was introduced by Shamir [31] and the first constructions were proposed in [11,4]. In order to reduce the communication and computation overhead on the PKG, the notion of hierarchical IBE ([16,17]) was introduced. HIBE imposes a tree-like structure on entities within the system and provides the higher level entities the ability to delegate key generation to lower-level entities without the involvement of the PKG.

This work presents two new HIBE schemes called $\mathcal{H}_1$ and $\mathcal{H}_2$. The literature already contains several different HIBE schemes. So, the question arises as to why new ones are needed? We argue below that previous direct constructions of HIBE schemes had one or more drawbacks related to either efficiency or security.

S.S.M. Chow et al. (Eds.): ProvSec 2014, LNCS 8782, pp. 243–258, 2014.

The new schemes overcome all these issues and are the candidates of choice for any practical deployment. To understand this, discuss different security and efficiency issues that arise while designing HIBE schemes.

Practical constructions of HIBE schemes are obtained from *pairings*. In particular, we focus on *Type-3 pairings* that have the most efficient implementations, both in terms of computation and representation [6,33,15]. Less efficient alternatives are Type-1 pairings or composite-order pairings. In addition to using Type-3 pairings, we are interested in obtaining HIBE schemes with *constant-size ciphertexts* i.e., the length of the ciphertext is independent of the (variable) length of the corresponding identity tuple. The first construction for CC-HIBE was given by Boneh, Boyen and Goh [3]. This work introduced a way to hash identity vectors into the pairing groups. Almost all known CC-HIBE schemes that appeared later have either used this technique or a variant [7,8,22,30,12,25,20,28,9].

Several security-related issues crop up while building HIBE schemes: security model, hardness assumptions and security degradation. Our goal is to obtain HIBE secure against adaptive-identity attacks [4,16,32] without random oracles. Another important security notion is *anonymity* [1] which requires that a ciphertext does not reveal any information about the recipient's identity. Anonymous HIBE schemes are useful in constructing certain searchable encryption primitives [1]. We focus on hardness assumptions that have widespread use in cryptography (called *standard assumptions*). Examples of such problems are decisional Diffie-Hellman (DDH), decisional bilinear Diffie-Hellman (DBDH) and decisional linear (DLin) assumptions. These are unlike some other problems that are tailor-made to suit the requirements of the particular scheme or parameterised by some quantity (arising in the construction). The latter type are called non-static. Another point of interest is the tightness of the security reduction. Tighter reductions have lower degradation values. Designing schemes that have low degradation is important.

**Prefix Decryption.** In some HIBE schemes, a ciphertext for an identity vector can be decrypted by any entity possessing a secret key for a prefix of that identity. Let us name this property *prefix decryption*. In constructions with separate ciphertext elements corresponding to individual components of the identity tuple, such as the one in [16], prefix decryption is facilitated – the ciphertext can be truncated to obtain a valid ciphertext under the prefix identity vector and thus can be decrypted using the corresponding key. We note that achieving constant-size ciphertexts and anonymity simultaneously results in the loss of prefix decryption. Although it may seem that this restriction is somehow tied to the property of anonymity, we would like to emphasise that this is a definitional issue. That is, whether prefix decryption is allowed or not must reflect in the HIBE definition. The definition we provide does not explicitly allow prefix decryption. We stress that the prefix decryption property is absent in all known HIBE constructions that concurrently attain constant-size ciphertexts and anonymity. Furthermore, all known HIBE schemes possess at most two out of the three features – constant-size ciphertexts, anonymity and prefix decryption.

On the other hand, not having prefix decryption guards against key escrow to some extent. An entity has the power to delegate keys to lower level entities but cannot decrypt ciphertexts sent to the lower-level entities. This feature may be useful in applications such as email. If the higher level entities are key generating servers, user privacy will not be compromised in the event that any of these servers is corrupted. Further, in primitives such as identity-based searchable encryption obtained from anonymous HIBE schemes [1], this limitation does not make any difference. For related discussions on this issue, the reader is refered to [16] and [10].

## 1.1 Possible Approaches to the Construction of HIBE Schemes

We have argued above that among HIBE schemes, it is CC-HIBE which is of practical importance and among the known CC-HIBE schemes, $\mathcal{H}_1$ and $\mathcal{H}_2$ are the most suitable ones for practical deployment. As mentioned earlier, both schemes are based on the recently proposed IBE due to Jutla and Roy [19] (abbreviated JR-IBE).

It is quite natural that the construction of a HIBE scheme will be based on an IBE scheme. To start with, it is desirable to avoid a security degradation which is exponential in the depth of the HIBE. In the current state of the art, this means that one has to follow the dual-system approach. So, any attempt to construct a CC-HIBE should start with an IBE which has been proved secure using the dual-system technique. However, not all IBE constructions have the structure suitable for extension to CC-HIBE. The reason is that in the proof, a crucial step is to argue that certain information (such as ciphertexts and keys) are indepedently distributed in the attacker's view even if the simulator does not choose them independently. This is harder to ensure in a HIBE as the adversary has access to more information that enables delegation. Some dual-system IBE constructions [34,27] do not facilitate extension to a CC-HIBE. On the other hand, known dual-system CC-HIBE constructions are secure under non-standard assumptions [22,20,28].

HIBE schemes can also be obtained by specialising schemes for hierarchical inner product encryption or predicate encryption; the downside is that the resulting efficiencies are inferior to those of the schemes reported here. We believe that HIBE is an important enough primitive to warrant research on obtaining direct and efficient constructions of such schemes.

## 1.2 Extending JR-IBE to CC-HIBE

Schemes $\mathcal{H}_1$ and $\mathcal{H}_2$ extend the JR-IBE to anonymous and non-anonymous CC-HIBEs respectively. At a top level, the identity-hashing technique of Boneh-Boyen-Goh [3] (BBG-hash) is applied on JR-IBE. We work in the setting of asymmetric pairings where ciphertext components are elements of $\mathbb{G}_1$ and key components are elements of $\mathbb{G}_2$. BBG-hash of the identity is required to be computed in both $\mathbb{G}_1$ and $\mathbb{G}_2$. During encryption, the BBG-hash is required to be computed in $\mathbb{G}_1$ and this requires adding some elements of $\mathbb{G}_1$ to the public parameters.

In previous CC-HIBE schemes in the prime-order setting within the dual system framework [20,28], anonymity appears as a by-product of the HIBE extension. The basic difficulty in making it non-anonymous was due to the following dichotomy concerning key delegation. The BBG-hash for the key is computed in $\mathbb{G}_2$. The hash is defined using certain elements of $\mathbb{G}_2$. During key delegation, the hash has to be rerandomised and so the elements should be publicly available. On the other hand, information about these elements must not be leaked because they form the source of randomness used to generate the *semi-functional* components during simulation.

The problem described above does not arise in case of JR-IBE. The feature of JR-IBE that makes extension to the non-anonymous CC-HIBE $\mathcal{H}_2$ possible is as follows. The master secret consists of two elements whose linear combination is used to mask the message during encryption. This is unlike previous (H)IBE schemes where a single element was used for the purpose. The two elements would be information theoretically hidden from an attacker's view. So the secret randomness for the semi-functional ciphertext space is provided by one of the two elements.

Anonymity is achieved by keeping the elements required to compute the BBG-hash in $\mathbb{G}_2$ to be secret and instead provide suitably randomised copies of these elements in the user keys. Problems then arise while defining semi-functional components and arguing about their well-formedness during simulation. Fortunately, it turns out that the problems can be handled by using appropriate algebraic relations. The technique of keeping certain elements hidden and providing their randomised version in the user keys closely follow the ideas introduced in [5] to obtain anonymity. In $\mathcal{H}_1$ the elements that are kept hidden are exactly the ones required to create the BBG-hash in $\mathbb{G}_2$. As a result, an adversary is unable to create an identity hash in $\mathbb{G}_2$ and cancel it out with the BBG-hash of the same identity in $\mathbb{G}_1$. This naturally leads to the scheme $\mathcal{H}_1$ being anonymous.

We note that a single-level instantiation of $\mathcal{H}_2$ provides a non-anonymous variant of the JR-IBE with rerandomisable keys.

## 1.3   Comparison to Existing HIBE Schemes

Table 1 provides a comparison of $\mathcal{H}_2$ with all previously proposed non-anonymous CC-HIBE schemes. Table 2 compares $\mathcal{H}_1$ with all previously proposed anonymous HIBE schemes.

We fix some notation required to compare different parameters of HIBE constructions. $h$: maximum depth of the HIBE; $\ell$: length of the identity tuple; $q$: number of key extraction queries. In [7], $N$ is the number of bits in an identity and $k$ represents number of blocks of $N/k$ bits. #pp, #msk, #cpr and #key denote number of group elements in the public parameters, master secret, ciphertext and key respectively. Enc, Dec, KGen and Deleg indicate the efficiency of encryption, decryption, key generation and delegation algorithms. For Type-3 pairing based schemes, $\mathcal{PP}$ and ciphertexts consist elements of $\mathbb{G}_1$; $\mathcal{MSK}$ and keys consist elements of $\mathbb{G}_2$. #pp $= (a,b)$ means that there are $a$ elements from $\mathbb{G}_1$, $\mathbb{G}_2$ and $b$ elements of $\mathbb{G}_T$. #cpr $= (a,b)$ denotes $a$ elements from $\mathbb{G}_1$ and $b$ elements from $\mathbb{Z}_p$ where $p = |\mathbb{G}_1|$. We do not consider the $\mathbb{G}_T$ element that masks the message in our comparison as it is present in all constructions. Enc $= (a,b)$ indicates $a$ scalar multiplications in $\mathbb{G}_1$ and $b$ exponentiations in $\mathbb{G}_T$; 'Dec' is measured in terms of number of pairings; 'KGen' and 'Deleg' are given by number of scalar multiplications in $\mathbb{G}_2$; 'Assump' denotes the set of underlying complexity assumptions; Deg is a shorthand for security degradation. 'Prefix Dec' indicates whether or not the HIBE supports prefix decryption. 'Const #cpr' denotes constant-size ciphertext.

In terms of security, $\mathcal{H}_2$ is comparable to [23] and [9]. The security of the construction in [22] is based on sub-group decision assumptions that cannot be considered to be standard assumptions. $\mathcal{H}_2$ achieves the best efficiency compared to all other schemes. In terms of security and efficiency, there is no construction that is comparable to $\mathcal{H}_1$.

**Table 1.** Comparison of non-anonymous CC-HIBE schemes based on pairings without random oracles

| Scheme | [3] | [7] | [8] | [22] | [23] | [9] | $\mathcal{H}_2$ |
|---|---|---|---|---|---|---|---|
| Pairing | Type-1 | Type-1 | Type-1 | Composite | Type-1 | Type-3 | Type-3 |
| Security | selective-id | adaptive-id | selective⁺-id | adaptive-id | adaptive-id | adaptive-id | adaptive-id |
| Assump. | Decisional $h$-wBDHI | $h$-wDBDHI* | $h$-wDBDHI* | Subgroup Decision | DLin | $d$-Lin | SXDH |
| Deg. | 1 | $O((kq2^{N/k})^h)$ | 1 | $O(q)$ | $O(q)$ | $O(q)$ | $O(q)$ |
| #pp | $(h+4,0)$ | $(h+3+hk,0)$ | $(2h+3,1)$ | $(h+3,1)$ | $(32h^2+16h+25,1)$ | $(2d(d+1)(h+2),d)$ | $(3h+9,1)$ |
| #msk | 1 | 1 | 1 | 1 | 5 | $d+1$ | 2 |
| #cpr | $(2,0)$ | $(2,0)$ | $(3,0)$ | $(2,0)$ | $(13,0)$ | $(2(d+1),0)$ | $(3,1)$ |
| #key | $h-\ell+2$ | $(k+1)(h-\ell)+2$ | $2(h-\ell+1)$ | $h-\ell+2$ | $8h+5$ | $(d+1)(h-\ell+2)$ | $2(h-\ell)+5$ |
| Enc | $(\ell+2,1)$ | $(2,1)$ | $(\ell+2,1)$ | $(\ell+2,1)$ | $32h+23$ | $(d(d+1)(\ell+2),d)$ | $(\ell+4,1)$ |
| Dec | 2 | 2 | 2 | 2 | 13 | $2(d+1)$ | 3 |
| KGen | $h+2$ | $2(h-\ell+1)$ | $2h-\ell+2$ | $2h-\ell+4$ | $16h(h+\ell)+10$ | $d(d+1)(h+2)$ | $2h+7$ |
| Deleg. | $\ell+2$ | $2(h-\ell)$ | $2h-\ell+1$ | $2h-\ell+6$ | $16h(h+\ell+1)+10$ | $d(d+1)(h+2)+d+1$ | $2h+9$ |

In absolute terms, the composite-order pairing based HIBE scheme of [22] has fewer group elements compared to $\mathcal{H}_2$. But at reasonable security levels (say, 128 bits), the length of representations of elements would be at least 6 times that of Type-3 pairing groups. The wide difference in the length of representations of group elements more than adequately compensates for the absolute number of group elements in composite-order HIBE schemes being lesser than that in the newly proposed HIBE scheme.

From Table 1 and the previous discussion, the only non-anonymous HIBE scheme which is comparable in efficiency and security to $\mathcal{H}_2$ is the Chen-Wee scheme described in [9] for $d = 1$ whence $d$-Lin becomes DDH. But the scheme in [9] is still less efficient compared to $\mathcal{H}_2$ in terms of ciphertext size and decryption time. A ciphertext will consist of 4 $\mathbb{G}_1$-elements whereas $\mathcal{H}_2$-ciphertexts contain 3 $\mathbb{G}_1$-elements along with an element of $\mathbb{Z}_p$. If an element of $\mathbb{G}_1$ is represented using two elements of $\mathbb{Z}_p$, then $\mathcal{H}_2$ ciphertexts consist of 7 $\mathbb{Z}_p$ elements as opposed to 8 in [9]. Certainly, $\mathcal{H}_2$ has shorter ciphertexts. While $\mathcal{H}_2$ has shorter ciphertexts and faster encryption and decryption algorithms, the Chen-Wee scheme has shorter decryption keys and faster key generation and delegation algorithms. For an encryption scheme, encryption and decryption will be used more often than key generation and delegation, so, the advantage of $\mathcal{H}_2$ over the Chen-Wee scheme outweighs the disadvantages.

The reader is refered to the full version [29] for a more concrete comparison.

**Table 2.** Comparison of anonymous HIBE schemes based on pairings without random oracles

| Scheme | [5] | [30] | [12] | [25] | [20],[28] | [24] | $\mathcal{H}_1$ |
|---|---|---|---|---|---|---|---|
| Pairing | Type-3 | Composite | Composite | Type-1 | Type-3 | Type-1 | Type-3 |
| Security | selective-id | selective-id | adaptive-id | selective-id | adaptive-id | adaptive-id | adaptive-id |
| Assump. | DLin,DBDH | $\ell$-wBDH*, $\ell$-cDH | Subgroup Decision | $h$-BDHE Aug. $h$-DLin | LW1,LW2,DBDH [20]:3-DH,XDH [28]:A1 | DLin | SXDH |
| Deg. | $O(1)$ | $O(1)$ | $O(q)$ | $O(1)$ | $O(q)$ | $O(hq)$ | $O(q)$ |
| Prefix Dec. | No | No | No | No | No | Yes | No |
| Const #cpr | No | Yes | Yes | Yes | Yes | No | Yes |
| #pp | $(2(h^2+3h+2),1)$ | $(h+6,1)$ | $(h+4,1)$ | $(h+6,1)$ | $(3h+6,1)$ | $(4(9h+4),1)$ | $(h+4,1)$ |
| #msk | $h^2+5h+7$ | $h+4$ | $2$ | $4$ | $h+6$ | $18h+10$ | $2h+6$ |
| #cpr | $(2h+5,0)$ | $(3,0)$ | $(2,0)$ | $(4,0)$ | $(6,0)$ | $(9\ell+5,0)$ | $(3,1)$ |
| #key | $(h+3)(3h-\ell+5)$ | $3(h-\ell+3)$ | $2(h-\ell+2)$ | $3(h-\ell+4)$ | $6(h-\ell+2)$ | $(4h-2\ell+1)(9\ell+5)+36(h-\ell)$ | $4(h-\ell)+10$ |
| Enc | $(2(\ell+3)(h+2)+1,1)$ | $(\ell+6,1)$ | $(\ell+4,1)$ | $(\ell+5,1)$ | $(3(\ell+2),1)$ | $27\ell+15$ | $(\ell+4,1)$ |
| Dec | $2h+3$ | $4$ | $2$ | $4$ | $6$ | $9\ell+5$ | $3$ |
| KGen | $h^3+h^2(5-\ell)+ h(7-3\ell)-2\ell+2$ | $3h-2\ell+2$ | $4(h+2-3\ell)$ | $(h+2(h-\ell+8))$ | $6h-5\ell+12$ | $(2h+3)(27\ell+10)$ | $2(2h-2\ell+5)$ |
| Deleg. | $5(h+2)(h+3)+1$ | $6(h-\ell)+21$ | $4(h-\ell)+11$ | $(4(h-\ell)+25)$ | $2(h-\ell+3)$ | $(9\ell+5)(6h\ell+14h-2\ell^4-8\ell+5)$ | $4(h-\ell+5)$ |

It is clear from Table 2 that all anonymous HIBE schemes possess either constant-size ciphertexts or the prefix decryption property and not both. The Boyen-Waters HIBE [5] has none of the two properties. The Okamoto-Takashima scheme [24] supports prefix decryption and at the same time achieves anonymity but at the cost of non-constant size of the ciphertext (the size is linear in the depth of the identity). In addition, ciphertexts in their scheme reveal the length of the recipient identity unlike the Boyen-Waters HIBE. $\mathcal{H}_1$, on the other hand, is anonymous and has short ciphertexts but lacks prefix deryption. All other efficiency parameters are better in case of $\mathcal{H}_1$.

We conclude that among anonymous HIBE schemes, $\mathcal{H}_1$ is the most efficient scheme with all the standard provable properties. We emphasise that the efficiency and provable security properties achieved for $\mathcal{H}_1$ have not been simultaneously achieved earlier, either for composite-order pairings, or, for prime-order pairings. For use in practice, one may choose the Okamoto-Takashima scheme or $\mathcal{H}_1$ according to whether the application requires prefix decryption or not.

**Subsequent Work by Blazy et.al.** A recent work [2] presents HIBE schemes (both with and without anonymity) generically constructed via a tranformation from message authentication codes (MAC). Security is based on the $d$-Lin assumptions. Consider the case $d = 1$. For the schemes with public parameters comparable to our schemes ciphertexts are larger than that of $\mathcal{H}_1$ and $\mathcal{H}_2$. They also present a non-anonymous scheme with a tighter reduction and ciphertexts shorter than $\mathcal{H}_2$-ciphertexts. But the public paramters are $O(hn)$ where $n$ denotes the length (in bits) of each identity.

**A Note on Notation and Proof Technique.** We have used the JR-IBE [19] as the basic building block and consequently, our notation and proofs build on that of [19]. This makes it easier for a reader to see the connections between our work and the IBE construction in [19]. Frameworks for presenting dual-system constructions and proofs have been proposed [21,14]. Neither the JR-IBE nor the constructions in the present work appear to fall within these frameworks.

**Preliminaries.** Before proceeding further we fix some notation. $x_1, \ldots, x_k \xleftarrow{R} \mathcal{X}$ indicates that elements $x_1, \ldots, x_k$ are sampled independently from the set $\mathcal{X}$ according to some distribution R. The uniform distribution is denoted U. For a (probabilistic) algorithm $\mathcal{A}$, $y \longleftarrow \mathcal{A}(x)$ means that $y$ is chosen according to the output distribution of $\mathcal{A}$ on input $x$. $\mathcal{A}(x; r)$ denotes that $\mathcal{A}$ is run on input $x$ with its internal random coins set to $r$. For two integers $a < b$, the notation $[a, b]$ represents the set $\{x \in \mathbb{Z} : a \leq x \leq b\}$. If $\mathbb{G}$ is a finite cyclic group, then $\mathbb{G}^\times$ denotes the set of generators of $\mathbb{G}$. A bilinear pairing is given by a 7-tuple $\mathcal{G} = (p, \mathbb{G}_1, \mathbb{G}_2, \mathbb{G}_T, e, P_1, P_2)$ where $\mathbb{G}_1 = \langle P_1 \rangle$, $\mathbb{G}_2 = \langle P_2 \rangle$ are groups written additively and $\mathbb{G}_T$ is a multiplicatively written group, all having the same order $p$ and $e : \mathbb{G}_1 \times \mathbb{G}_2 \to \mathbb{G}_T$ is a bilinear, non-degenerate and efficiently computable map. In an asymmetric pairing, $\mathbb{G}_1 \neq \mathbb{G}_2$. If no efficiently computable isomorphisms between $\mathbb{G}_1$ and $\mathbb{G}_2$ are known, then such pairings are called Type-3 pairings. The terms 'Type-3 pairing' and 'asymmetric pairing' are used interchangeably in the rest of the paper.

Due to space constraints, we omit some basic definitions. Most of these are standard. The full version [29] provides the definition of HIBE as consisting of five probabilistic polynomial time algorithms – Setup, Encrypt, KeyGen, Delegate and Decrypt. Also described are two games ano-ind-cpa and ind-cpa capturing security against chosen plaintext attack for HIBE schemes [16]) with the former additionally taking into account anonymity [13,12].

## 2 Jutla-Roy IBE with Ciphertexts in $\mathbb{G}_1$

In the IBE scheme of Jutla-Roy [19] (JR-IBE), ciphertext consists of elements in $\mathbb{G}_2$ and keys contain elements from $\mathbb{G}_1$. For Type-3 pairings, elements of $\mathbb{G}_1$ have a shorter representation compared to the elements of $\mathbb{G}_2$. To reduce the length of the ciphertext, one has to interchange the roles of the two groups. In contrast, for a signature scheme, it would be advantageous to have the signature to consist of elements from $\mathbb{G}_1$. Since the JR-IBE is obtained from non-interactive zero knowledge (NIZK) proofs via the idea of signatures, the scheme results in ciphertext elements being in $\mathbb{G}_2$.

This section describes a "dual" of the Jutla-Roy [19] (JR-IBE-D) where ciphertexts live in $\mathbb{G}_1$ and keys in $\mathbb{G}_2$. We use a compact notation to denote normal and semi-functional ciphertexts and keys. The group elements shown in curly brackets { } are the semi-functional components. To get the scheme itself, these components should be ignored.

**Parameters:** Choose $P_1 \xleftarrow{U} \mathbb{G}_1^\times$, $P_2 \xleftarrow{U} \mathbb{G}_2^\times$, $\Delta_1, \Delta_2, \Delta_3, \Delta_4, c, d, u, e \xleftarrow{U} \mathbb{Z}_p$, $b \xleftarrow{U} \mathbb{Z}_p^\times$, and set $U_1 = (-\Delta_1 b + d)P_1$, $V_1 = (-\Delta_2 b + e)P_1$, $W_1 = (-\Delta_3 b + c)P_1$, $g_T = e(P_1, P_2)^{-\Delta_4 b + u}$. The parameters are given by
$$\mathcal{PP} : (P_1, bP_1, U_1, V_1, W_1, g_T)$$

$\mathcal{MSK} : (P_2, cP_2, \Delta_1, \Delta_2, \Delta_3, \Delta_4, d, u, e)$

**Ciphertext:** Consists of $(C_0, C_1, C_2, C_3, \mathsf{tag})$ where

$\mathsf{tag}, s \xleftarrow{\mathsf{U}} \mathbb{Z}_p, \{\mu \xleftarrow{\mathsf{U}} \mathbb{Z}_p\}$

$C_0 = m \cdot (g_T)^s \{e(P_1, P_2)^{u\mu}\},$

$C_1 = sP_1\{+\mu P_1\}, \ C_2 = sbP_1,$

$C_3 = s(U_1 + \mathsf{id}V_1 + \mathsf{tag}W_1)\{+\mu(d + \mathsf{id} \cdot e + \mathsf{tag} \cdot c)P_1\}.$

**Key:** Contains five elements $(K_1, \ldots, K_5)$ defined as follows.

$r \xleftarrow{\mathsf{U}} \mathbb{Z}_p, \{\gamma, \pi \xleftarrow{\mathsf{U}} \mathbb{Z}_p\}$

$K_1 = rP_2, \ K_2 = rcP_2\{+\gamma P_2\}, \ K_3 = (u + r(d + \mathsf{id}e)) P_2\{+\gamma\pi P_2\},$

$K_4 = -r\Delta_3 P_2\{-\frac{\gamma}{b}P_2\}, \ K_5 = (-\Delta_4 - r(\Delta_1 + \mathsf{id}\Delta_2)) P_2\{-\frac{\gamma\pi}{b}P_2\} \ .$

*Note.* In JR-IBE [19], $b$ is mentioned to be an element of $\mathbb{Z}_p$. This is an oversight and $b$ should be an element of $\mathbb{Z}_p^\times$ as we have mentioned above. This is because if $b$ is zero, then division by $b$ and consequently the definitions of the semi-functional components will not be meaningful. Security of JR-IBE-D will follow from the security of $\mathcal{H}_1$ we present in this work.

## 3   Our CC-HIBE Constructions

Both schemes $\mathcal{H}_1$ and $\mathcal{H}_2$ are based on a Type-3 prime-order pairing with group order $p$. Identities are variable length tuples of elements from $\mathbb{Z}_p^\times$ with maximum length $h$.

As is typical with BBG-type extensions the element $V_1$ is replaced with $h$ elements $V_{1,1}, \ldots, V_{1,h}$ – one for each level of an identity. The set $U_1, (V_{1,j})_{j\in[1,h]}$ is used to create the identity hash – for an identity $\mathsf{id} = (\mathsf{id}_1, \ldots, \mathsf{id}_\ell)$, the hash is given by $U_1 + \sum_{j=1}^\ell \mathsf{id}_j V_{1,j}$. Element $W_1$ will be retained to append the tag-component to the hash. This replaces the hash in JR-IBE-D ciphertext without affecting the number of elements in the ciphertext. Moreover, since the hash is embedded in a single ciphertext component, only one tag is required. Note that the keys in JR-IBE-D have two sub-hashes that when combined during decryption cancels with the hash of the ciphertext.

In JR-IBE-D, each of $U_1, V_1, W_1$ is split into two components kept as part of the master secret. The two sets of components determine the sub-hashes required in generating keys. Similarly, for the HIBE, we need to split $V_{1,j}$ for all $j \in [1, h]$ as $V_{1,j} = b\Delta_{2,j} + e_j$ where $\Delta_{1,j}, e_j \xleftarrow{\mathsf{U}} \mathbb{Z}_p$. So the sub-hashes are determined by the vectors $\mathbf{v}_1 = (d, e_1, \ldots, e_h)$ and $\mathbf{v}_2 = (\Delta_1, \Delta_{2,1}, \ldots, \Delta_{2,h})$. Rerandomisation of keys during delegation can be done in two possible ways – make the encodings of vectors $\mathbf{v}_1, \mathbf{v}_2$ along with $\Delta_3, c$ in $\mathbb{G}_2$ public; or provide appropriately randomised copies of these elements in the key.

The second method retains the anonymity property leading to the scheme $\mathcal{H}_1$. This is because the vectors $\mathbf{v}_1, \mathbf{v}_2$ can be used to test whether a given ciphertext is encrypted to a particular identity or not. Keeping them secret naturally leads to anonymity. The former method leads to the scheme $\mathcal{H}_2$ that has shorter keys and faster algorithms compared to $\mathcal{H}_1$. But the efficiency comes at the cost of losing anonymity. Due to space constraints we only describe $\mathcal{H}_1$ and discuss its security. A description of $\mathcal{H}_2$ followed by an outline of its security is provided in [29].

### 3.1  Scheme $\mathcal{H}_1$

We define $\mathcal{H}_1 = (\mathcal{H}_1.\text{Setup}, \mathcal{H}_1.\text{Encrypt}, \mathcal{H}_1.\text{KeyGen}, \mathcal{H}_1.\text{Delegate}, \mathcal{H}_1.\text{Decrypt})$ where the algorithms are as follows.

$\mathcal{H}_1.\text{Setup}(\kappa)$: Generate a Type-3 pairing $(p, \mathbb{G}_1, \mathbb{G}_2, \mathbb{G}_T, e, F_1, F_2)$ based on the security parameter $\kappa$. Compute parameters as follows.

$P_1 \xleftarrow{U} \mathbb{G}_1^{\times}$, $P_2 \xleftarrow{U} \mathbb{G}_2^{\times}$, $\Delta_1, \Delta_3, \Delta_4, c, d, u, (\Delta_{2,j}, e_j)_{j=1}^h \xleftarrow{U} \mathbb{Z}_p$, $b \xleftarrow{U} \mathbb{Z}_p^{\times}$,
$U_1 = (-\Delta_1 b + d)P_1$, $V_{1,j} = (-\Delta_{2,j} b + e_j)P_1$ for $j = 1, \ldots, h$,
$W_1 = (-\Delta_3 b + c)P_1$, $g_T = e(P_1, P_2)^{-\Delta_4 b + u}$,

$\quad \mathcal{PP} : (P_1, bP_1, U_1, (V_{1,j})_{j=1}^h, W_1, g_T)$
$\quad \mathcal{MSK} : (P_2, cP_2, \Delta_1, \Delta_3, \Delta_4, d, u, (\Delta_{2,j}, e_j)_{j=1}^h)$

$\mathcal{H}_1.\text{Encrypt}(\mathcal{PP}, M, \mathbf{id} = (\text{id}_1, \ldots, \text{id}_\ell))$: Pick $\mathbf{tag}, s \xleftarrow{U} \mathbb{Z}_p$ and set the ciphertext $\mathcal{C} = (C_0, C_1, C_2, C_3, \mathbf{tag})$ where

$\quad C_0 = M \cdot (g_T)^s$, $C_1 = sP_1$, $C_2 = sbP_1$, $C_3 = s(U_1 + \sum_{j=1}^\ell \text{id}_j V_{1,j} + \mathbf{tag} W_1)$.

$\mathcal{H}_1.\text{KeyGen}(\mathcal{MSK}, \mathbf{id} = (\text{id}_1, \ldots, \text{id}_\ell))$: Pick $r_1, r_2 \xleftarrow{U} \mathbb{Z}_p$ and compute the secret key $\mathcal{SK}_{\mathbf{id}} = (\mathcal{S}_1, \mathcal{S}_2)$ for $\mathbf{id}$, with $\mathcal{S}_1 = ((K_i)_{i \in [1,5]}, (D_{1,j}, E_{1,j})_{j \in [\ell+1, h]})$ and $\mathcal{S}_2 = ((J_i)_{i \in [1,5]}, (D_{2,j}, E_{2,j})_{j \in [\ell+1, h]})$ where

$\quad K_1 = r_1 P_2$, $K_2 = r_1 c P_2$, $K_3 = \left(u + r_1(d + \sum_{j=1}^\ell \text{id}_j e_j)\right) P_2$,
$\quad K_4 = -r_1 \Delta_3 P_2$, $K_5 = \left(-\Delta_4 - r_1(\Delta_1 + \sum_{j=1}^\ell \text{id}_j \Delta_{2,j})\right) P_2$,
$\quad D_{1,j} = r_1 e_j P_2$, $E_{1,j} = -r_1 \Delta_{2,j} P_2$ for $j = \ell + 1, \ldots, h$,

$\quad J_1 = r_2 P_2$, $J_2 = r_2 c P_2$, $J_3 = r_2 \left(d + \sum_{j=1}^\ell \text{id}_j e_j\right) P_2$,
$\quad J_4 = -r_2 \Delta_3 P_2$, $J_5 = -r_2(\Delta_1 + \sum_{j=1}^\ell \text{id}_j \Delta_{2,j}) P_2$,
$\quad D_{2,j} = r_2 e_j P_2$, $E_{2,j} = -r_2 \Delta_{2,j} P_2$ for $j = \ell + 1, \ldots, h$

$\mathcal{H}_1.\text{Delegate}(\mathbf{id} = (\text{id}_1, \ldots, \text{id}_\ell), \text{id}_{\ell+1})$: Let $\mathbf{id} : \text{id}_{\ell+1} = (\text{id}_1, \ldots, \text{id}_{\ell+1})$. $\mathcal{SK}_{\mathbf{id}:\text{id}_{\ell+1}}$ is generated from $\mathcal{SK}_{\mathbf{id}}$ as follows.

$\quad \tilde{r}_1, \tilde{r}_2 \xleftarrow{U} \mathbb{Z}_p^{\times}$,
$\quad K_1 \leftarrow K_1 + \tilde{r}_1 J_1$,
$\quad K_2 \leftarrow K_2 + \tilde{r}_1 J_2$, $K_3 \leftarrow (K_3 + \text{id}_{\ell+1} D_{1,\ell+1}) + \tilde{r}_1(J_3 + \text{id}_{\ell+1} D_{2,\ell+1})$,
$\quad K_4 \leftarrow K_4 + \tilde{r}_1 J_4$, $K_5 \leftarrow (K_5 + \text{id}_{\ell+1} E_{1,\ell+1}) + \tilde{r}_1(J_5 + \text{id}_{\ell+1} E_{2,\ell+1})$,
$\quad D_{1,j} \leftarrow D_{1,j} + \tilde{r}_1 D_{2,j}$, $E_{1,j} \leftarrow E_{1,j} + \tilde{r}_1 E_{2,j}$ for $j = \ell + 2, \ldots, h$,

$\quad J_1 \leftarrow \tilde{r}_2 J_1$, $J_2 \leftarrow \tilde{r}_2 J_2$, $J_3 \leftarrow \tilde{r}_2(J_3 + \text{id}_{\ell+1} D_{2,\ell+1})$,
$\quad J_4 \leftarrow \tilde{r}_2 J_4$, $J_5 \leftarrow \tilde{r}_2(J_5 + \text{id}_{\ell+1} E_{2,\ell+1})$,
$\quad D_{2,j} \leftarrow \tilde{r}_2 D_{2,j}$, $E_{2,j} \leftarrow \tilde{r}_2 E_{2,j}$ for $j = \ell + 2, \ldots, h$,

setting $r_1 \leftarrow r_1 + \tilde{r}_1 r_2$ and $r_2 \leftarrow \tilde{r}_2 r_2$. Note that the new values of $r_1$ and $r_2$ have uniform and independent distribution over $\mathbb{Z}_p$ given that $r_1, r_2 \xleftarrow{U} \mathbb{Z}_p$ and

$\tilde{r}_1, \tilde{r}_2 \xleftarrow{\text{U}} \mathbb{Z}_p^\times$. Hence the distribution of $\mathcal{SK}_{\text{id}:\text{id}_{\ell+1}}$ is same as that of a freshly generated key for $\text{id} : \text{id}_{\ell+1}$ via the $\mathcal{H}_1$.KeyGen algorithm.
$\mathcal{H}_1$.Decrypt($\mathcal{C}, \mathcal{SK}_{\text{id}}$): Return $M'$ computed as:

$$M' = \frac{C_0 \cdot e(C_3, K_1)}{e(C_1, \text{tag}K_2 + K_3)e(C_2, \text{tag}K_4 + K_5)}.$$

**Correctness:** It is rather straightforward to verify the correctness. We omit calculations due to lack of space. The full version [29] contains details.

**From a Dual System Perspective.** One can see in Section 4 that the scalar $u$, along with scalars $d, c, e_{j_{j \in [1,h]}}$, define the semi-functional ciphertext space for $\mathcal{H}_1$. These scalars provide the secret information for simulating semi-functional components. A crucial requirement for a dual system proof is that these scalars are statistically hidden from the adversary. Observe that the element $g_T$ in the public parameters, information theoretically hides the element $u$. Similarly, elements $U_1, V_{1,j}, W_1$ hide the scalars $d, e_j, c$ respectively. Further intuition with respect to the dual-system proof and a sketch of how the various scalars interact is provided in Section 4.

**Anonymity and Constant-Size Ciphertexts.** As mentioned in Section 1, a CC-HIBE scheme achieving anonymity will not possess prefix decryption property. In $\mathcal{H}_1$, it is not possible to decrypt the ciphertext for $\text{id}$ with $\mathcal{SK}_{\text{id}'}$ (where $\text{id}'$ is a prefix of $\text{id}$). The reason is that is no way to remove (or truncate) the randomised components corresponding $\text{id} \setminus \text{id}'$ from the ciphertext (here, $\text{id} \setminus \text{id}'$ denotes the suffix of $\text{id}'$ in $\text{id}$). More percisely, given the hash $s(U_1 + \sum_{j=1}^{\ell} \text{id}_j V_{1,j} + \text{tag}W_1)$ for $\text{id} = (\text{id}_1, \ldots, \text{id}_\ell)$ it is impossible to extract a hash for $\text{id}'$ since we have no knowledge of $sV_{1,j}$'s.

### 3.2   Scheme $\mathcal{H}_2$

This section presents the second (non-anonymous) HIBE construction. As discussed in Section 3, two sub-hashes in the key are combined to form the identity-hash required for cancellation with the ciphertext. The sub-hashes are determined by the vectors $\mathbf{v}_1 = (d, e_1, \ldots, e_h)$ and $\mathbf{v}_2 = (\Delta_1, \Delta_{2,1}, \ldots, \Delta_{2,h})$. In order to realise anonymity, these vectors are kept as part of the master secret in $\mathcal{H}_1$. It turns out that we can obtain a non-anonymous scheme by making these vectors public. The availablity of these vectors facilitates rerandomisation and hence the keys no longer need extra components for this purpose. As a result, keys are shorter and algorithms KeyGen, Delegate are more efficient in comparison to $\mathcal{H}_1$.

The method of followed here in obtaining a non-anonymous HIBE did not work out for previously known anonymous HIBE schemes [28,20]. This is due to the following reasons. The element $\mathbb{G}_T$ would be of the form $e(P_1, P_2)^\alpha$ where $\alpha$ is part of the master secret. $P_1$ and $P_2$ would be required for encryption and delegation respectively as a result of which both $P_1$ and $P_2$ would be present in $\mathcal{PP}$. However, this leaks $\alpha$ information theoretically thus revealing the message too! The splitting of $\alpha$ here in terms of $\Delta_4$ and $u$ precisely overcomes this problem. Furthermore, the public parameters information-theoretically hide these scalars thus providing sufficient randomness during simulation to generate semi-functional components.

We define $\mathcal{H}_2 = (\mathcal{H}_2.\text{Setup}, \mathcal{H}_2.\text{Encrypt}, \mathcal{H}_2.\text{KeyGen}, \mathcal{H}_2.\text{Delegate}, \mathcal{H}_2.\text{Decrypt})$ where the algorithms are as follows.

$\mathcal{H}_2.\text{Setup}(\kappa)$: Generate a Type-3 pairing $(p, \mathbb{G}_1, \mathbb{G}_2, \mathbb{G}_T, e, F_1, F_2)$ based on the security parameter $\kappa$. Compute parameters as follows.

$$P_1 \xleftarrow{U} \mathbb{G}_1^\times, \ P_2 \xleftarrow{U} \mathbb{G}_2^\times, \ \Delta_1, \Delta_3, \Delta_4, c, d, u, (\Delta_{2,j}, e_j)_{j=1}^h \xleftarrow{U} \mathbb{Z}_p, \ b \xleftarrow{U} \mathbb{Z}_p^\times,$$
$$U_1 = (-\Delta_1 b + d)P_1, \ (V_{1,j} = (-\Delta_{2,j}b + e_j)P_1)_{j\in[1,h]}, \ W_1 = (-\Delta_3 b + c)P_1,$$
$$g_T = e(P_1, P_2)^{-\Delta_4 b + u},$$

$$\mathcal{PP}: (P_1, bP_1, U_1, (V_{1,j})_{j=1}^h, W_1, P_2, \Delta_1 P_2, \Delta_3 P_2, dP_2, cP_2, (\Delta_{2,j}P_2, e_j P_2)_{j=1}^h, g_T)$$
$$\mathcal{MSK}: (\Delta_4, u)$$

$\mathcal{H}_2.\text{Encrypt}(\mathcal{PP}, M, \mathbf{id} = (\text{id}_1, \ldots, \text{id}_\ell))$: Identical to $\mathcal{H}_1.\text{Encrypt}$.

$\mathcal{H}_2.\text{KeyGen}(\mathcal{MSK}, \mathbf{id} = (\text{id}_1, \ldots, \text{id}_\ell))$: Pick $r \xleftarrow{U} \mathbb{Z}_p$ and compute the secret key $\mathcal{SK}_{\mathbf{id}} = ((K_i)_{i\in[1,5]}, (D_j, E_j)_{j\in[\ell+1,h]})$ for $\mathbf{id}$ where,

$$K_1 = rP_2, \ K_2 = rcP_2, \ K_3 = \left(u + r(d + \sum_{j=1}^\ell \text{id}_j e_j)\right)P_2,$$
$$K_4 = -r\Delta_3 P_2, \ K_5 = \left(-\Delta_4 - r(\Delta_1 + \sum_{j=1}^\ell \text{id}_j \Delta_{2,j})\right)P_2,$$
$$D_j = re_j P_2, \ E_j = -r\Delta_{2,j}P_2 \text{ for } j = \ell + 1, \ldots, h.$$

$\mathcal{H}_2.\text{Delegate}(\mathbf{id} = (\text{id}_1, \ldots, \text{id}_\ell), \text{id}_{\ell+1})$: Let $\mathbf{id} : \text{id}_{\ell+1} = (\text{id}_1, \ldots, \text{id}_{\ell+1})$. $\mathcal{SK}_{\mathbf{id}:\text{id}_{\ell+1}}$ is generated from $\mathcal{SK}_{\mathbf{id}}$ as follows.

$$\tilde{r} \xleftarrow{U} \mathbb{Z}_p^\times,$$
$$K_1 \leftarrow K_1 + \tilde{r}P_2,$$
$$K_2 \leftarrow K_2 + \tilde{r}cP_2, \ K_3 \leftarrow (K_3 + \text{id}_{\ell+1}D_{\ell+1}) + \tilde{r}(d + \sum_{j=1}^{\ell+1} \text{id}_j e_j)P_2,$$
$$K_4 \leftarrow K_4 - \tilde{r}\Delta_3 P_2, \ K_5 \leftarrow (K_5 + \text{id}_{\ell+1}E_{\ell+1}) - \tilde{r}(\Delta_1 + \sum_{j=1}^{\ell+1} \text{id}_j \Delta_{2,j})P_2,$$
$$D_j \leftarrow D_j + \tilde{r}e_j P_2, \ E_j \leftarrow E_j - \tilde{r}\Delta_{2,j}P_2 \text{ for } j = \ell + 2, \ldots, h,$$

setting $r \leftarrow r + \tilde{r}$. Note that the distribution of $\mathcal{SK}_{\mathbf{id}:\text{id}_{\ell+1}}$ is same as that of a freshly generated key for $\mathbf{id} : \text{id}_{\ell+1}$ via the KeyGen algorithm.

$\mathcal{H}_2.\text{Decrypt}(\mathcal{C}, \mathcal{SK}_{\mathbf{id}})$: Identical to $\mathcal{H}_1.\text{Decrypt}$.

*Note.* The encryption and decryption algorithms of $\mathcal{H}_1$ and $\mathcal{H}_2$ are identical and hence the correctness of decryption for $\mathcal{H}_2$ follows from that of $\mathcal{H}_1$. The KeyGen and Delegate algorithms for $\mathcal{H}_2$ are identical to the portion of the corresponding algorithms for $\mathcal{H}_1$ which modify the $\mathcal{S}_1$-components of the key. The $\mathcal{S}_2$ components of the key in $\mathcal{H}_1$ are not required in $\mathcal{H}_2$.

## 4   Security of $\mathcal{H}_1$

The scheme $\mathcal{H}_1$ is proved secure in the sense of ANO-IND-ID-CPA (described in [29]) following the dual system methodology introduced by Waters [34]. We first provide algorithms $\mathcal{H}_1.\text{SFEncrypt}$ and $\mathcal{H}_1.\text{SFKeyGen}$ that generate semi-functional ciphertexts and keys (respectively) required for a dual system proof. In addition, we need an algorithm PSFKeyGen that generates *partial semi-functional keys* (refer to [28,29] for the underlying intuition). These are required only in the security proof of $\mathcal{H}_1$ and not $\mathcal{H}_2$. The security of $\mathcal{H}_2$ is very similar to that of $\mathcal{H}_1$. A sketch of the proof is provided in the full version [29].

$\mathcal{H}_1$.SFEncrypt$(\mathcal{MSK}, \mathcal{C})$: Suppose that $\mathcal{C}$ is given by $(\mathcal{C} = (C_0, C_1, C_2, C_3)) \leftarrow \mathcal{H}_1$.Encrypt$(m, \mathbf{id} = (\mathsf{id}_1, \ldots, \mathsf{id}_\ell))$. Pick $\mu \xleftarrow{\mathsf{U}} \mathbb{Z}_p$ and modify the components of $\mathcal{C}$ as follows.

$$C_0 \leftarrow C_0 \cdot e(P_1, P_2)^{u\mu}, \; C_1 \leftarrow C_1 + \mu P_1, \; C_2 \leftarrow C_2,$$
$$C_3 \leftarrow C_3 + \mu(d + \textstyle\sum_{j=1}^{\ell} \mathsf{id}_j e_j + \mathsf{tag} \cdot c) P_1.$$

Return the modified ciphertext $\mathcal{C} = (C_0, C_1, C_2, C_3)$.

$\mathcal{H}_1$.SFKeyGen$(\mathcal{MSK}, \mathcal{SK}_{\mathbf{id}})$: This algorithm takes in a normal secret key $\mathcal{SK}_{\mathbf{id}} = (\mathcal{S}_1, \mathcal{S}_2)$ for identity $\mathbf{id} = (\mathsf{id}_1, \ldots, \mathsf{id}_\ell)$ and generates a semi-functional key as follows.

$$\gamma_1, \gamma_2, \pi, \sigma, (\pi_j, \sigma_j)_{j=1}^h \xleftarrow{\mathsf{U}} \mathbb{Z}_p,$$
$$K_1 \leftarrow K_1, \; K_2 \leftarrow K_2 + \gamma_1 P_2, \; K_3 \leftarrow K_3 + \gamma_1 \pi P_2,$$
$$K_4 \leftarrow K_4 - (\gamma_1/b) P_2, \; K_5 \leftarrow K_5 - (\gamma_1 \pi/b) P_2,$$
$$D_{1,j} \leftarrow D_{1,j} + \gamma_1 \pi_j P_2, \; E_{1,j} \leftarrow E_{1,j} - (\gamma_1 \pi_j/b) P_2 \quad \text{for } j = \ell+1, \ldots, h,$$
$$J_1 \leftarrow J_1, \; J_2 \leftarrow J_2 + \gamma_2 P_2, \; J_3 \leftarrow J_3 + \gamma_2 \sigma P_2,$$
$$J_4 \leftarrow J_4 - (\gamma_2/b) P_2, \; J_5 \leftarrow J_5 - (\gamma_2 \sigma/b) P_2,$$
$$D_{2,j} \leftarrow D_{2,j} + \gamma_2 \sigma_j P_2, \; E_{2,j} \leftarrow E_{2,j} - (\gamma_2 \sigma_j/b) P_2 \quad \text{for } j = \ell+1, \ldots, h,$$

The resulting key $\mathcal{SK}_{\mathbf{id}} = (\mathcal{S}_1, \mathcal{S}_2)$ is returned.

PSFKeyGen$(\mathcal{MSK}, \mathcal{SK}_{\mathbf{id}})$: Returns a key $\mathcal{SK}_{\mathbf{id}}$ for identity $\mathbf{id}$ with $\mathcal{S}_1$-components having semi-functional terms (generated according to $\mathcal{H}_1$.SFKeyGen algorithm) and $\mathcal{S}_2$-components being normal (as returned by $\mathcal{H}_1$.KeyGen algorithm).

It is straightforward to see that decryption of a semi-functional ciphertext by a normal key or that of a normal ciphertext with a semi-functional key succeeds. When both ciphertext and key are semi-functional, decryption results in an extra masking factor of $e(P_1, P_2)^{\gamma\mu(\mathsf{tag}+\pi)}$ on the message. Decryption is only successful if $\pi = -\mathsf{tag}$ whence the ciphertext and key become *nominally semi-functional*.

The following theorem states precisely the security guarantee we obtain for $\mathcal{H}_1$.

**Theorem 1.** *If $(\varepsilon_{\mathrm{DDH1}}, t_1)$-DDH1 and $(\varepsilon_{\mathrm{DDH2}}, t_2)$-DDH2 assumptions hold in $\mathbb{G}_1$ and $\mathbb{G}_2$ respectively, then $\mathcal{H}_1$ is $(\varepsilon, t)$-ANO-IND-ID-CPA-secure where $\varepsilon \leq \varepsilon_{\mathrm{DDH1}} + 2q \cdot \varepsilon_{\mathrm{DDH2}} + (2q/p)$, $t_1 = t + O(h\rho)$ and $t_2 = t + O(h\rho)$. $\rho$ is the maximum time required for one scalar multiplication in $\mathbb{G}_1$ and $\mathbb{G}_2$.*

**Proof Sketch.** Fix any $t$-time adversary $\mathscr{A}$. Let $\mathsf{G}_{real}$ denote the HIBE security game ano-ind-cpa (described in [29]) and $\mathsf{G}_{final}$ be a game where all keys are semi-functional and the challenge ciphertext is a semi-functional encryption of a random message to a random identity vector. The probability that $\mathscr{A}$ wins in $\mathsf{G}_{final}$ is $1/2$. To prove the theorem, we need to show a bound on $\mathsf{Adv}_{\mathcal{H}_1}^{\mathsf{ano-ind-cpa}}(\mathscr{A}) = |\Pr[\mathscr{A} \text{ wins in } \mathsf{G}_{real}] - (1/2)|$ which is equivalent to bounding $|\Pr[\mathscr{A} \text{ wins in } \mathsf{G}_{real}] - \Pr[\mathscr{A} \text{ wins in } \mathsf{G}_{final}]|$. In order to obtain this bound, we first define a sequence of games starting from $G_{real}$ and making small changes until we reach $G_{final}$. Define $G_{k,0}$, $1 \leq k \leq q$ similar to $G_{real}$ except that challenge ciphertext is semi-functional, first $k-1$ keys are semi-functional and $k$-th key is partial semi-functional. In $G_{k,1}$, $0 \leq k \leq q$, the challenge ciphertext is semi-functional and first $k$ keys are semi-functional. The game sequence is $G_{real}$, $G_{0,1}$, $(G_{k,0}, G_{k,1})_{k=1}^{q}$, $G_{final}$. The advantage of $\mathscr{A}$ in winning $G_{real}$ can now be bounded in terms of its advantage in distinguishing between successive games. This is done via reductions from the SXDH problem to the task of distinguishing between successive games. Essentially, there are two kinds of reductions - first and second. In the first reduction, we show that $\mathscr{A}$'s ability to distinguish between $G_{real}$ and $G_{0,1}$ can be used to solve a DDH1 instance. The second reduction shows that an algorithm $\mathscr{A}$ that can distinguish between $G_{k-1,1}$ and $G_{k,0}$ for some $k \in [1, q]$, can be used to construct an algorithm $\mathscr{B}_2$ solving DDH2. Similar arguments hold for all values of $k$ and also for the transition from $G_{k,0}$ to $G_{k,1}$. The final transition i.e, $G_{q,1}$ to $G_{final}$ is done just by changing the way information provided to $\mathscr{A}$ is generated so that the distribution of $\mathscr{A}$'s view in the two games are statistically indistinguishable except with probability $2q/p$.. We now provide an outline of each stage in the proof.

**First Reduction:** Suppose that $\mathscr{B}_1$ is a DDH1-solver. $\mathscr{B}_1$ simulates the game using a DDH1 instance $(\mathcal{G}, P_1, bP_1, sbP_1, P_2, (s+\mu)P_1)$. The element $b$ of the instance corresponds to the scalar $b$ of the scheme. $\mathscr{B}_1$ sets up the system normally since it has all information required to do so. The master secret is also known since none of its components depend on $b$. Furthermore, it cannot create semi-functional keys as no encoding of $b$ in $\mathbb{G}_2$ is provided. All the key extract queries are answered normally. $\mathscr{B}_1$ sets the randomiser for the challenge ciphertext $\widehat{\mathcal{C}}$ to be $s$ (from the instance). $\widehat{\mathcal{C}}$ will be normal or semi-functional depending on whether the instance is real i.e., $\mu = 0$, or random ($\mu \xleftarrow{U} \mathbb{Z}_p$).

**Second Reduction:** Suppose $(\mathcal{G}, P_1, P_2, rP_2, cP_2, (rc + \gamma)P_2)$ is provided as instance to the DDH2-solver $\mathscr{B}_2$. Here $c$ corresponds to the scalar $c$ in $\mathcal{MSK}$. Elements $d, (e_j)_{j \in [1,h]}$ are set to random degree-1 polynomials in $c$. Scalar $b$ is chosen randomly from $\mathbb{Z}_p^{\times}$. Let $\mathbf{y} = (d, e_1, \ldots, e_h)$. The public parameters are created differently since $\mathbf{y}$ is not known. Only its encoding in $\mathbb{G}_2$ i.e, $\mathbf{y}P_2$ is known. Specifically $U_1, V_{1,j}, W_1$ are chosen at random from $\mathbb{G}_1$. Depending on these and $\mathbf{y}$, the corresponding $\Delta$'s are implicitly set. Encodings of $\Delta$'s can be computed only in $\mathbb{G}_2$. This enables normal key generation as well as semi-functional key generation. In its response to the $k$-th key extract query, $\mathscr{B}_2$ maps $r$ from the instance to the randomiser $r_1$ in the key. Accordingly it generates the key choosing $r_2$ at random. If $\gamma = 0$, the key will be normal. Otherwise the key is partial semi-functional and $\gamma$ corresponds to the randomiser $\gamma_1$ in the semi-functional part. Moreover, a linear polynomial $f(\mathbf{id}_k)$ in $\mathbf{id}_k$-components is embedded in the semi-functional scalar $\pi$. This polynomial is determined by the co-efficients of $c$ in $\mathbf{y}$. The coefficients of $c$ in $e_j$ also determine $\pi_j$ respectively. For the challenge ciphertext, $\mathscr{B}_2$ has to create semi-functional components which depend on $\mathbf{y}$. But $\mathbf{y}$ depends on $c$ and encoding of $c$ in $\mathbb{G}_1$ is not known. The only way out is to set $\mathsf{tag} = -f(\widehat{\mathsf{id}}_\beta)$ so that terms depending on $c$ vanish. A consequence is that $\mathscr{B}_2$ can only generate nominally semi-functional ciphertext for $\mathsf{id}_k$. We then argue that the simulation is perfect.

**Final Transition:** It is required to show that $\mathsf{G}_{q,1}$ and $\mathsf{G}_{final}$ are statistically indistinguishable from the attacker's point of view except for probability at most $2q/p$. The generation of public parameters and keys provided to $\mathscr{A}$ are changed ensuring that their form is equivalent to that in $\mathsf{G}_{q,1}$ and they are independent of the scalars $u, d, (e_j)_{j \in [1,h]}$. Consequently the challenge ciphertext is the only place where these scalars come into play, especially in those components that consist of the identity-hash and the message. Basically, the message and the id-hash are masked by random quantities so that $\mathsf{G}_{final}$ is simulated. Refer to the full version [29] for details of the proof.

## 5   Conclusion

We obtain two HIBE schemes with constant-size ciphertexts and full security from the IBE scheme of Jutla and Roy. One achieves anonymity while the other is non-anonymous with shorter keys. Compared to previous HIBE schemes, our constructions provide very good efficiency with just 3 pairings for decryption and 3 group elements in the ciphertext. These are also the only CC-HIBEs achieving security under standard assumptions and degradation independent of the HIBE depth. In HIBE-related literature focussed on either constant-size ciphertexts or anonymity or both, we believe that our constructions complete the picture.

**Acknowledgement.** We thank reviewers of a previous version of this paper for providing useful comments.

## References

1. Abdalla, M., et al.: Searchable encryption revisited: Consistency properties, relation to anonymous IBE, and extensions. In: Shoup, V. (ed.) CRYPTO 2005. LNCS, vol. 3621, pp. 205–222. Springer, Heidelberg (2005)
2. Blazy, O., Kiltz, E., Pan, J.: (Hierarchical) identity-based encryption from affine message authentication. In: Garay, J.A., Gennaro, R. (eds.) CRYPTO 2014, Part I. LNCS, vol. 8616, pp. 408–425. Springer, Heidelberg (2014)
3. Boneh, D., Boyen, X., Goh, E.-J.: Hierarchical identity based encryption with constant size ciphertext. In: Cramer, R. (ed.) EUROCRYPT 2005. LNCS, vol. 3494, pp. 440–456. Springer, Heidelberg (2005)
4. Boneh, D., Franklin, M.K.: Identity-based encryption from the Weil pairing. SIAM J. Comput. 32(3), 586–615 (2003), Earlier version appeared in the proceedings of CRYPTO 2001
5. Boyen, X., Waters, B.: Anonymous hierarchical identity-based encryption (without random oracles). In: Dwork, C. (ed.) CRYPTO 2006. LNCS, vol. 4117, pp. 290–307. Springer, Heidelberg (2006)

6. Chatterjee, S., Menezes, A.: On cryptographic protocols employing asymmetric pairings – the role of $\psi$ revisited. Discrete Applied Mathematics 159(13), 1311–1322 (2011)

7. Chatterjee, S., Sarkar, P.: New constructions of constant size ciphertext HIBE without random oracle. In: Rhee, M.S., Lee, B. (eds.) ICISC 2006. LNCS, vol. 4296, pp. 310–327. Springer, Heidelberg (2006)

8. Chatterjee, S., Sarkar, P.: Constant size ciphertext HIBE in the augmented selective-id model and its extensions. J. UCS 13(10), 1367–1395 (2007)

9. Chen, J., Wee, H.: Fully, (almost) tightly secure IBE and dual system groups (2013), https://sites.google.com/site/jchencrypto/publications

10. Chow, S.S.M.: Removing Escrow from Identity-Based Encryption. In: Jarecki, Tsudik (eds.) [18], pp. 256–276

11. Cocks, C.: An identity based encryption scheme based on quadratic residues. In: Honary, B. (ed.) Cryptography and Coding 2001. LNCS, vol. 2260, pp. 360–363. Springer, Heidelberg (2001)

12. De Caro, A., Iovino, V., Persiano, G.: Fully secure anonymous HIBE and secret-key anonymous IBE with short ciphertexts. In: Joye, M., Miyaji, A., Otsuka, A. (eds.) Pairing 2010. LNCS, vol. 6487, pp. 347–366. Springer, Heidelberg (2010)

13. Ducas, L.: Anonymity from asymmetry: New constructions for anonymous HIBE. In: Pieprzyk, J. (ed.) CT-RSA 2010. LNCS, vol. 5985, pp. 148–164. Springer, Heidelberg (2010)

14. Escala, A., Herold, G., Kiltz, E., Ràfols, C., Villar, J.: An algebraic framework for diffie-hellman assumptions. In: Canetti, R., Garay, J.A. (eds.) CRYPTO 2013, Part II. LNCS, vol. 8043, pp. 129–147. Springer, Heidelberg (2013)

15. Galbraith, S.D., Paterson, K.G., Smart, N.P.: Pairings for cryptographers. Discrete Applied Mathematics 156(16), 3113–3121 (2008)

16. Gentry, C., Silverberg, A.: Hierarchical ID-based cryptography. In: Zheng, Y. (ed.) ASIACRYPT 2002. LNCS, vol. 2501, pp. 548–566. Springer, Heidelberg (2002)

17. Horwitz, J., Lynn, B.: Toward hierarchical identity-based encryption. In: Knudsen, L.R. (ed.) EUROCRYPT 2002. LNCS, vol. 2332, pp. 466–481. Springer, Heidelberg (2002)

18. Jarecki, S., Tsudik, G. (eds.): PKC 2009. LNCS, vol. 5443. Springer, Heidelberg (2009)

19. Jutla, C.S., Roy, A.: Shorter Quasi-Adaptive NIZK Proofs for Linear Subspaces. In: Sako, K., Sarkar, P. (eds.) ASIACRYPT 2013, Part I. LNCS, vol. 8269, pp. 1–20. Springer, Heidelberg (2013)

20. Lee, K., Park, J., Lee, D.: Anonymous HIBE with short ciphertexts: full security in prime order groups. Designs, Codes and Cryptography, 1–31 (2013)

21. Lewko, A.B.: Tools for Simulating Features of Composite Order Bilinear Groups in the Prime Order Setting. In: Pointcheval, Johansson [26] (eds.), pp. 318–335

22. Lewko, A., Waters, B.: New Techniques for Dual System Encryption and Fully Secure HIBE with Short Ciphertexts. In: Micciancio, D. (ed.) TCC 2010. LNCS, vol. 5978, pp. 455–479. Springer, Heidelberg (2010)

23. Okamoto, T., Takashima, K.: Achieving Short Ciphertexts or Short Secret-Keys for Adaptively Secure General Inner-Product Encryption. In: Lin, D., Tsudik, G., Wang, X. (eds.) CANS 2011. LNCS, vol. 7092, pp. 138–159. Springer, Heidelberg (2011)

24. Okamoto, T., Takashima, K.: Adaptively Attribute-Hiding (Hierarchical) Inner Product Encryption. In: Pointcheval, Johansson (eds.) [26], pp. 591–608

25. Park, J.H., Lee, D.H.: Anonymous HIBE: Compact construction over prime-order groups. IEEE Transactions on Information Theory 59(4), 2531–2541 (2013)

26. Pointcheval, D., Johansson, T. (eds.): EUROCRYPT 2012. LNCS, vol. 7237. Springer, Heidelberg (2012)
27. Ramanna, S.C., Chatterjee, S., Sarkar, P.: Variants of waters' dual system primitives using asymmetric pairings - (extended abstract). In: Fischlin, M., Buchmann, J., Manulis, M. (eds.) PKC 2012. LNCS, vol. 7293, pp. 298–315. Springer, Heidelberg (2012)
28. Ramanna, S.C., Sarkar, P.: Anonymous constant-size ciphertext HIBE from asymmetric pairings. In: Stam, M. (ed.) IMACC 2013. LNCS, vol. 8308, pp. 344–363. Springer, Heidelberg (2013)
29. Ramanna, S.C., Sarkar, P.: Efficient (anonymous) compact hibe from standard assumptions. Cryptology ePrint Archive, Report 2013/806 (2013), http://eprint.iacr.org/
30. Seo, J.H., Kobayashi, T., Ohkubo, M., Suzuki, K.: Anonymous hierarchical identity-based encryption with constant size ciphertexts. In: Jarecki, Tsudik (eds.) [18], pp. 215–234
31. Shamir, A.: Identity-based cryptosystems and signature schemes. In: Blakely, G.R., Chaum, D. (eds.) CRYPTO 1984. LNCS, vol. 196, pp. 47–53. Springer, Heidelberg (1985)
32. Shi, E., Waters, B.: Delegating capabilities in predicate encryption systems. In: Aceto, L., Damgård, I., Goldberg, L.A., Halldórsson, M.M., Ingólfsdóttir, A., Walukiewicz, I. (eds.) ICALP 2008, Part II. LNCS, vol. 5126, pp. 560–578. Springer, Heidelberg (2008)
33. Smart, N.P., Vercauteren, F.: On computable isomorphisms in efficient asymmetric pairing-based systems. Discrete Applied Mathematics 155(4), 538–547 (2007)
34. Waters, B.: Dual System Encryption: Realizing Fully Secure IBE and HIBE under Simple Assumptions. In: Halevi, S. (ed.) CRYPTO 2009. LNCS, vol. 5677, pp. 619–636. Springer, Heidelberg (2009)

# Computationally Efficient Ciphertext-Policy Attribute-Based Encryption with Constant-Size Ciphertexts

Yinghui Zhang[1,2], Dong Zheng[1], Xiaofeng Chen[3], Jin Li[4], and Hui Li[3]

[1] National Engineering Laboratory for Wireless Security,
Xi'an University of Posts and Telecommunications, Xi'an 710121, P.R. China
yhzhaang@163.com, zhengdong@xupt.edu.cn
[2] State Key Laboratory of Information Security, Institute of Information Engineering,
Chinese Academy of Sciences, Beijing 100096, P.R. China
[3] State Key Laboratory of Integrated Service Networks (ISN),
Xidian University, Xi'an 710071, P.R. China
xfchen@xidian.edu.cn, lihui@mail.xidian.edu.cn
[4] School of Computer Science, Guangzhou University,
Guangzhou 510006, P.R. China
jinli71@gmail.com

**Abstract.** Ciphertext-policy attribute-based encryption (CP-ABE) is extremely suitable for cloud computing environment in that it enables data owners to make and enforce access policies themselves. However, most of the existing CP-ABE schemes suffer severe efficiency drawbacks due to large computation cost and ciphertext size, both of which linearly increase with the complexity of access policies. Aiming at tackling the challenge above, in this paper, we propose a CP-ABE scheme which features constant computation cost and constant-size ciphertexts. The proposed CP-ABE scheme is proven selective-secure in the random oracle model under the decision $n$-Bilinear Diffie-Hellman Exponent ($n$-BDHE) assumption, where $n$ represents the total number of attributes in universe. In particular, the proposed scheme can efficiently support AND-gate access policies with multiple attribute values and wildcards. Performance comparisons indicate that the proposed CP-ABE scheme is promising in real-world applications, especially for the scenarios where computation and bandwidth issues are major concerns.

**Keywords:** Attribute-based encryption, Constant computation, Constant-size ciphertexts, Cloud computing.

# 1 Introduction

Cloud computing is an increasingly popular computing paradigm and it can provide flexible, inexpensive, and quality services. Furthermore, cloud computing realizes the pay as you go environment in which various resources are made available to users as they pay for what they use. Although the advantages of

S.S.M. Chow et al. (Eds.): ProvSec 2014, LNCS 8782, pp. 259–273, 2014.
© Springer International Publishing Switzerland 2014

the new technology are desirable, data privacy and security issues have become major concerns for individuals and organizations using such services. In order to prevent potential threats to their data such as improper use by the cloud storage server and unauthorized access by outside users, people would like to make their private data only accessible to users authorized by them. However, in traditional mechanisms based on access control lists, it is required that the storage server should be in the same security domain as data owners and enforce access policies himself. Therefore, those traditional methods are no longer suitable for cloud-based data sharing, where the server is not fully trusted by users. In particular, fine-grained data access control is necessary for cloud-based data sharing and different levels of access privileges should be granted to different users according to their attributes and roles. With the rapid development of cloud computing technology, the above security issues are thrown into sharp focus. This motivates researchers to consider a paradigm shift, where instead of trusting and being dependent on service providers, data owners can make and enforce fine-grained access policies themselves.

As a one-to-many public-key primitive, attribute-based encryption (ABE) is very promising in implementing fine-grained data sharing systems in cloud computing. In ABE systems, descriptive attributes and access policies, which are associated with attribute secret keys and ciphertexts, are used to enable fine-grained access control over encrypted data. A particular attribute secret key can decrypt a ciphertext if and only if associated attributes and the access policy match each other. ABE comes in two flavors called key-policy ABE (KP-ABE) and ciphertext-policy ABE (CP-ABE). In KP-ABE, the access policy is enforced in secret keys and ciphertexts are labeled with a set of attributes. In CP-ABE, the roles of the attribute set and the access policy are swapped from what we described for KP-ABE: every ciphertext is associated with an access policy, and every secret key is associated with a set of attributes. Compared with KP-ABE, CP-ABE is more suitable for cloud-based data sharing in that it enables data owners to make and enforce access policies themselves.

Nevertheless, there remain several challenges to the application of CP-ABE in cloud-based data sharing. On the one hand, in most of existing CP-ABE schemes, the decryption cost incurred by bilinear pairing (**pair**) and exponentiation (**exp**) operations linearly grows with the complexity of the access policy. On the other hand, most of existing CP-ABE constructions have large-size ciphertexts, which leads to a large communication cost in data sharing. Therefore, before wide deployments on cloud computing platforms, it is indispensable to reduce the computation cost and ciphertext length of CP-ABE while keeping its expressiveness.

To the authors' knowledge, the AND-gate CP-ABE construction due to Chen et al. [6] is most efficient[1]. It only needs three **exp** in encryption phase and two

---

[1] Although the CP-ABE scheme in [26] has smaller ciphertexts than [6], it only supports AND-gate policy on positive and negative values without wildcards in essence, which is denoted by $\mathbf{AND}_{+,-}$. It easily follows that the wildcards used in the ciphertext policy of [26] cannot play the role of "don't care".

**pair** in decryption phase, and has constant-size ciphertexts. However, the AND-gate policy in scheme [6] only supports three values of attributes: positive value, negative value, and wildcards[2], and we denote the policy by $\mathbf{AND}^*_{+,-}$. In this paper, we aim to give a more efficient CP-ABE scheme supporting AND-gate policy with multiple values and wildcards, which is denoted by $\mathbf{AND}^*_m$. It is worth noting that $\mathbf{AND}^*_m$ is indeed more expressive than $\mathbf{AND}^*_{+,-}$. In other words, in the sense of the same expressiveness, $\mathbf{AND}^*_m$ based scheme is more efficient than $\mathbf{AND}^*_{+,-}$ based one. We show this in the following.

Assume there are $n$ attributes in universe and the attribute set is $\mathcal{U} = \{\omega_1, \omega_2, \cdots, \omega_n\}$. Each attribute has multiple values, and suppose $S_i = \{v_{i,1}, v_{i,2}, \cdots, v_{i,n_i}\}$ is the multi-value set for $\omega_i$ and $|S_i| = n_i$. In Table 1, we consider an $\mathbf{AND}^*_m$ policy $\mathbf{CP1} = v_{1,1} \wedge v_{2,1} \wedge v_{3,3} \wedge *$, where the attribute $\omega_4$ associated with "Gender" is not cared for. In other words, if someone's attributes match $\mathbf{CP1}$ in terms of the first three attributes, he/she can decrypt the ciphertexts under $\mathbf{CP1}$ regardless of the gender. Note that $n = 4$, $n_1 = 4$, $n_2 = 3$, $n_3 = 3$, $n_4 = 2$ in Table 1, and IS, CS and CE represent "Information Security", "Computer Science" and "Communication Engineering", respectively. In order to realize the same expressiveness as $\mathbf{CP1}$ based on $\mathbf{AND}^*_{+,-}$ policy, the ciphertext policy $\mathbf{CP2}$ in Table 2 has to be adopted, where $\mathbf{CP2} = \omega_1^+ \wedge \omega_2^{-1} \wedge \omega_3^{-1} \wedge \omega_4^{-1} \wedge \omega_5^+ \wedge \omega_6^{-1} \wedge \omega_7^{-1} \wedge \omega_8^{-1} \wedge \omega_9^{-1} \wedge \omega_{10}^+ \wedge * \wedge *$. Obviously, the total number of attributes associated with $\mathbf{AND}^*_{+,-}$ is significantly larger than that of $\mathbf{AND}^*_m$, and this often leads to more storage overheads at users' side because of attribute secret keys and public system parameters.

**Table 1.** An example of $\mathbf{AND}^*_m$

| Attributes | $\omega_1$ | $\omega_2$ | $\omega_3$ | $\omega_4$ |
|---|---|---|---|---|
| Description | Institution | Department | Duty | Gender |
| Values | Univ. A | IS | Administrator | Male |
| | Univ. B | CS | Teacher | Female |
| | Univ. C | CE | Student | / |
| | Univ. D | / | / | / |
| **CP1** | Univ. A | IS | Student | * |

**Table 2.** An example of $\mathbf{AND}^*_{+,-}$

| Attributes | $\omega_1$ | $\omega_2$ | $\omega_3$ | $\omega_4$ | $\omega_5$ | $\omega_6$ | $\omega_7$ | $\omega_8$ | $\omega_9$ | $\omega_{10}$ | $\omega_{11}$ | $\omega_{12}$ |
|---|---|---|---|---|---|---|---|---|---|---|---|---|
| Description | Univ. A | Univ. B | Univ. C | Univ. D | IS | CS | CE | Administrator | Teacher | Student | Male | Female |
| Values | $\omega_1^+$ | $\omega_2^+$ | $\omega_3^+$ | $\omega_4^+$ | $\omega_5^+$ | $\omega_6^+$ | $\omega_7^+$ | $\omega_8^+$ | $\omega_9^+$ | $\omega_{10}^+$ | $\omega_{11}^+$ | $\omega_{12}^+$ |
| | $\omega_1^-$ | $\omega_2^-$ | $\omega_3^-$ | $\omega_4^-$ | $\omega_5^-$ | $\omega_6^-$ | $\omega_7^-$ | $\omega_8^-$ | $\omega_9^-$ | $\omega_{10}^-$ | $\omega_{11}^-$ | $\omega_{12}^-$ |
| **CP2** | $\omega_1^+$ | $\omega_2^-$ | $\omega_3^-$ | $\omega_4^-$ | $\omega_5^+$ | $\omega_6^-$ | $\omega_7^-$ | $\omega_8^-$ | $\omega_9^-$ | $\omega_{10}^+$ | * | * |

---

[2] After a simple analysis, we know that the ciphertext policy of scheme [6] successfully supports wildcards.

In summary, to realize practical fine-grained data sharing systems, it is of importance to construct CP-ABE schemes, which support $\mathbf{AND}_m^*$ policy and enjoy constant computation cost and constant-size ciphertexts.

**Our Contribution.** We propose a CP-ABE scheme and prove its selective security against chosen plaintext attacks (CPA) in the random oracle model under the decision $n$-Bilinear Diffie-Hellman Exponent ($n$-BDHE) assumption, where $n$ denotes the total number of attributes in universe. The proposed scheme enjoys desirable properties of small and constant computation cost and ciphertext length. It can efficiently support $\mathbf{AND}_m^*$ policy and hence is more preferable than previous CP-ABE constructions. Performance comparisons indicate that the proposed CP-ABE scheme is extremely suitable for real-world applications, especially for the scenarios where computation and bandwidth issues are major concerns.

**Related Work.** In order to improve the flexibility of users to share their data, Sahai and Waters [25] introduced ABE as a fuzzy version of identity-based encryption (IBE). Goyal et al. [10] further extended this idea and defined two complementary notions of ABE: KP-ABE and CP-ABE. The first KP-ABE construction [10] realized the monotonic access structure for key policies. To increase the expressiveness, Ostrovsky et al. presented a KP-ABE scheme that supports non-monotone key policies [22]. The first construction of CP-ABE supporting tree-based access structure was proposed by Bethencourt et al. [4]. However, the construction [4] was proven to be secure in generic group models. To overcome this weakness, Cheung and Newport presented another CP-ABE construction [7] and its security proof was given in the standard model. The construction supports the $\mathbf{AND}_{+,-}^*$ ciphertext policy. Since ABE is promising in realizing fine-grained data sharing systems, recent years have witnessed a number of variants of ABE. Such as accountable ABE [18,20], ABE with recipient-anonymity [14,16,21,27], etc.

However, most of the previous ABE systems suffer severe efficiency drawbacks in terms of the computation cost in encryption and decryption phases and the size of ciphertexts, which usually grow with the number of attributes the user has to hold for successful decryption. Considering the practical application scenarios where users are resource-constrained with respect to computing power and bandwidth, ABE schemes with low computation and communication costs have received a lot of attention in recent years. The schemes [3,5,19,23] belong to KP-ABE and those in [2,6,8,9,12,13,24,26,28] are CP-ABE. The results in [1] merge the schemes in [3,13]. As the first ABE scheme with constant-size ciphertexts, the CP-ABE construction proposed by Emura et al. [8] only supports $\mathbf{AND}_m$ policy without wildcards, where $\mathbf{AND}_m$ denotes the AND-gate policy supporting multiple values without wildcards. Decryption is enabled only if the decryptor's attributes are identical to the access policy. Therefore, their scheme can be simply implemented based on IBE schemes with the same efficiency by using each user's attribute list as his/her identity. Similarly, the CP-ABE schemes [24] supporting $\mathbf{AND}_m$ and [12] supporting $\mathbf{AND}_+$ have the same disadvantage as the scheme [8], where $\mathbf{AND}_+$ represents the AND-gate policy supporting single positive value without wildcards. Herranz et al. [13] proposed a $(\ell, n)$-threshold

CP-ABE scheme with constant-size ciphertexts. However, their scheme requires $n+\ell+1$ **exp** in encryption phase and 3 **pair** and $\mathcal{O}(\ell^2)$ **exp** in decryption phase. Ge et al. [9] proposed a new $(\ell, n)$-threshold CPA-secure CP-ABE scheme with constant-size ciphertexts, and then extended it to a CCA2-secure one. However, their schemes have quadratic attribute secret key size based on $\ell$ and the decryption cost still linearly grows with the number of normal attributes in universe in accordance with **exp**. Attrapadung et al. [2] proposed an inner product encryption with constant-size ciphertexts and the decryption cost is linearly proportional to the number of attributes involved in the access policy. Zhou et al. [28] presented a CP-ABE scheme with constant-size ciphertexts and $\mathbf{AND}^*_{+,-}$ policy while the decryption cost linearly grows with the number of attributes in universe. Although outsourced ABE [11,15,17] can reduce the computation cost of users, the systems have to introduce additional servers. Currently, the CP-ABE construction proposed by Chen et al. [6] is most efficient. They constructed a CPA-secure CP-ABE scheme and then get a security-enhanced one. Both schemes admit $\mathbf{AND}^*_{+,-}$ policy and enjoy constant computation cost and constant-size ciphertexts.

**Organization.** The remaining of this work is organized as follows. Some preliminaries are reviewed in Section 2. We then present the definition and security model of attribute-based encryption in Section 3. Our CP-ABE construction together with its security results are described in Section 4. Security and efficiency comparisons are given in Section 5. Finally, we conclude this paper in Section 6.

# 2   Preliminaries

In this section, we first define the notations used in this paper and review some cryptographic background. Then access policies are explained.

## 2.1   Notations

## 2.2   Cryptographic Background

**Definition 1 (Bilinear Pairing).** *Let $\mathbb{G}$ be a cyclic multiplicative group of some large prime order $p$, $g \in_R \mathbb{G}$ be a generator, and $\mathbb{G}_T$ be a cyclic multiplicative group of the same order, whose identity we denote as 1. We call $\hat{e}$ a bilinear pairing if $\hat{e} : \mathbb{G} \times \mathbb{G} \to \mathbb{G}_T$ is a map with the following properties:*

**Table 3.** Notations used throughout this paper

| Notations | Meanings |
|---|---|
| $\mathbf{AND}_+$ | AND-gate policy supporting single positive value without wildcards |
| $\mathbf{AND}_{+,-}$ | AND-gate policy supporting positive and negative values without wildcards |
| $\mathbf{AND}^*_{+,-}$ | AND-gate policy supporting positive and negative values with wildcards |
| $\mathbf{AND}_m$ | AND-gate policy supporting multiple values without wildcards |
| $\mathbf{AND}^*_m$ | AND-gate policy supporting multiple values with wildcards |

1. *Bilinear:* $\hat{e}(g^a, g^b) = \hat{e}(g,g)^{ab}$ *for all* $a, b \in \mathbb{Z}_p^*$.
2. *Non-degenerate: There exists* $g_1, g_2 \in \mathbb{G}$ *such that* $\hat{e}(g_1, g_2) \neq 1$.
3. *Computable: There is an efficient algorithm to compute* $\hat{e}(g_1, g_2)$ *for all* $g_1, g_2 \in \mathbb{G}$.

**Definition 2 (Decision $(t, \epsilon, \ell)$-BDHE assumption).** *Security of our construction is based on a complexity assumption called the Bilinear Diffie-Hellman Exponent (BDHE) assumption. Let* $\mathbb{G}$ *be a bilinear group of prime order* $p$*, and* $g, h$ *two independent generators of* $\mathbb{G}$*. Denote* $\overrightarrow{y}_{g,\alpha,\ell} = (g_1, g_2, \cdots, g_\ell, g_{\ell+2}, \cdots, g_{2\ell}) \in \mathbb{G}^{2\ell-1}$*, where* $g_i = g^{(\alpha^i)}$ *for some unknown* $\alpha \in \mathbb{Z}_p^*$*. An algorithm* $\mathcal{B}$ *that outputs* $\mu \in \{0, 1\}$ *has advantage* $\epsilon$ *in solving the decision* $\ell$*-BDHE problem if*

$$|Pr[\,\mathcal{B}(g, h, \overrightarrow{y}_{g,\alpha,\ell}, \hat{e}(g_{\ell+1}, h)) = 1\,] - Pr[\,\mathcal{B}(g, h, \overrightarrow{y}_{g,\alpha,\ell}, Z) = 1\,]| \geq \epsilon,$$

*where the probability is over the random choice of* $g, h$ *in* $\mathbb{G}$*, the random choice* $\alpha \in \mathbb{Z}_p^*$*, the random choice of* $Z \in \mathbb{G}_T$*, and the random bits consumed by* $\mathcal{B}$*. We say that the decision* $(t, \epsilon, \ell)$*-BDHE assumption holds in* $\mathbb{G}$ *if no t-time algorithm has advantage at least* $\epsilon$ *in solving the decision* $\ell$*-BDHE problem in* $\mathbb{G}$*.*

### 2.3    Access Policy

An access policy $W$, namely a ciphertext policy in CP-ABE, is a rule that returns either 0 or 1 given a set $L$ of attributes. We say that $L$ satisfies $W$ if and only if $W$ answers 1 on $L$. Usually, notation $L \models W$ is used to represent the fact that $L$ satisfies $W$, and the case of $L$ does not satisfy $W$ is denoted by $L \not\models W$. In our construction, we consider AND-gate policy $\mathbf{AND}_m^*$. As a generalization of the access policy $\mathbf{AND}_{+,-}^*$ in [7], $\mathbf{AND}_m^*$ is also adopted in [21]. Formally, given an attribute list $L = [L_1, L_2, \cdots, L_n]$ and an access policy $W = [W_1, W_2, \cdots, W_n] = \bigwedge_{i \in \mathcal{I}_W} W_i$, where $\mathcal{I}_W$ is a subscript index set and $\mathcal{I}_W = \{i | 1 \leq i \leq n, W_i \neq *\}$, we say $L \models W$ if $L_i = W_i$ or $W_i = *$ for all $1 \leq i \leq n$ and $L \not\models W$ otherwise. It is noted that the wildcard $*$ in $W$ plays the role of "don't care" value.

## 3    Syntax and Security Model

In this section, we review the syntax of attribute-based encryption and present its security models.

### 3.1    Syntax of CP-ABE

In a practical ABE system, there are four entities: AA (Attribute Authority), CSP (Cloud Service Provider), DO (Data Owner) and DU (Data User). AA is in charge of issuing attribute secret keys for DO and DU. CSP is an entity that hosts the encrypted files of DO. A CP-ABE system consists of four algorithms **Setup**, **KeyGen**, **Encrypt** and **Decrypt**. They are detailed as follows:

- **Setup**$(1^\lambda) \to (PK, MK)$: The setup algorithm is run by AA. On input a security parameter $\lambda$, it returns the system public key $PK$ which is distributed to DO and DU, and the master key $MK$ which is kept private.
- **KeyGen**$(PK, MK, L) \to SK_L$: The key generation algorithm is run by AA. On input the system public key $PK$, the master key $MK$ and an attribute list $L$, it outputs $SK_L$ as the attribute secret key associated with $L$.
- **Encrypt**$(PK, M, W) \to CT_W$: The encryption algorithm is run by DO. On input the system public key $PK$, a message $M$ and an access policy $W$ specified by DO, it generates a ciphertext $CT_W$ as the encryption of $M$ with respect to $W$, which is outsourced to CSP.
- **Decrypt**$(PK, CT_W, SK_L) \to M$ or $\perp$: The decryption algorithm is run by DU. On input the system public key $PK$, a ciphertext $CT_W$ of a message $M$ under $W$, and a secret key $SK_L$ associated with $L$, it outputs the message $M$ if $L \models W$, and the error symbol $\perp$ otherwise.

### 3.2 Formalized Security Model for CP-ABE

Following schemes in [4,7,10], we use a notion called indistinguishability against selective ciphertext-policy and chosen-plaintext attacks (IND-sCP-CPA) in the proof of our construction. The formal definition is given based on the following IND-sCP-CPA game, as shown in Fig. 1. The game involves an adversary $\mathcal{A}$ and a challenger $\mathcal{S}$.

---

**Init:** The adversary $\mathcal{A}$ commits to a challenge ciphertext policy $W^*$.

**Setup:** The challenger $\mathcal{S}$ chooses a sufficiently large security parameter $\lambda$, and runs the **Setup** algorithm to get a master key $SK$ and the corresponding system public key $PK$. It retains $SK$ and gives $PK$ to $\mathcal{A}$.

**Phase 1:** In addition to hash queries, the adversary $\mathcal{A}$ issues a polynomially bounded number of queries to the following key generation oracle:

- **KeyGen Oracle** $\mathcal{O}_{KeyGen}$: The adversary $\mathcal{A}$ submits an attribute list $L$, if $L \not\models W^*$, the challenger $\mathcal{S}$ gives $\mathcal{A}$ the secret key $SK_L$ and outputs $\perp$ otherwise.

**Challenge:** Once $\mathcal{A}$ decides that **Phase 1** is over, it outputs two equal length messages $M_0$ and $M_1$ from the message space, on which it wishes to be challenged with respect to $W^*$. The challenger $\mathcal{S}$ randomly chooses a bit $b \in \{0, 1\}$, computes $CT_{W^*} = \textbf{Encrypt}(PK, M_b, W^*)$ and sends $CT_{W^*}$ to $\mathcal{A}$.

**Phase 2:** The same as **Phase 1**.

**Guess:** The adversary $\mathcal{A}$ outputs a guess bit $b' \in \{0, 1\}$ and wins the game if $b' = b$.

The advantage of an adversary $\mathcal{A}$ in the IND-sCP-CPA game is defined as follows:

$$\text{Adv}_{\text{CP-ABE}}^{\text{IND-sCP-CPA}}(\mathcal{A}) = |\Pr[b' = b] - \frac{1}{2}|.$$

---

**Fig. 1.** The IND-sCP-CPA game

**Definition 3.** *A CP-ABE scheme is said to be IND-sCP-CPA secure if no probabilistic polynomial-time adversary can break the IND-sCP-CPA game with non-negligible advantage.*

# 4   Proposed CP-ABE Scheme

## 4.1   Construction

- **Setup($1^\lambda$):** Let $\mathbb{G}$ and $\mathbb{G}_T$ be two cyclic multiplicative groups of a large prime order $p$. Suppose $g$ is a generator of $\mathbb{G}$ and $\hat{e} : \mathbb{G} \times \mathbb{G} \to \mathbb{G}_T$ is a bilinear map. Assume there are $n$ attributes in universe and the attribute set is $\mathcal{U} = \{\omega_1, \omega_2, \cdots, \omega_n\}$. Each attribute has multiple values, and suppose $S_i = \{v_{i,1}, v_{i,2}, \cdots, v_{i,n_i}\}$ is the multi-value set for $\omega_i$ and $|S_i| = n_i$. Define two collision-resistant hash functions $H_0 : \mathbb{Z}_p^* \times \{0,1\}^{\log_2 n} \times \{0,1\}^{\log_2 m} \to \mathbb{Z}_p^*$ and $H_1 : \mathbb{Z}_p^* \to \mathbb{G}$, where we assume that the universe of attribute values can be encoded as elements in $\mathbb{Z}_p^*$ and $m = \max_{i=1}^n n_i$. Also, AA chooses $x, y \in_R \mathbb{Z}_p^*$, and computes $X_{i,k_i} = g^{-H_0(x||i||k_i)}$, $Y_{i,k_i} = \hat{e}(g,g)^{H_0(y||i||k_i)}$ for $1 \le i \le n$ and $1 \le k_i \le n_i$. Finally, the system public key is published as $PK = \langle g, \{X_{i,k_i}, Y_{i,k_i}\}_{1 \le i \le n, 1 \le k_i \le n_i}\rangle$, and the master key is $MK = \langle x, y\rangle$.
- **KeyGen($PK, MK, L$):** Let $L$ be the attribute list for the user who obtains the corresponding attribute secret key. AA chooses $sk \in_R \mathbb{Z}_p^*$ for the user. Then for $1 \le i \le n$, suppose $L_i = v_{i,k_i}$, AA computes:

$$\overline{\sigma}_i = \sigma_{i,k_i} = g^{H_0(y||i||k_i)} H_1(sk)^{H_0(x||i||k_i)}.$$

Finally, the corresponding attribute secret key is $SK_L = \langle sk, \{\overline{\sigma}_i\}_{1 \le i \le n}\rangle$.
- **Encrypt($PK, M, W,$):** To encrypt a message $M \in \mathbb{G}_T$ under a ciphertext policy $W = \bigwedge_{i \in \mathcal{I}_W} W_i$, where suppose $W_i = v_{i,k_i}$, DO computes $\langle X_W, Y_W\rangle = \langle \prod_{i \in \mathcal{I}_W} \overline{X}_i, \prod_{i \in \mathcal{I}_W} \overline{Y}_i\rangle$ with $\langle \overline{X}_i, \overline{Y}_i\rangle = \langle X_{i,k_i}, Y_{i,k_i}\rangle$. Then, DO chooses $s \in_R \mathbb{Z}_p^*$ and sets $CT_W = \langle W, C_0, C_1, C_2\rangle$, where $C_0 = M \cdot Y_W^s$, $C_1 = g^s$, and $C_2 = X_W^s$.
- **Decrypt($PK, CT_W, SK_L$):** The ciphertext $CT_W = \langle W, C_0, C_1, C_2\rangle$ is decrypted by DU with an attribute secret key $SK_L = \langle sk, \{\overline{\sigma}_i\}_{1 \le i \le n}\rangle$ as follows. DU first checks whether $L \models W$. If not, the decryption algorithm returns $\bot$. Otherwise, DU computes $\sigma_W = \prod_{i \in \mathcal{I}_W} \overline{\sigma}_i$. Then, the message is recovered as

$$M = \frac{C_0}{\hat{e}(\sigma_W, C_1) \cdot \hat{e}(H_1(sk), C_2)}.$$

## 4.2   Correctness

If $L \models W$, the message can be successfully recovered according to the decryption algorithm. Indeed, suppose the indexes satisfy $L_i = v_{i,k_i}$, we have

$$\frac{C_0}{\hat{e}(\sigma_W, C_1) \cdot \hat{e}(H_1(sk), C_2)}$$

$$= \frac{M \cdot Y_W^s}{\hat{e}(\sigma_W, g^s) \cdot \hat{e}(H_1(sk), X_W^s)}$$

$$= \frac{M \cdot (\prod_{i \in \mathcal{I}_W} \overline{Y}_i)^s}{\hat{e}\left(\prod_{i \in \mathcal{I}_W} \overline{\sigma}_i, g^s\right) \cdot \hat{e}\left(H_1(sk), \left(\prod_{i \in W} \overline{X}_i\right)^s\right)}$$

$$= \frac{M \cdot \left(\prod_{i \in \mathcal{I}_W} \hat{e}(g,g)^{H_0(y||i||k_i)}\right)^s}{\hat{e}\left(\prod_{i \in \mathcal{I}_W} g^{H_0(y||i||k_i)} H_1(sk)^{H_0(x||i||k_i)}, g^s\right) \cdot \hat{e}\left(H_1(sk), \left(\prod_{i \in \mathcal{I}_W} g^{-H_0(x||i||k_i)}\right)^s\right)}$$

$$= M.$$

## 4.3 Security Analysis

**Theorem 1.** *Assume that $\mathcal{A}$ makes at most $q_{H_1}$ queries to the random oracle $H_1$, and at most $q_K$ queries to the key generation oracle. If the decision $(\tau, \epsilon, n)$-BDHE assumption holds in $\mathbb{G}$, then the proposed construction is $(\tau', \epsilon, n)$-secure, where $\tau' = \tau + \mathcal{O}(q_{H_1} + nq_K + m)\tau_1 + \mathcal{O}(m)\tau_2$ with $m = \sum_{i=1}^{n} n_i$. Here, $\tau_1$ and $\tau_2$ denotes the time complexity to compute an exponentiation in $\mathbb{G}$ and $\mathbb{G}_T$, respectively.*

*Proof.* Suppose that there exists a $\tau$-time adversary $\mathcal{A}$, which breaks the proposed scheme with $\text{Adv}_{\text{CP-ABE}}^{\text{IND-sCP-CPA}}(\mathcal{A}) \geq \epsilon$. We build a simulator $\mathcal{S}$ that has advantage $\epsilon$ in solving the decision $n$-BDHE problem in $\mathbb{G}$. $\mathcal{S}$ takes as input a random decision $n$-BDHE challenge $(g, h, \overrightarrow{y}_{g,\alpha,n}, Z)$, where $\overrightarrow{y}_{g,\alpha,n} = (g_1, g_2, \cdots, g_n, g_{n+2}, \cdots, g_{2n})$ and $Z$ is either $\hat{e}(g_{n+1}, h)$ or a random element in $\mathbb{G}_T$. The simulator $\mathcal{S}$ plays the role of the challenger in the IND-sCP-CPA game, and interacts with the adversary $\mathcal{A}$ as follows.

**Init.** The simulator $\mathcal{S}$ receives a challenge access structure $W^* = \bigwedge_{i \in \mathcal{I}_{W^*}} W_i$ specified by the adversary $\mathcal{A}$, where $\mathcal{I}_{W^*} = \{i_1, i_2, \cdots, i_w\}$ with $\omega \leq n$ represents the attribute index set specified in $W^*$. During the game, $\mathcal{A}$ will consult $\mathcal{S}$ for answers to the random oracles $H_0$ and $H_1$. Roughly speaking, these answers are randomly generated, but to maintain the consistency and to avoid collision, $\mathcal{S}$ keeps two tables $\mathcal{L}_1$ and $\mathcal{L}_2$ to store the answers used.

**Setup.** The simulator $\mathcal{S}$ needs to generate a system public key $PK$. $\mathcal{S}$ chooses $j^* \in_R \{1, 2, \cdots, w\}$ and $x, x', y, y' \in_R \mathbb{Z}_p^*$. Then, it does the following:

1. If $i_j \in \mathcal{I}_{W^*} - \{i_{j^*}\}$, suppose $W_{i_j} = v_{i_j, k_{i_j}}$, then $\mathcal{S}$ computes:

$$\left(X_{i_j, k_{i_j}}, Y_{i_j, k_{i_j}}\right) = \left(g^{-H_0(x||i_j||k_{i_j})} g_{n+1-i_j}^{-1}, \hat{e}(g,g)^{H_0(y||i_j||k_{i_j})}\right).$$

Also, for $k \neq k_{i_j}$, $\mathcal{S}$ computes:

$$\left(X_{i_j, k}, Y_{i_j, k}\right) = \left(g^{-H_0(x'||i_j||k)}, \hat{e}(g,g)^{H_0(y'||i_j||k)}\right).$$

2. For $i_{j^*}$, suppose $W_{i_{j^*}} = v_{i_{j^*}, k_{i_{j^*}}}$, then $\mathcal{S}$ does the following:

$$(X_{i_{j^*}, k_{i_{j^*}}}, Y_{i_{j^*}, k_{i_{j^*}}}) = (g^{-H_0(x||i_{j^*}||k_{i_{j^*}})} \prod_{t \in \mathcal{I}_{W^*} - \{i_{j^*}\}} g_{n+1-t}, \hat{e}(g,g)^{H_0(y||i_{j^*}||k_{i_{j^*}})} \hat{e}(g,g)^{\alpha^{n+1}}).$$

Also, for $k \neq k_{i_{j^*}}$, $\mathcal{S}$ computes:

$$(X_{i_{j^*}, k}, Y_{i_{j^*}, k}) = (g^{-H_0(x'||i_{j^*}||k)}, \hat{e}(g,g)^{H_0(y'||i_{j^*}||k)}).$$

3. If $i_j \notin \mathcal{I}_{W^*}$, for $1 \leq k_{i_j} \leq n_{i_j}$, $\mathcal{S}$ computes

$$(X_{i_j, k_{i_j}}, Y_{i_j, k_{i_j}}) = (g^{-H_0(x||i_j||k_{i_j})}, \hat{e}(g,g)^{H_0(y||i_j||k_{i_j})}).$$

Then $PK = \langle g, \{X_{i,k_i}, Y_{i,k_i}\}_{1 \leq i \leq n, 1 \leq k_i \leq n_i} \rangle$ and $\mathcal{S}$ sends $PK$ to $\mathcal{A}$.

**Phase 1.** The adversary $\mathcal{A}$ makes the following queries.

- **Hash Oracle** $\mathcal{O}_{H_0}(\cdot)$: When there is a query on $H_0$ for input '$\cdot$', $\mathcal{S}$ first looks if there is an item containing '$\cdot$' in $\mathcal{L}_0$. If it is, the previous defined value is returned. Otherwise, it chooses $r \in_R \mathbb{Z}_p^*$, adds the entry $\langle \cdot, r \rangle$ to $\mathcal{L}_0$ and returns $r$.
- **Hash Oracle** $\mathcal{O}_{H_1}(sk)$: When there is a query on $H_1$ for input $sk$, $\mathcal{S}$ first looks if there is an item containing $sk$ in $\mathcal{L}_1$. If it is, the previous defined value is returned. Otherwise, it proceeds as follows:
  - If $sk$ corresponds to an attribute list $L$ in the key generation oracle, $\mathcal{S}$ adds the entry $\langle sk, g_{i_j} g^z \rangle$ to $\mathcal{L}_1$ and returns $g_{i_j} g^z$, where $z \in_R \mathbb{Z}_p^*$ and $i_j$ is associated with $L$ and satisfies $L_{i_j} \notin W_{i_j}$.
  - Otherwise, $\mathcal{S}$ randomly chooses $i_j \in_R \{1, 2, \cdots, n\}$, $z \in_R \mathbb{Z}_p^*$, adds the entry $\langle sk, g_{i_j} g^z \rangle$ to $\mathcal{L}_1$ and returns $g_{i_j} g^z$.
- **KeyGen Oracle** $\mathcal{O}_{KeyGen}(L)$: Suppose $\mathcal{A}$ summits an attribute list $L$ in a secret key query. If $L \not\models W^*$, there must exist $i_j \in \mathcal{I}_{W^*}$ such that $L_{i_j} \notin W_{i_j}$. Without loss of generality, assume $L_{i_j} = v_{i_j, \hat{k}_{i_j}}$ and $W_{i_j} = v_{i_j, k_{i_j}}$. $\mathcal{S}$ chooses $sk \in_R \mathbb{Z}_p^*$. Also, $\mathcal{S}$ computes $\overline{\sigma}_{i_j} = \sigma_{i_j, \hat{k}_{i_j}} = g^{H_0(y'||i_j||\hat{k}_{i_j})}(g_{i_j} g^z)^{H_0(x'||i_j||\hat{k}_{i_j})}$. For $t \neq i_j$, $\mathcal{S}$ chooses $z \in_R \mathbb{Z}_p^*$ and computes $\overline{\sigma}_t$ as follows:

  **Case 1.** If $t \in \mathcal{I}_{W^*} - \{i_{j^*}\}$, suppose $L_t = v_{t, k_t}$, $\mathcal{S}$ computes

  $$\overline{\sigma}_t = \sigma_{t, k_t} = g^{H_0(y||t||k_t)}(g_{i_j})^{H_0(x||t||k_t)} g_{n+1-t+i_j}(\overline{X}_t)^{-z}.$$

  **Case 2.** If $t = i_{j^*}$, suppose $L_{i_{j^*}} = v_{i_{j^*}, k_{i_{j^*}}}$, $\mathcal{S}$ computes $\overline{\sigma}_{i_{j^*}}$ as

  $$\overline{\sigma}_{i_{j^*}} = \sigma_{i_{j^*}, k_{i_{j^*}}} = g^{H_0(y||i_{j^*}||k_{i_{j^*}})}(g_{i_j})^{H_0(x||i_{j^*}||k_{i_{j^*}})} \Big( \prod_{k \in \mathcal{I}_{W^*} - \{i_{j^*}, i_j\}} g_{n+1-k+i_j}^{-1} \Big)(\overline{X}_{i_{j^*}})^{-z}.$$

  **Case 3.** If $t \notin \mathcal{I}_{W^*}$, suppose $L_t = v_{t, k_t}$, $\mathcal{S}$ computes

  $$\overline{\sigma}_t = \sigma_{t, k_t} = g^{H_0(y||t||k_t)}(g_{i_j} g^z)^{H_0(x||t||k_t)}.$$

Finally, $\mathcal{S}$ returns $SK_S = \langle sk, \{\overline{\sigma}_i\}_{1 \leq i \leq n}\rangle$.

**Challenge.** The simulator $\mathcal{S}$ sets

$$x_{W^*} = \sum_{t \in \mathcal{I}_{W^*}} H_0(x\|t\|k_t) = \sum_{j=1}^{w} H_0(x\|i_j\|k_{i_j}), y_{W^*} = \sum_{j=1}^{w} H_0(y\|i_j\|k_{i_j}),$$

and defines $\langle X_{W^*}, Y_{W^*}\rangle$ as follows:

$$
\begin{cases}
X_{W^*} & = \overline{X}_{i_{j^*}} \prod_{t \in \mathcal{I}_{W^*} - \{i_{j^*}\}} \overline{X}_t \\
& = \left(g^{-H_0(x\|i_{j^*}\|k_{i_{j^*}})}\right) \prod_{t \in \mathcal{I}_{W^*} - \{i_{j^*}\}} g_{n+1-t} \cdot \prod_{t \in \mathcal{I}_{W^*} - \{i_{j^*}\}} g^{-H_0(x\|t\|k_t)} g_{n+1-t}^{-1} \\
& = g^{-x_{W^*}}, \\
Y_{W^*} & = \overline{Y}_{i_{j^*}} \prod_{t \in \mathcal{I}_{W^*} - \{i_{j^*}\}} \overline{Y}_t \\
& = \hat{e}(g,g)^{H_0(y\|i_{j^*}\|k_{i_{j^*}})} \hat{e}(g,g)^{\alpha^{n+1}} \cdot \prod_{t \in \mathcal{I}_{W^*} - \{i_{j^*}\}} \hat{e}(g,g)^{H_0(y\|t\|k_t)} \\
& = \hat{e}(g,g)^{\sum_{j=1}^{w} H_0(y\|i_j\|k_{i_j}) + \alpha^{n+1}}.
\end{cases}
$$

The adversary $\mathcal{A}$ summits two messages $M_0$ and $M_1$ of equal length. The simulator $\mathcal{S}$ can challenge $\mathcal{A}$ as follows. $\mathcal{S}$ chooses $b \in_R \{0, 1\}$, and computes $C_0^* = M_b \cdot Y_{W^*}^s = M_b Z \hat{e}(g, h)^{y_{W^*}}$, $C_1^* = h$, and $C_2^* = h^{-x_{W^*}}$.

It's noted that the challenge ciphertext $CT_{W^*} = \langle W^*, C_0^*, C_1^*, C_2^*\rangle$ is a valid encryption of $M_b$ whenever $Z = \hat{e}(g_{n+1}, h)$. On the other hand, when $Z$ is a random element in $\mathbb{G}_T$, $CT_{W^*}$ is independent of $b$ in the adversary's view.

**Phase 2:** The same as **Phase 1**.

**Guess:** The adversary $\mathcal{A}$ outputs a guess bit $b'$ of $b$. If $b' = b$, the simulator $\mathcal{S}$ outputs 1 in the decision $n$-BDHE game to guess that $Z = \hat{e}(g_{n+1}, h)$. Otherwise, it outputs 0 to indicate that $Z$ is a random element in $\mathbb{G}_T$. Therefore, if $Z = \hat{e}(g_{n+1}, h)$, then $CT_{W^*}$ is a valid ciphertext and we have

$$\Pr[\mathcal{S}(g, h, \overrightarrow{y}_{g,\alpha,n}, \hat{e}(g_{n+1}, h)) = 1] = \frac{1}{2} + \mathsf{Adv}_{\mathsf{CP\text{-}ABE}}^{\mathsf{IND\text{-}sCP\text{-}CPA}}(\mathcal{A}) \geq \frac{1}{2} + \epsilon.$$

If $Z$ is a random element in $\mathbb{G}_T$, the message $M_b$ is completely hidden from $\mathcal{A}$, and we have

$$\Pr[\mathcal{S}(g, h, \overrightarrow{y}_{g,\alpha,n}, Z) = 1] = \frac{1}{2}.$$

Therefore, $\mathcal{S}$ has advantage at least $\epsilon$ in solving the decision $n$-BDHE problem in $\mathbb{G}$ within time $\tau$. It easily follows that the time complexity of $\mathcal{S}$ is $\tau' = \tau + \mathcal{O}(q_{H_1} + nq_K + \sum_{i=1}^{n} n_i)\tau_1 + \mathcal{O}(\sum_{i=1}^{n} n_i)\tau_2$. $\qquad \square$

## 5    Performance Analysis

In this section, the previous CP-ABE schemes [1,2,6,8,9,12,13,24,26,28] with constant-size ciphertexts and the proposed scheme are compared from the aspects of security and efficiency. The ciphertext size of schemes [1,2,6,8,9,12,13,24,28] and ours is $2|\mathbb{G}| + |\mathbb{G}_T|$ and that of scheme [26] is $|\mathbb{G}| + |\mathbb{G}_T|$. In Table 4, performance comparisons are made in terms of the attribute private key size, the size of system public key and master key, the computation overheads of encryption and decryption, the expressiveness of access policy, the adopted security model, and assumptions. For simplicity, the multiplication cost over groups is ignored in Table 4, where **exp** and **pair** represent an exponentiation operation and a pairing operation, respectively. Let $n$ be the total number of attributes in universe, $\ell$ be the number of attributes the user has, $s$ be the number of attributes the user has to hold in order to match the access policy, and $N$ be the total number of attribute values in the system. We denote the bit length of an element in a group $\mathbb{G}$ by $|\mathbb{G}|$. For asymmetric bilinear pairings [1,13], we use $|\mathbb{G}|$ to represent the average length of $|\mathbb{G}_1|$ and $|\mathbb{G}_2|$. In Table 4, SK, PK, and MSK stand for the attribute secret key, the system public key, and the master secret key. The notation IP represents inner product policy. Furthermore, s-STdM, f-STdM, s-ROM, aMSE-DDH, DBDH, and $q$-BDHE stand for selective security in the standard model, full-security in the standard model, selective-security in the random oracle model, the augmented multi-sequence of exponents decisional Diffie-Hellman assumption, the decisional bilinear Diffie-Hellman assumption, and the decisional bilinear Diffie-Hellman exponent assumption, respectively. Note that $q$ has different values in different schemes.

**Table 4.** Comparisons of CP-ABE schemes with constant-size ciphertexts

| Schemes | Parameter Size | | | Computation Cost | | Policy | Model | Assumption |
|---|---|---|---|---|---|---|---|---|
| | SK | PK | MSK | Enc. | Dec. | | | |
| HLR [1,13] | $(n+s-1)|\mathbb{G}|$ | $(2m+1)|\mathbb{G}|+|\mathbb{G}_T|$ $+(m-1)|\mathbb{Z}_p^*|$ | $|\mathbb{G}|+2|\mathbb{Z}_p^*|$ | $(n+\ell+1)$ exp | 3 pair+$(\ell^2)$ exp | Threshold | s-STdM | aMSE-DDH |
| GZC [9] | $2n(n+s)|\mathbb{G}|$ | $(2n+2)|\mathbb{G}|+|\mathbb{G}_T|$ | $|\mathbb{Z}_p^*|$ | 3 exp | 2 pair+$(2n)$ exp | Threshold | s-STdM | $q$-BDHE |
| AL [2] | $(2n+5)|\mathbb{G}|$ | $(n+2)|\mathbb{G}|+|\mathbb{G}_T|$ | $|\mathbb{G}|$ | 4 exp | 3 pair+$(n-1)$ exp | IP | s-STdM | $q$-BDHE |
| ZHW [28] | $(2n+1)|\mathbb{G}|$ | $(6n+1)|\mathbb{G}|$ | $2|\mathbb{Z}_p^*|$ | 2 exp | $(2\ell+1)$ pair | $\mathbf{AND}_{+,-}^*$ | s-STdM | $q$-BDHE |
| HSM [12] | $(s+2)|\mathbb{G}|$ | $(n+4)|\mathbb{G}|$ | $|\mathbb{Z}_p^*|$ | 3 exp | 2 pair | $\mathbf{AND}_+$ | s-STdM | DBDH |
| TDM [26] | $(2s+1)|\mathbb{G}|$ | $2|\mathbb{G}|+3n|\mathbb{G}_T|$ | $3n|\mathbb{Z}_p^*|$ | 2 exp | 2 pair | $\mathbf{AND}_{+,-}$ | s-STdM | DBDH |
| EM [8] | $2|\mathbb{G}|$ | $(N+2)|\mathbb{G}|+|\mathbb{G}_T|$ | $(N+1)|\mathbb{Z}_p^*|$ | 3 exp | 2 pair | $\mathbf{AND}_m$ | s-STdM | DBDH |
| RD [24] | $2|\mathbb{G}|$ | $(N+2)|\mathbb{G}|+|\mathbb{G}_T|$ | $2|\mathbb{G}|$ | 3 exp | 2 pair | $\mathbf{AND}_m$ | f-STdM | New |
| CZF [6] | $(n+1)|\mathbb{G}|$ | $2n|\mathbb{G}|+2n|\mathbb{G}_T|$ | $4n|\mathbb{Z}_p^*|$ | 3 exp | 2 pair | $\mathbf{AND}_{+,-}^*$ | s-STdM | $q$-BDHE |
| Proposed | $n|\mathbb{G}|+|\mathbb{Z}_p^*|$ | $(N+1)|\mathbb{G}|+N|\mathbb{G}_T|$ | $2|\mathbb{Z}_p^*|$ | 3 exp | 2 pair | $\mathbf{AND}_m^*$ | s-ROM | $q$-BDHE |

In Table 4, all the CP-ABE schemes have small and constant-size ciphertexts. However, the schemes in [1,2,9,13,28] suffer an efficiency drawback that the decryption cost is not constant in terms of the the number of **exp** or **pair**. Although enjoying constant computation costs, one drawback of schemes [8,12,24,26] is that the access policy fails to support wildcards. To decrypt a ciphertext, DU's attributes need to be completely identical to the access policy. In essence, the wildcards used in the ciphertext policy of [26] fail to play the role of "don't care". The CP-ABE scheme [6] is very efficient in terms of ciphertext length and computation costs while it only supports $\mathbf{AND}_{+,-}^*$. The proposed CP-ABE construction is comparable to other schemes and the access policy supports $\mathbf{AND}_m^*$. On the other hand, in all the schemes, only the scheme [24] achieves full security, and the schemes [1,2,6,8,9,12,13,26,28] and ours are selective-secure. However, the scheme [24] is proven secure under four new assumptions in composite order bilinear groups, which are denoted by **New**. The others are based on groups of prime order. Notice that a fully-secure scheme is also presented in [2], and it is proven secure under DBDH and D-Linear assumptions, where D-Linear represents the decisional linear assumption. However, the ciphertext length is $9|\mathbb{G}| + |\mathbb{G}_T|$ and the decryption phase involves nine **pair**. The proposed scheme is proven secure in the random oracle model, and others are proven secure in the standard model. In addition, the scheme [1,13] is proven secure under the aMSE-DDH assumption, which is not a standard one, and the schemes [2,6,9,28] and ours are proven secure under the decisional BDHE assumption. The schemes [8,12,26] are proven secure under the DBDH assumption. In general, the proposed CP-ABE scheme enjoys desirable properties of small and constant computation cost and constant-size ciphertexts, which is very suitable for practical scenarios where computation and bandwidth issues are major concerns.

## 6  Conclusion

In this paper, to realize secure and efficient attribute-based data sharing systems, we propose a CP-ABE scheme, which features small and constant computation cost and constant-size ciphertexts and it can efficiently support $\text{AND}_m^*$ policy. The proposed scheme is proven selective-secure in the random oracle model under the decision $n$-BDHE assumption, where $n$ denotes the total number of attributes in universe. In addition, extensive performance comparisons indicate that the proposed CP-ABE scheme is extremely suitable for real-world applications.

**Acknowledgements.** We are grateful to the referees for their invaluable suggestions. This work is supported by the National Natural Science Foundation of China (Grant Nos. 61402366, 61272455, 61272457, 61472091, 61472472, 61272037, and 61100224), the Ministry of Industry and Information Key Project Fund (Grant No. 2013ZX03002004), the National Science and Technology Major Projects (Grant No. 2012ZX03002003), the Natural Science Foundation of Shaanxi Province (Grant No. 2013JZ020), and the Fundamental Research Funds for the Central Universities (Grant Nos. K50511010001, and JY10000901034).

## References

1. Attrapadung, N., Herranz, J., Laguillaumie, F., Libert, B., De Panafieu, E., Ràfols, C.: Attribute-based encryption schemes with constant-size ciphertexts. Theoretical Computer Science 422, 15–38 (2012)
2. Attrapadung, N., Libert, B.: Functional encryption for inner product: Achieving constant-size ciphertexts with adaptive security or support for negation. In: Nguyen, P.Q., Pointcheval, D. (eds.) PKC 2010. LNCS, vol. 6056, pp. 384–402. Springer, Heidelberg (2010)
3. Attrapadung, N., Libert, B., de Panafieu, E.: Expressive key-policy attribute-based encryption with constant-size ciphertexts. In: Catalano, D., Fazio, N., Gennaro, R., Nicolosi, A. (eds.) PKC 2011. LNCS, vol. 6571, pp. 90–108. Springer, Heidelberg (2011)

4. Bethencourt, J., Sahai, A., Waters, B.: Ciphertext-policy attribute-based encryption. In: IEEE Symposium on Security and Privacy 2007, pp. 321–334. IEEE Press, Los Alamitos (2007)
5. Chen, C., Chen, J., Lim, H.W., Zhang, Z., Feng, D., Ling, S., Wang, H.: Fully secure attribute-based systems with short ciphertexts/signatures and threshold access structures. In: Dawson, E. (ed.) CT-RSA 2013. LNCS, vol. 7779, pp. 50–67. Springer, Heidelberg (2013)
6. Chen, C., Zhang, Z., Feng, D.: Efficient ciphertext policy attribute-based encryption with constant-size ciphertext and constant computation-cost. In: Boyen, X., Chen, X. (eds.) ProvSec 2011. LNCS, vol. 6980, pp. 84–101. Springer, Heidelberg (2011)
7. Cheung, L., Newport, C.: Provably secure ciphertext policy abe. In: ACM Conference on Computer and Communication Security 2007, pp. 456–465. ACM, New York (2007)
8. Emura, K., Miyaji, A., Nomura, A., Omote, K., Soshi, M.: A ciphertext-policy attribute-based encryption scheme with constant ciphertext length. In: Bao, F., Li, H., Wang, G. (eds.) ISPEC 2009. LNCS, vol. 5451, pp. 13–23. Springer, Heidelberg (2009)
9. Ge, A., Zhang, R., Chen, C., Ma, C., Zhang, Z.: Threshold ciphertext policy attribute-based encryption with constant size ciphertexts. In: Susilo, W., Mu, Y., Seberry, J. (eds.) ACISP 2012. LNCS, vol. 7372, pp. 336–349. Springer, Heidelberg (2012)
10. Goyal, V., Pandey, O., Sahai, A., Waters, B.: Attribute-based encryption for fine-grained access control of encrypted data. In: ACM Conference on Computer and Communication Security 2006, pp. 89–98. ACM, New York (2006)
11. Green, M., Hohenberger, S., Waters, B.: Outsourcing the decryption of abe ciphertexts. In: USENIX Conference on Security 2011. USENIX Association, Berkeley (2011), http://static.usenix.org/event/sec11/tech/full_papers/Green.pdf
12. Han, J., Susilo, W., Mu, Y., Yan, J.: Attribute-based oblivious access control. The Computer Journal 55(10), 1202–1215 (2012)
13. Herranz, J., Laguillaumie, F., Ràfols, C.: Constant size ciphertexts in threshold attribute-based encryption. In: Nguyen, P.Q., Pointcheval, D. (eds.) PKC 2010. LNCS, vol. 6056, pp. 19–34. Springer, Heidelberg (2010)
14. Katz, J., Sahai, A., Waters, B.: Predicate encryption supporting disjunctions, polynomial equations, and inner products. In: Smart, N. (ed.) EUROCRYPT 2008. LNCS, vol. 4965, pp. 146–162. Springer, Heidelberg (2008)
15. Lai, J., Deng, R.H., Guan, C., Weng, J.: Attribute-based encryption with verifiable outsourced decryption. IEEE Transactions on Information Forensics and Security 8(8), 1343–1354 (2013)
16. Lai, J., Deng, R.H., Li, Y.: Expressive cp-abe with partially hidden access structures. In: ACM Symposium on Information, Computer and Communications Security 2012, pp. 18–19. ACM, New York (2012)
17. Li, J., Chen, X., Li, J., Jia, C., Ma, J., Lou, W.: Fine-grained access control system based on outsourced attribute-based encryption. In: Crampton, J., Jajodia, S., Mayes, K. (eds.) ESORICS 2013. LNCS, vol. 8134, pp. 592–609. Springer, Heidelberg (2013)
18. Li, J., Ren, K., Zhu, B., Wan, Z.: Privacy-aware attribute-based encryption with user accountability. In: Samarati, P., Yung, M., Martinelli, F., Ardagna, C.A. (eds.) ISC 2009. LNCS, vol. 5735, pp. 347–362. Springer, Heidelberg (2009)

19. Li, Q., Xiong, H., Zhang, F., Zeng, S.: An expressive decentralizing kp-abe scheme with constant-size ciphertext. International Journal of Network Security 15(3), 161–170 (2013)
20. Liu, Z., Cao, Z., Wong, D.S.: Blackbox traceable cp-abe: how to catch people leaking their keys by selling decryption devices on ebay. In: ACM Conference on Computer and Communication Security 2013, pp. 475–486. ACM, New York (2013)
21. Nishide, T., Yoneyama, K., Ohta, K.: Attribute-based encryption with partially hidden encryptor-specified access structures. In: Bellovin, S.M., Gennaro, R., Keromytis, A.D., Yung, M. (eds.) ACNS 2008. LNCS, vol. 5037, pp. 111–129. Springer, Heidelberg (2008)
22. Ostrovsky, R., Sahai, A., Waters, B.: Attribute-based encryption with non-monotonic access structures. In: ACM Conference on Computer and Communication Security 2007, pp. 195–203. ACM, New York (2007)
23. Rao, Y.S., Dutta, R.: Computationally efficient dual-policy attribute based encryption with short ciphertext. In: Susilo, W., Reyhanitabar, R. (eds.) ProvSec 2013. LNCS, vol. 8209, pp. 288–308. Springer, Heidelberg (2013)
24. Rao, Y.S., Dutta, R.: Recipient anonymous ciphertext-policy attribute based encryption. In: Bagchi, A., Ray, I. (eds.) ICISS 2013. LNCS, vol. 8303, pp. 329–344. Springer, Heidelberg (2013)
25. Sahai, A., Waters, B.: Fuzzy identity-based encryption. In: Cramer, R. (ed.) EUROCRYPT 2005. LNCS, vol. 3494, pp. 457–473. Springer, Heidelberg (2005)
26. Tran, P.V.X., Dinh, T.N., Miyaji, A.: Efficient ciphertext-policy abe with constant ciphertext length. In: IEEE Conference on Computing and Convergence Technology 2012, pp. 543–549. IEEE Press, Los Alamitos (2012)
27. Zhang, Y., Chen, X., Li, J., Wong, D.S., Li, H.: Anonymous attribute-based encryption supporting efficient decryption test. In: ACM Symposium on Information, Computer and Communications Security 2013, pp. 511–516. ACM, New York (2013)
28. Zhou, Z., Huang, D., Wang, Z.: Efficient privacy-preserving ciphertext-policy attribute based encryption and broadcast encryption. IEEE Transactions on Computers (2013), doi:10.1109/TC.2013.200

# Attribute-Based Signcryption : Signer Privacy, Strong Unforgeability and IND-CCA2 Security in Adaptive-Predicates Attack

Tapas Pandit[1], Sumit Kumar Pandey[2], and Rana Barua[1]

[1] Indian Statistical Institute, Kolkata, India
[2] C R RAO AIMSCS, Hyderbad, India

**Abstract.** An Attribute-Based Signcryption (ABSC) is a natural extension of Attribute-Based Encryption (ABE) and Attribute-Based Signature (ABS), where we have the message confidentiality and authenticity together. Since the signer privacy is captured in security of ABS, it is quite natural to expect that the signer privacy will also be preserved in ABSC. In this paper, first we propose an ABSC scheme which is *weak existential unforgeable, IND-CCA2* secure in *adaptive-predicates* attack and achieves *signer privacy*. Secondly, by applying strongly unforgeable one-time signature (OTS), the above scheme is lifted to an ABSC scheme to attain *strong existential unforgeability* in *adaptive-predicates* model. Both the ABSC schemes are constructed on common setup, i.e the public parameters and key are same for both the encryption and signature modules. Our first construction is in the flavor of $Ct\mathcal{E}\&\mathcal{S}$ paradigm, except one extra component that will be computed using both signature components and ciphertext components. The second proposed construction follows a new paradigm (extension of $Ct\mathcal{E}\&\mathcal{S}$), we call it "Commit then Encrypt and Sign then Sign" ($Ct\mathcal{E}\&St\mathcal{S}$). The last signature is done using a strong OTS scheme. Since the non-repudiation is achieved by $Ct\mathcal{E}\&\mathcal{S}$ paradigm, our systems also achieve the same.

**Keywords:** Attribute-based encryption, Attribute-based signature, Attribute-based signcryption, Commitment scheme.

## 1 Introduction

In the last couple of years, attribute-based encryption (ABE) has become a privilege way for encrypting a message for many users. In this encryption, a message is encoded with a policy and a key is labeled with a set of attributes. This form of ABE is known as ciphertext-policy attribute-based encryption (CP-ABE) and in its dual form, key-policy attribute-based encryption (KP-ABE), the role of policy and the set of attributes are interchanged. Since its introduction (Fuzzy Identity-Based Encryption) [35] till to date many schemes have been proposed, some of them are CP-ABE [4,22,30,39,21], some of them are KP-ABE [16,33,22,30,2], most of them are selectively secure under chosen plaintext attack (CPA) [16,39,33,2], few of them are adaptively secure under CPA [30,22,32] and

S.S.M. Chow et al. (Eds.): ProvSec 2014, LNCS 8782, pp. 274–290, 2014.

very few of them are secure under chosen ciphertext attack (CCA) [30] for general policies. But, there are techniques [9,7,40] to convert a CPA secure scheme to CCA secure scheme. However, the schemes that are adaptively secure under CCA in the standard model seem to be more powerful.

Side by side with ABE, attribute-based signature (ABS) also draws much attention due to its versatility. Unlike the traditional signature scheme, it captures unforgeability for a policy (group of users) and signer privacy. Similar to ABE, in attribute-based signature a message is signed under a policy and a key is associated with a set of attributes. We call this form of ABS as CP-ABS [31,26,23,27] and its dual form, where the role of the policy and the set of attributes are reversed, is called KP-ABS [36]. Similar to the traditional signature, ABS can be weak existential unforgeable[1] [31,26,27,23] or strong existential unforgeable under chosen message attack (CMA). Most of the ABS [36] proposed so far are weak existential unforgeable. But, by a simple technique [20] one can obtain strongly unforgeable signature scheme from weak unforgeable scheme. Since here the message is signed under a policy, similar to ABE there are two types of unforgeability, selective-predicate [36,23] and adaptive-predicate [31,26,27].

Zheng [41] introduced the concept of signcryption that provides an efficient way of achieving the message confidentiality and an authenticity together as compared to "Sign then Encrypt" approach. But they have not given any formal security proof as no formal security model was known to them. Then J.Baek et al. [3] first formalized the security notion for signcryption. Later An et al. [1] proposed the generic constructions of signcryption in three paradigm, "Sign then Encrypt $(St\mathcal{E})$", "Encrypt then Sign $(\mathcal{E}tS)$" and "Commit then Encrypt and Sign $(Ct\mathcal{E}\&S)$". As compared to $St\mathcal{E}$ and $\mathcal{E}tS$ paradigms, $Ct\mathcal{E}\&S$ has an advantage that in Signcrypt (resp. Unsigncrypt) both the routines, Encrypt and Sign (resp. Decrypt and Ver) can be executed in parallel, i.e., in $Ct\mathcal{E}\&S$ paradigm both Signcrypt and Unsigncrypt run faster as compared to other two paradigms. The generic constructions in [1] were proven in two users model in PKI setting, but using some minor modification one can have the same security in multi user setting. Since it's debut several signcryption schemes [29,28,24,25,13,11,8] have been proposed either in PKI setting or in IBE setting.

Meanwhile S.Haber et al. [17] first proposed the idea of combining public-key schemes, where an encryption scheme and a signature scheme are combined to have the common public parameters and the key. But the Encrypt and Decrypt (resp. Sign and Ver) of the encryption (resp. signature) scheme were kept unchanged in the combined scheme. The security model is called joint security of the combined public-key schemes, where in message confidentiality the adversary is given only the encryption component of the challenge message but not the signature and in authenticity the adversary is has to forge a signature. In both cases, the adversary will get access to some oracles. Later, Vasco et al. showed in [37] that the IBE scheme [6] and the IBS scheme [19] can be combined in the joint security model. However, in this joint security model semantic

---

[1] Unless stated, existential unforgeable means weak existential unforgeable throughout this paper.

security of the message is not possible if the signature of the challenge message is additionally given with the challenge ciphertext.

It is natural to ask whether signcryption can be extended to the context of attribute-based cryptography. It was Gagné et. al. [15] who first answered the question but the policy considered in their construction (called attribute-based signcryption) was a threshold policy. Basically in their construction, the structure of Fuzzy IBE in [35] and a new efficient threshold ABS were used as encryption primitive and signature primitive respectively. Subsequently, Emura et al. [14] proposed a dynamic attribute-based signcryption (ABSC), where access structures of encryptors can be changed without re-issuing the secret keys of the users. Both the signcryption scheme were shown to be secure (confidentiality and authenticity) under selective-predicate attack. Since ABSC is a natural

**Table 1.** Performance of our CP-ABSC scheme

| Scheme | CS | Key size | Signcryption size | Signcrypt time | Unsigncrypt time |
|--------|----|----------|-------------------|----------------|------------------|
| [15] | No | $2|A_s|, 3|A_e|$ | $\mathcal{O}(|\omega_s| + |\omega_e|)$ | $\mathcal{O}(|\omega_s| + |\omega_e|)$ | $\mathcal{O}(|\omega_s| + d)$ |
| [14] | No | $2|A_s|, \theta_e$ | $\mathcal{O}(\ell_s + |\mathcal{U}_e| + \mathfrak{S})$ | $\mathcal{O}(\ell_s + |\mathcal{U}_e| + \mathfrak{S})$ | $\mathcal{O}(\ell_s + |\mathcal{U}_e| + \mathfrak{S})$ |
| [10] | Yes | $\mathfrak{M}|A| + 2$ | $2\ell_s + \ell_e + 4$ | $\mathcal{O}(\ell_s) + \mathcal{O}(\ell_e)$ | $\mathcal{O}(\ell_s) + \mathcal{O}(|\mathcal{I}_B|)$ |
| Our | Yes | $\mathfrak{M}|A| + 2$ | $2\ell_s + 2\ell_e + 5 + \wp$ | $Max\{\mathcal{O}(\ell_s), \mathcal{O}(\ell_e)\}$ | $Max\{\mathcal{O}(\ell_s), \mathcal{O}(|\mathcal{I}_B|)\}$ |

*In table 1, CS and |A| stand for the common setup and cardinality of the set A respectively. The schemes supporting the common setup have the single key extraction algorithm and in this case, we use A to indicate the user set of attributes. Otherwise two set of attributes, $A_s$ and $A_e$ are used respectively for signcryption and unsigncryption. In later case, the individual key sizes are separated by comma (,). Let $\ell_s$ and $\ell_e$ respectively denote the size of the signer policy $\Gamma_s$ and receiver policy $\Gamma_e$. $\mathfrak{M}$ stands for maximum # repetition of an attribute in an access policy. Let $\omega_s$, $\omega_e$ and d respectively represent the signing set of attributes, encryption set of attributes and threshold value in [15]. $\mathcal{U}_e$ and $\mathfrak{S}$ respectively denote the attribute universe involved in encryption and length of verification key for OTS. $\theta_e = 2|A_e| + 2\mathfrak{S} + 1$. The sizes of the commitment and the one-time signature are described by $\wp$. Let $|\mathcal{I}_B|$ be the minimum # row in the receiver policy $\Gamma_e$ labeled by the set B to compute the target vector $\mathbf{1}$. The key size and signcryption size are measured by # group elements involved in the key and signcryption respectively. The time for signcrypt is # exponentiations to construct a signcryption, whereas the time for unsigncrypt is both # exponentiations and # pairings.*

**Table 2.** Security features of our CP-ABSC scheme

| Scheme | Type | SAS | EAS | Auth. | Conf. | NR | SP | APM |
|--------|------|-----|-----|-------|-------|----|----|-----|
| [15] | KP | Threshold | Threshold | wEUF-CMA | IND-CCA2 | No | NK | No |
| [14] | CP | MAT | AGW | sEUF-CMA | IND-CCA2 | Yes | No | No |
| [10] | CP | MSP | MSP | sEUF-CMA | IND-CCA2 | Yes | Yes | No |
| Our | CP | MSP | MSP | sEUF-CMA | IND-CCA2 | Yes | Yes | Yes |

*In table 2, the abbreviations SAS, EAS, Auth., Conf., NR, SP, APM, NK, MAT, MSP, AGW, KP and CP stand for signing access structure, encryption access structure, signcryption unforgeability, confidentiality of message, non-repudiation, signer-privacy, adaptive-predicates model, not known, monotone access tree, monotone span program, AND-gate with wildcard respectively, key-policy and ciphertext-policy.*

extension of both ABE and ABS, and the signer privacy is preserved in ABS, so the signer privacy property is supposed to be inherited in ABSC as well. But the later ABSC scheme lacks the property of signer privacy.

Recently Chen et al. [10] proposed a scheme in combined public-key framework but in attribute-based flavor. In their scheme the ABE and ABS modules have the same public parameters and the key distribution. Their scheme is based on the construction of Waters [39] and was shown to be secure (selectively) in the joint security model. Then they extended it to have a combined attribute-based signcryption ($St\mathcal{E}$ paradigm).

## 1.1   Our Approach and Contribution

Our constructions are almost in the flavor of $Ct\mathcal{E}\&S$ paradigm. In $Ct\mathcal{E}\&S$ paradigm, a message $m$ is first committed to $(\check{c}, \check{d})$, then the commitment part $\check{c}$ and decommitment part $\check{d}$ are respectively signed to $\sigma$ and encrypted to $\varrho$ in parallel to produce the signcryption $\Upsilon := (\check{c}, \sigma, \varrho)$. Similarly, in unsigncryption the verification (to verify $\sigma$) and the decryption (to get the $\check{d}$) run in parallel to extract the message as $m := \mathsf{Open}(\check{c}, \check{d})$. But this generalized construction [1] never achieves strong unforgeability (resp. CCA2 security) in the insider security model as long as the primitive encryption algorithm (resp. the primitive sign algorithm) is probabilistic.

Our first CP-ABSC construction achieves *signer privacy, adaptive-predicates weak unforgeability*, and *adaptive-predicates IND-CCA2* security in the standard model. Moreover, our constructions support the combined public-key environment of "Combined Public-Key scheme", viz, both the primitives, encryption and signature have a common setup, i.e., the public parameters and key are identical. Suppose we want a signcryption for a message $m$ under the policies[2] $(\Gamma_s, \Gamma_e)$. Let $\sigma := (\boldsymbol{S}_0, \ldots, \boldsymbol{S}_{\ell_s})$ be the signature for $(\check{c}, \Gamma_s)$, generated by a primitive CP-ABS, where $(\check{c}, \check{d}) \longleftarrow \mathsf{Commit}(m)$. Let $\varrho_0 := (\boldsymbol{C}_0, \ldots, \boldsymbol{C}_{\ell_e})$ be the ciphertext generated by a primitive CP-ABE that conceals $\check{d}$ under a policy $\Gamma_e$. To achieve the CCA2 security, we first bind all the components $\boldsymbol{S}_i$'s and $\boldsymbol{C}_i$'s through a collision resistant hash function $H_e : \{0, 1\}^* \longrightarrow \mathbb{Z}_N$ to $h_e := H_e(\Gamma_e, \Gamma_s, \check{c}, \varrho_0, \sigma)$. Then we encode $h_e$ using a secret $s_e$ involved in the encryption of the primitive CP-ABE and Boneh-Boyen hash technique [5] to an additional ciphertext component $C_{\ell_e+1}$. This basically prevents the adversary $\mathscr{A}$ from changing the challenge signcryption except the component $C_{\ell_e+1}$, but if it gets changed then it will be recognized via a verification process. If the primitive CP-ABS scheme is weak unforgeable and the commitment scheme has relaxed-binding property, then proposed CP-ABSC scheme is shown to be weak unforgeable.

---

[2]  $\Gamma_s$ and $\Gamma_e$ are respectively signer policy (i.e., on whom behalf, signer signs m) and receiver policy (i.e., who will be eligible for this plaintext $m$).

Our second CP-ABSC scheme additionally achieves *strong unforgeability* in *adaptive-predicates* attack[3]. First notice that in the former scheme the adversary can modify the replied signcryption for a message $(m, \Gamma_s, \Gamma_e)$ : since $\mathscr{A}$ has access to key $\mathcal{SK}_A$ with $\Gamma_e(A) = \mathsf{True}$, so it can extract $\breve{d}$ from $\varrho$ and then re-encrypts it to get modified (new) signcryption for the same message $(m, \Gamma_s, \Gamma_e)$. Therefore, the former scheme does not achieve the strong unforgeability. The later scheme is obtained by combining the former scheme and a strong one-time signature (OTS) scheme. Essentially, we sign $h_e \| C_{\ell_e + 1}$ using strong OTS scheme to guarantee that the signcryption for a message can not be altered even if the adversary knows the unsigncryption key. Surprisingly, the strong unforgeability of this CP-ABSC scheme relies only on the weak unforgeability of the primitive CP-ABS scheme and the strong unforgeability of the primitive strong OTS scheme, i.e., no more relaxed-binding property of the primitive commitment scheme is required.

The primitive CP-ABE scheme considered here is a (CCA2) variant[4] of CP-ABE scheme of Lewko et al. in [22]. Our primitive CP-ABS scheme (in section 3) has the similar structure as of ABS scheme in the combined public-key framework [10] except - (a) the encoding from hash of message to group element, and (b) the bilinear pairing groups. The ABS scheme of [10] was proven in selective-predicate model, whereas ours is shown to be secure in adaptive-predicate model. Since the adaptive security (confidentiality and authenticity) is one of the main motivations of our work, we must require the adaptive-unforgeability of the primitive CP-ABS scheme. Therefore, the ABS of [10] can not be applied directly to our CP-ABSC schemes. Another reason for moving prime to composite order pairing groups is to fit the ABS scheme to CP-ABE scheme of [22]. There are many commitment schemes [12,18,34] suitable for our systems, but we use them as a black box in our constructions.

**Summary of Our Contribution.** To the best of our knowledge, this is the first scheme having strong unforgeability and IND-CCA2 security in adaptive-predicates model. Since our solution supports $\mathcal{CtE\&S}$ paradigm, Signcrypt and Unsigncrypt run faster as compared to other paradigms, viz, $\mathcal{EtS}$ and $\mathcal{StE}$. Our system is based on the common setup, i.e the public parameters and key are same for both the encryption and signature module. In addition it supports non-repudiation, dynamic property and signer privacy. A details comparisons of performance and the security features between our scheme and others are given in table 1 and table 2. The proofs of confidentiality and unforgeability are based on the dual system methodology of [38]. Due to space restriction, all the missing proofs will be given in full version of this paper.

**Discussion.** We remark that our proposed solution is not generic. One may think that applying the generic construction [1] it is possible but this is not the

---

[3] We remark that adaptive-predicates IND-CCA2 security (resp. existential unforgeability) and IND-CCA2 security (resp. existential unforgeability) in adaptive-predicates attack both carry the same meaning.

[4] This is not explicitly given but the signcryption scheme implicitly contains it.

case. Indeed, $\mathcal{CtE\&S}$ paradigm preserves only weak unforgeability and[5] IND-gCCA2. But here our proposed scheme attains both strong unforgeability and IND-CCA2 security in adaptive-predicates attack. Further, our solution supports the common setup for encryption and signature, so the security proof can not carry through as in $\mathcal{CtE\&S}$ paradigm. For our system, the considered form of ABS, where a signature is associated with a policy and key is labeled by a set of attributes, is called CP-ABS.

## 1.2    Organization

This paper is organized as follows. Section 2 contains the preliminaries. A CP-ABS scheme and its security are provided respectively in section 3 and 4. A adaptive-predicates weak unforgeable and IND-CCA2 secure CP-ABSC scheme and its security are given respectively in section 5 and 6. In section 7, our adaptive-predicates strongly unforgeable and IND-CCA2 secure CP-ABSC scheme and its security are demonstrated.

# 2    Preliminaries

Basic notation, definitions and hardness assumptions are provided in this section. For definition and security model of commitment scheme, ABS, strongly unforgeable OTS and CP-ABSC, refer to [1], [26], [30] and appendix A respectively. For access structure and linear secret sharing scheme, see [22].

*Notation.* Let $[\ell] := \{i \in \mathbb{N} : 1 \leq i \leq \ell\}$, $g_T := e(g, g)$, where $e$ is a bilinear pairing. Let the vectors $\mathbf{1}$ and $\mathbf{0}$ respectively denote $(1, 0, \ldots, 0)$ and $(0, 0, \ldots, 0)$, where the length of the vectors will be understood from the context. Let $\mathbf{Y} := (y_1, \ldots, y_n)$ and $\mathbf{W} := (w_1, \ldots, w_n)$ be two vectors, then $\mathbf{Y}.\mathbf{W}$ denotes the dot product of $\mathbf{Y}$ and $\mathbf{W}$, i.e., $\mathbf{Y}.\mathbf{W} := \sum_{i=1}^{n} y_i w_i$. For $S \subset \mathbb{Z}_N^{\ell_s}$ and $\boldsymbol{\alpha} \in \mathbb{Z}_N^{\ell_s}$, we define $\boldsymbol{\alpha} + S := \{\boldsymbol{\alpha} + \boldsymbol{\beta} \mid \boldsymbol{\beta} \in S\}$. For a set $X$, $x \xleftarrow{\text{R}} X$ denotes that $x$ is randomly picked from $X$ according to the distribution $R$. Likewise, $x \xleftarrow{\text{U}} X$ indicates $x$ is uniformly selected from $X$. To better understand the schemes, we use two subscripts, $s$ and $e$ respectively for encryption and signature. Through out this paper, we will use the symbol $\Gamma := (M, \rho)$ for monotone span programs, where $\ell \times n$ stands for the order of the matrix $M$. For an access structure $\Gamma$ and a set attributes $A$, $\Gamma(A)$ stands for boolean variable, i.e, $\Gamma(A) = \mathsf{True}$ if $A$ satisfies $\Gamma$, else $\Gamma(A) = \mathsf{False}$. For a matrix $M_e$ (resp. $M_s$), the symbol $\boldsymbol{M}_e^{(i)}$ (resp. $\boldsymbol{M}_s^{(i)}$) represents the $i^{th}$ row of the matrix $M_e$ (resp. $M_s$).

*Composite Order Bilinear Groups.* Let $\mathcal{G}$ be an algorithm which takes $1^\kappa$ as a security parameter and returns a description of a composite order bilinear groups, $\mathcal{J} := (N := p_1 p_2 p_3, \mathbb{G}, \mathbb{G}_T, e)$, where $p_1, p_2, p_3$ are three distinct primes and $\mathbb{G}$ and $\mathbb{G}_T$ are cyclic groups of order $N$ and $e : \mathbb{G} \times \mathbb{G} \to \mathbb{G}_T$ is a map such that

---

[5] IND-gCCA2 is a weaker security notion than IND-CCA2. For details refer to [1].

1. (Bilinear) $\forall g, h \in \mathbb{G}, a, b \in \mathbb{Z}_N, e(g^a, h^b) = e(g, h)^{ab}$
2. (Non-degenerate) $\exists g \in \mathbb{G}$ such that $e(g, g)$ has order $N$ in $\mathbb{G}_T$

Let $\mathbb{G}_{p_1}, \mathbb{G}_{p_2}$ and $\mathbb{G}_{p_3}$ respectively denote the subgroups of $\mathbb{G}$ of order $p_1, p_2$ and $p_3$. Let $h_i \in \mathbb{G}_{p_i}$ and $h_j \in \mathbb{G}_{p_j}$ be arbitrary elements with $i \neq j$, then $e(h_i, h_j) = 1$. This property is called orthogonal property of $\mathbb{G}_{p_1}, \mathbb{G}_{p_2}, \mathbb{G}_{p_3}$.

*Hardness Assumptions.* We describe here three Decisional SubGroup (DSG) assumptions [22] for 3 primes, DSG1, DSG2 and DSS3 in composite order bilinear groups. Let $\mathcal{J} := (N = p_1 p_2 p_3, \mathbb{G}, \mathbb{G}_T, e) \xleftarrow{\text{U}} \mathcal{G}(1^\lambda)$ be the common parameters for each assumptions.

[DSG1]. Let $g \xleftarrow{\text{U}} \mathbb{G}_{p_1}, X_3 \xleftarrow{\text{U}} \mathbb{G}_{p_3}, T_0 \xleftarrow{\text{U}} \mathbb{G}_{p_1}, T_1 \xleftarrow{\text{U}} \mathbb{G}_{p_1 p_2}$. Define $\mathcal{D} := (\mathcal{J}, g, X_3)$

[DSG2]. Let $g, X_1 \xleftarrow{\text{U}} \mathbb{G}_{p_1}, X_2, Y_2 \xleftarrow{\text{U}} \mathbb{G}_{p_2}, X_3, Y_3 \xleftarrow{\text{U}} \mathbb{G}_{p_3}, T_0 \xleftarrow{\text{U}} \mathbb{G}_{p_1 p_3}, T_1 \xleftarrow{\text{U}} \mathbb{G}$. Then set $\mathcal{D} := (\mathcal{J}, g, X_1 X_2, Y_2 Y_3, X_3)$

[DSG3]. Let $\alpha, s \xleftarrow{\text{U}} \mathbb{Z}_N, g \xleftarrow{\text{U}} \mathbb{G}_{p_1}, X_2, Y_2, Z_2 \xleftarrow{\text{U}} \mathbb{G}_{p_2}, X_3 \xleftarrow{\text{U}} \mathbb{G}_{p_3}, T_0 := e(g,g)^{\alpha s}, T_1 \xleftarrow{\text{U}} \mathbb{G}_T$. Define $\mathcal{D} := (\mathcal{J}, g, g^\alpha X_2, g^s Y_2, Z_2, X_3)$

The advantage of an algorithm $\mathscr{A}$ in breaking DSGi, for $i = 1, 2, 3$ is defined by

$$\text{Adv}_{\mathscr{A}}^{\text{DSGi}}(\kappa) = |Pr[\mathscr{A}(\mathcal{D}, T_0) = 1] - Pr[\mathscr{A}(\mathcal{D}, T_1) = 1]|$$

We say that the DSGi assumption holds if for every PPT algorithm $\mathscr{A}$, the advantage $\text{Adv}_{\mathscr{A}}^{\text{DSGi}}(\kappa)$ is at most negligible in security parameter $\kappa$.

# 3    Basic Ciphertext-Policy Attribute-Based Signature

Illustrated here is a basic ciphertext-policy attribute-based signature (CP-ABS) scheme for monotone span program (MSP) in the composite order pairing groups $(N := p_1 p_2 p_3, \mathbb{G} := \mathbb{G}_{p_1} \times \mathbb{G}_{p_2} \times \mathbb{G}_{p_2}, \mathbb{G}_T, e)$, for 3 distinct primes $p_1$, $p_2$ and $p_3$. The subgroup $\mathbb{G}_{p_2}$ has no role in this scheme but it will be used to prove the security. As we mentioned earlier that the proposed CP-ABS scheme has the similar structure to that of [10] except some minor modifications, viz., the encoding function from hash of messages to group elements and pairing groups. To have the unforgeability of the ABS scheme in adaptive-predicate model, we allow such modifications. In this basic CP-ABS construction, the policies, i.e., MSPs are restricted to have each entry of row labeling function $\rho_s$ to be distinct. In other word, the row labeling functions $\rho_s$ of the monotone span programs $\Gamma_s := (M_s, \rho_s)$ are injective. From this basic CP-ABS construction one can easily lift to full CP-ABS construction by a mechanism described in appendix B.

Setup$(1^\kappa, \mathcal{U})$: It executes $\mathcal{G}(1^\kappa)$ to have composite order bilinear groups descriptor, $\mathcal{J} := (N := p_1 p_2 p_3, \mathbb{G}, \mathbb{G}_T, e)$ with known factorization $p_1, p_2$ and $p_3$ of $N$. It chooses $g \xleftarrow{\text{U}} \mathbb{G}_{p_1}, X_3 \xleftarrow{\text{U}} \mathbb{G}_{p_3}, a, a_s, b_s, \alpha \xleftarrow{\text{U}} \mathbb{Z}_N$ and $t_i \xleftarrow{\text{U}} \mathbb{Z}_N$ for each attribute $i \in \mathcal{U}$. It then sets $u_s := g^{a_s}, v_s := g^{b_s}, T_i := g^{t_i}$ for $i \in \mathcal{U}$. Let $H_s : \{0,1\}^* \longrightarrow \mathbb{Z}_N$ be a hash function. The public parameters and master secret are given by

$$\mathcal{PP} := (\mathcal{J}, g, g^a, u_s, v_s, g_T^\alpha, \{T_i\}_{i \in \mathcal{U}}, X_3, H_s)$$
$$\mathcal{MSK} := (\alpha).$$

KeyGen$(\mathcal{PP}, \mathcal{MSK}, A)$: It picks $t \xleftarrow{\text{U}} \mathbb{Z}_N, R, R_0' \xleftarrow{\text{U}} \mathbb{G}_{p_3}$. For each attribute $i \in A$, the algorithm chooses $R_i \xleftarrow{\text{U}} \mathbb{G}_{p_3}$ and outputs the secret key
$$\mathcal{SK}_A := [A, \ K := g^{\alpha+at}R, \ L := g^t R_0', \ K_i := T_i^t R_i, \ \forall i \in A].$$

Sign$(\mathcal{PP}, m, \mathcal{SK}_A, \Gamma_s := (M_s, \rho_s))$: Let $M_s$ be an $\ell_s \times n_s$ matrix. Suppose $\Gamma_s(A) = \text{True}$, then there exist $\mathcal{I}_A \subseteq [\ell_s]$ and $\{\alpha_s^{(i)}\}_{i \in \mathcal{I}_A}$ such that $\sum_{i \in \mathcal{I}_A} \alpha_s^{(i)} M_s^{(i)} = 1$. It selects $\beta \xleftarrow{\text{U}} \{\beta = (\beta_1, \ldots, \beta_{\ell_s}) \in \mathbb{Z}_N^{\ell_s} \mid \sum_{i \in [\ell_s]} \beta_i M_s^{(i)} = 0\}$. Suppose $\mathcal{SK}_A := [A, \ K := g^{\alpha+at}R, \ L := g^t R_0', \ K_i := T_i^t R_i, \ \forall i \in A]$, then it re-randomizes the key $\mathcal{SK}_A$ as follows: it picks $\hat{t} \xleftarrow{\text{U}} \mathbb{Z}_N$ and sets $\tilde{t} := t + \hat{t}$

$$\tilde{\mathcal{SK}}_A := [A, \ \tilde{K} := K.g^{a\hat{t}}, \ \tilde{L} := L.g^{\hat{t}}, \ \tilde{K}_i := K_i.T_i^{\hat{t}}, \ \forall i \in A]$$
$$:= [A, \ \tilde{K} := g^{\alpha+a\tilde{t}}R, \ \tilde{L} := g^{\tilde{t}} R_0', \ \tilde{K}_i := T_i^{\tilde{t}} R_i, \ \forall i \in A]$$

It picks $r_s, \tau \xleftarrow{\text{U}} \mathbb{Z}_N, \bar{R}, \bar{R}_0 \xleftarrow{\text{U}} \mathbb{G}_{p_3}$ and for each $i \in [\ell_s]$, it chooses $\bar{R}_i \xleftarrow{\text{U}} \mathbb{G}_{p_3}$. Then it computes $h_s := H_s(m||\Gamma_s)$. The components of signature are given by (for $i \notin \mathcal{I}_A$, it sets $\alpha_s^{(i)} := 0$)

$$S_0 := \left( \tilde{K}(u_s^{h_s} v_s)^{r_s} \bar{R}, \ g^{r_s} \bar{R}_0 \right)$$
$$S_i := \left( \tilde{L}^{\alpha_s^{(i)}} (g^\tau)^{\beta_i} \bar{R}_i, \ (\tilde{K}_{\rho_s(i)})^{\alpha_s^{(i)}} (T_{\rho_s(i)})^{\tau \beta_i} \bar{R}'_i \right) \text{ for } i \in [\ell_s].$$

After simplification, it gives

$$S_0 := \left( g^{\alpha+a\tilde{t}} (u_s^{h_s} v_s)^{r_s} \tilde{R}, \ g^{r_s} \tilde{R}_0 \right), \text{ where } \tilde{R} := R\bar{R}, \ \tilde{R}_0 := \bar{R}_0$$
$$S_i := \left( (g^{\tilde{t}})^{\alpha_s^{(i)}} (g^\tau)^{\beta_i} \tilde{R}_i, \ (T_{\rho_s(i)}^{\tilde{t}})^{\alpha_s^{(i)}} (T_{\rho_s(i)}^\tau)^{\beta_i} \tilde{R}'_i \right),$$

where $\tilde{R}_i := (R_0')^{\alpha_s^{(i)}} \bar{R}_i, \ \tilde{R}'_i := R_{\rho_s(i)}^{\alpha_s^{(i)} + \tau \beta_i} \bar{R}'_i$
The final output (signature) is $\sigma := (S_0, \{S_i\}_{i \in [\ell_s]})$
Ver$(\mathcal{PP}, m, \sigma, \Gamma_s)$: It first computes a verification text, then using this verification text it will verify the signature. The following is the construction of verification text: It picks $u_s := (s, u_2, \ldots, u_{n_s}) \xleftarrow{\text{U}} \mathbb{Z}_N^{n_s}$ and $r_s^{(i)} \xleftarrow{\text{U}} \mathbb{Z}_N$ for $i \in [\ell_s]$. It computes $h_s := H_s(m||\Gamma_s)$. Let $M_s^{(i)}$ denote the $i^{th}$ row of the matrix, $M_s$ and let $\lambda_s^{(i)} := M_s^{(i)}.u_s$. The verification text is given by

$$V_0 := \left( g^s, (u_s^{h_s} v_s)^s, g_T^{\alpha s} \right)$$
$$V_i := \left( g^{a\lambda_s^{(i)}} T_{\rho_s(i)}^{-r_s^{(i)}}, \ g^{r_s^{(i)}} \right), \text{ for } i \in [\ell_s]$$

The final verification text is $\mathcal{V} := (V_0, \{V_i\}_{i \in [\ell_s]})$

Now, it computes $\Delta_s := \dfrac{e(S_{01}, V_{01})}{e(S_{02}, V_{02}) \prod_{i=1}^{\ell_s} (e(S_{i1}, V_{i1}) e(S_{i2}, V_{i2}))}$ and checks $\Delta_s \overset{?}{=} V_{03}$. It returns 1 if $\Delta_s = V_{03}$, else returns 0.

*Correctness.*

$$\Delta_s = \frac{e(S_{01}, V_{01})}{e(S_{02}, V_{02}) \prod_{i=1}^{\ell_s} (e(S_{i1}, V_{i1}) e(S_{i2}, V_{i2}))}$$

$$= \frac{g_T^{\alpha s + a\tilde{s}} . e(u_s^{h_s} v_s, g)^{sr_s}}{e(u_s^{h_s} v_s, g)^{sr_s} \prod_{i=1}^{\ell_s} (e(S_{i1}, V_{i1}) e(S_{i2}, V_{i2}))}$$

$$= \frac{g_T^{\alpha s + a\tilde{s}}}{\prod_{i=1}^{\ell_s} (e(g^{\tilde{t}\alpha_s^{(i)} + \tau\beta_i}, g^{a\lambda_s^{(i)} - r_s^{(i)} t_{\rho_s(i)}}) . e(g^{\tilde{t}\alpha_i t_{\rho_s(i)} + \tau\beta_i t_{\rho_s(i)}}, g^{r_s^{(i)}}))}$$

$$= \frac{g_T^{\alpha s + a\tilde{s}}}{\prod_{i=1}^{\ell_s} g_T^{a\tilde{t}\lambda_s^{(i)} \alpha_s^{(i)} + a\tau\lambda_s^{(i)} \beta_i}} = \frac{g_T^{\alpha s + a\tilde{s}}}{g_T^{a\tilde{t} \sum_{i=1}^{\ell_s} \lambda_s^{(i)} \alpha_s^{(i)} + a\tau \sum_{i=1}^{\ell_s} \lambda_s^{(i)} \beta_i}} = g_T^{\alpha s}$$

## 4    Security Proof of CP-ABS

**Theorem 1.** *The proposed attribute-based signature scheme in section 3 is perfectly private.*

**Theorem 2.** *The proposed basic CP-ABS scheme is adaptive-predicate existential unforgeable if DSG1, DSG2 and DSG3 assumptions hold and $H_s$ is a collision resistant hash function.*

## 5    Basic Ciphertext-Policy Attribute-Based Signcryption

In this section, we present our basic ciphertext-policy attribute-based signcryption (CP-ABSC) supporting monotone span programs. The scheme is based on the composite order bilinear pairing groups. Here we consider two policies, sender policy $\Gamma_s := (M_s, \rho_s)$ and receiver policy $\Gamma_e := (M_e, \rho_e)$. Similar to section 3, in our basic CP-ABSC scheme, both the row labeling functions $\rho_s$ and $\rho_e$ are assumed to be injective. By applying the mechanism illustrated in appendix B, a full CP-ABSC construction is easily obtained.

This construction is almost in the flavor of $\mathcal{CtE\&S}$ paradigm. To construct our scheme, we use any commitment scheme with hiding and relaxed-binding properties, CCA2 version encryption scheme of [22] and the ABS scheme described in section 3. Let $\Pi_{\mathsf{ABS}} := (\mathsf{ABS.Setup}, \mathsf{ABS.KeyGen}, \mathsf{ABS.Sign}, \mathsf{ABS.Ver})$ and $\Pi_{\mathsf{Commit}} := (\mathsf{C.Setup}, \mathsf{Commit}, \mathsf{Open})$ be respectively the ABS scheme described in section 3 and commitment scheme.

Setup($1^\kappa, \mathcal{U}$): It runs $\mathcal{CK} \longleftarrow \mathsf{C.Setup}(1^\kappa)$, $(\mathcal{ABS.PP}, \mathcal{ABS.MSK}) \longleftarrow \mathsf{ABS.Setup}(1^\kappa, \mathcal{U})$. It chooses $a_e, b_e \xleftarrow{\mathsf{U}} \mathbb{Z}_N$ and sets $u_e := g^{a_e}, v_e := g^{b_e}$. Let $H_e : \{0,1\}^* \longrightarrow \mathbb{Z}_N$ be a hash functions. The public parameters (combining $\mathcal{ABS.PP}, \mathcal{CK}$ and $u_e, v_e, H_e$) and master secret are given by

$\mathcal{PP} := (\mathcal{I}, g, g^a, u_s, u_e, v_s, v_e, g_T^\alpha, \{T_i\}_{i \in \mathcal{U}}, X_3, H_s, H_e, \mathcal{CK})$

$\mathcal{MSK} := \mathcal{ABS.MSK} = (\alpha)$

KeyGen($\mathcal{PP}, \mathcal{MSK}, A$): $\mathcal{SK}_A \longleftarrow$ ABS.KeyGen($\mathcal{ABS.PP}, \mathcal{MSK}, A$)

Signcrypt($\mathcal{PP}, m, \mathcal{SK}_A, \Gamma_s := (M_s, \rho_s), \Gamma_e := (M_e, \rho_e)$): Let $M_s$ (resp. $M_e$) be an $\ell_s \times n_s$ (resp. $\ell_e \times n_e$) matrix. It runs $(\check{c}, \check{d}) \longleftarrow$ Commit($m$) (see footnote [6]). The Signcrypt algorithm has two part, Sign and Encrypt, both run in parallel except the part $C_{\ell_e+1}$.

**Sign:** $\sigma := (S_0, \{S_i\}_{i \in [\ell_s]}) \longleftarrow$ ABS.Sign($\mathcal{ABS.PP}, (\check{c} \| \Gamma_e), \mathcal{SK}_A, \Gamma_s := (M_s, \rho_s)$), where the components are given by

$$S_0 := (g^{\alpha + a\tilde{t}}(u_s^{h_s} v_s)^{r_s} \tilde{R}, g^{r_s} \tilde{R}_0), \text{ where } h_s := H_s((\check{c} \| \Gamma_e) \| \Gamma_s)$$

$$S_i := ((g^{\tilde{t}})^{\alpha_s^{(i)}}(g^\tau)^{\beta_i} \tilde{R}_i, (T_{\rho_s(i)}^{\tilde{t}})^{\alpha_s^{(i)}}(T_{\rho_s(i)}^\tau)^{\beta_i} \tilde{R}'_i)$$

**Encrypt:** It picks $u_e := (s_e, u_2, \ldots, u_{n_e}) \xleftarrow{\text{U}} \mathbb{Z}_N^{n_e}$ and $r_e^{(i)} \xleftarrow{\text{U}} \mathbb{Z}_N$ for $i \in [\ell_e]$. Let $M_e^{(i)}$ denote the $i^{th}$ row of the matrix, $M_e$ and let $\lambda_e^{(i)} := M_c^{(i)}.u_e$. The ciphertext components of the signcryption are given by

$$C_0 := (g^{s_e}, \check{d}.g_T^{\alpha s_e})$$

$$C_i := (g^{a\lambda_e^{(i)}} T_{\rho_e(i)}^{-r_e^{(i)}}, g^{r_e^{(i)}}), \text{ for } i \in [\ell_e]$$

It sets $\varrho_0 := (C_0, \{C_i\}_{i \in [\ell_e]})$ and computes $h_e := H_e(\Gamma_e, \Gamma_s, \check{c}, \varrho_0, \sigma)$. Then, it calculates the last component $C_{\ell_e+1} := (u_e^{h_e} v_e)^{s_e}$. Then it sets the ciphertext part of the signcryption as $\varrho := (\varrho_0, C_{\ell_e+1})$.

It outputs the signcryption $\Upsilon := (\check{c}, \sigma, \varrho)$

Unsigncrypt($\mathcal{PP}, \Upsilon, \mathcal{SK}_B, \Gamma_s := (M_s, \rho_s), \Gamma_e := (M_e, \rho_e)$): Let $M_s$ (resp. $M_e$) be an $\ell_s \times n_s$ (resp. $\ell_e \times n_e$) matrix. This algorithm consists of two routines, Ver and Decrypt run in parallel.

Ver: flag $\longleftarrow$ ABS.Ver($\mathcal{PP}, (\check{c} \| \Gamma_e), \sigma, \Gamma_s$). If flag $= 0$, it returns $\perp$.

Decrypt: It computes $h_e := H_e(\Gamma_e, \Gamma_s, \check{c}, \varrho_0, \sigma)$. Then it checks $e(g, C_{\ell_e+1}) \stackrel{?}{=} e(u_e^{h_e} v_e, C_{01})$ and if the equality does not hold, it returns $\perp$. If $\Gamma_e(B) \neq$ True, it returns $\perp$, else there exist $\mathcal{I}_B \subset [\ell_e]$ and $\{\alpha_e^{(i)}\}_{i \in \mathcal{I}_B}$ such that $\sum_{i \in \mathcal{I}_B} \alpha_e^{(i)} M_e^{(i)} = \mathbf{1}$. Then, it picks $r \xleftarrow{\text{U}} \mathbb{Z}_N$, $R_0 \xleftarrow{\text{U}} \mathbb{G}_{p_3}$ and computes

$$\Delta_e := \frac{e(K.(u_e^{h_e} v_e)^r, C_{01})}{e(g^r R_0, C_{\ell_e+1}) \prod_{i \in \mathcal{I}_B}(e(L, C_{i1}).e(K_{\rho_e(i)}, C_{i2}))^{\alpha_e^{(i)}}}$$

Finally it returns the message $m := $ Open($\check{c}, C_{02}/\Delta_e$)

*Correctness.* It follows from the correctness of Ver and Decrypt routines. Since, the correctness of Ver is immediate from that of ABS in section 3, we illustrate here only the correctness of Decrypt.

---

[6] For brevity, we just omit $\mathcal{CK}$ in Open and Commit algorithm throughout this paper.

$$\Delta_e = \frac{e(K.(u_e^{h_e} v_e)^r, C_{01})}{e(g^r, C_{\ell_e+1}) \prod_{i \in \mathcal{I}_B} (e(L, C_{i1}).e(K_{\rho_e(i)}, C_{i2}))^{\alpha_e^{(i)}}}$$

$$= \frac{g_T^{\alpha s_e + a t s_e} . e(u_e^{h_e} v_e, g)^{r s_e}}{e(u_e^{h_e} v_e, g)^{r s_e} \prod_{i \in \mathcal{I}_B} ((g_T^{a t \lambda_e^{(i)} - t \rho_e(i) r_e^{(i)}})(g_T^{t \rho_e(i) r_e^{(i)}}))^{\alpha_e^{(i)}}}$$

$$= \frac{g_T^{\alpha s_e + a t s_e}}{\prod_{i \in \mathcal{I}_B} g_T^{a t \alpha_e^{(i)} \lambda_e^{(i)}}} = \frac{g_T^{\alpha s_e + a t s_e}}{g_T^{a t \sum_{i \in \mathcal{I}_B} \alpha^{(i)}_e \lambda_e^{(i)}}} = g_T^{\alpha s_e}$$

$$\mathsf{Open}(\check{c}, C_{02}/\Delta_e) = \mathsf{Open}(\check{c}, \check{d}) = m$$

*Non-Repudiation (Publicly Verifiability).* Since it is achieved by $\mathcal{CtE\&S}$ paradigm, our systems also achieve the same.

*Dynamic property.* In dynamic attribute-based system, a new attribute can be added dynamically to the system without re-issuing the whole secret key of the user. Here a user sends it's one secret key component, viz, $L := g^t R_0'$ to the PKG and then PKG will send the secret key component corresponding to the new attribute : Suppose $att$ is a new attribute, then PKG computes $T_{att} := g^{t_{att}}$ by choosing $t_{att} \xleftarrow{\mathsf{U}} \mathbb{Z}_N$, keeps $t_{att}$ to itself and adds $T_{att}$ to $\mathcal{PP}$. Then, it sets $K_{att} := L^{t_{att}} R_{att}$ by picking $R_{att} \xleftarrow{\mathsf{U}} \mathbb{G}_{p_3}$ and returns it to the user.

## 6    Security Proof of CP-ABSC

**Theorem 3.** *The proposed attribute-based signcryption scheme in section 5 is perfectly private. (The Signer Privacy for CP-ABSC can be defined in similar manner as in CP-ABS. The details will be found in full version.)*

**Theorem 4.** *If DSG1, DSG2 and DSG3 assumptions hold, $H_e$ is a collision resistant hash function and $\Pi_{\mathsf{Commit}}$ has hiding property, then our proposed basic CP-ABSC scheme in section 5 is adaptively secure.*

**Theorem 5.** *If DSG1, DSG2 and DSG3 assumptions hold for $\mathcal{J}$, the primitive commitment scheme $\Pi_{\mathsf{Commit}}$ has relaxed-binding property and $H_s$ is a collision resistant hash function, then the proposed basic CP-ABSC scheme in section 5 is adaptive-predicates existential unforgeable.*

## 7    Extension to Strongly Unforgeable CP-ABSC

Here in this section, we describe our strongly unforgeable and IND-CCA2 secure CP-ABSC scheme for access policies represented by the monotone span programs. This scheme follows almost the same structure of weak unforgeable and IND-CCA2 secure CP-ABSC described in section 5. But to protect the signcryption from forging, we bind all the components by a strongly unforgeable OTS scheme which we call "Commit then Encrypt and Sign then Sign" ($\mathcal{CtE\&StS}$)

paradigm. Although the similar type of generic constructions using strongly un-forgeable OTS scheme are available in the literature [9,20] in the context of ABE and ABS, here we do not apply the OTS scheme in straightforward way because of the following reasons: (a) we no more assume the relaxed-binding property of the commitment scheme for strong unforgeability, and (b) to reuse the part of IND-CCA2 security proof of the construction described in section 5 for the current CP-ABSC construction.

We just give a short description of our strongly unforgeable and IND-CCA2 secure CP-ABSC construction, since it follows the CP-ABSC in section 5 and the idea of strongly unforgeable CP-ABS stated above. Let $\Pi_{\mathsf{Commit}} := (\mathsf{C.Setup}, \mathsf{Commit}, \mathsf{Open})$ be a commitment scheme. Let $\Pi_{\mathsf{wABS}} := (\mathsf{wABS.Setup}, \mathsf{wABS.KeyGen}, \mathsf{wABS.Sign}, \mathsf{wABS.Ver})$ and $\Pi_{\mathsf{ABE}} := (\mathsf{ABE.Setup}, \mathsf{ABE.KeyGen}, \mathsf{ABE.Encrypt}, \mathsf{ABE.Decrypt})$ be the CP-ABS scheme and CP-ABE scheme respectively used in section 5. Let $\Pi_{\mathsf{OTS}} := (\mathsf{Gen}, \mathsf{OTS.Sign}, \mathsf{OTS.Ver})$ be a strong unforgeable OTS scheme. Demonstrated below are only two routines, Signcrypt and Unsigncrypt as rest are same as in section 5.

−Signcrypt$(\mathcal{PP}, m, \mathcal{SK}_A, \Gamma_s, \Gamma_e)$ : It first runs $(\check{c}, \check{d}) \longleftarrow \mathsf{Commit}(m)$, $(\mathsf{verk}, \mathsf{signk}) \longleftarrow \mathsf{Gen}(1^\kappa)$. Then, it executes in parallel $\sigma_w := (S_0, \ldots, S_{\ell_s}) \longleftarrow \mathsf{wABS.Sign}(\mathcal{PP}, \check{c}||\mathsf{verk}||\Gamma_e, \mathcal{SK}_A, \Gamma_s)$ and $\varrho_0 := (C_0, \ldots, C_{\ell_e}) \longleftarrow \mathsf{ABE.Encrypt}(\mathcal{PP}, \check{d}, \Gamma_e)$. Then it computes $h_e := H_e(\Gamma_e, \Gamma_s, \check{c}, \mathsf{verk}, \varrho_0, \sigma_w)$, $C_{\ell_e+1} := (u_e^{h_e} v_e)^{s_e}$ and $\sigma_o \longleftarrow \mathsf{OTS.Sign}(h_e||C_{\ell_e+1}, \mathsf{signk})$. Now it sets the signature part of the sign-cryption $\sigma_s := (\sigma_w, \sigma_o, \mathsf{verk})$ and the ciphertext part of the signcryption $\varrho := (\varrho_0, C_{\ell_e+1})$. It returns the signcryption $\Upsilon := (\check{c}, \sigma_s, \varrho)$.

−Unsigncrypt$(\mathcal{PP}, \Upsilon, \mathcal{SK}_B, \Gamma_s, \Gamma_e)$ : It first parses $\Upsilon$ as $(\check{c}, \sigma_s, \varrho)$, where $\sigma_s := (\sigma_w, \sigma_o, \mathsf{verk})$. Then it runs in parallel $\mathsf{flag}_o \longleftarrow \mathsf{OTS.Ver}(\sigma_w, \sigma_o, \mathsf{verk})$, $\mathsf{flag}_w \longleftarrow \mathsf{wABS.Ver}(\mathcal{PP}, \check{c}||\mathsf{verk}||\Gamma_e, \sigma_w, \Gamma_s)$ and $\check{d} \longleftarrow \mathsf{ABE.Decrypt}(\mathcal{PP}, \varrho, \mathcal{SK}_B, \Gamma_e)$. If $\mathsf{flag}_o = 1$ and $\mathsf{flag}_w = 1$, it returns $\mathsf{Open}(\check{c}, \check{d})$ else $\perp$.

*Correctness, Dynamic property and Non-repudiation.* These are immediate from that of section 5.

**Theorem 6.** *The proposed CP-ABSC scheme in section 7 is perfectly private.*

**Theorem 7.** *If DSG1, DSG2 and DSG3 assumptions hold, $H_e$ is a collision resistant hash function, $\Pi_{\mathsf{Commit}}$ has hiding property and $\Pi_{\mathsf{OTS}}$ is a strong unforgeable OTS scheme, then our proposed CP-ABSC scheme in section 7 is adaptively secure.*

*Proof.* The proof can be obtained by the similar approach as in proof of theorem 4 and the argument used for proving CCA2 security in [9].

**Theorem 8.** *If DSG1, DSG2 and DSG3 assumptions hold for $\mathcal{J}$, $\Pi_{\mathsf{OTS}}$ is a strong unforgeable OTS scheme and $H_s, H_e$ are collision resistant hash functions, then the proposed basic CP-ABSC scheme in section 7 is existential strong existential unforgeable.*

**Acknowledgements.** One of the authors would like to thank R C Bose Centre for Cryptology and Security, ISI Kolkata for the financial support. Moreover, authors pay their sincere thanks to Dr. Mridul Nandi, ISI Kolkata and anonymous reviewers for their comments and suggestions that helped in polishing the technical and editorial content of this paper.

# References

1. An, J.H., Dodis, Y., Rabin, T.: On the security of joint signature and encryption. In: Knudsen, L.R. (ed.) EUROCRYPT 2002. LNCS, vol. 2332, pp. 83–107. Springer, Heidelberg (2002)
2. Attrapadung, N., Libert, B., de Panafieu, E.: Expressive key-policy attribute-based encryption with constant-size ciphertexts. In: Catalano, D., Fazio, N., Gennaro, R., Nicolosi, A. (eds.) PKC 2011. LNCS, vol. 6571, pp. 90–108. Springer, Heidelberg (2011)
3. Baek, J., Steinfeld, R., Zheng, Y.: Formal proofs for the security of signcryption. In: Naccache, D., Paillier, P. (eds.) PKC 2002. LNCS, vol. 2274, pp. 80–98. Springer, Heidelberg (2002)
4. Bethencourt, J., Sahai, A., Waters, B.: Ciphertext-policy attribute-based encryption. In: IEEE Symposium on Security and Privacy, pp. 321–334. IEEE Press (2007)
5. Boneh, D., Boyen, X.: Efficient selective-ID secure identity-based encryption without random oracles. In: Cachin, C., Camenisch, J.L. (eds.) EUROCRYPT 2004. LNCS, vol. 3027, pp. 223–238. Springer, Heidelberg (2004)
6. Boneh, D., Franklin, M.: Identity-Based Encryption from the Weil Pairing. In: Kilian, J. (ed.) CRYPTO 2001. LNCS, vol. 2139, pp. 213–229. Springer, Heidelberg (2001)
7. Boneh, D., Katz, J.: Improved efficiency for CCA-secure cryptosystems built using identity-based encryption. In: Menezes, A. (ed.) CT-RSA 2005. LNCS, vol. 3376, pp. 87–103. Springer, Heidelberg (2005)
8. Boyen, X.: Multipurpose identity-based signcryption. In: Boneh, D. (ed.) CRYPTO 2003. LNCS, vol. 2729, pp. 383–399. Springer, Heidelberg (2003)
9. Canetti, R., Halevi, S., Katz, J.: Chosen-ciphertext security from identity-based encryption. In: Cachin, C., Camenisch, J.L. (eds.) EUROCRYPT 2004. LNCS, vol. 3027, pp. 207–222. Springer, Heidelberg (2004)
10. Chen, C., Chen, J., Lim, H.W., Zhang, Z., Feng, D.: Combined public-key schemes: The case of ABE and ABS. In: Takagi, T., Wang, G., Qin, Z., Jiang, S., Yu, Y. (eds.) ProvSec 2012. LNCS, vol. 7496, pp. 53–69. Springer, Heidelberg (2012)
11. Chen, L., Malone-Lee, J.: Improved identity-based signcryption. In: Vaudenay, S. (ed.) PKC 2005. LNCS, vol. 3386, pp. 362–379. Springer, Heidelberg (2005)
12. Damgård, I., Fujisaki, E.: A statistically-hiding integer commitment scheme based on groups with hidden order. In: Zheng, Y. (ed.) ASIACRYPT 2002. LNCS, vol. 2501, pp. 125–142. Springer, Heidelberg (2002)
13. Dent, A.W., Fischlin, M., Manulis, M., Stam, M., Schröder, D.: Confidential signatures and deterministic signcryption. In: Nguyen, P.Q., Pointcheval, D. (eds.) PKC 2010. LNCS, vol. 6056, pp. 462–479. Springer, Heidelberg (2010)
14. Emura, K., Miyaji, A., Rahman, M.S.: Dynamic attribute-based signcryption without random oracles. International Journal of Applied Cryptography 2(11), 199–211 (2012)

15. Gagné, M., Narayan, S., Safavi-Naini, R.: Threshold attribute-based signcryption. In: Garay, J.A., De Prisco, R. (eds.) SCN 2010. LNCS, vol. 6280, pp. 154–171. Springer, Heidelberg (2010)

16. Goyal, V., Pandey, O., Sahai, A., Waters, B.: Attribute-based encryption for fine-grained access control of encrypted data. In: ACM Conference on Computer and Communications Security, pp. 89–98. ACM (2006)

17. Haber, S., Pinkas, B.: Securely combining public-key cryptosystems. In: ACM Conference on Computer and Communications Security, pp. 215–224. ACM (2001)

18. Halevi, S., Micali, S.: Practical and provably-secure commitment schemes from collision-free hashing. In: Koblitz, N. (ed.) CRYPTO 1996. LNCS, vol. 1109, pp. 201–215. Springer, Heidelberg (1996)

19. Hess, F.: Efficient identity based signature schemes based on pairings. In: Nyberg, K., Heys, H.M. (eds.) SAC 2002. LNCS, vol. 2595, pp. 310–324. Springer, Heidelberg (2003)

20. Huang, Q., Wong, D.S., Zhao, Y.: Generic transformation to strongly unforgeable signatures. In: Katz, J., Yung, M. (eds.) ACNS 2007. LNCS, vol. 4521, pp. 1–17. Springer, Heidelberg (2007)

21. Lewko, A., Waters, B.: New proof methods for attribute-based encryption: Achieving full security through selective techniques. In: Safavi-Naini, R., Canetti, R. (eds.) CRYPTO 2012. LNCS, vol. 7417, pp. 180–198. Springer, Heidelberg (2012)

22. Lewko, A., Okamoto, T., Sahai, A., Takashima, K., Waters, B.: Fully secure functional encryption: Attribute-based encryption and (hierarchical) inner product encryption. In: Gilbert, H. (ed.) EUROCRYPT 2010. LNCS, vol. 6110, pp. 62–91. Springer, Heidelberg (2010)

23. Li, J., Au, M.H., Susilo, W., Xie, D., Ren, K.: Attribute-based signature and its applications. In: ACM Conference on Computer and Communications Security, pp. 60–69. ACM (2010)

24. Libert, B., Quisquater, J.-J.: Efficient signcryption with key privacy from gap diffie-hellman groups. In: Bao, F., Deng, R., Zhou, J. (eds.) PKC 2004. LNCS, vol. 2947, pp. 187–200. Springer, Heidelberg (2004)

25. Libert, B., Quisquater, J.-J.: Improved signcryption from $q$-diffie-hellman problems. In: Blundo, C., Cimato, S. (eds.) SCN 2004. LNCS, vol. 3352, pp. 220–234. Springer, Heidelberg (2005)

26. Maji, H., Prabhakaran, M., Rosulek, M.: Attribute-based signatures: Achieving attribute-privacy and collusion-resistance. Cryptology ePrint Archive, Report 2008/328 (2008), http://eprint.iacr.org/

27. Maji, H., Prabhakaran, M., Rosulek, M.: Attribute-based signatures. Cryptology ePrint Archive, Report 2010/595 (2010), http://eprint.iacr.org/

28. Malone-Lee, J., Mao, W.: Two birds one stone: Signcryption using RSA. In: Joye, M. (ed.) CT-RSA 2003. LNCS, vol. 2612, pp. 211–226. Springer, Heidelberg (2003)

29. Matsuda, T., Matsuura, K., Schuldt, J.C.N.: Efficient constructions of signcryption schemes and signcryption composability. In: Roy, B., Sendrier, N. (eds.) INDOCRYPT 2009. LNCS, vol. 5922, pp. 321–342. Springer, Heidelberg (2009)

30. Okamoto, T., Takashima, K.: Fully secure functional encryption with general relations from the decisional linear assumption. In: Rabin, T. (ed.) CRYPTO 2010. LNCS, vol. 6223, pp. 191–208. Springer, Heidelberg (2010)

31. Okamoto, T., Takashima, K.: Efficient attribute-based signatures for non-monotone predicates in the standard model. In: Catalano, D., Fazio, N., Gennaro, R., Nicolosi, A. (eds.) PKC 2011. LNCS, vol. 6571, pp. 35–52. Springer, Heidelberg (2011)

32. Okamoto, T., Takashima, K.: Fully secure unbounded inner-product and attribute-based encryption. In: Wang, X., Sako, K. (eds.) ASIACRYPT 2012. LNCS, vol. 7658, pp. 349–366. Springer, Heidelberg (2012)

33. Ostrovsky, R., Sahai, A., Waters, B.: Attribute-based encryption with non-monotonic access structures. In: ACM Conference on Computer and Communications Security, pp. 195–203 (2007)

34. Pedersen, T.P.: Non-interactive and information-theoretic secure verifiable secret sharing. In: Feigenbaum, J. (ed.) CRYPTO 1991. LNCS, vol. 576, pp. 129–140. Springer, Heidelberg (1992)

35. Sahai, A., Waters, B.: Fuzzy identity-based encryption. In: Cramer, R. (ed.) EUROCRYPT 2005. LNCS, vol. 3494, pp. 457–473. Springer, Heidelberg (2005)

36. Shahandashti, S.F., Safavi-Naini, R.: Threshold attribute-based signatures and their application to anonymous credential systems. In: Preneel, B. (ed.) AFRICACRYPT 2009. LNCS, vol. 5580, pp. 198–216. Springer, Heidelberg (2009)

37. Vasco, M.I.G., Hess, F., Steinwandt, R.: Combined (identity-based) public key schemes. Cryptology ePrint Archive, Report 2008/466 (2008), http://eprint.iacr.org/

38. Waters, B.: Dual system encryption: Realizing fully secure IBE and HIBE under simple assumptions. In: Halevi, S. (ed.) CRYPTO 2009. LNCS, vol. 5677, pp. 619–636. Springer, Heidelberg (2009)

39. Waters, B.: Ciphertext-policy attribute-based encryption: An expressive, efficient, and provably secure realization. In: Catalano, D., Fazio, N., Gennaro, R., Nicolosi, A. (eds.) PKC 2011. LNCS, vol. 6571, pp. 53–70. Springer, Heidelberg (2011)

40. Yamada, S., Attrapadung, N., Hanaoka, G., Kunihiro, N.: Generic constructions for chosen-ciphertext secure attribute based encryption. In: Catalano, D., Fazio, N., Gennaro, R., Nicolosi, A. (eds.) PKC 2011. LNCS, vol. 6571, pp. 71–89. Springer, Heidelberg (2011)

41. Zheng, Y.: Digital signcryption or how to achieve cost (signature & encryption) << cost(signature) + cost(encryption). In: Kaliski Jr., B.S. (ed.) CRYPTO 1997. LNCS, vol. 1294, pp. 165–179. Springer, Heidelberg (1997)

# A    Ciphertext-Policy Attribute-Base Signcryption

## A.1    Definition

A ciphertext-policy Attribute-Base Signcryption(CP-ABSC) scheme consists of four PPT algorithms - Setup, KeyGen, Signcrypt and Unsigncrypt.

Setup: Input: a security parameter $\kappa$ and a universe of attributes $\mathcal{U}$. Output: public parameters $\mathcal{PP}$ and a master secret $\mathcal{MSK}$.

KeyGen: Input: a set of attributes $A$, $\mathcal{PP}$ and $\mathcal{MSK}$. Output: a secret key $\mathcal{SK}_A$ corresponding to $A$.

Signcrypt: Input: $\mathcal{PP}$, a message $m$, $\mathcal{SK}_A$, a predicate $\Gamma_s$ (signer policy) with $\Gamma_s(A) = \mathsf{True}$ and another predicate $\Gamma_e$ (receiver policy). Output: a signcryption $\Upsilon$ for $(\Gamma_e, \Gamma_s)$.

Unsigncrypt: Input: $\mathcal{PP}$, a signcryption $\Upsilon$, $\mathcal{SK}_B$, $\Gamma_s$ and $\Gamma_e$ with $\Gamma_e(B) = \mathsf{True}$. Output: a message $m$ if $\Upsilon$ is valid else $\perp$.

## A.2   Adaptive-Predicates IND-CCA2 Security of CP-ABSC

A CP-ABSC scheme is *adaptively secure (adaptive-predicates IND-CCA2 secure)* if no PPT adversary A has non-negligible advantage in this game:

**Setup:** The challenger $\mathscr{B}$ runs $(\mathcal{PP}, \mathcal{MSK}) \longleftarrow \mathsf{Setup}(1^\kappa, \mathcal{U})$ and gives $\mathcal{PP}$ to $\mathscr{A}$.

**Query:** The adversary $\mathscr{A}$ is given access to the oracles $\mathsf{KeyGen}(\mathcal{PP}, \mathcal{MSK}, .)$, $\mathsf{Signcrypt}(\mathcal{PP}, ., .)$ and $\mathsf{Unsigncrypt}(\mathcal{PP}, ., .)$.

**Challenge:** $\mathscr{A}$ provides two equal length messages $m_0, m_1$ and the challenge access policies $(\Gamma_s^*, \Gamma_e^*)$ s.t for each set of attributes $A$ queried to $\mathsf{KeyGen}(\mathcal{PP}, \mathcal{MSK}, .)$ oracle, $\Gamma_e^*(A) = \mathsf{False}$. $\mathscr{B}$ picks $b \xleftarrow{\mathrm{U}} \{0,1\}$. Then, it signcrypts the challenge message $m_b$ using the challenge policies $\Gamma_s^*$ and $\Gamma_e^*$ and gives the challenge signcryption $\Upsilon_b$ to $\mathscr{A}$.

**Query:** Again, $\mathscr{A}$ is given access to $\mathsf{KeyGen}(\mathcal{PP}, \mathcal{MSK}, .)$, $\mathsf{Signcrypt}(\mathcal{PP}, ., .)$ and $\mathsf{Unsigncrypt}(\mathcal{PP}, ., .)$ oracles but if $A$ is a set of attributes queried to $\mathsf{KeyGen}(\mathcal{PP}, \mathcal{MSK}, .)$ oracle and $\Upsilon$ is a unsigncryption query to $\mathsf{Unsigncrypt}(\mathcal{PP}, ., .)$ oracle, then $\Gamma_e^*(A) = \mathsf{False}$ and $\Upsilon \neq \Upsilon_b$.

**Guess:** $\mathscr{A}$ sends a guess $b'$ to $\mathscr{B}$.

The advantage of $\mathscr{A}$ in above is $\mathsf{Adv}_{\mathscr{A}}^{\mathrm{ABSC-CCA}}(\kappa) = \left| \Pr[b = b'] - \frac{1}{2} \right|$.

## A.3   Adaptive-Predicates Unforgeability of CP-ABSC

A CP-ABSC scheme is *adaptive-predicates strong existential unforgeable* if no PPT adversary A has non-negligible advantage in this game:

**Setup:** Same as in A.2.

**Query:** The adversary $\mathscr{A}$ is given access to the oracles $\mathsf{KeyGen}(\mathcal{PP}, \mathcal{MSK}, .)$ and $\mathsf{Signcrypt}(\mathcal{PP}, ., .)$.

**Forgery:** The adversary outputs a signcryption $\Upsilon^*$ for $(m^*, \Gamma_s^*, \Gamma_e^*)$.

$\mathscr{A}$ succeeds in this game if $(\Upsilon^*, m^*, \Gamma_s^*, \Gamma_e^*) \neq (\Upsilon^{(i)}, m^{(i)}, \Gamma_s^{(i)}, \Gamma_e^{(i)})$, where $\Upsilon^{(i)}$ is the reply by $\mathsf{Signcrypt}$ oracle for $(m^{(i)}, \Gamma_s^{(i)}, \Gamma_e^{(i)})$, $\Gamma_s^*$ does not accept any set of attributes queried to $\mathsf{KeyGen}$ oracle and $\mathsf{Unsigncrypt}(\mathcal{PP}, \Upsilon^*, SK_B, \Gamma_s^*, \Gamma_e^*) = m^*$, where $\Gamma_e^*(B) = \mathsf{True}$.

The advantage of $\mathscr{A}$ in above game is the success probability of $\mathscr{A}$.

# B   Mechanism for Full Construction

Although the technique is available in [22] but for self-containment, in this section we briefly demonstrate it. The mechanism described here is for both CP-ABS and CP-ABSC supporting MSPs. For full construction, the row labeling functions of span programs are not assumed to be injective. If we allow an attribute to repeat in the span programs at most $\mathfrak{M}$ time and the size of the universe $\mathcal{U}$ is $n$, then the size of new universe $\mathcal{U}'$ for the full construction will be $n\mathfrak{M}$. Basically in this full construction, for each attribute $\chi \in \mathcal{U}$, we consider $\mathfrak{M}$ copies of $\chi$ in $\mathcal{U}'$. To enumerate each copy, we assign a label say $j$ to the attribute say $\chi$, i.e., $\mathcal{U}' := \{(\chi, j) | \chi \in \mathcal{U}, j \in [\mathfrak{M}]\}$. Similarly, for any access policy $\Gamma := (M, \rho)$ if $\rho(i) = \chi$ and the attribute $\chi$ appears $j^{th}$ time, then we label the $i^{th}$ row by $(\chi, j)$, i.e., we have a new row labeling function $\rho'$ defined by $\rho'(i) := (\chi, j)$. Likewise if $A$ is a set of attributes corresponding to $\mathcal{U}$, then $A' := \{(\chi, j) | \chi \in A, j \in [\mathfrak{M}]\}$ is the set of attributes for $\mathcal{U}'$. Then, we have that the set of attributes $A$ satisfies the policy $(M, \rho)$ if and only if $A'$ satisfies $(M, \rho')$. Due to this technique, the sizes of public parameters and key increase by a factor linear to $\mathfrak{M}$, but the sizes of signature (resp. signcryption) and the cost of sign and ver (resp. signcrypt and unsigncrypt) for CP-ABS (resp. CP-ABSC) remain unchanged.

# How to Use Pseudorandom Generators in Unconditional Security Settings

Koji Nuida

National Institute of Advanced Industrial Science and Technology (AIST),
Tsukuba, Ibaraki 305-8568, Japan
k.nuida@aist.go.jp

**Abstract.** Cryptographic pseudorandom generators (PRGs) can reduce the randomness complexity of computationally secure schemes. Nuida and Hanaoka (IEEE Trans. IT 2013) developed a security proof technique against computationally unbounded adversaries under the use of cryptographic PRGs. However, their proof assumed unproven hardness of the underlying problem for the cryptographic PRG. In the paper, we realize a *fully unconditional* security proof, by extending the previous result to "non-cryptographic" PRGs such as the one by Impagliazzo, Nisan and Wigderson (STOC 1994) based on graph theory rather than one-way functions. In fact, our proof technique is effective only for some restricted class of schemes; then we also propose a "dual-mode" modification of the PRG to prove computational security even for schemes outside the class, while keeping the unconditional security for schemes in the class.

**Keywords:** Pseudorandom generators, information-theoretic security.

## 1 Introduction

Cryptographic pseudorandom generators (PRGs) can generate randomness for computationally secure schemes. On the other hand, when the original scheme is information-theoretically secure, it was expected that the security is degraded to computational. Recently, Nuida and Hanaoka [14] developed a security proof technique under the use of a cryptographic PRG, *where the computational power of adversaries are not assumed to be bounded*. However, their proof still assumed *the unproven hardness of an underlying computational problem for the PRG* (e.g., the hardness of the Decisional Diffie–Hellman (DDH) problem, for the PRG in [4] used in the numerical example of [14]). The aim of the work is to remove the latter kind of assumptions, realizing a *fully unconditional* security proof.

### 1.1 Our Contributions

In the paper, we remove the unproven assumptions in the previous result and realize a fully unconditional security, by extending the result in [14] to "non-cryptographic" PRGs. We use the PRG by Impagliazzo, Nisan and Wigderson

S.S.M. Chow et al. (Eds.): ProvSec 2014, LNCS 8782, pp. 291–299, 2014.

[7], hereafter called an *INW PRG*, whose indistinguishability is based on *unconditionally provable* graph-theoretic properties rather than one-way functions associated to cryptographic PRGs.

In fact, our proof technique (as well as the previous result in [14]) is effective only for some restricted class of schemes, and no security is guaranteed for schemes outside the class. To resolve the issue, we also propose a technique of combining the INW PRG with a cryptographic PRG, in such a way that the security under the use of the resulting PRG is at least computational even for schemes outside the class, while the unconditional security is kept for schemes in the class. We call the resulting PRG a *dual-mode PRG*. Such a hybrid property is also potentially useful when the security notion for the original scheme involves both information-theoretically secure parts and computationally secure parts.

One may feel that, whenever the randomness complexity of an information-theoretically secure scheme can be reduced by our technique using the INW PRGs, the randomness complexity could also be reduced by modifying the individual scheme directly. We emphasize that, even if it is true, our result provides a *unified* way to reduce the randomness complexity, hence is still meaningful.

## 1.2    Related Work

Dubrov and Ishai (Sect. 3.2.1 of [3]) also mentioned that the randomness complexity of some cryptographic processes can be unconditionally decreased by using PRGs proposed in the same paper. However, the possible applications of their result are restricted in comparison to our result; indeed, their result only corresponds to Theorem 1 in the paper, but not to more general Theorem 2.

Our construction of dual-mode PRGs has in fact a flavor similar to several "indistinguishability amplification" results such as Yao's XOR lemma (e.g., [10]). However, in contrast to those *quantitative* security improvements, our dual-mode PRGs focus on *qualitative* properties (i.e., hybrid security property).

## 1.3    Organization of the Paper

In Sect. 2, we summarize the proof technique of the previous work [14] and its problem, and then propose a solution by using the INW PRG. In Sect. 3, we summarize the construction and properties of the INW PRGs. In Sect. 4, we give a numerical example of our result. In Sect. 5, we propose the dual-mode PRGs. Finally, in Sect. 6, we discuss other potential applications of our proposed techniques. See the full version of the paper for some omitted details.

## 1.4    Notations and Terminology

A *directed edge* of an (undirected) graph is an edge, with distinction of the two end vertices as the source and the destination. We say that a graph is $\delta$-*regular*, if each vertex is adjacent to precisely $\delta$ edges. For a binary rooted tree $T$, let $r(T)$, $V(T)$ and $L(T)$ denote the root of $T$, the set of vertices of $T$, and the set of leaves of $T$ ordered from left to right, respectively. For each $v \in V(T)$, let $v^{\uparrow}$, $v_{\leftarrow}$ and $v_{\rightarrow}$ denote its parent vertex, left child vertex and right child vertex (if exist), respectively. For two random variables $\mathcal{R}_1, \mathcal{R}_2$, let $\Delta(\mathcal{R}_1, \mathcal{R}_2)$ denote their statistical distance; $\Delta(\mathcal{R}_1, \mathcal{R}_2) := (1/2) \sum_x |\Pr[x \leftarrow \mathcal{R}_1] - \Pr[x \leftarrow \mathcal{R}_2]|$. For any map $F$, let $[F]$ denote an algorithm to compute the value of $F$.

## 2  A Framework for Our Unconditional Security Proof

Here we explain the previous proof technique in [14] on which our result is based. We consider the following abstract security game for a cryptographic scheme:

1. The *challenger* generates an object $\alpha$ by using an output of a random source $r \leftarrow \mathcal{R}$. We denote the function to compute $\alpha$ by $F_1$; i.e., $F_1(r) = \alpha$.
2. The *adversary* obtains some information $\beta \in B$ on $\alpha$ and give it to the attack algorithm $\mathcal{A}$. We denote the function to compute $\beta$ by $F_2$; i.e., $F_2(\alpha) = \beta$. Then the adversary sends the output $\gamma \in C$ of $\mathcal{A}(\beta)$ to the challenger.
3. The challenger decides, from $\gamma$ and $\alpha$, whether the adversary wins or not. We denote the function to make the decision by $F_3$; i.e., $F_3(\alpha, \gamma) = 1$ if the adversary wins, and $F_3(\alpha, \gamma) = 0$ otherwise.

The success probability of the adversary's attack (i.e., the winning probability of the adversary in the game above) relative to random source $\mathcal{R}$ is defined by

$$\mathsf{Succ}_{\mathcal{A}, \mathcal{R}} := \Pr_{r \leftarrow \mathcal{R}}[\alpha = F_1(r); \beta = F_2(\alpha); \gamma \leftarrow \mathcal{A}(\beta); \delta = F_3(\alpha, \gamma) : \delta = 1]$$

$$= \Pr_{r \leftarrow \mathcal{R}}[\beta = F_2(F_1(r)); \gamma \leftarrow \mathcal{A}(\beta); \delta = F_3(F_1(r), \gamma) : \delta = 1] .$$

Let $\mathcal{R}_U$ denote the uniformly random source, and let $\mathcal{R}_P$ denote the output distribution of a given PRG. We suppose that the scheme is secure if $\mathcal{R}_U$ is used, i.e., $\mathsf{Succ}_{\mathcal{A}, \mathcal{R}_U}$ is sufficiently small for any possible attack algorithm $\mathcal{A}$. Our goal here is to prove that the scheme is still secure if the PRG $\mathcal{R}_P$ is used; i.e., $\mathsf{Succ}_{\mathcal{A}, \mathcal{R}_P}$ is sufficiently small. For the purpose, it suffices to show that $|\mathsf{Succ}_{\mathcal{A}, \mathcal{R}_U} - \mathsf{Succ}_{\mathcal{A}, \mathcal{R}_P}|$ is sufficiently small for any possible $\mathcal{A}$. For each $\beta_0 \in B$ and $\gamma_0 \in C$, let $\mathcal{F}_{\beta_0, \gamma_0}$ denote the map with input $r$ that outputs 1 if $F_2(F_1(r)) = \beta_0$ and $F_3(F_1(r), \gamma_0) = 1$, and outputs 0 otherwise. Then the argument in [14] implies that $\mathsf{Succ}_{\mathcal{A}, \mathcal{R}} = \sum_{\beta_0 \in B, \gamma_0 \in C} \Pr[\gamma_0 \leftarrow \mathcal{A}(\beta_0)] \Pr[\mathcal{F}_{\beta_0, \gamma_0}(\mathcal{R}) = 1]$ and

$$|\mathsf{Succ}_{\mathcal{A}, \mathcal{R}_U} - \mathsf{Succ}_{\mathcal{A}, \mathcal{R}_P}|$$
$$\leq \sum_{\beta_0 \in B, \gamma_0 \in C} \Pr[\gamma_0 \leftarrow \mathcal{A}(\beta_0)] \left| \Pr[\mathcal{F}_{\beta_0, \gamma_0}(\mathcal{R}_U) = 1] - \Pr[\mathcal{F}_{\beta_0, \gamma_0}(\mathcal{R}_P) = 1] \right| .$$

Now we introduce the following two conditions, where we fix values $T$ and $\varepsilon$:

**Condition 1.** The PRG is indistinguishable in the following sense; if the complexity of an algorithm $\mathcal{D}$ with 1-bit output is bounded by $T$, then we have

$$\Delta(\mathcal{D}(\mathcal{R}_U), \mathcal{D}(\mathcal{R}_P)) = \left| \Pr[\mathcal{D}(\mathcal{R}_U) = 1] - \Pr[\mathcal{D}(\mathcal{R}_P) = 1] \right| \leq \varepsilon .$$

**Condition 2.** The map $\mathcal{F}_{\beta_0,\gamma_0}$ for any $\beta_0 \in B$ and $\gamma_0 \in C$ above satisfies that the complexity of the algorithm $[\mathcal{F}_{\beta_0,\gamma_0}]$ is bounded by $T$.

Note that *these two conditions are independent of the choice of the adversary's attack algorithm* $\mathcal{A}$; e.g., $\mathcal{A}$ *may have unbounded complexity.* From now, suppose that the two conditions above are satisfied. Then we have the following bound:

$$|\mathsf{Succ}_{\mathcal{A},\mathcal{R}_U} - \mathsf{Succ}_{\mathcal{A},\mathcal{R}_P}| \le \sum_{\beta_0 \in B,\, \gamma_0 \in C} \Pr[\gamma_0 \leftarrow \mathcal{A}(\beta_0)] \cdot \varepsilon$$

$$= \varepsilon \sum_{\beta_0 \in B} \sum_{\gamma_0 \in C} \Pr[\gamma_0 \leftarrow \mathcal{A}(\beta_0)] = \varepsilon \sum_{\beta_0 \in B} 1 = |B| \cdot \varepsilon , \tag{1}$$

which is *independent of the attack algorithm* $\mathcal{A}$, and is effective if $|B| \cdot \varepsilon$ is sufficiently small (note that $|B|$ depends heavily on the individual scheme).

## 2.1  Our First Contribution: Using "Non-Cryptographic" PRGs

We point out that, the argument in [14] supposed to use cryptographic PRGs against distinguishers with bounded *time complexity*; consequently, *Condition 1 requires some unproven assumptions* (cf., P=NP? Problem), though (1) itself was derived without any assumptions on the complexity of the attack algorithm $\mathcal{A}$. In other words, *the security proof in [14] will be ineffective if an efficient algorithm to distinguish the cryptographic PRG from random is found.*

To resolve the issue, we use "non-cryptographic" PRGs (less frequently used in cryptography), especially the one by Impagliazzo, Nisan and Wigderson [7] based on expander graphs, hereafter called an *INW PRG*. The underlying complexity measure is close to the space complexity rather than the time complexity, and *the hardness to distinguish the PRG from random is unconditionally provable* by graph-theoretic facts. Now Condition 1 becomes provable as well, therefore our security proof under the use of the PRG is also made unconditional.

## 3  Impagliazzo–Nisan–Wigderson PRG

In the section, we summarize the construction and properties of the INW PRGs denoted by $G^{\mathrm{INW}}$. Let $\ell_{\mathrm{INW}}$ denote its seed length. The output set of $G^{\mathrm{INW}}$ is $\mathbf{R} = \prod_{v \in L(T)} R_v$ where $R_v$ is some set indexed by the leaves $v$ of a binary rooted tree $T$. For each $v \in V(T) \setminus L(T)$, let $\Gamma_v$ be a $\delta_v$-regular graph with $\nu_v$ vertices, and define $R_v$ to be the set of the directed edges of $\Gamma_v$ ($\delta_v \nu_v$ edges in total). See Sect. 1.4 for some notations. We say that a map $f \colon X \to Y$ is *most balanced*, if $|f^{-1}(y_1)| - |f^{-1}(y_2)| \in \{-1, 0, 1\}$ for any $y_1, y_2 \in Y$. Then for each $v \in V(T) \setminus L(T)$, we define a map $G_v^{\mathrm{INW}} \colon R_v \to R_{v_\leftarrow} \times R_{v_\rightarrow}$ in the following manner. Given a directed edge $x_v \in R_v$ of $\Gamma_v$, let $y_{v_\leftarrow}$ and $y_{v_\rightarrow}$ denote its source and destination vertices, respectively. Then we map $y_{v_\leftarrow}$ and $y_{v_\rightarrow}$ to an element $x_{v_\leftarrow} \in R_{v_\leftarrow}$ and an element $x_{v_\rightarrow} \in R_{v_\rightarrow}$ by fixed, most balanced maps $V(\Gamma_v) \to R_{v_\leftarrow}$ and $V(\Gamma_v) \to R_{v_\rightarrow}$, respectively. Now we define $G_v^{\mathrm{INW}}(x_v) := (x_{v_\leftarrow}, x_{v_\rightarrow})$.

Then $G^{\mathrm{INW}}$ is constructed as follows. Given a seed $s \in \{0, 1\}^{\ell_{\mathrm{INW}}}$, first we map $s$ to an element $x_{r(T)} \in R_{r(T)}$ by a fixed, most balanced map $\{0, 1\}^{\ell_{\mathrm{INW}}} \rightarrow R_{r(T)}$. Secondly, we determine the elements $x_v \in R_v$ for $v \in V(T) \setminus \{r(T)\}$ by successively applying the maps $G_u^{\mathrm{INW}}$ for $u \in V(T) \setminus L(T)$ in an ascending order with respect to the depth of $u$. Finally, we define $G^{\mathrm{INW}}(s) := (x_v)_{v \in L(T)} \in \boldsymbol{R}$.

To evaluate the indistinguishability of the INW PRG quantitatively, here we fix a concrete computational model associated to the tree $T$ as follows:

- In the model, an algorithm is equipped with a common memory $M$ which can take one of $|M|$ possible states, as well as a processor associated to each leaf of $T$ (identified with the leaf itself) that has unbounded computational power and unbounded local memory. Given an input $\boldsymbol{r} = (r_v)_{v \in L(T)}$ for the algorithm, the component $r_v$ is distributed to $v \in L(T)$ at the beginning.
- The execution of the algorithm consists of $\mu$ rounds, where $\mu$ is a parameter. For each round, the first (leftmost) leaf is activated first, and each leaf is activated after the execution of the previous leaf ends. Each leaf first reads the current state of the common memory $M$, decides the new memory state by using the current state of $M$ and the local memory state of the leaf, and updates the state of $M$ accordingly (the local memory state is also updated).
- Finally, after the final round ends, the output of the algorithm is decided according to the final state of the common memory $M$.

The *adjacency matrix* of graph $\Gamma_v$ is a symmetric $\{0, 1\}$-matrix of size $\nu_v$, where the $(i, j)$-entry is 1 if and only if the $i$-th and the $j$-th vertices of $\Gamma_v$ are adjacent. Since $\Gamma_v$ is a $\delta_v$-regular graph, if we order the eigenvalues of the adjacency matrix as $\lambda_1 \geq \lambda_2 \geq \cdots \geq \lambda_{\nu_v}$, then $\lambda_1 = \delta_{\nu_v}$. Now we define $\lambda(\Gamma_v) := \max\{|\lambda_2|, |\lambda_{\nu_v}|\}$. On the other hand, it is known that, for any integers $n, m \geq 1$, the statistical distance between the uniform random variable on $[m] := \{1, \ldots, m\}$ and the output of any most balanced map $[n] \rightarrow [m]$ with uniformly random input is $\rho(n, m) := (n \bmod m) \cdot (m - (n \bmod m))/(nm)$, where $(n \bmod m)$ is the remainder of $n$ modulo $m$ (see Lemma VI.1 of [14]). Now we have the following results (whose proofs are similar to the original paper [7] and are omitted due to the page limitation; see the full version for details):

**Theorem 1.** *Let $\mathcal{R}_U$ denote the uniform distribution on $\boldsymbol{R}$, and let $\mathcal{R}_P$ denote the output distribution of $G^{\mathrm{INW}}$ with uniformly random seed $s \in \{0, 1\}^{\ell_{\mathrm{INW}}}$. Then for any algorithm $\mathcal{D}$ described in the computational model above, we have*

$$\Delta(\mathcal{D}(\mathcal{R}_U), \mathcal{D}(\mathcal{R}_P)) \leq |M|^{\mu} \sum_{v \in V(T) \setminus L(T)} \frac{\lambda(\Gamma_v)}{2\delta_v} + \Delta_{\mathrm{dist}} ,$$

$$\Delta_{\mathrm{dist}} := \rho(2^{\ell_{\mathrm{INW}}}, \nu_{r(T)}\delta_{r(T)}) + \sum_{\substack{v \in V(T) \setminus L(T) \\ v \neq r(T)}} \rho(\nu_{v\uparrow}, \nu_v \delta_v) + \sum_{v \in L(T)} \rho(\nu_{v\uparrow}, |R_v|) .$$

**Theorem 2.** *Let $\mathcal{R}_U$ and $\mathcal{R}_P$ be as in Theorem 1. In the situation of Sect. 2, suppose that the algorithm $[\mathcal{J}_{\beta_0, \gamma_0}]$ can be described in the computational model above with common memories of size bounded by $|M|$ and at most $\mu$ rounds*

**Table 1.** Comparison of seed lengths (here "Our result" shows the seed lengths by our result; "Plain" shows the originally used random bits; "[14]" shows the seed lengths in the previous result [14]; and the approximate values are written in scientific E notation)

| $N$ | $10^3$ | $10^4$ | $10^5$ | $10^6$ | $10^7$ | $10^8$ | $10^9$ |
|---|---|---|---|---|---|---|---|
| $m$ | 614 | 702 | 789 | 877 | 964 | 1052 | 1139 |
| Plain | 9.21E6 | 1.05E8 | 1.18E9 | 1.31E10 | 1.44E11 | 1.57E12 | 1.70E13 |
| [14] | 6.87E6 | 9.72E6 | 1.33E7 | 1.75E7 | 2.25E7 | 2.83E7 | 3.51E7 |
| Our result | 3.09E5 | 4.90E5 | 6.65E5 | 8.67E5 | 1.14E6 | 1.40E6 | 1.68E6 |

for any $\beta_0 \in B$ and $\gamma_0 \in C$. Then, without any assumption on hardness of computational problems nor on the complexity of the algorithm $\mathcal{A}$, we have the following, where $\Delta_{\mathsf{dist}}$ is defined as in Theorem 1:

$$|\mathsf{Succ}_{\mathcal{A},\mathcal{R}_U} - \mathsf{Succ}_{\mathcal{A},\mathcal{R}_P}| \leq |B| \cdot \left( |M|^\mu \sum_{v \in V(T) \setminus L(T)} \frac{\lambda(\Gamma_v)}{2\delta_v} + \Delta_{\mathsf{dist}} \right)$$

We note that the bounds in Theorems 1 and 2 become better when $\lambda(\Gamma_v)$ becomes smaller. A graph $\Gamma_v$ is called a *Ramanujan graph*, if $\lambda(\Gamma_v) \leq 2\sqrt{\delta_v - 1}$; this is known to almost attain the theoretical lower bound of $\lambda(\Gamma_v)$ (see e.g., Sect. 5.3 of [6]). For example, we can use Ramanujan graphs given by a part of the result by Morgenstern [12] (see the full version of the paper for details):

**Proposition 1 ([12]).** *For any positive integers $L, D$, there is an explicit construction of a $(2^D + 1)$-regular Ramanujan graph with $2^{6DL} - 2^{2DL}$ vertices.*

## 4    Example: Collusion-Secure Codes

In the section, we give a numerical example of our technique applied to a collusion-secure code in [13] (with the number $c = 3$ of corrupted users), which is the same as the example in [14] and has information-theoretic security. Roughly speaking, in the abstract security game in Sect. 2, $\alpha$ is the collection of $m$-bit words, one per each of the $N$ users; $\beta$ is the collection of the three words for the corrupted users; $\gamma$ is a word of length $m$ on an expanded alphabet $\{0, 1, ?\}$, where '?' means a bit erasure; and $F_3(\alpha, \gamma) = 1$ if and only if the "most suspicious" user determined from $\alpha$ and $\gamma$ is not a corrupted user. See the numerical example in [14] for details. Then an analysis shows that, to bound the difference $|\mathsf{Succ}_{\mathcal{A},\mathcal{R}_U} - \mathsf{Succ}_{\mathcal{A},\mathcal{R}_P}|$ by a value $\varepsilon_{\mathsf{diff}}$, the seed length for the INW PRG becomes $\ell_{\mathsf{INW}} \sim 12 \log_2 N (\log_2 N + 4m + \log_2(1/\varepsilon_{\mathsf{diff}}))$ when $N \to \infty$ (see the full version of the paper), while $\ell_{\mathsf{org}} := 15mN + m$ random bits are originally used in total. On the other hand, for the choices of $\varepsilon_{\mathsf{diff}} := 10^{-6}$ and other parameters as the numerical example in [14], the seed lengths $\ell_{\mathsf{INW}}$ are calculated as in Table 1. This table shows that our seed lengths are much shorter than the originally required random bits and also significantly smaller than those in [14].

## 5  Our Second Contribution: Dual-Mode PRGs

We note that, in the situation of Sect. 2, no security is guaranteed if the set $B$ (hence the right-hand side of (1)) is too large (though (1) itself holds unconditionally). To resolve the issue, in the section we propose a technique to modify the INW PRG in such a way that, by using the resulting PRG, the information-theoretic security is kept if $B$ is sufficiently small, while at least computational security is guaranteed even if $B$ is too large. For two random variables $\mathcal{R}_1, \mathcal{R}_2$ on the output set $R$ of the INW PRG $G^{\mathrm{INW}}$, let $\mathcal{R}_1 * \mathcal{R}_2$ denote the random variable on $R$ computing the component-wise group operation $*$ for values of $\mathcal{R}_1$ and $\mathcal{R}_2$. We call $\mathcal{R}_P * \mathcal{R}_C$ the *dual-mode PRG*, where $\mathcal{R}_C$ denotes the output distribution of a cryptographic (computationally secure) PRG $G^{\mathrm{comp}}$. Then we have the following result (deduced from the fact that both $\mathcal{R}_U * \mathcal{R}_C$ and $\mathcal{R}_P * \mathcal{R}_U$ are identical to $\mathcal{R}_U$; see the full version of the paper for details):

**Theorem 3.** *Under the same assumptions as Theorem 2, we have:*

- *The value* $|\mathrm{Succ}_{\mathcal{A}, \mathcal{R}_U} - \mathrm{Succ}_{\mathcal{A}, \mathcal{R}_P * \mathcal{R}_C}|$ *satisfies the same inequality as the value* $|\mathrm{Succ}_{\mathcal{A}, \mathcal{R}_U} - \mathrm{Succ}_{\mathcal{A}, \mathcal{R}_P}|$ *in Theorem 2.*
- *Suppose that the maps* $F_1$, $F_2$ *and* $F_3$ *in Sect. 2,* $G^{\mathrm{INW}}$ *and the operator* $*$ *in* $R$ *are all polynomial-time computable. Then* $|\mathrm{Succ}_{\mathcal{A}, \mathcal{R}_U} - \mathrm{Succ}_{\mathcal{A}, \mathcal{R}_P * \mathcal{R}_C}|$ *is negligible for any probabilistic polynomial-time algorithm* $\mathcal{A}$.

As an example, we apply the dual-mode PRG to Shamir's $k$-out-of-$n$ secret sharing scheme [17] over the field $\mathbb{F}_q$. Let $k'$, $1 \leq k' < k$, denote the number of corrupted users. Then an analysis (see the full version of the paper) shows that, to bound the bias of the $k'$ corrupted shares from uniform by $\varepsilon_{\mathrm{diff}} = k^{-\omega(1)}$ (negligible in $k$), the seed length for the part $G^{\mathrm{INW}}$ of the dual-mode PRG is

$$\ell_{\mathrm{INW}} \sim 12 \log_2 k (k' \log_2 q + \omega(1) \log_2 k) \quad (\text{when } k \to \infty) ,$$

having lower order than the number $\ell_{\mathrm{org}} \sim k \log_2 q$ of the originally used random bits if $k' = o(k / \log_2 k)$. Now the corrupted shares are statistically close to uniform (information-theoretic security) when at most $k'$ users are corrupted, while these are computationally indistinguishable from uniform (at least computational security) even if more than $k'$ (and at most $k - 1$) users are corrupted.

## 6  Other Potential Applications

Finally, in this section, we discuss a possible application of our result to lossy encryption [1,9,15] with small randomness space. In [5], Hemenway and Ostrovsky showed that any lossy encryption scheme for which the randomness space for encryption is smaller than the plaintext space can be converted into a (slightly) lossy trapdoor function (e.g., [16]); and the latter is further converted (via other results in [8,11]) into various cryptographic primitives such as CCA-secure encryption and adaptive trapdoor functions. However, construction of such schemes with small randomness spaces is difficult; the only known construction so far (to the author's best knowledge) is the one based on the Damgård–Jurik cryptosystem [2]. Indeed, since the ciphertexts under a lossy key should be *statistically* indistinguishable, a naive strategy of reducing the randomness space by cryptographic PRGs is not effective. The author hopes that our *unconditional* proof technique using "non-cryptographic" PRGs is effective to resolve the problem; a detailed study is a future research topic.

**Acknowledgments.** The author thanks Takeshi Koshiba for a fruitful discussion on a previous version of the work; thanks the members of Shin-Akarui-Angou-Benkyo-Kai, especially Takahiro Matsuda for his suggestion of the content in Sect. 6 and many comments, Keita Emura and Goichiro Hanaoka for their precious comments; and thanks the anonymous referees for their comments.

# References

1. Bellare, M., Hofheinz, D., Yilek, S.: Possibility and impossibility results for encryption and commitment secure under selective opening. In: Joux, A. (ed.) EUROCRYPT 2009. LNCS, vol. 5479, pp. 1–35. Springer, Heidelberg (2009)
2. Damgård, I., Jurik, M., Nielsen, J.B.: A generalization of Paillier's public-key system with applications to electronic voting. Int. J. Inform. Sec. 9(6), 371–385 (2010)
3. Dubrov, B., Ishai, Y.: On the randomness complexity of efficient sampling. In: Proceedings of STOC 2006, pp. 711–720 (2006)
4. Farashahi, R.R., Schoenmakers, B., Sidorenko, A.: Efficient pseudorandom generators based on the DDH assumption. In: Okamoto, T., Wang, X. (eds.) PKC 2007. LNCS, vol. 4450, pp. 426–441. Springer, Heidelberg (2007)
5. Hemenway, B., Ostrovsky, R.: Building injective trapdoor functions from oblivious transfer. Electronic Colloquium on Computational Complexity, TR10-127, Revision 1 (2010), http://eccc.hpi-web.de/report/2010/127/
6. Hoory, S., Linial, N., Wigderson, A.: Expander graphs and their applications. Bull. Amer. Math. Soc. 43(4), 439–561 (2006)
7. Impagliazzo, R., Nisan, N., Wigderson, A.: Pseudorandomness for network algorithms. In: Proceedings of STOC 1994, pp. 356–364 (1994)
8. Kiltz, E., Mohassel, P., O'Neill, A.: Adaptive trapdoor functions and chosen-ciphertext security. In: Gilbert, H. (ed.) EUROCRYPT 2010. LNCS, vol. 6110, pp. 673–692. Springer, Heidelberg (2010)
9. Kol, G., Naor, M.: Cryptography and game theory: Designing protocols for exchanging information. In: Canetti, R. (ed.) TCC 2008. LNCS, vol. 4948, pp. 320–339. Springer, Heidelberg (2008)
10. Levin, L.A.: One-way functions and pseudorandom generators. Combinatorica 7(4), 357–363 (1987)
11. Mol, P., Yilek, S.: Chosen-ciphertext security from slightly lossy trapdoor functions. In: Nguyen, P.Q., Pointcheval, D. (eds.) PKC 2010. LNCS, vol. 6056, pp. 296–311. Springer, Heidelberg (2010)
12. Morgenstern, M.: Existence and explicit constructions of q+1 regular Ramanujan graphs for every prime power q. J. Combin. Theory, Series B 62, 44–62 (1994)

13. Nuida, K., Fujitsu, S., Hagiwara, M., Kitagawa, T., Watanabe, H., Ogawa, K., Imai, H.: An improvement of discrete Tardos fingerprinting codes. Des. Codes Cryptography 52(3), 339–362 (2009)
14. Nuida, K., Hanaoka, G.: On the security of pseudorandomized information-theoretically secure schemes. IEEE Trans. Inform. Theory 59(1), 635–652 (2013)
15. Peikert, C., Vaikuntanathan, V., Waters, B.: A framework for efficient and composable oblivious transfer. In: Wagner, D. (ed.) CRYPTO 2008. LNCS, vol. 5157, pp. 554–571. Springer, Heidelberg (2008)
16. Peikert, C., Waters, B.: Lossy trapdoor functions and their applications. In: Proceedings of STOC 2008, pp. 187–196 (2008)
17. Shamir, A.: How to share a secret. Commun. ACM 22(11), 612–613 (1979)

# Equivalence between MAC, WCR and PRF for Blockcipher Based Constructions

Nilanjan Datta and Mridul Nandi

Indian Statistical Institute, Kolkata, India 700108
nilanjan_isi_jrf@yahoo.com, mridul.nandi@gmail.com

**Abstract.** In FSE'10, Nandi proved a sufficient condition of pseudo random function (PRF) for affine domain extensions (ADE), a wide class of blockcipher based domain extensions. This sufficient condition is satisfied by all known ADE, however, it is not a characterization of PRF. In this paper we completely characterize the ADE and show that weaker security notions *message authentication code (MAC) and weakly collision resistant (WCR) are indeed equivalent to PRF*.

**Keywords:** Affine Domain Extension, Blockcipher, MAC, PRF, WCR.

## 1 Introduction

During a message exchange protocol in the symmetric key setting, sender sends a message $M$ to the receiver along with a tag $T = \mathcal{G}_K(M)$ where $\mathcal{G}_K$ denotes a message authentication code (MAC) with a shared key $K$. The pair $(M, T)$ is called a *valid pair*. This ensures the "integrity" of the message and the "authenticity" of the sender by verifying validness of the received pair. $\mathcal{G}$ is called $(t, q, \sigma, \epsilon)$-mac if for any $(t, q, \sigma)$-forgery adversary $\mathcal{F}$, i.e. it makes at most $q$ queries having at most $\sigma$ blocks (inputs of the underlying blockcipher) with (time) complexity at most $t$, has **mac-advantage**

$$\mathbf{Adv}_{\mathcal{G}}^{\mathrm{mac}}(\mathcal{F}) := \mathbf{Pr}_{\mathrm{rand}(\mathcal{F}), K}[(M, T) \leftarrow \mathcal{F}^{\mathcal{G}_K}, \ (M, T) \text{ is a fresh valid pair}]$$

at most $\epsilon$. Here, $\mathrm{rand}(A)$ denotes the random coin of an algorithm $A$. Weak Collision Resistant (WCR) [1] is a variant of collision security property of $\mathcal{G}_K(\cdot)$. It is called $(t, q, \sigma, \epsilon)$-wcr if any $(t, q, \sigma)$-collision adversary $\mathcal{C}$ has *wcr-advantage*

$$\mathbf{Adv}_{\mathcal{G}}^{wcr}(\mathcal{C}) := \mathbf{Pr}_{\mathrm{rand}(\mathcal{C}), K}[\mathcal{C}^{\mathcal{G}_K} = (M, M'), \ \mathcal{G}_K(M) = \mathcal{G}_K(M'), \ M \neq M']$$

at most $\epsilon$. A Pseudo Random Function (PRF) [9] over $\mathcal{M}$ is a keyed function $\mathcal{G}_K$ over $\mathcal{M}$, whose output distribution is "indistinguishable" from that of random function $\mathcal{R}$ (output is uniformly distributed for every fresh queries) for any computational adversary. More formally, it is called $(t, q, \sigma, \epsilon)$-*pseudorandom function* if for every $(t, q, \sigma)$-distinguisher $\mathcal{D}$, the **prf-advantage**

$$\mathbf{Adv}_{\mathcal{G}}^{\mathrm{prf}}(\mathcal{D}) := \mathbf{Pr}_{\mathrm{rand}(\mathcal{D}), \mathcal{R}}[\mathcal{D}^{\mathcal{R}} = 1] - \mathbf{Pr}_{\mathrm{rand}(\mathcal{D}), K \in_R \{0,1\}^k}[\mathcal{D}^{\mathcal{G}_K} = 1]$$

is at most $\epsilon$. One can similarly define prp-advantage $\mathbf{Adv}_{\mathcal{G}}^{\mathrm{prp}}(\mathcal{D})$ when $\mathcal{G}$ is distinguished from a random permutation $\Pi$. Without loss of generality, throughout the paper, we simplify distinguisher which makes **exactly** $q$ **distinct queries**.

S.S.M. Chow et al. (Eds.): ProvSec 2014, LNCS 8782, pp. 300–308, 2014.

## 1.1    (Affine) Domain Extension

A domain extension based on a keyed blockcipher $E_K$ (a keyed family of permutation usually modeled to be PRP [13] or PRF) invokes $E_K$ several times sequentially. In case of an affine domain extension (or ADE) [16], the inputs (called *intermediate inputs*) to $E_K$ are determined by some *affine functions* of the previous outputs (called *intermediate outputs*) of $E_K$. The output of the last invocation of the blockcipher is the final output. We denote a vector $a$ by $(a_1, \ldots, a_t)$. Let $a^{\mathrm{tr}}$ denote its transpose (column) vector and $\bar{a} := (1, a_1, \ldots, a_t)$. A matrix $C_{l \times l} = ((c_{i,j}))$ over $\mathbb{F}_{2^n}$ (or $\{0,1\}^n$ is said to be *lower-triangular* if $c_{i,j} = 0$ for all $1 \leq i \leq j \leq l$.

**Definition 1.** *A domain extension $\mathcal{G}$ is called* Affine Domain Extension *(ADE) over $\mathcal{M}$ if for each message $M \in \mathcal{M}$, we associate a lower-triangular matrix $C_{l \times l}$ and $m_{l \times 1}$, such that $\mathcal{G}_K(M) = y_l$ where $y_i$'s are defined recursively as (1) $(x_1, \ldots, x_l)^{\mathrm{tr}} = A \cdot (1\ y_1\ \ldots\ y_l)^{\mathrm{tr}}$, $A = (m\ C)$ and (2) $E_K(x_i) = y_i$, $1 \leq i \leq l$. The matrix $A$ is called* **coefficient matrix** *of $M$ and the integer $l := l(M)$ is called the length of $M$. Similarly, we define $\mathcal{G}^\pi(M)$ where $\pi$ is a permutation.*

A class of popular constructions like CBC-MAC [6], GCBC* [18], OMAC [10], PMAC [8] etc. are some of such examples. For example, in case of CBC-MAC applied to a three block message $M = (m_1, m_2, m_3)$ the corresponding coefficient matrix is $(M^{\mathrm{tr}} C)$ where $c_{2,1} = c_{3,2} = 1$ and all other entries are zero. The original PRF bounds for the above were about $\frac{\sigma^2}{2^n}$ or $\frac{l^2 \cdot Q^2}{2^n}$ [4,5,11,12,19,21] and later [3,14,15,16,17,21,22] have been improved where $\ell$ and $\sigma$ are the longest and total number of blocks present in all queries.

## 1.2    Our Contribution

We know that a PRF implies a message authentication code and weakly collision resistant. However, the converse is not true in general. In this paper, we show that **message authentication code (MAC) and weakly collision resistant (WCR) are indeed equivalent to PRF for ADE based on blockcipher modeled to be a PRP.** Thus, we have a complete characterization of ADE. The previously known sufficient condition [16] is not necessary.

**Theorem** [Main theorem of the paper]. Let $\mathcal{G}$ be a ADE based on a random permutation $\Pi$ over $\{0,1\}^n$. Then for any $(t, q, \sigma)$-distinguisher $\mathcal{D}$ there is a $(t', q, \sigma)$-forgery and $(t', q, \sigma)$-collision adversaries $\mathcal{F}$ and $\mathcal{C}$ respectively such that $\mathbf{Adv}_{\mathcal{G}^\Pi}^{\mathrm{prf}}(\mathcal{D}) \leq \frac{4\sigma^2}{2^n} + 2\min\{\mathbf{Adv}_{\mathcal{G}^\Pi}^{\mathrm{wcr}}(\mathcal{C}), \mathbf{Adv}_{\mathcal{G}^\Pi}^{\mathrm{mac}}(\mathcal{F})\}$ where $t' \approx t$.

## 2    Estimation of Probability of a View

Suppose we have $q$ messages (queried by an adversary), $M_i \in \mathcal{M}$ of length $l_i$ in $n$-bit blocks, $1 \leq i \leq q$ and their corresponding co-efficient matrix is given by $A_i = (m_i\ C_i)$. Then the joint co-efficient matrix $A := A^{M_1, \ldots, M_q}$ of the $q$ messages is given by the following partition matrix.

$$\begin{pmatrix} m_1 & C_1 & 0 & \cdots & 0 \\ m_2 & 0 & C_2 & \cdots & 0 \\ \cdot & \cdot & \cdot & \cdot & \cdot \\ \cdot & \cdot & \cdot & \cdot & \cdot \\ m_q & 0 & 0 & \cdots & C_q \end{pmatrix}_{t\times(t+1)}.$$

Here $t = t_q$ and $t_i = \sum_{j=1}^{i} l_j$. To each $\pi$ we associate an intermediate input and output vectors are $x^\pi := (x_1, \ldots, x_t)$ and $y^\pi := (y_1, \ldots, y_t)$ respectively, where (I) $A \cdot \overline{y} = x$ and (II) $\pi(x_i) = y_i$, $i \in [1..t] := \{1, \ldots, t\}$. Let $\mathbb{P}_n[y]$ denote the set of all permutations $\pi$ with $y = y^\pi$. So

$$\mathbb{P}_n[y] = \{\pi : \pi(x_i) = y_i, 1 \le i \le t, x = A \cdot \overline{y}\}, \quad |\mathbb{P}_n[y]| = (2^n - s)! \quad (1)$$

where $s$ denotes the number of distinct values of the output vector $y$. Let us define **collision relation** $\mathsf{coll}(y) :=\sim$ over $[1..t]$ of a vector $y$ as $i \sim j$ if $y_i = y_j$. It is an equivalence relation capturing the collisions of the elements of the vector $y$. We define $\mathsf{coll}_\pi = \mathsf{coll}(y^\pi)$. We identify the tuples of distinct elements $w = (w_1, \ldots, w_t)$ as set $\{w_1, \ldots, w_t\}$. From the context it must be clear. Given a subset $T = \{t_1, \ldots, t_q\} \subseteq [1..t]$ we define $w[T]$ by the sub-tuple $(w_{t_1}, \ldots, w_{t_q})$. For a matrix $A$, $A[i, \cdot]$ and $A[\cdot, j]$ denote the $i$th row and $j$th column respectively. Similarly we define the sub-matrices $A[1..i, \cdot]$ or $A[\cdot, 1..j]$ etc.

Let $\mathcal{V}$ be the set of all tuples $w = (w_1, \ldots, w_q)$. The view of $D^\mathcal{O}$, denoted $\mathsf{view}(D^\mathcal{O})$, by the tuple $(w_1, \ldots, w_q) \in \mathcal{V}$ where $w_i$ denotes the response of the $i$th query, $1 \le i \le q$. We say that a view $w$ is *realizable* if $\mathbf{Pr}_\mathcal{O}[\mathsf{view}(D^\mathcal{O}) = w]$ is positive. The set of all realizable views is denoted by $\mathcal{V}_\mathcal{O}$. We denote the *truncated view* $\mathsf{view}(D^\mathcal{O})[i]$ by the $i$-tuple $(w_1, \ldots, w_i)$ where $\mathsf{view}(D^\mathcal{O}) = (w_1, \ldots, w_q)$, $i \le q$.

$$\mathbf{Pr}[\mathsf{view}(D^\mathcal{O})[i] = w] = \sum_{v \in \mathcal{V}: v[1..i] = w} \mathsf{Pr}[\mathsf{view}(D^\mathcal{O}) = v].$$

Note that, for $v \in \mathcal{V}$, we have, $\mathbf{Pr}_\mathcal{R}[\mathsf{view}(D^\mathcal{R})[i] = v[1..i]] = 2^{-ni}$. In this section we provide an estimate of probability of realizing views where the oracle is an affine domain extension $\mathcal{G}$ based on a random permutation $\Pi$ on $\{0,1\}^n$.

**Lemma 1.** *Let $w = (w_1, \ldots, w_q) = v[1..q]$ for some $v \in \mathcal{V}$. Then either $w$ is not realizable (i.e. the probability of realizing $w$ is zero) or*

$$\mathbf{Pr}_\Pi[\mathsf{view}(D^{\mathcal{G}^\Pi})[q] = w] = \sum_{s \ge 1} \frac{N_{w,s}}{P(2^n, s)} \quad (2)$$

*where $P(2^n, s) = 2^n(2^n - 1)\ldots(2^n - s + 1)$ and $N_{w,s}$ denotes the number of output vectors $y$ with $s$ many distinct elements and $y_{t_i} = w_i$, $1 \le i \le q$.*

Due to page limit, we skip the proof of the above and also some of the results mentioned later. The proof can be found in [7]. To use the above lemma we need to provide an estimate of $N_{v,s}$ which can be done by identifying a special equivalence relation $\sim^*$, called *forced relation*, such that there are sufficient number of output vectors $y$ inducing the forced collision relation, i.e., $\mathsf{coll}(y) =\sim^*$. Since for all these output vectors the $s$ value is same with the number of equivalence classes of $\sim^*$, we will immediately have a lower bound of the probability of the view. More precisely, if we can show the following: there is a relation, called forced relation, with $s + q$ many classes such that the number

of output vectors $y$ with $y_{t_i} = w_i$ for all $i$ is at least $2^{ns}(1 - \epsilon)$, then we have
$\mathbf{Pr}_\Pi[\text{view}(D^{\mathcal{G}^\Pi})[q] = w] = \sum_{s \geq 1} \frac{N_{w,s}}{P(2^n, s)} \geq \frac{2^{ns}(1-\epsilon)}{P(2^n, s+q)} \geq \frac{1-\epsilon}{2^{nq}}$.

## 2.1   Forced Relation

Let $\mathcal{V}_{\text{dist}} = \{(w_1, \ldots, w_q) \in \mathcal{V} : w_i\text{'s are distinct}\}$, $\mathcal{V}_{\text{coll}} = \mathcal{V} \setminus \mathcal{V}_{\text{dist}}$. We study the following problem motivated from the probability computation of realizing a view $w = (w_1, \ldots, w_q) \in \mathcal{V}_{\text{dist}}$ as discussed above. Let $A = (m \ C)$ be a coefficient matrix with a strictly lower triangular matrix $C_{t \times t}$ and a vector $m_{t \times 1}$ whose elements are from $\mathbb{F}_{2^n}$. Let $\sim$ be an equivalence relation over $[t]$.

*Problem 1.* Reduce the affine function $A : y \mapsto A(y) := C \cdot y + m$, given that
(i) $\text{coll}(y) =\sim$ and
(ii) $y[T] = w$ where $T = (t_1, \ldots, t_q)$, $t_i$'s are distinct element from $[t]$.

There may be different ways to reduce a system of affine equations. We reduce the affine function by incorporating the given constraints as much as possible. The equivalence relation is considered not to have any collision on $T$, i.e. for all $i \neq j \in T$, $i \nsim j$, as we fix distinct final outputs $w_i$'s. Let the leader set (consists of one element from each equivalence class) of $\sim$ be $L \sqcup T$. We choose elements of $L := \{i_1, \ldots, i_s\}$ to be the minimum elements of the equivalence classes.

$$C \cdot y + m = m + (C[\cdot, 1] \cdot y_1 + \ldots + C[\cdot, t]y_t)$$
$$= (m + \sum_{t_i \in L_f} w_i \sum_{j \sim t_i} C[\cdot, j]) + \sum_{i \in L}(\sum_{j \sim i} C[\cdot, j])y_i$$
$$= A^{\text{rd}}[., 0] + \sum_{i \in L} A^{\text{rd}}[., i]y_i$$

where $\text{rd} = (\sim, T, w)$ to denote that we reduce the matrix $A$ using the triple rd. We can complete the matrix $A^{\text{rd}}_{t \times (t+1)}$ by defining $A^{rd}[., i] = \mathbf{0}$ for all $i \notin \{0\} \cup L$. Thus, we have
$$A(y) = x, \ \text{coll}(y) =\sim, \ y[T] = w$$

$$\Leftrightarrow \ A^{\text{rd}}[., 0] + \sum_{i_j \in L} A^{\text{rd}}[., i_j]z_j = x, \ z_j\text{'s are distinct and different from } w'_i s$$

where $z_j = y_{i_j}$, $1 \leq j \leq s$. In fact, given a solution $z$, we construct an unique solution $y$ as $y[L] = z$, $y[T] = w$ and the other $y_i$'s are defined through the relation $\sim$, i.e. $y_i = w_j$ if $i \sim t_j$ or $y_i = z_j$ if $i \sim i_j$. This reduction helps to solve $y$ for the following equations:

$$\text{coll}(y) = \text{coll}(m + C \cdot y) = \sim, \ y[T] = w. \tag{3}$$

If we denote $y[L] = z$ then the above equation is equivalently written as (i) $\text{coll}(A^{\text{rd}}(z)) =\sim$, (ii) $z_i$'s are distinct and different from $m_j$'s. Note that $\sim$ is fixed for which no collision on $T$. To have a solution we have the following immediate necessary condition:

$$A^{rd}[i,.] = A^{rd}[j,.] \Rightarrow i \sim j.$$

In fact, there are other different necessary conditions. However, we consider a special equivalence relation which would satisfy all necessary conditions and also gives several solutions of $z$ and hence $y$.

**Definition 2.** *We say that an equivalence relation $\sim$ over $[t]$ is* **forced relation** *w.r.t $A$, $T$ and $w$ if*

$$A^{rd}[i,.] = A^{rd}[j,.] \Leftrightarrow i \sim j, \quad \text{where } rd = (\sim, T, w). \tag{4}$$

Note that there may not exist forced relation with no collision in $T$. Clearly, if $\sim$ is a forced relation with no collision in $T$ then we have (i) $(A^{rd}[i,.] - A^{rd}[j,.])\bar{z} \neq 0$ for all $i \nsim j$ and (ii) $z_i$'s are distinct and different from $w_j$'s. The number of such $z$, equivalently $y$, is at least

$$2^{ns} \times (1 - \frac{\binom{s}{2} + \binom{t}{2} + st}{2^n}).$$

This can be easily seen as total possible choices without any constraint is $2^{ns}$ and number of $z$ which does not satisfy a given constraint is $2^{n(s-1)}$. The number of constraint is at most $\binom{s}{2} + \binom{t}{2} + st$ which includes the distinct choices of $z$, the number of pairs $(i,j)$ for which $i \nsim j$ and different from $w_i$'s. Now we prove the existence of forced collision which may or may not have collisions in $T$. In fact, we prove a more general statement which says the existence of extending a given relation to a forced relation.

**Lemma 2 (Extension Lemma).** *Given any relation $\sim$ satisfying the property $i \sim j \Rightarrow A^{rd}[i,\cdot] = A^{rd}[j,\cdot]$ where $rd = (\sim, T, w)$ then there is a forced relation $\sim'$, denoted $\text{Ext}_A(\sim)$, containing $\sim$.*

*Moreover, $\text{Ext}$ can be defined in a way such that whenever $\sim$ is a forced collision w.r.t $A[1..t', \cdot]$, $T$ and $w$ for some $t' \leq t_q$ then $\sim' = \sim$ on $[1..t']$.*

**Corollary 1.** *If we choose $\sim$ to be an empty relation then from the above lemma: there is always a forced collision relation.*

## 3   Reducing Distinguishing to Forgery

A distinguisher $D$, distinguishing an ADE $\mathcal{G}^{\Pi}$ based on a random permutation $\Pi$ from a random function $\mathcal{R}$, a forgery $\mathcal{F}^{\mathcal{G}^{\Pi}}$ is defined as follows: $D$ initially keeps an equivalence relation $\sim_0$, an empty coefficient matrix $A_0$ and an empty forbidden set $F_0$. In addition with these, it also stores a vector $w$ and $t$, initialized to empty. Now, it runs $D$ and responses as described below.

§ **On $i^{\text{th}}$ query $M_i$ from $D$:** It updates (i) the coefficient matrix $A_i$ and $t_i$ from $M_i$, $A_{i-1}$ and $t[1..i-1]$, (ii) the equivalence relation $\sim_i$ by running $\text{Ext}_{A_i}(\sim_{i-1})$ for $w[1..i-1] = (w_1, \ldots, w_{i-1})$ and $t[1..i-1] = (t_1, \ldots, t_{i-1})$ and (iii) computes the forbidden set

$$F_i = \{ \frac{A_i[a,0] - A_i[b,0]}{A_i[a,k] - A_i[b,k]} : \exists k, a, b < t_i, A_i[a,k] \neq A_i[b,k], A_i[a,z] = A_i[b,z] \forall z \neq k \}.$$

1. If $t_i \sim_i t_j$ for some $j < i$ then forge event sets true and forge by the pair $(M_i, w_j)$ and stop.[1]
2. Otherwise, it forwards the query and obtains a response $w_i$. If $w_i \in F_i$ then abort (this can happen with low probability as the size of the forbidden set would be bounded). The reason of considering forbidden set is to have consistence update of forced collision pattern.

§ **Finalization:** If it neither aborts nor forges then it aborts and we would be able to prove that, in this case, $D$ can not distinguish $\mathcal{G}^\Pi$ from random function. The more details of the above description is given below.

## 3.1   Computation of of Forging Probability of $\mathcal{F}$

---

**Input:** $A, T, W, \sim$

**Extension Algorithm $Ext_A(\sim)$**
1   let $T$ be the set of final output indexes, $L$ is the set of smallest indexes corresponding to an equivalence class which are not $\sim$-related to any element of $T$.
2   If $k \in T$ (Case : 1)
3        Add $A^\sim[*, j].w_k$ to $A^\sim[*, 0]$
4        Make $A^\sim[*, j] = 0$
5        Add the pair $(t_k, j)$ to $\sim$
6   If $k \in L$ (Case : 2)
7        Add $A^\sim[*, j]$ to $A^\sim[*, k]$
8        make $A^\sim[*, j] = 0$
9        Add the pair $(k, j)$ to $\sim$

---

**Algorithm 1:** Extension Algorithm

**Lemma 3.** *If $\sim_i$ is force collision relation with respect to $A$, $w = (w_1, \ldots, w_{i-1})$ and $T = (t_1, \ldots, t_{i-1})$. Then if $w_i \notin F_i$, then force collision relation doesn't change.*

We categorize the possible views of $\mathcal{D}$ into the following four classes - (i) collision view $\mathcal{V}_{\text{coll}}$ (collisions in $w_i$ values), (ii) random view $\mathcal{V}_{\text{rand}} = \{(w_1, w_2, \cdots, w_q) : \forall i, j \neq i, w_i \notin F_i$ and $t_i \not\sim^* t_j \}$ (iii) forbidden view $\mathcal{V}_{\text{forb}} = \{(w_1, w_2, \cdots, w_i) : w_i \in F_i$ and $\forall j \leq i, k < j, t_k \not\sim^* t_j \}$ and (iv) forge view $\mathcal{V}_{\text{forge}} = \{(w_1, w_2, \cdots, w_i) : \forall k < i, w_k \notin F_k$ and $\exists j < i, t_i \sim^* t_j \}$. It is easy to see that, $\mathcal{F}$ forges whenever the view of $D^{\mathcal{G}^\Pi}$ is a forge view and the probability that a random view is forbidden has low probability. We skip the proofs as these are more or less straightforward.

**Lemma 4.** $\Pr[view(D^{\mathcal{G}^\Pi})$ *sets* forge *true*$] = \Pr[\mathcal{F}$ *forges*$] \leq \Pr[\mathcal{C}$ *wins WCR*$]$.

**Lemma 5.** $\Pr[view(\mathcal{D}^\mathcal{R}) \in \mathcal{V}_{\text{forb}}] \leq \varepsilon_1$ *where* $\varepsilon_1 = \frac{\binom{t}{2}}{2^n}$

---

[1] Note that when we reduce for WCR game we can have the collision for this event as $\mathcal{G}^\Pi(M_i) = \mathcal{G}^\Pi(M_j)$.

**Theorem 1 (Main theorem of the paper).** *Let $\mathcal{G}$ be a ADE based on a random permutation $\Pi$. Then for any distinguisher $\mathcal{D}$ there is a forgery and collision adversaries $\mathcal{F}$ and $\mathcal{C}$ respectively such that*

$$\mathbf{Adv}_{\mathcal{G}}^{\mathrm{prf}}(\mathcal{D}) \leq \frac{4\sigma^2}{2^n} + 2 \cdot \mu$$

*where $\mu = \min\{\mathbf{Adv}_{\mathcal{G}}^{\mathrm{wcr}}(\mathcal{C}),\ \mathbf{Adv}_{\mathcal{G}}^{\mathrm{mac}}(\mathcal{F})\}$.*

**Proof.** Note that $t \leq \sigma$ the maximum number of blocks in all queries. Recall that we have four types of disjoint views $\mathcal{V}_{\mathrm{coll}}, \mathcal{V}_{\mathrm{forb}}, \mathcal{V}_{forge}$ and $\mathcal{V}_{\mathrm{rand}}$. Since for all random views $v \in \mathcal{V}_{\mathrm{rand}}$, we have $\Pr[\mathsf{view}(\mathcal{D}^{\mathcal{G}}) = v] \geq (1 - \epsilon) \times \Pr[\mathsf{view}(\mathcal{D}^{\mathcal{R}}) = v]$ where $\epsilon \leq 2\sigma^2/2^n$ (as shown before). Using the idea of coefficient H-technique we have $\mathbf{Adv}_{\mathcal{G}}^{\mathrm{prf}}(\mathcal{D}) \leq \epsilon + \Pr[\mathsf{view}(\mathcal{D}^{\mathcal{R}}) \in \mathcal{V}_{\mathrm{forb}} \cup \mathcal{V}_{\mathrm{coll}}] + \Pr[\mathsf{view}(\mathcal{D}^{\mathcal{R}}) \in \mathcal{V}_{\mathrm{forge}}]$. Now from counting of $\mathcal{V}_{\mathrm{coll}}$ and lemma 5, we know that $\Pr[\mathsf{view}(\mathcal{D}^{\mathcal{R}}) \in \mathcal{V}_{\mathrm{forb}} \cup \mathcal{V}_{\mathrm{coll}}] \leq \frac{\binom{q}{2} + \binom{\sigma}{2}}{2^n}$. Now we need to bound $\Pr[\mathsf{view}(\mathcal{D}^{\mathcal{R}}) \in \mathcal{V}_{\mathrm{forge}}]$. Since the oracle of the distinguisher is random function, not the ADE, we use the following relationship for all forge views $v = (w_1, \ldots, w_i)$ (note that the first $(i - 1)$-tuple determines the forge event and $w_i$ can be chosen freely) :

$$\Pr[\mathsf{view}(\mathcal{D}^{\mathcal{G}})[i - 1] = v[1..i - 1]] \geq (1 - \epsilon) \times \Pr[\mathsf{view}(\mathcal{D}^{\mathcal{R}})[i] = v[1..i - 1]].$$

Since the view $(w_1, \ldots, w_{i-1})$ is actually a random view (as both forge and forbidden did not occur before) we have the above inequality. So combining this, we have

$$\mathbf{Adv}_{\mathcal{G}}^{\mathrm{prf}}(\mathcal{D}) \leq \frac{2\sigma^2}{2^n} + \frac{2\sigma^2}{2^n} + \frac{1}{1 - \frac{2\sigma^2}{2^n}} \times \Pr_{\Pi}[\mathsf{view}(\mathcal{D}^{\mathcal{G}}) \in \mathcal{V}_{\mathrm{forge}}] \leq \frac{4\sigma^2}{2^n} + 2 \cdot \mathbf{Adv}_{\mathcal{G}}^{\mathrm{mac}}(\mathcal{F})$$

Since we can assume that $4\sigma^2 \ll 2^n$, this proves our main theorem. Similarly we have the result for weak collision resistant. $\qquad\square$

## 4    Conclusion and Acknowledgement

In this paper we showed that message authentication code (MAC) and weakly collision resistant (WCR) are indeed equivalent to PRF for all PRP based Affine Domain Extension. This work is supported by the Centre of Excellence in Cryptology (CoEC) and R.C. Bose Centre, for Cryptology and Security, Indian Statistical Institute, Kolkata.

## References

1. Bellare, M.: New Proofs for NMAC and HMAC: Security Without Collision-Resistance. In: Dwork, C. (ed.) CRYPTO 2006. LNCS, vol. 4117, pp. 602–619. Springer, Heidelberg (2006). Citations in this document: §1.
2. Bellare, M., Guérin, R., Rogaway, P.: XOR MACs: New Methods for Message Authentication Using Finite Pseudorandom Functions. In: Coppersmith, D. (ed.) CRYPTO 1995. LNCS, vol. 963, pp. 15–28. Springer, Heidelberg (1995)

3. Bellare, M., Pietrzak, K., Rogaway, P.: Improved Security Analyses for CBC MACs. In: Shoup, V. (ed.) CRYPTO 2005. LNCS, vol. 3621, pp. 527–545. Springer, Heidelberg (2005)

4. Bellare, M., Kilian, J., Rogaway, P.: The security of cipher block chaining. In: Desmedt, Y.G. (ed.) CRYPTO 1994. LNCS, vol. 839, pp. 341–358. Springer, Heidelberg (1994)

5. Bernstein, D.J.: A short proof of the unpredictability of cipher block chaining (2005), http://cr.yp.to/papers.html#easycbc

6. Black, J.A., Rogaway, P.: CBC MACs for arbitrary-length messages: The three-key constructions. In: Bellare, M. (ed.) CRYPTO 2000. LNCS, vol. 1880, p. 197. Springer, Heidelberg (2000). Citations in this document: §1.1.

7. Datta, N., Nandi, M.: Equivalence between MAC and PRF for Blockcipher based Constructions, ePrint Archive, 2013/575 (2013). Citations in this document: §2.

8. Black, J.A., Rogaway, P.: A Block-Cipher Mode of Operations for Parallelizable Message Authentication. In: Knudsen, L.R. (ed.) EUROCRYPT 2002. LNCS, vol. 2332, pp. 384–397. Springer, Heidelberg (2002). Citations in this document: §1.1.

9. Goldreich, O., Goldwasser, S., Micali, S.: How to construct random functions. JACM, 792–807 (1986). Citations in this document: §1.

10. Iwata, T., Kurosawa, K.: OMAC: One-Key CBC MAC. In: Johansson, T. (ed.) FSE 2003. LNCS, vol. 2887, pp. 129–153. Springer, Heidelberg (2003). Citations in this document: S1.1.

11. Iwata, T., Kurosawa, K.: Stronger Security Bounds for OMAC, TMAC, and XCBC. In: Johansson, T., Maitra, S. (eds.) INDOCRYPT 2003. LNCS, vol. 2904, pp. 402–415. Springer, Heidelberg (2003)

12. Jutla, C.S.: PRF Domain Extension using DAG. In: Halevi, S., Rabin, T. (eds.) TCC 2006. LNCS, vol. 3876, pp. 561–580. Springer, Heidelberg (2006)

13. Luby, M., Racko, C.: How to construct pseudorandom permutations from pseudorandom functions. SIAM Journal of Computing, 373–386 (1988). Citations in this document: §1.1.

14. Minematsu, K., Matsushima, T.: New Bounds for PMAC, TMAC, and XCBC. In: Biryukov, A. (ed.) FSE 2007. LNCS, vol. 4593, pp. 434–451. Springer, Heidelberg (2007)

15. Mandal, A., Nandi, M.: Improved Security Analysis of PMAC. Journal of Mathematical Cryptology, 149–162 (July 2008)

16. Nandi, M.: A Unified Method for Improving PRF Bounds for a Class of Blockcipher Based MACs. In: Hong, S., Iwata, T. (eds.) FSE 2010. LNCS, vol. 6147, pp. 212–229. Springer, Heidelberg (2010). Citations in this document: §1.1, §1.2.

17. Nandi, M.: Improved security analysis for OMAC as a pseudorandom function. Journal of Mathematical Cryptology, 133–148 (2009)

18. Nandi, M.: Fast and Secure CBC-Type MAC Algorithms. In: Dunkelman, O. (ed.) FSE 2009. LNCS, vol. 5665, pp. 375–393. Springer, Heidelberg (2009). Citations in this document: §1.1.

19. Nandi, M.: A Simple and Unified Method of Proving Indistinguishability. In: Barua, R., Lange, T. (eds.) INDOCRYPT 2006. LNCS, vol. 4329, pp. 317–334. Springer, Heidelberg (2006)

308    N. Datta and M. Nandi

20. Patarin, J.: Etude des Générateurs de Permutations Basés sur le Schéma du D.E.S., Phd Thésis de Doctorat de l'Université de Paris 6 (1991)
21. Petrank, E., Racko, C.: CBC MAC for real-time data sources. Journal of Cryptology 13, 315–338 (2000)
22. Pietrzak, K.: A Tight Bound for EMAC. In: Bugliesi, M., Preneel, B., Sassone, V., Wegener, I. (eds.) ICALP 2006. LNCS, vol. 4052, pp. 168–179. Springer, Heidelberg (2006)
23. Sarkar, P.: Pseudo-Random Functions and Parallelizable Modes of Operations of a Block Cipher (2009), http://eprint.iacr.org/2009/217
24. Vaudenay, S.: Decorrelation over infinite domains: The encrypted CBC-MAC case. In: Stinson, D.R., Tavares, S. (eds.) SAC 2000. LNCS, vol. 2012, pp. 189–201. Springer, Heidelberg (2001)

# A Short Fail-Stop Signature Scheme
# from Factoring*

Takashi Yamakawa[1,3], Nobuaki Kitajima[2], Takashi Nishide[2],
Goichiro Hanaoka[3], and Eiji Okamoto[2]

[1] The University of Tokyo, Japan
yamakawa@it.k.u-tokyo.ac.jp
[2] University of Tsukuba, Japan
kitajima@cipher.risk.tsukuba.ac.jp, {nishide,okamoto}@risk.tsukuba.ac.jp
[3] National Institute of Advanced Industrial Science and Technology (AIST), Japan
hanaoka-goichiro@aist.go.jp

**Abstract.** Fail-stop signature (FSS) is information theoretically secure digital signature in the sense that even if a signature is forged, the signer can prove the forgery with overwhelming probability. There are many known constructions of FSS schemes based on various assumptions. Among them, factoring-based schemes are important due to their high reliability. However, known factoring-based FSS schemes generally suffer from their large signature sizes, which are larger than $|N|$, where $|N|$ is the length of an underlying composite number.

In this paper, we propose a new factoring-based FSS scheme. For this purpose, we propose a variant of the generic construction of FSS schemes based on a bundling homomorphism. Specifically, we introduce a notion of a *collision resistant group generator*, which can be seen as a variant of a bundling homomorphism, and propose a generic construction of FSS schemes based on it. Then we propose a construction of a collision resistant group generator based on the factoring assumption. This yields the first factoring-based FSS scheme whose signature size is smaller than $|N|$.

# 1 Introduction

## 1.1 Background

Digital signatures are analogues of handwritten signatures in the digital world that ensure the validity of digital documents. Many researchers have attempted to construct secure and efficient digital signature schemes. One main approach to ensure security of digital signature schemes is to reduce them to computationally difficult problems. However, such computational security becomes weaker as time goes on due to developments of algorithms and hardware. On the other hand, there exist documents for which we require digital signatures with strong and long-term security such as official or financial documents.

* The first author is supported by a JSPS Fellowship for Young Scientists.

S.S.M. Chow et al. (Eds.): ProvSec 2014, LNCS 8782, pp. 309–316, 2014.
© Springer International Publishing Switzerland 2014

Fail-stop signatures (FSS) [13] are proposed to ensure such strong and long-term security. An FSS scheme satisfies not only the computational unforgeability as an ordinary digital signature scheme but also information theoretical security in the following sense: even if a signature is forged, the signer can prove the forgery with overwhelming probability *without assuming the adversary's computational power.*

Many FSS schemes have been constructed based on various assumptions such as the discrete logarithm assumption [12], the RSA assumption [9] and the factoring assumption [13,7,4]. Among them, factoring-based schemes are important due to their high reliability. However, though many factoring-based FSS schemes have been proposed thus far, they are not very efficient. Specifically, their signature sizes are larger than $|N|$, where $|N|$ is the length of an underlying composite number. This is because they use an element of $\mathbb{Z}_N^*$ as a component of a signature, and $|N|$-bit string is needed to represent an element of $\mathbb{Z}_N^*$. Therefore, we cannot construct an FSS scheme whose signature size is smaller than $|N|$ as long as we use an element of $\mathbb{Z}_N^*$ as a component of a signature.

### 1.2    Our Contribution

In this paper, we propose the first FSS scheme which satisfies the following two properties simultaneously:

1. A signature size smaller than $|N|$,
2. Security reducible to the factoring assumption.

**Technical Overview.** As mentioned above, it is impossible to construct an FSS scheme whose signature size is smaller than $|N|$ as long as we use an element of $\mathbb{Z}_N^*$ as a component of a signature. To overcome this barrier, we use an element of $\mathbb{Z}$ as a signature instead of an element of $\mathbb{Z}_N^*$. However, this idea does not work in the existing framework to construct FSS schemes based on a bundling homomorphism [5]. This is because this framework requires a signature to be an element of a finite group due to the domain of bundling homomorphism being a finite group. Then we introduce a new primitive that we call a *collision resistant group generator*, which can be seen as a variant of a bundling homomorphism where the domain is $\mathbb{Z}$. We propose a generic construction of FSS schemes based on it as a variant of the existing framework. Finally, we construct a collision resistant group generator based on the factoring assumption with respect to a special type of RSA moduli, called semi-smooth RSA moduli [3]. As a result, we obtain an FSS scheme based on the factoring assumption with respect to semi-smooth RSA moduli whose signatures are short.

**Variant Scheme.** As a side result, we propose an FSS scheme that is secure under the factoring assumption with respect to a more widely used type of RSA moduli. Specifically, we consider $N = PQ$ where $P$ and $Q$ are distinct strong primes, i.e., $(P-1)/2$ and $(Q-1)/2$ are also primes. To the best of our knowledge, this is the first FSS scheme under the factoring assumption with respect to this type of RSA moduli.

## 1.3   Related Work

The notion of FSS was first proposed by Waidner and Pfitzmann [13] in 1989. In 1992, van Heyst and Pedersen [12] proposed an efficient FSS scheme based on the discrete logarithm assumption, that is still the most efficient known FSS scheme even now. On the other hand, there had been no known efficient FSS scheme based on the factoring assumption. Thus, in 2004, Schmidt-Samoa [7] proposed an efficient FSS scheme based on the factoring assumption with respect to an RSA modulus with the form $N = P^2 Q$ where $P$ and $Q$ are primes. In 2011, Mashatan and Ouafi [4] proposed a more efficient FSS scheme by considering RSA modulus with the form $N = PQ$ such that $a|P-1$ and $\gcd(a, Q-1) = 1$ for an odd integer $a$. Theirs is the most efficient known FSS scheme whose security is reduced to the factoring assumption.

In this paper, we do not consider schemes of [11] (which was later repaired by [7]) , [10] and [8] since their security was not reduced to the factoring assumption and they rely on stronger assumptions.

## 2   Preliminaries

*Notation* We use $[n]$ to denote the set $\{1, \ldots, n\}$ for $n \in \mathbb{N}$. If $S$ is a finite set, then we use $x \xleftarrow{\$} S$ to denote that $x$ is chosen uniformly at random from $S$. If $\mathcal{A}$ is an algorithm, we use $x \leftarrow \mathcal{A}(y)$ to denote that $x$ is output by $\mathcal{A}$ whose input is $y$. We say that a function $f(\cdot) : \mathbb{N} \to [0, 1]$ is negligible if for all positive polynomials $p(\cdot)$ and all sufficiently large $\lambda \in \mathbb{N}$, we have $f(\lambda) < 1/p(\lambda)$. We say $f$ is overwhelming if $1 - f$ is negligible. We say that a randomized algorithm $\mathcal{A}$ runs in probabilistic polynomial time (PPT) if there exists a polynomial $p$ such that execution time of $\mathcal{A}$ with input length $\lambda$ is less than $p(\lambda)$. For $x, y \in \mathbb{Z}$, we use $x|y$ to mean that $x$ divides $y$. For $N \in \mathbb{N}$, we denote bit-length of $N$ by $|N|$.

*Fail-Stop Signatures* Intuitively, FSS is a digital signature scheme where even if a signature is forged, the signer can prove the forgery. That is, compared with an ordinary digital signature scheme, which consists of (PreKeyGen, KeyGen, Sign, Verify) an FSS scheme has two additional algorithm ProveForgery which proves that a signature is forgery and VerifyProof which verifies if a proof of forgery is valid or not. There is a two security requirement for a fail-stop signature scheme: *verifier's security* and *signer's security*. Signer's security requires that for any computationally unbounded cheating forger, a signer can prove its forgery with overwhelming probability. Verifier's security requires that any PPT cheating signer cannot produce a proof of forgery for a signature produced by the signer. We refer to [4] for the formal definition and omit it due to the page limitation.

## 3   Generic Construction of Fail-Stop Signature

A generic construction of an FSS scheme based on a *bundling homomorphism* [5] is known. However, we do not use the generic construction directly in this paper. Instead, we propose a variant of the generic construction. Specifically, we introduce a new primitive which we call a *collision resistant group generator*, and propose a generic construction of FSS schemes based on it.

### 3.1   Collision Resistant Group Generator

Here, we define our new primitive, a collision resistant group generator. It is a PPT algorithm that outputs a description of group $G$ and an element $g \in G$ with an upper bound $S$ of $\mathrm{ord}(g)$ so that $h(x) := g^x$ is collision resistant. The formal definition is as follows.

**Definition 1** *Let* GGen *be a PPT algorithm which is given a security parameter* $1^\lambda$ *and outputs a description of a group* $G$, *an element* $g \in G$ *and an integer* $S$ *such that* $S > \mathrm{ord}(g)$. *We say that* GGen *is a collision resistant group generator if for any PPT algorithm* $\mathcal{A}$, *there exists a negligible function* negl *such that*

$$\Pr[g^x = g^y, x \neq y, \ x, y \in \mathbb{Z} : (x, y) \leftarrow \mathcal{A}(G, g, S), (G, g, S) \leftarrow \mathsf{GGen}(1^\lambda)] < \mathsf{negl}(\lambda).$$

*We say that* $\mathcal{A}$ *breaks the collision resistance of* GGen *if the above probability is non-negligible.*

### 3.2   Proposed Generic Construction of Fail-Stop Signature Schemes

In this section, we construct an FSS scheme based on a collision resistant group generator. The construction is as follows. We let a message space $\mathcal{M}$ be $[M]$ for an integer $M$.

PrekeyGen($1^\lambda, 1^\sigma$): It runs $(G, g, S) \leftarrow \mathsf{GGen}(1^\lambda)$ and outputs a public parameter $PP := (G, g, S)$.

KeyGen($PP$): It chooses $sk_1 \xleftarrow{\$} [2^{2\sigma+3}(M+2)S]$ and $sk_2 \xleftarrow{\$} [2^{\sigma+1}S]$ and sets $pk_1 := g^{sk_1}$ and $pk_2 := g^{sk_2}$. It outputs a secret key $sk := (sk_1, sk_2)$ and a public key $pk := (pk_1, pk_2)$.

Sign($PP, sk, m$): It computes a signature $s := sk_1 + m sk_2$ and outputs it. We note that this is computed on $\mathbb{Z}$.

Verify($PP, pk, m, s$): It outputs 1 if $m \in \mathcal{M}$, $s \in \mathbb{Z}$ and $g^s = pk_1 pk_2^m$ hold. Otherwise it outputs 0.

ProveForgery($PP, sk, m^*, s^*$): It computes $s := \mathsf{Sign}(PP, sk, m^*) = sk_1 + m^* sk_2$. If $s^* = s$, then it outputs $\bot$, and otherwise outputs pr $:= s$ as a proof of forgery.

VerifyProof($PP, pk, m^*, s^*,$ pr): It outputs 1 if $g^{\mathsf{pr}} = g^{s^*}$ and pr $\neq s^*$ hold, and otherwise outputs 0.

### 3.3   Security

Our generic construction is one-time secure if an underlying algorithm GGen is a collision resistant group generator. Note that the formal security definition is given in [4].

**Theorem 1** *Our generic construction is one-time secure if* GGen *is a collision resistant group generator.*

We can divide this theorem to the following two lemmas.

**Lemma 1** *Our generic construction is secure for a verifier if* GGen *is a collision resistant group generator.*

**Lemma 2** *Our generic construction is one-time secure for a signer.*

It is clear that Theorem 1 follows from Lemmas 1 and 2. Then we prove the above two lemmas. Here, we give only a proof sketch due to the page limitation. First, we prove the verifier's security. Let $\mathcal{A}$ be a PPT adversary that breaks the verifier's security of the scheme. That is, $\mathcal{A}$ is given $PP$ and outputs $(s^*, \mathsf{pr})$ such that $g^{\mathsf{pr}} = g^{s^*}$. This clearly breaks the security of the collision resistance group generator. Thus, such $\mathcal{A}$ does not exist.

Next, we move on to the signer's security. A forger against the one-time security of our scheme obtains a public parameter $PP = (G, g, S)$, public key $(pk_1 = g^{sk_1}, pk_2 = g^{sk_2})$ and a signature $s = sk_1 + msk_2$ for an arbitrary chosen message $m$. We observe that conditioned on $(pk_1 = g^{sk_1}, pk_2 = g^{sk_2})$, $sk_1$ and $sk_2$ have exponentially many possible values (in $\sigma$) since they are chosen from an exponentially larger range than $S > \mathrm{ord}(g)$. Moreover, we want to claim that $sk_1$ and $sk_2$ still have exponentially many possible values conditioned on $s = sk_1 + msk_2$ in addition to $(pk_1 = g^{sk_1}, pk_2 = g^{sk_2})$ since there is two variables $sk_1$ and $sk_2$ whereas only a single linear combination of them is given. This is a similar idea to what is used in the construction based on bundling-homomorphism. However, this idea cannot be applied to our case so simply. It is true that if $s$ has a "medium" value, then the number of possible values of $sk_1$ and $sk_2$ is exponentially large. However, if $s$ is extremely small or large, then it may reveal much information on $sk_1$ and $sk_2$. For example, if $m = 1$, and $s = 2$, then we must have $sk_1 = sk_2 = 1$. Thus, to complete the proof, we prove that $s$ has a "medium" value (i.e., $2^{\sigma+1}MS < s \leq 2^{2\sigma+3}(M+2)S$) with overwhelming probability.

## 4 Constructions of Collision Resistant Group Generators

In this section, we give concrete constructions of collision resistant group generators. In our main construction, the underlying group is $\mathbb{Z}_N^*$ for an RSA modulus $N$ of special form which we call a semi-smooth RSA modulus [3]. By using this collision resistant group generator in the above generic construction, we obtain an FSS scheme whose signature size is small under the factoring assumption. We also propose a variant of the above construction. Our variant is secure under a more standard type of the factoring assumption that a product of strong primes cannot be factorized. However, the signature size of the resulting FSS scheme is larger than that in the above construction. Then we give the concrete constructions of collision resistant group generators in the following.

**Main Construction.** Our basic idea is to generate an RSA modulus $N$ and $g \in \mathbb{Z}_N^*$ so that $x \mapsto g^x$ is collision resistant. This idea is used in constructions of factoring-based identification schemes and digital signature schemes in the random oracle model [2,6]. To reduce the signature size, it is needed to keep $\mathrm{ord}(g)$ small. For the purpose, we use a *semi-smooth RSA modulus* [3]. First, we describe the definition and properties of semi-smooth RSA moduli.

An integer $N = PQ$ is called a semi-smooth RSA modulus if $P = 2pp' + 1$ and $Q = 2qq' + 1$ are distinct odd primes with same length, where $p'$ and $q'$ are distinct odd primes and $p$ and $q$ are products of some distinct odd primes smaller than a polynomially bounded integer $B$ which satisfy $\gcd(p, q) = 1$. Let $\mathsf{IGen}(1^\lambda)$ be an efficient algorithm which outputs a random semi-smooth RSA modulus $N$. We assume that the bit-length of $p'q'$ is public and fixed regardless of randomness of $\mathsf{IGen}$.

We say that the factoring assumption holds with respect to $\mathsf{IGen}$ if for any efficient adversary $\mathcal{A}$, there exists a negligible function $\mathsf{negl}$ such that

$$\Pr[A \in \{P, Q\} : N \leftarrow \mathsf{IGen}(1^\lambda), A \leftarrow \mathcal{A}(N)] < \mathsf{negl}(\lambda).$$

For 80-bit security, [3] proposed to set $B = 2^{15}$ and $|p'q'| = 320$. Note that the attack described in [1] cannot be applied in this parameter setting.

We consider the structure of a multiplicative group $\mathbb{Z}_N^*$ for a semi-smooth RSA modulus $N$. We define the group of quadratic residues as $\mathbb{QR}_N := \{u^2 \bmod N : u \in \mathbb{Z}_N^*\}$. $\mathbb{QR}_N$ is a cyclic group of order $(P - 1)(Q - 1)/4 = p'q'pq$. It follows that there exists a unique subgroup of $\mathbb{QR}_N$ of order $p'q'$, which we call the semi-smooth subgroup and denote it by $G_{ss}$. Let $P_B$ be the product of all odd primes smaller than $B$. Then we have $pq|P_B$. Therefore if we set $u \xleftarrow{\$} \mathbb{Z}_N^*$ and $g := u^{2P_B} \bmod N$, then $g$ is distributed uniformly in $G_{ss}$, and $g$ is a generator of $G_{ss}$ with overwhelming probability.

The following Lemma is essential in the construction of a collision resistant group generator. We omit the proof due to the page limitation.

**Lemma 3** *Let $N = PQ = (2pp' + 1)(2qq' + 1)$ be a semi-smooth RSA modulus and $g$ be a generator of $G_{ss}$. There exists an efficient algorithm* Fact *which is given $N$, $g$ and $x, y \in \mathbb{Z}$ such that $g^x = g^y \bmod N$.*

Then we construct a collision resistant group generator GGen based on the factoring assumption with respect to semi-smooth RSA moduli.

GGen($1^\lambda$): It runs $N \leftarrow \mathsf{IGen}(1^\lambda)$, chooses $u \xleftarrow{\$} \mathbb{Z}_N^*$ and sets $g := u^{2P_B} \bmod N$ and $S := 2^{|p'q'|}$. Then it outputs $(N, g, S)$. (Here, $N$ is interpreted as a description of the group $\mathbb{Z}_N^*$.)

The following Lemma can be proven by using Lemma 3. The full proof is omitted due to the page limitation.

**Lemma 4** *If the factoring assumption holds with respect to* IGen, *then* GGen *is a collision resistant group generator.*

We let $\mathsf{FSS}_{\mathsf{Ours}}$ be the proposed FSS scheme where $\mathsf{GGen}$ is plugged in.

**Variant Construction.** In our main construction, we assume that semi-smooth RSA moduli cannot be factorized. However, we cannot say that this is a standard type of the factoring assumption and it might weaken the security of the scheme. Here, we construct a collision resistant group generator based on the factoring assumption for more standard type of RSA modulus: $N = PQ$ where $P$ and $Q$ are strong primes (i.e., $(P-1)/2$ and $(Q-1)/2$ are also primes). This type of RSA modulus is widely used in the literatures. The idea is similar to that of our main construction: If we choose $g \in \mathbb{Z}_N^*$ appropriately, then it is difficult to find $x$ and $y$ such that $g^x = g^y$. The concrete construction is omitted due to the page limitation. We let $\mathsf{FSS}_{\mathsf{Var}}$ be the proposed FSS scheme where the variant construction is plugged in.

# 5 Discussion

Here, we discuss the efficiency and security of the proposed FSS schemes. We compare our schemes with MO11 [4] since it is the most efficient known FSS scheme based on the factoring assumption. The comparisons are given in Table 1. We consider 80-bit security (i.e., $\lambda = \sigma = 80$), and we set $M = 2^{160}$ since we may compress a message by using a collision resistant hash function. In $\mathsf{FSS}_{\mathsf{Ours}}$, we set $|N| = 1024$, $|p'q'| = 320$ and $S = 2^{320}$, and in $\mathsf{FSS}_{\mathsf{Var}}$ we set $|N| = 1024$ and $S = 2^{1022}$. We assume that $g^\alpha$ for $k$-bit integer $\alpha$ can be computed by $1.5k$ multiplications.

In $\mathsf{FSS}_{\mathsf{Ours}}$, a signature size is smaller and a signing is more efficient than in MO11 though verification is less efficient. Specifically, $\mathsf{FSS}_{\mathsf{Ours}}$ is the first FSS scheme based on the factoring assumption whose signature size is smaller than $|N|$. In $\mathsf{FSS}_{\mathsf{Var}}$, though the signature size is not smaller than that of MO11, the signing is still more efficient. Note that the multiplication in signing is done on $\mathbb{Z}$ in $\mathsf{FSS}_{\mathsf{Ours}}$ and $\mathsf{FSS}_{\mathsf{Var}}$ but on $\mathbb{Z}_N^*$ in MO11. Therefore, we cannot simply compare them. However, in our schemes, $m$ and $sk_2$ are smaller than $N$, and thus, the multiplication cost is smaller than that on $\mathbb{Z}_N^*$.

**Table 1.** Comparison of the efficiency among factoring-based FSS schemes, where $\lambda = \sigma = 80$, $M = 2^{160}$, in MO11, $N = PQ = (2ap + 1)(2q + 1)$ where $P, Q, p, q$ are primes and $a$ is an odd integer such that $p > 2a$ and $\mathsf{Sign}(\#\text{mult.})$ and $\mathsf{Verify}(\#\text{mult.})$ denote the number of multiplications on $\mathbb{Z}_N^*$ (or $\mathbb{Z}$ in signing of our proposed schemes) required for signing and verification, respectively.

| | Size of $sk$ (bits) | Size of $pk$ (bits) | Size of $s$ (bits) | Sign (#mult.) | Verify (#mult.) | Form of $N$ |
|---|---|---|---|---|---|---|
| MO11 [4] | 2,048 | 2,048 | 1,024 | 240 | 320 | $(2ap + 1)(2q + 1)$ |
| $\mathsf{FSS}_{\mathsf{Ours}}$ | 1,044 | 2,048 | 643 | 1 | 1,205 | semi-smooth RSA modulus |
| $\mathsf{FSS}_{\mathsf{Var}}$ | 2,448 | 2,048 | 1,345 | 1 | 2,258 | product of strong primes |

The underlying assumption of all of these schemes is the factoring assumption. However, the settings of $N$ are different, and we cannot simply compare their strengths. Nevertheless, we can say that the underlying assumption of $\mathsf{FSS_{Var}}$ (that a product of strong primes cannot be efficiently factorized) is the most standard among them.

**Acknowledgment.** We would like to thank the anonymous reviewers and members of the study group "Shin-Akarui-Angou-Benkyou-Kai" for their helpful comments.

# References

1. Coron, J.-S., Joux, A., Mandal, A., Naccache, D., Tibouchi, M.: Cryptanalysis of the RSA subgroup assumption from TCC 2005. In: Catalano, D., Fazio, N., Gennaro, R., Nicolosi, A. (eds.) PKC 2011. LNCS, vol. 6571, pp. 147–155. Springer, Heidelberg (2011)
2. Girault, M.: Self-certified public keys. In: Davies, D.W. (ed.) Advances in Cryptology - EUROCRYPT 1991. LNCS, vol. 547, pp. 490–497. Springer, Heidelberg (1991)
3. Groth, J.: Cryptography in subgroups of $\mathbb{Z}_n^*$. In: Kilian, J. (ed.) TCC 2005. LNCS, vol. 3378, pp. 50–65. Springer, Heidelberg (2005)
4. Mashatan, A., Ouafi, K.: Efficient fail-stop signatures from the factoring assumption. In: Lai, X., Zhou, J., Li, H. (eds.) ISC 2011. LNCS, vol. 7001, pp. 372–385. Springer, Heidelberg (2011)
5. Torben, P.: Pedersen and Birgit Pfitzmann: Fail-stop signatures. SIAM J. Comput. 26(2), 291–330 (1997)
6. Pointcheval, D.: The composite discrete logarithm and secure authentication. In: Imai, H., Zheng, Y. (eds.) PKC 2000. LNCS, vol. 1751, pp. 113–128. Springer, Heidelberg (2000)
7. Schmidt-Samoa, K.: Factorization-based fail-stop signatures revisited. In: López, J., Qing, S., Okamoto, E. (eds.) ICICS 2004. LNCS, vol. 3269, pp. 118–131. Springer, Heidelberg (2004)
8. Susilo, W.: Short fail-stop signature scheme based on factorization and discrete logarithm assumptions. Theor. Comput. Sci. 410(8-10), 736–744 (2009)
9. Susilo, W., Mu, Y.: Provably secure fail-stop signature schemes based on RSA. IJWMC 1(1), 53–60 (2005)
10. Susilo, W., Safavi-Naini, R.: An efficient fail-stop signature scheme based on factorization. In: Lee, P.J., Lim, C.H. (eds.) ICISC 2002. LNCS, vol. 2587, pp. 62–74. Springer, Heidelberg (2003)
11. Susilo, W., Safavi-Naini, R., Gysin, M., Seberry, J.: A new and efficient fail-stop signature scheme. Comput. J. 43(5), 430–437 (2000)
12. van Heyst, E., Pedersen, T.P.: How to make efficient fail-stop signatures. In: Rueppel, R.A. (ed.) Advances in Cryptology - EUROCRYPT 1992. LNCS, vol. 658, pp. 366–377. Springer, Heidelberg (1993)
13. Waidner, M., Pfitzmann, B.: The dining cryptographers in the disco - unconditional sender and recipient untraceability with computationally secure serviceability (abstract). In: Quisquater, J.-J., Vandewalle, J. (eds.) Advances in Cryptology - EUROCRYPT 1989. LNCS, vol. 434, p. 690. Springer, Heidelberg (1990)

# Computational Soundness of Asymmetric Bilinear Pairing-Based Protocols

Kazuki Yoneyama

NTT Secure Platform Laboratories
3-9-11 Midori-cho Musashino-shi Tokyo 180-8585, Japan
yoneyama.kazuki@lab.ntt.co.jp

**Abstract.** Asymmetric bilinear maps using Type-3 pairings are known to be advantageous in several points (e.g., the speed and the size of a group element) to symmetric bilinear maps using Type-1 pairings. Kremer and Mazaré introduce a symbolic model to analyze protocols based on bilinear maps, and show that the symbolic model is computationally sound. However, their model only covers symmetric bilinear maps. In this paper, we propose a new symbolic model to capture asymmetric bilinear maps. Our model allows us to analyze security of various protocols based on asymmetric bilinear maps (e.g., Scott's client-server ID-based key exchange). Also, we show computational soundness of our symbolic model under the decisional bilinear Diffie-Hellman assumption.

**Keywords:** formal method, computational soundness, asymmetric bilinear pairing.

## 1 Introduction

**Formal Methods, and Computational Soundness.** The *formal method* is a useful tool to analyze security of cryptographic protocols in the error-less and automatic manner. Since the original work by Dolev and Yao [1], many protocols have been analyzed by formal methods. In the Dolev-Yao (DY) model all values and operations are represented *symbolically*. For example, a message is defined as a symbolic term $t$, and symmetric-key encryption (SKE) of $t$ with a key $sk$ is defined as a term $\{t\}_{sk}$. If $sk$ is unknown, then $\{t\}_{sk}$ is regarded as symbol $\{\Box\}_{sk}$ that means the undeducible term regardless of the encrypted term. Thus, the symbolic model is easier to analyze security than the ordinary cryptographic way because it is highly-abstracted. This approach is mainly interested in authentication and confidentiality properties, and has been used in the analysis of several practical protocols. Conversely, the basic symbolic analysis does not a priori carry any cryptographic *computational security* guarantees. That is, it is not trivial whether a secure protocol in the symbolic model is also secure in the computational setting. Since security of cryptographic protocols is often proved under some computational assumption, there is a gap between security in the symbolic model and in the computational model.

Abadi and Rogaway [2] give a bridge to the gap. They show that if a protocol based on a strongly secure SKE is secure in their symbolic model, it is also secure in the computational model. This property is called as *computational soundness*.

S.S.M. Chow et al. (Eds.): ProvSec 2014, LNCS 8782, pp. 317–325, 2014.

Hence, to prove computational soundness is very important when introducing a new symbolic model.

**Cryptographic Bilinear Maps.**   For upwards of ten years, cryptographic protocols based on *bilinear maps* are widely studied. A bilinear map allows us to compute element $g_T^{ab}$ in the target group from two distinct elements $g^a$ and $g^b$ in the source group in the secure and efficient manner thanks to the power of pairings. It is a fundamental tool to construct various high-functional protocols. There are two types of bilinear maps: one is *symmetric*, and the other is *asymmetric*. Symmetric bilinear maps are implemented with Type-1 pairings, and asymmetric bilinear maps are implemented with Type-2 or Type-3 pairings. Most previous cryptographic schemes based on bilinear maps adopt the symmetric setting because of its simplicity. However, it is pointed out that Type-3 pairings are much faster and more compact to implement than Type-1 parings. Additionally, some recent works like [3] indicate that Type-1 parings cannot be securely implemented with practical parameters as follows: The known way to implement type-1 pairings is to use supersingular curves. The attacks to discrete logarithm computations for popular supersingular curves for pairings show that using fields of characteristic 2 or 3 must be considered insecure. Thus, the remaining way to securely and efficiently implement Type-1 parings is using supersingular curves embedding degree 2 or 3 over $GF(p)$ with large characteristics. Concretely, for 128-bit security, while asymmetric pairings are achieved by 256-bit elliptic curves with embedding degree 12, symmetric pairings need 1024-bit elliptic curves with embedding degree 3. Hence, asymmetric bilinear maps are more desirable than symmetric bilinear maps to construct efficient protocols. Indeed, recently, it is considered important to use the asymmetric setting when designing protocols using bilinear maps.

Kremer and Mazaré [4] introduce a symbolic model to analyze protocols based on bilinear maps, and show that the symbolic model is computationally sound. Their model can be seen as an extension of the symbolic model with modular exponentiation [5]. The soundness is proved under the decisional bilinear Diffie-Hellman (DBDH) assumption and the semantic security of SKE. They show Joux's tripartite key exchange, and TAK-2 and TAK-3 protocols as applications of their model. However, their model only covers symmetric bilinear maps.

## 1.1   Our Contribution

In this paper, we give a new symbolic model for asymmetric bilinear maps and its computational soundness.

First, we define the symbolic model by extending the model for modular exponentiation [5] and symmetric bilinear maps [4]. We adjust the syntax of symbolic messages, capacity of the symbolic adversary, and symbolic equivalence to the asymmetric bilinear map setting.

Next, we show computational soundness of our symbolic model under the DBDH assumption. We modify the DBDH assumption for asymmetric bilinear maps to the more generalized form (called the expanded DBDH assumption,

Exp-DBDH). Based on the Exp-DBDH and a special semantic security of SKE, we can prove computational soundness.

Finally, we give an example protocol based on asymmetric bilinear maps to examine usefulness of our model. We consider a client-server ID-based authentication [6], and show the very simple (computational) security proof of the protocol with the combination of our symbolic model and soundness result.

This work can be seen as a milestone to analyze security of various protocols based on asymmetric bilinear maps in simple and rigorous ways.

## 2    Extension of DBDH Assumption

In this section, we introduce an extension of the DBDH assumption. Such an extension is useful to prove that the symbolic equivalence implies computational indistinguishability.

### 2.1    Expanded Decisional Bilinear Diffie-Hellman Assumption for Asymmetric Bilinear Group

First, we formulate the new assumption (called the expanded DBDH assumption, Exp-DBDH). The "expansion" means that a distinguisher receives multiple exponents and DH instances in $G_1$ and $G_2$, and is only required to distinguish one of multiple challenges, while in the DBDH assumption just a single instance and a challenge are given. To properly define such a situation, we must care about whether some of multiple challenges are trivially derived from instances. For example, if $a' \in \mathbb{Z}_p$, $g_1^{b'} \in G_1$ and $g_2^{c'} \in G_2$ are given as a part of instances, and $e(g_1, g_2)^{a'b'c'} \in G_T$ is contained in challenges, then the distinguisher can trivially distinguish the challenge from the random value. Thus, a condition to avoid such a trivial case must be considered. The following is our definition:

Let $\kappa$ be the security parameter and $(G_1, G_2, G_T, g_1, g_2, p)$ be an asymmetric bilinear group. As the DBDH assumption, we define two experiments, $\mathsf{Exp}^{\text{edbdh-real}}(\mathcal{D})$ and $\mathsf{Exp}^{\text{edbdh-rand}}(\mathcal{D})$. Let $X = (x_i)_{1 \leq i \leq \alpha}$, $Y = (y_i)_{1 \leq i \leq \beta}$ and $Z = (z_i)_{1 \leq i \leq \gamma}$ be sets of elements which are randomly chosen from $\mathbb{Z}_p$. Let $F = (f_i)_{1 \leq i \leq \delta}$ be the set of polynomials based on power-free 3-monomials consisting of elements of $X$, $Y$ and $Z$, where each $f_i$ and the set of monomials $\{a'b'c'|a', b', c' \in X\} \cup \{a'b'c'|a', b' \in X, c' \in Y\} \cup \{a'b'c'|a', b' \in X, c' \in Z\} \cup \{a'b'c'|a' \in X, b' \in Y, c' \in Z\}$ have no linear relation. A distinguisher $\mathcal{D}$ is given inputs $(x_1, \ldots, x_\alpha, g_1, g_1^{y_1}, \ldots, g_1^{y_\beta}, g_2, g_2^{z_1}, \ldots, g_2^{z_\gamma}, R_1, \ldots, R_\delta)$. $R_i = g_T^{f_i}$ in $\mathsf{Exp}^{\text{edbdh-real}}(\mathcal{D})$, and $R_i = g_T^{r_i}$ in $\mathsf{Exp}^{\text{edbdh-rand}}(\mathcal{D})$, where $g_T = e(g_1, g_2)$ and $r_i \in_R \mathbb{Z}_p$. We define advantage $\mathbf{Adv}^{\text{Exp-DBDH}}(\mathcal{D}) = |\Pr[\mathsf{Exp}^{\text{edbdh-real}}(\mathcal{D}) = 1] - \Pr[\mathsf{Exp}^{\text{edbdh-rand}}(\mathcal{D}) = 1]|$, where the probability is taken over the choices of $X, Y, Z, (r_i)_{1 \leq i \leq \delta}$ and the random tape of $\mathcal{D}$.

**Definition 1 (Exp-DBDH Assumption).** *We say that the Exp-DBDH assumption in $(G_1, G_2, G_T)$ holds if for any PPT distinguisher $\mathcal{D}$ the advantage $\mathbf{Adv}^{\text{Exp-DBDH}}(\mathcal{D})$ is negligible in security parameter $\kappa$.*

## 2.2  Relation between Assumptions

Next, we show that the Exp-DBDH assumption holds if the DBDH assumption holds. The result is meaningful when $\delta$ is polynomially bounded in $\kappa$ asymptotically. Since $\alpha$, $\beta$, and $\gamma$ are some constant numbers, $\delta$ can be polynomially bounded.

**Theorem 1.** *If for any distinguisher* $\mathcal{D}_1$ *of the DBDH assumption in* $(G_1, G_2, G_T)$, $\mathbf{Adv}^{\mathrm{DBDH}}(\mathcal{D}_1)$ *is negligible in* $\kappa$, *then for any distinguisher* $\mathcal{D}_2$ *of the Exp-DBDH assumption in* $(G_1, G_2, G_T)$, $\mathbf{Adv}^{\mathrm{Exp\text{-}DBDH}}(\mathcal{D}_2)$ *is negligible in* $\kappa$.

The proof of Theorem 1 uses the game hopping technique [7]. The initial game is the same as $\mathsf{Exp}^{\mathrm{edbdh\text{-}real}}(\mathcal{D}_2)$, and the final game is the same as $\mathsf{Exp}^{\mathrm{edbdh\text{-}rand}}(\mathcal{D}_2)$. We consider intermediate games that challenges of $\mathcal{D}_2$ are gradually changed from real values to random values. Specifically, in an intermediate game, $g_T^{f_i}$ is replaced with $g_T^{r_i}$. We can prove that the game and the previous game are indistinguishable with the DBDH assumption. We construct $\mathcal{D}_1$ of the DBDH assumption such that $R$ in the DBDH assumption is set as $R_i$ in the Exp-DBDH assumption. If $R$ is the real value (i.e., $R = g_T^{abc}$), then $R_i$ is also the real value (i.e., $R_i = g_T^{f_i}$). Otherwise, $R_i$ is a random value (i.e., $R_i = g_T^{r_i}$). We note that since $f_i$ and $(X, Y, Z)$ are linear independent because of the definition of the Exp-DBDH assumption, $\mathcal{D}_1$ can perfectly simulate the environment for $\mathcal{D}_2$. This change is indistinguishable thanks to the DBDH assumption. Since all intermediate changes (i.e., $\delta$ games) are indistinguishable, the initial game and the final game is also indistinguishable.

## 3  Our Symbolic Model

In this section, we introduce a symbolic model that covers asymmetric bilinear maps. It is an extension of previous symbolic models for modular exponentiations [5] and symmetric bilinear maps [4]. As such symbolic models our model follows the Abadi-Rogaway logic [2].

### 3.1  Syntax

First, we formulate the syntax of symbolic messages.

Let **Nonce**, **Key** and **Exponent** be countable disjoint sets of symbols for messages, nonces, secret keys and exponents. DH instances appeared in the DBDH and Exp-DBDH assumption (e.g., $g_1^a$, $g_2^{bc}$, $g_2^{abc}$) are represented using power-free monomials or polynomials. Let **Poly** be a set of power-free polynomials based on power-free 3-monomials with variables in **Exponent** and coefficients in $\mathbb{Z}$. Term $(t_1, t_2)$ represents the composition of terms $t_1$ and $t_2$, term $\{t\}_{sk}$ represents the ciphertext of $t$ with secret key $sk$ for SKE, and term $g_T^{\mathbf{Poly}}$ represents the set of modular exponentiations of $g_T$ to the power of polynomials in **Poly**. The set of message expressions **Msg** is defined by the following grammar: $\mathbf{Msg} ::= \mathbf{Nonce} \mid \mathbf{Key} \mid (\mathbf{Msg}, \mathbf{Msg}) \mid \{\mathbf{Msg}\}_{\mathbf{Key}} \mid g_1^{\mathbf{Poly}} \mid g_2^{\mathbf{Poly}} \mid g_T^{\mathbf{Poly}} \mid \{\mathbf{Msg}\}_{g_T^{\mathbf{Poly}}}$. For simplicity, we use a notation $\{\mathbf{Msg}\}_{g_T^{\mathbf{Poly}}}$ to represent the set of encryption with $g_T^P$ for $P \in \mathbf{Poly}$ where $g_T^P$ is directly used as an element of **Key**. Indeed, some key extraction algorithm like a hash function is applied to $g_T^P$, but we omit it.

## 3.2   Symbolic Adversary

Next, we define capacity of the symbolic adversary. In this paper, we focus on passive adversaries as in [5,4].

We use deduction relation $\vdash$. For a finite set of terms $E \subseteq \mathbf{Msg}$ and a term $t \in \mathbf{Msg}$, $E \vdash t$ means that $t$ can be deduced from $E$ by an eavesdropper. Our deduction relation $\vdash$ contains some extension of the basic DY inference system [1]. By the following rules we can formulate the power of adversaries:

$$(1): \frac{t \in E}{E \vdash t} \quad (2): \frac{E \vdash (t_1, t_2)}{E \vdash t_1} \quad (3): \frac{E \vdash (t_1, t_2)}{E \vdash t_2} \quad (4): \frac{E \vdash t_1 \quad E \vdash t_2}{E \vdash (t_1, t_2)}$$

$$(5): \frac{E \vdash t \quad E \vdash sk}{E \vdash \{t\}_{sk}} \quad (6): \frac{E \vdash \{t\}_{sk} \quad E \vdash sk}{E \vdash t} \quad (7): \frac{E \vdash x \quad E \vdash g_1^y \quad E \vdash g_2^z}{E \vdash g_T^{xyz}}$$

$$(8): \frac{E \vdash x \quad E \vdash y \quad E \vdash g_1^z}{E \vdash g_T^{xyz}} \quad (9): \frac{E \vdash x \quad E \vdash y \quad E \vdash g_2^z}{E \vdash g_T^{xyz}} \quad (10): \frac{E \vdash x \quad E \vdash y \quad E \vdash z}{E \vdash g_T^{xyz}}$$

$$(11): \frac{E \vdash g_T^P \quad E \vdash g_T^Q}{E \vdash g_T^{\lambda P + Q}} \quad (12): \frac{E \vdash \{t\}_{g_T^P} \quad E \vdash g_T^P}{E \vdash t}$$

where $sk \in \mathbf{Key}$, $x, y, z, \lambda \in \mathbb{Z}_p$, and $P, Q \in \mathbf{Poly}$.

Rules $(1), (2), (3), (4), (5)$ and $(6)$ are the same as the DY rules, and these guarantee security of SKE. Rules $(7), (8), (9)$ and $(10)$ correspond to four possible ways to obtain an exponentiation $g_T^{xyz}$ using asymmetric bilinear maps. The different point from the setting of symmetric bilinear maps is in the rule $(7)$. In the symmetric setting, if $(E \vdash x \quad E \vdash g_1^y \quad E \vdash g_1^z)$ holds, $E \vdash g_T^{xyz}$ holds. It does not holds in the asymmetric setting because $g_T^{yz}$ cannot be derived from $g_1^y$ and $g_1^z$. Thus, such a rule is not contained, and the case $g_1 \neq g_2$ is allowed (i.e., $(7)$). Rule $(11)$ handles linear relations between polynomials. An adversary can obtain $g_T^{PQ}$ by multiplying $g_T^P$ and $g_T^Q$, and can obtain $g_T^{\lambda P}$ by the exponentiation of $y_T^P$ to the power of $\lambda$. Rule $(12)$ corresponds to the syntax of SKE when the secret key is an element of $g_T^{\mathbf{Poly}}$.

## 3.3   Symbolic Equivalence

Next, we show a symbolic expression to represent information revealed via $\vdash$. We use *patterns* as the Abadi-Rogaway logic. If an adversary cannot deduce a key $sk$ from term $t$, and $\{t'\}_{sk}$ is contained in $t$, then the pattern of $\{t'\}_{sk}$ is expressed with symbol $\{\square\}_{sk}$ (i.e., cannot be decrypted). The pattern of term $t \in \mathbf{Msg}$ and a finite set $\mathbf{K}$ is defined by the following inductive rules:

$$pattern((t', t''), \mathbf{K}) = (pattern(t', \mathbf{K}), pattern(t'', \mathbf{K}))$$

$$pattern(\{t'\}_{sk}, \mathbf{K}) = \begin{cases} \{pattern(t', \mathbf{K})\}_{sk} & (\text{if } (t \vdash sk) \vee (sk \in \mathbf{K})) \\ \{\square\}_{sk} & (\text{otherwise}) \end{cases}$$

$$pattern(\{t'\}_{y_T^P}, \mathbf{K}) = \begin{cases} \{pattern(t', \mathbf{K})\}_{g_T^P} & (\text{if } (t \vdash g_T^P) \vee (g_T^P \in \mathbf{K})) \\ \{\square\}_{g_T^P} & (\text{otherwise}) \end{cases}$$

$$pattern(t', \mathbf{K}) = t' \quad (\text{if } t' \in \mathbf{Nonce} \cup \mathbf{Key} \cup g_T^{\mathbf{Poly}})$$

where $t'$ and, $t''$ are sub-expressions of $t$. We say that two expressions $t_1$ and $t_2$ are *symbolically equivalent* (written $t_1 \equiv t_2$) if and only if $pattern(t_1, \mathbf{K}_1) = pattern(t_2, \mathbf{K}_2)$.

### 3.4  Renaming of Expressions

If we try to connect symbolic equivalence and computational indistinguishability, the definition of symbolic equivalence is too strong. For example, expressions $(t_1, \{t_1\}_{sk_1})$ and $(t_2, \{t_2\}_{sk_2})$ are different in the sense of symbolic equivalence. However, if $t_1$ and $t_2$, and $sk_1$ and $sk_2$ are chosen from the same distributions, respectively, these two expressions must be indistinguishable in the sense of computational indistinguishability. Thus, we must consider the renaming of expressions to remain equivalence.

For SKE the renaming rule is very simple. It is solved by allowing renaming of key and nonce symbols. However, the renaming of exponents in polynomials is not very easy because if we apply some simple rule, then it may make symbolic equivalence too weak. For example, we consider term $(g_1^X, g_2^Y, g_2^{XY})$, and renaming rule $\{XY \mapsto w\}$ where $X$, $Y$, and $w$ are elements in **Poly**, and $w$ is not contained in the terms. In this case, if $w$ can be $X + Y$, then it means that $(g_1^X, g_2^Y, g_2^{X+Y})$ is equivalent with $(g_1^X, g_2^Y, g_2^{XY})$. However, actually, an adversary can distinguish two terms by computing $e(g_1^X, g_2) \cdot e(g_1, g_2^Y)$ and $e(g_1, g_2^{X+Y})$. To avoid such a situation, the renaming rule must preserve linear dependence of expressions.

We recall the definition of *linear dependence preserving injective renamings* of polynomials. We denote the set of all polynomials in term $t$ by $poly(t)$.

**Definition 2 (Linear Dependence Preserving Injective Renamings).** *Let* $\sigma : poly(t) \to \mathbf{Poly}$ *be an injective renaming of the polynomials in term $t$. We say that $\sigma$ is linear dependence preserving if* $\forall P_1, \ldots, P_n \in poly(t)$, $\forall a_1, \ldots, a_n, b \in \mathbb{Z}$, $\Sigma_{i=1}^n a_i P_i = b \Leftrightarrow \Sigma_{i=1}^n a_i P_i \sigma = b$.

We say that two expressions $t_1$ and $t_2$ are *equivalent up to renaming* (written $t_1 \cong t_2$) if there exists renaming $\sigma$ such that $t_1 \sigma \equiv t_2$.

## 4  Computational Soundness

In this section, we show computational soundness of our symbolic model. Computational soundness guarantees that if a protocol using asymmetric bilinear maps is secure in our symbolic model, then the protocol is also secure in the computational model.

### 4.1  Well-Formedness

First, we need to restrict the use of bilinear maps only to produce *well-formed terms*. Intuitively, it does not occur that for $P$ and $Q$ such that $g_T^P$ and $g_T^Q$ occur in term $t$ exponents in $P$ and $Q$ contain a common exponent, and an exponent in $P$ or $Q$ directly appears in $t$. Such a situation is an incorrect use of bilinear maps, and should be avoided. If such expressions are contained, then even if the renaming of terms are equivalent up to renaming, it is easily distinguishable by erasing the exponent that directly appears in $t$ from $P$ or $Q$. Thus, we forbid such an incorrect use of bilinear maps.

The definition of well-formed terms is as follows:

**Definition 3 (Well-Formed Terms).** *We say that term $t$ is well-formed if for any pair of $P$ and $Q$ such that $g_T^P$ and $g_T^Q$ occur in $t$, $P$ and $Q$ have no common exponent, or for any $P$ such that $g_T^P$ occurs in $t$, any exponent in $P$ does not directly appear in $t$.*

### 4.2 Acyclicity

Next, we need to assume that for any term there is no *encryption cycle* (e.g., a secret key is encrypted by the same key). Such an assumption can be removed by strengthening IND-CPA* of SKE to add the key-dependent message security [8]. However, in this paper, we forbid symbolic terms to contain key cycles for simplicity.

The definition of acyclic terms is as follows:

**Definition 4 (Acyclic Terms).** *We say that term $t$ is acyclic if polynomial $P$ occurs as a secret key in $t$ and is not a linear combination of other polynomials that occur in $t$, and there exists a total order $\prec$ among keys used in $t$ such that for any subterm $\{t'\}_{Key}$ (e.g., $Key$ is $sk$ or $g_T^P$) either $Key$ is deducible from $t$ or for another key $Key'$ in $t'$ $Key' \prec Key$ holds.*

### 4.3 Soundness Result

Our main theorem states that distributions related to equivalent terms are computationally indistinguishable.

**Theorem 2.** *Let $t_1$ and $t_2$ be two acyclic well-formed terms, and $t_1 \cong t_2$. The underlying SKE satisfies IND-CPA*, and the Exp-DBDH assumption in $(G_1, G_2, G_T)$ holds. Then, $t_1$ and $t_2$ are computational indistinguishable (written $t_1 \approx t_2$).*

The proof of Theorem 2 uses (a constant number of) transitivity of computational indistinguishability. First, we show that term $t_i$ and $pattern(t_j, \mathbf{K}_j)$ are computationally indistinguishable using IND-CPA* of SKE. If we assume that there exists a computational distinguisher between $t_j$ and $pattern(t_j, \mathbf{K}_j)$, we can construct an adversary to break IND-CPA* and derive a contradiction. Next, we show that $pattern(t_1, \mathbf{K}_1)$ and $pattern(t_2, \mathbf{K}_2)$ are computationally indistinguishable using the Exp-DBDH assumption. If we assume that there exists a computational distinguisher between $pattern(t_1, \mathbf{K}_1)$ and $pattern(t_2, \mathbf{K}_2)$, we can construct a solver of the Exp-DBDH problem and derive a contradiction. Finally, by transitivity we have $t_1 \approx pattern(t_1, \mathbf{K}_1) \approx pattern(t_2, \mathbf{K}_2) \approx t_2$.

# 5 Application

In this section, we show an application of our symbolic model and soundness result.

## 5.1 Scott's Client-Server ID-Based Authentication

Scott [6] firstly studied the design and security of key exchange protocols with asymmetric bilinear maps. This paper is well known because the external Diffie-Hellman (XDH) assumption is firstly introduced. As one of proposed protocols in the paper, he introduces a client-server ID-based authentication protocol based on asymmetric bilinear maps. We show the security of this protocol with our symbolic model.

**Protocol.** $(G_1, G_2, G_T, g_1, g_2, p)$ is an asymmetric bilinear group. Let $ID_C$ be a client's ID, and $ID_S$ be the server's ID. In initialization, the server generates and keeps a master secret key $z$. The client privately keeps a short PIN $\alpha \in \mathbb{Z}_p$. For the secret key generation, the client registers his PIN $\alpha$ to the server, then the server computes $C = H_1(ID_C)$, $S = H_2(ID_S)$ and $C^{z-\alpha}$, where $H_1$ is a hash function $\{0,1\}^* \to G_1$ and $H_2$ is a hash function $\{0,1\}^* \to G_2$. The server sends a hardware token containing $C^{z-\alpha}$ to the client.

In an authentication session, the client chooses $x \in_R \mathbb{Z}_p$, inputs $\alpha$ and $x$ to his hardware token. The token computes and outputs $X = e(C^{z-\alpha} \cdot C^\alpha, H(ID_S))^x$. The client sends $X$ to the server. The server chooses $y \in_R \mathbb{Z}_p$, computes $Y = e(C,S)^{yz}$, and sends $Y$ to the client.

On receiving $Y$, the client computes the session key $SK = Y^x$. Also, on receiving $X$, the server computes the session key $SK = X^y$.

**Security.** We show that any passive adversary cannot distinguish the session key and a random key; that is, any information of the session key is not leaked.

Since ranges of $H_1$ and $H_2$ are $G_1$ and $G_2$ respectively, $C$ can be represented as $g_1^c$ for an exponent $c$, and $S$ can be represented as $g_2^s$ for an exponent $s$. Then, $e(C,S)$ is also represented as $g_T^{cs}$. Since generators $g_1$, $g_2$ and $g_T$ are not directly used in the protocol, we can deal with $C$, $S$ and $e(C,S)$ as new generators (i.e., $g_1' := C$, $g_2' := S$ and $g_T' := e(C,S)$). A passive adversary can see terms $(g_1', g_2', g_T', g_T'^{xz}, g_T'^{yz})$. From our symbolic equivalence, we have $(g_1', g_2', g_T', g_T'^{xz}, g_T'^{yz}, SK) \cong (g_1', g_2', g_T', g_T'^{xz}, g_T'^{yz}, g_T'^P)$, where $P$ is a random and linear independent polynomial from $(xz, yz)$. Moreover, by Theorem 2 these terms are also computationally indistinguishable, and the protocol is secure against passive adversaries.

# References

1. Dolev, D., Yao, A.C.C.: On the Security of Public Key Protocols. In: FOCS 1981, pp. 350–357. IEEE (1981)
2. Abadi, M., Rogaway, P.: Reconciling Two Views of Cryptography (The Computational Soundness of Formal Encryption). In: Watanabe, O., Hagiya, M., Ito, T., van Leeuwen, J., Mosses, P.D. (eds.) IFIP TCS 2000. LNCS, vol. 1872, pp. 3–22. Springer, Heidelberg (2000)
3. Granger, R., Kleinjung, T., Zumbrägel, J.: Breaking e128-bit Securef Supersingular Binary Curves (or how to solve discrete logarithms in $\mathbb{F}_{2^{4\cdot1223}}$ and $\mathbb{F}_{2^{12\cdot367}}$). In: Garay, J.A., Gennaro, R. (eds.) CRYPTO 2014, Part II. LNCS, vol. 8617, pp. 126–145. Springer, Heidelberg (2014)
4. Kremer, S., Mazaré, L.: Computationally sound analysis of protocols using bilinear pairings. Journal of Computer Security 18(6), 999–1033 (2010)
5. Bresson, E., Lakhnech, Y., Mazaré, L., Warinschi, B.: A Generalization of DDH with Applications to Protocol Analysis and Computational Soundness. In: Menezes, A. (ed.) CRYPTO 2007. LNCS, vol. 4622, pp. 482–499. Springer, Heidelberg (2007)
6. Scott, M.: Authenticated ID-based Key Exchange and remote log-in with simple token and PIN number. In: Cryptology ePrint Archive: 2002/164 (2002)
7. Shoup, V.: Sequences of games: A tool for taming complexity in security proofs. In: Cryptology ePrint Archive: 2004/332 (2004)
8. Black, J., Rogaway, P., Shrimpton, T.: Encryption-Scheme Security in the Presence of Key-Dependent Messages. In: Nyberg, K., Heys, H.M. (eds.) SAC 2002. LNCS, vol. 2595, pp. 62–75. Springer, Heidelberg (2003)

# Timed-Release Computational Secret Sharing Scheme and Its Applications

Yohei Watanabe and Junji Shikata

Graduate School of Environment and Information Sciences,
Yokohama National University, Japan
watanabe-yohei-xs@ynu.jp, shikata@ynu.ac.jp

**Abstract.** A secret sharing scheme is an important cryptographic primitive. In this paper, we focus on a computational secret sharing (CSS) scheme, which is a practical, simple secret sharing scheme, with timed-release functionality, which we call a timed-release computational secret sharing (TR-CSS) scheme. In TR-CSS, participants more than or equal to a threshold number can reconstruct a secret by using their shares only when the time specified by a dealer has come. Our TR-CSS can be regarded as a natural extension of Krawczyk's CSS, and we finally succeed to add timed-release functionality to Krawczyk's CSS with small overhead, which seems to be almost optimal. Moreover, we show our proposal of TR-CSS is important for constructing threshold encryption and multiple encryption with timed-release functionality in a generic and efficient way.

## 1 Introduction

Shamir [12] and Blakley [2] independently proposed secret sharing schemes. Krawczyk [7] proposed more practical secret sharing scheme, which is called a *computational secret sharing* (CSS for short) scheme, under the assumption that the adversary's computational power is bounded. The share size of CSS is significantly smaller than that in traditional secret sharing schemes (i.e. with information-theoretic security).

Meanwhile, "time" is intimately related to our lives. As protocols associated with "time", *timed-release cryptographic protocols* introduced in [8] are well-known. Informally, the goal of timed-release cryptography is *to securely send certain information into the future*. For instance, in timed-release public key encryption (TR-PKE for short), a sender transmits a ciphertext so that a receiver can decrypt it when the time which the sender specified has come, and the receiver cannot decrypt it before the time. So far, various researches on timed-release cryptography have been studied (e.g., [10,4,3]).

From the above discussion, it is useful and important to consider a secret sharing scheme with timed-release security, which is called a *timed-release secret sharing* (TR-SS) scheme. Recently, Watanabe and Shikata proposed a TR-SS scheme in the information-theoretic security setting [13]. They show that the share size of their scheme must be also larger than or equal to the secret size as

S.S.M. Chow et al. (Eds.): ProvSec 2014, LNCS 8782, pp. 326–333, 2014.
© Springer International Publishing Switzerland 2014

in traditional secret sharing schemes. In this paper, we deal with a CSS scheme with timed-release functionality, which we call a *timed-release computational secret sharing* (TR-CSS) scheme, from the aspect of efficiency. Specifically, as in the case of TR-SS [13], we aim to achieve TR-CSS with the share size (almost) equivalent to that of traditional CSS. TR-CSS is useful when one wants to add timed-release property to any application of secret sharing schemes. In addition to this, TR-CSS can also be used for adding timed-release functionality to other cryptographic protocols.

**Our Contribution.** Our main purpose in this paper is *to realize a secret sharing scheme with timed-release functionality in a generic and efficient way* in terms of the share size. Specifically, we begin with newly formalizing a model and a security notion of $(k, n)$-TR-CSS. In addition, we propose two kinds of constructions of $(k, n)$-TR-CSS starting from identity-based encryption (IBE), and we finally succeed to add timed-release functionality to traditional CSS — especially for Krawczyk's scheme [7]— with small overhead, which seems to be *almost optimal.* Therefore, our study on TR-CSS can be regarded as a natural extension of Krawczyk's CSS in terms of both a model and constructions.

Moreover, we show TR-CSS can provide threshold encryption with timed-release functionality from TR-CSS in a generic and efficient way. To realize this, we consider constructing multiple encryption with timed-release functionality from TR-CSS based on Dodis–Katz paradigm [6], since Dodis and Katz [6] showed threshold encryption can be constructed from multiple encryption in a generic and simple way.

## 2   Preliminaries

**Notation.** If we write $(y_1, \ldots, y_m) \leftarrow A(x_1, \ldots, x_n)$ for an algorithm $A$ having $n$ inputs and $m$ outputs, it means to input $x_1, \ldots, x_n$ into $A$ and to get the resulting output $y_1, \ldots, y_m$. If $\mathcal{X}$ is a set, we write $x \overset{U}{\leftarrow} \mathcal{X}$ to mean the operation of picking an element $x$ of $\mathcal{X}$ uniformly at random, and $|\mathcal{X}|$ denotes its cardinality. If $x$ is a string, then $|x|$ denotes its bit-length. We use $\kappa$ as a security parameter. When we write negligible $\epsilon$ in $\kappa$, it means a function $\epsilon : \mathbb{N} \to [0, 1]$ where $\epsilon(\kappa) < 1/g(\kappa)$ for any polynomial $g$ and sufficiently large $\kappa$. Furthermore, in this paper "probabilistic polynomial-time" is abbreviated as PPT. Let $\mathcal{P} := \{P_1, P_2, \ldots, P_n\}$ be a set of IDs of all participants and $\mathcal{W}$ be a set of corrupted participants. For any subset of participants $\mathcal{J} = \{P_{i_1}, \ldots, P_{i_j}\} \subseteq \mathcal{P}$, $u_{\mathcal{J}} := (u_{i_1}, \ldots, u_{i_j})$ denotes shares held by $\mathcal{J}$. In addition, we consider a $(k, n)$-*threshold access structure* $\Gamma := (\mathcal{Q}, \mathcal{F})$, where $\mathcal{Q} := \{\mathcal{Q} \subseteq \mathcal{P} \mid |\mathcal{Q}| \geq k\}$ and $\mathcal{F} := \{F \subseteq \mathcal{P} \mid |F| \leq k - 1\}$. $\mathcal{S}$ is a set of possible secrets with a probability distribution $P_S$, and we assume $|\mathcal{S}| = 2^\lambda$ for simplicity (i.e. the length of a secret is $\lambda$ bit), where $\lambda$ is a polynomial in $\kappa$.

**Secret Sharing and Information Dispersal Algorithm.** A secret sharing scheme [12,2] and an information dispersal algorithm [9] with $(k, n)$-threshold access structures ($(k,n)$-SS and $(k,n)$-IDA for short, respectively)[1] are used for the distribution of a piece of information among $n$ participants, in such a way that the recovery of the information is possible in presence of $k$ ($\leq n$) participants. In $(k,n)$-SS, $k$ participants can reconstruct the secret while any $k-1$ participants obtain no information on the secret from their shares. On the other hand, in $(k,n)$-IDA, there are no restriction whatsoever about the sets which are not in $\mathscr{Q}$. Therefore, we can consider $(k,n)$-IDA as $(k,n)$-SS without considering its security. $(k,n)$-SS (resp. $(k,n)$-IDA) $\Pi$ consists of two-tuple algorithms, $SS.Share$ and $SS.Recon$ (resp. $IDA.Share$ and $IDA.Recon$). $SS.Share$ (resp. $IDA.Share$) takes a $(k,n)$-threshold access structure $\Gamma = (\mathscr{Q}, \mathscr{F})$ and a secret (called as a file in the context of IDA) $s \in \mathcal{S}$ as input and then outputs $n$ shares $(u_1, \dots, u_n)$. $SS.Recon$ (resp. $IDA.Recon$) takes at least $k$ shares $u_Q$ for $Q \in \mathscr{Q}$ as inputs and outputs a secret $s$. We say that $\Pi$ has the *perfect correctness* property if it meets the following condition: For all $\kappa \in \mathbb{N}$, all $s \in \mathcal{S}$, and for all $(u_1, \dots, u_n) \leftarrow X.Share(1^\kappa, \Gamma, s)$, it holds that $s \leftarrow X.Recon(1^\kappa, u_Q)$ for any $Q \in \mathscr{Q}$, where $X \in \{SS, IDA\}$. Then, we can define $\Pi$ as $(k,n)$-IDA if it meets the above perfect correctness property. A lower bound on share size required for $(k,n)$-IDA is $|u_i| \geq \frac{\lambda}{k}$, where $\lambda$ is the bit-length of the file.

To give security formalization of $(k,n)$-SS, we consider the following *Privacy game* as in [11]: $\mathcal{W} \leftarrow \emptyset$; $(s^{(0)}, s^{(1)}, st) \leftarrow A(\mathsf{chal})$; $b \overset{U}{\leftarrow} \{0,1\}$; $(u_1, \dots, u_n) \leftarrow SS.Share(1^\kappa, \Gamma, s^{(b)})$; $b' \leftarrow A^{Corrupt(\cdot)}(\mathsf{guess}, st)$. Here, we require $|s^{(0)}| = |s^{(1)}| = \lambda$, and $st$ is state information. In addition, $Corrupt(\cdot)$ is a *corrupt oracle* which takes an ID $P_i$ as input, and then $\mathcal{W} \leftarrow \mathcal{W} \cup \{P_i\}$ and returns $u_i$. $A$ can query to $Corrupt(\cdot)$ until $|\mathcal{W}| = k-1$. We define the advantage of $A$ in the above game as $Adv_{\Pi,A}^{\mathsf{Privacy}}(\kappa) := \left| \Pr[b = b'] - \frac{1}{2} \right|$.

Based on the above game, we consider two security notions, *perfect privacy* and *computational privacy*. These notion mean that *no* information is leaked from subthreshold shares in an information-theoretic sense or in a complexity-theoretic sense. Hereafter, we call $(k,n)$-SS with perfect privacy $(k,n)$-*perfect secret sharing* ($(k,n)$-PSS for short), and we also call $(k,n)$-SS with computational privacy $(k,n)$-*computational secret sharing* ($(k,n)$-CSS for short). Formally, $(k,n)$-PSS is defined as follows. For $\exists \kappa_0 \in \mathbb{N}$ and $\forall \kappa \geq \kappa_0$, $(k,n)$-SS $\Pi$ is said to be $(k,n)$-PSS if it has perfect correctness and $Adv_{\Pi,A}^{\mathsf{Privacy}}(\kappa) = 0$ for any computationally-unbounded adversary $A$. $(k,n)$-CSS is also defined as follows. For $\exists \kappa_0 \in \mathbb{N}$ and $\forall \kappa \geq \kappa_0$, $(k,n)$-SS $\Pi$ is said to be $\epsilon$-$(k,n)$-CSS if it has perfect correctness and there exists a negligible $\epsilon$ in $\kappa$ such that $Adv_{\Pi,A}^{\mathsf{Privacy}}(\kappa) < \epsilon$ for any PPT adversary $A$. Krawczyk proposed $\epsilon$-$(k,n)$-CSS [7] and successfully reduced the share size, which is $\frac{\lambda}{k} + |K|$, where $|K|$ means the key size of the underlying $\epsilon$-FTG-CPA secure symmetric encryption[2] used in the construction, respectively.

---

[1] Secret sharing schemes with the $(k,n)$-threshold access structure is traditionally called $(k,n)$-threshold secret sharing schemes.

[2] As in [7], for simplicity, we also assume that the ciphertext-overhead is zero in the following, since it can be achieved by carefully selecting symmetric encryption. The notion of FTG-CPA is defined in [1] and we also use $\epsilon$-FTG-CPA secure symmetric encryption as a building block of TR-CSS.

**Identity-Based Encryption (IBE).** IBE $\Sigma$ consists of four-tuple algorithms (*IBE.Setup, IBE.KeyGen, IBE.Enc, IBE.Dec*) defined. *IBE.Setup* generates a public parameter $prm$ and a master secret key $mk$. *IBE.KeyGen* takes the master secret key $mk$ and an identity $ID \in \mathcal{ID}_{IBE}$ as input and outputs a secret key $sk_{ID}$ for $ID$. *IBE.Enc* takes the public parameter $prm$, an identity $ID$, and a plaintext $m \in \mathcal{M}_{IBE}$ as input and then outputs a ciphertext $c_{ID}$. *IBE.Dec* takes a secret key $sk_{ID}$ for $ID$ and a ciphertext $c_{ID}$ as input and then outputs a plaintext $m$ or $\perp$.

**Symmetric Encryption (SE).** SE $\Phi$ consists of three-tuple algorithms (*SE.KGen, SE.Enc, SE.Dec*). *SE.KGen* generates a secret key $K \in \mathcal{K}_{SE}$. *SE.Enc* takes a secret key $K$ and a plaintext $M \in \mathcal{M}_{SE}$ as input and then outputs a ciphertext $C$. *SE.Dec* takes a secret key $K$ and a ciphertext $C$ as inputs and then outputs a plaintext $M$ or $\perp$.

# 3 Timed-Release Computational Secret Sharing

We propose a timed-release computational secret sharing (TR-CSS for short) scheme. As in TR-PKE, we consider the presence of a *time-server*, whose role is to periodically generate and broadcast *time-signals*. The time-server executes a setup algorithm and a time-signal generation algorithm in TR-PKE, hence, it is natural and reasonable that we assume these algorithms in TR-CSS. The time-server do not have any interaction with any other entities, namely, it independently generates time-signals and only broadcasts them as in the case of TR-PKE.

## 3.1 The Model of $(k, n)$-TR-CSS

We consider a TR-CSS with a $(k, n)$-threshold access structure ($(k, n)$-TR-CSS for short). Informally, $(k, n)$-TR-CSS is executed as follows. First, a time-server $TS$ generates a master public key and a master secret key. Next, a dealer $D$ specifies future time, as $D$ wants, when a secret can be reconstructed by at least $k$ participants (we call the time *the specified time*), and he generates $n$ shares from the secret by using the master public key. And, $D$ sends shares to corresponding participants, respectively, via secure channels. The time-server $TS$ periodically broadcasts a time-signal which is generated by using his secret key. When the specified time has come, at least $k$ participants can compute the secret by using both their shares and the time-signal of the specified time. Let $\mathcal{T}$ be a set of time. For any subset of participants $\mathcal{J} = \{P_{i_1}, \ldots, P_{i_j}\} \subseteq \mathcal{P}$, $u_{\mathcal{J}}^{(t)} := (u_{i_1}^{(t)}, \ldots, u_{i_j}^{(t)})$, where $u_i^{(t)}$ is $P_i$'s share at the specified time $t$.

A $(k, n)$-TR-CSS $\Psi$ consists of four-tuple algorithms (*Setup, Release, Share, Recon*) defined as follows: $(mpk, msk) \leftarrow Setup(1^{\kappa})$ takes a security parameter $\kappa$ as input and outputs a master public key $mpk$ and a master secret key $msk$. $ts^{(t)} \leftarrow Ext(msk, t)$ takes the master secret key $msk$ and time $t \in \mathcal{T}$ as input and outputs a time-signal $ts^{(t)}$ at time $t$. $(u_1^{(t)}, \ldots, u_n^{(t)}) \leftarrow Share(\Gamma, mpk, s, t)$ takes a

**Table 1.** Left side: the *Type-I Privacy game*. Right side: the *Type-II Privacy game*.

| | |
|---|---|
| $\mathcal{W} \leftarrow \emptyset$; $(mpk, msk) \leftarrow Setup(1^\kappa)$; | $\mathcal{W} = \mathcal{P}$; $(mpk, msk) \leftarrow Setup(1^\kappa)$; |
| $(s^{(0)}, s^{(1)}, t^*, st) \leftarrow A(\text{chal}, mpk, msk)$; | $(s^{(0)}, s^{(1)}, t^*, st) \leftarrow A^{Release(msk, \cdot)}(\text{chal}, mpk)$; |
| $b \overset{U}{\leftarrow} \{0, 1\}$; | $b \overset{U}{\leftarrow} \{0, 1\}$; |
| $(u_1^{(t^*)}, \dots, u_n^{(t^*)}) \leftarrow Share(\Gamma, mpk, s^{(b)}, t^*)$; | $(u_1^{(t^*)}, \dots, u_n^{(t^*)}) \leftarrow Share(\Gamma, mpk, s^{(b)}, t^*)$; |
| $b' \leftarrow A^{Corrupt(\cdot)}(\text{guess}, st)$. | $b' \leftarrow A^{Release(msk, \cdot)}(\text{guess}, u_1^{(t^*)}, \dots, u_n^{(t^*)}, st)$. |

$(k, n)$-threshold access structure $\Gamma = (\mathcal{Q}, \mathcal{F})$, a master public key $mpk$, a secret $s \in \mathcal{S}$ and a specified time $t$ as input, and then outputs $n$ shares $(u_1^{(t)}, \dots, u_n^{(t)})$ at time $t$ . $s \leftarrow Recon(u_{\mathcal{Q}}^{(t)}, ts^{(t)})$ takes at least $k$ shares $u_{\mathcal{Q}}^{(t)}$ for $\mathcal{Q} \in \mathcal{Q}$ and a time-signal $ts^{(t)}$ at specified time $t$ as inputs, and outputs a secret $s$. We say that $\Psi$ has the *perfect correctness* property if it meets the following condition: For all $\kappa \in \mathbb{N}$, all $s \in \mathcal{S}$, $(mpk, msk) \leftarrow Setup(1^\kappa)$, all $t \in \mathcal{T}$, all $ts^{(t)} \leftarrow Ext(msk, t)$, and all $(u_1^{(t)}, \dots, u_n^{(t)}) \leftarrow Share(\Gamma, mpk, s, t)$, it holds that $s \leftarrow Recon(u_{\mathcal{Q}}^{(t)}, ts^{(t)})$ for any $\mathcal{Q} \in \mathcal{Q}$.

*Remark 1.* In the case that a time-server does not exist (i.e., $\mathcal{T} = \emptyset$, $mpk$ is a security parameter $\kappa$, and $msk$ is an empty string), the model of $(k, n)$-TR-CSS can be regarded as that of traditional $(k, n)$-SS. Namely, our model of TR-CSS includes the model of traditional secret sharing schemes.

### 3.2 Security Definition of $(k, n)$-TR-CSS

To discuss security, we convert security notions of TR-PKE into those of CSS: Even a curious time-server who colludes with at most $k - 1$ participants can obtain no information on the secret; and all participants can obtain no information on the secret without a time-signal at the specified time. Hence, we consider the following two notions: privacy against a curious time-server (Type-I Privacy) and privacy against participants (Type-II Privacy). To formalize these notion, we consider the *Type-I Privacy game* and the *Type-II Privacy game* (see Table 1). In both games, we require $|s^{(0)}| = |s^{(1)}| = \lambda$, and $st$ is state information. $Corrupt(\cdot)$ is a *corrupt oracle*, which is the same as that of the *Privacy* game in $(k, n)$-SS. $Release(msk, \cdot)$ is a *time-signals generation oracle* which takes time $t$ as input, and returns $Ext(msk, t)$. $A$ is allowed to access the above oracle at most $q_t$ times at any time, however, it cannot submit the target time $t^*$ to $Release(msk, \cdot)$ after the chal stage. We define the advantages of $A$ in the above games as $Adv_{\Psi, A}^{\text{Type-I Privacy}}(\kappa) := |\Pr[b = b'] - \frac{1}{2}|$ and $Adv_{\Psi, A}^{\text{Type-II Privacy}}(\kappa) := |\Pr[b = b'] - \frac{1}{2}|$, respectively. Then, we define Type-I Privacy and Type-II Privacy as follows.

**Definition 1 (Type-I Privacy).** *For $\exists \kappa_0 \in \mathbb{N}$ and $\forall \kappa \geq \kappa_0$, $(k, n)$-TR-CSS $\Psi$ meets $\epsilon$-*Type-I Privacy* if there exists a negligible $\epsilon$ in $\kappa$ such that $Adv_{\Psi, A}^{\text{Type-I Privacy}}(\kappa) < \epsilon$ for any PPT adversary $A$.*

**Definition 2 (Type-II Privacy).** *For $\exists \kappa_0 \in \mathbb{N}$ and $\forall \kappa \geq \kappa_0$, $(k, n)$-TR-CSS $\Psi$ meets $(q_t, \epsilon)$-Type-II Privacy if there exists a negligible $\epsilon$ in $\kappa$ such that $Adv_{\Psi, A}^{Type-II\ Privacy}(\kappa) < \epsilon$ for any PPT adversary A, where $q_t$ is the number of queries that A can issue to the oracle in the Type-II Privacy game.*

**Definition 3 (Security).** *$(k, n)$-TR-CSS $\Psi$ is said to be $(q_t, \epsilon_1, \epsilon_2)$-$(k, n)$-TR-CSS if it has perfect correctness, $\epsilon_1$-Type-I Privacy and $(q_t, \epsilon_2)$-Type-II Privacy.*

### 3.3   Constructions of $(k, n)$-TR-CSS

We propose two kinds of constructions of $(k, n)$-TR-CSS. First, we propose a generic construction. Our generic construction can be regarded as extension of Krawczyk's CSS [7]. The idea of our construction is to combine Krawczyk's CSS and IBE. Let $\Pi_1$ be $(k, n)$-SS, $\Pi_2$ be $(k, n)$-IDA, $\Sigma$ be IBE, and $\Phi$ be SE. Suppose that $\mathcal{T} \subseteq \mathcal{ID}_{IBE}$. Then, $(k, n)$-TR-CSS $\Psi=\{Setup, Ext, Share, Recon\}$ is constructed as follows. **Setup**: It computes $(prm, mk) \leftarrow IBE.Setup(1^\kappa)$, and then outputs $(mpk, msk) := (prm, mk)$. **Ext**: It computes $sk_t \leftarrow IBE.KeyGen(mk, t)$, and then outputs $ts^{(t)} := sk_t$. **Share**: First, it computes $K \leftarrow SE.Gen(1^\kappa)$ and $C \leftarrow SE.Enc(K, s)$, and then it calculates $c_t \leftarrow IBE.Enc(prm, t, K)$. Finally, it generates $(\tilde{u}_1, \ldots, \tilde{u}_n) \leftarrow IDA.Share\ (1^\kappa, \Gamma, C)$ and $(\hat{u}_1, \ldots, \hat{u}_n) \leftarrow SS.Share(1^\kappa, \Gamma, c_t)$, and then it outputs $u_i^{(t)} := (\tilde{u}_i, \hat{u}_i)$ $(1 \leq i \leq n)$. **Recon**: It computes $c_t \leftarrow SS.Recon(1^\kappa, \hat{u}_{\mathcal{Q}})$ and $C \leftarrow IDA.Recon(1^\kappa, \tilde{u}_{\mathcal{Q}})$. Then, it computes $K \leftarrow IBE.Dec(sk_t, c_t)$ and $s = SE.Dec(K, C)$.

We can show that the resulting $(k, n)$-TR-CSS in the above construction is secure, if given $(k, n)$-SS is $(k, n)$-PSS, IBE meets IND-ID-CPA [14], and SE meets FTG-CPA [1], as follows (see [14] and [1] for security definitions of IBE and SE, respectively). Due to space limitation, the proof will be given in the full paper.

**Theorem 1.** *If given SE $\Phi$ is $\epsilon_1$-FTG-CPA secure, $(k, n)$-SS $\Pi_1$ is $(k, n)$-PSS, and IBE $\Sigma$ is $(q_{ID}, \epsilon_2)$-IND-ID-CPA secure, then the resulting $(k, n)$-TR-CSS $\Psi$ in the above construction is $(q_t, \delta_1, \delta_2)$-$(k, n)$-TR-CSS, where $q_t = q_{ID}$, $\delta_1 \leq \epsilon_1$ and $\delta_2 \leq \epsilon_1 + 2\epsilon_2$.*

Then, the share size in our generic construction of $(k, n)$-TR-CSS is given by $|u_i^{(t)}| = \frac{\lambda}{k} + |K| + \mathrm{COH}_{IBE}(\kappa)$, where $\mathrm{COH}_{IBE}(\kappa)$ is the ciphertext-overhead in IBE $\Sigma$. Note that the share size in our construction is only $\mathrm{COH}_{IBE}(\kappa)$-bits longer than that in Krawczyk's CSS. It means that we successfully added the timed-release functionality to CSS with only the underlying IBE's ciphertext-overhead.

Next, we consider improving the above construction by focusing on currently known efficient IBE. Our idea is to use the Waters's IBE [14] and to slightly modify the above generic construction as follows: For the three components of the ciphertext of IBE, shares are generated by applying $(k, n)$-PSS to only one component and by applying $(k, n)$-IDA to other ones to reduce the share size.

Let $\mathbb{G}$ and $\mathbb{G}_T$ be groups of prime order $p$ in which a generator is denoted by $g$ and $e : \mathbb{G} \times \mathbb{G} \rightarrow \mathbb{G}_T$ be a bilinear map. We assume that each time $t := (t_1, t_2, \ldots, t_\ell) \in \{0, 1\}^\ell$ is an $\ell$ bit string, where $t_i$ $(1 \leq i \leq \ell)$ is $i$-th bit of $t$. $\Pi_1$, $\Pi_2$ and $\Phi$ are the same as those in the above generic construction. **Setup**: $\alpha \xleftarrow{U} \mathbb{Z}_p$ and $g, g_2, u', u_1, \ldots, u_\ell \xleftarrow{U} \mathbb{G}$. Then, it outputs $mpk := (g, g_1(:= g^\alpha), g_2, u', u_1, \ldots, u_\ell)$ and $msk := g_2^\alpha$. **Ext**: $r_1 \xleftarrow{U} \mathbb{Z}_p$. Then, the time-signal $ts^{(t)}$ at time $t$ is constructed as $ts^{(t)} := (ts_1^{(t)}, ts_2^{(t)}) = (g_2^\alpha(u' \prod_{i=1}^\ell u_i^{t_i})^{r_1}, g^{r_1})$. **Share**: First, it computes $K \leftarrow SE.Gen(1^\kappa)$ and $C \leftarrow SE.Enc(K, s)$. Next, it computes $c_t^{(0)} := K \cdot e(g_1, g_2)^{r_2}$, $c_t^{(1)} := g^{r_2}$ and $c_t^{(2)} := (u' \prod_{i=1}^\ell u_i^{t_i})^{r_2}$, where $r_2 \xleftarrow{U} \mathbb{Z}_p$. Then, it computes $(\tilde{u}_1, \ldots, \tilde{u}_n) \leftarrow IDA.Share(1^\kappa, \Gamma, C)$, $(\hat{u}_1^{(0)}, \ldots, \hat{u}_n^{(0)}) \leftarrow SS.Share(1^\kappa, \Gamma, c_t^{(0)})$, $(\hat{u}_1^{(1)}, \ldots, \hat{u}_n^{(1)}) \leftarrow IDA.Share(1^\kappa, \Gamma, c_t^{(1)})$, and $(\hat{u}_1^{(2)}, \ldots, \hat{u}_n^{(2)}) \leftarrow IDA.Share(1^\kappa, \Gamma, c_t^{(2)})$. Finally, it outputs $(u_1^{(t)}, \ldots, u_n^{(t)})$, where $u_i^{(t)} := (\tilde{u}_i, \hat{u}_i^{(0)}, \hat{u}_i^{(1)}, \hat{u}_i^{(2)})$ $(1 \leq i \leq n)$. **Recon**: First, it computes $C \leftarrow IDA.Recon(1^\kappa, \tilde{u}_\mathcal{Q})$, $c_t^{(0)} \leftarrow SS.Recon(1^\kappa, \hat{u}_\mathcal{Q}^{(0)})$, $c_t^{(1)} \leftarrow IDA.Recon(1^\kappa, \hat{u}_\mathcal{Q}^{(1)})$, and $c_t^{(2)} \leftarrow IDA.Recon(1^\kappa, \hat{u}_\mathcal{Q}^{(2)})$. Then, it computes $K = c_t^{(0)} \frac{e(ts_2^{(t)}, c_t^{(2)})}{e(ts_1^{(t)}, c_t^{(1)})}$ and $s = SE.Dec(K, C)$.

Since Waters's IBE meets IND-ID-CPA, then we immediately obtain the following theorem.

**Theorem 2.** *Let $q$ be the number of queries and $\epsilon$ be an upper bound of the advantage of an adversary in IND-ID-CPA game of Waters's IBE. If given SE $\Phi$ is $\epsilon'$-FTG-CPA secure and $(k, n)$-SS $\Pi_1$ is $(k, n)$-PSS, then the resulting $(k, n)$-TR-CSS $\Psi$ in the above construction is $(q_t, \delta_1, \delta_2)$-$(k, n)$-TR-CSS, where $q_t = q$, $\delta_1 \leq \epsilon'$ and $\delta_2 \leq \epsilon' + 2\epsilon$.*

Then, the share size of the above construction of $(k, n)$-TR-CSS is given by $|u_i^{(t)}| = \frac{\lambda}{k} + |K| + \frac{2|\mathbb{G}|}{k}$, where $|\mathbb{G}|$ denotes the length of the element of $\mathbb{G}$. Namely, we can achieve the share size which is close to that of Krawczyk's CSS when $k$ is sufficiently large. Moreover, Waters's IBE is a simple, elegant and efficient construction under the standard assumption. Hence, in the sense of the share-overhead compared with Krawczyk's CSS, we can say that this construction is *almost optimal*.

### 3.4   Application to Construction of Threshold Encryption and Multiple Encryption with Timed-Release Functionality

TR-CSS can provide threshold encryption [5] with timed-release functionality (TR-TE for short). Since Dodis and Katz showed that multiple encryption can be transformed to threshold encryption [6] and multiple encryption has many other applications, we first consider multiple encryption with timed-release functionality (TR-ME). In [6], multiple encryption is constructed from $n$ PKEs, one-time signature and $(k, n)$-CSS. We can construct TR-ME by replacing $(k, n)$-CSS with $(k, n)$-TR-CSS in the above construction. This construction is more efficient than a construction by replacing PKEs with TR-PKEs. Moreover, TR-ME from $(k, n)$-TR-CSS can realize *a combining algorithm with timed-release functionality*, whereas TR-ME from TR-PKE can realize *a partial decryption algorithm with timed-release functionality*. Considering a scenario such that each secret key of TR-ME is co-located in different locations, the former has more *suitable* timed-release functionality than the latter. In addition, TR-ME can be also transformed to TR-TE as in the case of multiple encryption, since timed-release functionality have little or no effect on traditional security of multiple encryption and threshold encryption. Due to space limitation of this paper, we will explain the above results in details in a full version of this paper. Furthermore, we expect that TR-CSS can be used in various applications of multiple encryption.

**Acknowledgements.** We would like to thank Goichiro Hanaoka and Keita Emura for helpful suggestions to improve the preliminary version of this paper. The first author is supported by JSPS Research Fellowships for Young Scientists.

# References

1. Bellare, M., Desai, A., Jokipii, E., Rogaway, P.: A concrete security treatment of symmetric encryption. In: Proceedings of the 38th Annual Symposium on Foundations of Computer Science, pp. 394–403 (1997)
2. Blakley, G.: Safeguarding cryptographic keys. In: Proceedings of the 1979 AFIPS National Computer Conference, pp. 313–317. AFIPS Press, Monval (1979)
3. Cathalo, J., Libert, B., Quisquater, J.-J.: Efficient and non-interactive timed-release encryption. In: Qing, S., Mao, W., López, J., Wang, G. (eds.) ICICS 2005. LNCS, vol. 3783, pp. 291–303. Springer, Heidelberg (2005)
4. Chan, A.F., Blake, I.: Scalable, server-passive, user-anonymous timed release cryptography. In: Proceedings of the 25th IEEE International Conference on Distributed Computing Systems, ICDCS 2005, pp. 504–513 (2005)
5. Desmedt, Y.G., Frankel, Y.: Threshold cryptosystems. In: Brassard, G. (ed.) Advances in Cryptology - CRYPTO 1989. LNCS, vol. 435, pp. 307–315. Springer, Heidelberg (1990)
6. Dodis, Y., Katz, J.: Chosen-ciphertext security of multiple encryption. In: Kilian, J. (ed.) TCC 2005. LNCS, vol. 3378, pp. 188–209. Springer, Heidelberg (2005)
7. Krawczyk, H.: Secret sharing made short. In: Stinson, D.R. (ed.) Advances in Cryptology - CRYPTO 1993. LNCS, vol. 773, pp. 136–146. Springer, Heidelberg (1994)
8. May, T.: Timed-release crypto (1993)
9. Rabin, M.O.: Efficient dispersal of information for security, load balancing, and fault tolerance. J. ACM 36(2), 335–348 (1989)
10. Rivest, R.L., Shamir, A., Wagner, D.A.: Time-lock puzzles and timed-release crypto. Tech. Rep. Technical memo MIT/LCS/TR-684, MIT Laboratory for Computer Science (1996) (revision October 3, 1996)
11. Rogaway, P., Bellare, M.: Robust computational secret sharing and a unified account of classical secret-sharing goals. In: Proceedings of the 14th ACM Conference on Computer and Communications Security, CCS 2007, pp. 172–184. ACM, New York (2007)
12. Shamir, A.: How to share a secret. Commun. ACM 22(11), 612–613 (1979)
13. Watanabe, Y., Shikata, J.: Timed-release secret sharing scheme with information theoretic security. ArXiv e-prints (January 2014), http://arxiv.org/abs/1401.5895
14. Waters, B.: Efficient identity-based encryption without random oracles. In: Cramer, R. (ed.) EUROCRYPT 2005. LNCS, vol. 3404, pp. 114–127. Springer, Heidelberg (2005)

# Deniable Version of SIGMA Key Exchange Protocol Resilient to Ephemeral Key Leakage*

Łukasz Krzywiecki

Wrocław University of Technology, Poland
lukasz.krzywiecki@pwr.wroc.pl

**Abstract.** We propose modifications of SIGMA key exchange protocol that provide the deniability property. Our proposition, based on ring signatures, provide the possibility that a single party alone can produce a simulated transcripts of the protocol without the peer participation. Moreover we strengthen the SIGMA resulting session keys by additional using of long-term keys in the Diffie-Hellman key exchange phase of the protocol. Our proposition preserves the modular construction of the protocol, and does not change the number of the protocol rounds.

**Keywords:** authentication, key exchange, deniability, simultability, privacy, AKE protocol.

## 1 Introduction

In this paper we propose some modifications to SIGMA - Authenticated Key Exchange (AKE) protocol - that provide the deniability property, and strengthen the security of the resulting session keys. AKE protocols allow parties mutually identify themselves in order to establish a secretly share encryption key, used to secure subsequent communication. SIGMA family of key exchange protocols from IPsec [1] and the Internet Key Exchange (IKE) standards [2] is an elegant example of AKE modular construction, that use cryptographic primitives: signatures, message authentication codes, and pseudorandom functions, in such a way that security of the established session key can be proved formally, provided that underlying primitives are secure. However the signatures in SIGMA transcripts may be used as undeniable proofs for third parties (other than those running the protocol) that the communication with the signers took place. This in some scenarios, could be regarded as a drawback. The *deniability* property for AKE protocols guarantees that parties still can mutually identify themselves, but the transcript of the protocol is not a proof that parties partake in the protocol execution. Due to undeniable character of regular signatures in SIGMA, only a different context of its deniability was studied in [3], where it was shown that SIGMA is partially independent - so called *peer-independent*, i.e.: parties cannot deny their participation in the protocol, but those, which sign their messages

---

* Partially supported by funding from Polish National Science Center decision number DEC-2013/09/B/ST6/02251.

S.S.M. Chow et al. (Eds.): ProvSec 2014, LNCS 8782, pp. 334–341, 2014.
© Springer International Publishing Switzerland 2014

first, can deny their peer identity. Therefore, in this paper we take another approach, suggested in [3], for transforming the regular SIGMA into its deniable version, by replacing regular signatures with ring signatures. Another aspect of SIGMA analysed in the paper regards the security of the session key established via protocol execution. SIGMA is proven to be secure in the Canetti-Crawczyk (CK) model [4] assuming the ephemeral keys were not compromised. However there are possible scenarios in which the ephemeral keys are leaked to the adversary, e.g. (via badly implemented pseudorandom generators). Thus we strengthen the session key security via long term static keys, preserving at the same time compatibility with original SIGMA. Our contribution in this short paper is the following:

- We extend the deniability notion model from [3] to capture the possibility of a distinguisher algorithm to obtain the secret keys of parties. The knowledge of those keys can change the distinguisher's view, and influence its decisions.
- We propose a modified 3-round SIGMA, which uses ring signatures to provide the deniability (in our stronger model) for the protocol initiator. Similarly, propose a modified 4-round SIGMA, which provides the deniability for the protocol responder. Therefore we complement the results from [3], for 3-round and 4-round versions of SIGMA.
- We strengthen the SIGMA resulting session key by additional using of long term certified keys in the Diffie-Hellman (DH) key exchange phase of the protocol. We provide a security discussion in our slightly extended model of CK [4], which additionally allows the adversary to query for ephemeral keys.
- Our extensions can be done optionally by the communicating parties providing compatibility with original SIGMA (unlike other deniable protocols e.g. SKEME [5]).

## 2 Building Blocks and Background

Presented AKE protocols are based on Diffie-Hellman (DH) key exchange, so we assume that corresponding computations are done within a group $G = \langle g \rangle$ of prime order $q$, where computational Diffie-Hellman assumption (CDH) holds. We follow the general notation from [6]. Let $I$ and $R$ be two peer parties of the key exchange protocol, then: $(\mathsf{sk}_I, \mathsf{pk}_I)$ and $(\mathsf{sk}_R, \mathsf{pk}_R)$ denotes pairs of long-term secret/public keys of $I$ and $R$ respectively, randomly chosen according to the key generating algorithm KGEN; $\mathrm{SIG}_{\mathsf{sk}_I}(m)$ denotes a signature of $m$ computed by the means of a secret key $\mathsf{sk}_I$ of $I$; PRF is a pseudo-random function. $\mathrm{MAC}_k(m)$ denotes a message authentication code of $m$ computed by the means of a key $k$. Moreover $\mathrm{RSIG}_{\mathsf{sk}_I, \{\mathsf{pk}_I, \mathsf{pk}_R\}}(m)$ denotes a ring signature of $m$ computed by the means of a secret key $\mathsf{sk}_I$ of $I$, and verifiable with public keys $\{\mathsf{pk}_I, \mathsf{pk}_R\}$ of parties $I$ and $R$ (we further describe ring signatures in Section 2.2).

### 2.1 Review of SIGMA Protocol

Let us briefly review the SIGMA protocol - the 3-round version denoted as $\Sigma_0$ in [6]. The parties: an initiator $I$, and a responder $R$ exchange messages (build on top of a predefined secure building blocks: signature schema SIG, message authentication code MAC, and pseudorandom function PRF), in order to identify themselves and to establish a secret session key.

---

**The protocol messages for 3-round version of SIGMA**:

      M1 ($I \rightarrow R$): $s, g^x$

      M2 ($I \leftarrow R$): $s, g^y, ID_R, \text{SIG}_{\text{sk}_R}("1", s, g^x, g^y), \text{MAC}_{k_1}("1", s, ID_R)$

      M3 ($I \rightarrow R$): $s, ID_I, \text{SIG}_{\text{sk}_I}("0", s, g^x, g^y), \text{MAC}_{k_1}("0", s, ID_I)$

**The protocol steps:**

1. An initiator $I$ chooses a session id $s$. Picks at random $x \leftarrow_\$ \mathbb{Z}_q$. Computes ephemeral DH public key $g^x$. Sends $s, g^x$ in Message 1 to a responder party.

2. The responder $R$ picks at random $y \leftarrow_\$ \mathbb{Z}_q$. Computes ephemeral DH public key $g^y$. Computes a key $(g^x)^y = g^{xy}$. Derives two keys $k_0 = \text{PRF}_{g^{xy}}(0)$, and $k_1 = \text{PRF}_{g^{xy}}(1)$. Erases $y, g^{xy}$ from its memory. Computes $\text{MAC}_{k_1}("1", s, ID_R)$, and $\text{SIG}_{\text{sk}_R}("1", s, g^x, g^y)$. Sends the session id $s$, its own identifier $ID_R$, the DH public key $g^y$, the signature, and the mac in the message ("M2") to $I$.

3. $I$ computes the key $(g^y)^x = g^{xy}$. Derives $k_0 = \text{PRF}_{g^{xy}}(0)$, and $k_1 = \text{PRF}_{g^{xy}}(1)$. Erases $y, g^{xy}$ from its memory. Verifies $\text{MAC}_{k_1}("1", s, ID_R)$. Retrieves the public key of the party identified by $ID_R$. Verifies $\text{SIG}_{\text{sk}_R}("1", s, g^x, g^y)$. If one of the above verifications fails, $I$ aborts the session and outputs "failure". Otherwise $I$ computes $\text{MAC}_{k_1}("0", s, ID_I)$, and $\text{SIG}_{\text{sk}_I}("0", s, g^x, g^y)$. Sends $s, ID_I$, the signature, and the mac in the message ("M3") to $R$. $I$ completes the session with public output $(ID_I, s, ID_R)$ and the secret session key $k_0$.

4. $R$ verifies $\text{MAC}_{k_1}("0", s, ID_I)$. Retrieves the public key $\text{pk}_I$ of the party identified by $ID_I$. Verifies the signature $\text{SIG}_{\text{sk}_I}("0", s, g^x, g^y)$. If one of the above verifications fails, $R$ aborts the session and outputs "failure". Otherwise $R$ completes the session with public output $(ID_R, s, ID_I)$ and the session key $k_0$.

---

As it was shown in [3], the protocol can be only considered as partially deniable for the responder, because his signature is produced before seeing the identity of the initiator. The responder cannot deny his participation in the protocol, however he can deny its peer identity. Similarly, partial deniability for the initiator was shown in [3] for 4-round version of SIGMA.

---

**The protocol messages for 4-round version of SIGMA**:

      M1 ($I \rightarrow R$): $s, g^x$

      M2 ($I \leftarrow R$): $s, g^y$

      M3 ($I \rightarrow R$): $s, ID_I, \text{SIG}_{\text{sk}_I}("0", s, g^x, g^y), \text{MAC}_{k_1}("0", s, ID_I)$

      M4 ($I \leftarrow R$): $s, ID_R, \text{SIG}_{\text{sk}_R}("1", s, g^x, g^y), \text{MAC}_{k_1}("1", s, ID_R)$

---

## 2.2 Review of Ring Signatures

**Definition 1.** *A ring signatures* RING *is defined as a 4-tuple of the following procedures:* (STR, KGEN, RSIG, RVER): STR – *structure generation – is a randomized algorithm that takes a security parameter $\xi$, creates an algebraic structure $G$.* KGEN – *key generation – is a randomized algorithm that takes an algebraic structure $G$, and produces a pair* (sk, pk) *over $G$ interpreted as private/public keys.* RSIG – *signing procedure – is a randomized algorithm that takes a message*

$m$, the secret key $\mathsf{sk}_j$, and the set of public keys $\mathbf{pk} = \{\mathsf{pk}_1, \ldots, \mathsf{pk}_n\}$. It returns a signature $\sigma$. We write $\sigma \leftarrow \mathrm{RSIG}_{\mathsf{sk}_j,\mathbf{pk}}(m)$. RVER – signature verification – is a deterministic algorithm that takes a message $m$, a signature $\sigma$ for $m$, and the set of public keys $\mathbf{pk}$. It returns a bit: 1 or 0 to indicate whether the signature $\sigma$ is valid, i.e. someone having a public key in a set $\mathbf{pk}$ indicated by $\sigma$ has signed $m$. We write $d \leftarrow \mathrm{RVER}(m, \sigma, \mathbf{pk})$.

We assume that the ring schema is secure RING in the same sense in which SIG is secure, i.e. no forger without the secret key should produce a verifiable ring signature in the *chosen-message* scenario.

We define the anonymity of ring signatures by the game ExpAnon between a challenger $\mathcal{C}$ and a distinguisher algorithm $\mathcal{D}$. The challenger $\mathcal{C}$ setups the system, knows all secret keys $\{\mathsf{sk}_1, \ldots \mathsf{sk}_n\}$ and corresponding public keys $\Omega = \{\mathsf{pk}_1, \ldots \mathsf{pk}_n\}$ of all users $\{u_1, \ldots u_n\}$. We analyze the strongest adversary possible, which knows all the private keys of the users.

---

Experiment ExpAnon

1. $\mathcal{D}$ is given all private and public keys. $\mathcal{D}$ choses a ring, which is a subset $Y \subset \Omega$.
2. $\mathcal{D}$ choses two public keys from $Y$ (say $pk_0$ and $pk_1$), and a test message $m$ (this message could be the same or different from messages from query stage). The challenger $\mathcal{C}$ draws a bit $b$ at random, and creates a signature $\sigma_b = \mathrm{RSIG}_{sk_b,Y}(m)$. The signature $\sigma_b$ is given to $\mathcal{D}$.
3. $\mathcal{D}$ outputs a bit $\hat{b}$.

We say that $\mathcal{D}$ wins in the experiment if $b = \hat{b}$.

---

**Definition 2.** *We define* $\mathbf{Adv}(\mathcal{D}) = |\Pr[\mathcal{D}(\sigma_1) = 1] - \Pr[\mathcal{D}(\sigma_0) = 1]|$ *as the advantage of* $\mathcal{D}$ *in* ExpAnon. *We say that the ring signatures is anonymous if the advantage* $\mathbf{Adv}(\mathcal{D})$ *is negligible.*

In this definition the adversary knows all parameters, including secrets, which should not help him in winning in ExpAnon. The only unknown is the bit $b$ drawn in step 2).

## 3 Proposed Deniable Versions of SIGMA Protocol

In order to make SIGMA protocol deniable we observe the following: Suppose we have two users with the following roles: a signer $u_s$, and a verifier $u_v$. Let the signer creates the ring signature $\sigma = \mathrm{RSIG}_{\mathsf{sk}_s,\{\mathsf{pk}_s,\mathsf{pk}_v\}}(m)$ over the ring consisted of both the signer $u_s$, and the verifier $u_v$. The verifier $u_v$ can check the validity of the resulting signature, and is convinced that it was really the signer $u_s$ who produced $\sigma$, hence the ring $\{\mathsf{pk}_s, \mathsf{pk}_v\}$ without element $\mathsf{pk}_v$ consists with only one public key $\mathsf{pk}_s$ belonging to the signer. Note that for the external observer the resulting ring signature $\sigma$, validated by both public keys, is anonymous in the sense of Definition 2.

In order to strengthen the session key security we assume that the ring signature scheme used in the protocol is defined in the same group $G$, in which DH key exchange computations of the protocol are done (we propose to use the ring signature scheme from [7] which is unconditionally anonymous even if signing keys are leaked). Thus we assume that each pair of secret/public keys $(\mathsf{sk}, \mathsf{pk})$ is of the form $(\mathsf{sk}, g^{\mathsf{sk}})$. For simplicity we denote by $(\mathsf{sk}_I, g^{\mathsf{sk}_I})$, $(\mathsf{sk}_R, g^{\mathsf{sk}_R})$ the pairs of secret/public keys of the parties $I$ and $R$ respectively.

### 3.1   Initiator Deniability - Detailed Description

> **The protocol messages:**
> M1 $(I \to R)$: $s, g^{\mathsf{sk}_I x}$
> M2 $(I \leftarrow R)$: $s, g^{\mathsf{sk}_R y}, ID_R$, $\text{SIG}_{\mathsf{sk}_R}("1", s, g^{\mathsf{sk}_I x}, g^{\mathsf{sk}_R y})$, $\text{MAC}_{k_1}("1", s, ID_R)$
> M3 $(I \to R)$: $s, ID_I$, $\text{RSIG}_{\mathsf{sk}_I, \{\mathsf{pk}_I, \mathsf{pk}_R\}}("0", s, g^{\mathsf{sk}_I x}, g^{\mathsf{sk}_R y})$, $\text{MAC}_{k_1}("0", s, ID_I)$

The protocol steps are analogous the the original 3-round SIGMA protocol. Therefore we highlight only the differences.

1. M1, M2: Parties exchange DH keys $g^{\mathsf{sk}_I x}$ and $g^{\mathsf{sk}_R y}$ and the responder commits to its identity with a regular signature SIG.
2. M3: The initiator commits to his identity with a ring signature RSIG.

### 3.2   Responder Deniability - Detailed Description

Here we propose the modified 4-round SIGMA protocol, which provides the deniability property to the responder only.

> **The protocol messages:**
> M1 $(I \to R)$: $s, g^{\mathsf{sk}_I x}$
> M2 $(I \leftarrow R)$: $s, g^{\mathsf{sk}_R y}$
> M3 $(I \to R)$: $s, ID_I$, $\text{SIG}_{\mathsf{sk}_I}("0", s, g^{\mathsf{sk}_I x}, g^{\mathsf{sk}_R y})$, $\text{MAC}_{k_1}("0", s, ID_I)$
> M4 $(I \leftarrow R)$: $s, ID_R$, $\text{RSIG}_{\mathsf{sk}_R, \{\mathsf{pk}_I, \mathsf{pk}_R\}}("1", s, g^{\mathsf{sk}_I x}, g^{\mathsf{sk}_R y})$, $\text{MAC}_{k_1}("1", s, ID_R)$

1. M1, M2: Parties exchange DH keys,
2. M3: the initiator commits to its identity by regular signature SIG,
3. M4: the responder commits to its identity with ring signature RSIG.

## 4   Extended Deniability Model

We extend the formall definition of deniability property from [3] which follows the general idea from [8]. Let $\pi$ be a key-exchange protocol defined by a key generation algorithm KGEN and interactive machines $I$ and $R$. Consider an adversary $\mathcal{M}$ which runs on input of a number of public keys $\mathsf{pk} = (\mathsf{pk}_1, \ldots, \mathsf{pk}_\ell)$, randomly chosen according to the key generating algorithm KGEN, and some auxiliary input $aux$. The adversary can run concurrently a number of executions with the honest parties, some as an initiator, others as a responder. The view of $\mathcal{M}$ consists of: its internal randomness, the transcript of the entire interaction, and the session keys computed in all the protocols in which $\mathcal{M}$ participated. We denote this view as $\text{View}_{\mathcal{M}}(\textbf{pk}, aux)$. In our definitions we separate the deniability feature for the initiator and the responder. Note that in some scenario it suffices to provide the possibility of denying for one party only, e.g. an initiator – a client to some Internet service.

**Definition 3.** *We say that* $(\text{KGEN}, I, R)$ *is an* Initiator-strongly-deniable *key exchange protocol with respect to the class $AUX$ of auxiliary inputs if for any adversary $\mathcal{M}$ in the role of the responder, for any input of public keys* $\textbf{pk} = (\textsf{pk}_1, \ldots, \textsf{pk}_\ell)$ *and any auxiliary input $aux \in AUX$, there exists a simulator $SIM_{\mathcal{M}}$ in the role of the initiator that, running on the same inputs as $\mathcal{M}$, produces a simulated view which is indistinguishable from the real view of $\mathcal{M}$.*

*That is, consider the following two probability distributions, denoted as $\mathcal{R}$ for real, and $\mathcal{S}$ for simulated, where* $\textbf{pk} = (\textsf{pk}_1, \ldots, \textsf{pk}_\ell)$ *is the set of public keys of the honest parties:*

$$\mathcal{R}^I = [(\textsf{sk}_i, \textsf{pk}_i) \leftarrow \text{KGEN}(1^n); (aux, \textbf{pk}, \text{View}^I_{\mathcal{M}}(\textbf{pk}, aux)]$$

$$\mathcal{S}^I = [(\textsf{sk}_i, \textsf{pk}_i) \leftarrow \text{KGEN}(1^n); (aux, \textbf{pk}, SIM^I_{\mathcal{M}}(\textbf{pk}, aux)]$$

*then for all probabilistic poly-time machines* Dist, *secret keys* $\textbf{sk} = (\textsf{sk}_1, \ldots, \textsf{sk}_\ell)$, $\textsf{sk}_{\mathcal{M}}$ *and all $aux \in AUX$*

$$|\Pr_{x \in \mathcal{R}^I}[\textsf{Dist}(x, \textbf{sk}, \textsf{sk}_{\mathcal{M}}) = 1]| - |\Pr_{x \in \mathcal{S}^I}[\textsf{Dist}(x, \textbf{sk}, \textsf{sk}_{\mathcal{M}}) = 1]| \leq \textsf{negl}(n).$$

**Definition 4.** *We say that* $(\text{KGEN}, I, R)$ *is an* Responder-strongly-deniable *key exchange protocol with respect to the class $AUX$ of auxiliary inputs if for any adversary $\mathcal{M}$ in the role of the initiator, for any input of public keys* $\textbf{pk} = (\textsf{pk}_1, \ldots, \textsf{pk}_\ell)$ *and any auxiliary input $aux \in AUX$, there exists a simulator $SIM_{\mathcal{M}}$ in the role of the responder that, running on the same inputs as $\mathcal{M}$, produces a simulated view which is indistinguishable from the real view of $\mathcal{M}$.*

*That is, consider the following two probability distributions, denoted as $\mathcal{R}$ for real, and $\mathcal{S}$ for simulated, where* $\textbf{pk} = (\textsf{pk}_1, \ldots, \textsf{pk}_\ell)$ *is the set of public keys of the honest parties:*

$$\mathcal{R}^R = [(\textsf{sk}_i, \textsf{pk}_i) \leftarrow \text{KGEN}(1^n); (aux, \textbf{pk}, \text{View}^R_{\mathcal{M}}(\textbf{pk}, aux)]$$

$$\mathcal{S}^R = [(\textsf{sk}_i, \textsf{pk}_i) \leftarrow \text{KGEN}(1^n); (aux, \textbf{pk}, SIM^R_{\mathcal{M}}(\textbf{pk}, aux)]$$

*then for all probabilistic poly-time machines* Dist, *secret keys* $\textbf{sk} = (\textsf{sk}_1, \ldots, \textsf{sk}_\ell)$, $\textsf{sk}_{\mathcal{M}}$ *and all $aux \in AUX$*

$$|\Pr_{x \in \mathcal{R}^R}[\textsf{Dist}(x, \textbf{sk}, \textsf{sk}_{\mathcal{M}}) = 1]| - |\Pr_{x \in \mathcal{S}^R}[\textsf{Dist}(x, \textbf{sk}, \textsf{sk}_{\mathcal{M}}) = 1]| \leq \textsf{negl}(n).$$

In the above definitions we propose the stronger notion of deniability: the distinguisher algorithm Dist takes as an input not only the distribution instance $x$ but is also given the set of secret keys, including the one of the denying party, and the one of the adversary $\mathcal{M}$. We want to stress that these keys, could really change the way the Dist decides. Note, that in our approach we propose to use the ring signatures from [7] (which are unconditionally anonymous) as a method for providing deniability. Now, if we use ring signatures which anonymity breaks on signing key leakages, e.g. the scheme from [9] based on the proof of equation of discrete logarithms, then the resulting AKE protocol is only deniable in the sense of definition 1 from [3], but is not deniable in the sense of our stronger definitions of deniability.

**Theorem 1.** *The modified 3-round SIGMA protocol proposed in Section 3.1 is initiator-strongly-deniable in the sense of Definition 3.*

*Proof.* We build the simulator for some identity $ID_I$ with the public key $\mathsf{pk}_I$. The simulator runs on the same input as $\mathcal{M}$, according to the protocol till the step 3, where it computes the message M3': $s, ID_I, \mathrm{RSIG}_{\mathsf{sk}_{\mathcal{M}},\{\mathsf{pk}_I,\mathsf{pk}_{\mathcal{M}}\}}("0", s, \mathsf{pk}_I^x, g^{\mathsf{sk}_{\mathcal{M}}y}),$ $\mathrm{MAC}_{k_1}("0", s, ID_I)$, instead of the regular message M3: $s, ID_I, \mathrm{RSIG}_{\mathsf{sk}_I,\{\mathsf{pk}_I,\mathsf{pk}_{\mathcal{M}}\}}("0", s, g^{\mathsf{sk}_I x}, g^{\mathsf{sk}_{\mathcal{M}}y}), \mathrm{MAC}_{k_1}("0", s, ID_I)$. Note that the simulator easily computes $k_0, k_1$ because it computes $g^{\mathsf{sk}_I x \mathsf{sk}_{\mathcal{M}} y}$ as $\mathsf{pk}_I^{x \mathsf{sk}_{\mathcal{M}} y}$. Now the only difference between distributions $\mathcal{S}^I$ and $\mathcal{R}^I$ are signatures: $\mathrm{RSIG}_{\mathsf{sk}_{\mathcal{M}},\{\mathsf{pk}_I,\mathsf{pk}_{\mathcal{M}}\}}("0", s, g^{\mathsf{sk}_I x}, g^{\mathsf{sk}_{\mathcal{M}}y})$ vs. $\mathrm{RSIG}_{\mathsf{sk}_I,\{\mathsf{pk}_I,\mathsf{pk}_{\mathcal{M}}\}}("0", s, g^{\mathsf{sk}_I x}, g^{\mathsf{sk}_{\mathcal{M}}y})$. So, if the distinguisher Dist distinguishes between the two distributions with non negligible probability, it could be immediately used as the distinguisher $\mathcal{D}$ to break the anonymity of the underlying ring signature scheme. $\square$

**Theorem 2.** *The modified 4-round SIGMA protocol proposed in Section 3.2 is responder-strongly-deniable in sense of Definition 4.*

Due to space constrains we omit the rest of proofs. We will present them in the full version of the paper.

## 5  Extended Session Key Security

In order to strengthen security of the session key we slightly modify the CK model (in the manner of eCK from [10]). We add two additional queries to the CK model from [4]: *Ephemeral Key Reveal*$(P_i, s)$ - reveals the ephemeral secret key of the party. *Long-Term Key Reveal*$(P_i, s)$ - reveals the static long-term secret of the party. Note, that we are unable to prove the security of the proposed modifications in eCK, hence the modified deniable protocol with ring signatures, is not immune to key-compromise impersonation (KCI) attacks in which the adversary reveals a long-term secret key of a party and then impersonates others to this party. Indeed in the proposed modified deniable version of SIGMA any initiator $I$ knowing the long term secret key of the responder can produce ring signature $\mathrm{RSIG}_{\mathsf{sk}_R,\{\mathsf{pk}_A,\mathsf{pk}_R\}}("0", s, \mathsf{pk}_A^x, g^{\mathsf{sk}_R y})$ which is indistinguishable from $\mathrm{RSIG}_{\mathsf{sk}_A,\{\mathsf{pk}_A,\mathsf{pk}_R\}}("0", s, \mathsf{pk}_A^x, g^{\mathsf{sk}_R y})$, thus making the responder party $R$ believe it communicates with the party $A$. To capture this, we modify the security definition from [4] to cover uncorrupted parties for which *Long-Term Key Reveal* queries were not issued. We subsequently modify the definition of the exposed session. We say that a session $s$ is **exposed** if the adversary $\mathcal{A}$ makes *Long-Term Key Reveal*$(P, s)$ query for a party in the session $s$. We have:

**Definition 5.** *A protocol $\pi$ provides the session key security if for all adversaries $\mathcal{A}$ the following properties holds*

*P1 if two uncorrupted parties $P_i$ and $P_j$, for which Long-Term Key Reveal queries were not issued, complete matching session and $\mathcal{O}_{s,P_i}$ and $\mathcal{O}_{s,P_j}$ with output $(P_i, s, P_j)$ and $(P_j, s, P_i)$ respectively then the session key $K$ output in these sessions is the same except with a negligible probability.*

*P2 $\mathcal{A}$ succeeds in distinguishing the output from its test query for not exposed sessions with probability not more than $\frac{1}{2}$ plus a negligible fraction.*

**Theorem 3.** *Under the DDH assumption in $G$, and assuming the security of the underlying cryptographic functions* SIG, RSIG, MAC, PRF *the proposed 3-round protocol from section 3.1 is secure in the sense of definition 5.*

**Theorem 4.** *Under the DDH assumption in $G$, and assuming the security of the underlying cryptographic functions* SIG, RSIG, MAC, PRF *the proposed 4-round protocol from section 3.2 is secure in the sense of definition 5.*

# References

1. Kent, S., Atkinson, R.: Security Architecture for the Internet Protocol. RFC 2401 (Proposed Standard,) Obsoleted by RFC 4301, updated by RFC 3168 (November 1998)
2. Harkins, D., Carrel, D.: The Internet Key Exchange (IKE). RFC 2409 (Proposed Standard), Obsoleted by RFC 4306, updated by RFC 4109 (November 1998)
3. Raimondo, M.D., Gennaro, R., Krawczyk, H.: Deniable authentication and key exchange. In: Juels, A., Wright, R.N., di Vimercati, S.D.C. (eds.) ACM Conference on Computer and Communications Security, pp. 400–409. ACM (2006)
4. Canetti, R., Krawczyk, H.: Analysis of key-exchange protocols and their use for building secure channels. In: Pfitzmann, B. (ed.) EUROCRYPT 2001. LNCS, vol. 2045, pp. 453–474. Springer, Heidelberg (2001)
5. Krawczyk, H.: Skeme: a versatile secure key exchange mechanism for internet. In: Ellis, J.T., Neuman, B.C., Balenson, D.M. (eds.) NDSS, pp. 114–127. IEEE Computer Society (1996)
6. Canetti, R., Krawczyk, H.: Security analysis of ike's signature-based key-exchange protocol. IACR Cryptology ePrint Archive 2002, 120 (2002)
7. Herranz, J., Sáez, G.: Forking lemmas for ring signature schemes. In: Johansson, T., Maitra, S. (eds.) INDOCRYPT 2003. LNCS, vol. 2904, pp. 266–279. Springer, Heidelberg (2003)
8. Dwork, C., Naor, M., Sahai, A.: Concurrent zero-knowledge. In: Proceedings of the Thirtieth Annual ACM Symposium on Theory of Computing, STOC 1998, pp. 409–418. ACM, New York (1998)
9. Kumar, S., Agrawal, S., Venkatesan, R., Lokam, S.V., Rangan, C.P.: Forcing out a confession - threshold discernible ring signatures. In: Katsikas, S.K., Samarati, P. (eds.) SECRYPT, pp. 379–388. SciTePress (2010)
10. LaMacchia, B., Lauter, K., Mityagin, A.: Stronger security of authenticated key exchange. In: Susilo, W., Liu, J.K., Mu, Y. (eds.) ProvSec 2007. LNCS, vol. 4784, pp. 1–16. Springer, Heidelberg (2007)

# Complete Robustness
# in Identity-Based Encryption

Hui Cui, Yi Mu, and Man Ho Au

School of Computer Science and Software Engineering,
University of Wollongong, Wollongong, NSW 2522, Australia
hc892@uowmail.edu.au, ymu,aau@uow.edu.au

**Abstract.** Complete robustness (CROB) was proposed to guarantee
that for a public key encryption scheme, decryption attempts will fail
with high probability if the wrong decryption key is used to decrypt
a ciphertext, even if the keys are maliciously generated by the adversary. In this paper, we extend the notion of complete robustness to the
identity-based setting. We firstly formalize the CROB for identity-based
encryption, and present a generic construction achieving CROB from an
arbitrary identity-based encryption scheme. After that, we investigate
whether there exist some kind of relations between CROB and related-
key attack (RKA) security for the case of identity-based encryption. We
conclude that these two notions (CROB and RKA security) are separable for identity-based encryption, but with a slight modification to
our generic construction, an identity-based encryption scheme offering
complete robustness with security against related-key attacks can be
constructed from any identity-based encryption scheme.

**Keywords:** Identity-based encryption, CROB, RKA security.

## 1 Introduction

A crucial security requirement of encryption is providing privacy of the encrypted data, i.e. data privacy. To capture various requirements of data privacy,formalizations like indistinguishability or non-malleability [13] under either
chosen plaintext attacks (CPA) or chosen ciphertext attacks (CCA) [15] are presented. In recent years, user privacy has become an equally relevant concern,
which leads to anonymity, to be another pursued goal in encryption schemes.
Anonymity, also known as key privacy in public-key encryption, was introduced
in [4], meaning that a ciphertext does not leak any information about the public
key (or user identity) under which it was created, thereby making the communication anonymous. Under this scenario, a fundamental question was raised in
[1]: how does a legal user know whether an anonymous ciphertext is intended
for him or not? Furthermore, what will happen if a legal user uses its decryption
key on a ciphertext was not created for it? To address this issue, robustness was
put forward in [1], which guarantees that decryption fails with high possibility
if the "wrong" decryption key is used.

S.S.M. Chow et al. (Eds.): ProvSec 2014, LNCS 8782, pp. 342–349, 2014.

**Robust Encryption.** Robustness (ROB), which has been implicitly applied to applications such as bid privacy [20], consistency in searchable encryption [11], anonymous broadcast encryption [3,17], and anonymous hybrid encryption [19], ensures the property that a ciphertext cannot be correctly decrypted under two different decryption keys. [1] detailed the formal definition of robustness, which introduced two kinds of robustness in encryption: weak robustness (WROB) and strong robustness (SROB), as well as the generic construction to obtain them under the setting called general encryption, which includes both public-key encryption (PKE) and identity-based encryption (IBE). Later, a stronger notion called complete robustness (CROB) in [14] was put forward to provide robustness guarantees in more challenging settings such as the encryption of key-dependent messages [10] or messages encrypted under related keys [6], where the adversary should not be able to find "collisions" in the scheme beyond those which are already implied by the correctness property of the scheme. Also, [14] introduced other robustness notions and explored their relationships.

**RKA Security.** In practice, an attacker might induce modifications in a hardware-stored key by fault injection [9] or other means. When the attacker can subsequently observe the outcome of the cryptographic primitive under this modified key, we have a related-key attack (RKA). RKA was first conceived as tools for the cryptanalysis of blockciphers [16,8], but the ability of attackers to modify keys stored in memory via tampering [12,9] raises concerns that RKA can actually be mounted to a master key of identity-based encryption, a signing key of a certificate authority, or a decryption key, making RKA security important for a wide variety of primitives. Efforts to achieve RKA security have been made on a variety of cryptographic primitives [18,2,5,21,7] such as identity-based encryption, public-key encryption, symmetric encryption, signature.

In this paper, the primitive we target is identity-based encryption, of which the RKA security was firstly defined in [5], and we will consider it under chosen ciphertext attack (CCA) security model, called CC-RKA.

**Our Contributions.** We give the definition of complete robustness in the identity-based setting. In a CROB security game under public-key setting [14], the honest key generation requirement is removed and it is viewed in the term of the behavior of the encryption of decryption algorithms with respect to each other. Roughly speaking, in CROB the adversary should not be able to find "collisions" in the scheme beyond those already implied by the correctness of the scheme. In identity-based encryption, the identities (like the public keys in public-key encryption) are already chosen maliciously, so the natural extension of considering complete robustness would allow the adversary to also choose the master keys maliciously. Specifically, we require that in completely robust identity-based encryption the adversary should not be able to "explain" a ciphertext $C$ of its choice as an encryption under: (1) with the same master keys, two different maliciously generated decryption keys $DK[id_0]$, $DK[id_1]$ by revealing the plaintext for $id_0$ and the decryption key $DK[id_1]$ for $id_1$; or (2) with the different master keys, two different maliciously generated decryption keys $DK[id_0]$, $DK'[id_1]$ by revealing the plaintext for $id_0$ and the decryption key $DK'[id_1]$ for

$id_1$ or two different maliciously generated decryption keys DK[$id_0$], DK'[$id_0$] by revealing the plaintext for $id_0$ and the decryption key DK'[$id_0$] for $id_0$. The reason we consider the second case is that in practice, users may apply decryption keys from different Private Key Generators using the same or different identities, and later decrypt the incoming ciphertexts with them.

Besides, we show that CROB for identity-based encryption does not imply security against related key attacks. In [14], it is implied that there exist some relations between CROB and RKA security under public-key setting. We try to explore whether such implication exists in IBE as well, and then we found that in identity-based setting CROB does not inherit this property. To sustain our claim, we demonstrate that an CROB secure IBE scheme could fail to achieve RKA security under chosen ciphertext attacks.

Lastly, we present a generic construction of IBE scheme that achieves both CROB-CCA security and CC-RKA security. Previously, we have discussed that a CROB secure IBE scheme does not imply RKA security. Here we start from a generic transform that takes a CCA secure IBE scheme and returns a CROB-CCA scheme, followed by modifications to allow this generic construction to provide CC-RKA security as well.

## 2   Preliminaries

In this section, we recall some basic notions and definitions about identity-based encryption schemes and commitment schemes.

### 2.1   Identity-Based Encryption Scheme

An identity-based encryption scheme $\mathcal{IBE}$ is composed of the following four algorithms [5]: parameter generation algorithm PG, master key generation algorithm MPG, key generation algorithm KG, encryption algorithm Enc, and decryption algorithm Dec. (Please see the full version of this paper for details.)

**AI-CCA Security.** Following the definition described in [1], we briefly revisit the game of AI-CCA security, which models the usual indistinguishability and anonymity under chosen ciphertext attacks (IND-CCA and ANON-CCA) of an IBE scheme $\mathcal{IBE}$ in a single game. (Please see the full version of this paper for details.)

### 2.2   Commitment Scheme

A commitment scheme $\mathcal{CME}$ is composed of the following three algorithms [5]: parameter generation algorithm CPG, committal algorithm Com and deterministic verification algorithm Ver. (Please see the full version of this paper for details.)

## 3   Modeling RKA Security and Robustness

In this section, we briefly revisit the security models of related-key attack security and three kinds of robustness security, respectively.

## 3.1   RKA Security

**Related-Key Deriving Functions.** Let $\mathcal{K}$ be the key space. Our definition follows the notion of related-key deriving (RKD) functions given in [6]. (Please see the full version of this paper for this part.)

*Restricted related-key deriving functions.* We define a few classes of functions over the key space $\mathcal{K}$. A set $\Phi^c = \{\phi_c\}_{c\in\mathcal{K}}$ with $\phi_c(dk) = c$ is a set of constant functions. A set $\Phi^a = \{\phi_a\}_{a\in\mathcal{K}}$ with $\phi_a(dk) = a * dk$ is a set of linear functions where $*$ is multiplication or addition. A set $\Phi^{\mathrm{aff}} = \{\phi_{a,b}\}_{a,b\in\mathcal{K}}$ with $\phi_{a,b}(dk) = a * dk + b$ is a set of affine functions where $*$ is multiplication. A set $\Phi^{\mathrm{poly}(d)} = \{\phi_q\}_{q\in\mathcal{K}_d[x]}$ with $\phi_q(dk) = q(dk)$ is a set of polynomial functions, where $q$ ranges over the set $\mathcal{K}_d[x]$ of polynomials over $\mathcal{K}$ of degree at most $d$.

**CC-RKA Security.** On the basis of the games describing RKA security under the chosen ciphertext attacks in [5], we define the games of CC-RKA security for an identity-based encryption scheme $\mathcal{IBE} = $ (PG, MPG, KG, Enc, Dec) in the full version of this paper.

## 3.2   Robustness

As in identity-based setting, the identities are already chosen by the adversary, we extend it to also allow the adversary to choose master keys maliciously. Since it is possible that the adversary chooses the same master keys for two distinct identities, in the Finalize procedure we divide the outputs of the adversary into two cases. These modifications result in our complete robustness under chosen ciphertext attacks (CROB-CCA), which we formalize under an identity-based encryption scheme $\mathcal{IBE}$ in Fig.1.

The CROB advantage of an adversary, in this case, is $\mathbf{Adv}_{\mathcal{IBE}}^{\mathrm{CROB\text{-}CCA}} = \Pr[\mathrm{CROB\text{-}CCA}_{\mathcal{IBE}}^{A} \Rightarrow \mathrm{true}]$.

| proc Initialize | proc Finalize() |
|---|---|
| List $\leftarrow \emptyset$ | For each pair $(mpk_0, id_0, M_0, C_0)$, |
| $pars \leftarrow \mathrm{PG}(1^\lambda)$ | $(mpk_1, id_1, M_1, C_1) \in$ List |
| Return $pars$ | If $(mpk_0 = mpk_1)$ |
| proc Enc$(mpk, id, M, r)$ | If $(C_0 = C_1 \neq \perp) \wedge (id_0 \neq id_1) \wedge$ |
| $C \leftarrow \mathrm{Enc}(pars, mpk, id, M; r)$ | $(M_0 \neq \perp \wedge M_1 \neq \perp)$    return true |
| List $\leftarrow (mpk, id, M, C) \cup$ List | If $(mpk_0 \neq mpk_1)$ |
| proc Dec$(mpk, id, \mathrm{DK}[id], C)$ | If $(C_0 = C_1 \neq \perp) \wedge (M_0 \neq \perp \wedge M_1 \neq \perp)$ |
| $M \leftarrow \mathrm{Dec}(pars, mpk, id, \mathrm{DK}[id], C)$ | return true |
| List $\leftarrow (mpk, id, M, C) \cup$ List | Return false |

**Fig. 1.** Game defining CROB-CCA for $\mathcal{IBE} = $ (PG, MPG, KG, Enc, Dec)

# 4   A Framework for CROB-Secure IBE Schemes

In this section, we describe a framework for creating completely robust IBE schemes, and demonstrate that it cannot resist related-key attacks.

## 4.1   Generic Construction

Given an identity-based encryption scheme $\mathcal{IBE}$ = (PG, MPG, KG, Enc, Dec) and a commitment scheme $\mathcal{CMT}$ = (CPG, Com, Ver), we transform them to an identity-based encryption scheme $\overline{\mathcal{IBE}}$ = ($\overline{\text{PG}}$, $\overline{\text{MPG}}$, $\overline{\text{KG}}$, $\overline{\text{Enc}}$, $\overline{\text{Dec}}$) of which the algorithms are depicted in Fig.2 without the first line and the last line in Algorithm $\overline{\text{Dec}}$(Pars, $mpk$, $id$, DK[$id$], $c$)).

## 4.2   Complete Robustness

**Theorem 1.** *Let $\mathcal{IBE}$ = (PG, MPG, KG, Enc, Dec) be a secure identity-based encryption scheme, and let $\overline{\mathcal{IBE}}$ = ($\overline{\text{PG}}$, $\overline{\text{MPG}}$, $\overline{\text{KG}}$, $\overline{\text{Enc}}$, $\overline{\text{Dec}}$) be the identity-based encryption scheme resulting from applying the complete robustness transform to $\mathcal{IBE}$ and a commitment scheme $\mathcal{CMT}$ = (CPG, Com, Ver). Then (1) CROB-CCA: Let $\mathcal{A}$ be an adversary algorithm against the CROB-CCA security of $\overline{\mathcal{IBE}}$. Then there is an adversary algorithm $\mathcal{B}$ against the the biding security of $\mathcal{CMT}$ such that $\mathbf{Adv}_{\overline{\mathcal{IBE}}}^{\text{CROB-CCA}}(\mathcal{A}) \leq \mathbf{Adv}_{\mathcal{CMT}}^{\text{Binding}}(\mathcal{B})$. (2) $\overline{\mathcal{IBE}}$ cannot resist related-key attacks: Let $\mathcal{A}$ be an adversary algorithm against the CC-RKA security of $\overline{\mathcal{IBE}}$. Then algorithm $\mathcal{A}$ wins in the CC-RKA security game.*

**Proof.** The proof is straightforward. Please see the full version of this paper for the details.

# 5   A Framework for RKA-Secure and Completely Robust IBE Schemes

Here, we present a generic construction for creating completely robust IBE schemes that can resist related-key attacks.

## 5.1   Construction

Let Verify be an algorithm checking the validity of DK[$id$] for $id$, which firstly runs Enc($pars$, $mpk$, $id$, $m$) under a randomly chosen message $m$ to generate a ciphertext $C$, then decrypts $C$ with DK[$id$]. If Dec($pars$, $mpk$, $id$, DK[$id$], $C$) = $m$, it returns 1. Actually, Verify($pars$, $mpk$, $id$, DK[$id$]) implies the correctness of an identity-based encryption scheme.

Given an identity-based encryption scheme $\mathcal{IBE}$ = (PG, MPG, KG, Enc, Dec) and a commitment scheme $\mathcal{CMT}$ = (CPG, Com, Ver), we transform them to an identity-based encryption scheme $\overline{\mathcal{IBE}}$ = ($\overline{\text{PG}}$, $\overline{\text{MPG}}$, $\overline{\text{KG}}$, $\overline{\text{Enc}}$, $\overline{\text{Dec}}$) of which the algorithms are depicted in Fig.2.

Note that it is required that $mpk$ of $id\|mpk$ in KG($pars$, $mpk$, $msk$, $id\|mpk$) should be recomputed with the corresponding private master key $msk$.

Algorithm $\overline{\text{PG}}(1^\lambda)$
$pars \leftarrow \text{PG}(1^\lambda)$
$cpars \leftarrow \text{CPG}(1^\lambda)$
Return Pars $= (pars, cpars)$
Algorithm $\overline{\text{MPG}}(pars)$
$(msk, mpk) \leftarrow \text{MPG}(pars)$
Return $(msk, mpk)$
Algorithm $\overline{\text{Enc}}(\text{Pars}, mpk, id, \overline{M})$
$(com, dec) \leftarrow \text{Com}(cpars, id\|mpk)$
$C \leftarrow \text{Enc}(pars, mpk, id\|mpk, \overline{M}\|dec)$
Return $c = (C, com)$

Algorithm $\overline{\text{KG}}(\text{Pars}, mpk, msk, id)$
$\text{DK}[id] \leftarrow \text{KG}(pars, mpk, msk, id\|mpk)$
Return $(id, \text{DK}[id])$
Algorithm $\overline{\text{Dec}}(\text{Pars}, mpk, id, \text{DK}[id], c)$
If Verify$(pars, mpk, id, \text{DK}[id]) = 1$ then
  $M \leftarrow \text{Dec}(pars, mpk, id\|mpk, \text{DK}[id], C)$
  If $M = \perp$ then return $\perp$
  $\overline{M}\|dec \leftarrow M$
  If (Ver$(cpars, id\|mpk, com, dec) = 1$)
  then return $\overline{M}$
  Else return $\perp$
Else return $\perp$

**Fig. 2.** An identity-based encryption scheme $\overline{\mathcal{IBE}} = (\overline{\text{PG}}, \overline{\text{MPG}}, \overline{\text{KG}}, \overline{\text{Enc}}, \overline{\text{Dec}})$ resulting from an identity-based encryption scheme $\mathcal{IBE} = (\text{PG}, \text{MPG}, \text{KG}, \text{Enc}, \text{Dec})$ and a commitment scheme $\mathcal{CMT} = (\text{CPG}, \text{Com}, \text{Ver})$

### 5.2   Security Proof

**Theorem 2.** *Let $\mathcal{IBE} = (\text{PG}, \text{MPG}, \text{KG}, \text{Enc}, \text{Dec})$ be a secure identity-based encryption scheme, and let $\overline{\mathcal{IBE}} = (\overline{\text{PG}}, \overline{\text{MPG}}, \overline{\text{KG}}, \overline{\text{Enc}}, \overline{\text{Dec}})$ be the identity-based encryption scheme resulting from applying the complete robustness transform to $\mathcal{IBE}$ and a commitment scheme $\mathcal{CMT} = (\text{CPG}, \text{Com}, \text{Ver})$. Then (1) AI-CCA: Let $\mathcal{A}$ be an adversary algorithm against the AI-CCA security of $\overline{\mathcal{IBE}}$. Then there is an adversary algorithm $\mathcal{W}$ against the WROB-CCA security of $\mathcal{IBE}$, an adversary algorithm $\mathcal{H}$ against the the hiding security of $\mathcal{CMT}$, and an adversary algorithm $\mathcal{B}$ against the AI-CCA security of $\mathcal{IBE}$ such that $\mathbf{Adv}_{\overline{\mathcal{IBE}}}^{\text{AI-CCA}}(\mathcal{A}) \leq 2 \cdot \mathbf{Adv}_{\mathcal{IBE}}^{\text{WROB-CCA}}(\mathcal{W}) + 2 \cdot \mathbf{Adv}_{\mathcal{CMT}}^{\text{Hiding}}(\mathcal{H}) + 3 \cdot \mathbf{Adv}_{\mathcal{IBE}}^{\text{AI-CCA}}(\mathcal{B})$. (2) CROB-CCA: Let $\mathcal{A}$ be an adversary algorithm against the CROB-CCA security of $\overline{\mathcal{IBE}}$. Then there is an adversary algorithm $\mathcal{B}$ against the the biding security of $\mathcal{CMT}$ such that $\mathbf{Adv}_{\overline{\mathcal{IBE}}}^{\text{CROB-CCA}}(\mathcal{A}) \leq \mathbf{Adv}_{\mathcal{CMT}}^{\text{Binding}}(\mathcal{B})$. (3) CC-RKA: Let $\mathcal{A}$ be an adversary algorithm against the CC-RKA security of $\overline{\mathcal{IBE}}$ under the restricted RKD functions. Then there is an adversary algorithm $\mathcal{I}$ against the the AI-CCA security of $\overline{\mathcal{PKE}}$ such that $\mathbf{Adv}_{\overline{\mathcal{IBE}}}^{\text{CC-RKA}}(\mathcal{A}) \leq \mathbf{Adv}_{\overline{\mathcal{IBE}}}^{\text{AI-CCA}}(\mathcal{I})$.*

**Proof of Part 1 of Theorem 2.** This part is the same as the first part of Theorem 4.2 in [1], so we omit the proof here. For more details, please see that in [1]. Note that it was observed in [14] that under public-key encryption, the weak robustness assumption can be removed with a slight modification to the original transform in [1].

**Proof of Part 2 of Theorem 2.** The same as that in Theorem 1.

**Proof of Part 3 of Theorem 2.** The proof proceeds with a sequence of games. We start with Game 0 which is the real game, because complete robustness makes more sense in the anonymous background, we modify the original

CC-RKA security game according to our construction as showed in the full version of this paper.

Game 1 is the same as Game 0 with the difference in the Dec procedure that we modify "If Verify($pars$, $mpk$, $id$, DK'$[id]$) = 1 then" to "If DK'$[id]$ = DK$[id]$ then". Due to the correctness of the Verify algorithm, Verify($pars$, $mpk$, $id$, DK'$[id]$) will fail with high probability if DK'$[id] \neq$ DK$[id]$. From this point of view, related-key decryption queries can be reduced to normal decryption queries. Game 2 to Game 5 are the same as Game 1 with the difference in the description of the Dec procedure, which can be found in Figure 12 in [1] (See proc Dec(($C$, $com$), $id$) of $G_1$, $G_2$, $G_3$, $G_4$). Game 6 and Game 7 are exactly like Game 5 with the difference in the decryption of the LR procedure, which can be found in Figure 12 in [1] (See proc LR($id_0^*$, $id_1^*$, $\overline{M}_0^*$, $\overline{M}_1^*$) of $G_5$, $G_6$). For the detailed analysis of Game 2 to Game 7, please see [1]. As a result, we have $\mathbf{Adv}_{\mathcal{IBE}}^{\text{CC-RKA}}(\mathcal{A}) \leq \mathbf{Adv}_{\mathcal{IBE}}^{\text{AI-CCA}}(\mathcal{I})$.

# 6    Conclusions

Complete robustness was firstly achieved in [14] in public-key encryption providing robustness in the more challenging environment such as messages encrypted under related-key. However, robustness was formalized in [1] to guarantee that in both public-key and identity-based encryption, decryption attempts fail with high probability if the wrong decryption key is used to decrypt a ciphertext. Due to this observation, in this paper, we extend the notion of complete robustness to identity-based setting. After describing the security model of CROB in identity-based encryption, we put forward a generic construction achieving CROB from an arbitrary identity-based encryption scheme. Then we try to explore whether CROB implies RKA security for identity-based encryption. Unfortunately, we fail to find the existence of such kind of relationship for an underlying identity-based encryption scheme. Nevertheless, with a slight modification to our generic transform to achieve CROB from any identity-based encryption scheme, we can achieve RKA security in completely robust identity-based encryption.

# References

1. M. Abdalla, M. Bellare, and G. Neven. Robust encryption. In *TCC*, volume 5978 of *Lecture Notes in Computer Science*, pages 480–497. Springer, 2010.
2. B. Applebaum, D. Harnik, and Y. Ishai. Semantic security under related-key attacks and applications. In *ICS*, volume 2011 of *Tsinghua University Press*, pages 45–60. Tsinghua University Press, 2011.
3. A. Barth, D. Boneh, and B. Waters. Privacy in encrypted content distribution using private broadcast encryption. In *Financial Cryptography*, volume 4107 of *Lecture Notes in Computer Science*, pages 52–64. Springer, 2006.
4. M. Bellare, A. Boldyreva, A. Desai, and D. Pointcheval. Key-privacy in public-key encryption. In *ASIACRYPT*, volume 2248 of *Lecture Notes in Computer Science*, pages 566–582. Springer, 2001.

5. M. Bellare, D. Cash, and R. Miller. Cryptography secure against related-key attacks and tampering. In *ASIACRYPT*, volume 7073 of *Lecture Notes in Computer Science*, pages 486–503. Springer, 2011.

6. M. Bellare and T. Kohno. A theoretical treatment of related-key attacks: Rka-prps, rka-prfs, and applications. In *EUROCRYPT*, volume 2656 of *Lecture Notes in Computer Science*, pages 491–506. Springer, 2003.

7. M. Bellare, K. G. Paterson, and S. Thomson. Rka security beyond the linear barrier: Ibe, encryption and signatures. In *ASIACRYPT*, volume 7658 of *Lecture Notes in Computer Science*, pages 331–348. Springer, 2012.

8. E. Biham. New types of cryptoanalytic attacks using related keys (extended abstract). In *EUROCRYPT*, volume 765 of *Lecture Notes in Computer Science*, pages 398–409. Springer, 1993.

9. E. Biham and A. Shamir. Differential fault analysis of secret key cryptosystems. In *CRYPTO*, volume 1294 of *Lecture Notes in Computer Science*, pages 513–525. Springer, 1997.

10. J. Black, P. Rogaway, and T. Shrimpton. Encryption-scheme security in the presence of key-dependent messages. *IACR Cryptology ePrint Archive*, 2002:100, 2002.

11. D. Boneh, G. D. Crescenzo, R. Ostrovsky, and G. Persiano. Public key encryption with keyword search. In *EUROCRYPT*, volume 3027 of *Lecture Notes in Computer Science*, pages 506–522. Springer, 2004.

12. D. Boneh, R. A. DeMillo, and R. J. Lipton. On the importance of checking cryptographic protocols for faults (extended abstract). In *EUROCRYPT*, volume 1233 of *Lecture Notes in Computer Science*, pages 37–51. Springer, 1997.

13. D. Dolev, C. Dwork, and M. Naor. Non-malleable cryptography (extended abstract). In *STOC*, pages 542–552. ACM, 1991.

14. P. Farshim, B. Libert, K. G. Paterson, and E. A. Quaglia. Robust encryption, revisited. In *Public Key Cryptography*, volume 7778 of *Lecture Notes in Computer Science*, pages 352–368. Springer, 2013.

15. S. Goldwasser and S. Micali. Probabilistic encryption. *J. Comput. Syst. Sci.*, 28(2):270–299, 1984.

16. L. R. Knudsen. Cryptanalysis of loki91. In *AUSCRYPT*, volume 718 of *Lecture Notes in Computer Science*, pages 196–208. Springer, 1992.

17. B. Libert, K. G. Paterson, and E. A. Quaglia. Anonymous broadcast encryption: Adaptive security and efficient constructions in the standard model. In *Public Key Cryptography*, volume 7293 of *Lecture Notes in Computer Science*, pages 206–224. Springer, 2012.

18. S. Lucks. Ciphers secure against related-key attacks. In *FSE*, volume 3017 of *Lecture Notes in Computer Science*, pages 359–370. Springer, 2004.

19. P. Mohassel. A closer look at anonymity and robustness in encryption schemes. In *ASIACRYPT*, volume 6477 of *Lecture Notes in Computer Science*, pages 501–518. Springer, 2010.

20. K. Sako. An auction protocol which hides bids of losers. In *Public Key Cryptography*, volume 1751 of *Lecture Notes in Computer Science*, pages 422–432. Springer, 2000.

21. H. Wee. Public key encryption against related key attacks. In *Public Key Cryptography*, volume 7293 of *Lecture Notes in Computer Science*, pages 262–279. Springer, 2012.

# Author Index